The Corbetts

Rab Anderson

Scottish Mountaineering Club
Hillwalkers' Guides

Published by the Scottish Mountaineering Press

Third Edition 2025

ISBN 978-1-907233-57-9
A catalogue record of this book is available from the British Library

SMC ® and Munro's Tables ® are registered trade marks
Some maps are derived from Ordnance Survey OpenData™ © Crown copyright and database right 2021

Front Cover: Cir Mhòr from the summit of Caisteal Abhail, Arran; Scott Wanstall
This Page: Baosbheinn & Beinn an Eòin from Beinn Alligin, with the Fisherfield
          Corbetts and Munros beyond & distant An Teallach; Robert Durran

Layout Rab: Anderson
Maps: Helen Stirling & Rab Anderson
Proofing: Sophie Nicholson

Printed and bound in China by Latitude Press Ltd
Distributed by Cordee Ltd (t) 01455 611185 (w) www.cordee.co.uk

MIX
Paper | Supporting
responsible forestry
FSC® C010256

Foinaven from Arkle's South Top (Rab Anderson)

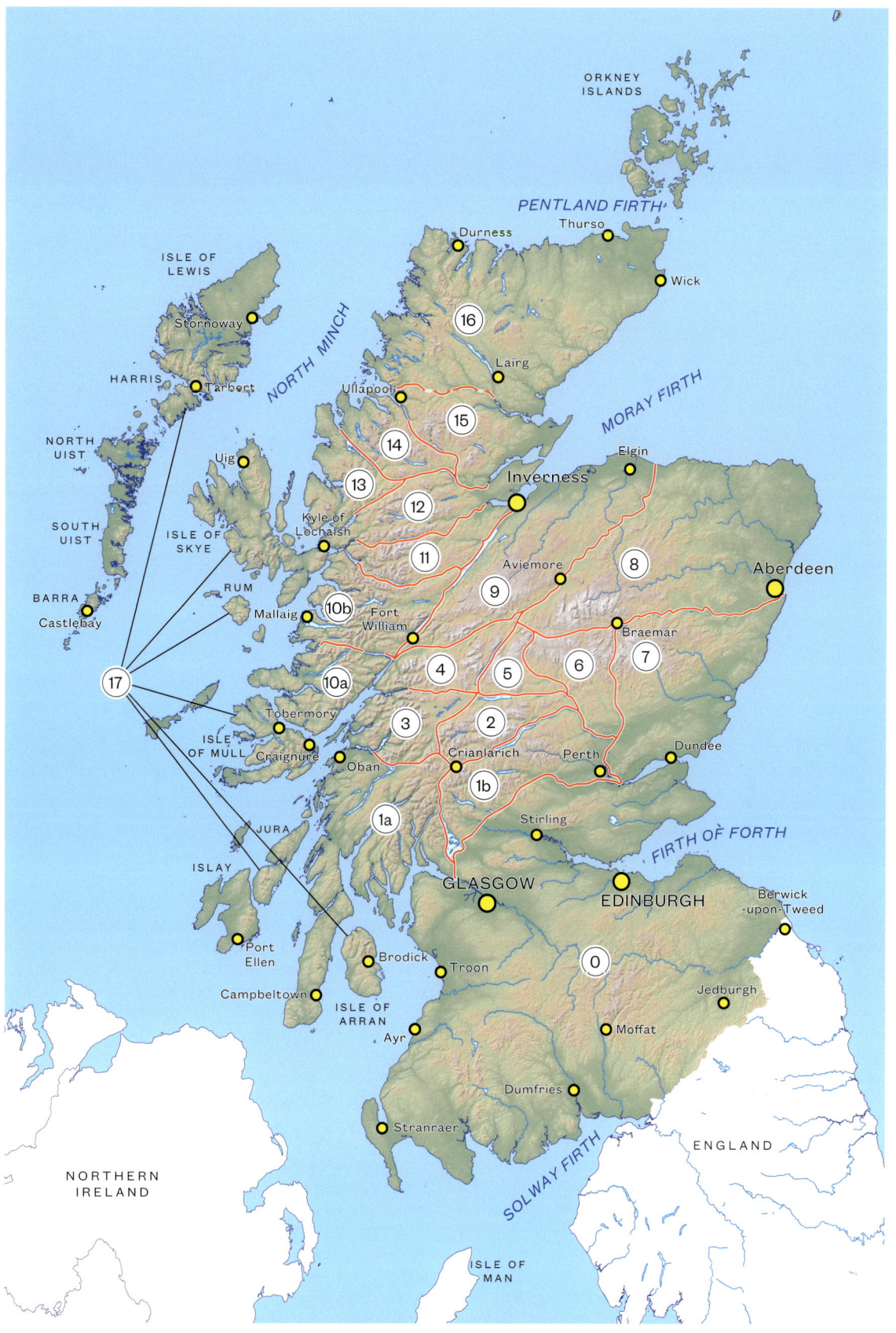

ORKNEY
ISLANDS

PENTLAND FIRTH

Durness
Thurso
Wick

ISLE OF
LEWIS

NORTH MINCH

Stornoway

HARRIS
Tarbert

NORTH
UIST

Uig

SOUTH
UIST

ISLE OF
SKYE

BARRA
Castlebay

RUM

Mallaig

Lairg

16

Ullapool

15

14

13

12

11

Kyle of
Lochalsh

MORAY FIRTH

Elgin

Inverness

Aviemore

8

Aberdeen

10b

Fort
William

9

Braemar

7

6

5

4

3

Tobermory

ISLE
OF MULL

Craignure

Oban

10a

Crianlarich

2

1b

Perth

Dundee

17

JURA

ISLAY

1a

Stirling

FIRTH OF FORTH

Port
Ellen

Brodick

Troon

GLASGOW

EDINBURGH

Berwick
-upon-Tweed

Campbeltown

ISLE OF
ARRAN

Ayr

0

Jedburgh

Moffat

NORTHERN
IRELAND

Stranraer

Dumfries

SOLWAY FIRTH

ENGLAND

ISLE OF
MAN

Beinn an Aodainn and the River Carnach, with Sgùrr a' Choire-bheithe to the left (Derek Sime)

The Corbetts

This is the collective name given to the 222 Scottish mountains of between 2500 feet (762m) and 3000 feet (914.4m) in height that have a reascent of 500 feet (152m) on all sides, giving them a distinct separation from neighbouring mountains. These hills were identified, climbed and listed by Scottish Mountaineering Club (SMC) member John Rooke Corbett and, as with earlier hill listings by Sir Hugh Munro (The Munros) and Percy Donald (The Donalds), the hills on his list have taken his name.

This guidebook describes how to climb the Corbetts in natural day walks, which could be either the ascent of a single Corbett, or the traverse of two or more. The 500 foot height separation criterion that has been applied to these hills means that their standalone nature makes linking multiple Corbetts into longer expeditions difficult, unlike the Munros, which have no separation criterion, thereby enabling multiple Munros on long ridges to be conveniently linked. As a result, the majority of Corbetts provide shorter, single day outings. However, there are many instances where it is possible to ascend one Corbett, return to the road, then drive to another location to ascend another one. These single day descriptions should not be seen as a discouragement to multi-day bothy or tent-based exploration, which has its own rewards.

Routes are described as starting and finishing at convenient points on public roads, since it recognised that most walkers use cars to reach their chosen hills. This should not deter walkers from exploring the use of public transport to reach the hills, although it is realised that bus stops and railway stations are not so conveniently placed

to enable this.

Descriptions and walk times apply to summer ascents, although they can be applied in winter as well, bearing in mind the hazards that snow and ice can bring, the shorter daylight hours, as well as the need for additional skills and equipment, such as ice axe and crampons.

John Rooke Corbett

John Rooke Corbett was born in Handforth, Manchester, in 1876, the son of Christopher Corbett, a Manchester surveyor and sanitary engineer. Educated at Hulme and Manchester Grammar Schools, he attended St John's College Cambridge where he graduated with First Class Honours in Maths; a distinguished 20th Wrangler.

Whilst at university, he was known on at least one occasion to have walked from Cambridge to the family home in Manchester at the end of term. Following his graduation, he worked in his father's business as a surveyor and valuer before taking up a salaried position in 1911 as District Valuer in Manchester's Inland Revenue Valuation Department. He subsequently moved to Bristol where he was the District Valuer responsible for war damage following the First World War.

Corbett was an original member of the Manchester-based Rucksack Club, formed in 1902, and took on the role of Convenor of Rambles where he arranged weekend activities. He is noted for introducing the Moonlight Ramble, a tradition that the Club has continued to maintain. Corbett also joined the Fell and Rock Climbing Club in 1919, and was noted as a regular attendee at their Dinner meets, as well serving on their Committee and becoming a Vice President and Honorary Member.

In 1923, Corbett joined the SMC, and despite living in Bristol he became an active member, also managing to attend most of the Club meets. He served on the SMC's Committee and was a joint editor of the second edition of the SMC's 1932 guidebook to the Northern Highlands.

Corbett's interest in the Scottish Hills saw him, in 1930, become the fourth person to compleat The Munros, and the second to compleat the full listing of both Munros and Tops. His sister drove him around Scotland for his final six Munros and she accompanied him on the ascent of his final one, Buachaille Etive Mòr, whilst two maiden aunts apparently sat in the car awaiting their return; the reason he could not celebrate his achievement with champagne on the summit.

It is said that Corbett went on to climb all of Scotland's 2000 foot hills, which would have been a remarkable achievement. However, there has been some speculation over this statement and whether it is a simple mistake that should perhaps have been 2500 foot hills, which would be the listing of hills between 2500 and 3000 feet that he was compiling; what we now know of as The Corbetts. It would have been a mammoth undertaking to have climbed all of the eminences above 2000 feet, which number well-over 2000 if a 100 foot drop is applied. If a 500 foot drop is applied, which would include what we now know of as The Grahams, then it is perhaps more realistic, but still a large number. However, the facts remain unclear. Regardless of this anomaly, Corbett's walking exploits are impressive, especially given that he lived in Bristol at the time he appeared to be most active in Scotland.

Corbett completed his list of Scottish hills in 1939. Unfortunately his exploits were curtailed in 1943 when he suffered a heart attack aged 65. Although he returned to work for a time, his health declined and he died in 1949.

In his final years he lived with his sister Catherine Louisa Corbett, who was also a keen walker and climber. As only the second female to gain a medical degree from Manchester University, she was a founding member of The Pinnacle Club and also a member of the Fell and Rock Climbing Club. It was her who provided the SMC with her brother's work on his list of Scottish 2500ft hills, subsequently published in the 1952 SMC Journal.

Corbetts List

Following the publication of Sir Hugh Munros tables of Scottish 3000ft mountains, the roots for Corbett going on to compile the list of Scottish Hills in the 2500 to 3000ft bracket could be said to come from Rucksack Club and Fell & Rock Climbing Club member Philip Minor who, in Corbetts words,''was the first to take up the idea of ascending every mountain top in England and Wales over 2500ft.''

Corbett took on the role of identifying, cataloguing and climbing these hills, which Minor completed in 1911 at the time Corbett published a list of 130 of these hills. They were called the Twenty-Fives; now referred to as The Corbett Twenty-Fives. Corbett called this 'a new craze or hobby, which may be looked upon as a special form of the old passion for peak bagging which has long been known to mountaineers.' One has to assume that someone as thorough as Corbett went on to complete the list himself.

Originally there was no separation criterion applied and the list simply included all raised areas of ground above 2500ft, or eminences as they were called then. Corbett subsequently revised the list in 1929 when it ran to 148 tops, with a basic separation criterion that all tops had to have a separate 50ft contour ring. Revised again in 1933, the current listing contains 158 Twenty-Fives.

So, having joined the SMC in 1923, Corbett turned his attention to Scotland and its hills in the 2500 to 3000ft bracket, to which he applied a more rigid separation criterion that each hill should have a reascent of at least 500 feet (152.4m) on all sides between it and any adjacent higher hill, what is now known as a hill's prominence, or drop. In this way the separation between Corbetts is more clearly defined than is the case with Munros, with the fairly large height drop between them ensuring that they are distinct hills, unlike the Munros where the criterion for separation does not involve a rigidly fixed drop between adjacent summits.

Having been first published in the 1952 SMC Journal, the importance of Corbetts List was realised and it was included in the SMC's Munros Tables book in 1953. As has been the case with the Munros, the list of Corbetts has been amended over the years as a result of changes in hill and col heights. Corbett's original geographical sections were also reorganised to make them coterminous with those adopted in Munros Tables. Additionally, for ease of use, the entries in the current version of Corbetts List, which appears on page 390 here, have been laid out to run in the same order as the hills appear in the text of this guidebook.

The SMC holds a record of those who have compleated the Munros, Munro Tops, Furths, Corbetts, Grahams and Donalds; see www.smc.org/hills/compleators. In keeping with the historic nature of these hill listings, the archaic spelling of complete has been used. Corbett compleators are called Corbeteers and at the time of writing there are 920 people who have registered as Corbeteers, compared to 8150 Munroists.

Within the ranks of the Corbetts there are many hills of great interest, character and beauty that are the equal of all but a few Munros, their lower height offering a different perspective of the surrounding landscape. There are Corbetts whose ascent will take the hillwalker into remote and unfamiliar parts of Scotland. The Corbetts should not in be looked upon as lesser hills, but visited and enjoyed in their own right as part of the wealth and diversity of the Scottish landscape.

Acknowledgements

Thanks are due to all those involved in the 1990 and 2002 editions of The Corbetts. Also to Chris Anderson, Davie Black, Dave Johnson, Tom Prentice and all those who have provided valuable information and feedback.

West from the summit of Beinn Enaiglair to Slioch, the Fisherfield hills and An Teallach (Hugh Munro)

ROUTE DESCRIPTIONS

Hill Heights and Summit Locations

Corbetts are referenced C1 (Beinn a' Chlaidheimh) to C222 (Beinn na h-Uamha), depending upon height. A list of Corbetts in order of height is given on page 392 at the back of the book.

Height and summit location information has been taken from the Ordnance Survey (OS) as the national mapping authority and producers of the most widely-used maps for hillwalkers. The SMC recognises that independent surveys are being performed, and while not all of this information is submitted to the OS, it is held in the Database of British and Irish Hills (DoBIH). Heights from the DoBIH that differ from, or are more accurate than, OS heights are included in the Table of Corbetts starting on page 386. This Table is laid out in order of the standard SMC Sections, which matches the chapters in this book.

A number of summit locations also differ to those shown on maps, albeit most only slightly, and the relevant information on these is noted at the end of the Table, as well as in the walk description.

Mapping

Route maps illustrate route descriptions and serve as aids to planning. The detail on these maps is not complete and they should not take the place of a proper OS or Harvey map.

Continuous red lines on the route maps indicate the principal routes whilst red dashed lines indicate some alternatives or extensions. Yellow lines and yellow dashed lines generally indicate secondary routes together with their variations. These colours correspond with the overall route distance, height and timings in the descriptions.

Information on these maps should be self-explanatory. For the avoidance of doubt, FB and WB stand for Foot-bridge and Wire Bridge. Not all such bridges are shown, or mentioned, and there is no guarantee that a bridge will still be in place on the day of your visit.

The recommended maps for hillwalking are the Ordnance Survey 1:50k Landranger Series and in the heading for each walk the letter L followed by a number, denotes the relevant OS map. The OS also produce an Explorer Series of maps at a larger scale of 1:25k. The heights of features in this guide are generally taken from either the OS 1:50k map series or the 1:25k series.

Harvey Maps' 1:25k Superwalker and 1:40k British Mountain Maps series are on waterproof and tearproof paper and cover a number of popular mountain areas. Harvey also publish a number of summit map enlargements.

UK mapping uses metric measurements, so distances and heights in the text are in kilometres *(km)* and metres *(m)*. Distances when approaching by car are sometimes in miles to aid measurement via a car mileometer.

Six figure grid references identify certain locations and are preceded by two OS grid letters to provide a unique reference to within 100m. The Tables on page 386 give eight figure grid references for summits.

The maps in this book use the following symbols to indicate the status of a summit:

● **Corbett** (222); 2500ft (762m) to below 3000ft (914.4m); minimum 500ft (152.4m) drop

▲ **Munro** (282); 3000ft (914.4m) and higher

△ **Munro Top** (226); 3,000ft (914.4m) and higher, less distinct summit heights

◆ **Graham** (231); 600m (1968.5ft) to below 762m (2500ft), minimum 150m drop.

■ **Donald** (89); Lowlands, over 2000ft (609.6m).
Note: Seven Donalds are also Corbetts.

☐ **Donald Tops** (52); Lowlands, less-distinct summit heights over 2000ft (609.6m).

⊗ Other summit

Distances, Height Gain & Time

Distances and height gains have generally been rounded up to the nearest 0.25km and 5m respectively. Ascent times are calculated on the basis of 4.5km per hour for distance walked, plus 10m per minute (1 hour per 600m) for climbing uphill. Times have generally been rounded up to the nearest 5 minutes.

These timings are a close metric approximation to Naismith's Rule. No allowance has been made for stops, but an allowance has made for difficult ground and for steep or difficult descents during the walk. Descent times are based on Langmuir's method of adding 10 minutes per 300m of difficult or steep descent; a timing which has been applied a little more liberally, and is particularly relevant to long descents at the end of the day.

Where descriptions relate to the traverse of two or more hills, the distance, height gain and time at selected summits are cumulative from the start. This data is shown in bold text. The overall distance, height gain and time has been highlighted at the end of each route description - in red for primary routes and in yellow for secondary routes.

The objective of this book is to describe routes to the Corbetts. However, it is often possible to extend routes to take in nearby hills, and routes have been described with this in mind. Without stating it every time, it will often be possible to shorten a walk after the principal objective has been climbed, either by returning via the route of ascent, or by some other route. Whilst routes have been described in a specific direction, this is only a suggestion and on the day a reverse approach to the one described might better suit the conditions, or the individual(s).

Bikes

It is normal practice for many walkers to use bikes on longer approaches. Arriving at a standard bike time is more difficult than it is for walking, so timings given are likely to vary more from individual to individual, especially for those who are more used to biking and are prepared to put more speed and effort into uphill sections and speedier downhill returns at the end of the day.

Where bikes are an advantage this is mentioned and a reasonable but rough indication of the time is given, together with an approximate saving on the day. In cases where a bike approach is fairly lengthy (generally 6km or more), then both a bike distance/time and a walk distance/time are given to the point that bikes are left. Times and distances are then given on foot, from and back to that point, with the final red and yellow full distance/time figures indicating *with a bike* and *on foot*, so it is clear what the difference is. Many hillwalkers are now using battery assisted bikes, but suggested times

given are for leg power only bikes.

Bikes can cause erosion on paths and open hillsides, so should only be used on prepared surfaces such as tracks for vehicular access and some stalkers' paths.

Parking, Roads, Tracks & Paths

Three levels of parking have been identified on the maps. ℙ indicates an official, or publicly maintained car park, or a parking area such as a layby. ℙ indicates there is adequate off-road parking. ℙ indicates parking is limited, or restricted, such as in small pull-offs or verge parking.

Throughout the text, *road* means a tarmac surface, usually public. Where a surfaced road is private, as in some estate roads, this is mentioned. *Track* means any unsurfaced way such as used by forestry or estate vehicles; usually private. An *ATV track* is any less distinct route on the hill used by all-terrain-vehicles such as quad bikes. Tracks can usually be biked, whereas it is unlikely that ATV tracks can be. *Path* means a clear pedestrian route on the ground, often a stalkers' or hillwalkers' path.

MOUNTAIN SAFETY & USEFUL INFORMATION

Participation Statement

Mountaineering Scotland, the representative body for climbers and hillwalkers in Scotland, recognises that hill-walking, climbing and mountaineering are activities with a danger of personal injury or death. Participants in these activities should be aware of and accept these risks, and be responsible for their own actions and involvement.

Navigation, Equipment & Planning

Good mountain craft, navigation skills, equipment and clothing, together with forward planning can all help ones enjoyment of the hills and help reduce the chance of an accident. In the event of an emergency an understanding of First Aid, even at a basic level, and its application in the mountain environment is useful. Although mobile phones and GPS are used for navigational and communication purposes, there are places in the hills where there is no signal. Both rely on batteries and electronics, which can fail, or be easily damaged. Consequently, they should never be a substitute for navigation skills with a map and compass. The potential hazards of winter conditions, river crossings (particularly in spate), or challenging conditions resulting from changes in the weather should always be borne in mind.

Weather Forecasting

Although weather forecasting has improved over the years, it is not a precise science. There are many weather forecasts available, but a few are worth mentioning. The Mountain Weather Information Service (MWIS) has forecasts covering Scotland in five areas. The Meteorological Office (Met Office) also has specialist Mountain Weather forecasts covering the main mountain areas of Scotland in four areas, within which there are individual forecasts for most of the major hills; mainly Munros. In addition, BBC TV and Radio forecasts, which at times include an

▶

Sgùrr Dubh from Sgòrr nan Lochaine Uaine, with Sgùrr Bàn and Sgurr nan Fhir Duibhe on Beinn Eighe beyond, then

outdoor activities forecast, also have regularly updated web-based forecasts. These are all available for mobile phones, together with other mobile phone app forecasts.

Avalanches

Avalanches occur with great regularity in the Scottish hills and can happen wherever there is snow lying on ground of sufficient angle. Winter walkers should familiarise themselves with the principles of snow structure and avalanche prediction.

While the ability to make your own assessment of risk is vital, snow and avalanche predictions for the major mountain areas are produced by the Sportscotland Avalanche Information Service (SAIS) and are readily available throughout the winter.

As well as on the SAIS website, which can be linked to from the Mountaineering Scotland website, these reports can be found at police stations, sports shops, tourist information centres and on display boards in mountain areas. The About Avalanches section on the SAIS website makes useful reading.

A Chance in a Million? is the classic work on avalanches and is recommended reading for anyone venturing onto the Scottish hills in winter.

Mountain Rescue

In the event of an accident, contact the police, either by phone (999), or in person. It is often better to stay with a casualty, but in a party of two, one may have to leave to summon help. If the casualty has to be left, leave them in a warm, comfortable, sheltered, and well-marked place.

Further information is available on the Mountain Rescue Scotland website.

Midges, Clegs, Deer Ked & Ticks

Biting insects such as midges, clegs and deer ked can make things unpleasant at times. Ticks however can carry Lyme disease, and incidents of this appear to be on the increase, so it is worth checking oneself after trips and reading up on them. Mountaineering Scotland, the BMC and Lyme Disease Action UK all have relevant information.

Access

The Land Reform (Scotland) Act 2003 gives everyone statutory access rights to most land and inland water including mountains, moorland, woods and forests, grassland, paths and tracks, and rivers and lochs. People only have these rights if they exercise them responsibly by respecting people's privacy, safety and livelihoods, and Scotland's environment.

Equally, land managers have to manage their land and water responsibly in relation to access rights. The Outdoor Access Scotland website and the Scottish Outdoor Access Code provide detailed guidance on these responsibilities. Whilst access rights apply to pedestrians and cyclists, they do not extend to vehicles being driven up private roads without permission.

Stalking, Shooting & Lambing

Deer stalking can take place all year round, but the key busier periods are in the autumn (particularly the first three weeks of October) and the winter (late January to mid

the Fisherfield hills and Creag Rainich (Robert Durran)

February). During these periods more stalking activity takes place during the working week (Monday to Friday) and hill-walkers are more likely to be asked to use alternative routes. The hills are still accessible during these periods, but it is worth planning ahead in case a different route, or objective, has to be taken.

Fewer routes will be affected by stalking on Saturdays, and stalking does not usually take place on Sundays, although requests to avoid disturbing deer may still be made. Information sources such as the Heading for the Scottish Hills website and Mountaineering Scotland website provide general access information and details of stalking activities on specific estates.

There should be no stalking access issues on Forestry and Land Scotland, National Trust for Scotland and John Muir Trust lands, but check Heading for the Scottish Hills.

The grouse shooting season is from 12th August until 10th December.

If you are heading onto the hills with a dog, disturbance to sheep should be avoided, especially during the lambing season between March and May.

Footpath Erosion, Cairns & Memorials

It is the responsibility of all walkers to minimise their as regards to route-finding. The indiscriminate building of cairns and memorials on the hills should be discouraged.

Public Transport

Most walkers will arrive by car. For those using public transport, timetables are best found via the internet.

Bothies

The Mountain Bothies Association maintains about 80 bothies on various estates throughout Scotland. None of these are owned by the MBA, but belong to estates which generously allow their use. A number of bothies are closed during the Stalking Season. Visit the MBA's website for further information.

Mountaineering Scotland

This is the representative body for climbers and hill-walkers in Scotland. One of its primary concerns is the continued free access to the hills. Information about bird restrictions, stalking and access issues can be obtained from them. Any hill user encountering problems regarding access should contact Mountaineering Scotland.

Scottish Mountaineering Club

The SMC produces guidebooks for Hillwalkers, Scramblers and Climbers. All profits from these guidebooks go to the Scottish Mountaineering Trust (*SMT*) and provide much of the SMT's revenue.

Scottish Mountaineering Trust

The Scottish Mountaineering Trust (*SMT*) is a Scottish charity that provides grants to projects, people and organisations promoting recreation, education and safety in the hills and mountains, especially those of Scotland.

The Scottish Mountaineering Trust supports:

- Publication of guides to, and information about, the hills and mountains of Scotland.
- Footpath construction and maintenance for public access.
- Mountaineering education and training, especially that aimed at young people and disadvantaged communities.
- Mountain rescue teams and organisations that promote mountain safety.
- Renovation of club huts available to the mountaineering community.
- Development of knowledge and the appreciation of our mountains, their history and culture.

In all these activities the Trust seeks to ensure the conservation of the environment.

In the past 35 years the SMT has provided over £2m to people and organisations working in these areas.

The SMT is funded by donations from individuals and organisations who share its values. It is also funded from the publication of climbing, scrambling and walking guidebooks, together with other books about the Scottish mountains, by its wholly owned subsidiary the Scottish Mountaineering Press.

If you would like to find out more about how the SMT can help you, or your organisation, or to support the SMT with a donation, please visit *www.thesmt.org.uk*.

Corserine with Carlin's Cairn to its left, seen between Mullwharchar, left, and Dungeon Hill, right, across Loch Enoch from Redstone Rig on The Merrick (Rab Anderson)

SECTION 0
Galloway & The Borders

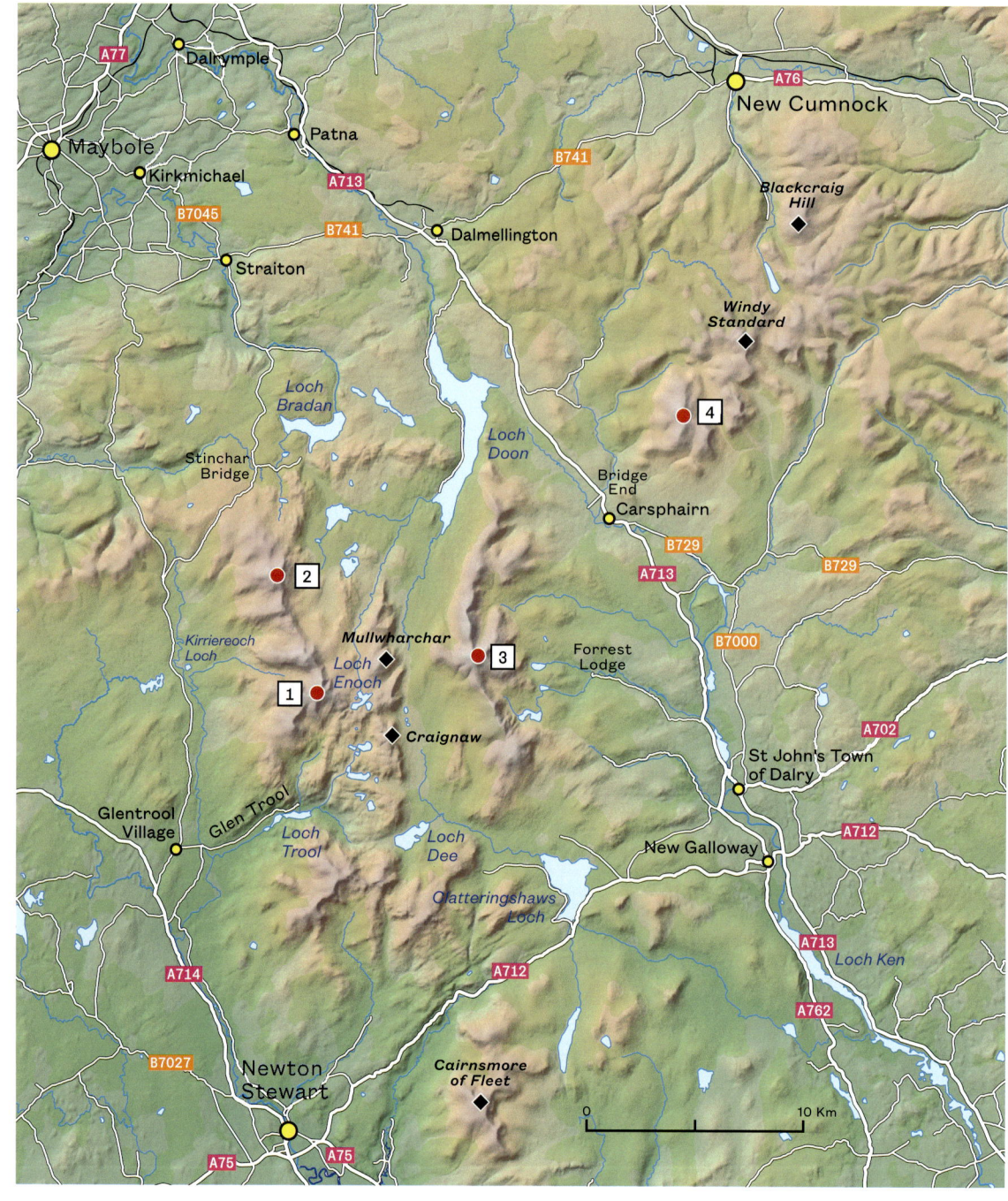

SECTION 0

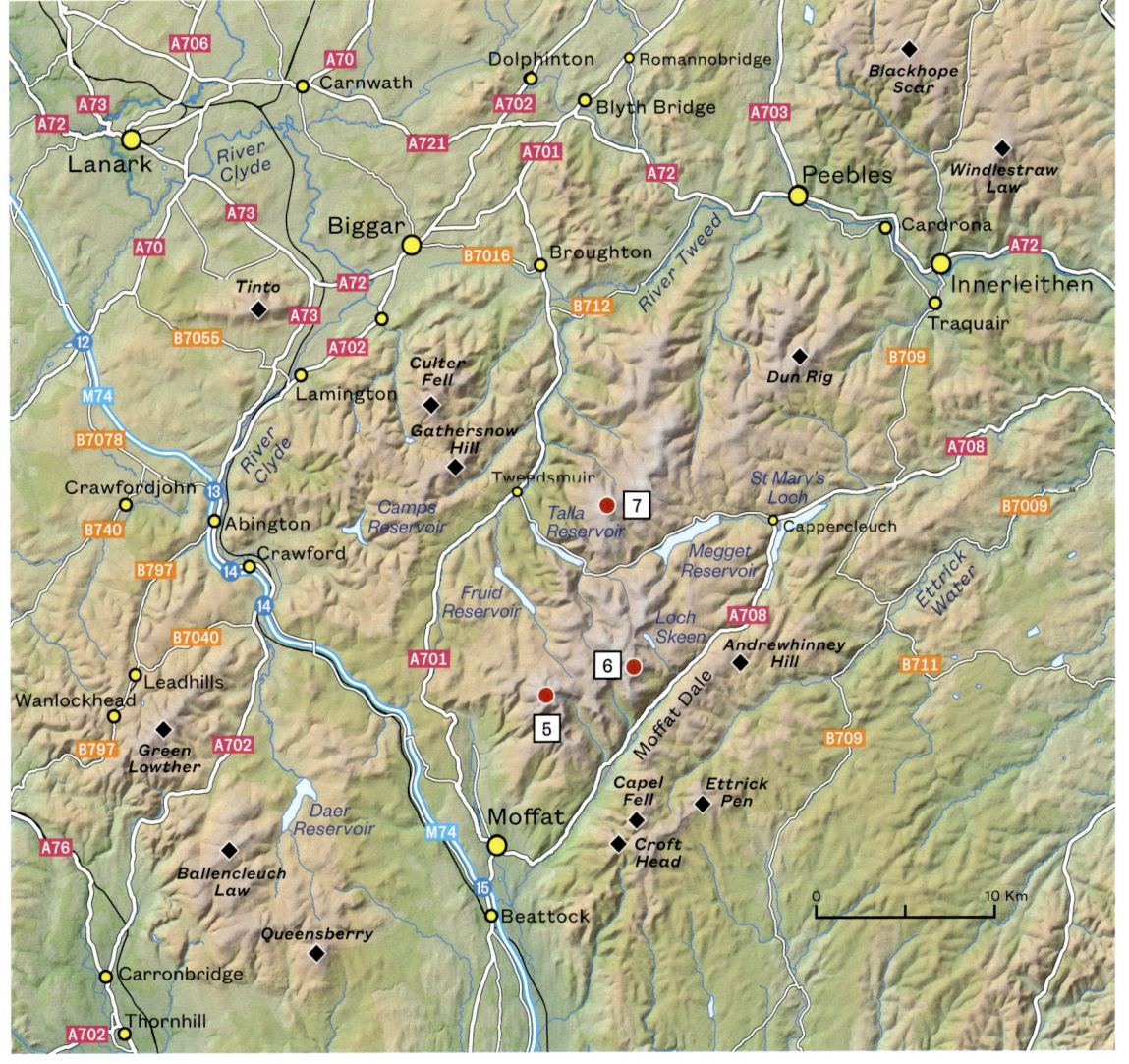

SECTION 0

The Merrick; 843m; (C98); L77; NX427855; branched, spreading, or fingered hill

Located in the Galloway Forest Park, and forming the south-western highpoint of the Southern Uplands, The Merrick is also the highest hill in that range, albeit by only 3m over Broad Law.

Lying to the north of Loch Trool, and the through route followed by the Southern Upland Way eastwards to Loch Dee, The Merrick is one of the North Galloway Hills. These hills form a series of three northwards running parallel ridgelines with The Merrick sitting on the left-hand ridgeline, which also includes the other Corbett here; Shalloch on Minnoch.

Due to its resemblance to a giant hand when viewed from above, this ridgeline is known as The Awful Hand, with The Merrick being the forefinger. The central ridgeline is made up of a series of lower hills and is known as the Dungeon Range, whilst the right-hand ridgeline is known as The Rhinns of Kells, on which sits Corserine, the third of the North Galloway Corbetts.

Mainly comprised of granite, these hills lie in a rugged and beautiful part of Scotland. A number of sandy-shored lochans lie trapped in the glacial hollows between The Merrick and the central ridgeline, further enlivening the scenery. The exploration of these hills, their ridgelines and their lochans, is a delightful revelation.

The Merrick is generally climbed on its own, taking in the minor summit of Benyellary on the way, and this is the principal route described here. However, The Merrick can be paired with Shalloch on Minnoch for a more demanding outing, as described in the panel on page 19. It can also form part of a longer extension taking in the three principal hills of the Dungeon Range, as described in the SMC's guidebook *The Grahams & The Donalds*. This route shown in yellow on the map on page 18, but not described (20km; 1260m; 7h 45min).

With two cars, the western ridge-line can be traversed from north to south by leaving one car in a track entrance to the north of Cairnadloch, and another at the road end in Glen Trool; see end of panel on page 19.

The start point for the ascent of The Merrick is reached from the south-west, along forested Glen Trool, via a single-track road which ends in oak woods above Loch Trool. There are two car parks, one 200m before the road ends, and another one at the road end. To the south of the upper car park is Bruce's Stone: a large boulder on a pedestal, inscribed to commemorate Robert the Bruce's victory over a superior English army in 1307, prior to him becoming King.

Leave the upper car park by a path through the bushes, signed The Merrick Trail, and follow this to, then up the west bank of the Buchan Burn, which tumbles down the hillside in a series of waterfalls and cascades. The forest on the initial section has been felled, and there are open views ahead to Benyellary and The Merrick.

Continue along a flatter section through younger trees to reach the bothy at Culsharg. Pass to the left of the bothy and begin the ascent proper up the side of the Whiteland Burn past some mature trees to

The Merrick and Little Spear from Kirrireoch Hill (Rab Anderson)

emerge onto a forest track.

Turn right across the burn then take the path on the left, uphill through a gate into the forest. It is a fairly steep climb, which although stony, is wet in places. Emerge into the open onto drier ground and follow

the path uphill through another gate, swinging rightwards to climb beside a drystane dyke to gain the cairn on the flat summit of Benyellary (719m).

Continue alongside the wall, gently downhill along the Neive of the Spit, above a steep slope on the right, the Scars of Benyellary, which drops into the bowl of a grassy south-east facing corrie. The slope ahead is known as the Broads of Merrick, and the ascent passes through the wall twice before swinging away from it north-east at a pleasant angle across the upper slope.

A trig point marks the summit towards the northern end of an expanse of flat, mossy ground, studded with granite boulders left behind by the ice ages and embedded due to frost heaving of the surrounding soil (6.5km; 780m; 2h 45min).

To the north is The Merrick's north ridge, known as the Little Spear, which provides the link to Kirriereoch Hill, then Tarfessock and Shalloch on Minnoch beyond. On a clear day, it is possible to see the Scottish Highlands, Ireland's Mourne Mountains and England's Lake District.

The simplest return is back the same way (13km; 860m; 4h 30min).

A good circuit, albeit longer and on rougher terrain, can be achieved by crossing the flat summit area south-eastwards to descend the broad and rocky, but easy, south-east ridge, known as Redstone Rig. There is a rough path, and the line generally

heads towards the middle of Loch Enoch in the basin below and an island with a small inset loch. Partway down, veer towards the southern end of Loch Enoch, onto a more prominent spur, from where there are two options:

(i) The first option is to drop steeply south to a col above the south-west end of the loch, then make a short climb across a wall onto the ridgeline beyond. A path runs all the way along the crest of this undulating ridge, known as the Rig of Loch Enoch, and it provides a splendid highway leading to the top of Buchan Hill (493m) overlooking Loch Trool. The highpoint is at the northern end, and beyond that there are a number of other knolls.

The original route continues to a prominent cairn on the far south-western highpoint. From there, it heads briefly west to drop south-west down a wide gully between candy-striped rocks to the west of the crags of the Black Gairy. There is a vague path to follow. The grassy slope below this gully, all the way to the wall at the bottom, had been churned up by cattle and was full of holes, making it uncomfortable to descend. In summer the lower slopes are also covered in bracken. If this descent is chosen, there is a gate in the wall at NX418805 close to the Buchan Burn, beyond which the track is gained, leading over the bridge across the   ▶

Crossing the Neive of the Spit from Benyellary to The Merrick, with Corserine beyond (Rab Anderson)

The Merrick and its south-east ridge, Redstone Rig, from Rig of Loch Enoch (Rab Anderson)

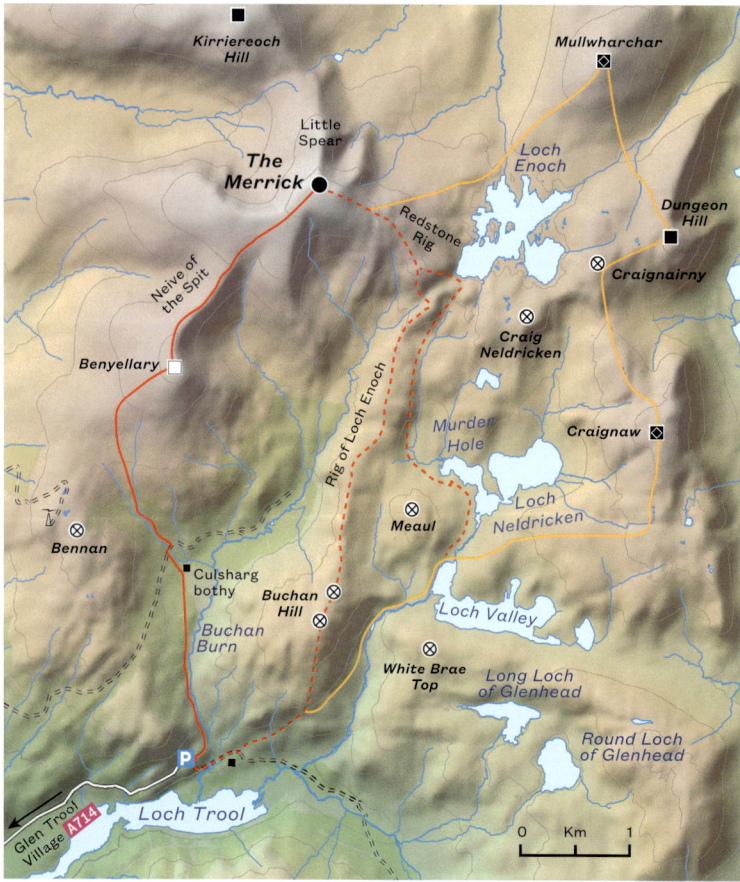

burn and back up to the car park (14.5km; 930m; 5h 15min).

An alternative is to descend southwards from the south-east top of Buchan Hill (NX427816) to meet the path coming down from Loch Valley. This path runs alongside a wall, then passes through it to descend across the slope to reach the track leading to the bridge over the Buchan Burn.

(ii) The second option descends to the sandy bay at the south-west end of Loch Enoch. From there, a path goes east above the loch for a short way before heading south beneath Craig Neldricken to pass the west end of Loch Arron. The path follows the outflow from this loch to pass the west end of Loch Neldricken, a spot known as The Murder Hole. It then continues above the loch, between it and a knoll named Meaul, to reach Loch Valley. From there, the path follows the outflow, the Gairland Burn, for a way before cutting across the southern flanks of Buchan Hill. The path runs alongside a wall, then passes through it to descend across the slope to reach the track leading to the bridge over the Buchan Burn (14.5km; 830m; 4h 55min).

Shalloch on Minnoch & The Merrick
Both of these hills can be climbed as an extended circuit starting from Forestry and Land Scotland's Kirrieroch car park at NX358867 beside the Water of Minnoch. The route to Shalloch on Minnoch is the same as described on page 20, (7.5km; 560m; 2h 40min), and then south across Tarfessock to Kirrierioch Hill, (11.5km; 850m; 4h 10min).

From Kirriereoch Hill, descend south-east to the col with The Merrick at 637m, then climb the fine ridge of Little Spear to gain the trig point on the summit of The Merrick (13.25km; 1060m; 4h 55min).

To descend, drop south-west off the summit close to the edge overlooking the corrie, Black Gairy, then traverse the edge to gain the wall coming up from Benyellary. Follow the wall to where it drops off north, then continue west down the crest to cross another wall and descend rough ground. This leads to a forest break at NX387853, reached by crossing a wall. Go through the overgrown break to a track, and turn left along this, then left across the Kirriemore Burn to regain the track used in the approach, 800m from the start (22.5km; 1090m; 7h 15min).

Continuing to Benyellary from The Merrick, then descending west down Kirn Brae adds about 1km, 60m, 20min to this route.

Including Caerloch Dhu from Shalloch on Minnoch adds a further 3.5km, 180m, 1h 15min there-and-back for anyone taking on the challenge of climbing all the Donalds and Donald Tops in the range.

If transportation between the start and finish points can be arranged, then a full north-to-south traverse of the Awful Hand range is perhaps a better option. The traverse starts via a path from the passing place at NX394948 (see page 20), and climbs over Shalloch on Minnoch (4.75km; 420m; 1h 45min) to The Merrick (10.5km; 920m, 4h). The descent to Glen Trool is made by the standard ascent route from there, over Benyellary, as described on page16 (17km; 1000m; 5h 45min).

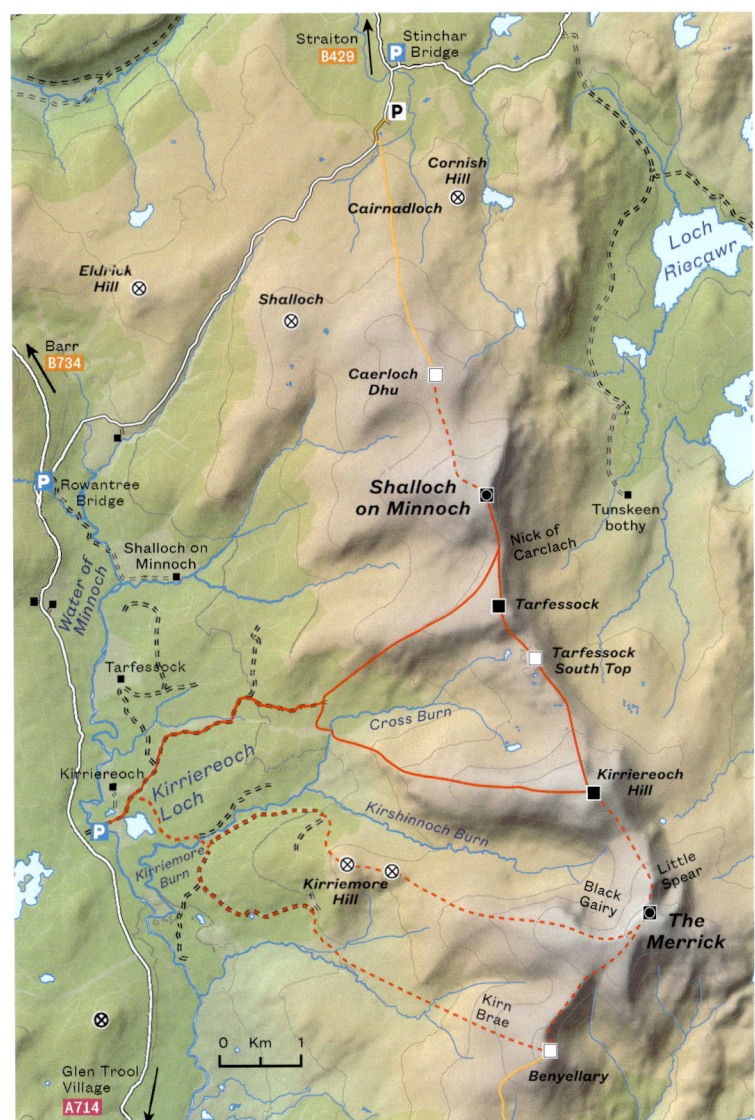

Shalloch on Minnoch; *775m; (C200); L77; NX407905; middle heel*

Shalloch on Minnoch is the north-ernmost of the three hills forming the ridge that extends northwards from The Merrick. Closest to The Merrick is Kirriereoch Hill, the highest of the three and formerly a Corbett, whilst Tarfessock is the middle hill. All three hills are easily linked to form the circuit described here, which can be extended to include The Merrick; see panel opposite.

The full ridgeline is known as The Awful Hand due to its resemblance to a giant hand when viewed from above: The Merrick being the forefinger. With the use of two vehicles it is possible to traverse the full ridgeline by leaving one vehicle at a track entrance to the north of Cairnadloch and the other at the Glen Trool road end; see panel opposite.

Since Shalloch on Minnoch lies to the east of the unclassified minor road between Straiton in the north and Glentrool Village in the south, it can be approached from the Forestry Commission's Kirriereoch car park at NX358867 beside the Water of Minnoch. This is accessed by a ▶

signed track which leaves the road some 2.5 miles (4km) south of the Barr road junction at Rowantree Bridge and 4.5 miles (7.5km) north of Glentrool Village.

Walk along the track towards Kirriereoch Loch, then turn left and right to pass Kirriereoch Farm. In a further 300m a track joins from the right: the return route if The Merrick is included; see panel on page 19. Continue ahead past a branch off left, then, 250m after crossing the bridge over the Pillow Burn, take a fork off right and follow this to its end at NX389881. If The Merrick is not going to be included, a bike can be used for the 4km to this point, giving a saving of at least 1h on the day.

Just before the track end, follow a path north-east up a clearing beside old fence posts. It is worth noting that the return route ascends the continuation of the clearing and fence posts immediately below the track. The route leads onto the west ridge of Tarfessock, across which a rising traverse is made to gain the col with Shalloch on Minnoch: the Nick of Carclach (628m). A broad ridge is climbed onto the plateau where the summit lies near the corrie edge of the Maiden's Bed, about 300m to the south-east of the lower trig point

(7.5km; 560m; 2h 40min).

For those interested in The Donalds, Caerloch Dubh, a Donald Top to the north, can be included; an added 3.5km, 180m, 1h 15min there and back.

Return to the Nick of Carclach and continue up onto Tarfessock (697m). From there, descend north-east, then cross the small rise of Tarfessock South Top (620m) and the ensuing rough ground, studded with lochans, to reach a fence at the col below Kirriereoch Hill's screes. Avoid these on the left by steep grass, then climb to a wall straddling the hill and continue south-east for about 180m to the top of Kirriereoch Hill (786m) (11.5km; 850m; 4h 10min).

This was on Corbett's original list, but the reascent from the col with The Merrick falls short of the required 500 feet. More recent measurements give a reascent of 150.2m (493 feet) making this a Marilyn, but not a Corbett.

Return to the wall and follow it down the west ridge to where it turns south. Pass through the wall and continue down the ridge on a rough path beside metal fence posts to gain a fence around forestry in the glen. Follow the fence west to an old stile on the right and cross over to reach

the Cross Burn. Ford the burn and continue between a fence on the left and forestry on the right to where the plantation ends, then cross a marshy clearing to regain the end of the track used on the approach, which is followed back (19.5km; 870m; 6h 15min).

Shalloch on Minnoch can also be climbed from the north via a path that starts from a passing place at NX394948. There is limited verge parking here. Track entrances about 250m and 350m to the north provide space, whilst the Stinchar Bridge car park is a further 750m to the north. Follow the path up Cairnadloch, then over Caerloch Dhu to the trig point, then to the summit of Shalloch on Minnoch about 300m to the south-east (4.75km; 420m; 1h 45min).

Return the same way (9.5km; 460m; 3h).

Whilst it is possible to continue over Tarfessock to Kirriereoch Hill for those interested in collecting The Donalds, a return all the way along the ridge is required (17.5km; 1020m; 6h). Better would be to undertake this as a full traverse of the Awful Hand over The Merrick and Benyellary (see panel on page 19), although a vehicle would be required at either end (17km; 1000m; 5h 45min).

Tarfessock with Shalloch on Minnoch beyond, seen from the south-east, en route to Kirriereoch Hill (Rab Anderson)

Corserine from Millfire (Tom Prentice)

Corserine; *814m; (C134); L77; NX497870; crossing point of the Rhinns (of Kells)*

The central and highest point of the long, curving ridge known as the Rhinns of Kells, which runs from north to south between Loch Doon and Clatteringshaws Loch, is Corserine, the second highest of the Galloway hills.

The normal route of ascent is from the east, from a car park at NX552862 near Forrest Lodge. This is gained by following the single-track road which leaves the A713 at Polharrow Bridge just over 2 miles (3.5km) to the north of St John's Town of Dalry.

Walk north towards Forrest Lodge and turn left before the bridge, then follow a track named Birger Natvig Road west along the south side of the Polharrow Burn, past the house at Fore Bush. When the track splits after 2km near Loch Harrow, follow the right branch (Robert Watson Road) north-west across the Polharrow Burn, and continue straight ahead for a further 1km to where the track starts to swing right at NX525874.

Take the track on the left here and follow it across a bridge over the Folk Burn. In a further 300m, turn left

onto a waymarked track, which becomes a prepared path, and emerge from the forestry at an information board with a route map. Ascend the path west onto Craigrine, the north-east ridge of Corserine, to reach the cairn and stone wall of Hennessy's Shelter, then continue up to the summit plateau. The trig point lies towards the west end, at the far side

of the fine north-facing corrie (**6.5km; 690m; 2h 35min**).

Returning the same way is simplest (**13km; 690m; 4h 5min**).

However, it is better to extend the route along the ridge south-south-east to pass over craggy Millfire (716m) and climb onto Milldown (738m) beside a drystane dyke. Drop to the ►

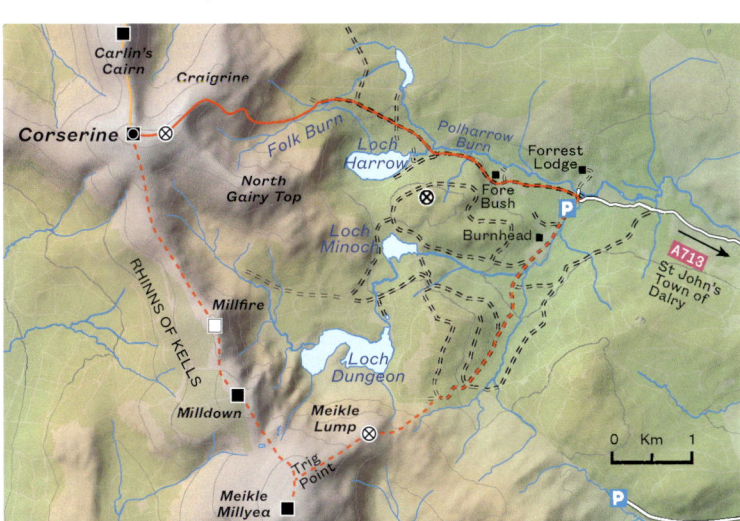

Milldown and Corserine from the Rhinns of Kells ridge (Rab Anderson)

Lochans of Auchniebut, and follow the wall onto Meikle Millyea. The northern top has a trig point and is shown as the 746m highpoint by the OS. However, a more recent OS confirmed survey shows the 749m summit to be located at NX516825, a further 400m along the wall to the south-west (**11.5km; 920m; 4h 10min**).

Return to the trig point, then, just beyond this, cross the wall that joins the one followed on the ascent, and follow it down the north-east ridge.

The wall turns east over Meikle Lump, and is followed down to where the path leaves it to descend north-east past a tiny lochan. Continue steeply down the path, out to the side of the wall, to reach a prominent information board.

Beyond this, a prepared path leads through the forest to a track. Turn right, then right again down the main track, named Prof. Hans Heilberg Road, and follow this for 3km, keeping straight on at all junctions and passing Burnhead, to reach the car park (**17km; 920m; 5h 40min**).

The northern part of the Rhinns of Kells ridge can be climbed from the parking for Cairnsmore of Carsphairn at Bridge-end and Green Well of Scotland. This is described in the SMC's guidebook *The Grahams & The Donalds,* and climbs Corran of Portmark, Bow, Meaul, Carlin's Cairn and Cairnsgarroch. Corserine is included by a there-and-back from Carlin's Cairn, across the col at 708m known as the Riders' Gap (**26km; 1190m; 8h**).

The traverse of the whole Rhinns of Kells ridge is a fine expedition. However, the start and finish are a long way apart, so suitable transport arrangements are necessary. A start can be made from Green Well of Scotland, with a finish either at NX503781 north of Craigencallie House, or at NX558826 at the end of the road along the Garroch Burn from Glenlee.

Corserine seen from between Tarfessock South Top and Kirriereoch Hill to the west (Rab Anderson)

Cairnsmore of Carsphairn across Holm of Daltallochan from the south-west (Tom Prentice)

Cairnsmore of Carsphairn; *797m; (C164); L77; NX594980; moor of cairns, above Carsphairn (carse of alders)*

Rising to the north of the village of Carsphairn, Cairnsmore of Carsphairn forms the highest point of a range of grassy hills that runs north-eastwards from there. Carsphairn is located in the upper valley of The Glenkens, through which the Water of Deugh flows to be met by the Water of Ken before becoming the River Dee and emptying into the Solway Firth.

The main A713 from Ayr to Castle Douglas runs through The Glenkens, and it is from Bridge-end and Green Well of Scotland, about 1km north of Carsphairn and some 10 miles (16km) south of Dalmellington, that the principal approach for the ascent of Cairnsmore of Carsphairn begins.

Immediately to the south of the bridge over the Water of Deugh on the south side of the road opposite the entrance to the approach track past Bridge-end, there is a section of old road where there is ample parking for some 15 or so cars. This is on a bend in the road, so care should be taken on entering and leaving the parking, especially the latter, when anyone wishing to head southwards is perhaps best turning left to head

north first, to either turn left just over the bridge to turn around, or turn around in a track entrance on the opposite side of the road 50m further on.

Leave the parking and carefully cross the road, then go up the track on the opposite side past the cottage. Follow the main track up the floor of the glen alongside the Water of Deugh, shortly passing a curious pool on the left named the Green Well of

Scotland, which folklore reputes to be bottomless and to contain gold guarded by the Devil. Cairnsmore of Carsphairn can be seen in the distance ahead, beyond its foothills, Willieanna and Dunool. Continue past a barn, then follow the stony track uphill, away from the river to pass to the left of a stand of trees and through a gate in a wall across the hillside.

▶

The wall leading to the top of Cairnsmore of Carsphairn (Tom Prentice)

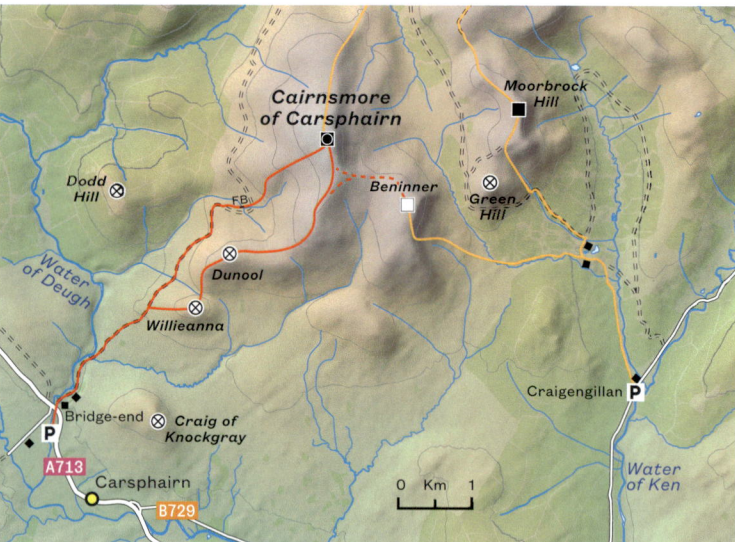

descending the broad south ridge to Black Shoulder (688m), taking care to follow the rough ATV track that swings south-west to meet a fence, rather than go south-east to Beninner (although this could be included by a there-and-back across the Nick of the Lochans col; an added 2km, 125m, 45min. The fence soon meets a wall, which is followed downhill to the south-west then west to Dunool (541m).

Drop steeply into the col with Willieanna, the Nick of Disgee, and go through a gate in a fence. Either follow the fence rightwards downhill to regain the track, or climb steeply up the other side onto the top of Willieanna (430m), then leave the wall and descend rough ground south-westwards to rejoin the track where it passes through the gate in the wall across the hillside. Follow the track back (**12km; 665m; 4h**).

An ascent can also be made from Craigengillan beside the Water of Ken to the south-east, via Moorbrock, as for the circuit described in the SMC's guidebook *The Grahams & The Donalds*; shown on the map but not described here.

Continue on the track past Willieanna and Dunool to where the original track ended at a drystane dyke to the north of Dunool. The track has been extended for tree planting operations, and now curves around the head of the valley ahead, down which the Polsue Burn runs. It is better to leave the track here and follow a rough path alongside the drystane dyke to cross the burn by a footbridge at NX582970.

Continue uphill on the rough path beside the wall, crossing the track extension and passing through bouldery ground higher up, to reach the trig point with an adjacent large cairn on the flat summit of Cairnsmore of Carsphairn (**6km; 610m; 2h 20min**).

The quickest return is back the same way (**12km; 615m; 3h 50min**).

A good circuit can be made by

Cairnsmore of Carsphairn from Dunool (Tom Prentice)

Hart Fell, left, and Under Saddle Yoke from Saddle Yoke (Rab Anderson)

Hart Fell; *808m; (C146); L78; NT113135; hill of the stag*

Located on the east side of the M74 corridor, and well seen from there to those travelling north, is a range of hills that rises above Moffat and extends north-east to include three Corbetts. These are Hart Fell, White Coomb then Broad Law, which is separated from the others by the pass between Talla and Megget Reservoirs. They are mostly steep-sided hills with rounded grassy tops, which give good high-level walking.

Hart Fell occupies a large area of ground in the triangle to the north of Moffat, between the A701 to the Devil's Beef Tub and the A708 up Moffat Dale. These roads provide the start points for the two routes of ascent to Hart Fell.

The standard route starts from the A708 in Moffat Dale, where Hart Fell's south-east aspect rises above the deep subsidiary valley, or corrie, of Black Hope. The route described is a very fine horseshoe around Black Hope, which includes the subsidiary summits of Nether Coomb Craig, Swatte Fell, Falcon Rig, Hartfell Rig, Under Saddle Yoke and Saddle Yoke; the latter two being the steepest and most distinctive peaks in the area.

Start from Blackshope cottage, or Capplegill itself, in Moffat Dale, 5.5 miles (8.8km) to the north-east of Moffat. Blackshope is the white cottage on the north side of the road, just east of the farm at Capplegill and the bridge over the Blackhope Burn. Limited parking is possible at the east side of this cottage, only on the east side of the entrance to the gated track into the Black Hope valley. Take care not to block access to the track, or the garage. There is space by the wall on the opposite verge, and also space on the grass in front of the white building opposite the entrance to Capplegill, some 350m to the west.

From either parking spot, walk along the road to a gate into a field on the west side of a small building on the right bank of the Hang Burn.

Go through the gate and walk up the side of a fence towards the cleft of Hang Gill on the hillside. Climb over a gate and zigzag steeply up the side of Hang Gill. At the top, above a waterfall, go through a sliding gate in an electrified fence, then right through another sliding gate. Continue on a rough path, initially to the side of the burn, then bearing right onto the broad

ridge running up the side of Black Craig to gain the top of Nether Coomb Craig (724m). The slope on the right here plunges steeply into Black Hope, and there are fine views over the corrie to Hart Fell and across to Under Saddle Yoke and Saddle Yoke.

Now following an ATV track, cross the dip and ascend onto the flat top of Swatte Fell. Head across left to the fence and an old wall, then go through a gate to find the highest point, which is some 250m to the south-west along the wall. The OS 1:50k map gives a height of 728m there, whilst the 1:25k map gives a height of 729m some 300m further north-east along the wall where there is a small cairn. The DoBIH confirms the former as being the highest point, but with a height of 730m.

Go back through the gate to follow the wall and fence over Falcon Craig (724m); a cairn on the other side of the fence marks the top. At the narrow neck to the north, the Hass o' the Red Roads, the wall turns and goes down a valley, down which the Auchencat Burn flows into the River Annan. Continue uphill beside the ▶

Hart Fell and the Black Hope valley from Nether Coomb Craig (Rab Anderson)

fence and along the flat top to reach the trig point on Hart Fell (**6.75km; 760m; 2h 45min**).

Swing around the head of the Black Hope valley alongside the fence and descend over Hartfell Rig. Follow the path as it moves away from the fence, which continues north-east to the col with Cape Law, and swing southwards across the head of Whirly Gill. Ascend across the slope then up the broad ridge onto 745m-high Under Saddle Yoke (**10.75km; 910m; 3h 55min**).

Descend steeply to a narrow col then back up the narrow ridge on the other side onto Saddle Yoke (736m). Savour the view to the Ettrick Hills in front, Carrifran Gans and White Coomb to the side, with the Eildons and The Cheviot in the far distance, then plunge down the long south ridge into Moffat Dale. Just before the foot of the ridge, head right to reach the track at a gate, then follow this back (**14.25km; 960m; 5h 10min**).

Another good circuit starts from the A701 to the west, some 5 miles (8km) north of Moffat, at a height of 395m at the top of the Devil's Beef Tub. The Beef Tub is a natural, steep-sided corrie bowl at the head of Annandale, where Border reivers hid stolen cattle.

There is space to park considerably around the entrance to a gated track at NT055128. There is further parking downhill a little. The initial part of the route, to just beyond Chalk Rig Edge, is followed by the Annandale Way long-distance footpath.

Cross the fences to the side of the gate by stiles and climb to the trig point on top of Annanhead Hill (478m) then continue over to Great Hill (466m) with the slopes below falling steeply into the Beef Tub. Continue along the grassy crest of the ridge beside the fence, over Chalk Rig Edge (500m), then drop slightly and climb towards the top of Whitehope Heights, a Donald. Cross the stile in the deer fence to gain the cairn, then return back over the fence. Hart Fell's vast bulk dominates the view east here.

Drop gently north-east through an odd corridor created by a sheep fence on the left and a deer fence on the right, then more steeply east to a narrow col (527m). A long and steep 280m ascent beside the fence gains the flat summit of Hart Fell with its fine panoramic views (**7.5km; 710m; 2h 55min**).

Follow the fence south for 200m, and when this swings away south-east, head south-west on an ATV track down a long, grassy shoulder over Arthur's Seat. Go through a gate in the deer fence and continue down the narrow spur of Well Rig, through the gap between the burns, to pass above Hartfell Spa, a chalybeate

spring thought to have health-giving iron salt properties. At the bottom, go right and through gates to gain a track leading to the minor road up the floor of the glen at Newton.

Turn right and follow the road around the east side of the buildings at Ericstane, then on to the buildings at Corehead, which are rounded in an anti-clockwise direction. A number of gates are passed through to gain an indistinct path which rises up the side of the Devil's Beef Tub to the heights above. This is certainly one of the highlights of the walk, and the final airy traverse to reach the col proves somewhat of a surprise, and not just for weary knees weakened by the ascent! All that remains is a short reascent of Annanhead Hill, beyond which lies the road (**17.5km; 1020m; 5h 55min**).

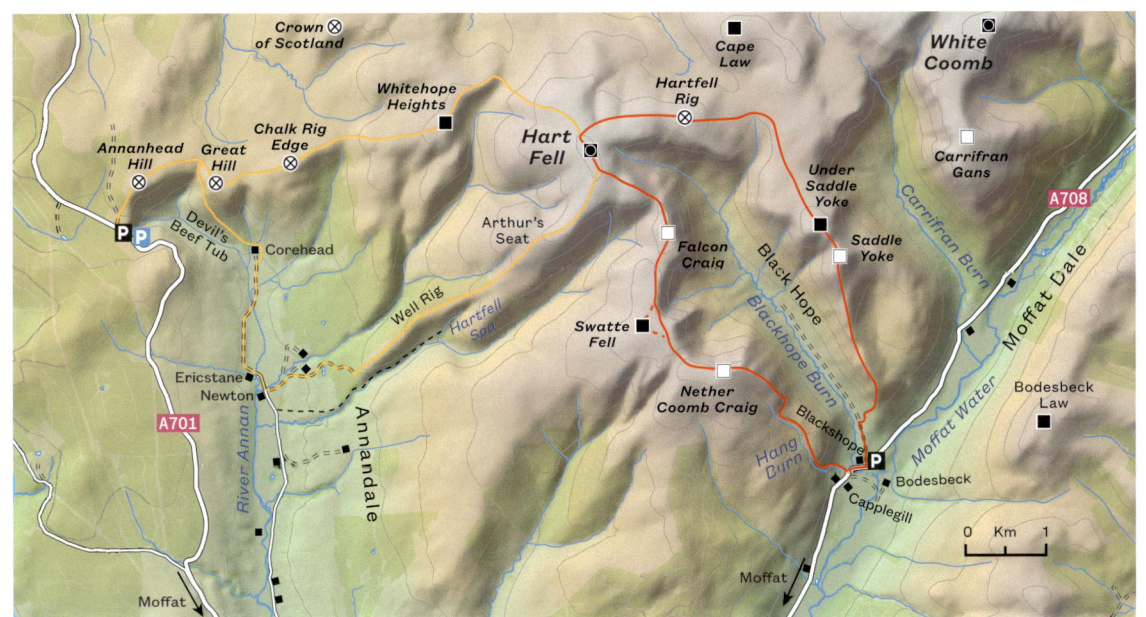

Across Annandale to Whitehope Heights, left, and Hart Fell, centre, from the A701 to the west (Tom Prentice)

White Coomb; *821m; (C123); L79; NT163150; white arched ridge*

To the north-east of Moffat, the high ground rises steeply from the A708 through Moffat Dale to form an extensive area of rounded hills, cut by deep and surprisingly craggy valleys. Hart Fell is the highest of the first group of hills and forms a horseshoe around the Black Hope valley, whilst White Coomb is the highest of the second group and forms part of a horseshoe around the valley enclosing the Grey Mare's Tail waterfall and picturesque Loch Skeen.

The route for White Coomb starts from the National Trust for Scotland pay-and-display car park below the Grey Mare's Tail waterfall.

Ascend the path up and across the steep slope to the north-east of the waterfall. Above the fall, where the path levels off, a wall on the other side of the burn descends from White Coomb high to the left. This leads to a crossing of the burn and is the return route. It can be used as a quick there-and-back route, but it is better to continue along the path beside the Tail Burn to its outflow from idyllic Loch Skeen, where there are two options:

(i) The first option is the shorter, and crosses the outflow via stepping stones, then follows a rough path up the prominent spur of Mid Craig above the loch. Pass over the top at 729m, drop slightly, then ascend via rough paths and sheep tracks to gain the broad ridgeline crest between Firthybrig Head and Donald's Cleuch head. Turn left (south), then climb over Donald's Cleuch Head alongside a fence and an old wall onto Firthhope Rig, where there is a junction of fences and walls. The top actually lies on the other side of the southern fence, where it turns south-west. Follow the south-eastern fence and wall across a dip, then up onto the flat top of White Coomb, and when these diverge, head south for 120m to the summit cairn (**6.75km; 650m; 2h 35min**).

(ii) The second option is a longer traverse of the high ground around Loch Skeen, which includes Lochcraig Head, a Donald. This is shown dashed in red on the map. Go along the east side of the loch for about 200m, then break off right across heather to pick up a fence, which is followed across some boggy ground towards Lochcraig Head. Any other line is likely to prove more difficult. The fence and an old wall running beside it lead up the right side of the steep slope before swinging round and traversing across the flat summit area a short distance south of the actual top itself, which is gained alongside another fence. Drop to the col above the head of the loch, Talla Nick, then climb over Firthybrig Head to join option (i) and follow this to White Coomb. This longer route adds 2km, 100m, 45min to the day.

To descend, return to the wall, then follow this, and a rough path beside it, down the broad eastern spur, encountering a steep section, onto Upper Tarnberry. Continue down to cross the Tail Burn and return down the main path (**9.75km; 660m; 3h 35min**).

The SMC's book *The Grahams & The Donalds* describes the longer route with the inclusion of three

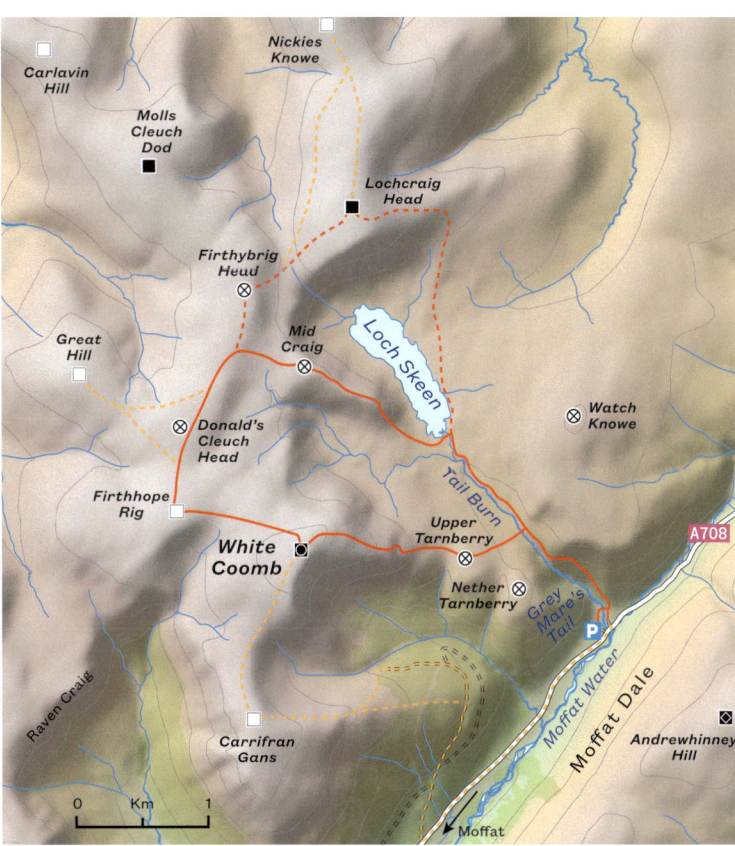

White Coomb and Lochcraig Head from Nowtrig Head (Rab Anderson)

outlying Donald Tops. These are Nickies Knowe, to the north of Lochcraig Head, Great Hill, off to the west, and Carrifran Gans, to the south of White Coomb. The route taking

these in is shown on the map dashed in yellow, and gives a much longer outing (**20.5km; 900m; 6h 30min**).

The SMC's *The Grahams & The Donalds* book also describes a big

round from Talla Linnfoots to the north, which includes all the Donalds and Donald Tops around the Games Hope Burn and valley, together with White Coomb.

White Coomb from the Tail Burn, above the Grey Mare's Tail (Rab Anderson)

> **Broad Law; 840m; (C105); L72; NT146235; broad (flat-topped) hill**

The highest hill in the Scottish Borders, but the second highest hill in the Southern Uplands after The Merrick, Broad Law forms part of a range of high hills between Moffat and Peebles. The range lies between the A701 alongside the River Tweed, and the A708, which runs along St Mary's Loch and the Yarrow Water. The hills here are generally rounded, grassy and dissected into ridges and spurs, giving good walking terrain.

One route ascends the hill from near the Crook Inn, one of Scotland's oldest coaching inn, dating back to 1604, and the place where the newly formed Scottish Mountaineering Club held its first meet in 1891 to climb Broad Law. It may be possible to park at the inn, but there is parking on the River Tweed side of the verge 400m to the south, at NT109260, where the route starts across the bridge to Hearthstane.

Cross the bridge and follow the road, which loops round over the Hearthstane Burn into the farmyard. Continue on a track up the valley and follow it up the side of Glenheurie Rig past forestry, then on up the broad, exposed slope above. In winter, the track fills with snow and gives arduous walking. When the track

forks at the top, go right to the circular-canopied NATS (National Air Traffic Services) building, then on to the trig pillar 100m to the south (**5.75km; 610m; 2h 15min**).

The only other distinguishing features on the summit are the aerial to the north-east and the fence. The view, however, is expansive, although the summit is set too far back to be able to see into the valleys.

Returning the same way is quickest (**11.5km; 610m; 3h 45min**).

However, it is much better to make a horseshoe traverse of the Hearthstane valley. To do this, descend the broad ridge southwards by the fence to where it splits, then go right and descend across the head of the Hearthstane valley, above the steep slope dropping to Talla Reservoir to the south. Climb onto Talla Cleuch Head (690m), a Donald, still following the fence, then descend north and north-west to Mathieside Cairn (669m).

Leave the fence and follow a rough ATV track northwards down the long ridge onto the minor rise of Snout Hill (511m). Continue beside a fence and above forestry, passing over Manyleith Head (475m) and onto the final rise of Hog Hill (487m). Drop down into the Tweed valley beside the fence

onto a track to the south of a communications aerial. Go along the track to just before the aerial, then drop down left across an old wall and through a gate to descend beside another wall to gain a lower track. Turn right along this back to Hearthstane and the start (**14.75km; 740m; 4h 45min**).

Talla Cleuch Head and Broad Law from Laird's Cleuch Rig to the south-west (Rab Anderson)

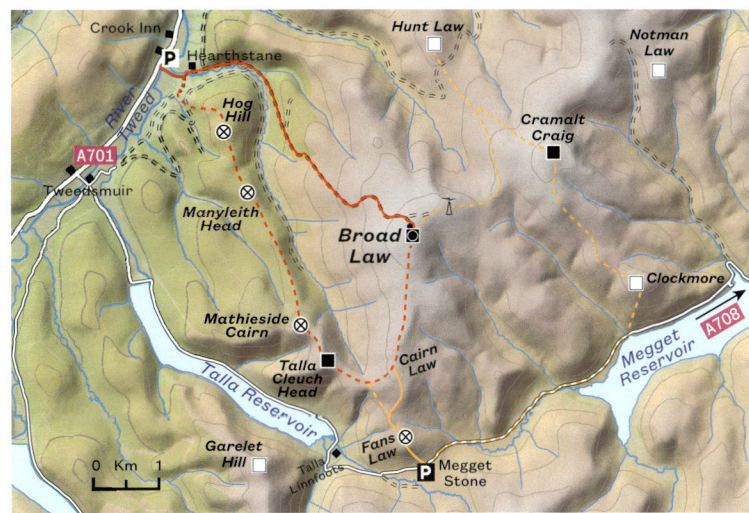

Broad Law across Hearthstane and the Tweed Valley from Crook Hill (Rab Anderson)

A much shorter route starts from the highpoint of the road at 450m between Talla Reservoir and Megget Reservoir. The road crosses from the A701 at Tweedsmuir to the A708 at St Mary's Loch. Parking is limited, but there is space for a few well-parked cars at the cattle grid beside the Megget Stone boundary marker.

Ascend an ATV track up the hillside to the right of the fence above the cattle grid onto Fans Law. Cross flat ground and swing round beside the fence. Continue uphill for a short distance before crossing the fence and cutting north-west up and across the slope to reach another fence coming down off Cairn Law. Make a gradual 2km ascent beside this fence to gain the trig point (**3.75km; 400m; 1h 30min**).

Return the same way (7.5km; 410m; 2h 30min).

The SMC guidebook *The Grahams & The Donalds* describes a route from here over Broad Law, which includes all the Donalds and Donald Tops, with a return up the road from Megget Reservoir. This route is shown dashed in yellow on the map, but not described (20.5km; 970m; 6h 30min).

The National Air Traffic facility on the summit of Broad Law (Rab Anderson)

The Cobbler's South Peak, Centre Peak
and North Peak from the south-east ridge
(Rab Anderson)

SECTION 1a
Loch Fyne to Loch Lomond

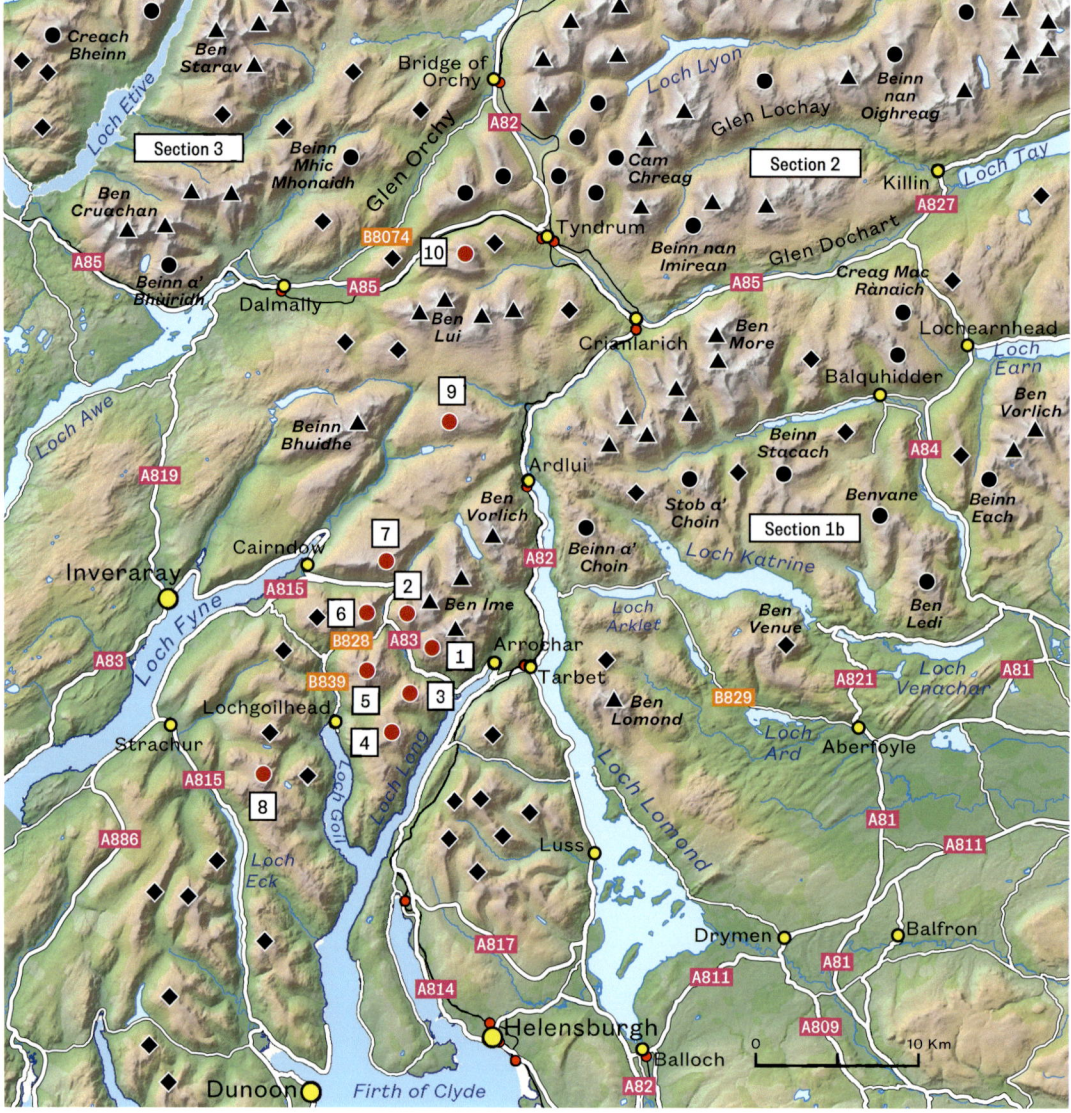

SECTION 1a

The Cobbler's South Peak, Centre Peak and North Peak from above the Allt a' Bhalachain (Rab Anderson)

The Cobbler (Ben Arthur); 884m; (C43); L56; NN259058

To the west of the village of Arrochar at the head of Loch Long, there is a rugged group of mountains known as The Arrochar Alps, which contains seven closely-grouped Corbetts. Undoubtedly, the most distinctive of these, probably of any Corbett, is The Cobbler, whose three jagged rock peaks create a magnificent spectacle. The Cobbler has long been regarded as one of Scotland's finest mountains and its proximity to Glasgow also makes it one of the most popular.

Despite The Cobbler's formidable appearance, the ascent is easy, apart from the last few metres onto the spectacular summit block, where some rock climbing ability and a good head for heights is called for.

The ascent is made from one of two pay-and-display car parks at the head of Loch Long. The east one is run by the Loch Lomond & the Trossachs National Park and the west one by Argyll & Bute District Council. These can be busy and they are expensive; in 2025 the cost was £1.20 per hour. Note that route times given here do not include for stops.

Leave the south end of the west car park and cross the road to follow a prepared path, which zigzags up the hillside onto a forestry track. Go left and cross over to ascend the zigzag continuation path, and emerge from the trees to reach a small dam on the Allt a' Bhalachain (Buttermilk Burn).

Continue beside the burn into Coire a' Bhalachain to the large Narnain Boulders, then on for 350m or so to where the path forks. The left-hand path ascends into the east-facing corrie below the North Peak to gain the col between it and the Centre Peak, whilst the main right-hand path continues by the burn to the col with Beinn Narnain, then ascends up the back via the north ridge.

It is possible to go up one path and return by the other. The left-hand option, as well as being shorter, is more scenic earlier in the day due to the light. However, it is steeper and rockier, and although not difficult, it is much easier in ascent than descent. The right-hand option is longer but easier, especially in descent.

To ascend via the left-hand path, cross the burn and follow the path up through the lower rocks, then climb into the upper corrie past more rocks. The spectacular prows and rock faces of the North Peak soar above, and are home to many rock and winter climbs. Continue up past these rocks ▶

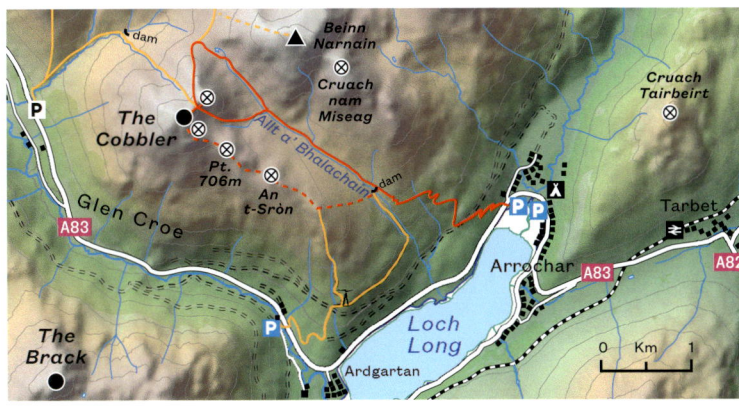

The Cobbler's exposed summit pedestal, with Ben Lomond, left (Tom Prentice)

to the col between the peaks.

The route to the Centre Peak now climbs south-west up the side of a broad ridge to a flat top opposite the distinctive summit rock pedestal. Most people are content to go no higher (**5.25km; 890m; 2h 40min**).

Those who wish to attain the highest point can slide through a polished hole, then follow an exposed ledge on the south side and make a potentially awkward move to climb onto this most airy of perches.

Return to the col, then make the short ascent, with a little easy scrambling, to the top of the spectacular North Peak. Regain the col, then follow the path northwards onto the north ridge and down the side of this in zigzags to the col with Beinn Narnain. Those with time and energy could climb either Beinn Ìme or Beinn Narnain, or both. Otherwise, simply follow the main path down into Coire a' Bhalachain, back past the Narnain Boulders, to return as for the ascent route (**11.75km; 930m; 4h 30min**).

A variation, which also makes a good circuit, is to ascend the south-east ridge. This is gained from the dam on the Allt a' Bhalachain, either crossing below or above it. A path leads up a grassy slope onto the start of the ridge. Continue over the minor knolls of An t-Sròn (614m) and Pt.706m, then climb to and beneath the South Peak's South Face. Gain the col between the peaks, then continue steeply up the side of the

Centre Peak's south ridge to the top (**5km; 920m; 2h 40min**).

Climb the North Peak, then return via the main path down the north ridge (**11.5km; 960m; 4h 30min**).

The south-east ridge can also be climbed by a tougher circuit starting from Forestry and Land Scotland's car park (NN269036) at Ardgartan at the foot of Glen Croe.

Leave the south end of the car park, following the Cowal Way path, and cross the A83. The path makes a long traverse, then zigzags uphill into the forest. Just inside the conifers, and before a bench at the start of a track, follow a rough path uphill through the trees to emerge onto a higher track. Go left, then right along

another track to a communications mast, then ascend the grassy track opposite, which leads out of the trees. Climb tussocky ground above the treeline to gain the south-east ridge at the point the path from the dam arrives, then continue up this to the top (**5km; 910m; 2h 40min**).

Traverse to the North Peak, then go down the north ridge path and descend past the Narnain Boulders to the dam. Cross above or below the dam, then follow an old path down through the trees between the main burn on the left and a parallel-running burn on the right. Leave this path at the 170m contour, just before the burn on the right joins and creates an awkward rocky section. Gain a clearing on the right, then the start of a grassy track, and follow this back to the communications mast to return as for the ascent down through the trees (**12km; 950m; 4h 40min**).

The summit of The Cobbler's South Peak can only be attained by a rock climb. The easiest way is from the col with the Centre Peak. It is a short, exciting, but polished and slippery climb, graded Moderate, on which many use a rope to abseil back down.

The panel on page 38 describes a circuit around Coire Croe. The descent from The Cobbler to the parking on this route can be used as an ascent route. However, this is not an attractive way, and with a 2h 50min there-and-back time, it is simply a means of ticking the peak quickly.

North Peak with Ben Vane, Ben Vorlich and Beinn Narnain (Rab Anderson)

Across Glen Croe from Ben Donich to Beinn Luibhean and Beinn Ìme, with Stob Coire Creagach, left (Tom Prentice)

Beinn Luibhean; 858m; (C80); L56; NN242079; hill of the little plants

Rising steeply above the Rest and be Thankful pass at the head of Glen Croe, Beinn Luibhean is the south-western outlier of Beinn Ìme, the highest of The Arrochar Alps. A high col separates the pair: the Bealach a' Mhargaidh (c.675m).

The usual route up Beinn Luibhean is via its south ridge, which catches the sun, even in the winter. This is also the most direct route, as well as a good start for a longer traverse around the corrie, Coire Croe, which includes Beinn Ìme and The Cobbler, and perhaps even Beinn Narnain; see panel on page 38.

Start from a small car park at NN242060 in Glen Croe, on the east side of the road immediately south of a bridge the A83 crosses before the landslip zone and stabilisation works.

Go through a gate, cross a bridge over the burn, then ascend a path and go up through a gate in the deer fence above onto the open hillside.

Continue a short way, then leave the main path by the burn to climb north up the broad and grassy ridge, which leads directly to the summit; a short and easy ascent (**2km; 700m; 1h 35min**).

The view to the north-east is blocked by pointed Beinn Ìme, but in an arc from north to south all six of the other Arrochar Corbetts can be seen, whilst to the right of Cnoc Còinnich, and beyond Arran, Ailsa Craig floats in the sea on the horizon.

Return by the route of ascent (**4km; 700m; 2h 20min**).

A more satisfactory ascent can be made via the north ridge. Either park at a track entrance at NN236092 on the east side of the A83, or at the Butterbridge parking area around the bend to the north.

From the track entrance, pass through a walkers' gate and follow a short section of track to where it turns right then go up a path on the left to a communications mast. Cross

the deer fence by a stile, then follow a path up the side of the fence for a short way before dropping to the burn to follow the path beside this, thereby avoiding boggy ground next to the fence.

The same point is reached from the Butterbridge parking area by walking ▶

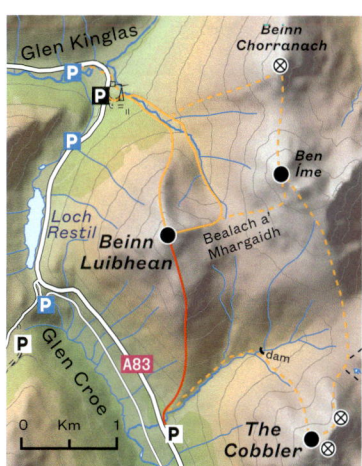

along the road to the end of the crash barrier, then going through a gate to ascend past a ruined building.

Just beyond the top edge of the forestry plantation, go through a gate in the deer fence which cuts across the hillside on its way to the col between Beinn Luibhean and Beinn Ìme. Climb up and slightly right to gain a depression, and follow this steeply up left onto a little flattening on a crest. Continue above to gain the north ridge proper, then zigzag up this on an intermittent rough path to the summit (**2.25km; 660m; 1h 45min**).

Descend the east ridge, which is rocky in places, to gain the Bealach a' Mhargaidh, then go left and through a gate in the deer fence at NN249080.

Drop to the main burn and follow a rough path down beside this. If the more direct line to the left of the burn is taken, there are some small drops to negotiate, and the terrain is steeper than the map suggests. Continue down by the burn to rejoin the ascent route below the gate in the deer fence, and return to the start (5.25km; 670m; 2h 45min).

The north ridge route can be extended to include Beinn Ìme from

---

Beinn Luibhean, Beinn Ìme and The Cobbler
This is a fine circuit around Coire Croe taking in Beinn Luibhean, Beinn Ìme, and The Cobbler, and possibly Beinn Narnain.

*Climb Beinn Luibhean by its south ridge, as described on page 37 (**2km; 680m; 1h 35min**).*

*Descend the east ridge, rocky in places, to gain the Bealach a' Mhargaidh. There is a deer fence across the hillside here, which prevents a more direct route unless one climbs the fence. There is a gate at NN249080, down to the left. Once through this, follow the fence uphill to where it veers off right, then ascend the slope to gain a path on the shoulder, then Beinn Ìme's summit (**4.5km; 1020m; 2h 50min**).*

*Descend to the Bealach a' Mhàim, then go through a gate and continue past the two paths off up to Beinn Narnain to gain another col. Ascend the path that zigzags up The Cobbler's north ridge to gain the col with the North Peak, then turn right and climb to the top (**7.75km; 1280m; 4h 15min**).*

Return to the col and climb the North Peak, then go back down the path for a short way before descending north-west by the burn that drains the corrie on this side of the mountain; there is a rough path. Cross the burn in the floor of the corrie just below a dam, then follow the path on the other side back to the start (10.75km; 1320m; 5h 25min).

Including Beinn Narnain, via the paths up and down its north-west ridge, is an additional 2.5km, 290m, 1h 20min there and back.

---

the Bealach a' Mhargaidh. Either detour slightly and go through the gate in the deer fence at NN249080, or take a more direct route and climb the fence. Beyond the fence, the steepening slope leads to the path up Beinn Ìme, then its summit (**4.75km; 1000m; 3h**).

Descend north to the Glas Bhealach (c.750m) with Beinn Chorranach, then either descend west beside the Allt Beinn Ìme, or better, climb Beinn Chorranach (888m), then descend the slope to the west, and return to the start (7.75km; 1135m; 4h 30min).

Beinn Luibhean and its north ridge from Butterbridge, with Beinn Ìme left (Rab Anderson)

The Brack across Glen Croe, with Loch Long, left, Cnoc Còinnich's summit, centre, and Beinn Bheula, right (Rab Anderson)

The Brack; *787m; (C178); L56; NN245030; speckled hill*

Together with Ben Donich and Cnoc Còinnich, The Brack is one of three Corbetts located on the Ardgoil Peninsula. The estate here was purchased by Archibald C. Corbett (no relation to John R. Corbett) in 1905 and gifted to the citizens of Glasgow as an area of mountain landscape for recreation. Now in public ownership, it forms part of the Argyll Forest Park, managed by Forestry and Land Scotland.

Overlooking Ardgartan and Arrochar at the head of Loch Long, The Brack is a rugged hill that sits opposite The Cobbler at the entrance to Glen Croe. Its north face above this glen is particularly steep and rocky, holding an impressively dark and gloomy crag high up beneath the summit. The long and broad east ridge, Cruach Fhiarach, extends towards Ardgartan, but its flanks are extensively forested and there are no ascent routes on that part of the hill.

The standard route is via the steep northern corrie between Cruach Fhiarach and The Brack, starting from the Forestry and Land Scotland car park, building and toilets at the foot of Glen Croe at NN269036. There is further parking on the other side of the bridge over the Croe Water.

Cross the Croe Water, then turn right and go along the forest track for some 2km to where another track goes off left after a bend. Continue along the right-hand track for a further 100m to just before the burn that cascades down from The Brack. Turn off left and follow a signed path steeply uphill to the left of the burn. There is a brief scramble at the start.

Exit the forest and step over a fence to gain the open hillside, then continue on the path, which crosses to the other side of the burn. The steep ascent continues beside the cascading burn, passing to the left of a lower crag, then on up between some huge boulders at the foot of the larger crags of the north face.

Continue up a shallow grassy corrie, below some smaller crags and pinnacles, to gain the east ridge at an idyllic little lochan with some large boulders in it. Turn right here and follow the path up, then left above the lochan into a grassy depression.

At the top of the depression, a left traverse is followed by a further steep climb and a sudden finish to gain the trig point (**4km; 760m; 2h 15min**).

Return the same way (**8km; 770m; 3h 30min**).

Another option is to descend the northern ridge. On reaching the top of a deep gully cleft, break left off the ridge to avoid rocks lower down and descend a grassy watercourse. At the Bealach Dubh-lic, cross a fence to pick up a rough path with marker posts then follow this down into the forest at NN240045. Drop to a track, then turn right to regain the upward route and return (**10km; 780m; 4h**).

This option would enable Ben Donich to be included from the bealach by climbing up and back down its east ridge; an added 4.5km, 470m, 2h. However, the combination of the two hills is probably better undertaken, and a little quicker, from the Rest and Be Thankful, as described for Ben Donich on page 43

Another descent option is to go down the broad and hummocky

▶

The south-west ridge of The Brack, with The Cobbler beyond (Tom Prentice)

south-west ridge to a small lochan. Go through the gap beyond this lochan, then drop left off the ridge and descend below the crags on the knoll at the bottom to join the Cowal Way path from Lochgoilhead to Ardgartan. This path passes through the col with Cnoc Còinnich on the far side of a small lochan, and is followed down to the east to enter the forestry area by a gate.

Descend to a track, then either go left then down this, or take the path to its side, which joins the track lower down. Continue down Coilessan Glen, keeping right at a fork, to cross the Coilessan Burn by a bridge and carry on downhill to a T-junction. Turn left over the burn again to reach the Coilessan parking area, then follow the access road back for 3km (**12.5km; 780m; 4h 30min**).

This option enables Cnoc Còinnich to the south to be included by crossing the col between the hills, then ascending its northern ridge and returning to the col; an added 3.5km, 280m, 1h 30min.

However, the two hills are probably better, and quicker, climbed from the Coilessan Glen parking area used for the ascent of Cnoc Còinnich, as described opposite.

Map on opposite page

Cnoc Còinnich, The Brack & Ben Donich

These three closely-grouped Corbetts on the Ardgoil Peninsula can be climbed together in a fine single outing from Lochgoilhead, starting from the public car park at NN200013 on the east shore of Loch Goil. The initial part of the route follows the Cowal Way, which passes through the col between Cnoc Còinnich and The Brack.

From the north end of the car park, cross diagonally left over the road and turn right into a lane. Follow it past public toilets and the Scout Centre, continuing ahead onto a path which swings right to a junction with a track. Turn left onto the track, then take the right fork (a path also cuts the corner), and ascend north, then east, beside forestry into Donich Glen, to a bridge over the Allt Airigh na Creige at NN213017.

Just after this, turn right onto a path signed Coilessan Hill Path, and follow it to a forest break. Ascend this to the right of a burn, boggy in places and with occasional white posts, to cross a stile onto the open hillside. Continue on a vague grassy path which veers up and left, following posts towards the col between The Brack and Cnoc Còinnich. Leave the path as it levels out, then climb Cnoc Còinnich's broad north ridge, passing a small lochan near the top, to gain the summit cairn perched on a crag (**4.5km; 760m; 2h 15min**).

Return to the col, then climb The Brack by its south-west ridge, bypassing craggy Pt.578m to its east (**8km; 1060m; 3h 45min**).

Descend the north-west ridge and the slope to its left to gain the Bealach Dubh-lic, then ascend the east ridge of Ben Donich (**11.75km; 1525m; 5h 40min**).

To make the long descent to Lochgoilhead, go down the south ridge; the Sròn Coire Caorach. Lower down, head for the corner of a fence below a large boulder: Clach a' Bhreatunnaich. Traverse right along the fence above the forestry then cross the fence and go down a path onto a forest track. Turn left and go along this for 150m then go down a path on the right to cut across the head of track and cross a bridge over the Allt Coire Odhar (Donich Water on some maps) to rejoin the upward route and follow this over the bridge across the Allt Airigh na Creige back to the start (**17.75km; 1525m; 7h 15min**).   **Map on opposite page**

*Cnoc Còinnich; 764m; (C220);
L56; NN233007; mossy knoll*

Formerly one of the highest Grahams, Cnoc Còinnich was surveyed in 2016 and found to be 3m higher than previously thought, and therefore promoted to Corbett status.

Located on the Ardgoil Peninsula between Loch Goil to the west and Loch Long to the east, Cnoc Còinnich can be climbed from either of those sides. Since it lies to the south of The Brack, and is connected to the latter by a col at c.485m, it can easily be combined with that mountain. Together with Ben Donich and The Brack, Cnoc Còinnich forms a closely-grouped trio of Corbetts, and if the ascent is made from the west, all three can be climbed; see panel on the opposite page.

The eastern approach to Cnoc Còinnich is via Coilessan Glen, and starts from a parking area at NN258011, at the end of the narrow forestry road along the west side of Loch Long. This is accessed from the Forestry and Land Scotland car park, building and toilets at the foot of Glen Croe, just off the A83 at Ardgartan, where the normal route to The Brack

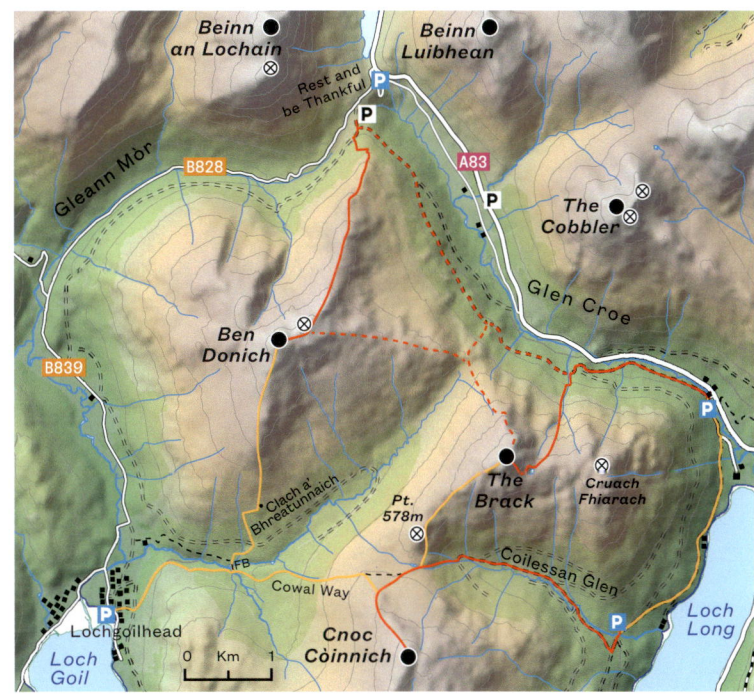

starts. Much of the route follows the Cowal Way, which passes through the col between the hills on the way to Lochgoilhead.

Go through a gate (often locked) at the start of a forest track, and cross the Coilessan Burn, then turn right at the first junction, following the

Coilessan Glen Road sign. Ascend the main track past a track off left, then cross the burn and continue uphill past another track which cuts back sharply right.

Higher, towards the head of the glen, where a track breaks off right to ▶

The Brack and Cnoc Còinnich above Lochgoilhead (Tom Prentice)

contour below The Brack. Either follow the track straight ahead, which swings left across a burn to reach a path up through the trees, or take the path on the left beside the burn, which crosses the track further up.

Either way, continue uphill on the path to exit the forestry area by a gate and climb past occasional white posts to gain the col with The Brack, where there is a small lochan. Head off left at some point to pick the least boggy route onto the north ridge of Cnoc Còinnich, then ascend this ridge, passing above some crags.

Higher up, a small lochan is passed just before the summit cairn, which is perched on a crag overlooking the east face high above Loch Long (**4.75km; 665m; 2h 5min**).

Return by the same route (**9.5km; 665m; 3h 30min**).

The western approach starts from a large public car park at NN200013 in Lochgoilhead on the east shore of Loch Goil. Much of the route follows the Cowal Way, which passes through the col between the hills on the way to Ardgartan.

From the north end of the car park, cross diagonally left over the road and turn right onto a tarmac lane. Follow it past public toilets and the Scout Centre, continuing ahead onto a path which swings right to a junction with a track. Turn left onto the track, then take the right fork (a path also cuts the corner), which ascends north then east beside forestry into Donich Glen, to reach a bridge over the Allt Airigh na Creige at NN213017.

Just after this, turn right onto a path signposted Coilessan Hill Path and continue to a forest break. Ascend this to the right of the burn, boggy in places and with occasional white posts, to cross a stile and gain the open hillside. Continue on an ill-defined grassy path which veers up and left, following posts towards the col between The Brack and Cnoc Còinnich. Leave the path as it starts to level out, then climb the broad north ridge of Cnoc Còinnich, passing a small lochan, to gain the summit cairn perched on a crag above the east face (**4.5km; 760m; 2h 15min**).

Return the same way (**9km; 760m; 3h 35min**).

From either of these routes, it is straightforward enough to include The Brack by ascending its south-west ridge from the small lochan at the connecting col at c.485m. Craggy Pt.578m is normally bypassed to its east to gain a small lochan at the start of the ridge proper. Return the same way; an added 3.5km, 300m, 1h 35min.

If the ascent of The Brack is made via the Ardgartan route, then Cnoc Còinnich can also be included from there, with a return made via Coilessan Glen; see page 39.

Ben Donich; 847m; (C95); L56; NN218043; brown hill

Cnoc Còinnich from Ben Donich (Tom Prentice)

Ben Donich occupies a commanding position in the angle between Lochgoilhead, Gleann Mòr and Glen Croe, overlooking the Rest and be Thankful pass. Ridges radiate from the summit to the four compass points and the hill is almost entirely surrounded by forest, some of which has been felled and replanted.

The normal route of ascent is via the north ridge, which provides a direct route from the B828 at the head of Gleann Mòr, 500m south of the Rest and be Thankful. There is parking for about 12 cars just inside the entrance to a forest track on the south side of the road. If busy, the car park at the Rest and be Thankful can be used. With a starting height of 290m, and a path following the ridge,

The rock step on Ben Donich's north ridge – Beinn Luibhean, Beinn Ìme, Beinn Narnain and The Cobbler behind (Rab Anderson)

it is a short and quite easy outing.

Walk along the track past a track off left, then take a path on the left signed to Ben Donich, and zigzag up through the trees to exit the forestry area by a gate and climb steeply onto the start of the north ridge. Continue up the ridge and traverse along the side of some grassy knolls. There is a fine view ahead of the ridge rising up the side of a shallow corrie, which is topped by a line of cliffs from which an impressive jumble of boulders has slipped.

On reaching the rise, there are some rock fissures, typical of the mica schist in this area, and care should be taken if there is snow on the ground covering these, since some of the fissures are quite deep.

At the top of the rise, the path reaches a step where the ridge has slipped on three sides, and a climb

has to be made down a short wall to pass through the boulders. The bottom step down should be the only tricky bit, and, whilst not difficult, it is unavoidable. Beyond this, a steeper climb leads over easy-angled ground, then across a slight dip with a final short climb to the trig point on the summit (**4km; 580m; 1h 50min**).

Return the same way (**8km; 600m; 3h 5min**).

This route can be extended to climb The Brack by returning to the dip to the north-east, then descending the indistinct east ridge to reach the col between the hills; the Bealach Dubh-lic (384m). At the bottom of this descent, the natural lie of the land leads towards two bands of crags on the right (south) side, so these need to be avoided.

Cross a fence, then ascend the steepening slope to the right of The

Brack's indistinct north-west ridge to gain an easing and fine viewpoint overlooking the corrie to the east. From there, make the final ascent to the trig point (**7.5km; 990m; 3h 30min**).

Return to the Bealach Dubh-lic and cross it to pick up the line of a rough path marked with white posts. Follow this northwards and drop through some boulders to gain a forest break at NN240045, then the main forest track. The track is followed northwards through the forest for 2.5km to regain the start (**12.25km; 1100m; 5h 10min**).

These ridges above the Bealach Dubh-lic can also be used to include Ben Donich following an ascent of The Brack via its normal route from Ardgartan; see page 39.

The panel on page 40 describes the ascent of Cnoc Còinnich, The Brack and Ben Donich from Lochgoilhead.

Map on page 41

Beinn an Lochain rising above Loch Restil, from Beinn Luibhean (Rab Anderson)

Beinn an Lochain; *901m; (C19): L56; NN218079; hill of the little loch*

Rising prominently above the road through the Rest and be Thankful pass at the head of Glen Croe, Beinn an Lochain presents an impressive sight. Its rocky east face rises steeply above Loch Restil in a succession of rocky crags and grass terraces, whilst the eye is drawn to the long and elegant north-east ridge which falls towards Glen Kinglas. It is this ridge that provides the route of ascent.

Park in a layby on the west side of the road, 600m beyond the north end of Loch Restil; there is also a pull-off on the other side of the road. Step over the crash barrier and cross the burn, normally straightforward. If the water is a little high, it may be better to cross at an island just upstream by a step and a jump.

Two paths cross boggy ground to join at a boulder, from where the base of the north-east ridge is gained. The route up the ridge has become rutted and boggy, and there are a numerous little eroded-out rock steps to negotiate, with bypass options on steep grass to the side. In the wet, some care is required. Despite this, the ridge provides a splendid and scenic highway.

The initial section of the ridge rises to a knoll (637m), beyond which the path drops slightly before cutting steeply up right above a line of crags to avoid the rocky crest. Exit the traverse by a slabby rock groove, then traverse back up left onto the crest. Under cover of snow, this section requires care, especially in descent.

Easier-angled ground follows for a way, above a boulder-strewn and steep north-facing corrie, heading towards the mountain's upper crags named The Old Man's Face; note the impressive boulder on a pedestal over to the right. The path steepens again for the ascent of the summit pyramid, initially on the crest, then traversing up and left to exit onto easier grassy ground leading to a cairn on a grassy knoll. A survey in 2015 determined that the highest point is the next knoll, 100m to the south-west, on the far side of a slight dip (**3km; 700m; 2h**).

Although the usual return is made by the route of ascent, it is better to drop southwards off the summit pyramid, almost to the col with the south top (834m), then traverse back north beneath the pyramid, following a rough path along a grass terrace. Regain the north-east ridge and follow the path back down, which can be surprisingly time-consuming (**6.5km; 725m; 3h 15min**).

A descent can also be made from the south top (834m), eastward towards the Rest and be Thankful pass, then northwards alongside Loch Restil.

Stob Coire Creagach; 817m; (C128); L56; NN230109; peak of the craggy corrie

The north side of Glen Kinglas is dominated through its 10km length down to Loch Fyne by a high ridge, whose southern slopes drop in a single sweep from the summits down to the glen. There are a number of tops on the ridge, of which Stob Coire Creagach (unnamed on the OS 1:50k map) is the highest.

Sitting centrally on the ridge, Stob Coire Creagach rises steeply above the bend in Glen Kinglas, at the point it is joined by the glen of the Bealach an Easain Duibh coming down from the Rest and be Thankful at the head of Glen Croe. As a result, Stob Coire Creagach features prominently in the view ahead when travelling north on the A83 coming down from the Rest and be Thankful, where it also becomes apparent that the climb will be steep and relentless.

The ascent is made from a large parking area directly beneath the summit, and just west of the bridge over the Kinglas Water where the A83 bends west into Glen Kinglas near Butterbridge. To the south of the parking, there is a fine, arched stone bridge over the Kinglas Water, built in 1743 under the direction of Major Caulfield, General Wade's successor.

Turn right out of the car park and walk along the verge, then cross the road to a track entrance. Go through

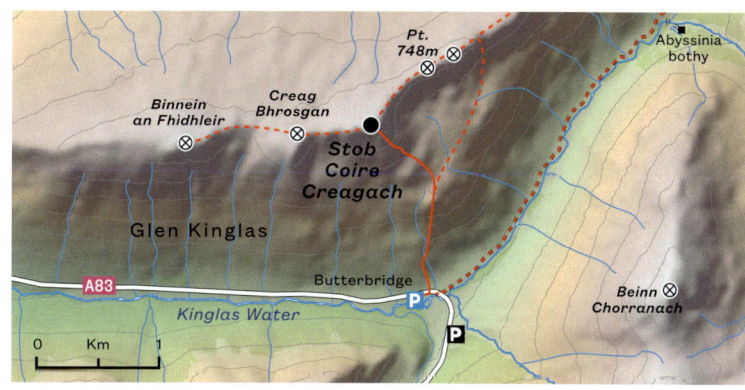

a side gate, then leave the track to go through a gate on the left. Ascend to the right of the fence, through an area planted with native trees such as birch, rowan and Scots pine. At the top of this area, move right over the burn to cross a deer fence by a stile.

Ascend rightwards through boulders to gain, then climb a shallow grassy gully, which gives an obvious way through a broken line of crags to gain an easing on the shoulder of the north-east ridge. Bear north-west up the grassy ridge to the final steepening, where a few small crags are bypassed to gain the summit (**1.75km; 640m; 1h 30min**).

Return the same way (**3.5km; 640m; 2h 15min**).

To lengthen what is a short outing, there are two options:

(i) Traverse west over Creag Bhrosgan (771m) to Binnein an Fhìdhleir (811m) with its trig point to enjoy the view out to Loch Fyne. It is probably best to return to Stob Coire Creagach and descend; an added 3.5km, 265m, 1h 20min.

(ii) Traverse north-east over Pt.748m above Coire Creagach and along the undulating ridge above a line of crags. This leads in 3km to Pt.596m at the end of the hill, where a less steep descent can be made into the head of Glen Kinglas for a return by the track down the glen; an added 8km, 70m, 2h 15min.

Beyond Pt.748m, it is possible to descend a gully and traverse a shelf beneath the crags to regain the approach route above the shallow grassy gully.

Creag Bhrosgan, left, and Stob Coire Creagach from the foot of Beinn an Lochain (Rab Anderson)

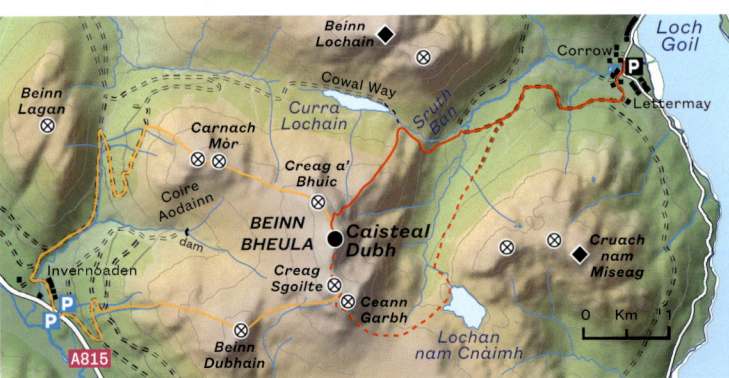

Beinn Bheula across Loch Goil, with Caisteal Dubh, centre, and Beinn Lochain, far right (Tom Prentice)

BEINN BHEULA, *hill of mouths or ford*
Caisteal Dubh; *779m; (C190); L56; NS154983; black castle*

West of Lochgoilhead is an area of steep and craggy hills with dense coniferous forests along their lower slopes, of which Beinn Bheula is the highest. Its east face is well seen from Lochgoilhead and is quite rocky, with many crags and escarpments above the forested glen of the Lettermay Burn. It is from this side that the hill is usually climbed. An ascent can also be made from the west side, from Invernoaden.

The ascent from Lochgoilhead is made from Lettermay, a short way down the west side of Loch Goil from its head. Parking is limited, but after leaving the side of the loch and passing the Drimsynie Estate Office entrance at Corrow, the single-track road widens to two lanes, and it is possible to park off the road on the left-hand verge. This is just before the road narrows and crosses the bridge over the Lettermay Burn.

Walk across the bridge over the Lettermay Burn, then turn up the track on the right and take the first track off left. The initial part of the route follows the Cowal Way, which is signed in places. Swing up right past the access track to some houses and a track off left, following the main track up into the Lettermay Forest past a gate. Continue uphill past a track off left, with Beinn Lochain filling the view ahead, and swing around into the glen past a minor track off right, where the view expands to take in the Sruth Bàn waterfall and Beinn Bheula.

Take the main track downhill to the right and cross the bridge over the Lettermay Burn. Turn off left here and follow a path up a clearing to a rougher path, then out into the open. Continue more steeply uphill on the south side of the Sruth Bàn and its waterfalls, which flow from Curra Lochain. A left then a right traverse leads to level ground near the top of

summit crest between Caisteal Dubh and its northern termination, Creag a' Bhuic (739m). Turn left (south) and make the final climb to the trig pillar on smooth, short-cropped grass (**5.5km; 800m; 2h 30min**).

The simplest option is to return the same way (11km; 830m; 4h 10min).

However, a traverse can be made by continuing south along the broad ridge for 750m onto Creag Sgoilte (767m). Drop off this, then, just before the rise to Ceann Garbh at the end of the ridge, descend south-south-west to avoid crags below. Once on less steep ground, the scattered remains of a Royal Navy Grumman Wildcat Martlet fighter, which crashed in 1940, may be seen. Before reaching the broad col with Cnoc na Trì Crìche, bear east, then north-east across grassy slopes to a path shown on OS maps, which has almost disappeared, and continue down to Lochan nan Cnàimh and its outflow.

A rough path appears and is followed across a fence into the forest and down the left side of the burn for a short way before crossing to the right bank. If the water is high, cross somewhere between the lochan and the fence along the forest, then go down the far side. Continue north-north-east along a firebreak on a descending line, crossing wet and muddy sections. Towards the end, go under a fallen tree, then up right onto a better path leading to a track, which is followed back (12.5km; 830m; 4h 30min).

The route from the west is a circuit

of Coire Aodainn. Extensive planting and a deer fence are likely to make any route into this corrie impractical.

Start from Forestry and Land Scotland's Lauder Monument Car Park at NS122975, off the A815 to the south of Glenbranter and Invernoaden.

Go up a forest track, turning right (signed Lochgoilhead) to follow the main track, which turns left, then back right to a junction. Leave the track and go up the left side of a wide forest break to exit the forest. Step over the old fence above and climb to Beinn Dubhain (649m). Descend north-west between crags to the col, then climb to Creag Sgoilte and Caisteal Dubh (**5.5km; 880m; 2h 45min**).

Continue north onto Creag a' Bhuic, then descend north-west to a col and climb to Carnach Mòr (634m). Head westwards for 200m to another slight rise (Pt.628m), then descend north-west down grassy slopes, keeping above the steep ground dropping to the basin below the impressive landslip of the Tùr nan Calman (*doocot or tower of pigeons*) with its boulders, fissures and caves.

On reaching the edge of the forestry at NS132996, marked as Carnach Beag on the OS 1:25k map, step over the fence to gain a new track. Follow the track down left, southwards, then sharply back right to join the main track up the glen. Turn left down this track, then, at the bottom, turn left and go through Invernoaden to reach the main road, 200m from the start (12.5km; 990m; 5h).

the waterfalls.

Leave the Cowal Way at a small burn before a forestry plantation and climb south-south-west, initially beside a fence, then up the broad and indistinct ridge. Higher up, as a line of crags is approached, make a rising leftward traverse up a grassy rake, then go up a grassy gully beside the burn. This leads easily up between the crags to gain a dip in the

Caisteal Dubh and Glas Choire from Creag Sgoilte (Rab Anderson)

Meall an Fhùdair; 764m; (C218); L50 or L56; NN270192; hill of the powder

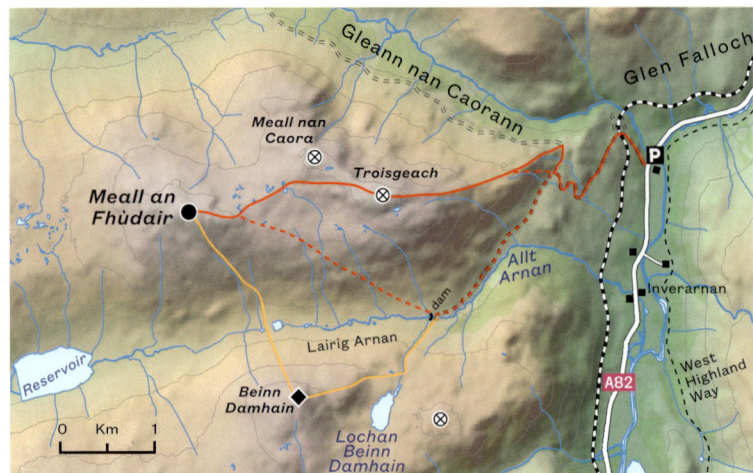

Together with Meall nan Caora and Troisgeach, its eastern tops, Meall an Fhùdair forms a large area of high ground that extends west from Glen Falloch at the head of Loch Lomond.

Meall an Fhùdair itself is a shapeless lump, obscured from general view by Meall nan Caora and Troisgeach, the latter having a fine and rocky eastern ridge, which is the line of ascent from Glen Falloch. The summit area between Troisgeach and Meall an Fhùdair is a flat, broad ridge, more like a plateau, dotted with numerous small lochans.

Despite its relative closeness to the Central Belt, and the popularity of nearby hills, Meall an Fhùdair is a hill that is largely overlooked. As well as its retiring nature, this may also be due to the lack of parking for the usual route of ascent via the hydro track that leaves the A82 opposite the entrance to Glen Falloch Farm at NN319196, about 2.5 miles (4km) north of Ardlui at the head of Loch Lomond. There is limited space at the track entrance; don't block the gate, or park in the entrance to the farm opposite. A few cars can be parked on the verges about 150m further north, on the north side of the bridge.

Cross a locked gate and walk up the hydro track, taking the shorter old track over the railway to shortcut the newer loop. Rejoin the newer track and follow it across the hillside, then zigzag up beneath the power line.

When the new track swings right back beneath the power line, and another track goes left, there are two options. One is to climb the hillside ahead by the burn to gain the crest of Troisgeach's east-north-east ridge. The other is to go right on the track, back beneath the power line, to where it rounds the corner over the ridge, then go up the ridge passing beneath the power line again. Ascend the fine rocky ridge, passing some small lochans on the flat top to gain the summit of Troisgeach (733m).

Head down west-north-west onto a broad ridge. Either continue along

Meall an Fhùdair and Troisgeach from Beinn Chabhair, with Beinn Bhuidhe beyond (Tom Prentice)

Across Inverarnan and Glen Falloch to Troisgeach and its fine eastern ridge (Rab Anderson)

this ridge past some more small lochans and make the short climb onto Meall nan Caora (721m) then drop south-west to a flat col, or take a more direct westward line down to the col, bypassing Meall nan Caora.

From the col, head south-west on rough and featureless ground with numerous rocky knolls, peaty hollows and small lochans, which could make it confusing in poor visibility, but otherwise easy. This area has a curiously large number of boulders perched precariously on embedded stones. Swing westwards as the ridge becomes more defined, then follow it up to the summit of Meall an Fhùdair (6.5km; 830m; 2h 50min).

There is a fine view across Glen Fyne to Beinn Bhuidhe, whilst to the north there is an unusual view of the Ben Lui group. To the east are the Crianlarich hills, with Ben More and Stob Binnein rising behind.

Return the same way (13km; 910m; 4h 50min), or by a slightly easier and perhaps 5min quicker route that makes a long descending east-south-east traverse to reach the hydro track in the Làirig Arnan, which is followed back to the approach and Glen Falloch.

Another option is to include Beinn Damhain, the Graham to the south, on the other side of the Làirig Arnan.

To do this, return east down the summit ridge for a way, then make a steep descent south following the left (east) side of a burn to reach the broad col at the head of the Làirig Arnan. Pass between a larger lochan and a smaller one, then continue directly up the steep slope ahead to ascend a depression between two ribs of rock and gain the top of Beinn Damhain (9km; 1130m; 4h 10min).

Descend the north-east ridge to gain the hydro track, and follow this back (15km; 1130m; 5h 45min).

Glen Falloch, Beinn Damhain, Troisgeach and Meall an Fhùdair (Rab Anderson)

Beinn Chùirn across Cononish (Tom Prentice)

Beinn Chùirn; 880m; (C48); L50; NN280292; cairn hill

Viewed on the approach from the east up the glen of the River Cononish, Beinn Chùirn creates an attractive sight. It forms the north side of a great amphitheatre, at whose head sits the bigger and more elegant Ben Lui, with another two Munros, Ben Oss and Beinn Dubhchraig forming the south side.

Rising above the farm at Cononish, Beinn Chùirn's flank is split by the distinctive cleft of the Eas Anie and its waterfall, to the side of which is the former Cononish Gold Mine. Falling steeply to the east of its summit is the attractive Coire na Saobhaidhe, whilst to the north, steep slopes drop to Glen Lochy, with Beinn Udlaidh rising on the other side.

The route up the River Cononish from the east starts either from Tyndrum, approached by track from Tyndrum Lower Station (gained from the Green Welly car park by the West Highland Way or Lower Station Road), or from Dalrigh to the south, where there is a sizeable three-part car park

at NN34329, just off the A82 at the start of the track to Cononish.

From Dalrigh, turn right out of the car park entrance, then left on a track past the access to the houses. Just beyond the houses, keep right on the main track and cross a bridge over a burn, then pass where the West Highland Way heads off right; it having joined at the fork.

Follow the track under the railway, then alongside the River Cononish, where it is soon joined by the track from Tyndrum. In a further 1.5km, when the track forks at Cononish, take the left fork (the right leads to

Beinn Chùirn from Meall Odhar, with Ben Lui beyond (Rab Anderson)

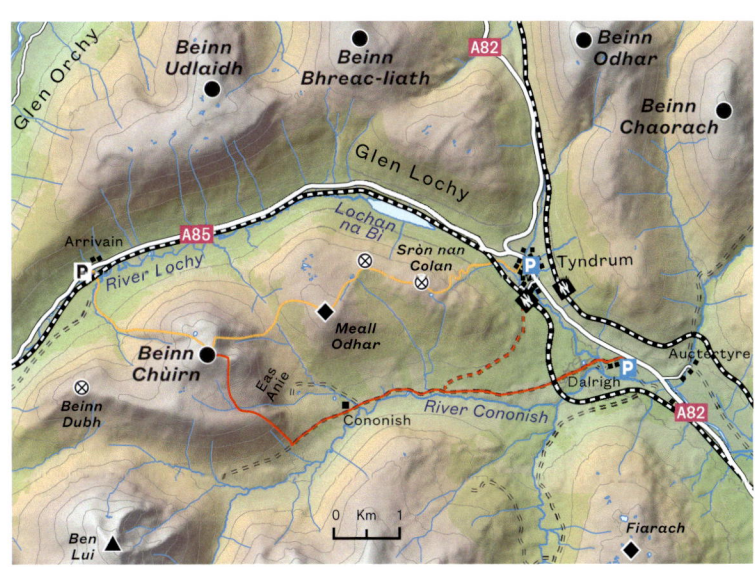

the gold mine) and continue through two gates.

About 300m beyond the second gate, break off up the hillside to follow a vague path and ATV track up onto the shoulder above Eas Anie. Cross the Allt Eas Anie; it may be necessary to head west for a way to cross near a tributary coming down from beneath the top. Once over, climb the slope ahead to gain the shoulder a little to the east of the summit.

Follow the edge of the steep drop into Coire na Saobhaidhe past the head of a gully, and ascend to the summit, which sits 100m back from the edge (**8km; 700m; 2h 55min**).

The easiest option is to return the same way (16km; 710m; 5h).

It is possible to link Beinn Chùirn with the Graham Meall Odhar, which rises above Cononish. This is best done by climbing the Graham first, as described in the SMC's *The Grahams & The Donalds* guidebook, either by the ascent route from Cononish, or from Tyndrum by ascending the descent route past the lead mines.

From the summit of Beinn Odhar,

drop north-west to follow a line of fence posts down a break in the trees, and climb a deer fence to gain the col. Head into Coire na Saobhaidhe, bypassing crags on their left side, then either break out onto the right-hand ridge, or continue up the corrie and break out right higher up. Both exits are on steep, but not difficult, ground. At the top, head south to the summit (**7.5km; 900m; 3h 20min**).

Descend via the standard ascent route (15.5km; 910m; 5h 30min).

For those fit and so inclined, this opens up the possibility of a Graham, Corbett and Munro combination.

A shorter route is possible from Glen Lochy to the north, where there are pull-offs either side of the A85, about 100m west of the cottages on

the south side of the road at Arrivain. This is opposite the bridge carrying the railway across the River Lochy.

To stay within the law, wade the River Lochy and go under the railway bridge, then ascend beside the Allt Garbh Choirean. Forestry operations have altered the appearance here.

Once above the forestry zone, bear east on the left (north) side of the northernmost burn in the corrie, and climb a grassy spur, which steepens near its top, but is not as craggy as the map suggests. This spur leads to a little lochan, from where the summit of Beinn Chùirn is a short climb 360m or so to the south-east (**2.75km; 665m; 1h 45min**).

Return the same way (5.5km; 700m; 2h 45min).

Beinn Chùirn and Beinn Dubh over Glen Lochy from Beinn na Sròine (Tom Prentice)

Across Loch Lubnaig to Benvane
(Rab Anderson)

SECTION 1b
Loch Lomond to Loch Tay

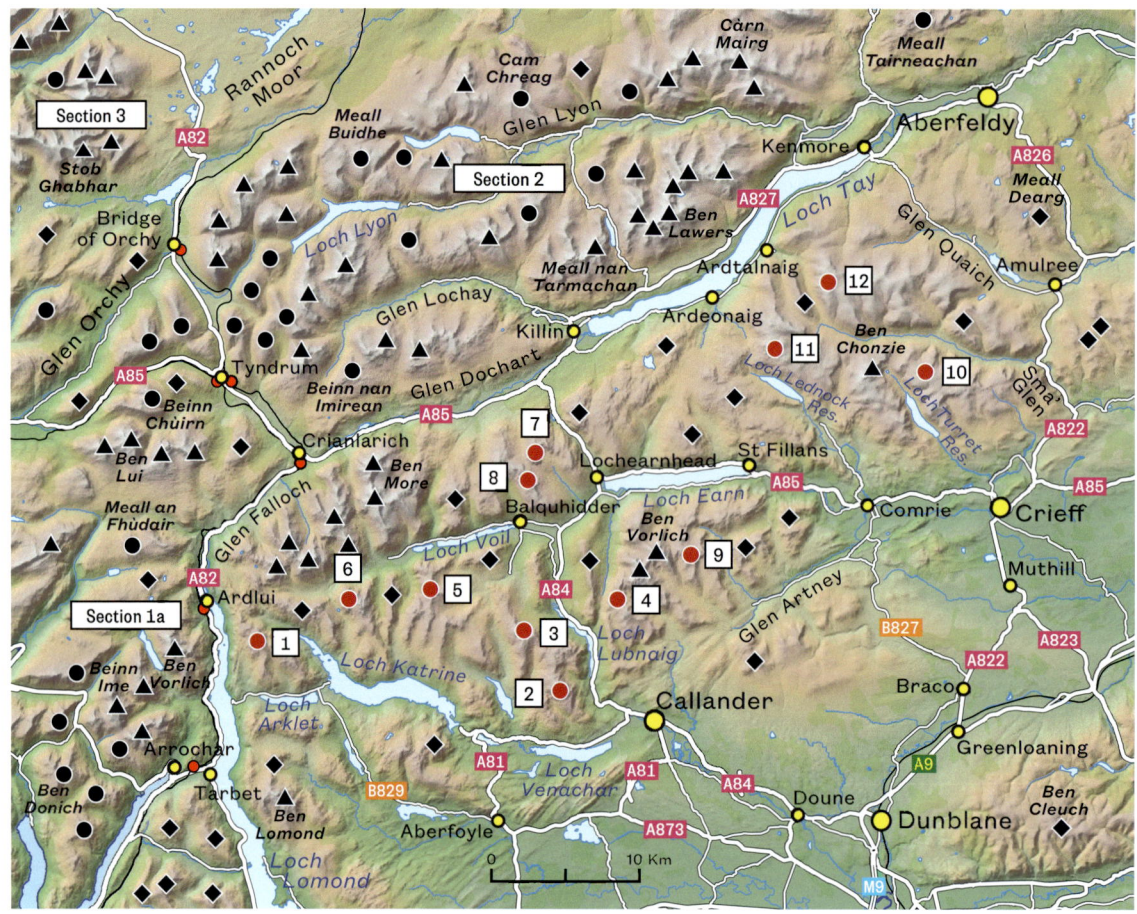

SECTION 1b

Beinn a' Choin across the Bealach a' Mheim from Stob an Fhàinne, with the Crianlarich Munros beyond (Tom Prentice)

Beinn a' Choin; *770m; (C208); L56; NN354130; hill of the dog*

Beinn a' Choin is the highest of a small group of hills enclosed within the triangle formed by Loch Lomond, Loch Katrine and Loch Arklet. From its summit, two long and broad grassy ridges drop southwards to Loch Arklet, enclosing Corriearklet Glen and the Corriearklet Burn.

The most direct way to the summit is from Garrison, just beyond the west end of Loch Arklet. However, a much better route is to make the longer circuit of Corriearklet Glen.

The direct route starts from the RSPB Inversnaid Nature Reserve's signposted car park (NN348096),

which is located behind Garrison Farm, accessed from the road about 800m west of the Loch Arklet dam.

In the aftermath of the 1719 Jacobite rising, a garrison was built here to control the route through Glen Arklet between Inversnaid on Loch Lomond and Callander. This was also the time when the legendary Highland outlaw Rob Roy MacGregor was active in these parts.

Go through a gate and follow a track north for 800m to a sheepfold. Continue on a grassy track for a further 600m or so, then take its right fork and climb north-east to reach a

burn: Allt Trosdain. Ascend by this burn and go through a gate in a deer fence, then continue uphill across a fenceline to gain the north side of a broad col: Bealach a' Mheim.

Climb through craggy ground to gain Beinn a' Choin's south-east ridge, then follow this to the top, crossing the fenceline and passing a tiny lochan in a hollow. The highest point is a flat-topped knoll with a cairn at the north end (**4.5km; 630m; 2h**).

Either return the same way (**9km; 630m; 3h 20min**), or via Stob an Fhàinne. For the latter, return down the ridge and cross the Bealach a' Mheim, following a rough path south along the high ground to meet the fenceline for the final climb onto Stob an Fhàinne (655m). One descent option is to follow the fenceline steeply down to the Great Trossachs Path, which leads back to the car park. The other option is to head south a short way to bypass a rocky prow, then make a steep descent south-west towards Garrison on rough and boggy ground. Go through a gate in a deer fence right of the ridgeline, then through a gate in the fields below (**8.5km; 700m; 3h 20min**).

Another descent from Beinn a'

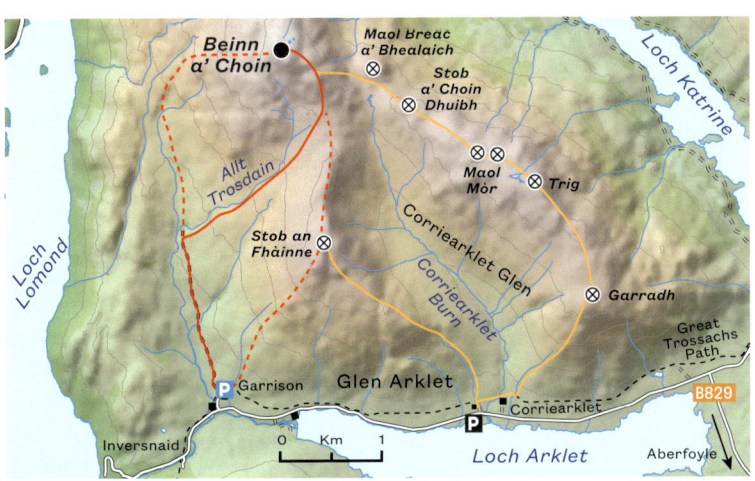

►

Choin can be made by following an old wall west from just below the summit knoll, then down south-west by a burn. Continue down beside the burn as it kinks north-west, then back south-west to bypass steep ground. Once opposite a stone shieling, head southwards to go down beside another burn to pick up the top of the grassy track, and follow this back (**9.25km; 630m; 3h 25min**).

The longer circuit of Corriearklet Glen starts where there is verge parking at N374094, to the west of Corriearklet: just west of a gate leading to a green barn. Go through the gate, and up a track to the barn. Go through another gate, then cross the Great Trossachs Path and follow a grassy ATV track up the hillside, heading for the crest of the ridge ahead. Climb more steeply up the crest onto Maol Odhar, then go through a gate in a deer fence and continue up to Stob a Fhàinne (655m).

Follow the fenceline north for a short way, then veer away from it on a rough path that cuts across higher ground and cross the Bealach a' Mheim. Climb onto Beinn a' Choin's south-east ridge and follow this to the top, crossing the fenceline and passing a tiny lochan to climb onto the flat-topped summit knoll (**4.5km; 700m; 2h 10min**).

Return down the south-east ridge for a way, then drop more steeply east to avoid some crags and cut across the south side of a knoll (Maol Breac a' Bhealaich) at the col with Maol Mòr. Ascend the ridge ahead and climb onto a prominent tooth-like craggy knoll called Stob a' Choin Dhuibh (645m). Drop off the back and climb to the top of Maol Mòr (694m). Continue along the crest for 700m, with numerous ups and downs, to reach the trig point (684m). Keep on down the crest, swinging south and crossing a stile over a deer fence, to reach the minor rise of Garradh (559m).

Now descend quite steeply south-west towards Corriearklet, passing down the side of a burn then a fence to gain the Great Trossachs Path. Follow this path behind Corriearklet back to the green barn and the start (**11km; 920m; 4h 25min**).

Ben Ledi from Kilmahog (Rab Anderson)

> **Ben Ledi;** *879m; (C50); L57; NN562097; hill of the gentle slope, or God's hill*

Rising some 8km to the north-west of the town of Callander, to which it forms a splendid backdrop, Ben Ledi occupies a prominent position on the southern edge of the Scottish Highlands. Together with Ben Lomond to its west, then Stùc a' Chroin and Ben Vorlich to its north-east, Ben Ledi forms a distinctive landmark in the view north from the lowlands of Central Scotland.

Lying to the south of Ben Ledi is Loch Venachar, and from there the mountain takes the form of a long northwards-running ridge that continues to Benvane, another Corbett. To the east of this ridge, steep, craggy and forested slopes fall to Loch Lubnaig and the A84, which runs northwards from Callander to Strathyre and Lochearnhead.

Whilst Ben Ledi can be paired with Benvane (see panel on page 59), it is generally climbed on its own, giving a fine and relatively short route. A start is made from parking at NN587091, on the west side of the bridge across the outflow from Loch Lubnaig: the

Garbh Uisge. This is at the point where the A84 exits the Pass of Leny just north of the Falls of Leny, and there is a sign for the Strathyre Forest Cabins. There is a small parking area immediately to the right and further parking down the road to the left.

Parking is limited, and it is usually busy. Please avoid parking along the road to the right, which is the access to the cottages and holiday cabins. If required, there is a long layby on the main road, a short distance to the north of the turn-off to the bridge.

Begin the ascent at the west end of the bridge by ascending a waymarked hill path, which soon passes an interpretive board for the Callander Commemorative Grove. Cross a forest track, then climb more steeply, swinging south-westwards to emerge from the trees beneath the steep upper slopes, where there are fine views up Loch Lubnaig to Beinn Each, with Stùc a' Chroin beyond.

Continue south-westwards onto the ridgeline, then turn sharply north and follow the path up the broad and

grassy crest of the ridge. Swing north-west and ascend to the minor highpoint of Meall Odhar, then on up the final slopes, passing an iron memorial cross, to reach the cairn and trig point on the summit of Ben Ledi (**4km; 770m; 2h 10min**).

It is a splendid viewpoint on the edge of the highland line, with many of the mountains of the Southern Highlands identifiable. In complete contrast, to the south there is an open view of the Forth Valley and the flatlands of Scotland's Central Belt.

The quickest return is back the same way (**8km; 780m; 3h 20min**).

However, it is much better to make a circuit and return via Stank Glen. Descend slightly north-west along the edge of a steep slope dropping into a hanging corrie (Coire an Fhaidhe), then out north beside a line of old fence posts to reach the end of the summit ridge, where the posts veer off left. Although it is possible to follow a path straight ahead here, down the ridge to the north, directly into Stank Glen, this is steep and rough. Instead, it is better to descend north-westwards by the fence posts, following a path down grassy slopes. Lower down, either take the first

path off right, or, perhaps better, continue ahead across a flattening beside a slight rise, then descend towards a grassy col between the hills: the Bealach nan Corp. Before reaching this col, leave the path to it, which continues on to Lochan nan Corp and Benvane beyond. Follow another path down rightwards into wetter ground at the very head of Stank Glen, just below and to the east of the Bealach nan Corp.

Descend into Stank Glen on the south side of the burn, on a path which is wet and eroded in places. Pass under the remaining wire of a fence to the left of an old gate, and drop down to gain the flat floor of the upper glen at the edge of the forest. Continue through the trees to stepping stones across the Stank Burn, where there are two options:

(i) Cross over and continue to meet a track, which is followed downhill to a junction, where the right branch is taken back across the burn by a bridge to rejoin the path on the other side.

(ii) Keep to the south side, and follow the path that curves around the edge of the flatter area, before descending south-eastwards to where it is joined by the route from the other

side, just beyond a small dam.

Descend the path, rough and eroded in places, through the bushes and trees to emerge onto a forest track. Cross over to the right, then take a waymarked path down left through a felled area, past a fine waterfall over to the left, to join another track. Either follow the track right then back left, or cut the corner on a path through the trees by the burn to rejoin the track. The track leads to the road on the west side of the river, where a right turn leads back to the start (**10.5km; 780m; 4h**).

A longer route starts from the Bochastle car park at NN607081, just off the A821 about 300m south of Kilmahog. A forest track, which can be biked, joins the standard route after 4km, where the hill path crosses the forest track (**7km; 810m; 2h 50min**); (**14km; 830m; 4h 40min**).

A circuit via Stank Glen can be made by traversing south along the forest track to where the hill path crosses it, then back to the start (**16.5km; 880m; 5h 25min**).

Sustrans Cycle Route 7 from Callander passes through the Bochastle car park and the parking for the principal route.

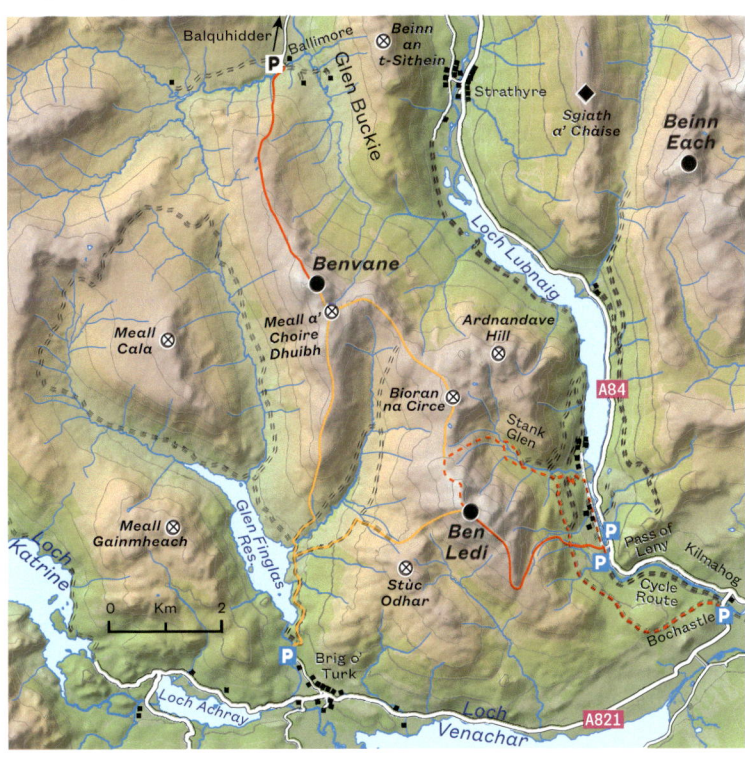

Benvane and its north ridge from Creag Mhòr (Tom Prentice)

Benvane; *821m; (C121); L57; NN535137; white hill*

Running parallel and to the west of Loch Lubnaig is a 5km-long high-level ridge that extends from the summit of Ben Ledi to Benvane. Although this ridge can be climbed as part of a fine traverse of both hills, a circuit of Gleann Casaig (see panel opposite), it is more common to climb both summits individually.

Steep, forested and craggy slopes rise above Loch Lubnaig, which effectively prevents direct access to these summits from there. So Ben Ledi is climbed by a route onto its south ridge, and Benvane either by a route onto its north ridge from Glen Buckie, or by its south ridge from Brig o' Turk and Glen Finglas Reservoir.

The Glen Buckie route starts from a parking area (NT529175) at the farm at Ballimore, at the end of a narrow road accessed from Balquhidder.

Walk across the bridge over the Calair Burn, then at the right of way signpost to Brig o' Turk and Glen Finglas, climb the banking and cross the field to pick up a grassy track. The track leads to the crossing of a stile next to a gate in a wall. Leave the grassy track here and climb uphill

beside the fence on an ATV track, following this and a path onto the north ridge just to the east of Mullach an t-Samhraidh (579m). Continue up the long north ridge to pick up a fence, which is followed for a way, then crossed by a stile on the final steepening. At the top, swing south-east to gain the summit, marked by a cairn (**4.5km; 640m; 2h**).

Ben Ledi lies to the south, with the Ochil Hills and the Forth Bridges visible to its left. Beinn Each then Stùc a' Chroin and Ben Vorlich sit on the opposite side of Loch Lubnaig. Close at hand to the north is Beinn Stacach, then a whole host of peaks on the long ranges above the glacial trenches formed by The Braes of Balquhidder and Loch Earn, then Glen Dochart and Loch Tay.

Return the same way (**9km; 655m; 3h 25min**).

For the route from Brig o' Turk, turn north off the A821 at the Brig o' Turk Tea Room and follow the road for 1km to a car park at NN531073 in woodland at the entrance to the Glen Finglas Reservoir and Hydro Electric Station. This is also the start point for

the traverse of Ben Ledi and Benvane; see panel opposite.

Walk up the road to through woodland to Glen Finglas Reservoir, and continue up the track on the east side of the reservoir, out into the open. Ignore the track up the east side of Gleann Casaig, and cross the bridge over the Allt Ghleann Casaig.

In front of a small hydro power station, turn right up the track on the west side of Gleann Casaig and follow it through a wall, then a fence. Leave the track here and climb steeply north onto the long ridge, which is followed over Pt.625m to Meall a' Choire Dhuibh (753m), then Benvane beyond (**7.5km; 740m; 2h 55min**).

Rather than return the same way, go back to Meall a' Choire Dhuibh, then turn north-east and follow the rough path along the crest. This swings around the head of Gleann Casaig, then drops south to the Bealach na Seann Làirige where a track arrives. Descend the track to regain the outward route above the reservoir and follow this back (**17.25km; 790m; 5h 30min**).

Map on page 57

Ben Ledi & Benvane

Brig o' Turk is the starting point for a fine traverse of both these hills, which takes in the 5km-long, high-level ridge that links them. Whilst the southern route to Benvane starts here, and Ben Ledi can also be climbed from this point, the circuit around Gleann Casaig, which takes in both hills, is a superior route.

Turn north off the A821 at the Brig o' Turk Tea Room and follow the road for 1km to a car park at NN531073 in woodland at the entrance to Glen Finglas Reservoir and Hydro Electric Station.

Walk uphill along the right-hand road (not the one to the Hydro Electric Station) through the woodland above Glen Finglas Reservoir and out into the open past a large shed and some cottages for 2km. Take the track on the right, up Gleann Casaig, past another large shed and on for about 1.5km until opposite the col up on the right (east) between Stùc Odhar and Ben Ledi.

*Just before a ford across the burn, either follow a rough ATV track for a way before leaving it to head to the col, or ford the burn, then take a slightly more direct route to the col, named An Cunglach (517m). From there, an old line of fence posts is followed north, then steeply east to arrive on the edge of the corrie about 200m to the north-west of the summit of Ben Ledi, which is easily gained (**6km; 790m; 2h 40min**).*

Return to the fence posts and follow them all the way down to the wide col at the head of Stank Glen, the Bealach nan Corp (c.650m), ignoring paths off right. Follow the ridgeline path up north, passing the west end of Lochan nan Corp, and climb onto Pt.722m (Bioran na Circe), passing between its highpoint and a small lochan. Continue along the ridge, dropping slightly to Stùc Dubh (662m) where a track arrives from Gleann Casaig.

*Descend a path to the right of the track to gain a wide col, named the Bealach na Seann Làirige (c.605m), the lowest point between the hills. Cross some haggy ground and ascend again, passing just below the little knoll of Creag Chaoruinneach, then swing west and south-west around the head of Gleann Casaig onto Pt.753m (Meall a' Choire Dhuibh). The path now turns northwards and leads up to Benvane's summit (**12.25km; 1090m; 4h 40min**).*

Return south to Meall a' Choire Dhuibh, then continue south down the ridge over Pt.625m and down above Creag na h-Airighe. Drop steeply down the nose at the end (Sròn Achaidh na h-Airde) to gain the track up the west side of Gleann Casaig, then follow this down to cross the river where it enters Glen Finglas Reservoir and return along the lochside track to the start (19.75km; 1130m; 6h 30min).

Map on page 57

Benvane from Ben Ledi, with Stob Binnein and Ben More, left (Tom Prentice)

Beinn Each; 813m; (C135); L57; NN601158; horse hill

Like the more prominent Ben Ledi to its west, Beinn Each stands on the southern edge of the Highlands. It is the main summit on the twisting, hummocky south-west ridge of Munro, Stùc a' Chroin, and together with that hill, and Ben Vorlich to its east, it forms part of the distinctive skyline when viewed from the Central Belt. There is, however, no sight of it from the main A84 road that runs past it up Loch Lubnaig.

The ascent is started from halfway up Loch Lubnaig, from a layby on the east side of the A84 at NN583137; there is also space just inside a forestry track entrance on the same side of the road 100m further north. This is the same start point as for Sgiath a' Chàise, a Graham, and since the initial part of the approach is the same, it is easy to include that hill.

From the south end of the layby, take the path signposted to Loch Earn via Glen Ample, up the side of the burn, Ardchullarie Burn, between it and the boundary fence around the grounds and house of Ardchullarie More. At the top corner of the fence, cross a burn then continue up through the trees, across a hydro track, to emerge onto the main forestry track. Exit the forestry by a gate and follow the track to where the main track turns left, then continue on the track through the glen to just beyond where it fords the burn, Eas an Eoin, that falls from Beinn Each up on the right.

Leave the track at a finger post signed to Beinn Each, and take a path that, in summer, ascends bracken-covered slopes. The path heads to a large boulder, crosses another burn, then zigzags uphill beside the burn before traversing the steep hillside up left, north, then north-east. A line of old fence posts is reached and followed to the summit on a small flat area (**3.5km; 690m; 1h 55min**).

Return the same way (**7km; 700m; 3h**).

Sgiath a' Chàise can be included on regaining the track by heading north along it for 600m to NN590156. Go through a gap in an old wall, then climb the heathery hillside to gain the crest just south of the pointed top of Creag a' Mhadaidh (557m). Climb over this top, cross a slight dip to gain an old fenceline then continue up the broad ridge to the top (645m). Return the same way; an added 4.75km, 325m, 1h 45min.

Beinn Each from Meall Mòr, with Stùc a' Chroin beyond (Rab Anderson)

North from the summit of Beinn Stacach to Stob Binnein and Ben More (Tom Prentice)

Beinn Stacach; *771m; (C205); L57; NN474163; peaky hill*

Unnamed on most maps at the time of writing, and simply shown as a 771m trig point, Beinn Stacach is the second hill in the chain that runs westwards along the south side of the Braes of Balquhidder. This chain also includes Stob a' Choin, The Corbett to the west, and three Grahams.

Beinn Stacach's summit sits above the head of Gleann Dubh, an offshoot of Glen Buckie, and it is from Glen Buckie that the ascent is made.

There is a small parking area (NT529175) at Ballimore farm, at the end of the narrow road south from Balquhidder. This is the start for the principal route to Benvane, as well as for the Graham Creag Mhòr, which can be included with Beinn Stacach.

A track on the north side of the Calair Burn appears to offer the best route. However, this passes through an area enclosed by a high deer fence with a locked gate. Instead, go south and cross the bridge over the Calair Burn, then climb the banking at the right of way signpost to Brig o' Turk and Glen Finglas and cross the field to pick up a grassy track. The track leads to the crossing of a stile next to a gate in a wall where the route to Benvane goes uphill to the left

following an ATV track.

Continue ahead on the rough path of the right of way, which can be very wet and muddy, for a further 1.75km, to just beyond some boulders, where the path turns south below a spur named Sròn a' Chonnaidh. Leave the path here and cross a gate in the fence to gain the burn, now the Allt a' Ghlinne Dhuibh, which can normally be forded. If not, continue upstream a little, to where the burn loops west, then cross the fence and a tributary to gain a bridge at NN508164, and use this to cross the burn.

Either way, cross the track on the other side, then climb west-north-west over moorland and the steepening grassy hillside to gain the broad east-north-east ridge of Beinn Stacach.

A rough path follows the undulating crest and passes over Pt.684m to reach a grassy col. Continue up the ridge and make a steeper short climb to arrive on the broad south ridge of the hill to the north of a prominent little rocky point, where there is a small lochan. An easy short climb to the north-north-west beside a line of fence posts gains the trig point on the summit (**7km; 640m; 2h 40min**).

▶

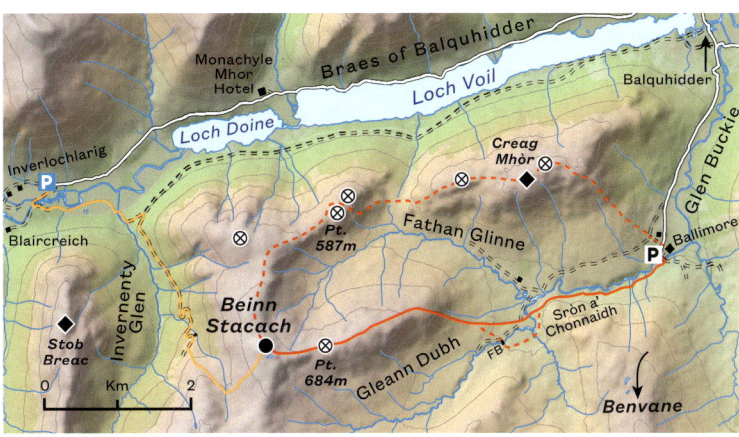

Returning the same way is perhaps easiest (12km; 700m; 4h 50min).

To make a fine circuit and include Creag Mhòr, descend the broad ridge to the north following the fenceline and swing around the head of the corrie: Fathan Glinne. Continue down the north-east ridge to the foot of the rise to Pt.587m, then drop off the ridge and cut across the south side of Pt.587m. Grassy slopes are then followed down to the north-east to the Bealach Driseach (365m). Ascend the broad west ridge of Creag Mhòr, passing over its west top (574m), to gain the summit at 658m (12.5km; 1020m; 4h 40min).

Drop northwards and climb east onto the next knoll, Pt.647m, then descend east towards a col before dropping south-east towards the corner of a conifer plantation. Step through the gap between the fence wires and continue down, passing a boulder with a rowan tree growing out of it, to go through an open gate in a stock fence to gain a track. This leads past a house to the road, then the car park (15.5km; 1035m; 5h 50min).

Another route climbs Beinn Stacach from the car park at Inverlochlarig at the end of the narrow road along the Braes of Balquhidder.

Walk southwards on the road to Blaircreich and cross two bridges, the second over the River Larig. Break off left through a gate, then follow a grassy track and path east beside the river. The path swings south-east through an old gate to reach the foot of Invernenty Glen between the hills.

At the edge of the forestry, cross the Invernenty Burn on stepping stones. Go up the far side next to a wall for 180m, and step over a fence to find the end of a track, which is followed up left to the main forestry track. Turn right and follow this track south up the glen to where it emerges from the forest at a wooden hut.

Leave the track just beyond the hut and climb onto the spur ahead to gain an old fenceline, which is followed south-east into Coire Odhar. Cross the burn, then turn north-east and follow the fence up to the top of Beinn Stacach (6.5km; 660m; 2h 35min).

Return by the route of ascent (13km; 670m; 4h 30min).

Across Loch Doine to Stob a' Choin (Tom Prentice)

Stob a' Choin; *869m; (C63); L56 & L57; NN417159; peak of the dog*

Situated opposite the Munro Beinn Tulaichean, some 3km to south-west of Inverlochlarig, Stob a' Choin is a fine hill and the highest point of the range that forms the south side of the Braes of Balquhidder. The range also contains Beinn Stacach, the Corbett further east, as well as three Grahams, and runs between the Braes of Balquhidder glacial trench containing Loch Voil, and Strath Gartney containing Loch Katrine.

Stob a' Choin's steep north ridge and pointed summit dominate the view as one approaches from Balquhidder along the narrow public road on the north side of Loch Voil. Its craggy north face rises steeply in a splendid single sweep from the River Larig to its castellated summit ridge of four tops.

A start is made from a car park at the end of the public road, 750m to the east of the farm at Inverlochlarig.

Walk west along the right of way, which leads eventually to Inverarnan in Glen Falloch, and was once the coffin route for the MacGregors on their way to Balquhidder Kirk. Pass through the farm and continue for 1.25km to a footbridge over the River Larig, then cross.

The best route is via the compelling north ridge. To gain this, head south-west up and across the slope, crossing the burns that drain the steep corrie to gain then follow a grassy rake between a lower broken band of crag (the Amar Stob a' Choin) and a narrower broken band of crag above. The aim is to gain a distinct flattening on the north ridge at 630m. Above this, the ridge is grassy, but steep, and leads to the north top, which gives fine views north across the glen to the Crianlarich Munros. The actual summit is 1m or so higher and lies a further 130m to the south

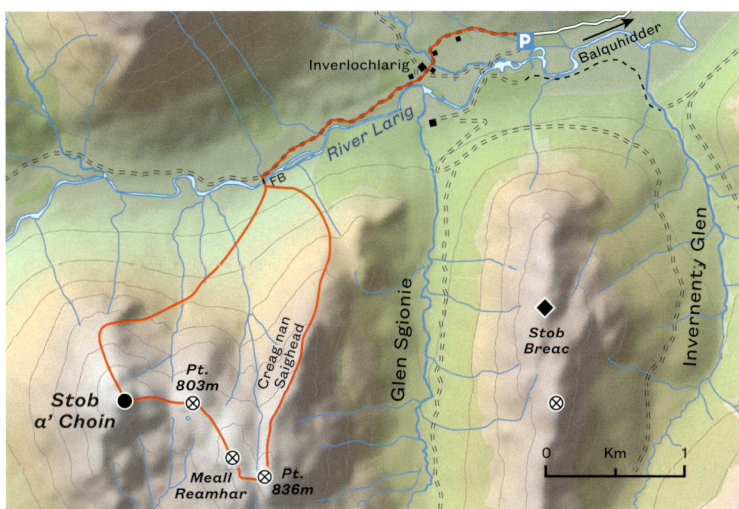

across a dip (**4.5km; 750m; 2h 15min**).

Traverse east and drop to a narrow col, Bealach Coire an Laoigh, then climb to the central top (803m); a fenceline runs along the tops here, aiding navigation in poor weather.

Descend slightly to the south-east, and climb onto the south-east top, Meall Reamhar (845m), before continuing south-east, then east across another narrow col to climb onto the far south-east top (836m).

Now descend the long north-north-east ridge, which forms the east side of the hill above Creag nan Saighead, following the fenceline down, then cutting across to regain the bridge over the River Larig and the track back (**10.5km; 900m; 4h 15min**).

There are times in winter when it may be prudent to go up and back down the north-north-east ridge above Creag nan Saighead (**6km; 900m; 2h 50min**), (**12km; 1050m; 4h 50min**).

Stob a' Choin's summit from the traverse over to Meall Reamhar (Rab Anderson)

Creag Mac Rànaich from the approach up the Glen Kendrum track (Rab Anderson)

Creag Mac Rànaich; *809m; (C144); L51; NN545255; Mac Rànaich's rock*
Meall an t-Seallaidh; *852m; (C90); L51; NN542234; hill of the view*

These two hills form the eastern part of a range that rises above Glen Ogle and Loch Earn to the east, and extends westwards between the Braes of Balquhidder and Glen Dochart, over The Stob, a Graham, to Ben More and the Crianlarich Munros.

Sat at the head of Glen Kendrum, Creag Mac Rànaich is seen when travelling north from Strathyre on the A84, midway between the Kingshouse Hotel and Lochearnhead. A distinctive feature is the large south-east facing rock buttress that sits below the top. However, on closer inspection this is revealed to be discontinuous and intersected by grass ledges.

Meall an t-Seallaidh forms the west side of Glen Kendrum and appears as a grassier hill whose uniformly steep southern flank rises above the road to Balquhidder. However, its northern top, Cam Chreag, and the steep slope above the shallow east-facing corrie in between are lined with small crags.

The hills are climbed together, with the car park at Lochearnhead being the normal starting place. This is 500m to the east of the junction of the A85 Crieff/Perth road with the A84 Callander/Crianlarich road.

Walk west on the pavement to the

junction and cross over. Turn right and walk north for 230m on the pavement and verge, then turn left onto the access road to the Scout Station. Go past the barrier and turn off right onto the signed Glen Ogle Trail and follow this uphill (a 90m climb) onto the former Edinburgh to Oban railway line, now the route of the Rob Roy Way and a cycle path. Turn left along this, and in 600m reach where the Rob Roy Way and the cycle path come up onto the old railway line from below past St Angus church. This is a longer route

by 600m, which is used on the return.

Continue south along the former railway line for 860m, then, before a bridge across it, go left and follow a grassy track up and across the bridge to join the track up Glen Kendrum. This track leads past one off left to a dam, then on up the glen to ford a burn. The track then zigzags steeply uphill, with craggy Creag Mac Rànaich filling the view, to reach its highpoint at the col between the hills (596m).

Leave the track and climb steeply north-east up the grassy gap in the

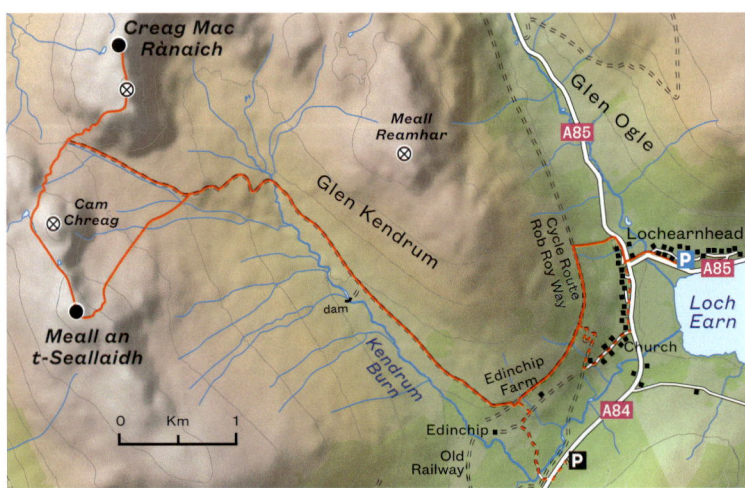

Creag Mac Rànaich's summit from the return to the south top, with the Ben Lawers group beyond (Tom Prentice)

craggy hillside. An indistinct path follows a line of intermittent fence posts and leads onto the flat summit of Creag Mac Rànaich. There are two tops about 260m apart. The northern one is a prominent little craggy knoll, shown by the OS as being 1m higher, but measured as being only 15cm higher (**9km; 770m; 3h 15min**).

Return to the col and go south-west across heather and peat, initially following a vague path beside the intermittent fence posts. A steeper ascent gains the col north-west of Cam Chreag, where there is a little lochan. Turn south, then either go over Cam Chreag (812m), or skirt around

its west side, and ascend the grassy ridge to the trig point on Meall an t-Seallaidh (**12.25km; 1055m; 4h 40min**).

To return to Glen Kendrum, drop to the south-east a very short way, then descend north-east, following grassy slopes down the edge of the shallow corrie. Cross heathery ground, then the burn, to regain the approach track above the zigzags, and follow this back to the former railway line.

After a further 900m, follow the slightly longer route back, down right via the zigzags of the Rob Roy Way and cycle path, then the road past St Angus Church. At the bottom, turn left along the A84 pavement to return to

the start (**20.5km; 1080m; 7h**).

It is possible to shorten the walk by 3km (40min), or so, by starting to the south of Lochearnhead, from limited parking at a track entrance on the east side of the A84 at NN583222.

Walk south on the wide verge for 150m, cross the road, and follow the Edinchip Estate access road, crossing the Rob Roy Way and cycle path, then the Kendrum Burn. Go right at a junction, then, before reaching Edinchip Farm, go left through a gate, signed to Glen Kendrum. Follow the left edge of the field, and go through a gate to join the principal route at the bridge over the former railway.

Meall an t-Seallaidh and Cam Chreag from Creag Mac Rànaich across Glen Kendrum (Chris Anderson)

Meall na Fearna; 809m; (C141); L51 & L57; NN650186; alder hill

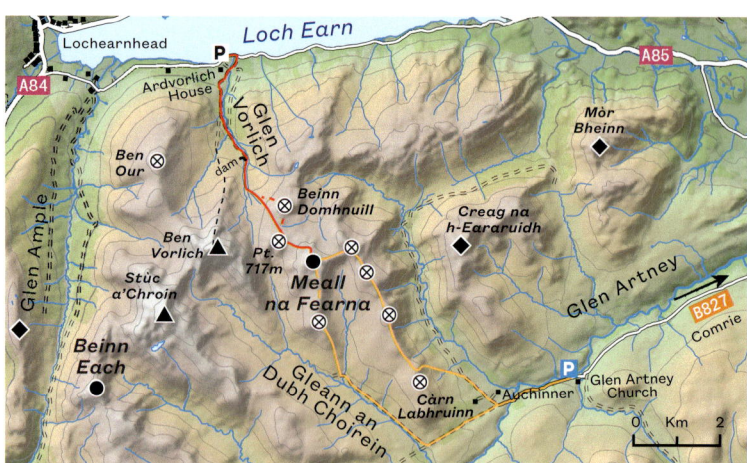

Rising above the Highland Boundary Fault, which runs through Glen Artney to its south, Meall na Fearna is one of a group of five principal hills that sit between the fault and the trench occupied by Loch Earn. Two Munros, Ben Vorlich and Stùc a Chroin, lie to its west, while two Grahams, Creag na h-Eararuidh and Mòr Bheinn, lie to its east.

It is a grassy hill with heather and peat bog, and from the two approaches to it, one from the north and the other from the south, its summit is hidden by smaller outlying tops.

The shortest approach is from the north, from Ardvorlich on the south side of Loch Earn, reached by leaving the A84 on the southern edge of Lochearnhead at the west end of the loch to go along the narrow south Loch Earn road for 4.5km.

There is ample roadside parking at NN633232 on the west side of the hump-backed bridge over the Ardvorlich Burn. This is the same parking for Ben Vorlich, so it can be busy.

The route follows the right of way from Ardvorlich to Callander for a way, and the initial section is the same as for the approach to Ben Vorlich. From the east side of the bridge over the Ardvorlich Burn, follow the access track towards Ardvorlich House, crossing back over the burn. Turn left, then follow a track uphill into Glen Vorlich, past several gates with stiles.

When the route to Ben Vorlich heads up the main right-hand track after 1.8km, branch off left on the track following the right of way. This joins a track coming in from the left, then crosses a concrete ford. Keep left at a fork, and follow the track across a bridge beside a small dam.

Continue on the rougher track, which climbs a narrow spur between two parallel running burns, heading south up Glen Vorlich for the Bealach Gliogarsnaich between Meall na Fearna and Ben Vorlich. Follow what is now an ATV track as it swings left across the left-hand burn, then climbs to a grassy area in front of a small outcrop on the north-west side of Beinn Domhnuill, where it heads left again, away from the line up the hill.

Now climb diagonally southwards across the pathless hillside, aiming for unnamed Pt.717m to avoid an area of peat hags at the col between it and Beinn Domhnuill. Once there, traverse across partway up Pt.717m to gain the col with Meall na Fearna, then ascend to the left of some craggy ground to

Meall na Fearna from the north-west, on the traverse beneath Pt.717m (Tom Prentice)

gain the left-hand ridge and follow this to the top (**6.25km; 800m; 2h 45min**).

There is a splendid view west to Ben Vorlich with Stùc a' Chroin beyond.

Return the same way (**12.5km; 830m; 4h 30min**), although both Pt.717m and Beinn Domhnuill (739m) are worth including; an added 0.3km, 90m, 15min.

A longer circuit, can be made from Glen Artney to the south, starting from the car park for Glenartney Church at NN711161, towards the end of the narrow road along the glen from the B827 south of Comrie to the east.

Walk south-westwards along the road and cross the bridge over the Water of Ruchill to where the road ends before Auchinner and Glenartney Lodge.

Whilst the quickest way is to go up Strath a' Ghlinne, which can be biked, and climb westwards to Meall na Fearna, the better route is to continue south-west on the track that swings around the foot of Sròn Aileach on Càrn Labhruinn. Branch off to take the rough track north-west up Gleann an Dubh Choirein for just over 2km, and cross the Allt na Fearna (there is a bridge upstream of the path) to gain the foot of Meall na Fearna's south ridge. Climb this ridge over a minor rise (Pt.686m) and continue up the ridge beyond to climb the summit cone (**9.5km; 700m; 3h 20min**).

Descend east to the head of Coire na Fearna, and climb onto Stob Chalum Mhic Griogair (742m). Drop south-east off this, then cross the dip and climb another rise, Pt.701m. Descend south-east to the col (592m) before another rise, Stùc Gharbh (636m), and pick up the line of an old stalkers' path on the edge of the corrie to the east.

Follow this path along the edge of the steep drop to the east, passing beneath the top of Stùc Gharbh, and continuing downhill along the edge to the hag-ridden col with Càrn Labhruinn. The path, which avoids the hags, then drops down by the burn, and is followed for a way before cutting across to go down the side of a fenced plantation. Gain the track in the floor of Strath a' Ghlinne, then follow it back to the road to regain the start (**18km; 860m; 5h 50min**).

Auchnafree Hill across Loch Turret Reservoir from Càrn Chois (Rab Anderson)

Auchnafree Hill; *789m; (C176); L52; NN808308; hill of the deer forest field*

Located on the southern edge of the Highland Boundary Fault, Auchnafree Hill is a vast, sprawling hill, the easternmost of the three principal summits that form the chain of hills extending along the south side of Glen Almond. The Munro Ben Chonzie is the highest point and lies to its west, with the Corbett Creag Uchdag further west again at the end.

The normal approach is from Loch Turret Reservoir, and since Auchnafree Hill sits across the head of Glen Turret from Ben Chonzie, it is often combined with that Munro for a splendid circuit of the reservoir.

The ascent starts from a car park at the Loch Turret Reservoir dam at NN821265, gained from Crieff by following the A85 north-west to Dalvreck, then turning north onto a minor road signposted to Monzie and Loch Turret Waterworks. Some 200m past the Glenturret Distillery, cross a bridge over the Turret Burn, then turn left and follow the road on the north side of the burn to the parking.

Walk up the road to the right of the dam, then follow the track for 600m and cross a bridge over the Allt Choinneachain. Leave the track here and ascend beside the burn for about 80m in height to pick up a rough path, which is followed up a leftwards-curving ridge above steeper ground named Creag Dhearg. The path leads to a large, well-built cairn then, a high-level track on the flat top of Choinneachain Hill, whose summit can be included by a short detour.

Follow the track down to the north, then up onto Tòn Eich, then drop down around the head of Gilbert's Burn, and break off right on another track. Follow this track north-west, then north up onto the flat top of Auchnafree Hill. Gain first one cairn then, in a further 100m, another one which marks the highest point (**6.25km; 590m; 2h 25min**).

Return to the main track and turn right downhill to reach a junction. Turn left here and follow the track above the reservoir back to the start (**13.75km; 570m; 4h 20min**).

The track used in the descent can be used as a slightly quicker, though duller, ascent route.

Another option (quicker by about 5min) is to go along the track above the loch, and leave it at NN807288 after crossing the Allt Bhaltair. Follow a short, grassy track that zigzags back up to the burn, then climb the spur of Tòn Eich to gain the track on top. Follow this around the head of Gilbert's Burn, as for the previous route.

▶

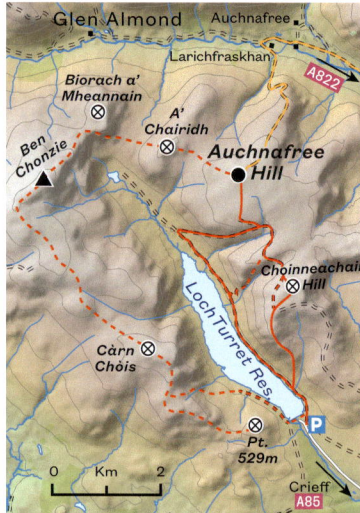

Creag Uchdag; 879m; (C51); L51 or L52; NN708323; crag of the hollows/slopes

Creag Uchdag forms the highest point at the west end of the chain of hills on the south side of Glen Almond that includes the Corbett Auchnafree Hill and the Munro Ben Chonzie. To its south and west, a traditional through route runs from Comrie to Ardeonaig on Loch Tay via Glen Lednock and Fin Glen. It is via these glens that the hill is generally approached.

The favoured approach is from the south, from a small parking area (NN743272) at Coishavachan towards the end of the narrow public road up Glen Lednock from Comrie. Since this is also the parking for one of the routes to Ben Chonzie, it can get busy, so parking on the verge just beyond this, or finding an alternative space without restricting passing places, or gate access points, may be required.

It used to be possible to drive up to the dam at Loch Lednock Reservoir and park there, but a gate has been placed across the road just beyond the last houses.

To continue to Ben Chonzie, cross to A' Chairidh (730m), then Biorach a' Mheannain (755m), then drop to the Bealach na Gaoith and climb to Ben Chonzie (931m); 4.5km, 500m, 2h from Auchnafree Hill.

Descend the south-east ridge over Meall na Sèide to Càrn Chòis. Follow the path off this and descend through the shallow corrie to the north-east of Beinn Liath to gain the end of a track above the loch. Follow the track to the dam and cross (**19.25km; 1240m; 7h**).

It is only slightly longer to stay high, following the fence across Beinn Liath to gain Pt.529m, then the dam.

An ascent can also be made from Newton Bridge in the Sma' Glen by walking up Glen Almond for 8.5km to cross the bridge to Larichfraskhan.

From there, the track that zigzags up onto the broad ridge above Crom Chreag is followed via its right branch onto the summit dome of Auchnafree Hill (**12.25km; 590m; 3h 40min**).

Return the same way (**24.5km; 610m; 6h 40min**).

The use of a bike to just beyond Larichfraskhan should save at least 2h on the day.

For the return to Newton Bridge on foot, Glen Almond can be regained by descending any of the deep corries, which are a notable feature on the south side of the glen. The corrie that the Allt Coire Chultrain flows down is perhaps the most interesting.

The crest eastwards to Meall Tarsuinn offers a high-level return, although broken and boggy in places.

![photograph]

Creag Uchdag and Meall Dubh Mòr over Loch Lednock Reservoir (Rab Anderson)

Walk up the road past the houses, and take the right fork, which leads to the east end of the impressive dam containing Loch Lednock Reservoir.

Opened in 1957, this is a diamond-headed buttress dam, one of only two in Scotland (the other being Errochty), designed to cope with the potential earth tremor hazard from the nearby Highland Boundary Fault. The dam forms part of the Breadalbane Hydro-electric Power Scheme of six dams and seven power stations, linked via a series of tunnels and pipelines to the surrounding major lochs. Loch Lednock being linked to St Fillans on Loch Earn.

Continue on a track above the reservoir for 300m and follow the main right fork uphill, then take its left fork through a gate in a fence to where it ends at the Allt Mòr. Cross the burn and continue north-west, diagonally up the hillside following an ATV track. Either leave the track and cut through an area of peat hags to gain the top of Meall Dubh Mòr (809m), or continue on the track beneath the hags then leave it to cross the line of a burn through a shallow basin, then gain this top.

An interesting alternative crosses the bridge over the Allt Mòr, just above the reservoir, then ascends beside the trees and through small rock outcrops onto the spur of Creag Liath. This provides a pleasant route to gain the ATV track.

From Meall Dubh Mòr, Creag Uchdag's prominent summit crest can be seen to the north-west. A vague path leads across the dip, then up to the trig point, which sits at the south-east end of the long and knobbly crest (**7km; 690m; 2h 40min**).

Either return the same way (**14km; 715m; 4h 50min**), or return to the dip with Meall Dubh Mòr, then drop south-west into the corrie, Coire an Eachdarra, and follow the left (south) side of the burn downhill. This, and the lower slopes, lead to a circular sheepfold above the reservoir. Rough terrain above the reservoir regains the dam and the road back; an added 500m, 10min.

A finer circuit starts at Ardeonaig, about 7 miles (11km) along the South Loch Tay road from Killin at the west end of Loch Tay, and 9 miles (15km) from Kenmore at the east end. With permission, it may be possible to park in the Ardeonaig Hotel car park, otherwise one may have to hunt around. There is a single space on the east side of the bridge over the Ardeonaig Burn.

Leave the road 100m to the east of the bridge over the Ardeonaig Burn, at a Right of Way signpost for Glen Lednock and Comrie. Go through the gate and ascend by the fence. Either step over a fence at the top right corner, or go through a gate in the top left corner. Either way, gain the Cill mo Chormaig ruined church and burial ground, then follow a fence and wall on its right onto a track. This leads through a gate, then past a farm building and through an open gateway in the upper wall onto the open hillside.

After a few initial zigzags, the grassy track swings below some trees into secluded Fin Glen with Creag Uchdag in view ahead. Follow the grassy track, boggy in places, up the glen to where the slope starts to rise and cross the Eas Domhain. Leave the right of way here and follow the slope to the right of the Eas Domhain uphill above some shielings. Continue up the right branch to a minor knoll before Tom a' Mhoraire then cross a

▶

Creag Uchdag and the Eas Domhain from the Fin Glen approach (Rab Anderson)

section of flat ground and climb steeply uphill to pass between two knolls. Finally, slant up right onto the long summit crest of Creag Uchdag, and follow this to the south-east for 350m to gain the trig point (**6.25km; 760m; 2h 40min**).

Return along the crest to gain the north-west top, then follow a line of intermittent old fence posts across the flat dip, passing through an area of peat hags, to gain Meall nan Oighreag (833m). There are some 19th century lead mine workings around the summit.

Now simply follow an ATV track down the broad north-west ridge beside a fence, with superb views up and down Loch Tay and across to the Ben Lawers massif. About halfway down, follow the ATV track which veers away from the fence around the side of Creag Liath, to descend through an upper boundary wall. Drop past a communications mast and weather station, then continue on down to rejoin the upwards route at the old graveyard (**13.5km; 820m; 4h 45min**).

A longer circuit can be made from Ardtalnaig, parking as for Creagan na Beinne; see opposite page. Walk up Ardtalnaig Glen on the road for 300m, then 100m beyond Ardtalnaig House, go through a metal gate on the right

and follow an old track (shown as a path on the OS 1:50k map), which zigzags up a field, then through lovely woodland to emerge onto the open hillside at NN707383.

Climb onto Sròn na Ceàrdaich and follow a fence along the ridge over Tullich Hill (682m), onto Meall nan Oighreag (833m), then Creag Uchdag (**8.25km; 870m; 3h 15min**).

Drop south-east and cross the dip to Meall Dubh Mòr (809m), then cross a bigger dip and climb to Creag nan Eun (852m). Descend to the east and climb onto a minor knoll (c.780m), then turn north and descend the ridge over Meall Aiteachain to cross the infant River Almond in the floor at the head of Glen Almond.

Now on the route of the Rob Roy Way, continue to the closed bothy at Dunan, then follow the track from there through the splendid moraine mounds, and down Gleann a' Chilleine between Shee of Ardtalnaig and Creagan na Beinne to return to Ardtalnaig (**21.75km; 1050m; 7h**).

From Dunan, those with additional energy might include either the Shee of Ardtalnaig, a Graham, or Creagan na Beinne, see opposite page.

> *Creagan na Beinne; 888m; (C36); L51 or L52; NN744368); little hill of the rocks/crags*

Creagan na Beinne forms the western highpoint of the chain of 800m summits that rise steeply above the north side of Glen Almond. On its south side, this glen rises steeply to the Munro Ben Chonzie and the Corbett Auchnafree Hill.

A traditional route runs west through Glen Almond from Newton Bridge to the east, from a section of the glen known as the Sma' Glen. This route runs past Dunan, then on through Gleann a' Chilleine, between Creagan na Beinne and the Graham Ciste Buide a' Claidheimh (Shee of Ardtalnaig), to reach the houses at Ardtalnaig midway down the south side of Loch Tay.

The Rob Roy Way long-distance route between Drymen and Pitlochry passes through Ardtalnaig, and from there an alternative loop runs through Gleann a' Chilleine to Glen Almond, then on to Glen Quoich and Aberfeldy.

The ascent of Creagan na Beinne is best made from Ardtalnaig. Since this lies almost midway along Loch Tay, it can either be approached from Killin to the west, or from Kenmore to the east, via the narrow road along the south side of the loch. Parking (best front-in, or rear-in) appears to be accepted on the loch side of the road at the cottages on the south side of the bridge over the Ardtalnaig Burn.

Walk north across the bridge over the burn, then go through a gate on the right and follow a track uphill by the trees. Continue on the main track, which bends left then right, to pass through a gate in a wall. A long traverse follows before the track zigzags steeply uphill through two gates to end beside an upper wall on the 360m contour. The views back over Loch Tay to the Ben Lawers group, and south-west along the Loch and Glen Dochart to Ben More and Stob Binnein, are splendid.

Go through a gap in the wall and continue on a rough track which runs beside the wall then a fence for a way. Initially grassy, then heathery, then grassy again, the track makes a long, rising and increasingly boggy traverse to cross the head of Coire Cruinneachan to meet a fence in the dip between Beinn Bhreac and Pt.658m.

Whilst the fence can be crossed and a direct route taken over Pt.658m, this entails crossing a dip then passing through an area of peat hags. The easier option is to simply follow the fence, which, after drop-ping slightly, swings round onto the crest of Creagan na Beinne's north shoulder. When the fence ends, continue up the broad crest beside intermittent fence posts to reach the summit cairn, which lies just off to the side (**8km; 790m; 3h 5min**).

The simplest return is back the same way (**16km; 810m; 5h 15min**).

The return can be varied by continuing northwards onto Beinn Bhreac (716m), with its trig point and fine views. From there, descend the broad ridge south-westwards to gain the start of the main track, which is followed back; an added 15min or so.

Another alternative is to descend the broad south ridge, known as Dunan Hill, to reach the watershed between Gleann a' Chilleine and Glen Almond at Dunan. There are some very fine post-glacial moraine mounds here. The easiest option from here is to follow the track through Gleann a' Chilleine, then down the road to Ardtalnaig (**18.5km; 790m; 5h 45min**).

Another option is to climb Ciste Buide a' Claidheimh (Shee of Ardtalnaig) and traverse its ridge, then descend to Ardtalnaig; an added ascent of 330m and 45min, or so.

Map on opposite page

Creagan na Beinne and Gleann a' Chilleine from the ascent track to the north-west (Rab Anderson)

Beinn Chaorach from the approach above
Auchtertyre, with Cam Chreag's south-east
top, centre, and Beinn Challuim, right
(Rab Anderson)

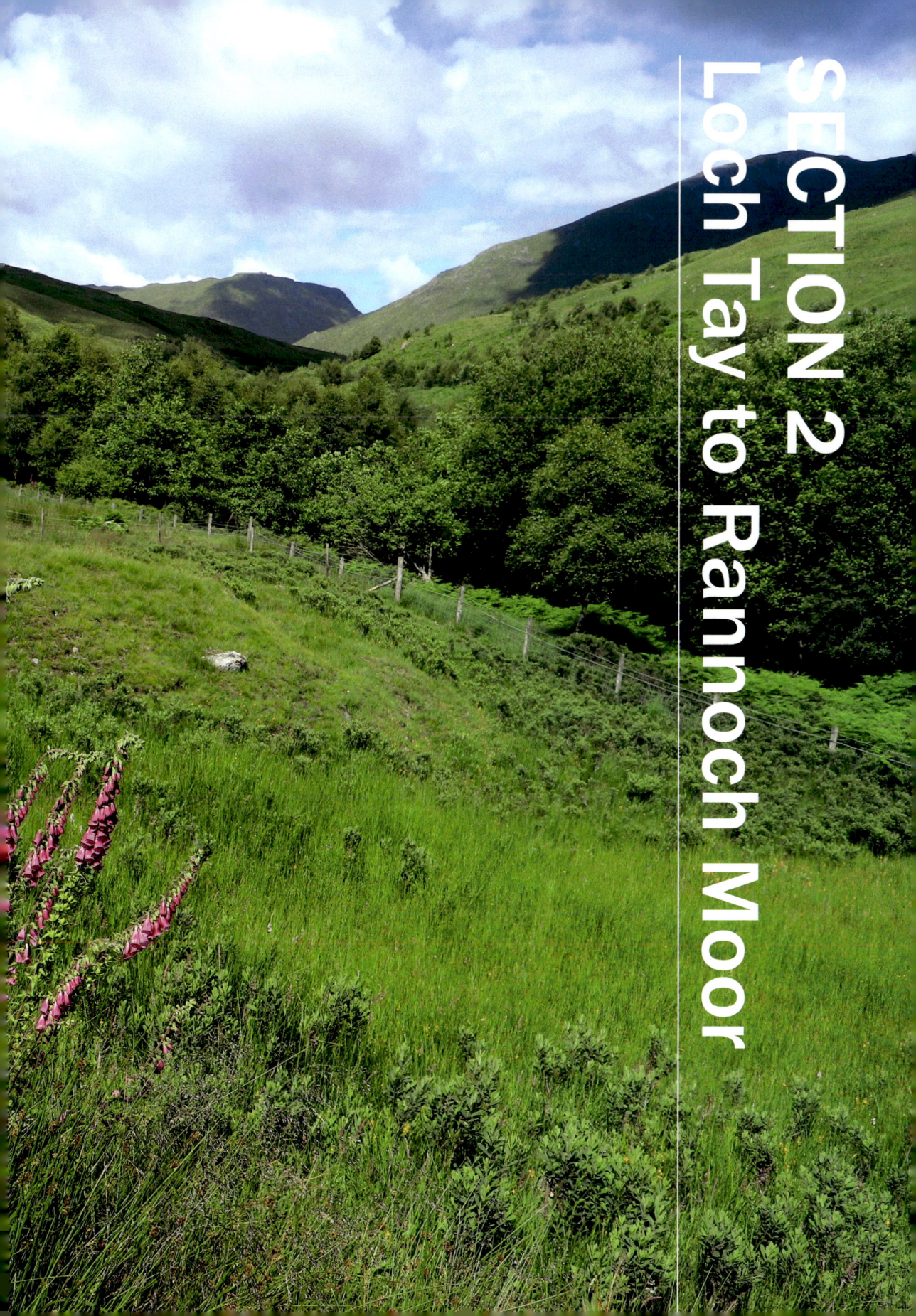

SECTION 2
Loch Tay to Rannoch Moor

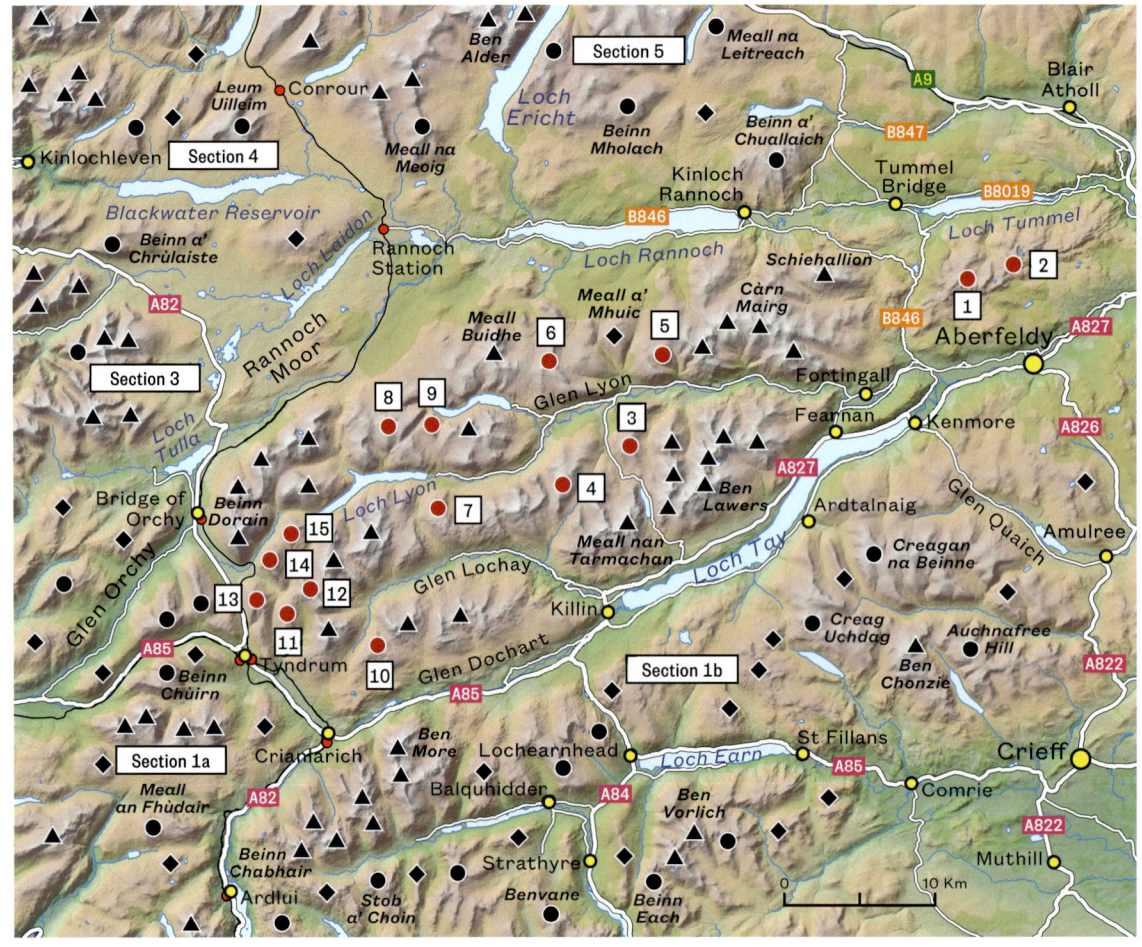

SECTION 2

Meall Tairneachan from Meall Odhar Mòr to the west (Rab Anderson)

Meall Tairneachan; *787m; (C181); L52; NN807543; hill of thunder*
Farragon Hill; *783m; (C186); L52; NN840553; St. Fergan's hill*

Stretching west from Pitlochry towards Schiehallion, and lying to the south of Loch Tummel, is a chain of hills, of which these two are the highest. Farragon Hill sits centrally and is the more prominent of the pair, its pointed shape visible from the A9 north of Dunkeld, whilst Meall Tairneachan, at the west end, is more rounded and less distinctive.

The range is known as a source for barytes (barium sulfate), a mineral currently used in the oil industry as a component of the lubrication pumped down well heads during drilling. There are various old and new workings.

The area that lies between Meall Tairneachan and Creag an Loch, an intermediary hill between the two Corbetts, is the site of the working Foss Mine. This consists of various opencast areas, shafts, spoil heaps and water catchment pools. Together with the mining infrastructure and the site tracks it is not an attractive area. Linking the two hills means that the mine area has to be passed through,

so care should be taken to obey any site instructions and signage. There should be no problem at weekends.

Although the access track to the mine can be used as an approach from the B846 to the west, parking is limited and the route is less aesthetic than that over Meall Odhar Mòr to the west of Meall Tairneachan.

The route over Meall Odhar Mòr starts from a car park on the east side of the B846, at NN777545, at Tomphubil, where there is an old limekiln.

Follow a short section of track and go through a gate in a deer fence then cut left across a flat area on a rough path beneath the overhead power line. Climb the hillside next to an old wall and the fence up the side of the forestry on the left. There are good views back to Schiehallion.

Cross a flattening, marked as Meall Odhar Beag on the OS 1:25k map, then go through a gate in another fence at the top edge of the trees.

Continue uphill beside the wall

onto the top of Meall Odhar Mòr (678m), where the twin humps of Meall Tairneachan's western tops rise ahead. Drop slightly and follow the wall across a flat area, then climb quite steeply up the hillside to a col between the humps on the horseshoe summit ridge.

It is worth climbing onto Cìoch Mòr (775m) to the right first, then returning to the col and following the curved ridge over Pt.780m to the stone trig point on the summit at the east end (**3.5km; 480m; 1h 35min**).

There is steep ground to the east here, so head northwards and drop to the highpoint of the track to the mine, then follow this along and zigzag down into the mine area. At the bottom, it is perhaps best to follow the southern track around the workings.

On the far side, the track swings north then east over the northern spur of Creag an Loch (736m) where it becomes grassier and drops into the corrie below Farragon Hill.

▶

At the bottom, when the track turns left to where it ends, head right past some large boulders and follow a rough path through the heather onto the high ground at a flat col. Swing north-east here and cross rough terrain on what is called Lick Hill on the OS1:25k map, then climb more steeply up the grassy summit cone of Farragon Hill; there are traces of path in places (**8.5km; 770m; 3h 15min**).

Return to the track, either the same way, or more directly, then follow it back through the mine area and up to its highpoint. Continue down the track, passing through a gate in a deer fence, for just over 1km to where the track levels out. Leave the track here and cross the flat corrie floor (Coire an t-Suidhe) on the left, then ascend to a gate in a deer fence. Go through the gate, or climb the wooden slats to its side, then follow the fence to rejoin the upwards route at the gate in the deer fence just above the Meall Odhar Beag flattening. Return to the start (**16.5km; 1060m; 6h**).

Creag an Loch could be included on the return, only adding 20min, or so, to the day.

For those who don't mind track walking, the track to the mine can be followed from verge parking on the B846 to its highpoint to climb Meall Tairneachan, then continue as for the principal route description.

Farragon Hill from the end of the track to the west (Rab Anderson)

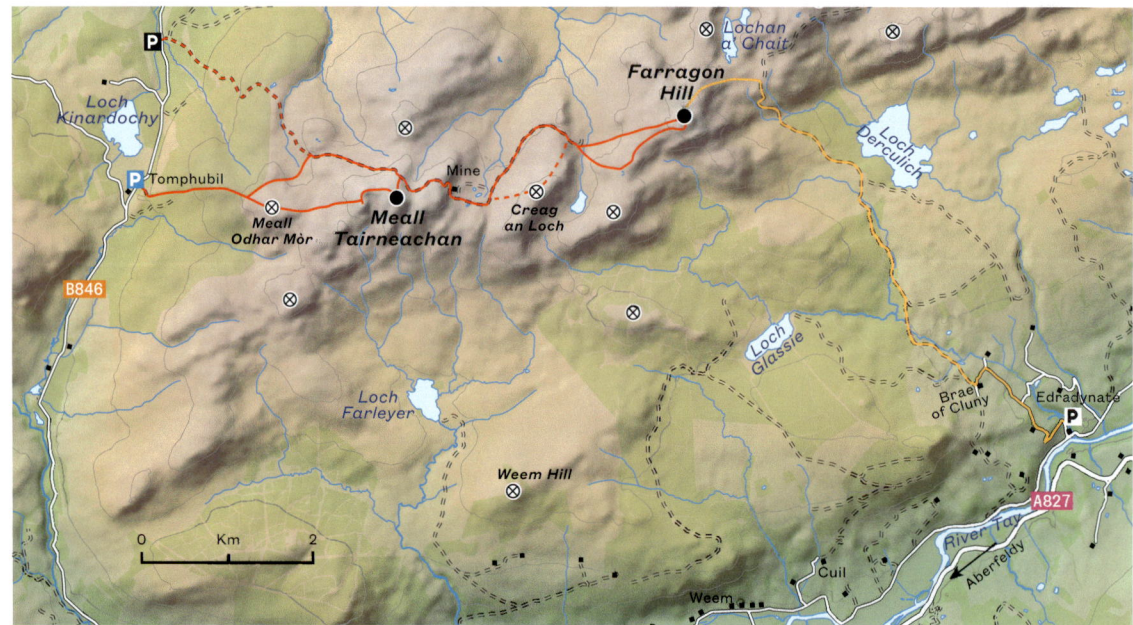

> *Meall nam Maigheach*; 779m; (C192); L51; NN586436; *hill of the hares*

Located at the north end of Lochan na Làirige, the reservoir that sits between Meall nan Tarmachan and the Ben Lawers group, Meall nam Maigheach displays little to impress when approached from there on the high road between Loch Tay and Glen Lyon. From much of Glen Lyon it is obscured by the lower Creag nan Èildeag, however, from the north-west, in the vicinity of Meggernie Castle, it reveals more of itself, seen rising above the ancient Caledonian pinewoods of Glen Lyon.

A route from Glen Lyon is the most enjoyable, especially via the long ridge from Creag nan Eildeag, which leads to its summit. However, parking is limited, and due to the road between Loch Tay and Glen Lyon climbing to a height of 549m to its north, Meall nam Maigheach is almost always climbed from there. It therefore provides a short ascent and can be conveniently paired with Beinn nan Oighreag, or one of the Innerwick Corbetts, or Meall nan Subh, with a drive along Glen Lyon and a break at the Bridge of Balgie cafe.

Most will want to take the shortest route by using the car parking spaces beneath the cairn just beyond the north end of Lochan na Làirige. However, this is also the parking for the ascent of the two Munros, Meall Corranaich and Meall a' Choire Lèith, so space is limited. The route from there over Meall nan Eun (635m) also crosses haggy and tussocky ground. As a result, it's better to park just over 1km to the west at NN582416, where there is room for two or three cars on the south side of the road at the point it turns the corner to descend to Glen Lyon. There is a green hut on the opposite side of the road with a ruin next to it.

Cross the road and walk past the hut to take a curving line northwards across the hillside of a shallow corrie (Corrie Buidhe). Initially this is well to the right of a wall that can be seen running up the far side of the corrie, and right of the burns that drain the corrie. This line gains the broad south-east ridge, then the summit, which is the first of two highpoints, the other being Meall Luaidhe (776m) to the north-west. A rock about 50m to the east-south-east of the cairn has been measured as the highest point (**2.25km; 280m; 55min**).

Return the same way (**4.5km; 280m; 1h 30min**). ▶

Useful for a short day, a quick ascent of Meall Tairneachan can be made from Tomphubil (**3.5km; 480m; 1h 35min**), returning the same way (**7km; 530m; 2h 40min**).

Farragon Hill can be climbed on its own from Edradynate, by turning off the road along the north side of the River Tay between Aberfeldy and Grandtully at Easter Cluny. There is good parking at the bend at NN884519 by the hydro building.

Walk up the road and turn left to pass Brae of Cluny (signed Farragon), then turn right along a track, and right again at a fork. This track leads past Loch Derculich (worth a detour), then on up the hillside to the east of Farragon Hill. Leave the track at the top of the zigzags, and climb onto the north-east ridge to gain the summit (**7.75km; 680m; 2h 50min**). Return the same way (**15.5km; 680m; 4h 45min**).

Meall nam Maigheach (Rab Anderson)

Meall nam Maigheach above the Glen Lyon Caledonian pinewoods (Rab Anderson)

Another route starts about 600m further down the road, from a two car space on the east side, just before the bridge over the burn draining the corrie. Walk down the road, then follow the wall up the left side of the shallow corrie to where it ends 100m to the south-west of the summit (**1.5km; 325m; 50min**).

Return the same way (3km; 325m; 1h 15min).

A more interesting walk can be had by starting at Camusvrachan where there is parking at the bridge over the River Lyon, a short way down a track signed to Roro.

Cross the bridge and go right to Roroyere. Pass a track off left, then cross the burn and go left up a grassy track onto the eastern prow of Creag nan Eildeag.

Look for the top of the unique rock feature of the 'Praying Hands of Mary' and follow a rough path to this. Continue up the crest beyond and go through a gap in a wall, then follow a fence up the crest to gain the top of Creag nan Èildeag (642m).

Drop to a col, then climb to Meall nam Maigheach (**6.75km; 700m; 2h 40min**).

Descend steeply east and cross the burn to gain a track, then follow this back down the glen (13.75km; 750m; 4h 30min).

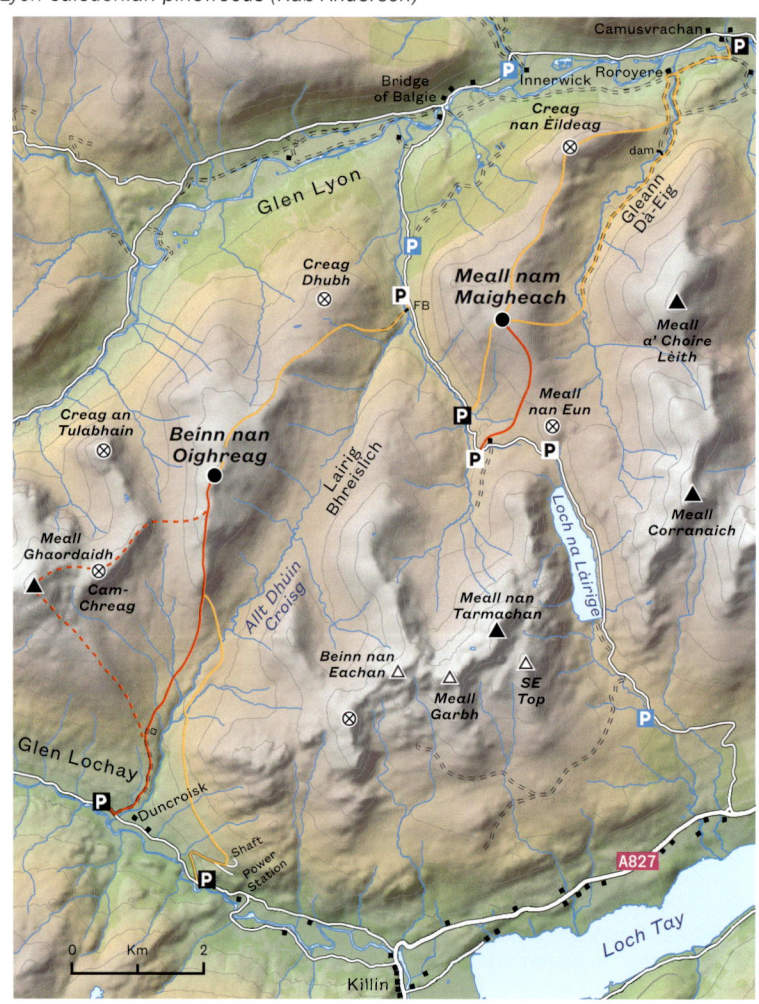

Beinn nan Oighreag; *909m; (C10); L51; NN541412; cloudberry hill*

Sitting between Meall Ghaordaidh to its west and the Meall nan Tarmachan range to its east, Beinn nan Oighreag is one of the higher Corbetts. In the 1930s, it was even suggested that it might just be a Munro, and as a result it attracted a flurry of attention.

Taking the form of a long and grassy whaleback ridge, Beinn nan Oighreag extends almost all of the way between Glen Lochay in the south and Glen Lyon to the north. The most direct route to and from Killin from these glens runs the length of its eastern flanks and passes through the Làirig Bhreislich. A large number of ruined sheilings are dotted along this route, which confirms that it must have seen much traffic from drovers and those on foot. Old descriptions state the pass as being 'a villainous bog, all peat hags and heathery hummocks'. Fortunately, the routes to the summit avoid this pass by climbing the hill's grassy ridges, although it can still be boggy in some places.

The ascent can be undertaken from either the Glen Lochay side, or the Glen Lyon side. The former gives the better route via its south ridge, to which there are two approaches, whilst the latter enables it to be conveniently paired with Meall nam Maigheach for a two-Corbett day, with a short drive up or down the road between the parking places.

From Glen Lochay, there are two approaches to the south ridge. Both are reached by a short drive along the glen via a narrow road with passing places, which leaves the A827 from the north side of the bridge over the River Lochay at the northern edge of Killin.

The shortest route starts some 3 miles (5km) along Glen Lochay, west of Duncroisk and about 200m beyond the bridge over the Allt Dhùin Croisk. There is space for six or so considerably parked cars at a widening on a bend in the road at NN526363. There are other places nearby where cars can be squeezed in off the road, as well as some space

on the right around the bend a little further on. This is the same parking as for the Munro Meall Ghaordaidh, so it can be busy; be prepared to drive back and use the parking and approach option described overleaf.

Walk back towards the bridge to a gate and a sign for Meall Ghaordaidh. Go through the gate into a field and follow a grassy track through another gate then on up the hillside; splendid views open out up the glen to Beinn Sheasgarnaich and Creag Mhòr. At a gate in a wall, cross by a stile on the right, then continue up the stony track over the lower ridge of Meall Ghaordaidh, passing the path off left to that hill.

With Beinn nan Oighreag now in sight ahead, continue past a stone sheepfold to cross a burn, the Allt an Fhaing. Follow the main, and increasingly rougher, ATV track to cross the major burn coming down from the col between Meall Ghaordaidh and Beinn nan Oighreag on stepping stones.

The ATV track now splits. The right-
▶

Beinn nan Oighreag on the approach above the Allt Dhùin Chroisg from Glen Lochay to the south (Rab Anderson)

hand branch leads in a few hundred metres to a slight crest and a cairn on a boulder. Leave the track here and climb the broad south ridge over tussocky ground to gain a grassy path running up a steepening to the right of some boulders.

A better route to the same point follows the left-hand ATV track, which becomes increasingly vague, to the left of the crest to where it effectively ends at a tall metal pole just below the boulders, from where the grassy path is gained.

The grassy path leads up to a boulder where a line of old fence posts is met and followed along a level section, then on up the final steepening for a short way. The posts pass west of and just below the summit, so cut up right to gain the summit, marked by a small cairn on a rock outcrop; the cairn to the north-east looks higher, but is actually lower (**6km; 780m; 2h 40min**).

The panorama is splendid. Meall Ghaordaidh to the west and the Ben Lawers massif to the east are close at hand, whilst in an arc from the north-west to the north-east, Buachaille Etive Mòr, Ben Nevis, the Northern Cairngorms and Ben Macdui stand out.

Return the same way (**12km; 790m; 4h 15min**).

This route allows Meall Ghaordaidh to be included by descending beside the fence posts to the col to the west (638m), then ascending over Cam-Chreag (890m) to the summit, from where the path down the long south-east ridge is descended; an additional 2.5km, 450m, 1h 45min.

A slightly longer route onto the south ridge of Beinn nan Oighreag starts some 2 miles (3.25km) along Glen Lochay where there is space for a few cars in the trees just before and at a hydro road off to the north at NN539352. This is 700m beyond a pipeline and a power station.

Follow the hydro road around a sharp bend and take the left-hand branch, then shortcut the bend on an ATV track, up and across a field, before the next bend in the track, which ends at an air shaft.

Continue on the rough track and path, which makes a rising traverse northwards across the hillside, through and alongside walls and fences. There are a number of small burns to cross, and it can be boggy in places, although there are railway sleepers across some bits. The route continues along above a wall, then on to a crossing of the Allt a' Choire Ghlais at NN538378 where what remains of the bridge is unsafe, but the crossing is normally dry. On the

other side, continue up the spur between the burns to reach the Allt Dhùin Croisg at a gravelly section at NN542387, where it can normally be crossed dry.

Briefly follow an ATV track, then follow the south ridge up to the summit, picking up the grassy path of the main route to the right of some boulders where it ascends a steeper section (**7.5km; 790m; 3h**).

Return by the same route (**15km; 800m; 5h**).

The ascent from the north is made from partway down the road between Loch Tay and Glen Lyon, from a small pull-off at NN571438, opposite a bridge across the Allt Baile a' Mhuilinn. This is about 2km down the road from the lower parking spot for Meall nam Maigheach, with which this hill could be combined.

Cross the bridge and follow an ATV track westwards then south-west-wards up the grassy hillside over a slight rise at 700m. The track continues up the broad ridge over Pt.899m where a line of fence posts is met and briefly followed. The posts pass west of and below the summit, which is the southernmost highpoint; a rock outcrop (**4.5km; 615m; 2h**).

Return the same way (**9km; 635m; 3h 15min**).

Map on page 78

Beinn nan Oighreag's summit ridge from the south (Tom Prentice)

Beinn Dearg and Glen Lyon from Ben Meggernie above Bridge of Balgie (Rab Anderson)

Beinn Dearg; 830m; (C115); L51; NN608497; red hill

Lying between Innerwick and Camusvrachan, Beinn Dearg is the easternmost of two Corbetts rising above the north side of Glen Lyon. The best-looking route would appear to be from the Camusvrachan side, via the forestry track and ridges either side of the Cùl Làirig, but there is nowhere to park at the start of the track. As a result, the only practicable way is from the Meggernie Estates car park (with toilets) at NN586475, at Innerwick near Bridge of Balgie.

It should be noted that the minor road between Loch Tay and Bridge of Balgie in Glen Lyon climbs to a height of 550m, and is not kept open in winter, so snow and ice regularly prevent access.

Between Beinn Dearg and Cam Chreag to the west are the obstacles of Meall a' Mhuic (745m), a Graham, and Meall nam Maigheach (741m). A high-level traverse between the Corbetts would be a tough under-taking, so anyone seeking to climb both in one outing is better returning towards Innerwick to utilise the hill tracks. The Graham, Meall a' Mhuic, is more easily included with Beinn Dearg, and a brief description for this is given at the end.

Walk back to the road then turn left and cross the Allt Ghallabhaich, passing the road off right to Innerwick itself and the kirk (one of numerous similar Thomas Telford Parliamentary Kirks throughout Scotland), then the Glen Lyon War Memorial cairn. Turn onto a track on the left known as the

Kirk Road, also an old drove road, which runs north through the Lairig Ghallabhaich to Dall on Loch Rannoch.

Follow the main track past tracks off to the right and left, and climb uphill to a junction where a track heads left downhill; the link to the

▶

Beinn Dearg above Camusvrachan in Glen Lyon (Grahame Nicoll)

Cam Chreag track for anyone seeking to add this in after an ascent of Beinn Dearg. Continue uphill, swinging right then left past a loop track off to the right, for 1.25km then turn up right and zigzag up through the trees to exit the forestry by a gate.

An ATV track leads to the top edge of the forestry, either follow this south for 120m to where a branch climbs onto the crest in the dip at the head of the Cùl Làirig, or climb eastwards up heathery ground to follow the broad and featureless slope to the top. A line of old fence posts is encountered, with the summit being located at the second cairn on the fenceline, about 100m beyond the first cairn. It is an otherwise bald and featureless flat summit with fine views across Glen Lyon to the Ben Lawers range (**5km; 615m; 2h 10min**).

The simplest return is back the same way (**10km; 615m; 3h 25min**).

An alternative is to swing around the head of the Cùl Làirig to Pt.741m, then to a cairn above Creag Àrd for the view east down Glen Lyon. Return towards Pt.741m then descend south-westwards to reach a fence, which is followed to the right to go through a gate. Follow the fence down beside the forestry to pass through another gate where rough ATV tracks are then followed downhill through a gate to gain the track used in the approach (**10.5km; 650m; 3h 40min**).

To include Meall a' Mhuic, return to where the ATV track enters the forestry, then cut straight down onto the main track. Head north for 750m then take another track, which doubles back downhill, and leave this before it reaches a dam. Cross the Allt Ghallabhaich and climb steeply north-west beside a burn on heathery ground that eases towards the summit (**9.5km; 925m; 3h 40min**).

Descend south to pick up a grassy track, which zigzags down to another track, and follow this across the Allt Ghallabhaich to return to the start (**14km; 925m; 4h 50min**).

Beinn Dearg and Cam Creag can be climbed together by utilising the link track across the Allt Ghallabhaich and Allt a' Mhuic between them (**21km; 1215m; 7h**).

Map opposite

Cam Chreag; 862m; (C75); L51; NN536491; crooked crag

Rising above the north side of Glen Lyon, Cam Chreag is the western-most of two Corbetts that are usually accessed from Innerwick near Bridge of Balgie. Between it and Beinn Dearg to the east are the obstacles of Meall nam Maigheach (741m) and Meall a' Mhuic (745m), a Graham. A high-level traverse between the Corbetts is likely to be a tough undertaking, so anyone seeking to climb both in one outing is better returning towards Innerwick to utilise the hill tracks.

The minor road between Loch Tay and Bridge of Balgie in Glen Lyon climbs to a height of 550m and is not kept open in winter, so snow and ice regularly prevent access.

Start from the Meggernie Estates car park (with toilets) at NN586475 at Innerwick. Leave the north-west corner of the car park and follow a

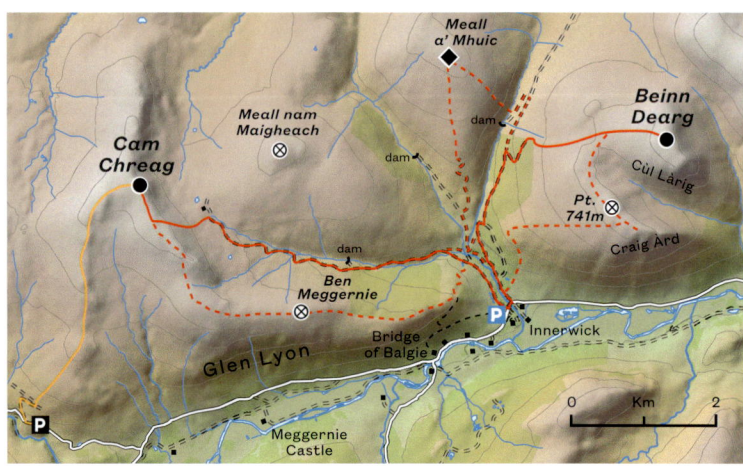

Cam Chreag's summit ridge, with the Ben Lawers massif and Meall nan Tarmachan beyond, and Meall nam Maigheach, centre (Rab Anderson)

track through a gate, then northwards along the base of a felled area of forestry, passing a path off left - one of the estate paths which can be used on an alternative return.

Continue along the track through another gate, then drop down across a bridge over the Allt a' Choire Uidhre and take the track on the left uphill above the burn. In a further 1km, the track crosses a bridge back over the burn and continues the westwards climb up Coire Odhar.

Follow the track almost to its end, then, at a bend at NN546486 about 100m short of a small hut, leave the track. Now follow a rough ATV track and path south-west then west up the steep slope, initially through heather then grass. There is no difficulty, however, in winter snow accumulates here, and the easterly nature of the slope means that an alternative route onto the ridgeline west of Ben Meggernie might be prudent. Under snow, the going can be tough here.

On gaining the long, level crest of the hill, turn right (north-west) for about 750m, then make a final short rise onto the rocky summit knoll (**6.5km; 650m; 2h 30min**).

The view to the north is open and extensive, and includes Ben Nevis, Ben Alder and Ben Macdui, whilst to the south, the Ben Lawers group and Meall nan Tarmachan lie closer at hand across Glen Lyon.

Return by the route of ascent (13km; 660m; 4h).

An alternative descent can be made along the crest to the south-south-east to gain Pt.754. From

there, the ridge is followed down over Ben Meggernie (662m). Although there are wooden marker posts in places on the line of rough ATV tracks, there is some quite rough going.

Just beyond the top of Creag an Fhaoraich above Bridge of Balgie, go through a gate in a fence and drop down to one of the Meggernie Estates paths. Follow this northwards, then steeply down through a felled area of forestry to regain the track used in the approach (14km; 660m; 4h 20min).

Climbing Cam Chreag and Beinn Dearg together and utilising the link track across the Allt a' Mhuic and the Allt Ghallabhaich, gives a much longer route (21km; 1215m; 7h).

A useful and perhaps more scenic route climbs the hill via its south ridge, starting from the road to the dam at Loch an Daimh, as used to access the Munros Stùc an Lochain and Meall Buidhe. Park on grass on the right at NN522459, just before a gate across the road.

Walk through the gate, then go up a track. At the second bend, go through a wall and follow a rough ATV track up its right side. When the wall ends, follow a line of iron fence posts over Creagan nan Gobhar and on up the ridge. The posts end in front of Pt.850m. Go over this and cross to the summit (**4.75km; 530m; 2h**).

Return the same way (9.5km; 570m; 3h 20min).

Cam Chreag across Coire Odhar from Ben Meggernie (Rab Anderson)

Meall nan Subh; 806m; (C151); L51; NN460397; hill of the soo (raspberry)

Occupying rugged ground between the Munros Beinn Sheasgarnaich and Meall Ghaordaidh, Meall nan Subh is a hill made up of a myriad of lumps and bumps, small crags, pools of water and bogs. It sits above the 505m highpoint of the road (marked on the OS 1:50k map as a track) that links the heads of Glen Lochay and Glen Lyon, which should make Meall nan Subh an easy, short hill. However, although there is parking at the high-point, the road between these glens is not maintained. Due to potholes and gouged-out bits, it is therefore pretty much unsuitable for anything other than four-wheel-drive vehicles with suitable clearance. It is also gated on the Loch Lochay side.

Whilst the road from Glen Lyon is marginally better and it may be possible to drive it, you are advised that you do so at your own risk.

In Glen Lochay, there is a car park at NN476368 (c.195m), 1km short of the road end at Kenknock. On foot, it is (**5.5km; 310m; 1h 40min**) to the start of the hill, with a return time and distance of (**11km; 310m; 2h 55min**), which should be added to those for the ascent of the hill and the return to the road.

In Glen Lyon, there are spaces to park in the vicinity of the bridge at NN459418 (c.310m), in front of the Lubreoch Dam across Loch Lyon just beyond Pubil. On foot, it is (**3km; 195m; 55min**) to the start of the hill, with a return time and distance of (**6km; 195m; 1h 35min**), which should be added to those for the ascent of the hill and the return to the road.

A bike will shorten these times considerably, especially on the downhill return. There is more ascent involved from Glen Lochay, and the initial climb above Kenknock is stiff.

Meall nan Subh can be paired with one of the other nearby Corbetts, with a drive along Glen Lyon between the hills, and perhaps a stop at the Bridge of Balgie cafe in between.

Whilst it is possible to strike off uphill to Meall nan Subh from various points on the road, it is perhaps best to continue to close to the 505m highpoint before commencing the ascent. Electricity lines cross the road here. Climb eastwards, crossing a fence, and head towards a small crag marked on the OS 1:25k map as Creag na h-Iolaire. Pass the left-hand side of this and continue uphill towards a knoll (795m), which at first

appears to be the top. The summit lies behind this, and is the central of three knolls, with a mass of peat and an island occupying the ground in the middle (**1.5km; 310m; 50min**).

North across Glen Lyon, the Corbett Sròn a' Choire Chnapanaich is prominent, with its partner Meall Buidhe to the west. However, it is the surrounding Munros that stand out: Stùc an Lochain to the north-east above Pubil, the vast bulk of Beinn Sheasgarnaich to the south-west, Meall Ghaordaidh to the east, and to the south Beinn Cheathaich and Sgiath Chùil's Top, Meall Churain, with Ben More and Stob Binnein between.

Head north-west to the northern knoll (c.790m), which is a slightly better viewpoint along Glen Lyon; there is a concrete survey pillar on its top. To return, head south-west to rejoin the ascent line and follow this back to the road (**3km; 325m; 1h 20min**).

If the approach up the road between the glens has been made on foot, or by bike, then those distances and times need to be added to the above time. On foot, it is possible to keep to the high ground to return to either glen.

Map opposite

Meall nan Subh showing its full height from the River Lyon in Glen Lyon (Rab Anderson)

Meall Buidhe from Sròn a' Choire Chnapanaich, with Buachaille Etive Mòr and Glen Coe, distant right (Tom Prentice)

Meall Buidhe; *910m; (C9); L51; NN427449; yellow hill*
Sròn a' Choire Chnapanaich; *837m; (C111); L51; NN456453; nose of the knobbly corrie*

These fairly remote Corbetts lie in the range of hills between Loch Lyon and Loch an Daimh. They form part of a twisting ridge to the west of the Munro Stùc an Lochain, which continues beyond Meall Buidhe and

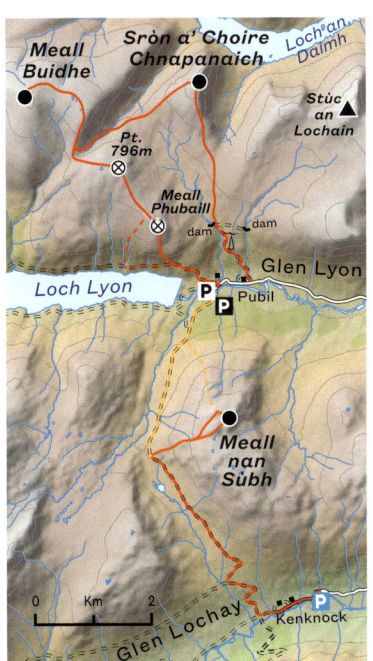

its western tops to the Bridge of Orchy Munros.

Although Meall Buidhe is one of the highest Corbetts, it is rather lost in the jumble of hills here, but from its summit there is an extensive view over Rannoch Moor. Sròn a' Choire Chnapanaich, a much smaller hill, is similarly lost, however, when seen from closer at hand, it reveals a steep and shapely upper pyramidal form.

The hills are climbed together and accessed from the upper reaches of Glen Lyon. Those with time and energy could incorporate the Munro Stùc an Lochain for a fine triptych.

There is ample verge parking where a track leaves the road at NN459419, just west of Pubil and before the access road to the Lubreoch Dam across Loch Lyon.

Walk up the track to pass above the dam and follow the track along the north side of Loch Lyon, where there are two options:

(i) Leave the track at its highpoint and climb steeply through the small rocky band of Creagan Deargain onto Meall Phubaill. Follow a rough path, which passes to the left of some peat

hags, and leads to unnamed Pt.796m.

(ii) Continue on the track for a further 750m, losing 50m in height, and go through a gate in a wall. Cross the first of two burns, which join below the track, then climb the hillside between the burns. Either continue up to the top of unnamed Pt.796m, or traverse beneath it; an added 15min or so to (i).

Meall Buidhe lies to the north-west here and Sròn a' Choire Chnapanaich to the north-east. Drop to the col (709m) with Meall Buidhe, where there is an isolated gate in a line of fence posts, then ascend the ridge to the right of the Allt nan Aighean, following the posts to a flat shoulder.

Continue past some small lochans, then curve around the head of grassy Coire nan Aighean to gain the flat and stony top. The southern of three cairns marks the summit of Meall Buidhe (**6km; 700m; 2h 30min**).

There is a spacious view north-west across Rannoch Moor and Loch Bà to Buachaille Etive Mòr and the Glen Coe mountains. Westwards is Beinn a' Chreachain and the Bridge of Orchy

▶

Sròn a' Choire Chnapanaich from Meall Buidhe, with Stùc an Lochain, right (Tom Prentice)

Hills, whilst to the south are Beinn Sheasgarnaich and Creag Mhòr.

Return to the col, then go down the left side of the burn, the Fèith Thalain, until it makes sense to cross over to gain the flat, peat-hagged, col between the hills. Cross the col on the left side, then ascend the broad, rounded slope ahead, picking up a line of fence posts, to a finish that eases off on short-cropped grass and heather. The fence posts veer off to the right just below the summit of Sròn a' Choire Chnapanaich (**10.5km; 930m; 4h 5min**).

There is now a good view east down Loch an Daimh, with the Munros Meall Buidhe to the left and Stùc an Lochain to the right.

Descend the ridge southwards towards a col (Bealach a' Mhàim, 631m), from where the Meall an Odhar ridge perhaps offers the Munro temptation for some. Angle down to the Allt Phubuill and follow this to a dam. Descend a track, which snakes down to Pubil, then go through a gate and continue down past the lodge to the road. Turn right back to the start (15.5km; 940m; 5h 30min).

Sròn a' Choire Chnapanaich from the descent alongside the Allt Phubuill (Rab Anderson)

Beinn nan Imirean; 849m; (C92); L51; NN419309; hill of the ridge

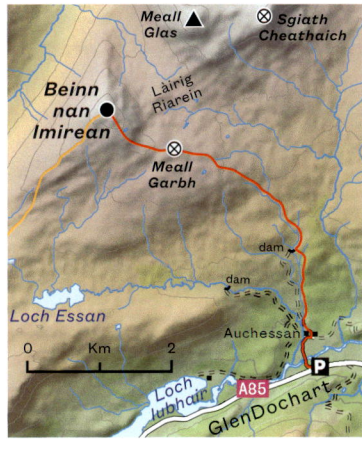

Like Meall Glas, to which it forms the western extension, and is separated from by the Làirig Riarein, Beinn nan Imirean rises gradually above Glen Dochart. To its west, across the River Lochay and the Làirig an Lochain, is the considerably bigger bulk of Beinn Challuim. Beinn nan Imirean is a modest hill, which can be glimpsed from the A85 when travelling west through Glen Dochart, appearing as an insignificant cone with a long south-west ridge.

The usual approach is from Glen Dochart, crossing the low skirt of gentle-angled moorland of peat hags and winding burns that rise north-wards above the glen. Verge parking is possible at NN448276 on the A85, on the east side of the access road to Auchessan; this is on a straight where traffic travels fast. This is also the parking for the Munros Meall Glas and Sgiath Chùil, so it can be busy. Much of the approach is the same as for that to Meall Glas.

Walk down the private road across the River Dochart, pass the first two houses, and go through a gate at the right-hand side of the next one - The Old Farmhouse. Follow a track up the side of the Allt Essan, ignoring the hydro track which crosses over, and continue beside the tributary coming down from Creag nan Uan ahead.

When the track ends at a sheep-fold after 300m, head uphill between the burn and a deer fence on a path which veers left to another fence. Cross this fence by a stile, then continue uphill by the burn, passing a dam and the end of the track on the other side. Follow the path beside the burn, crossing first one fork, then higher up another. Continue beside the left fork to where it disappears, then on for a short way onto the indistinct ridge of Meall Garbh, which sits below Beinn nan Imirean.

Leave the route to Meall Glas and climb onto the slight rise of Meall Garbh, whose top has a large boulder on it. Drop slightly to follow the high ground past a line of boulders, then continue more steeply up the ridge to a flattening with a small lochan. Another short climb leads over a false top to the small slab of rock marking the summit. It is a grand viewpoint (**5.5km; 710m; 2h 25min**). Return the same way (**11km; 730m; 4h**).

This route could be extended to include Meall Glas and Sgiath Chùil.

An ascent can also be made from Inverhaggernie in Strath Fillan, a little to the north-west of Crianlarich. There is a layby at NN367267 on the south side of the A82, 300m to the north of the access road to Inverhaggernie.

Follow the access road under the southern railway line and continue up the track to Inverhaggernie. Go left on the track that passes under the northern railway line and continue up the side of the Inverhaggernie Burn to a dam at NN385284. It is probably best to cross beneath this. On the other side, gain the foot of the long south-west ridge of Beinn nan Imirean, and follow this past a small lochan, then on up the main ridge to the top (**7.75km; 700m; 3h**). Return the same way (**15km; 700m; 5h**).

Beinn nan Imirean from Meall Garbh to the east on the approach from Glen Dochart - Ben Lui beyond (Rab Anderson)

Cam Chreag across Coreheynan from Beinn Chaorach (Tom Prentice)

Cam Chreag; 884m; (C44); L50; NN375346; crooked crag
Beinn Chaorach; 818m; (C125); L50; NN358328; sheep hill

These two hills form part of a compact cluster of five Corbetts that sit between Strath Fillan and the Bridge of Orchy Munros further north. They can be climbed together with the other Corbetts in the cluster as the only instance where such a grouping of Corbetts is practically possible in a single day. There is a grouping of four on Arran and four groups of three elsewhere.

However, the traverse of all five here is a demanding outing, so it is normal to split the group into three separate trips. It is reasonable to combine Cam Chreag and Beinn Chaorach with Beinn Odhar to the west for a round of three from the same starting point in Strath Fillan, and this option is covered at the end here, whilst the round of all five is described in the panel on page 91.

Beinn Chaorach is a mainly grassy hill, with an easy-angled grassy ridge falling south from its summit, and a similarly easy ridge to its north, which leads to a col at the apex of Coreheynan at the head of Gleann a' Chlachainn. From there, another grassy ridge rises eastwards to the summit of Cam Chreag, which sits at

the north-west end of an interesting 1km-long high-level summit ridge. This summit ridge contains another five or six knolls over 870m in height, with the 878m one at the south-east end appearing to look higher than the actual summit. At this south-east end, Cam Chreag is separated from the Munro Beinn Challuim by the Bealach Glas Leathaid, which forms the east side of Gleann a' Chlachainn.

For the straightforward round of two, leave the north side of the A82 in Strath Fillan, some 2km south of Tyndrum, and take the road to Auchtertyre (signed for a farm shop, wigwams & camping) and park on the right after a few hundred metres, beside some farm sheds.

Walk northwards and take the left-hand track uphill on the west side of the Allt Auchtertyre to pass beneath the Auchtertyre Viaduct carrying the West Highland Line railway. Continue on the easier-angled track, with the grassy south ridge of Beinn Chaorach in view ahead.

Loop around across a bridge over the Allt a' Chaol Ghlinne, which runs up Caol Ghleann, the glen separating Beinn Chaorach from Beinn Odhar,

and continue on the right-hand track. This zigzags steeply uphill before levelling off as it runs into Gleann a' Chlachainn, and is followed to a gate (often open) at NN361310 in a fence running up the hillside.

A decision needs to be made here

whether to climb Beinn a' Chaorach first, or to continue up the glen and climb Cam Chreag first. It is described here climbing Cam Chreag first, since following the track to its end to gain the col between the hills is perhaps easier than finding the end of the track in descent after climbing both hills.

Continue on the track, which after 1km becomes rougher and leads to a fenced area of planting entered by a stile. Follow this rougher track all the way to its end, crossing a fence out of the planted area, and continue uphill through haggy ground to the col (638m) to meet a rough path between the two hills. There is a line of very low (seemingly sawn-off) double wooden posts here that runs all the way up and over Beinn a' Chaorach, then on partway up Cam Chreag; the remains of an old electric fence system.

Follow the path to where the line of posts heads off north and continue up to gain the small cairn marking the summit, which sits at the north-west end of a long, elevated summit ridge containing several knolls of a slightly lesser height. This final section would not be straightforward in poor visibility (**8km; 710m; 3h**).

Return to the col, then follow the rough path, past the remains of the wind generator power source for the old electric fence and, at times, beside the remnants of the posts, up to the cylindrical trig pillar on Beinn Chaorach (**11km; 890m; 4h**).

To descend, simply follow the line of posts down the grassy south ridge to meet a gate in a fence running across the hillside at NN359313; there is a vague ATV track in places. Go through the gate, then descend beside another fence to regain the track in Gleann a' Chlachainn at the gate across it, and follow this back (**15.75km; 895m; 5h 15min**).

Whichever way Beinn a' Chaorach is climbed it is important to gain the gate in the fence running across the hillside at NN359313 since the fence has a top strand of barbed wire.

It is worth climbing the full length of the high-level ridge on Cam Chreag, which also makes this route into more of a circuit.

The best way of doing this is to leave the Gleann a' Chlachain track on the approach to Cam Chreag about 1km after crossing the stile into the planted area. This is at NN369326, on the other side of a burn. Cut downhill to gain a vague and overgrown ATV track, which leads across boggy ground to the Allt Gleann a' Chlachain, normally easily crossed just upstream.

Continue uphill to the north-east; if encountered, a line of low wooden posts from the redundant electric fence system can be followed. Cross the fence out of the planted area by a stile at NN376330 to gain the Bealach Ghlas Leathaid between Cam Chreag and Beinn Challuim.

Instead of following the old boundary fence posts, climb northwards up the steep and grassy spur, out to the left to avoid a craggy area, then swing north-east to meet the fence posts near the top. Gain the South-East Top (there are three high-points) then follow sheep tracks along the undulating broad crest to gain the main summit at the north-west end.

This circuit only adds about 20min or so to the standard ascent route via the col between the two Corbetts.

To include Beinn Odhar in the standard route for a threesome, from the summit of Beinn Chaorach, return northwards for 200m or so to pick up another line of low wooden posts from the redundant electric fence. Follow these posts west down a steep, but grassy, slope to gain the col (444m) between the hills.

Continue uphill to the west to gain the shoulder of Beinn Odhar, then a small lochan to the north-west: Lochan Choire Dhuibh. From there, make the final ascent north-west to the summit (**13.75km; 1340m; 5h 45min**).

Return to Lochan Choire Dhuibh, then follow a vague path along the crest, dropping to a height of 600m, and climb to Meall Buidhe (653m).

Descend the crest to the corner of a barbed wire fence, then go along its left side and through an open gate. There are now two options:

(i) Take a diagonal line south-east down the hillside to meet the track used on the approach up Caol Ghleann at NN355303, where it is gated and there is no fence to cross. Follow the track back.

(ii) Go through a gate on the right, then follow the fence and its decrepit continuation southwards to cross a bridge over the railway at NN350293. The far side has a low fence to climb, presumably to keep livestock from the open hill. Continue down to the access road and turn left back to the start (**20.25km; 1400m; 7h 45min**).

Beinn Chaorach from Beinn Challuim, with Ben Lui, left (Rab Anderson)

Map on page 91

Beinn Odhar from the West Highland Way above Tyndrum (Tom Prentice)

Beinn Odhar; *901m; (C22); L50; NN337338; dun-coloured hill*

Forming one of the cluster of five Corbetts that lie between Beinn Challuim and the Bridge of Orchy Munros, Beinn Odhar presents an attractive sight rising above the road north of Tyndrum. It can be climbed together with Cam Chreag and Beinn Chaorach (see page 89), or all of the others in the group (see panel opposite). However, it is described here on its own and provides an enjoyable ascent, which is stiffer than expected given a starting height of 235m.

Although there is limited space to park about 1km to the north of Tyndrum along the A82, it is better to park in Tyndrum itself, perhaps in the large car park for the Green Welly Stop (shop, cafe & toilets). This is on the north side of the road as one leaves Tyndrum heading north.

Walk past the fuel pumps, cross a footbridge over the Crom Allt burn, then turn right up the road past the village shop and post office. This is the route of the West Highland Way, which continues as a track between the main road and the Crom Allt, with Beinn Odhar rising splendidly ahead. Cross a bridge over the railway and go through a gate, then leave the track to gain the open hillside.

Head towards the Crom Allt and pick up a grassy track, which is followed up the hillside, initially just above the burn as it runs through a small gorge. Beyond the gorge, the track swings away and zigzags up the hillside. It is a little difficult to follow in places but despite appearing to traverse too far right at one point, it does traverse back left to end just beyond the walls of an old building at a distinctive patch of scree. This is, in fact, the spoil heap from an old lead mine trial, the shaft, or adit, for which is located on the other side of the rock rib a little higher beyond the spoil. This mine lies on the same vein as the old mine workings (c.1740) that can be seen to the south-west on Sròn nan Colan above Tyndrum.

The route continues by following a rough, grassy path up the side of the spoil patch to meet a line of old fence posts, then a small lochan on a level section on the shoulder of the ridge. Cross the level section, then continue up through a short boulder field and the rockier final slope before bearing left to gain the finely situated and scenic summit (**4.25km; 665m; 2h**).

The easiest return is back the same way (**8.5km; 665m; 3h 20min**).

A worthwhile alternative descent can be made by dropping south-east to another small lochan: Lochan Choire Dhuibh. From there, follow the crest, which swings southwards, and ascend Meall Buidhe (653m).

Return north for about 150m, then swing north-westwards off the crest and descend steep grassy slopes. Aiming for the Crom Allt above its gorge enables some minor slabby rocks to be avoided on grass to also gain a place where the burn can normally be easily crossed. Regain the grassy track used in the ascent and follow this back to Tyndrum (**10.25km; 715m; 3h 50min**).

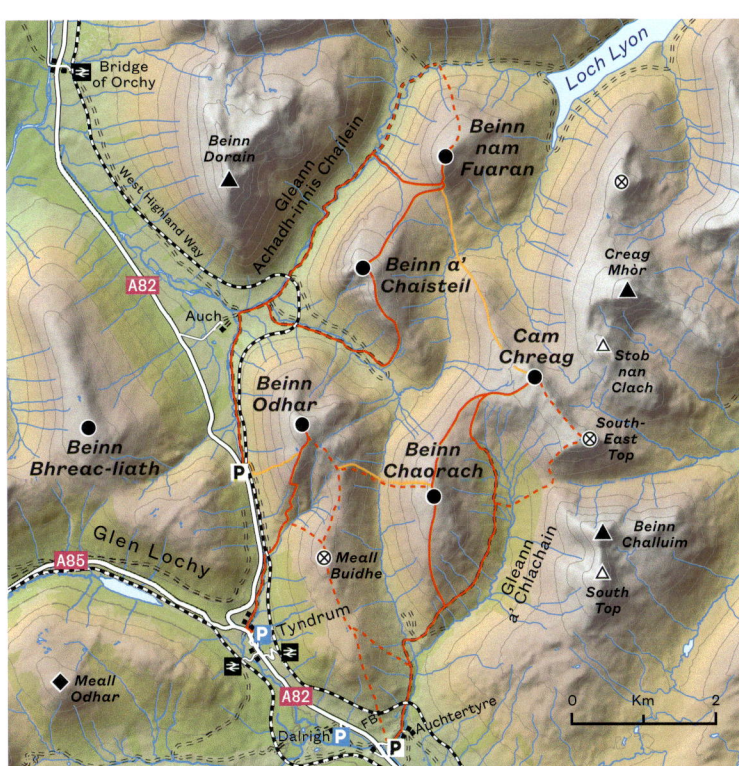

Beinn Odhar, Beinn Chaorach, Cam Chreag, Beinn nam Fuaran & Beinn a' Chaisteil

These five Corbetts can be climbed in one demanding outing for a unique Corbett 'hand'. Start at the highpoint of the road between Tyndrum and Bridge of Orchy, where there is a pull-off on the east side of the road at NN328331, where the northbound road veers away from the railway line as it passes beneath Beinn Odhar.

Go through a gate and walk down the track for 320m or so, then pass beneath the railway by a cattle creep. Now on the West Highland Way, walk back up the other side of the railway until just beyond the parking area, then take to the hillside. It is a brutal ascent alongside a fence, which leads to the small lochan at a flat section on the shoulder where the standard single hill route from Tyndrum arrives. Continuing south along the West Highland Way for about 1km leads to easier-angled slopes and that route, but lengthens the day. From the lochan, ascend through a small boulder field, then continue up the slope and bear left to the summit of Beinn Odhar (**2.5km; 600m; 1h 35min**).

Descend to the south-east, picking up a line of short wooden posts - the remnants of an electric fence system on some of these hills - to gain the small Lochan Choire Dhuibh. Still following the fenceline, continue south-east, then steeply east down to the col (444m). Ascend the steep slope on the other side next to the posts, then turn right (south) at the top to gain the cylindrical trig pillar on Beinn Chaorach (**5km; 975m; 3h**).

Return north to pick up the line of posts running down the north-north-east ridge and follow a rough path beside these, and out to their right, to gain the col (638m) with Cam Chreag. Ascend the path uphill beside the posts to where they head off north, then continue up to the summit, which sits at the north-west end of a high-level ridge with numerous knolls of a slightly lesser height (**7.5km; 1225m; 4h 10min**).

Descend the long northern ridge of Cam Chreag to where the Abhainn Ghlas is joined by the Allt a' Mhàim at about 400m. Cross the burn, then climb north up the east side of the Allt a' Mhàim, and on up the south ridge of Beinn nam Fuaran to meet a decrepit fenceline leading to the summit (**11.5km; 1630m; 5h 50min**).

Return partway down the ridge then drop south-westwards to cross the haggy col (the Màm Lorn, 546m), joining the decrepit fenceline again and following it up onto Beinn a' Chaisteil (**13.75km; 1970m; 7h 10min**).

The steep slopes and broken cliffs of Coire Gaothach and Creagan Liatha prevent a direct descent into Auch Glen or Glen Coralan, so head south-east down the ridge beside the fence. At about NN353355, leave the fence and drop southwards down a steep but grassy slope by the burn draining the hillside to gain the track in Glen Coralan.

Turn right (north-west) along the upper track, then take a track on the left to meet the lower track and follow this across a bridge over the Allt Coralan, and on beneath the smaller railway viaduct on the Auch Horseshoe. Turn left alongside the Allt Kinglass to meet the West Highland Way, then follow this up the left-hand track by the Allt Coire Chailein, back to the start (*21.5km; 2085m; 9h 15min*).

> **Beinn a' Chaisteil**; *886m; (C40); L50; NN347364; castle hill*
> **Beinn nam Fuaran**; *806m; (C149); L50; NN361381; hill of the springs*

Referred to as the Auch Corbetts, Beinn a' Chaisteil and Beinn nam Fuaran to its north sit opposite Beinn Dorain, overlooking Gleann Achaidh-innis Chailein, more commonly known as Auch Glen.

They form the northern pair of a cluster of five Corbetts which lie between Beinn Challuim above Strath Fillan and the Bridge of Orchy Munros. Whilst it is possible to climb all five Corbetts together, it is more usual to split them up into three separate walks; a description for the round of five is given on page 91.

When seen from the A82 as it descends past Auch, with its estate buildings and farm, Beinn a' Chais-teil's steep south-west and north-west faces present a distinctive sight rising above the West Highland Line railway's Auch Horseshoe and its nine-span viaduct. The railway makes a horseshoe here as it travels around the entrances to Glen Coralan and Gleann Achaidh-innis Chailein, and crosses viaducts spanning the two rivers flowing out of these glens: the Allt Coralan and the Allt Kinglass.

Beinn nam Fuaran is a smaller hill, tucked away behind Beinn a' Chaisteil at the head of Loch Lyon, with Beinn a' Chùirn and Beinn Mhanach to its north. It is only partly visible from the road when in the vicinity of the turn-off to Auch.

Since it gives a slightly shorter route, the preferred start would be where the private road to Auch leaves the A82. However, there is only limited verge parking here, which is on a straight where traffic travels fast. It is better, and safer, to park about 1.5 miles (2.5km) to the south, at the highpoint of the road between Tyndrum and Bridge of Orchy. There is a pull-off here, on the east side of the road at NN328331, where the northbound road veers away from the railway line as it passes beneath Beinn Odhar.

Go through a gate and follow a track downhill beside the railway. This is soon joined by the West Highland Way, which arrives beneath the railway. Continue downhill alongside the Allt Coire Chailein to meet the track from Auch. Leave the West Highland Way here and turn right along the Allt Kinglass, heading towards the viaduct. In a further 460m or so, before the ford across the Allt Coralan, turn right up another track.

With the well-defended and imposing sight of Beinn a' Chaisteil towering above, and living up to its name, follow this track beneath another viaduct on the horseshoe and continue up Glen Coralan. Cross the Allt Coralan by a bridge, then take a track on the left to gain a higher track, and turn right along this.

Leave the track at NN351348, just before it crosses a burn, then ascend the steep and grassy hillside on the west side of the burn to meet a decrepit fenceline on the south-east ridge. Follow the fenceline up the crest of the ridge, which provides a scenic route above Creagan Liatha and around the rim of Coire Gaothach, to reach the splendidly situated summit at the north-west end (**7.75km; 690m; 2h 50min**).

Descend north-east beside the fence towards conical Beinn nam Fuaran, down a broad grassy slope, then cross the broad and haggy col between the hills: the Màm Lorn (546m). The steep slope ahead is best climbed well to the right of the fence, rightwards onto the south ridge, which is followed to the top, meeting the fence again (**10.5km; 950m; 4h**).

Looking north-east up Loch Lyon, past the Corbetts Meall Buidhe and Sròn a' Choire Chnapanaich to Stùc an Lochain, and being surrounded by bigger hills, it is an interesting viewpoint.

The quickest return is to go back down the south ridge then cut across the fenceline to gain the north end of the Màm Lorn. From there, descend directly down the steep slope between the highest burns, then alongside another burn, heading towards the north end of a small

forestry plantation in the floor of the glen and the track.

Ford the Allt Kinglass to gain the track, and follow this down the glen, fording the river once more, then passing beneath the fine nine-span viaduct. Built in 1894, the viaduct has been recently refurbished. Ford the Allt Coralan to rejoin the approach route, and follow this back (**19km; 1065m; 6h 20min**).

A longer, and perhaps easier, descent can be made from Beinn nam Fuaran by descending north-wards beside the fenceline to gain the track at the foot of Beinn Mhanach. Follow the track west into Gleann Achaidh-innis Chailein, fording the burn twice to where it is joined to become the Allt Kinglass. In a further 600m or so, ford the Allt Kinglass to reach the small forestry plantation where the principal descent arrives, and continue as for this; an additional 2km, 30min.

Map on page 91

Beinn a' Chaisteil with the Auch Viaduct on the left (Tom Prentice)

Beinn nam Fuaran from Beinn a Chaisteil, with Beinn a' Chùirn and Beinn Mhanach, left (Rab Anderson)

Beinn Ceitlein and Stob Dubh across Glen Etive from Beinn Maol Chaluim, with Beinn Mhic Chasgaig, left, Creise behind, and Stob Coire an Albannaich, right (Rab Anderson)

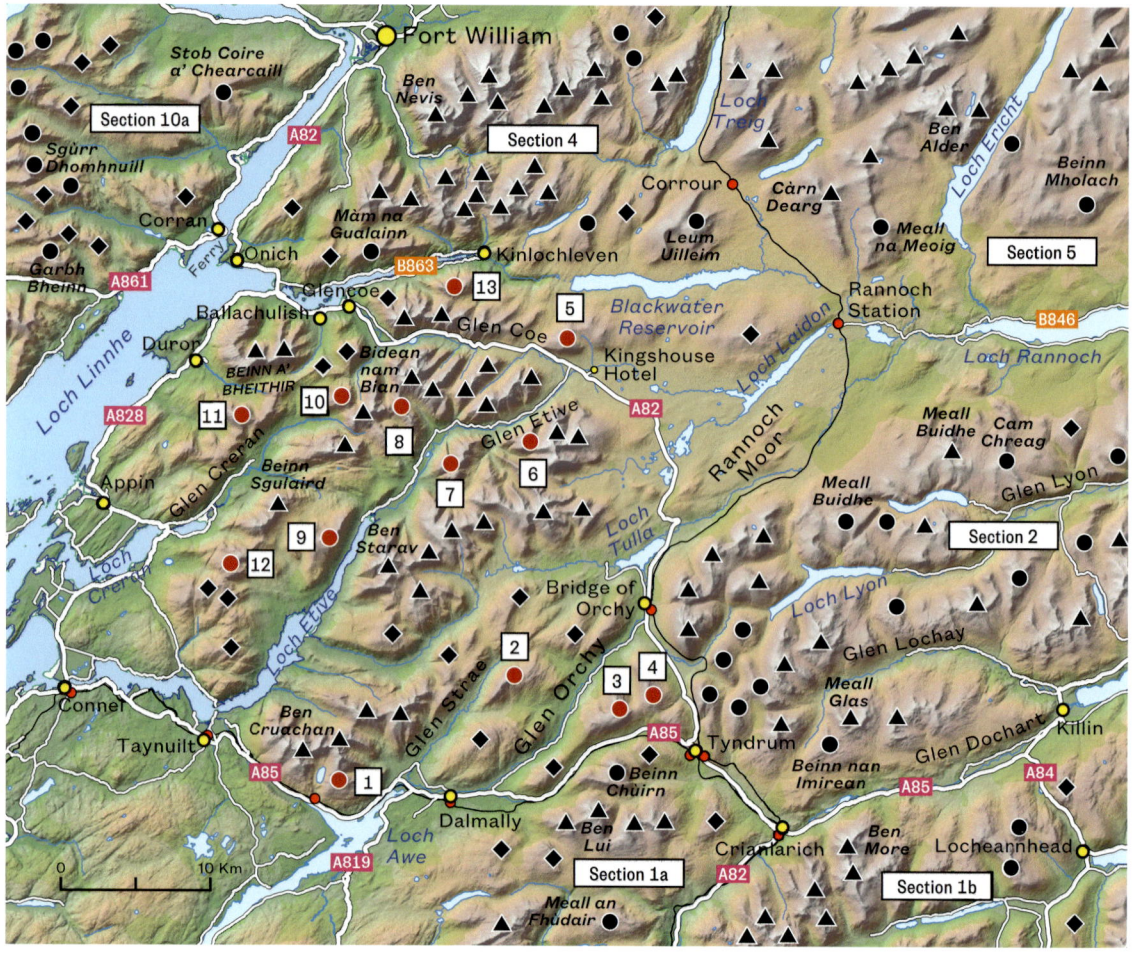

SECTION 3

Monadh Driseig and Beinn a' Bhùiridh from the east, with Coire Glas, right (Derek Sime)

Beinn a' Bhùiridh; 897m; (C26); L50; NN094283; *hill of roaring (of stags)*

Sitting in a commanding position overlooking Loch Awe, at the end of the Cruachan Horseshoe, Beinn a' Bhùiridh and its long east ridge create a compelling sight. Although often climbed as the final summit on the superb traverse of its higher Munro neighbours, it is a splendid summit in its own right. It can also be climbed as the first peak on the Dalmally Horseshoe, another equally fine traverse.

Start 25m up the B8077 from its junction with the A85, where there is a small pull-off opposite a gate at NN132283. The gate marks the start of a track which leads to some small quarries, an old lead mine and a small hydro scheme. There is also a pull-off on the A85, 110m to the east.

Follow the track north-west to a junction, then swing left and continue to the far side of a quarry. Leave the track here and climb southwards, passing either side of another quarry, to reach a col at 350m on the east ridge, to the side of a small knoll.

Continue up the ridge to reach Monadh Driseig (641m), where a trig point at the southern edge offers splendid views down Loch Awe.

Make a slight descent to the north-west then cross a col and ascend the fine ridge ahead, above a line of crags on its north side. Cross the north-east top and continue along the crest for 400m or so to the summit at the west end. A rock 20m to the north-north-east of the cairn is the highest point (**6.5km; 870m; 3h**).

Returning the same way is best, maintaining the splendid views. Cut across the north side of Monadh Driseig (**12.5km; 890m; 5h**).

Another option is to return to the dip before the north-east top, then make a steep descent north, mainly on grass, and avoiding as much of a

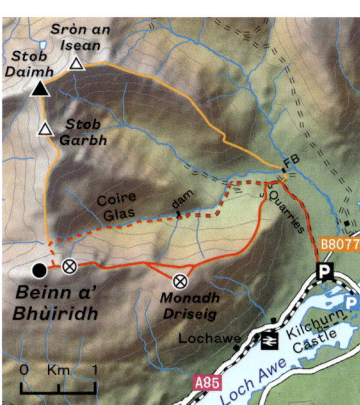

boulder field as is possible, to reach the Làirig Torran. If simply climbing Meall a' Bhùiridh, drop east into Coire Glas then descend by the Allt Coire Ghlais to reach the head of a track. Follow the track downhill and back to the start (**12.25km; 870m; 4h 45min**).

If continuing for the Dalmally Horseshoe, from the Làirig Torran ascend north to Stob Garbh (980m), a Munro Top, and cross the dip to Stob Daimh (998m), a Munro (**8.5km; 1200m; 4h 10min**).

Make an initially steep descent of the rocky north-east ridge to a col, then climb onto Sròn an Isean (966m), a Munro Top. Descend the long and easy-angled grassy east ridge. Towards the bottom, zigzag through a small band of rock outcrops, then descend steeper grass and continue to a bridge across the Allt Coire Chreachainn at NN128297, just before it joins the Allt Mhoille. Gain the track on the other side, then turn right up this to rejoin the track used in the approach, and follow this back (**14.5km; 1205m; 6h**).

For the ascent with the Cruachan Horseshoe see the SMC's guidebook *The Munros*.

Beinn Mhic Mhonaidh; 796m; (C165); L50; NN208350; hill of the son of the moor

Best seen in the view up Glen Strae, where it creates a bold rounded, profile, Beinn Mhic Mhonaidh is a shy hill, which from elsewhere lies hidden away in afforested country.

There are two routes to the hill; one from Glen Orchy, the other from Glen Strae. Both involve burn or river crossings, which could be difficult in spate, and both have approaches where a bike could be used.

The Glen Orchy route starts from the Eas Urchaidh (Falls of Orchy) car park at NN243320 in the middle of Glen Orchy, reached by the single-track road through the glen; either from the A82 at the north end near Bridge of Orchy, or from the A85 at the south end near Dalmally. The route to the Graham, Beinn Donachain, also starts here and follows the same initial approach.

Cross the bridge over the River Orchy beside the falls, and follow the main track straight ahead for 500m, then turn left up another track, which runs above the Allt Broighleachan.

After 2km, when the track ahead to Beinn Donachain enters a clearing, take the grassy fork on the right, and cross a bridge over the Allt Broigh-leachan.

Follow the grassy track across a burn and go up the side of a fence, past open ground on the left with fine, old Scots pines. Cross another two burns to reach where the track ends, then continue on a path by the burn to exit the forest by a gate. The ruined Àirigh Chailleach sheilings lie ahead, backed by the broad, open slopes of Beinn Mhic Mhonaidh, split by the drainage line of Coire Chailleach.

Cross the burn and follow the path northwards up the broad, grassy spur on the right side of the corrie. When the path and the right-hand burn fade higher up, break up left to gain the ridge close to a lochan, then go left onto the stony summit. A rock 50m to the east-south-east of the cairn is the highest point (**6.5km; 730m; 2h 40min**).

It is a grand viewpoint, featuring the massifs of Ben Cruachan, Ben Starav, Stob Ghabhar and Ben Lui. Across Glen Orchy to the east are Beinn Udlaidh and Beinn Bhreac-liath.

Return the same way (**13km; 740m; 4h 25min**).

The initial 4km or so could be biked, but there is 200m of ascent, and towards the end the track becomes rough.

The Glen Strae route starts at the entrance to the glen, gained by the B8077 loop road between Dalmally and Loch Awe. The approach track leaves the road on the west side of the bridge over the River Strae; park on the left about 50m up the track at NN145295.

Follow the track up the west side of the River Strae, keeping left at all forks and heading towards the foot of the south-west ridge of the hill. Once beyond the trees, either leave the track at NN171326 and follow an ATV track down to ford the river, or continue to NN175331 on the far side of a wall, then follow an ATV track down to ford the river. Either way, gain the ruins at Inbhir-nan-giubhas, then ford the Allt nan Giuthas to gain the south-west ridge. There is a bridge at NN186340, but one would have to double back around the trees to gain the ridge. Ascend the ridge, An Sgrìodan, passing some crags and going over the slight rise of the south-west top (Pt.736m) to gain the summit (**9.5km; 780m; 3h 30min**).

Simplest is to return the same way (**19km; 800m; 6h**).

A descent could be made as for the previous route to Àirigh Chailleach, to follow the Allt nan Giuthas back to Inbhir-nan-giubhas, then the track, but this is a little longer. The first 5km or so of this route provides a straight-forward cycle, which should save about 2h 20min on the day.

Map opposite

Beinn Mhic Mhonaidh's summit ridge from the south-west, with the Bridge of Orchy Hills beyond (Tom Prentice)

Beinn Udlaidh across the head of Coire Ghamhnain from Beinn Bhreac-liath (Tom Prentice)

Beinn Udlaidh; *840m; (C104); L50; NN280332; dark or gloomy hill*
Beinn Bhreac-liath; *802m; (C157); L50; NN302339; speckled grey hill*

Together with the Graham, Beinn na Sròine, these two hills occupy the triangle of ground bounded by Glen Lochy, Glen Orchy, and the A82 between Tyndrum and Bridge of Orchy. The Graham is climbed on its own, however, Beinn Udlaidh and Beinn Bhreac-liath are climbed together to give a pleasant and varied circuit. The hills are virtually surrounded by forestry, so access has to make use of the few gaps remaining. The best route is a circuit

of north facing Coire Ghamhnain between the hills, and starts at the entrance to the corrie at Invergaunan in Glen Orchy. There is space to park on the edges of a gated track entrance on the west side of the bridge over the Allt Ghamhnain. Avoid the track entrance to Invergaunan.

Climbing Beinn Udlaidh first, go through a gate next to the main gate and follow a rough track through the trees, past a branch off left. After 500m, and just beyond a sheep fank,

the track splits then rejoins. The right branch is boggy, so take the left branch and when they join continue through forestry to a gate across the track ahead.

One option is to go through the walkers' gate on the right and follow a rough path beside the fence on the right, up through an area planted with native trees, to go through a gate to gain the open hillside. The other option is to simply go up the right side

▶

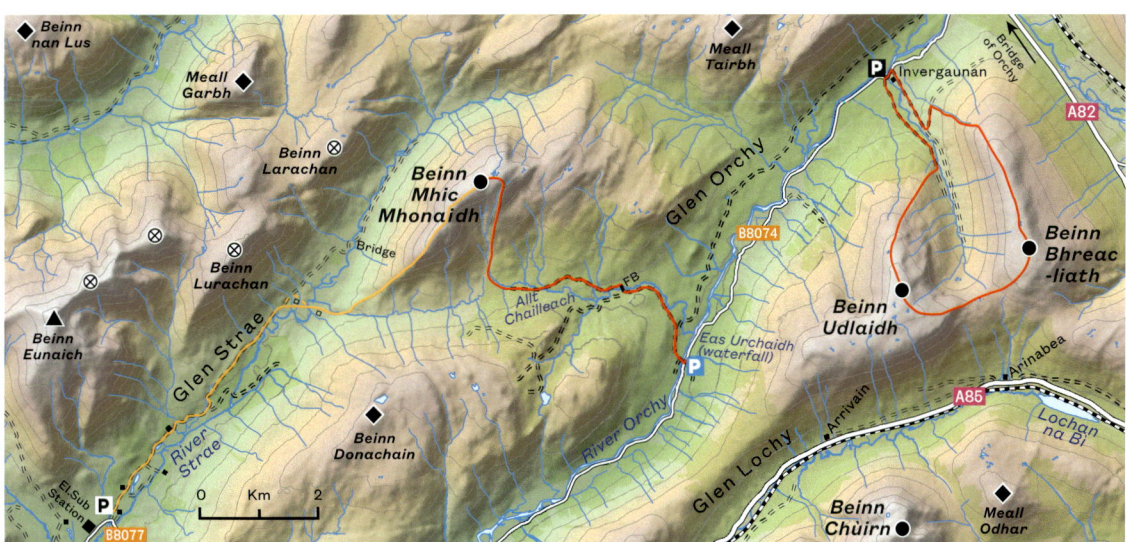

Beinn Bhreac-liath from Invergaunan in Glen Orchy (Tom Prentice)

of the fence and step over another fence to gain the same point. Continue alongside the fence for a short way to gain a remarkable quartz dyke. This is a prominent feature of the hill, and can be seen from the road between Loch Tulla and Bridge of Orchy.

Follow the line of quartz straight up the hillside for over 1km, onto the north ridge and past a small lochan to reach a flattening with another lochan. There is a splendid panorama to the west and north-west, from the Cruachan massif to Beinn Starav and Stob a' Choire Odhar. Continue up the broad and stony ridge onto the extensive flat summit, where the rock changes from the quartzite lower down to that of a thin, slate-like type (**4.25km; 710m; 2h 10min**).

To the south across Glen Lochy, the Corbett Beinn Chùirn is backed by magnificent Ben Lui and its attendants, whilst to the east Ben Challuim stands out.

The summit of Beinn Bhreac-liath lies on the opposite side of the corrie, and is reached by heading southwards over another quartz dyke, before swinging south-east to descend between some pools.

An old wall runs down the side of the ridge to the right here, and should not be followed, and neither should the obvious continuation of the ridge, for both end above steep, craggy ground. Instead, turn east-north-east to cross a broad col; a rough path gives the best line, although it does initially appear to head too far right.

Go through a gate in the fence to reach the lowest point (587m), then briefly head rightwards, before climbing north-east up the steep, grassy slope to the side of the burn that comes down from the obvious depression in the hillside. As the angle eases, turn north onto the flat top of Beinn Bhreac-liath (**7.25km; 925m; 3h 20min**).

More of the hills to the north-east are revealed; all five of the Corbetts opposite, with Beinn Odhar prominent and Beinn a' Chaisteall above the railway's Auch Horseshoe, then Beinn Dorain's long, water runnel-streaked western slope.

Descend the long and easy-angled north ridge for some 2km. A deer fence has been erected across the ridge, and at the time of writing there is no proper gate or crossing. Either climb it, or find the gap that has been created.

As the lower slopes begin, swing north-westwards to descend by the main burn draining the hillside. This provides a route down through an area that has been planted with native trees, to reach a track across the hillside. Turn left down this, then right at the bottom and follow the track past Invergaunan to the road, where a left turn leads back to the start (**12km; 925m; 4h 40min**).

The shortest ascent of both hills can be made from Arinabea in Glen Lochy, where the burns create breaks in the forest, by which it is quite easy to reach the col between them. This is simply a quick means of bagging both hills, and is an inferior route.

Descending Beinn Bhreac-liath's north ridge towards Glen Orchy (Tom Prentice)

Beinn a' Chrùlaiste across the River Coupall, from the south-west, with Altnafeadh, left (Rab Anderson)

Beinn a' Chrùlaiste; *857m; (C83); L41; NN246566; rocky hill*

Forming the gateway to Glen Coe opposite Buachaille Etive Mòr, Beinn a' Chrùlaiste appears as a somewhat disappointing lump in comparison. However, a relatively short ascent from a starting height of 290m comfortably takes one to a most rewarding viewpoint.

The best route starts at Altnafeidh, by a small forestry plantation at the foot of the west ridge, where there is ample parking. However, it does get very busy here, but there is normally space in a pull-off at the east end of the plantation, and at the entrance to a gate a little further east again.

Follow the West Highland Way east past the plantation and go through a walkers' gate in the fence, then climb uphill beside the fence on what can be a boggy path.

The path splits partway up the slope above the end of the fence. One path traverses left, whilst the other climbs the edge looking down on the road. The paths come together to the side of a rock step, above which the top of the minor rise of Stob Beinn a' Chrùlaiste (639m) should be gained.

From there, follow the path left (north) across a dip, before swinging eastwards up the long, easy-angled slope to the trig pillar marking the summit (**3.75km; 580m; 1h 50min**).

On the ascent, the views across to Buachaille Etive Mòr are superb.

Return the same way, with the peaks of Glen Coe laid out ahead, and to the right The Mamores with Ben Nevis beyond (**7.5km; 590m; 3h**).

Another route starts from the Kingshouse Hotel; either park there, or on the road to its north. It is not possible to drive across the bridge beside the hotel.

Go through a gate at the sharp bend to the north, then turn left up an ATV track and path on the west side of the Allt a' Bhalaich. Climb north for 1.5km to a height of about 420m, then climb westwards up a broad ridge. This is more rugged than the map suggests, with some rocky outcrops, and leads directly to the summit (**3.25km; 610m; 1h 45min**). Return the same way (**6.5km; 610m; 2h 45min**).

The return can be varied by descending the northern ridge to traverse east across the head of Coire Bhalach to climb the twin tops of Meall Bhalach, 708m and 705m, then descend to the Allt a' Bhalaich; an added 2.5km, 125m, 40min.

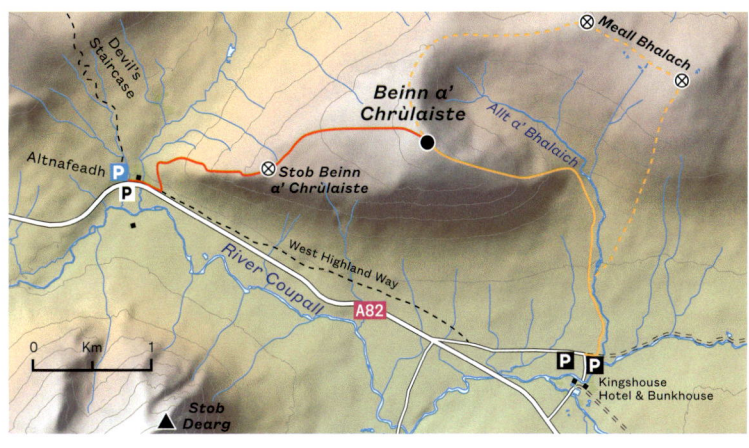

Beinn Mhic Chasgaig from Beinn Ceitlein, with Sròn na Crèise, left, and Clach Leathad, right (Rab Anderson)

Beinn Mhic Chasgaig; *864m; (C70); L41 & L50; NN221502; MacChasgaig's hill*

Hemmed in to the north, south and east by the much larger mountain ridges of Buachaille Etive Mòr and the Blackmount, Beinn Mhic Chasgaig still manages to present a bold front to Glen Etive, above which it extends for 3km from its attractive-looking northern ridge. Were it not for the barrier of the River Etive, this ridge would provide a good route.

From further down the glen at Alltchaorunn, it presents a less inspiring sight, with its west ridge terminating in a blunt nose ringed by crags. Although a direct route can be forced up this ridge, and the crags can be turned, a more circuitous and easier-angled route, which passes through a spectacular gorge, is better.

Start at the bridge over the River Etive at NN198512; there is space to park in a pull-off to the west. Cross the bridge and follow a hydro track to the right and around a bend. About 200m after passing the access track to Alltchaorunn, take a path on the right which leads down to the original stalkers' path alongside the Allt a' Chaorainn, upstream of a bridge. This provides a more pleasing route than that of the unsightly track. Follow the path upstream past lovely cascades and pools (if the hydro scheme has not dried these up) to gain the end of

the track, where the river forks at the entrance to Coire Ghiubhasain. There are hydro intakes on both rivers here.

The original route continued on a rough path up the side of the Allt Coire Ghiubhasain for 100m or so, to carefully descend some rock steps into the gorge, then cross a narrow plank-bridge over the river with the aid of wire handrails. Unfortunately, the rails have gone and the crossing is now dangerous. Instead, cross below the hydro intake and go up the far side to gain the path from the bridge. Follow this path up the side above the gorge, through a narrow and steep-sided glen.

On the left, a boulder gully runs up the hillside into Coire Aiteil, with the slopes to the right of this providing the descent route. Looking back, An Grianan is prominent, with Stob Coire Sgreamhach and Bidean nam Bian beyond.

Continue up the glen until above a fine cascade, then find a suitable place to cross, either below or above the fork. The crossing above is normally straightforward on slabs just upstream, and once over, the Allt Coire Odhair tributary can then be easily crossed. Continue up the side of this burn for a short way, then take a rising northwards diagonal line up

the very steep hillside. Higher up, aim for two boulders, then pass between these and continue to the col at 698m between Beinn Mhic Chasgaig and Crèise. Climb north-westwards from the col onto the flat summit. A boulder 60m to the north-east of the cairn at NN2211 5017 is the highest point (**5.25km; 770m; 2h 30min**).

This last section is not that straightforward and can feel exposed. It will be easier in ascent than descent. If unsure on such terrain, then the easier route is to cross the Allt Coire Ghiubhasain lower down, to go up and down the descent route to the side of the boulder gully.

Across Glen Etive, the full length of Buachaille Etive Mòr's summit ridge is prominent, as is the rocky profile of Crowberry Ridge and Crowberry Tower on Stob Dearg. On the descent, it is worth heading north, then west for a way for better views, before traversing back across the slope to descend south-westwards down the south side of Coire Aiteil. A couple of minor outcrops are easily avoided, and the slope steepens for the final descent down the side of the boulder gully. Cross the Allt Coire Ghiubhasain and return as for the approach (**9.5km; 785m; 3h 45min**).

Map on page 104

Stob Dubh; 883m; (C45); L41 & L50; NN166488; black peak

Encircled by the greater peaks of Glen Etive, Glen Coe and the Blackmount, Stob Dubh sits at the hub of a huge wheel of ridges, with the only break provided by Glen Etive. From anywhere in the glen Stob Dubh, and its subsidiary Beinn Ceitlein appear steep and intimidating, with few obvious lines of ascent. Situated at the bend in the glen opposite Dalness, the mountain's craggy slopes are riven by gully-clefts and rise steeply above the River Etive

When seen from the foot of Glen Etive, Stob Dubh presents a distinctive and particularly attractive pointed shape, with the U-shaped valley between the Munros Stob Dubh and Stob na Broige behind and to its left, and the cleft of the Garbh Allt gorge to its right.

There are two routes of ascent. One from upper Glen Etive to the north-east, which follows the ridge over Beinn Ceitlin via the south side of An Grianan, the very steep termination of the ridge. The other from lower Glen Etive by a direct and steep route up the south-west ridge.

The route from the north-east is a superb and scenic traverse over Beinn Ceitlein, which starts as for Beinn Mhic Chasgaig, from the pull-off to the west of the bridge over the River Etive at NN198512.

Cross the bridge and follow a hydro track to the right, then around a bend. About 200m after passing the access track to Alltchaorunn, take a path on the right which leads down to the original stalkers' path alongside the Allt a' Chaorainn, upstream of a bridge. Turn right down this path and cross the bridge.

Follow a rough path up the other side through the trees to emerge into the open, and cross a flat section. Go through a gate and climb steeply beside the burn to gain the fine col between Beinn Ceitlin and An Grianan. The top of An Grianan's rocky dome can be attained via its right-hand edge by a short climb, now or on the descent; an added 10min.

Continuing, climb steeply up the crest just left of rocks, then on up the ridge over a slight rise and across the dip above Coire Dubh-beag to climb

the right side of a steeper section.

The slope now broadens and is ascended past some small lochans; in poor visibility finding the right line across the rises and dips here might be awkward. The steep cone of Stob Dubh comes into view, and appears further away than expected, due to the great bulk of Beinn Ceitlein.

Cross above Coire Dubh-meadhonach to gain the 834m North-East Top then follow the crest across the dip and ascend to the 845m South-West Top above Coire Dubh-mòr. Drop to the col below, then ascend quite steeply through rocky ground to gain the splendid summit of Stob Dubh; a line close to the edge of Coire Dionachd on the right is best for the view, although the ground is easier to the left (**5.5km 910m; 2h 45min**).

The views are stunning and include Ben Nevis. Return the same way. It is probably easiest to go over the two tops of Beinn Ceitlein rather than find a lower line. Further down, after crossing the neck at the head of Coire Dubh-beag, where the top of An ▶

Stob Dubh from Beinn Trilleachan, with Buachaille Etive Mòr, left (Tom Prentice)

Beinn Maol Chaluim
Pt. 848m
Gleann Fhaolain
Stob na Broige
Glen Etive
River Etive
Dalness
Inbhir-fhaolain
Alltchaorunn
FB
An Grianan
Beinn Mhic Chasgaig
Gleann Chàrnan
Coire Dubh-beag
Coire Dubh-mheadhonach
Allt a' Chaorainn
Coire Odhar
Coire Ghiubhasan
Lochan Urr
Stob Dubh
Beinn Ceitlin
Coire Dubh-mòr
Inverchàrnan
Glen Ceitlin
P
0 Km 1

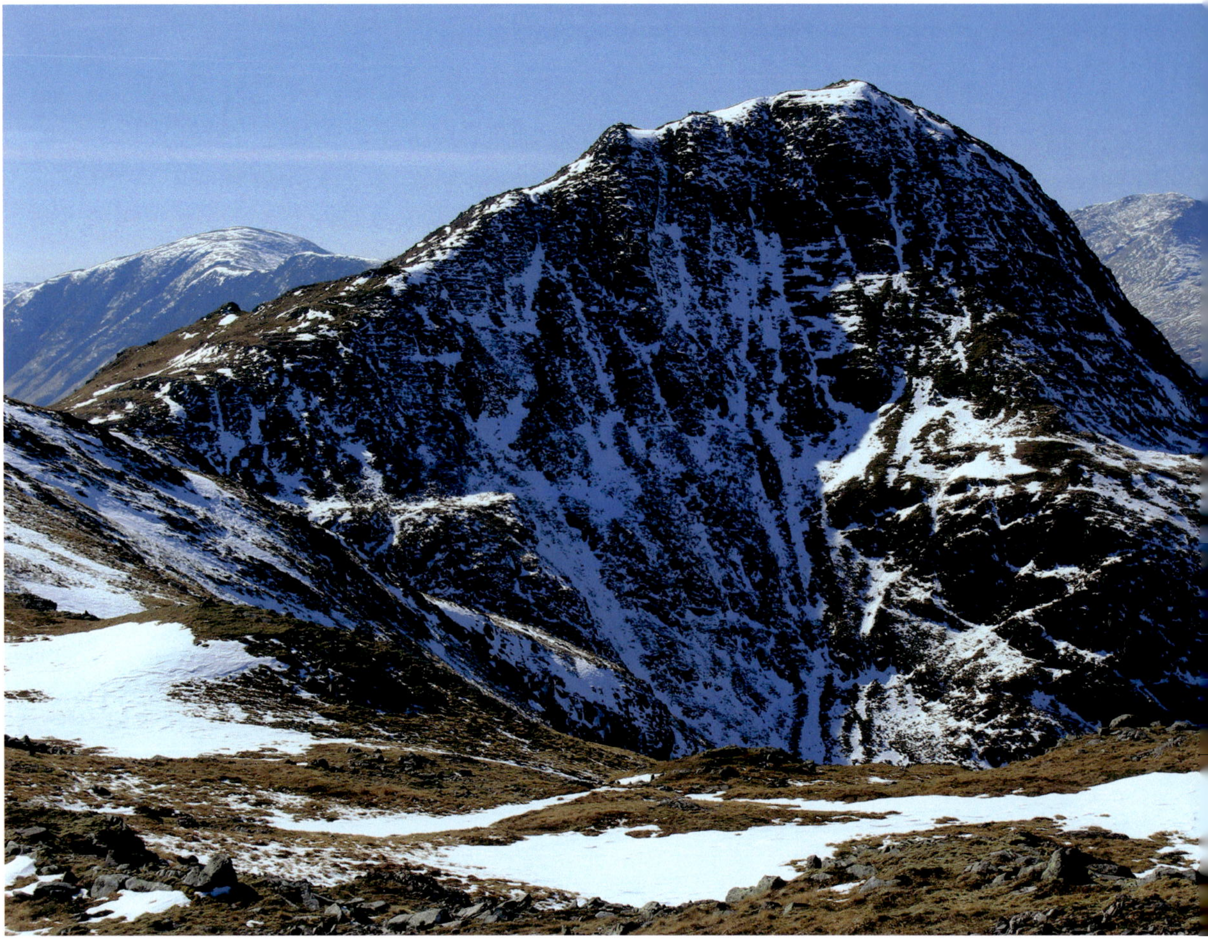

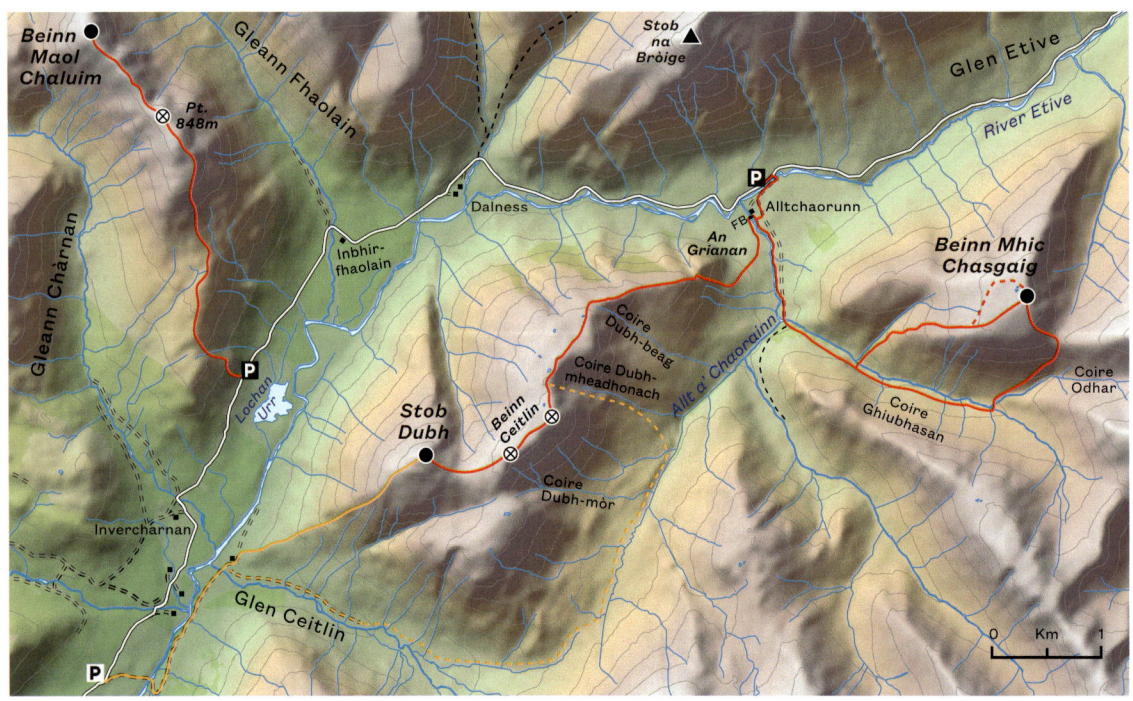

Grianan comes into view, it is possible to take a slanting line down to the right by the burn, to then traverse across and join the ascent route well below the An Grianan col, thereby avoiding the steeper slopes thereabouts (11km; 1060m; 4h 35min).

The route from lower Glen Etive starts at NN136468, opposite Coileitir, where a track leaves the road and goes down to the River Etive. This is the same start for Ben Starav and Stob Coire an Albannaich, and there are various places to park.

Walk down the track, cross the bridge over the River Etive, then turn left and follow the track northwards to cross the bridge over the Allt Ceitlein. The dauntingly steep south-west ridge of Stob Dubh looms above here.

Follow the track past the cottage, then go through a gate in the deer fence and follow a rough path up the ridge. Underfoot, the going is excellent on short grass, and the minor crags at roughly half height are easily turned, mainly on the right. Once above the last of these, the angle eases and the cairn is soon reached (4.5km; 880m; 2h 30min).

The simplest option is to return the same way, making sure that you have remembered the route through the crags (9km; 910m; 4h).

If continuing, it should be noted that there is no straightforward way off Beinn Ceitlein until on the far side of Coire Dubh-meadhonach, just over 1km along the ridge from the highest point. If it would be possible to arrange transportation at the north-east end, then it would be better to undertake this as a south-to-north traverse.

However, if returning to Coileitir and continuing to Beinn Ceitlein, make a steep descent east-south-east (easier further right) to a col, then ascend the broad ridge to the first and higher of Beinn Ceitlein's two tops at 845m. Continue over the North-East Top (834m), then drop down and traverse around the head of Coire Dubh-meadhonach, then descend slightly.

At NN180497, a descent can be made to the south-east, down grassy slopes and to the side of a boulder field. It is steep, and some crags are easily avoided. Cross the burn below a band of crags and descend south-wards to the floor of the glen. Pick up an old stalkers' path and follow this past the walled ruins of Fèith a' Chaorainn Mhòir, then on to gain the watershed. It is a fair trek back, but lovers of remote places should appreciate this glen. Continue down to join the path and ATV track alongside the Allt Ceitlein (the route to the Munro Meall nan Eun), and follow these back to the main track, then return along this (15km; 1030m; 5h 40min).

Stob Dubh from Beinn Ceitlein, with Beinn Trilleachan, left, and Beinn Sgulaird, right (Rab Anderson)

Buachaille Etive Mòr from Beinn Ceitlein (Rab Anderson)

Beinn Maol Chaluim; *907m; (C14); L41 & L50; NN135526); Malcolm's bare hill*

Another fine peak set amidst stunning scenery in Glen Etive, Beinn Maol Chaluim has a somewhat retiring nature, lying hidden behind the greater peaks of Glen Coe, between the Sgùrr na h-Ulaidh and Bidean nam Bian massifs.

Although its summit can be attained from Glen Coe via wild Fionn Ghleann, the going there is rough.

Much the better route is from Glen Etive, which gives a high-level ridge walk in splendid surroundings.

Start at NN149495, from a pull-off on the right (west) side of the road as

Beinn Maol Chaluim's summit ridge, with Bidean nam Bian, right (Rab Anderson)

of a small crag and continue up the steep hillside to gain the broad crest of the south ridge. Beyond a slight drop, there is a brief levelling before the angle steepens again and leads to a line of crags straddling the ridge at 650m. Either pass these on the left, or slant up right beneath them, then continue up the broad ridge to reach Pt.848m, the south-east top of Beinn Maol Chaluim.

With the splendid sight of Stob Coire Sgreamhach and Bidean nam Bian on the other side of Gleann Fhaolain, make a slight descent and follow the easy ridge for 1km to reach the white, quartz-capped summit (**4.5km; 830m; 2h 20min**).

To the north-west is Beinn a' Bheithir, then to the west and south-west Stob an Fhuarain, Sgùrr na h-Ulaidh and Beinn Fhionnlaidh. On the other side of Gleann Fhaolain, Bidean nam Bian and Stob Coire Sgreamhach dominate, and there is an interesting view of Buachaille Etive Mòr's ridge.

It is possible to make the link to Bidean nam Bian, but the slope on the other side is likely to deter most.

Return the same way, with Beinn Ceitlin and Stob Dubh on the other side of Glen Etive prominent (**9km; 870m; 3h 45min**).

Map on page 104

Beinn Maol Chaluim's summit ridge, with Sgùrr na h-Ulaidh and Stob an Fhuarain, left, and Beinn a' Bheithir, beyond (Rab Anderson)

one enters the open from the forestry south of Inbhir-faolain and Dalness. There is a small area of open hillside below Creag na Caillich, which is the only gap in the trees on the north-west side of the Glen Etive road. There are another two pull-offs in this gap.

Climb steeply up the hillside, out to the side of the trees and between the patches of bracken. Pass to the left

Bidean nam Bian and Stob Coire Sgreamhach across Gleann Fhaolain from Beinn Maol Chaluim (Rab Anderson)

Beinn Trilleachan; 840m; (C106); L50; NN086439; hill of the sandpipers/oystercatchers

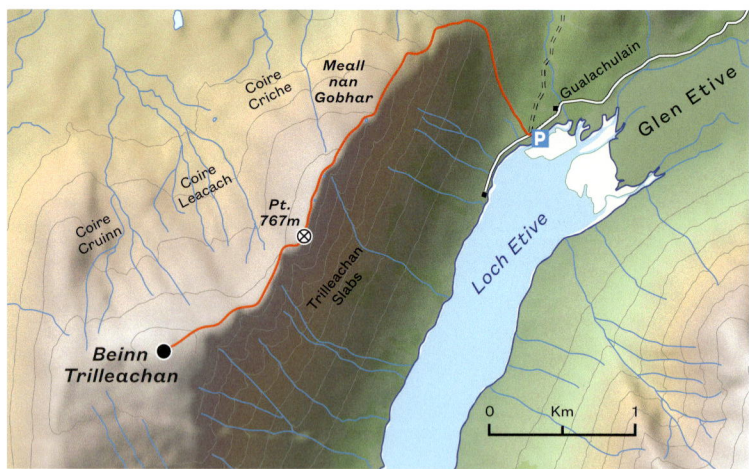

As one travels down lower Glen Etive, the view is increasingly dominated by Beinn Trilleachan, especially when highlighted by the morning sunshine glinting from the famous Etive, or Trilleachan Slabs; the great 200m sweep of granite on the east face of the hill above Loch Etive.

Beinn Trilleachan forms the west side of the deep trench that this narrow fjord-like sea loch sits in, and its slopes rise steeply to a long summit crest, which sits opposite the equally steep slope on the other side rising to the larger Ben Starav.

Start from the car park at NN111453, just beyond Gualachain at the head of Loch Etive, where the public road ends. An old cross-country route, not shown on any modern map, connects the heads of Loch Etive and Loch Creran and provides the first kilometre of the approach.

Pass to the side of the gate across the road, cross a track on the right, then follow the rough, and at times very wet, path up the side of the fence around the forestry. Leave this path at about the 150m contour and climb south-westwards up the broad ridge to pass over barely noticeable Meall nan Gobhar (590m), but from where the ridge becomes more rocky.

The sense of exposure on the left becomes increasingly felt here, and Ben Starav's mighty form on the other side of the loch holds the eye all the way along the crest of the ridge.

This section culminates at the granite-slabbed North-East Top (767m), where the cairn is perched directly above the great sweep of the Etive Slabs.

Make a short but steep descent of about 70m to a col at 693m at the head of a gully. On the other side, ascend a gentler slope across bare granite slabs, which lead to the top (**4.25km; 910m; 2h 35min**).

There is a grand view down Loch Etive to the Cruachan massif. Creach Bheinn is to the south-west, Beinn Sgulaird to the west, then Fraochaidh.

Return the same way, with the Glen Coe, Glen Etive and Blackmount peaks satisfyingly laid out ahead (**8.5km; 985m; 4h**).

Beinn Trilleachan from Ben Starav, with Beinn Sgulaird, right (Mike Dixon)

Meall Lighiche, right, from Meall Mòr, with Sgùrr na h-Ulaidh and Beinn Fhionnlaidh beyond (Rab Anderson)

Meall Lighiche; *772m; (C204); L41; NN094528; doctor's hill*

Tucked away at the head of Gleann-leac-na-muidhe, Meall Lighiche is a retiring hill encircled by a host of other hills. It can briefly be seen from the A82 towards the foot of Glen Coe, where it appears framed between Aonach Dubh a' Ghlinne and Meall Mòr.

Its western slopes are rounded and drop to the forests of Glen Creran, but its eastern flank falls precipitously from the outlying top Creag Bhàn to the head of Gleann-leac-na-muidhe.

Start from a small pull-off on the north side of the A82 at NN120563, at the apex of a bend where the road swings round over the Allt na Muidhe.

Traffic travels fast here and the bend is blind, so care is required. It is best to enter the pull-off in a south-bound direction, turning around in the NTS visitor centre entrance further north if required. Exit in a southbound direction, as well.

This is the same start point for the Munro Sgùrr na h-Ulaidh, which lies to the south-east of Meall Lighiche. Both hills can be climbed together starting with Meall Lighiche, and a description for this route is given in the SMC's guidebook *The Munros*.

For the ascent of Meall Lighiche on its own, access the Glencoe Greenway, which runs to the north of the parking,

then turn left along this to pass under the A82. This leads to the track up the west side of the Allt na Muidhe.

A layby further north on the A82 at NN115571 is perhaps a safer option, with a gate at its south end accessing the Greenway, which is followed south to the track.

Follow the track into Gleann-leac-na-muidhe and, after 1km, cross the bridge over to the east side. In a further 100m, beyond the driveway to a house and at the edge of the trees, take a path off on the left. The path bypasses the Glencoe Mountain Cottages and the house at Gleann-leac-na-muidhe to their south, and rejoins the track on the far side.

Follow the track for a further 1km to its end, where the glen turns south and Sgùrr na h-Ulaidh comes into view. Continue to the Allt na Muidhe and cross it at an island just above where it is joined by a tributary.

Head for a fence over to the right and follow a vague path uphill, soon leaving the fence to climb up to a small crag at the foot of the north ridge. Pass the crag on its right side, then climb the ridge to a small craggy domed knoll, bypassed to its right.

Continue up the terraced grassy slope to a small cairn (719m) at the

top of the Creag Bhàn ridge. Follow level ground for 200m, then turn west beside a line of old iron fence posts to reach the top of Meall Lighiche, where the cairn sits on a slab of quartz-embedded schist (**6km; 745m; 2h 45min**).

It is a splendid viewpoint. As well as the many higher peaks on show, the Corbetts, Fraochaidh and Creach Bheinn, stand out to the west.

Return by the route of ascent (**12km; 755m; 4h. 30min**).

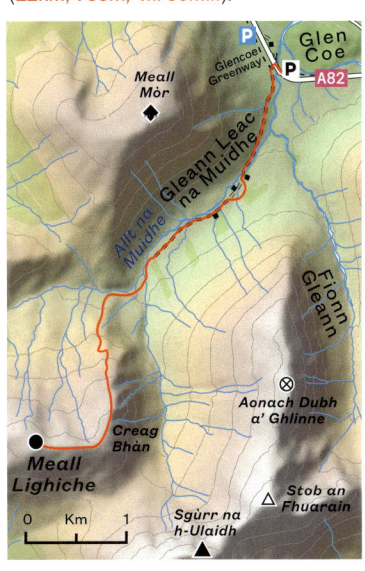

Fraochaidh from Beinn Fhionnlaidh – Fuar Bheinn, left, then Beinn Resipol, Garbh Bheinn and Sgùrr Dhomhnuill (Mike Dixon)

Fraochaidh; *879m; (C52); L41; NN029517; heathery hill*

Almost encircled by forestry in Appin, Fraochaidh is another retiring hill, similar to Meall Lighiche not far to the east. It sits tucked away behind the massive bulk of Beinn a' Bheithir, from which it is separated by Glen Duror and Gleann an Fhiodh, the two means of access to it. To the south is Glen Creran, which could also provide access, were it not for the extensive forestry there.

Each of the two approaches has its own merits. The route via Gleann an Fhiodh is long and follows a scenic ridge, whilst that via Glen Duror is shorter and overlooks Loch Linnhe.

The route via Gleann an Fhiodh starts at Ballachulish, from the car park at the visitor centre and Co-op store just off the A82. Much of the approach follows the traditional right of way to Duror.

Exit the car park either side of the visitor centre and turn right, then cross over and go left up Loanfern, past the playing fields, to cross the pedestrian bridge over the River Laroch. Turn left up a narrow road, signed as the Public Footpath to Glen Creran and Glen Duror, and pass the primary school.

When the road ends, continue through gates into the open, along firstly a track, then a path into Gleann an Fhiodh, with the shapely Graham Sgòrr a' Choise ahead and the Munro Top Sgòrr Bhàn on the right. Cross a number of burns and continue towards a large cairn and a signpost to Glen Creran at NN068548.

The sign points to the start of a diagonal path shown on maps, the line of the right of way to Glen Creran. However, the lower part of this route does not exist, and the sign should be ignored. Instead, follow the path below the cairn for about 350m to a small cairn, from where a rough path leads to the river where it flows through a flat area with shingle banks at NN066546.

On the other side, a green wooden post at the foot of a green strip on the hillside marks a path, which is followed directly up, past more marker posts, to reach the upper section of the right of way. This leads to the Màm Uchdaich col. Turn right at a rusty old gate (the fence and stile further on mark the top of the forest boundary), then follow a path and old fence posts up onto the crest

Step over a fence across the ridge and climb to Pt.626m, then drop to a col with a tiny lochan. Climb over a small knoll, passing above a lochan down to the right, and climb over Pt.718m to another col. Swing round over Pt.671m, then drop to another col, Bealach Dearg (c.645m). Now make the final ascent up the ridge, north-west above Coire Dearg, then south-west above Coire Dubh, to gain the summit cairn, adorned with fence ironmongery (**10.75km; 1090m; 4h 20min**).

The outlook is superb. West and north-west across Loch Linnhe to Kingairloch and Ardgour are the Corbetts Fuar Bheinn, Creach Bheinn and Garbh Bheinn, with Beinn Resipol and Rum beyond. North is Beinn a' Bheithir, whilst to the east is Glen Coe, with the Aonach Eagach and the Bidean nam Bian massif prominent.

Return the same way (**21.5km; 1290m; 7h 30min**).

The route via Glen Duror starts from the small Duror Forest car park (NN004551) at Achadh nan Darach (Achindarroch), gained by a short road off the A828. There is a fine view of the hill from the A828 at Duror, where it reveals itself rising high above the forest, with its two large north-facing corries.

Go through a side gate and follow the right-hand track through the forest and around the bend, to emerge into the open, with the hill ahead. In a further kilometre or so, the track crosses a burn between two tracks off left. This is the burn issuing from Eas nam Meirleach, an impressive gorge running up the hillside of Beinn a' Bheithir, which is visible from further up the route.

Continue for a few hundred metres and watch for a sign on the right giving notification of the bridge across the River Duror being removed. This is just before a weir and pond. Go down to the river and cross; normally straightforward, although the boulders can be slippery.

Follow a grassy path up the other side, left then up right, with some fallen trees to duck under or climb over. Emerge into a felled area, cross a small burn and continue across a short flat section to reach the end of a forestry track. Now climb uphill on a good felling track which, after a short steep section, traverses away right before climbing uphill again, steeply at times, to emerge from the forestry.

Leave the track a few metres from its end, then climb the hillside above and pass to the side of what the map shows as a lochan, but is normally a dried-up area of peat beside a small knoll named A' Chruach (485m). Pass a lochan in the hollow beyond and climb the grassy slope ahead, close to the edge on the left.

Cross a small rise, then the dip

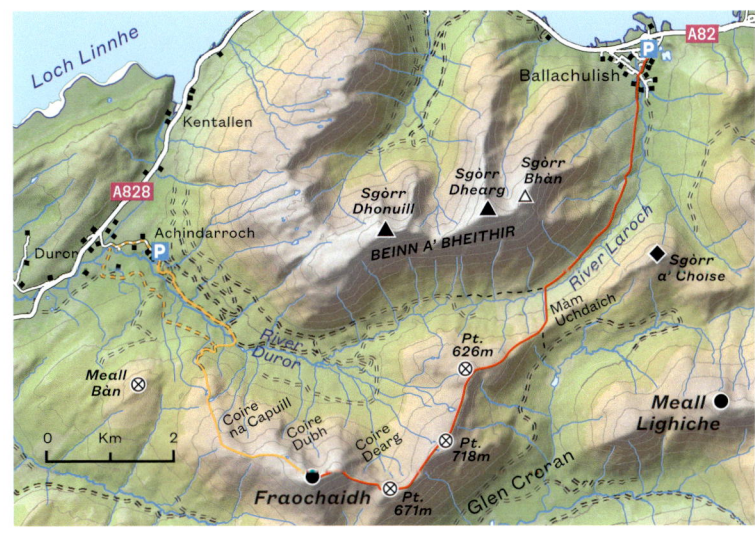

beyond at the head of the corrie, Coire nan Capuill, and ascend the broad ridge ahead on rockier ground to meet a line of fence posts. The posts run up a depression, but much the better route is to head up left to follow the rocky crest overlooking Coire Dubh. An idyllic small lochan is passed, then a point where the slope plunges dramatically into the corrie, before a short ascent leads to the level summit area and cairn (**6.5km; 840m; 2h 50min**).

Return by the route of ascent

(13km; 870m; 4h 40min).

At the start, if there is doubt about the crossing of the River Duror, walk back down the access road for 850m to a crossroads. Turn left here and go along a cycleway on a former railway line for 650m, then take the middle track, which swings left into forestry. Follow the main track, which curves round south into Glen Duror, then take the left fork, which leads into the felled area to end where the route arrives having forded the River Duror; an additional 1.5km, 40m, 20min.

Fraochaidh from Duror, with Coire Dubh, left, and Coire na Capuill, right (Rab Anderson)

> **Creach Bheinn**; *810m; (C139); L50; NN023422; hill of spoil*

Overshadowed by the bigger and more prominent Beinn Sgulaird, which adjoins it to the north, Creach Bheinn is an unassuming hill overlooking the head of Loch Creran. Both hills can be seen from the A828 when crossing the bridge over the narrows on Loch Creran, with Creach Bheinn's lower afforested slopes rising above the loch.

Start from the road around the east side of the head of Loch Creran, where there is a layby at NN009451, just beyond the northern of two entrances to Druimavuic. This is the same start as for the southern approach to Beinn Sgulaird, and the initial part of the route up the track is the same.

Walk back towards the northern entrance to Druimavuic and follow the track on the left through woodland behind the grounds of the house, passing through gates to reach the open hillside. The track swings left then back right over the crest of the lower part of the west ridge, heading towards the Allt Buidhe and the entrance to Coire Buidhe. This is where the route to Beinn Sgulaird heads off left up the ridge.

Continue on the track up the west

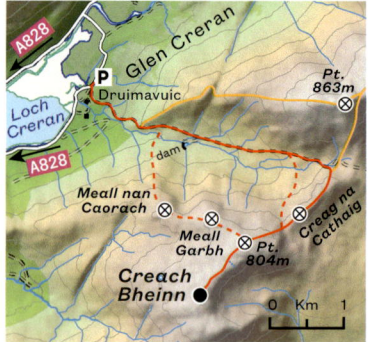

side of Coire Buidhe, with views across to Meall Garbh and Pt.804m (the north-east top), behind which Creach Bheinn's summit is hidden. Follow the track between crags on the left and those on Creag na Cathaig then, shortly after crossing a burn, leave it before the final section to the col ahead. Go up a short bit of old track, then cut up right onto the ridge and follow this over Creag na Cathaig (662m) to a col.

A steeper climb up either side of a depression leads up the rockier hillside to reach easier ground and Creach Bheinn's north-east top (Pt.804m). Continue across a slight dip for 1km to reach the trig pillar on the main summit (**7km; 880m; 3h**).

The outlook is splendid. North is Beinn Sgulaird, with Fraochaidh behind and to its left side. North-east up Glen Etive are the Glen Coe peaks, whilst to the east Beinn Trilleachan appears as a domed whaleback, showing a different perspective to that from Glen Etive, with Ben Starav beyond. To the west, the view extends across Loch Linnhe and south-west down the Firth of Lorn to Mull.

The simplest return is back the same way (**14km; 950m; 4h 50min**),

although from the col with Creag na Cathaig, it is possible to cut down and across the slope to follow a grassy spur dotted with boulders, then traverse across to the track, which is about 15min quicker.

A shorter, but steeper, alternative is to go down the west ridge from the north-east top to Meall Garbh (734m), then to Meall nan Caorach (c.620m), and descend from there to regain the track, which is about 30min quicker.

This descent over Meall Garbh and Meall nan Caorach could also be used as a quicker ascent route (**4.75km; 845m; 2h 30min**), and is perhaps best if Beinn Sgulaird is to be linked for a more demanding outing (**16.5km; 1510m 7h**).

Creach Bheinn across the head of Loch Creran from Beinn Churalain, with distant Ben Cruachan, right (Rab Anderson)

Garbh Bheinn across Loch Leven (Robert Durran)

> **Garbh Bheinn**; *867m; (C67); L41; NN169601; rough hill*

Being surrounded by higher and better-known peaks, and to some extent hidden by these, Garbh Bheinn is an isolated and largely neglected mountain. Sitting tucked in to the north of the great wall formed by Glen Coe's Aonach Eagach Ridge, it rises steeply above the head of Loch Leven. However, it is a very fine peak, and its enclosure by bigger peaks serves to make its summit an outstanding viewpoint.

The route to its conical summit ascends the attractive north-west ridge, which can be seen from the highest point on the B863 along the south side of Loch Leven, as well as from the other side of the loch.

Start at the foot of the north-west ridge, where there is a three car pull-off on the west side of the bridge (NN142607) over the Allt Gleann a' Chaolais, and a one car space on the other side. This is the second bridge, 300m east of the Caolasnacon caravan site.

From the east side of the bridge, follow a path up the Allt Gleann a' Chaolais for 60m, then take to a rough path on the left, which leads onto and up the initial rocky part of the ridge named Torran nan Crann. The path zigzags up the crest beyond to the slight rise of Stob Coire nan Sgoilte, where the upper cone is revealed.

Cross the slight dip at the head of Coire Sgoilte and continue up the ridge. A small pinnacle appears to block the way ahead, which can either be scrambled over or easily bypassed to its side. The summit is surprisingly spacious, and there are a number of cairns. The one of red igneous rock appears to be the higher, and it is worth moving around to take in the stunning views (**3km; 850m; 2h 5min**).

The best descent is to return via the ascent route, which allows the views to be further appreciated (6km; 865m; 3h 15min).

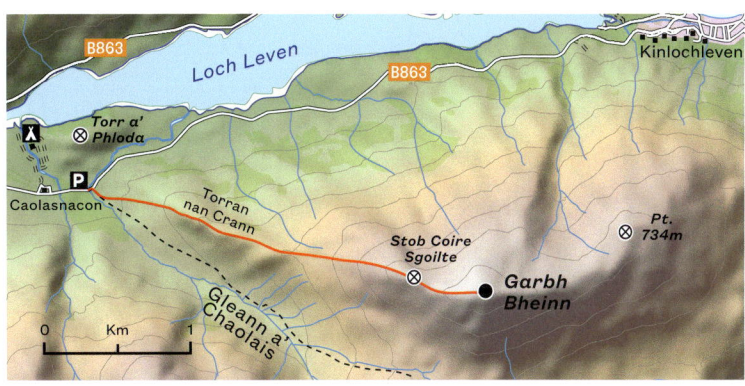

*Across Loch Coire a' Bhric Beag
and Corrour Station to Leum Uilleim
and Beinn a' Bhric (Derek Sime)*

SECTION 4
Loch Linnhe to Loch Ericht

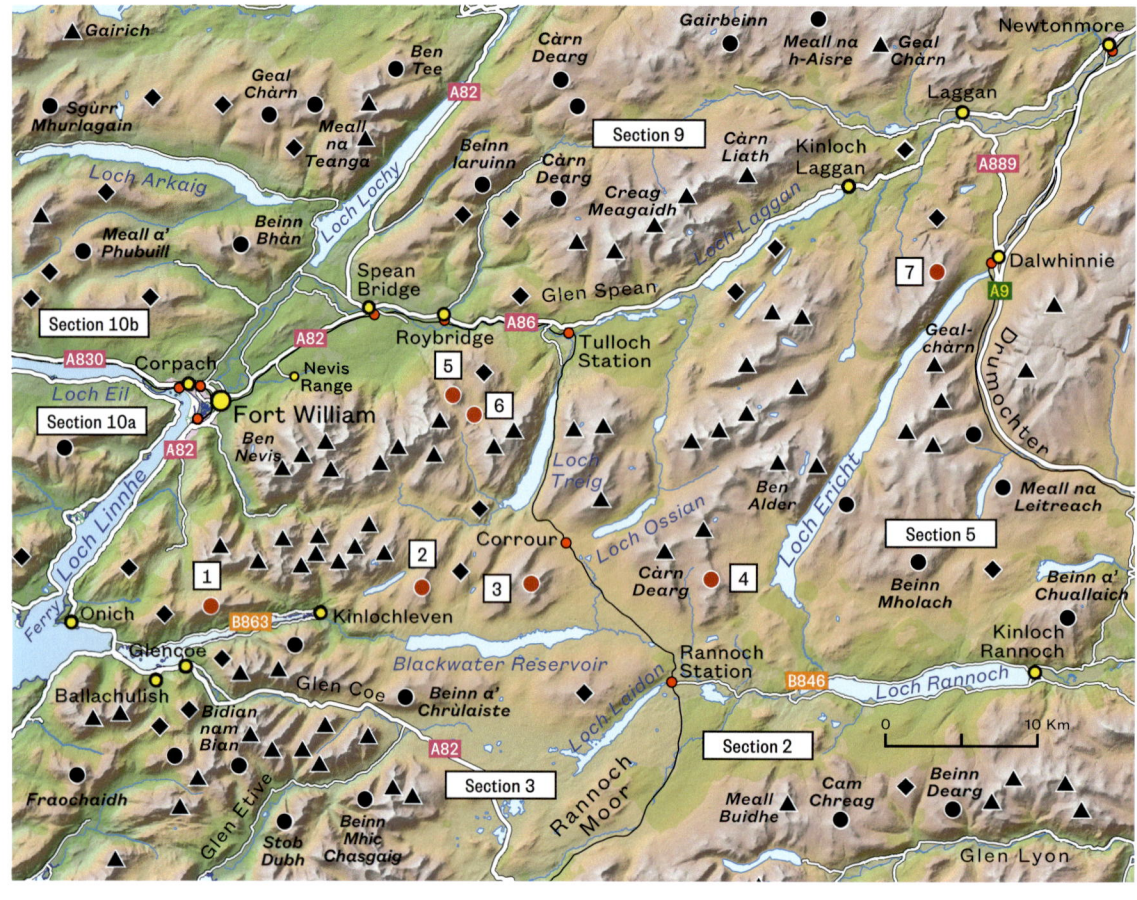

SECTION 4

Màm na Gualainn with Beinn na Caillich, right, across Loch Leven from Glencoe (Rab Anderson)

Màm na Gualainn; 796m; (C167); L41; NN115625; rise of the shoulder

Màm na Gualainn forms the highest point of a narrow ridge running along the north side of the fjord-like inlet of Loch Leven. The summit sits between the Pap of Glencoe on the opposite side of the loch and Meall a' Chaorainn, a subsidiary top of the Munro Mullach nan Coirean, at the west end of The Mamores range. To its west is the Graham Tom Meadhoin, with which Màm na Gualainn can be combined.

The best route is one that traverses the ridge westwards over Beinn na Caillich from Kinlochleven. This gives an excellent and highly scenic outing, best saved for a good day. The route can either be done as a circuit, or as a there-and-back the same way, or with transportation between the end and start points.

There is a public car park next to St Paul's Church in Wades Road. This is signed for the Grey Mare's Waterfall and is gained by leaving the main B863 (Lochaber Road) at the northern end of Kinlochleven, then either turning north-east along Kearan Road, or Wades Road itself.

Turn right out of the car park and go west along Wades Road with conical Beinn na Caillich visible ahead. Cross over the B863 and go right, then in 250m or so, cross back over to follow the West Highland Way ▶

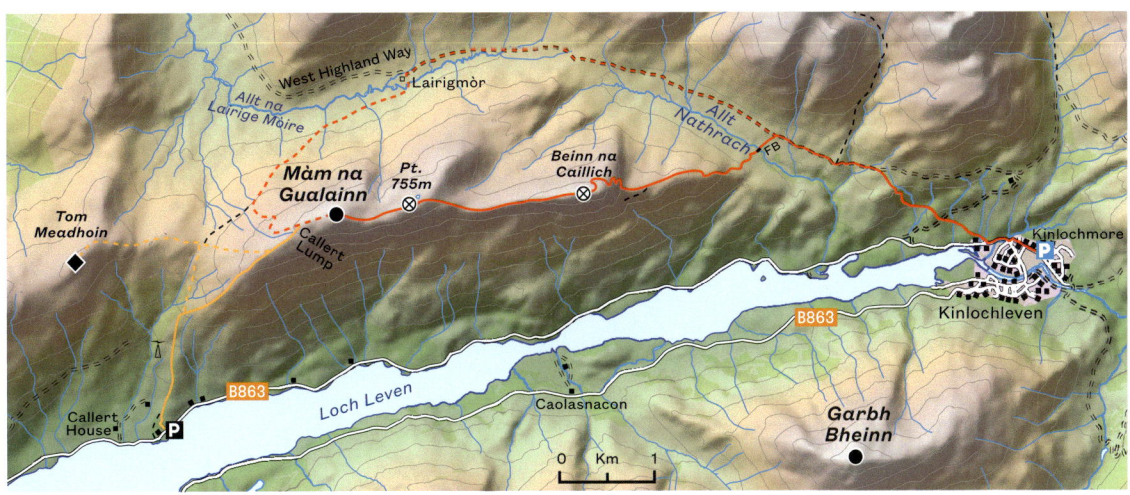

West along the ridge above Loch Leven from Beinn na Caillich to the summit of Màm na Gualainn (Rab Anderson)

path uphill through woodland. This crosses the access road to the former Mamore Lodge to join a track which traverses the hillside.

Follow the track west for just over 1km, then turn off left and descend a path to cross the bridge over the Allt Nathrach; the path is further west than shown on maps.

Ascend the path, which zigzags up onto the start of the ridge then along a level section. Take the right-hand path here and zigzag up to the top of Beinn na Caillich (764m). It is worth going to the cairn at the east end first for the view over Kinlochleven.

Descend the splendid high-level ridge to a narrow col, then take the lesser-travelled looking path on the right; not the bypass path on the left. The right-hand path leads over the East Top (755m) to reach a broad col with a small lochan, from where the final ascent is made to the trig pillar on top (9.25km; 1030m; 3h 50min).

The best return is back along the ridge to maintain the superb views. A traverse path avoids the climb over the East Top, although it is no hardship to go over it again (18.5km; 1260m; 6h 40min).

Another option is to follow the path down the west ridge by the fence, then go through a gate. Don't continue

down the path to Callert, which goes south-west beside the fence, but take the path just to the right, which passes to the north of Callert Lump. This leads towards the head of a burn running north-west. Pick up an old stalkers' path and follow this northwards as it zigzags down to meet the main path coming from Callert over the col between the hills. This then leads north-east to ford the Allt na Lairige Mòire and join the West Highland Way at the Lairigmòr ruins and walls. Follow the West Highland Way back to Kinlochleven (20.5km; 1150m; 6h 55min).

If descending to Callert, follow the ascent route described below.

A much shorter route starts at the west end of the hill, from the B863 to the east of Callert House on the opposite side of the loch from Glencoe village. There is a pull-off in the trees on the north side of the road at NN096603.

A signed Rights of Way path begins at the end of the woodland about 200m to the west. However, it is easier to follow the rough track which leaves the pull-off and follow this up the hillside to where it is joined by the Rights of Way path at the corner of an old wall. To the east there is a good view of Garbh Bheinn.

Continue on a rough ATV track running up the hillside, which has been marked with unsightly posts. Pass a communications aerial out to the left, well out from the edge of the forest. Although the ATV track can be followed all the way to the col, it is boggy in places and a bit of an eyesore. It is better to leave the track by breaking off right onto the south-west ridge at some point before reaching the top edge of the forest and the burn draining the hillside.

Ascend the ridge past some small outcrops, picking up traces of path, to reach a minor bump named Callert Lump, where a fence is met coming up the hillside on the right. Continue the ascent beside the fence, passing through a gate to the other side, then ascend up the side of a shallow depression to reach the trig pillar (3.25km; 4km; 790m; 2h).

Return by the route of ascent (6.5km; 785m; 3h 5min).

If Tom Meadhoin (621m), the Graham to the west, is included from this route, simply gain the col (466m) between the hills and climb onto a level spur, which leads to an ascent west onto the crest, where the summit is only a short distance to the south-west. Return to the col to descend (9.75km; 950m; 4h 5min).

Glas Bheinn; 792m; (C172); L41; NN259641; grey hill

In accordance with its name, Glas Bheinn is a rather undistinguished hill situated in the seldom-visited hill country to the east of the Mamores, that is bounded by Loch Eilde Mòr, Loch Treig, Loch Ossian and Blackwater Reservoir. To its east is the Graham Beinn na Cloiche, then the Corbett Leum Uilleim above Corrour.

Start in Kinlochleven, from a car park signed for the Grey Mare's Waterfall. This is gained by leaving the main B863 (Lochaber Road) at the northern end of Kinlochleven, then turning east along Wades Road. The car park is next to the white building of St Paul's Church, where Wades Road is joined by Kearan Road.

Head into woodland on the east side of the church, on a surfaced path to the waterfall. Follow this briefly left, then leave it and go right on a rougher path (signed to Loch Eilde Mòr), keeping left to cross a burn. Continue on the main path, which has become eroded, uphill through fine oak and birch woods to exit the woodland and skirt the northern flank of Meall an Doire Dharaich. On joining a track, go right along it for 480m, then leave it for a path that

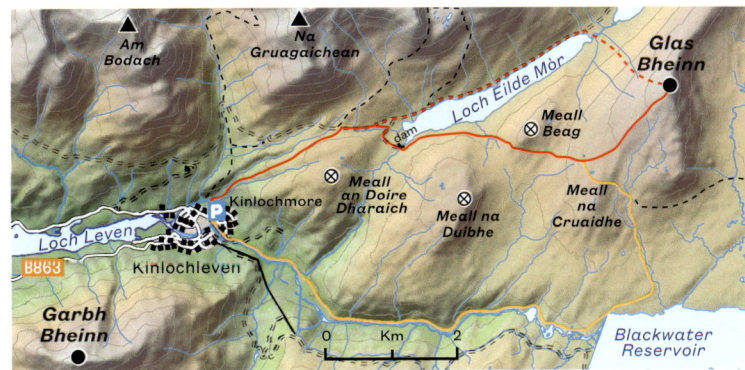

crosses a burn and cuts the corner to rejoin a branch of the track that runs across the head of Loch Eilde Mòr.

Follow this track across the dam and bridge over the outflow from the loch, then turn left onto a stalkers' path. Continue along the boggy path above the loch, soon swinging southeast away from the loch across a burn to make a rising traverse across the northern flank of Meall Beag (561m). Cross another small burn and ascend towards Meall na Cruaidhe on the broad south-west ridge of Glas Bheinn. Leave the path where it turns further south, and climb north-east up the ridge to the large cairn on the summit (**9km; 840m; 3h 20min**).

The Mamores range is prominent to the north-west with Sgùrr Chòinnich Mòr and the back of the Grey Corries beyond. South-westwards across Blackwater Reservoir dam, to the side of Beinn a' Chrùlaiste, there is an interesting view of Buachaille Etive Mòr and the Glen Coe peaks.

Return the same way (**18km; 900m; 5h 45min**).

An alternative is to make a steep descent west, then north-west from the summit to cross the causeway at the east end of Loch Eilde Mòr, and gain the track on the far side. This leads along the side of the loch to regain the approach route (**17.5km; 900m; 5h 35min**).

Another option is to regain the stalkers' path and follow it to the Blackwater Reservoir dam, then descend the path past Dubh Lochan and down the north side of the River Leven (**21km; 960m; 6h 35min**).

Across Blackwater Reservoir dam to Glas Bheinn (Rab Anderson)

Leum Uilleim from Beinn a' Bhric with Loch Ossian and distant Ben Alder (Rab Anderson)

Leum Uilleim; 909m; (C11); L41; NN330641; *William's leap*

Located on the northern edge of Rannoch Moor, Leum Uilleim occupies an isolated position in the heart of the Central Highlands. It rises south-west of remote Corrour Station on the West Highland Line, and were it not for the railway, the approach to it would require a considerable amount of effort. It is often referred to as the Trainspotting Hill following a clip in that iconic film; hopefully, everyone alighting from the train will be more successful with their proposed ascent!

Above the station, Leum Uilleim's slopes rise to what appears as an attractive conical summit, and when the ascent over this is combined with a traverse around its big north-east facing corrie, Coire a' Bhric Beag, it gives a rewarding and scenic circuit.

For the approach to Corrour by train, park at, or close to, whichever of the railway stations is used. Coming from the south, the train originates at Glasgow. Many people drive to Crianlarich to catch it, but it can also be caught at Tyndrum Upper Station, Bridge of Orchy and Rannoch Stations.

Coming from the north, the train originates at Fort William, but Spean Bridge, Roybridge and Tulloch Stations can all be used. Check the ScotRail website or phone 0845 601 5929 for the relevant train information – watch for seasonal variations, restricted Sunday service and request stopping.

For the southbound return, there are two evening trains, and for the northbound return, there is a mid-afternoon, then a late evening train. Plan well, and if required, take warm clothing for the wait. It is also worth checking the website for the seasonal Corrour Station House cafe and restaurant.

Hostelling Scotland has a hostel at Loch Ossian. As well as Leum Uilleim, there are four Munros and two Grahams that could be climbed from here. If approaching by rail, bikes can be taken on the train.

For anyone wishing to avoid the constraints of the approach by rail, it is possible to bike in on estate tracks from the south and from the north. Although both bike approaches are long, they make more of a day of it

and the journey is enjoyable.

The bike approach from the south starts some 2km to the east of Rannoch Station, where the track followed by the Road to the Isles leaves the B846 Rannoch road on the north side of Loch Eigheach. The track is signed as the Footpath to Fort William by Corrour, and there is parking on the south side of the road opposite it at NN446578. Follow the track for 3km to cross a bridge over the Allt Eigheach and keep left where the track splits to make an ascending traverse round the western flanks of Càrn Dearg to a height of 550m. Pass Corrour Old Lodge, then at Peter's Rock, drop west below Meall na Lice to the main track round Loch Ossian. Go left, then straight ahead to the station where bikes are left; take a bike lock (**16km**; **320m**; about **2h 20min**).

The bike approach from the north starts from a large layby at the south-west end of Loch Laggan on the south side of the A86 at NN433830, to the east of a bridge over the River Spean. Follow the estate track across the River Spean and go right past Luiblea to cross the Abhainn Ghuilbinn and pass Tòrgulbin. Continue south-west for 3.5km, then south on the main track past the west side of Meall Luidh Mòr to exit the forestry. Climb to a height of 430m above Loch Ghuilbinn, then descend south-west through Srath Ossian to reach the east end of Loch Ossian. Go around either side to Corrour Station (**24.5km; 240m;** about **3h**).

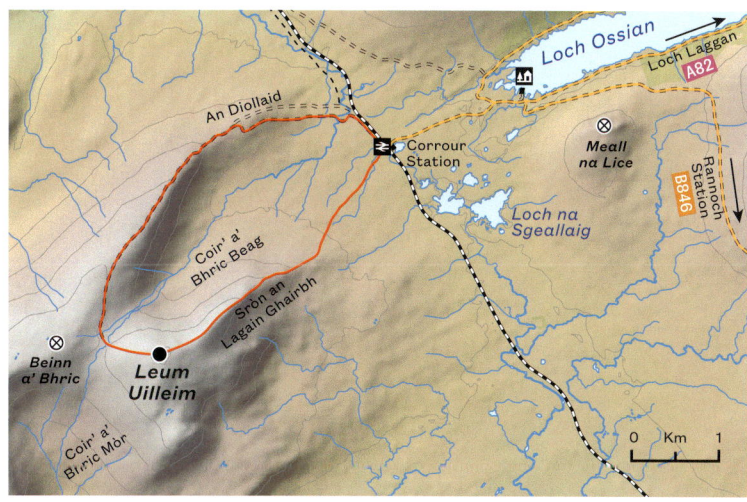

For the ascent of Leum Uilleim, cross the railway to the north of the platform, then pass a track on the right and take the track straight ahead, which becomes an ATV track. When this swings right on the line of the original stalkers' path, make your way as best you can across the lower boggy ground, heading directly for the base of the ridge ahead and drier ground. Climb this ridge, the Sròn an Lagain Ghairbh, over the minor rise that gives the hill its peak-like appearance, and continue to the broad and stony summit area. A large cairn marks the top; it is a grand viewpoint (**4km; 505m; 1h 45min**).

Descend westwards onto an ATV track and follow this north below the top of Beinn a' Bhric, across the head of Coire a' Bhric Beag, onto its north-east ridge. The top of Beinn a' Bhric could easily be included. Continue down the ridge on the ATV track, past Tom an Eòin, and on down the lower ridge of An Diollaid. When the track forks, keep left to continue down the lower part of the ridge and cross

wetter ground to meet a good path and a bridge across the Allt Coire a' Bhric Beag. The path leads back to the station (**10.5km; 530m; 3h 25min**).

If the approach has been made by bike, return the same way for an added bike distance and time of (**32km; 500m;** about **4h 30min**) for the southern route and (**49km; 380m;** about **5h 30min**) for the northern route.

Leum Uilleim from Corrour Station (Rab Anderson)

BEINN PHARLAGAIN; *perhaps grassy hollow*
Meall na Meoig; *868m; (C65); L42; NN448642; hill of whey*

A great south-facing horseshoe of ridges forms the north-eastern edge of Rannoch Moor, at the apex of which sit the Munros Càrn Dearg and Sgòr Gaibhre. Beinn Pharlagain is the multi-topped ridge that extends south-wards from Sgòr Gaibhre to form the eastern part of this horseshoe, and its highest point is Meall na Meoig,.

Although Beinn Pharlagain and Meall na Meoig can be climbed on their own, they are best climbed together with the two Munros for an excellent horseshoe traverse around Coire Eigheach.

The approach is made from near the end of the B846 along Loch Rannoch to Rannoch Station on the West Highland Line railway, from where the track on the line of the historic Road to the Isles leaves the road on the north side of Loch Eigheach. The track is signed as the Footpath to Fort William by Corrour, and there is parking on the south side of the road opposite it at NN446578.

It would be possible to approach by train to this station, but this would entail a 2.5km walk along the road to the start. However, by taking a bike on the train, the road could be biked, along with the initial 3.25km of track.

Follow the track for 3.25km to the bridge over the Allt Eigheach, then leave it and follow a rough ATV track north up the east side of the river. After 500m or so, the ATV track moves gradually away from the river, ascending the slope, then swinging right (north-east) to climb Leacann nan Giomach, where it disappears.

Continue up onto the ridge to gain the top of a minor rise (Pt.711m), then drop off this and climb onto Pt.799m. Descend to the dip with Beinn Pharlagain's South Top (807m), which is bypassed on its right, or climbed, then cross the dip to the north-east and bypass Garbh Mheall Mòr (838m) on its left, or climb it. Finally, climb to the summit of Meall na Meoig; a slab 40m to the north-north-west of the cairn is higher (**7.75km; 650m; 2h 45min**).

For the Corbett-only route, drop eastwards to pass between a larger lochan, Lochan Meoigeach, and a smaller one to its north-west, then descend north-west beside the outflow. Turn west, then south-west and cross the Allt Eigheach to pick up an ATV track, which is followed south to a dam. From there, a better track leads to the main Road to the Isles track,

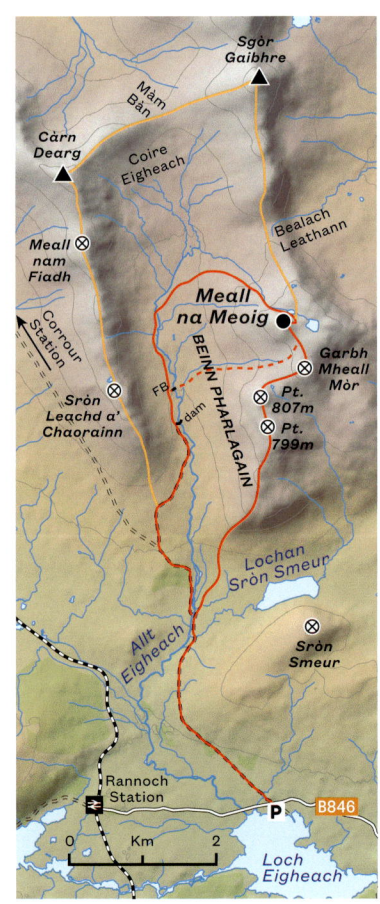

Meall na Meoig across Coire Eigheach, with Garbh Mheall Mòr, right, from Càrn Dearg (Tom Prentice)

> ***Cruach Innse***; 857m; (C84); L41; NN279763; *hill of the meadow or island hill*
>
> ***Sgùrr Innse***; 809m; (C142); L41; NN290748; *peak of the meadow or island peak*

Commonly referred to as The Innses, this pair of hills lies between the Munros of the Grey Corries and The Easains. The bigger Cruach is the northern of the pair, and rises above the Insh flats on the south side of the River Spean, with the shapely Sgùrr appearing over its east flank. Both are well seen from the area around Roy Bridge. They are steep and craggy hills lying above the Làirig Leacach pass, which runs through from Spean Bridge to the southern end of Loch Treig, separating them from the eastern end of the Grey Corries range. It is via this pass that the hills are reached.

The approach is by the narrow road signed to Corriechoille, which goes eastwards from the A82 just south of the bridge at Spean Bridge, up the south side of the River Spean. There is no parking at the end of this road, but it is acceptable to turn right and drive with care up the rough track past Corriechoille.

After 1.5km, a right branch enters the forestry area, where there is a small three-car parking space. A further 600m up the track past this right branch, there is a larger parking area for about nine cars at NN255788; there is also space at the bend just before this.

The track is the start of the right of way through the Làirig Leacach to Corrour and on to Rannoch. Follow the track uphill through a gate into a replanted area (passing the wooden statue of the Wee Minister, who offers good luck to travellers). Continue uphill past older trees to exit the forestry by a gate, then shortly cross the Allt Leachdach by a bridge. In a further 350m, leave the track at a small quarried area and climb eastwards to reach the broad north-west ridge of Cruach Innse. This gives a steeper ascent with rapidly expanding views, easing towards a flat and stony summit (**4.25km; 665m; 2h**).

▶

which is followed past a disguised hydro building, then over the bridge and back to the start (18.75km; 660m; 5h 30min).

This descent can be shortened by descending south from the summit of Meall na Meoig into the corrie, Coire na Bàin Lic, to follow a burn west and cross the Allt Eigheach lower down; 2.25km shorter and 30min quicker.

For the horseshoe extension, drop east off the summit of Meall na Meoig to pass between the lochans, then descend the ridge northwards and cross the Bealach Leathann (675m) and climb to Sgòr Gaibhre (**11.25km; 950m; 4h 10min**).

Follow the path down to the south-west, cross the Màm Bàn (c.725m) and climb to Càrn Dearg (**14.25km; 1180m; 5h 15min**).

Go down the long and undulating south ridge, passing over Meall nam Fiadh (861m) and Pt.821m to gain Sròn Leachd a' Chaorainn (737m) at the end of the ridge. Descend south to the hydro track from the dam, then follow this to the Road to the Isles track, which is followed past a disguised hydro building, then over the bridge and back to the start (24km; 1250m; 7h 55min).

Cruach Innse from the track to the Làirig Leacach (Mike Dixon)

Sgùrr Innse from the Làirig Leacach with Stob Coire Easain beyond (Mike Dixon)

Follow a path southwards down the broad ridge, which steepens and becomes rocky. At a brief levelling, follow the main path down left, then back right beneath a crag before weaving easily down the rocky ridge to easier ground leading to the broad col between the hills, the Bealach na Cruaiche (c.595m).

Cross a slight rise in the middle, then follow the path up easier ground past a large boulder, heading for a break in the scree and boulder slope beneath the craggy upper part of the hill. Ascend bouldery ground up the right side of the initial crag, then follow the path up and left via an obvious rake to bypass the main crag.

Climb back up right onto the broad crest above the crag, then traverse rightwards across the crest to where a path of sorts drops off the ridge down steeper ground to the right. Turn left here, and continue easily up the path to the top of Sgùrr Innse, marked by a small cairn on a rib of rock (**6.5km; 885m; 3h**).

It is worth heading south a short way, past a small lochan in the dip and across a flattening, to gain the top of the crags above the south-east face. There is a fine view across the gulf to The Easains, Stob a' Choire Mheadhoin and Stob Coire Easain, and beyond to Buachaille Etive Mòr and Buachaille Etive Beag, with Stob Bàn to the right.

Return to the col between the hills, ensuring that the correct turn is made to traverse across right to regain the rake. Slant down from the col to gain the track through the Làirig Leacach, opposite the large boulder of Clach Cartaidh, and follow the track back (**12.75km; 885m; 4h 45min**).

For anyone considering a descent to the south-west off Sgùrr Innse, perhaps to the bothy beneath Stob Bàn, the direct line is blocked by a line of crags. Begin by descending a short distance south-east, then follow a terrace west between the crags.

> **The Fara**; *911m; (C7); L42; NN598842; ladder hill*

Most people travelling the A9 corridor through the Drumochter Pass will have noted the elongated ridgeline of The Fara, which forms the western skyline above Dalwhinnie at the head of Loch Ericht. This ridgeline contains a number of tops, three of which are over 900m in height, with the highest point towards the northern end being only three metres short of Munro height.

The simplest route to the summit starts from the A889 to the north of Dalwhinnie, from the north side of the traffic-light-controlled bridge over the railway line just beyond the Dalwhinnie Distillery. There is a pull-off on the right at the start of the minor road to Crubenmore.

Walk along the verge of the A889 behind the distillery, and around the bend for 500m. Go through a gate signed for the Caochan Wood Trails and follow a track into the right side of the forestry plantation. Some 600m into the forest, leave the track at a small wooden bench on the left and go up the first break in the trees on a rough and boggy path. At the top, go left and through a gate in the deer fence around the forest, then cross rough ground for about 150m to gain a track coming up from the right. Follow this track to its end at NN607856. The track is not currently shown on the 1:50k map and goes further than shown on the 1:25k map.

Continue on a rough ATV track for about 50m or so, onto the crest of the north-east ridge, then ascend the ridge to the summit. There is a rough path for most of the way. The ridge kinks to the left at 840m, which should be watched for, especially in descent in poor visibility. A line of fence posts coming up from the Dirc Mhòr down to the right meets a huge built-up cairn at some boulders where a drystane dyke comes up from the Loch Ericht side. Although the OS map shows this as the summit, the highest point is a rock tor 100m to the south-south-west (**6km; 560m; 2h 15min**).

Returning the same way is the easiest (**12km; 565m; 3h 45min**).

For a fine extension, the ridge can be traversed southwards for another 4.25km to its end on 897m Meall Cruaidh (**10.25km; 720m; 3h 30min**).

To return, one option is to descend

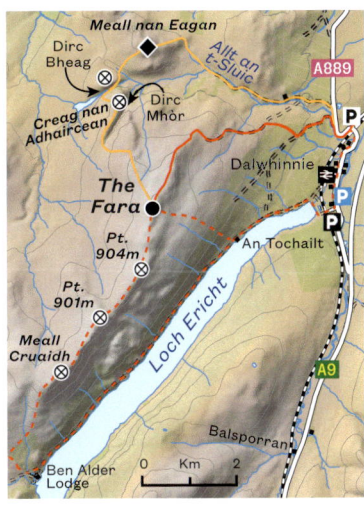

the south-west ridge, then go down the west end of the forest and drop to the track above Ben Alder Lodge. A lengthy walk beside the loch leads back to Dalwhinnie. Crossing the railway is prohibited at the time of writing, so cross the dam at the head of the loch and go through an underpass to the filling station, then follow the road back (**23.75km; 770m; 7h**).

This extended route can be shortened by some 3km, by parking next to the underpass, or the layby on the main road opposite the hotel. Approach through the underpass, cross the dam and go along the loch to An Tochailt, then steeply ascend the break in the trees and on directly to the summit. However, there is still the long walk back along the loch. It would probably be easier to use the principal start and traverse back along the ridge to descend as for the ascent route (**20.5km; 895m; 6h 15min**).

Perhaps a better option for a longer outing from the parking to the north of the distillery is to include Meall nan Eagan (658m), the Graham to the north, as described in the SMC's guidebook *The Grahams & The Donalds*. This includes the splendid glacial meltwater channels of the Dirc Bheag and Dirc Mhòr.

To do this, follow the Allt an t-Sluic

track to ascend Meall nan Eagan by its east ridge. Drop south-west, then go through the Dirc Bheag until it is possible to climb onto, then along, Creag nan Adhaircean above the Dirc Mhòr. Descend across the head of the Dirc Mhòr, then climb to the summit of The Fara up the ridge of Meall Liath beside a line of fence posts (**11.5km; 810m; 3h 45min**).

Descend by the north-east ridge and track, as described above (**17.5km; 815m; 5h 15min**).

A shortened version of this would be to omit Meall nan Eagan and climb up through the floor of the Dirc Mhòr.

Across Loch Ericht to The Fara (Rab Anderson)

South down Loch Ericht to Stob an Aonaich Mhòir, showing its full height, with distant Beinn Mhanach, Beinn a' Chreachain, centre, and Beinn Achaladair (Mike Dixon)

SECTION 5
Loch Ericht to Drumochter

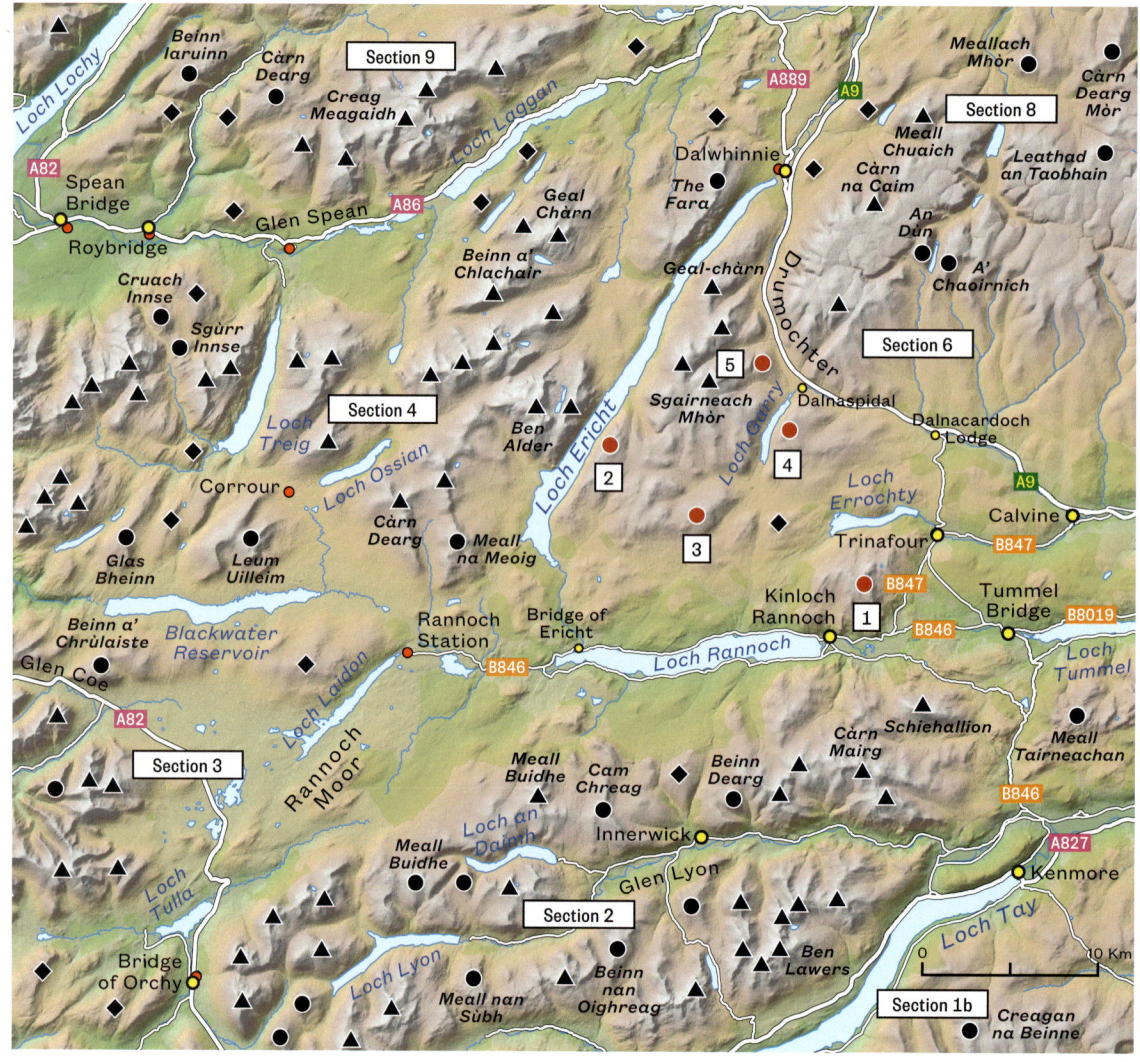

SECTION 5

Beinn a' Chuallaich across Dunalastair Reservoir (Rab Anderson)

Beinn a' Chuallaich; 892m; (C32); L42; NN684617; hill of the herding

---

This unassuming hill occupies the ground between the ends of Loch Rannoch and Dunalastair Water in the south, and Loch Errochty to the north. It gives a pleasant ascent when climbed via its long south ridge, and there are rewarding views from its summit.

Start from a pull-off at NN699589 in the trees above Dunalastair Reservoir. This is about 75m north from the junction of the B847 to Trinafour with the B846, which runs along Loch Tummel and Loch Rannoch.

Walk to the junction and go through a gate on the right. Follow a grassy track to the cottage at Drumglas and go through a gate to its right, then continue beneath the pylons on the track, which loops westwards uphill. The track passes through Creag Bhuidhe Wood, a gated area of hillside that has been planted with mixed trees. Beyond this, continue uphill onto the south ridge.

The track and an old stalkers' path run up the left side of the ridge to pass through a col to the west of, and below, the summit. However, it is

better to leave these to climb onto the ridge, crossing a tumbledown wall at its junction with another wall, then follow the crest with fine views. The Blackmount and Glen Coe lie to the west, Beinn a' Ghlo to the east and Schiehallion to the south across Dunalastair Water. Pass a small, stone windbreak just below the top to reach the substantial summit cairn, with a trig point just beyond (**4.5km; 680m; 2h 10min**).

With the hills to the north now in view, there is a splendid 360-degree panorama. A number of Corbetts lie fairly close and can be picked out; Beinn Mholach, Meall na Leitreach, The Sow of Atholl, Ben Vrackie, Meall Tairneachan and Farragon Hill.

The best return is back the same way, with the fine sight of Schiehallion ahead (**9km; 680m; 3h 30min**).

A circuit can be created by heading north from the summit to Meall nan Eun to descend east then south-east to the pick up a stalkers' path near the top corner of a forestry plantation. Follow the path through a gate, then go past a hut and down the side of the trees to go through another

gate to gain the B847. Walk down the road for 3km to regain the start (**11.5km; 705m; 4h**).

An ascent can be made via the descent described for the circuit above. There is parking on the B847 at NN707614 opposite the gate giving access past the hut to the hillside. However, this is shorter and not as scenic, nor as good as the route via the south ridge (**7km; 635m; 3h**).

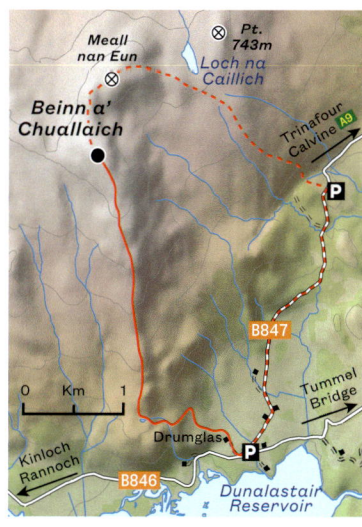

Distant Stob an Aonaich Mhòir from the hydro road (Rab Anderson)

Stob an Aonaich Mhòir; 855m; (C88); L42; NN537694; peak of the big crest

One of five Corbetts in the relatively unfrequented triangle of land bounded by Loch Rannoch, Loch Ericht, and the A9 corridor through Glen Garry and Drumochter, Stob an Aonaich Mhòir is an elusive and rather neglected hill. It sits opposite Ben Alder in a remote position, a long way down the east side of the glacial trench occupied by Loch Ericht.

There is a grand view of Stob an Aonaich Mhòir from the north, looking down Loch Ericht where it shows its full height, but there is no route to it from this direction. Fortunately, for the biker anyway, there is a surfaced hydro-road, which goes from near the west end of Loch Rannoch to the dam at the southern end of Loch Ericht, then on to Corrievarkie Lodge and a power station half way along Loch Ericht. This road climbs to a height of 635m, from where it is only a short climb north-west to Stob an Aonaich Mhòir. It would be feasible for those using bikes to also include Beinn Mholach in the day from this road.

Start at Bridge of Ericht, on the east side of the River Ericht where there is limited verge parking by the fence to the east of the access road, which starts beside a white cottage. The gate across the road is signed to Talladh-a-Bheithe Estate and Corrievarkie Lodge. There is also a

car park beside the loch, 1.3km to the east, just before the power station, which, for bikers, is no hardship.

Go through the side gate and follow the surfaced road gradually uphill to pass out in front of the dam across Loch Ericht, then on up beside the

Allt Ghlas, which is crossed higher up. Continue to the highpoint of the road where bikes can be left (**13km; 440m; about 1h 30min** by bike), (**3h 35min** on foot).

Simply climb north-west up slopes of grass and heather to gain the summit, which is perched above a steep slope overlooking the Loch Ericht trench, with Beinn Bheòil and Ben Alder opposite (**1.25km; 225m; 40min**).

Return to the road (**2.5km; 225m; 1h 5min**).

Return to Bridge of Ericht (**28.5km; 685m; 3h 35min** with a bike), (**7h 30min** on foot).

Beinn Mholach (opposite page) can be included by returning down the road over the bridge across the Allt Ghlas and crossing the Allt an Luib Bhàin to where an old stalkers' path leaves the road at NN537653. Climb east to pass just south of Pt.683m, then traverse east across the south side of Beinn Bhoidheach (790m) and drop to a broad, haggy col. From there, climb east to the trig point and large cairn on Beinn Mholach. Return the same way; an additional 10.5km, 470m, 3h 20min there and back.

Beinn Mholach's summit, with Loch Rannoch and Schiehallion beyond, and a distant Ben Vrackie, left (Rab Anderson)

Beinn Mholach; 841m; (C101); L42; NN587654; shaggy (rough) mountain

Sharing a desolate and neglected corner of the Central Highlands with Stob an Aonaich Mhòir, between Loch Ericht and Loch Rannoch, Beinn Mholach probably ranks as one of the lesser-visited summits in Scotland.

Whilst it is possible to approach the hill from Annat or Auchlich on Loch Rannoch, via tracks that join, finding suitable parking near the start of the tracks from the B846 is difficult. As a result, an approach from the north, from Dalnaspidal just off the A9 at Drumochter, is the best option. A bike can be used for 5.75km of track to the south end of Loch Garry for a saving of about 1h 30min on the times given.

Leave the A9 at Dalnaspidal and go right, then right again to reach a large parking area beside a cottage, over-looking the railway. Sustrans Route 7 cycle route runs through here. This is also the parking for Meall na Leitreach and The Sow of Atholl.

Walk back up the road past the access road to the lower cottage, then go down the road on the right and cross the railway. Take the track on the right opposite the Dalnaspidal Lodge estate buildings and follow it across the sluice dam on the Allt Dubhaig, then the bridge over the Allt Coire Luidhearnaidh to reach Loch Garry. The track runs along the west side of the loch beneath the steep slopes of An Cearcall, which rise to Meallan Buidhe then the Munro Sgairneach Mhòr, and those opposite, which rise to Meall na Leitreach.

Loch Garry is part of the Tummel Hydro Scheme, and when the water level is high it is fairly attractive. However, when the water is low, ugly bare tide lines show.

Pass a hydro pumping station building halfway along, which takes water from Loch Garry via a tunnel and feeds it downhill north-westwards for 7.6km through the mountains to a power station at the outfall halfway along Loch Ericht. The approach road to Stob an Aonaich Mhòir services this power station, and if a bike is used, Beinn Mholach can be included from there; see opposite page.

The track ends at the Allt Coire Easan where it flows into the south end of Loch Garry; bikes are best left here. Go through a gate and cross the burn on stepping stones to follow an ATV track across flat, boggy ground. When the track forks after 1km, go up right (a little shorter and drier) and continue to a hydro track running up the Allt Shallainn and two bridges across this. Continuing ahead on the line of the original path gains the end of the track at a small power station downstream of the bridges.

Cross the lower bridge and follow a hydro track on the other side for 270m. Immediately after crossing a small burn, which flows through pipes, it is probably best to leave the track and climb the hillside to gain some slabby rocks on an indistinct ridge to meet a rough ATV track. The ATV track leaves the main track 420m further along, at the point Duinish bothy comes into view on the left.

Follow the ATV track up the hillside past a small rocky knoll at 590m and continue up onto Creag nan Gabhar. The summit can now be seen, but is further away than it looks.

Cross flat ground and continue to where the track ends at a peaty col. Ascend south-west on a rough path to reach the summit, which is crowned by a remarkably large and well-built cairn, with the lower trig point just beyond (**11.75km; 480m; 3h 25min**).

Return the same way (**23.5km; 540m; 6h 25min**).

Map opposite

Meall na Leitreach across Loch Garry from Ceann Gorm (Rab Anderson)

Meall na Leitreach; *775m; (C197); L42; NN640703; hill of slopes*
The Sow of Atholl (Meall an Dobharchain); *803m; (C156); L42; NN625741; (watercress hill)*

Linking the south with the north, the Pass of Drumochter is an ancient and famous travellers' route, whose deep glacial trench breaks through the Grampian Mountains.

The first proper road through the pass was a military road constructed by General Wade in the early l8th century. Since then, the pass has been turned into one of the most important and busiest lines of communication in Scotland, carrying the A9 road, the railway, a cycle way, electricity pylons and the occasional RAF fly-through.

However, a climb up the hills at its sides soon shrinks man's work into perspective and when seen from the hillsides high above, the moraine-filled pass appears as if the work of the glaciers had been only yesterday.

Located on the west side of the pass at Dalnaspidal, and sitting opposite each other either side of the head of Loch Garry, are Meall na Leitreach and The Sow of Atholl. With the same start point, their close proximity to each other, and a height of 415m between them, they are conveniently climbed together.

The Sow of Atholl is the fanciful anglicised name given to balance it with its near neighbour to the north, An Torc, better known as the Boar of Badenoch. The original name given to The Sow was Meall an Dobharchain.

Leave the A9 at Dalnaspidal, going right, then right again to reach a large parking area beside a cottage, overlooking the railway. Sustrans Route 7 cycle route runs through here. This is also the parking for Beinn Mholach.

Walk back up the road past the access road to the lower cottage, then go down the road on the right and cross the railway. Take the track on the right opposite the Dalnaspidal Lodge estate buildings and follow it over a sluice dam bridge.

Climbing Meall na Leitreach first, turn left along a track beside a concrete waterway. At the bottom, cross to the other side by a narrow bridge, then cross a bridge over the River Garry and go up onto a track.

Go left along the track for 20m or so then leave it and follow an ATV track southwards up the hillside, passing through a gate to continue up the east side of a burn, the Allt nam Plaidean. As height is gained, there is a dramatic view northwards through the Pass of Drumochter, with The Sow of Atholl rising steeply to its west.

When the angle eases, follow the track as it swings westwards to cross a minor rise, Pt.748m, then turns south again for the final short climb

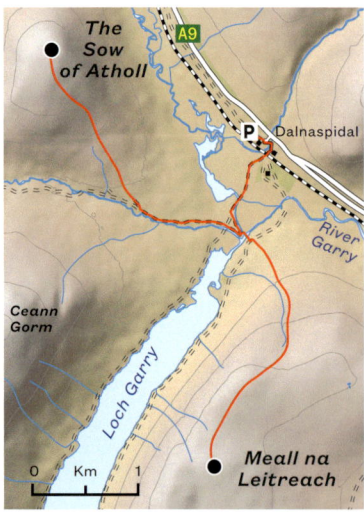

South to The Sow of Atholl, with Meall na Leitreach, Beinn a' Chuallaich and Schiehallion beyond (Rab Anderson)

to the flat summit of Meall na Leitreach. The highest point lies 100m to the east-south-east of the track and the point where the OS map shows it: a small cairn just before a larger cairn (**4km; 390m; 1h 35min**).

Return downhill and cross the bridge over the River Garry, then the narrow bridge over the concrete waterway. Go left and follow the track that runs up the side of the Allt Coire Luidhearnaidh, past a number of weirs, to cross the track leading to Loch Garry, and continue on a track by the burn for 900m. Turn right up a short section of track to a turning circle, then follow an ATV track up the hillside. When this veers right off the direct line, continue straight up to the flat top. The highest point has been surveyed as a cairn on a boulder, 40m east-south-east of where it's shown by the OS (**10km; 815m; 3h 45min**).

Return the same way and follow the track back over the sluice dam bridge to regain the start (**13.5km; 835m; 4h 45min**).

The Sow of Atholl is often climbed from further north as the first hill on the traverse around Coire Dhomhain over the Munros Sgairneach Mhòr and Beinn Udlamain, for an added time of 30min or so.

The Sow of Atholl from Dalnaspidal, with Sgairneach Mhòr, left, and A' Mharconaich, right (Rab Anderson)

Ben Vrackie's summit, with Schiehallion, left, and distant Ben Nevis, right of centre, then Ben Alder (Rab Anderson)

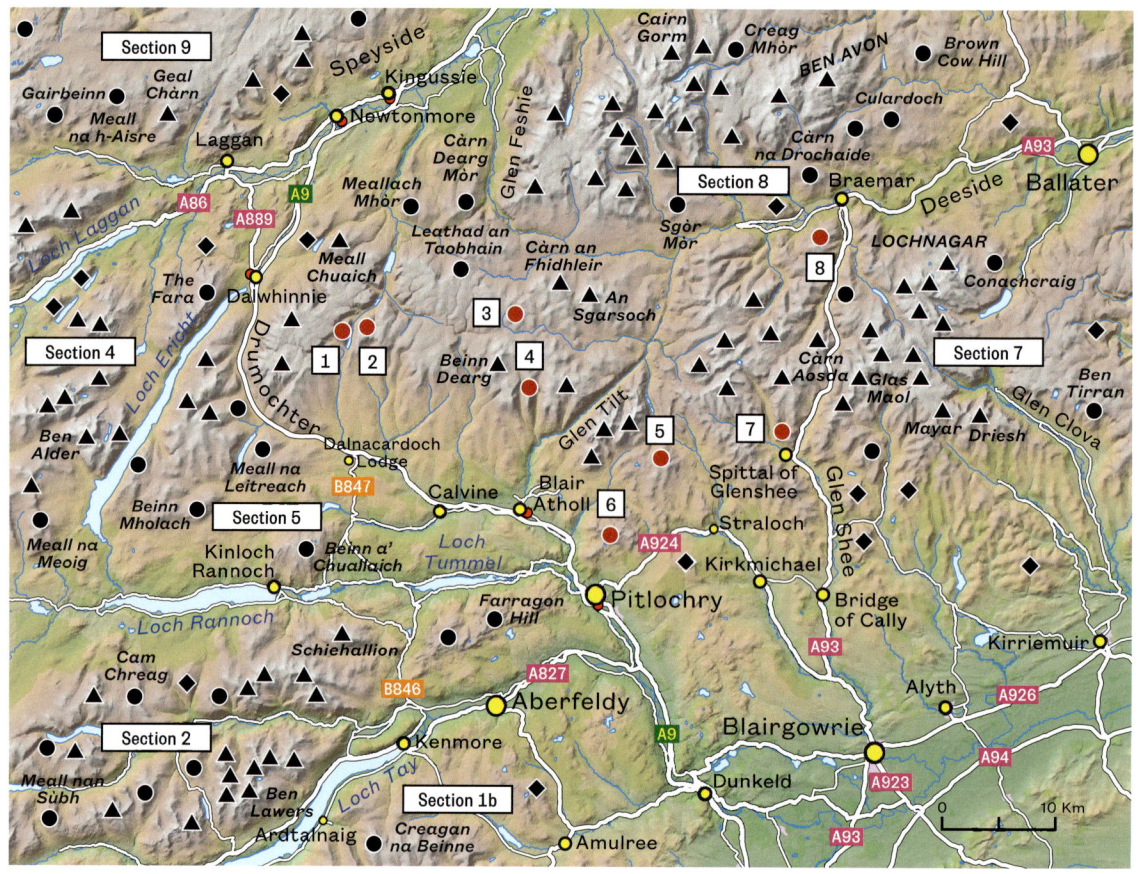

SECTION 6

An Dùn, left, and the craggy slope of Creag an Loch, right, from the Edendon Water (Anne Butler)

> ***An Dùn**; 827m; (C118); L42; NN716801 and NN717805; the fort*
> ***A' Chaoirnich (Maol Creag an Loch)**; 875m; (C56); L42; NN735807; (hill of the crag of the loch)*

Sitting in the middle of a large and remote tract of high ground to the south-west of the Cairngorms, these two hills stand astride one of the traditional routes through the Grampian Mountains to the east of the Pass of Drumochter. This is the Gaick Pass, which links Glen Garry with Strathspey.

Being separated by a distance of less than 2km, the hills are conveniently climbed together, but lying between them is a deep and very steep-sided glacial trench that has to be crossed, which is not so convenient. However, it is this separation and drop that make this such an interesting outing. The floor of the trench between the hills is filled by Loch an Dùin, and whilst tracks from the south and north lead to the loch, there is only a path alongside it linking the tracks.

The nearest road is the A9 to the south, and although this is some distance away, a track from there runs up the glen towards Loch an Dùin to provide a helpful means of access, especially if a bike is used.

Leave the A9 dual carriageway a short distance from its south-east end and take the turning off south for a minor road signed to Trinafour; Dalnacardoch Lodge sits just to the west of this. There is space to park a short way down the minor road.

Return to the A9 and cross via the cycle crossing point in the wide central reservation, then take the track on the opposite side into forestry; signed as the right of way to Speyside through the Gaick Pass. Take the left fork, which passes an aerial just before leaving the forestry, then keep right on the main track as it runs well-above the Edendon Water before descending past ruins and the disused cottage of Badnambiast to cross a bridge over the river.

Further on, the track crosses back again by a low concrete bridge, which becomes a ford in times of high water. An Dùn creates a compelling sight from here. Just before its base is reached, a fenced plantation is passed, within which is the derelict Sronphadruig Lodge.

Bikes are best left to the north of the lodge, where the track fords the river (**9km; 185m; 1h 10min** by bike), (**2h 15min** on foot). Distances and times are now given on foot, from and back to here.

Ascend the moraine ahead by the path closest to the river, onto level, boggy ground. The path becomes vague here as you head towards the south ridge of An Dùn, rising ahead like some gigantic motte, and very much reflecting its Gaelic name.

Pick up a better path that has come from a ford a little further up the river, then follow this for 60m or so before leaving it to ascend the ridge. The steepness, together with the firmness of the ground, enables height to be gained quickly, which is further aided by a path that appears partway up.

The ground soon gives way onto a surprisingly flat summit plateau with steep drops all around. It is certainly an unusual summit.

▶

There are two 827m highpoints some 400m apart. Surveys have, as yet, been unable to ascertain with certainty which is the higher, although one survey has determined that the southern cairned point at NN716801 might be the higher by 30mm. Continue along the plateau for a further 400m to the northern cairned highpoint at NN717805 (**2km; 345m; 1h**).

From the northern cairn, continue along the crest for another 500m, until just beyond the head of a burn which drops steeply to the floor of the glen. Descend steeply past a curious water-filled terrace to cross the foot of the burn and reach the floor of the glen, where the hillside opposite, known as the Bruthach nan Spàrdan (*steep slope of the hen roost*), presents a daunting prospect.

Cross the outflow from Loch an Dùin by stepping stones and continue up the grass slope ahead to a boulder fan where there are two options:

(i) Perhaps best, is to follow a deer path up left to traverse into a grassy runnel, which leads to a terrace. Above this, a series of terraces can be linked by a zigzag line using more

deer paths, before the ground gradually eases off to reach flat ground leading east to the small summit cairn on top of A' Chaoirnich.

(ii) Ascend deer paths up the right side of the burn and its ravine to reach the top of the steep slope, then head north-east to the small cairn marking the summit.

The eroded tableland characteristic of the Grampians is strikingly seen from here (**4.75km; 735m; 2h 30min**).

Head south across flat ground for 600m to a larger cairn, which is lower (867m), then descend gently southwest, aiming for the edge of the steep, craggy slope of Creag an Loch that drops to Loch An Dùin.

Pick up a deer path which leads across the slope and down a spur to the side of the main ridge. With the lodge in sight, continue on the path along the edge of the steep drop, almost to the col with Meall na Spianaig. Descend the steep slope by another deer path, which cuts back right, to gain the boggy flat ground to the north of the lodge, then the track (**8.25km; 735m; 3h 30min**).

Return along the track (**26.25km; 950m; about 5h 40min** with a bike), (**7h 45min** on foot).

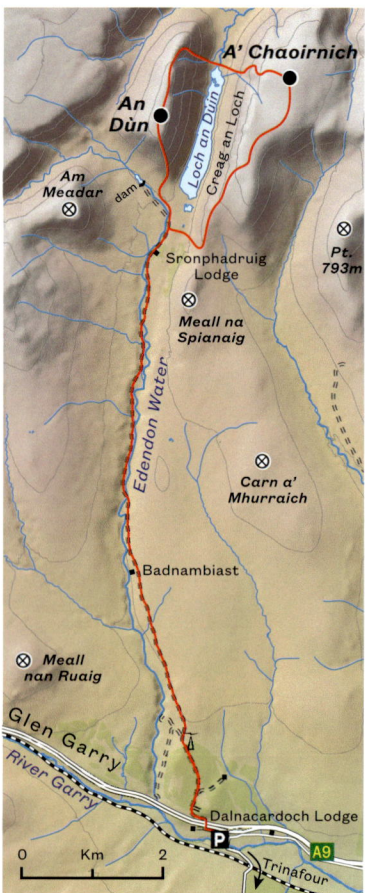

A' Chaornich from the descent off An Dùn, with Loch an Dùin below and craggy Creag an Loch, right (Rab Anderson)

Beinn Bhreac from the small unnamed lochan on the approach (Rab Anderson)

Beinn Bhreac; *912m; (C5); L43; NN868820; speckled hill*

As well as being one of the highest Corbetts, being only two and a bit metres short of Munro status, Beinn Bhreac is one of the most remote and inaccessible. It sits in the heart of an expanse of wild and featureless country to the south of The Cairngorms, between the headwaters of the River Feshie, the Tarf Water and the Bruar Water. Its ascent is more about the journey to get to it than the climb itself, which is easy once there.

The closest access point is from the A9 to the south, via Glen Bruar and the Bruar Water. For an ascent on foot, a start can be made from Bruar itself, but since most people are likely to bike in, then Calvine, just off the A9 to the west, provides a better start. An approach from Bruar is only some 600m shorter and 25m less in height gain, but it involves the fording of the Bruar Water, and is perhaps more awkward to follow. For these reasons, only the route from Calvine is described.

Those with more time, and wishing to explore this wild part of Scotland, might consider an approach from Glen Feshie, either via the River Feshie, or via a high-level traverse from Leathad an Taobhain, the Corbett to the north-west. However,

Beinn Dearg, a Munro, lies to the south of Beinn Bhreac, and if the approach is biked, then it is easy enough to include this to give a very

▶

The northern Cairngorm massif from Beinn Bhreac (Rab Anderson)

satisfying day.

In Calvine, there is parking on the south side of the road towards the eastern end of the hamlet; east of the telephone kiosk, and opposite the old petrol station. Walk west past the telephone kiosk, then go up a track on the right, signed as the Minigaig Pass to Speyside, an ancient right of way.

Cross the A9 and go up the track on the other side, crossing the line of General Wade's original military road. The track climbs up the edge of forestry to a height of 460m on Creag Bhagailteach before dropping towards an estate building at Cuilltemhuc in Glen Bruar, with Beinn Dearg rising beyond. By bike, some pushing is likely.

Continue north along the track above the Bruar Water and cross a bridge to reach Bruar Lodge. Carry on for a further 1km to cross a bridge over the Allt Beinn Losgarnaich, which flows down a gorge from between Beinn Losgarnaich and Beinn Dearg; this is opposite a dam. Bikes can be left here (**13.75km;**

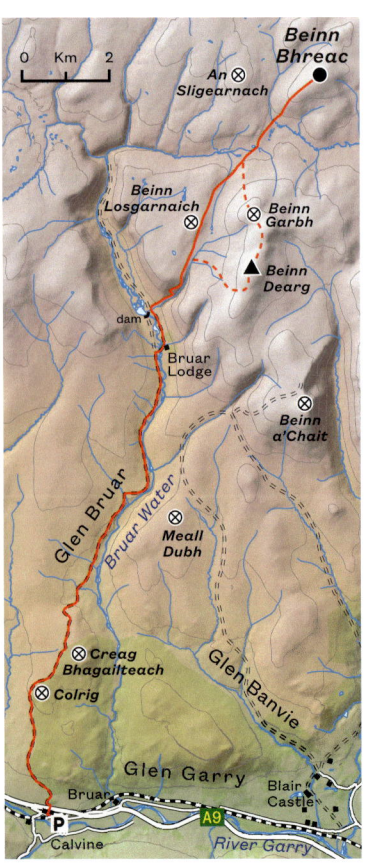

380m; **2h** by bike), (**3h 40min** on foot). Distances and times are now given on foot, from and back to this point.

Follow a vague path up the north side of the burn to join a stalkers' path where it has forded the burn, then follow this up the steep slopes of Beinn Losgarnaich. Above the gorge, the path levels out and follows the burn for a way before swinging left to avoid boggy ground at the watershed, then traversing the slope to pass just beneath the 786m summit of Beinn Losgarnaich. Beinn Bhreac is now in view ahead (with Cairn Toul in the distance), and the path, which becomes vague, descends gently down the other side to a burn - the Allt Mon' an Fhiadhain, a headwater of the Bruar Water.

Aiming for a small unnamed lochan, cross over, then head through some haggy ground and cross another burn to reach the lochan. Pass around its east side to pick up a rough path for a way, which follows the higher, dry ground above the watershed, then drop down to cross the meandering burn, which runs round the base of Beinn Bhreac - one of the headwaters of the Tarf Water.

Finally, climb to the top of Beinn Bhreac to be met by the sight of Ben Macdui and the northern Cairngorms laid out ahead (**7km; 520m; 2h 25min**).

Returning the same way is the easiest (**14km; 600m; 4h 15min**).

Return to Calvine (**41.5km; 1075m; 8h** with a bike), (**11h 15min** on foot).

On the return from Beinn Bhreac, it is relatively easy to include Beinn Dearg. From the small lochan, return partway towards the Allt Mon' an Fhiadhain, then climb the spur that projects from Beinn Garbh (932m), and gain its top. Cross a col and climb onto the northern end of Beinn Dearg's summit crest (Pt.973m), then drop down across a col and climb to the summit. To avoid the boulder field to the west of the summit, descend southwards for 400m or so, following the right-hand of two paths, then drop north-westwards to pick up the burn draining the hillside. Follow this down to gain the stalkers' path on the level ground at the top of the gorge, then return down this; an additional 1.75km, 290m, 1h.

Beinn Mheadhonach; 901m; (C21); L43; NN880759; middle hill

Glen Tilt, one of Scotland's most magnificent glens, slices through the hills to the north of Blair Atholl. It is a geological fault line along which the River Tilt flows, and it provides a traditional route through to Braemar and beyond. Steep slopes rise either side of the central part of the glen to the Munros of Càrn a' Chlamain on its north side and those of the Beinn a' Ghlo massif on its south side.

Beinn Mheadhonach sits between Càrn a' Chlamain and Beinn Dearg, another Munro to the west, and is well-seen from the A9 when looking into Glen Tilt across Blair Atholl. Contained by the deep glens of Gleann Diridh to its west and Gleann Mhairc to its east, it is a prominent conical hill with an elongated narrow ridge,

There is no road through Glen Tilt, which is one of its attractions, so those accessing the hills here either have to walk, or bike up the track beside the River Tilt, which in its lower part passes through lovely woodland. Whilst the approach to Beinn Mheadhonach is easily made on foot, one of the benefits of biking it is that afterwards there is the opportunity to bike further up the glen to explore the rapids on the river and the magnificent surroundings rising above it.

Distances and times are given on foot, but a bike should save at least 1h 20min on the day.

It is possible to include Beinn Mheadhonach with either of the Munros, Beinn Dearg or Càrn a' Chlamain, and the routes to do so are obvious on maps. However, the route described here, which is long enough as it is on foot, is simply the standard ascent of the hill on its own.

Blair Atholl lies just off the A9, and from there a narrow road, signed to Old Bridge of Tilt, is followed up the east side of the River Tilt to make a left turn across a narrow bridge over the river to a signposted car park.

Leave the car park entrance, then cross the road and follow the track on the opposite side through woodland well above the river. After 2.5km the track drops down to cross to the other side via the Cumhann-leum Bridge, and is followed for a further 1.75km.

Leave the track up the east side, then cross back over via Gilberts Bridge and go through a gate. Then, 50m from the bridge, go through a gate on the right. If this is unlocked it is possible to continue by bike; other-wise, leave bikes here. There is a diamond-shaped pedestrian gate to the left. Follow the grassy track for 1.5km to reach the Ach-mhairc Bridge, a small, stone bridge across the Allt Mhairc, which rushes through a dramatic narrow linn.

Cross to the other side and briefly follow the path along the glen before breaking off left uphill on a path. This passes a fine viewpoint looking up Glen Tilt over the ruins of the Ach Mhairc Mhòir township to lofty Bràigh Coire Chruinn-bhalgain in the Beinn a' Ghlo massif.

Continue on the path above the Allt Mhairc, with Beinn Mheadhonach in view ahead. When the path forks, take the slightly higher right fork and follow it into the mouth of Gleann Mhairc. The path traverses a steep slope before dropping to cross the Allt Mhairc by a splendid old, stone-arched bridge, actually named New Bridge.

A path on the other side is then followed up the long south ridge of Beinn Mheadhonach. When the path forks just below a tall cairn and stone windbreak on the right, take the left-hand path and keep to the crest of the ridge. If going to the cairn on the right-hand path, leave it just above the cairn to gain the left-hand path. The right-hand path is a deer track that simply contours the hillside, gradually petering out.

After crossing an old wall, the angle eases and the mossy summit ridge leads to a cairn. This looks and feels like the highest point, but the summit is in fact a further 400m or so to the north (**11.5km; 810m; 3h 50min**).

Return by the route of ascent (**23km; 870m; 6h 40min**).

Beinn Mheadhonach, centre, across Glen Tilt (Grahame Nicoll)

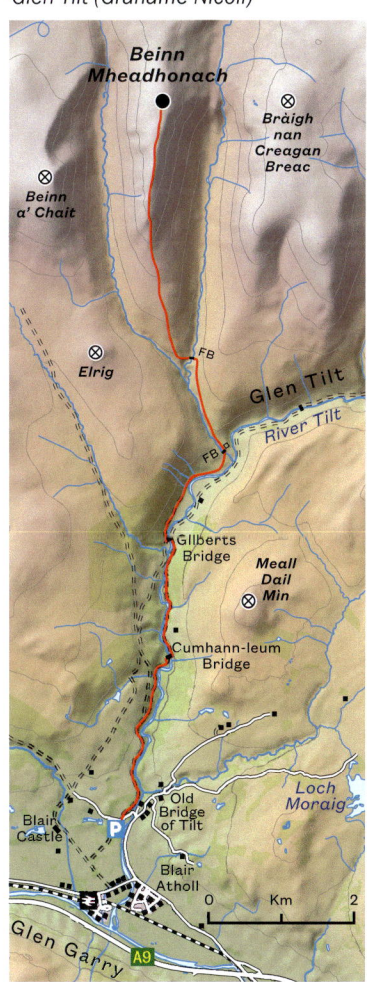

Ben Vuirich from the west near Loch Valigan (Rab Anderson)

Ben Vuirich; *903m; (C18); L43; NN997700; hill of roaring (of stags)*

Another lofty Corbett, Beinn Vuirich is the highest point of a large and fairly remote tract of high ground to the south-east of the Beinn a' Ghlo massif. It lies some distance from the nearest public road, and there are two approaches. One is the traditional route from Blair Atholl to the south-west, which is a route more suitable for an on-foot ascent. The other is from the south-east via a surfaced estate road up Gleann Fearnach, which with the aid of a bike, gives the easiest and perhaps the most enjoyable way of tackling the hill.

For the ascent from Blair Atholl, take the road to Old Bridge of Tilt and fork right, then right again at Fenderbridge, then continue to the end of the road above Loch Moraig, where there is a large pay-and-display car park. The route to Beinn a' Ghlo also starts here.

Walk up the track to where it swings left to Monzie farm, then go through a gate and follow a track, signed to Shinagag, across the southern slopes of Càrn Liath. At a fork, go right and descend south-east to cross a bridge over the Allt Girnaig.

About 100m or so before the derelict steading at Shinagag, turn left and head up the field on a grassy track to pass between two small

plantations, and go through a gate. Follow the track across the slope south of Meall Breac to where it peters out at a flattening at about NN971684 at the 590m contour.

Aiming for Creag nan Gobhar to the east, cut across Coire Buidhe Mòr on rough, heathery terrain with traces of the passage of animals and people in places, then climb onto Creag nan Gobhar. Continue along the ridge and climb to the stone wind shelter enclosing the trig point; the highest point is 20m or so to the north-east (**12km; 660m; 3h 45min**).

The view is splendid. Ben Vrackie lies to the south-west, with Schiehallion beyond, whilst the Beinn a' Ghlo massif fills the view north-west. North up Glen Loch into Glen Dee and the Làirig Ghru, The Devil's Point and Ben Macdui are prominent, whilst to the north-east, Càrn an Righ and Glas Tulaichean stand out, then the Glen Shee hills with a distant Lochnagar.

Either return the same way (**24km; 750m; 6h 50min**), or for added interest, descend south-west to the watershed and pass between some tiny lochans to reach nicely situated Loch Valigan, then regain the track, encountering some interesting rock formations.

An alternative is to descend heather and grass westwards then

north-west from the summit, aiming to cross the low ridge north of Stac nam Bodach (672m). From there, drop onto a track coming up from Glen Loch to the east and follow it south-west across the watershed.

Leave the track where it drops to some old sheilings by the burn, and continue south-west along a path above the Allt Coire Lagain. When the path forks on easier-angled ground, descend to the right and ford the burn where it has become the Allt Girnaig. A rough track leads to the point the improved path off Beinn a' Ghlo meets the end of track, which is followed to the track used in the approach (**23km; 685m; 6h 35min**).

If the water is high, continue south to Shinagag and cross via the bridge there; a detour of about 25min.

It is easy enough to bike the 5.25km to Shinagag for a return saving of about 1h 20min on the day. With persistence, or assisted power, the rougher track can be biked uphill for a further 2.5km to its end.

For the Gleann Fearnach route, follow the A924 which crosses the hills to the south of Ben Vuirich between Pitlochry and Bridge of Cally. The estate road up Gleann Fearnach begins just east of Straloch in Glen Brerachan, from the east side of the

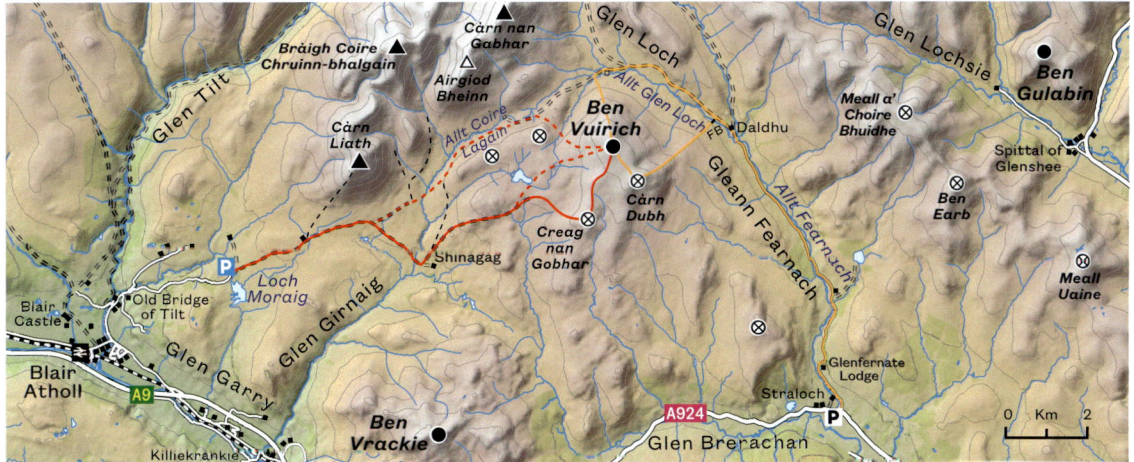

bridge over the Allt Fearnach. There is ample space to park at NO051638, just inside the entrance to the estate road. There is also a small layby on the west side of the bridge.

Follow the road past Glenfernate Lodge, then on up the glen above the Allt Fearnach, crossing this twice. Just beyond the second crossing, and in front of the isolated cottage at Daldhu, turn off left along a grassy track and go past the cottage then a small plantation. Bikes are best left at NO022706, above a bridge over what is now the Allt Glen Loch; (**8km; 135m; 50min** by bike), (**2h** on foot). Distances and time are now given on foot from and back to this point.

Continue along the undulating track, keeping left where a branch heads off north into Glen Loch and Loch Loch; there are good views to Càrn nan Gabhar, the highest of Beinn a' Ghlo's three Munros. Leave the track and cross the burn at a suitable point, then strike uphill to climb the north ridge of Beinn Vuirich. If the water is high, the track crosses the burn after it has forked twice, leaving a final narrower fork to cross.

There is a rough path in places on the ridge, and the ground becomes rockier higher up. A tall cairn is passed at the point the angle eases, and from there it is only a short distance to the stone wind shelter

enclosing the trig point; the highest point is 20m or so to the north-east (**5.5km; 590m; 2h 15min**).

To descend, head south-east across the dip to reach the top of Càrn Dubh and the end of an old wall and fence coming up from the south-east. Turn east here and descend the rocky east-north-east ridge, then cross flat ground to gain a fence. Follow the fence downhill on increasingly rough terrain, which is easier on the right side partway down where there is an ATV track. The fence leads to the bridge, which is crossed to regain the track (**9km; 610m; 3h 20min**).

Return to the start (**25km; 760m; 4h 50min** with a bike), (**7h** on foot).

Ben Vuirich from the road up Gleann Fearnach (Rab Anderson)

Ben Vrackie above Pitlochry (Rab Anderson)

Ben Vrackie; *841m; (C100); L43 & L52; NN950632; speckled hill*

Catching the eye of those travelling the A9, Ben Vrackie rises above Pitlochry and provides a splendid backdrop to the town. Its ease of access, a good path to its summit and the fact that it is one of the best viewpoints in the Southern Highlands, makes Ben Vrackie a popular hill.

There are two approaches; one from Moulin on the northern edge of Pitlochry, and the other from the National Trust for Scotland Visitor Centre at Killiecrankie.

The Pitlochry approach is the more popular and therefore the busiest, so parking can be a problem. From the centre of Pitlochry, follow the A924 uphill to Moulin and turn left immediately after the Moulin Hotel, along Baledmund Road. At a bend, continue straight ahead up a narrow lane to the Ben-y-Vrackie car park on the right, which can take some 20 cars. There is another small car park for 10 cars a little further on, off the fork on the right. If both are full, as they often can be, then you may have to hunt around for parking back along the road around Moulin.

From the lower car park, follow the road uphill and take the right fork past a cottage, then drop down right through the upper car park to follow a path uphill through the trees beside the Moulin Burn. Cross straight over a track and continue uphill on the path

by the burn to emerge onto the track again higher up. Follow the track for a short way to a bend, then continue on a path uphill through woodland and go through a gate onto the open hillside with Ben Vrackie in view ahead. Step over a burn, then continue to a

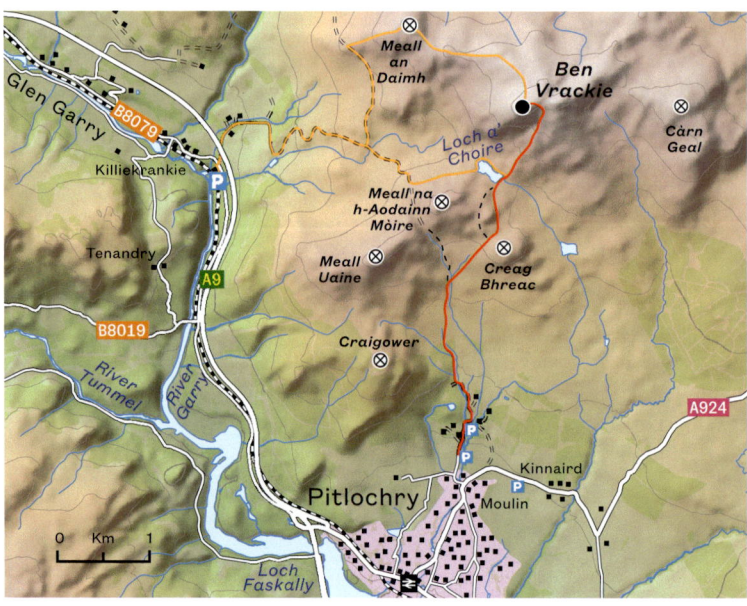

signposted fork and go right on the main route, passing between the knolls of Stac an Fheidh and Creag Bhreac, to gain the dam at the south-east end of Loch a' Choire.

The steep upper slopes of Ben Vrackie rise majestically above the loch and, after crossing the dam, are climbed by a well-constructed path that ascends a slight spur to the east of craggy ground. Height is gained quickly. At the top, a traverse up left gains the viewpoint indicator and adjacent trig point, perched on the edge above the steep drop to the loch (4.75km; 680m; 2h 10min).

To the west, is Schiehallion with Ben Lawers beyond it, then distant Ben More and Stob Binnein. The splendid northern aspect extends from The Mamores, past Ben Nevis and the Aonachs, to Ben Alder, then up Glen Garry to the Drumochter Hills with Beinn Dearg and the slender Corbett Beinn Mheadhonach to its right closer at hand. However, it is the view due north to the three Munros of the Beinn a' Ghlo massif that captures the eye, with the rolling hills of The Mounth extending eastwards across Glen Shee. To the south, the view extends down Strath Tay to The Lowlands, with the Lomond Hills above Loch Leven prominent.

To prolong the experience, it is worth taking in the other two minor summits to the north-east.

Return the same way (9.5km; 670m; 3h 35min).

The Killicrankie approach starts from the National Trust for Scotland Visitor Centre at the north end of the Pass of Killiecrankie; accessed along the B8079 to the north-west of Pitlochry, or south from Blair Atholl. As well as having better parking, this is a quieter and perhaps finer route, which also gives the option of a pleasant circuit. The parking is pay-and-display, but free to NTS members.

Walk north on the pavement, then cross carefully at the bend and go up the road to Old Faskally (signed to Ben-y-Vrackie). The road climbs uphill beneath the A9 then past the houses, where it loops right around the edge of a field to reach a signpost at the entrance to a Scottish Water treatment facility.

Take the grassy track on the left (signed to Ben-y-Vrackie) and follow it through the fields. Cross a fence by a step-over stile, then go through a gate, and further on, go right through a gate in a wall next to a ladder stile. Continue up the grassy track, which zigzags uphill with fine views north up Glen Garry to Blair Atholl and the Drumochter Hills beyond.

Pass through a final gate to gain the open hillside and, with Ben Vrackie now in view ahead, follow the track across a burn, then zigzag uphill to the south-east to reach a signpost. Turn left along the path signed to Ben-y-Vrackie and descend across Meall na h-Aodainn Mòire, taking the left-hand path at a fork, to reach the north-west end of Loch a' Choire. Follow the path along the far side to join the well-constructed path from Moulin, and continue up this to the top (6.5km; 760m; 2h 40min).

Returning the same way is perhaps simplest (13km; 820m; 4h 30min).

However, a good circuit can be had by descending north then north-west on an initially vague path that swings down the ridge then up onto Meall an Daimh (722m).

Drop north-west to the top corner of a wall then descend the path south-west beside this, steeply in places, through heather to reach a track. Follow the track southwards with a slight climb, then descend to meet the approach route just above the top gate and follow this back (13.75km; 800m; 4h 40min).

Ben Vrackie across Loch a' Choire (Rab Anderson)

Ben Gulabin from Spittal of Glenshee, with The Cairnwell beyond at the head of Gleann Beag (Rab Anderson)

Ben Gulabin; *806m; (C150); L43; NO100722; hill of the curlew (whimbrel), or hill of the beak*

Standing at the junction of Glen Shee with Gleann Beag, Ben Gulabin rises steeply above Spittal of Glenshee, and is prominent in the view when travelling north on the A93 between Blairgowrie and Braemar. It gives a short ascent and, with a short drive in between, is easily combined with one of the other nearby Corbetts: Monamenach, Creag nan Gabhar, Morrone or Càrn na Drochaid.

The ascent is made from just over 1km north of Spittal of Glenshee on the A93, where there are two places to pull off and park on the west side of the road. The northern one is beside a gate where a track climbs the hill. A grassy path links the southern pull-off with the northern one if it's busy.

Follow the track up to the col between Ben Gulabin and Creagan Bheithe to the north, crossing a burn, the Allt a' Charnaich. On the slopes of the latter hill are an old pylon and a ruined hut, which are the remains of an early ski development.

From the col, an ATV track climbs south-west up a strip of grass to provide the route to the top of Ben Gulabin, free from the heather that covers this side of the hill. When the angle eases, swing right along a path to the top (**2.75km; 445m; 1h 20min**).

It is worth going out to the south-east top (781m) for the view down Glen Shee. Return by the route of ascent (**6.25km; 460m; 2h 20min**).

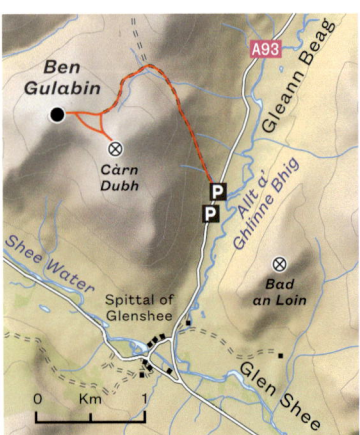

Morrone; 859m; (C77); L43; NO132886; big nose

Rising to the south-west above Braemar, Morrone is a rather featureless hill, which in winter takes much of the sun away from the village. However, its close proximity to Braemar makes it readily accessible and it provides a pleasant ascent with splendid views from the summit.

Unfortunately, the summit area is cluttered with some unsightly telecommunications towers and buildings, and one has to wander around these to appreciate the views.

At the turning circle roundabout on the road west out of Braemar, turn up Chapel Brae and continue ahead for 650m, then turn left into a large car park beside the duck pond.

Leave the south end of the car park, then drop down and follow a path through two gates in fences to reach a track, which is followed uphill past two houses. Either stay on the track where it swings right, or take the path straight ahead through birch

and juniper woodland to reach a view-point indicator and bench. Apparently, it was intended to site this 17m higher, so not all the points shown are visible from its present position.

Regain the track and cross it, following the path signed to Morrone, which climbs through more birch woodland to exit the planted area by a gate to gain the open hillside. The well-travelled path leads south-west up the hillside with ever expanding views, then past a line of cairns and on up to the summit, where a trig pillar stands forlornly beside a tall mast and ancillary building. The view is superb, especially north to The Cairngorms (**3.25km; 490m; 1h 30min**).

The best return is back the same way, giving more time to appreciate the view (**6.5km; 495m; 2h 35min**).

However, a longer circuit can be made by following the access track to the aerials, south-west and south-east over an unnamed top (824m),

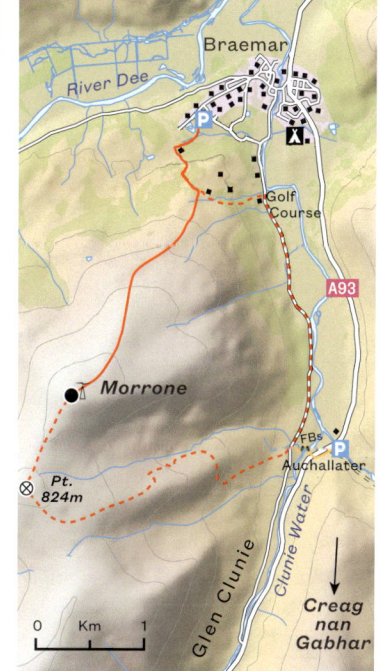

then downhill to the north-east to gain the minor road on the west side of the Cluny Water, opposite Auchallater. Walk north along the road for almost 2.5km, passing the golf course and clubhouse, then turn off left to follow a track which cuts sharply back. Continue on a path uphill through woodland to gain a track, which leads to the route of ascent beside the viewpoint indicator. Return down the path, or the track (**11km; 620m; 3h 45min**).

For anyone wishing to combine Morrone with Creag nan Gabhar in Section 7, and maximise the parking fee (as well as saving some time), an ascent can be made from the Auchallater pay-and-display car park.

Head south along the roadside verge for 200m, then follow a path to cross a footbridge over the Cluny Water. Go left across another foot-bridge, following a fence round, then up to the road on the other side. Ascend the access track to the aerials on Morrone, swinging right over an unnamed top (824m) to gain the summit (**4.5km; 520m; 1h 50min**).

Whilst returning the same way is quickest, it is perhaps better to reverse the principal route and walk along the road from the Braemar golf course (**10.5km; 560m; 3h 30min**).

Over Braemar to Morrone from Creag Choinnich (Rab Anderson)

Conachcraig's flat summit, left, from its central top, with Lochnagar beyond (Rab Anderson)

SECTION 7
Glen Shee to Glen Esk

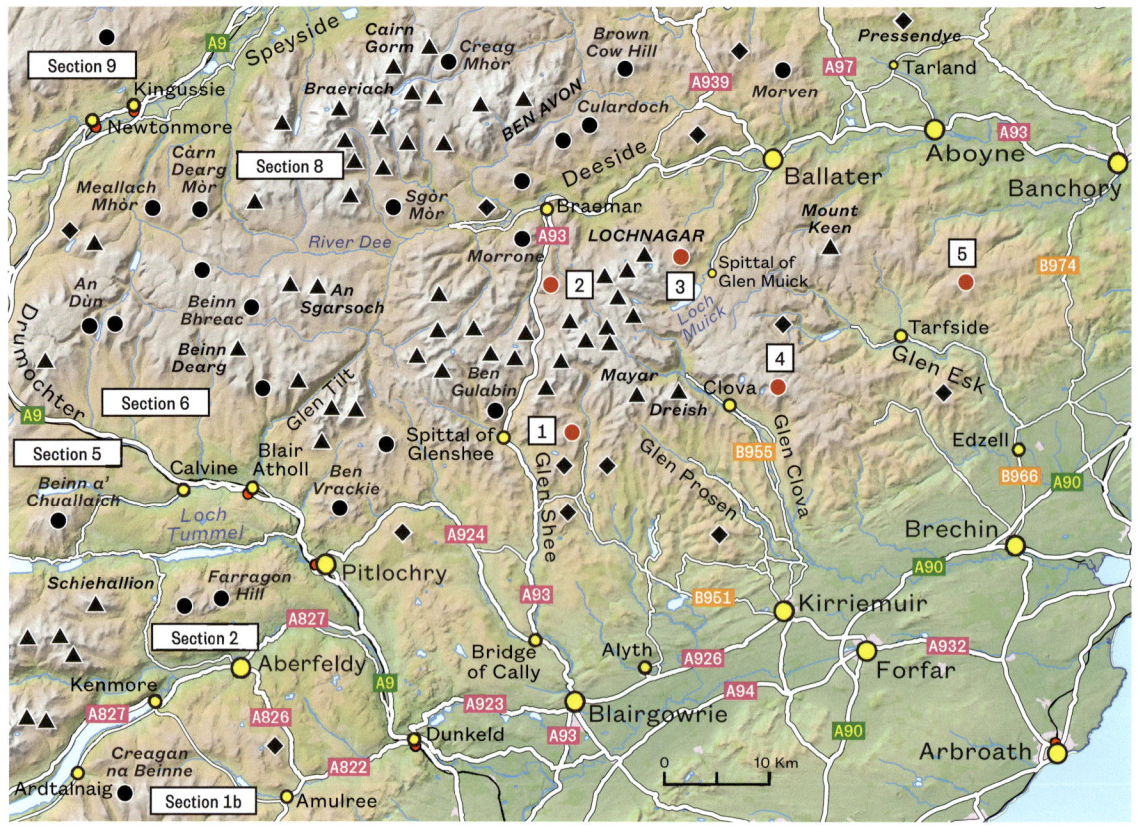

SECTION 7

Monamenach from Cairn Doos to the north-east (Rab Anderson)

Monamenach; 807m; (C148); L43; NO176706; middle hill

Arounded, grassy hill, Monamenach sits at the midpoint of the chain of hills between Glen Shee and Glen Isla that runs northwards from the Grahams Mount Blair and Mealna Letter, then on to the Munros Creag Leacach and Glas Maol.

It is best climbed from the end of the road up Glen Isla, and with a start at a height of 360m it gives an easy, short ascent, which could be combined with another nearby short Corbett such as Ben Gulabin.

Follow the road up Glen Isla to where it ends at Auchavan, then continue down right along a potholed track for 250m and park at NO192698, before a bridge over the River Isla.

Walk to the trees beyond the bridge, then go left to gain a track. Head down this for 100m, back towards Auchavan, then follow a grassy track across the field on the right. Pass through a gap in a wall and continue up the hillside on the track, crossing the Glack Burn. Just above the col at the head of the burn, where the track

loops down south, break off right and follow a grassy track up the steepening cone to the top of Monamenach (**2.5km; 445m; 1h 15min**).

Returning the same way is quickest (**5km; 445m; 2h**). However, it is worth making a short circuit by descending north-north-east and swinging round east across a haggy col onto Cairn Doos (629m). Follow the ridge down to the south a short way, then drop steeply down to the track alongside the River Isla, and follow this back (**6.25km; 470m; 2h 25min**).

A longer and more challenging day can be had by continuing from Monamenach, north-west over Black Hill, then Mallrenheskein to cut across Càrn Ait to gain the Munros Creag Leacach, then Glas Maol.

Descend eastwards to pick up the track on the line of the Monega Path, the historic route from Braemar to the eastern Lowlands, and follow this across Little Glas Maol, a Munro Top whose summit is crossed by a right fork in the track. The best route is the track above Caenlochan Glen, and

the branch over Monega Hill itself, before following the track down to Glen Isla and back to the start. This route is described in reverse in the SMC's guidebook *The Munros* (**20.5km; 1190m; 7h**).

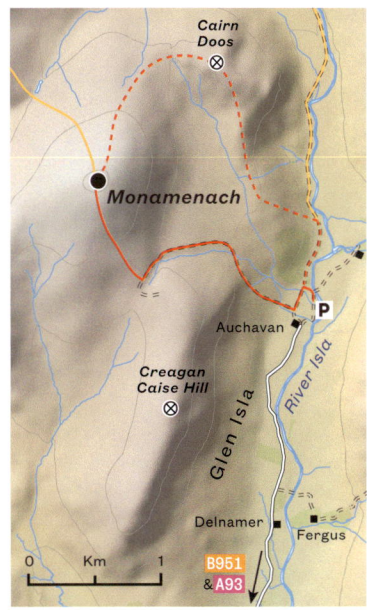

North down Glen Clunie to Creag nan Gabhar from Càrn Aosda's north ridge, with distant Culardoch (Rab Anderson)

Creag nan Gabhar; *834m; (C114); L43; NO154841; goat crag*

Located a few miles to the south of Braemar, and rising above the east side of the A93 through Glen Clunie, Creag nan Gabhar sits between that glen and Glen Callater. At its southern end, where the summit lies, it is quite a broad hill, filling the space between these glens as they diverge. A 3.5km-long, rounded ridgeline runs northwards from its summit, tapering down to where Glen Callater joins Glen Clunie at Auchallater.

The principal route of ascent is via this ridgeline from Auchallater, where there is a pay-and-display car park on the east side of the road, on the south side of the road bridge across the Callater Burn.

The nose of Sròn Dubh rises steeply to the south here, and the best route is to climb directly up this. Follow the track into Glen Callater for 180m and go through a gate. Leave the track and follow the fence for 200m, then go through an open gateway and follow a sheep track to exit the fenced area by another open gateway. Climb steeply up the nose of Sròn Dubh, through heather and past boulders, then on to the flat top to meet a rough track coming up from Glen Callater. An approach up this track is 1.5km longer.

Follow the track south up the ridge over the slight rise of Sròn nan Gabhar. Beyond this, the track becomes more of a path and leads on up the broadening ridge through scree patches to where it swings rightwards to gain the summit cairn. The cairn 100m to the south-west is lower (**4.75km; 485m; 1h 50min**).

It is a superb viewpoint ,with Lochnagar and its attendants to the east, the Glenshee hills to the south, and beyond Morrone to the north, the Cairngorm massif.

It is possible to make a circuit by heading east, then south-east off the summit over an unnamed top to pick up a track. Either follow the track to ford the Callater Burn (more of a river), and follow the main track back, or follow a rough path down close to the burn to cross a bridge over it then the bridge leading to Lochcallater Lodge, then follow the track back.

However, this is definitely a case where returning the same way is best, since it offers the spectacle of the Cairngorms spread out ahead. On

The north ridge – Morrone, left, then

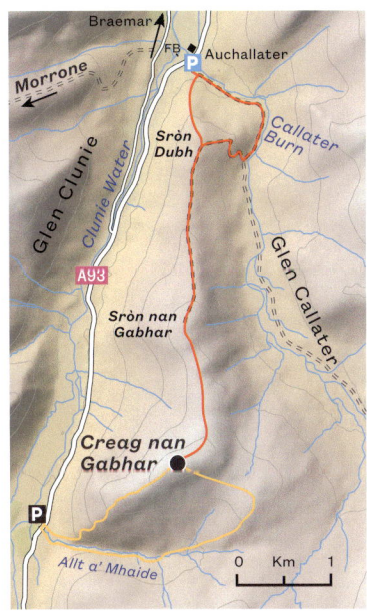

dangle hot feet in before returning to the start (**11km; 505m; 3h 20min**).

Another route from Alltamhait on the A93 to the south-west gives a good short circuit. There is space to park at NO141835 at the north end of a forestry plantation, to the north of the parking for the Munro An Socach. This is on the west side of the road, immediately to the north of a bridge over a burn, the Allt a' Mhaide, which flows down a deeply cut glen to the east of the road. A stalkers' path runs up the south side of the Allt a' Mhaide, though it is probably easier to return down this and to tackle the steep crest in ascent.

Go up the north side of the burn, following sheep tracks, then climb rightwards beneath scree before cutting left through the scree on a sheep track to gain the rounded crest. Continue up the crest, then through more scree to where the angle eases and a path appears, which is followed to the summit – the second of two cairns (**2km; 420m; 1h 10min**).

Head north-east along the summit crest for 150m, then follow another path which swings south-east and drops quite steeply off the summit area. Cross some boggy, flat ground

reaching Sròn Dubh it is probably easier to keep to the track, which swings right and zigzags down to the main track in Glen Callater.

On a warm day, the Callater Burn has some granite slabs and pools to

and climb slightly onto an unnamed rise. Either follow an ATV track south-east for a way to reach a stalkers' path, then follow this west, or cut the corner and descend south past a line of old stone shooting butts to gain the path. Either way, descend across the hillside on the path, over some burns, to cross the Allt a' Mhaide, then continue down above this, back to the road (**6.25km; 435m; 2h 15min**).

Càrn na Drochaide, Creag an Dail Bheag and Culardoch, with Beinn a' Bhuird and Ben Avon above (Rab Anderson)

Conachcraig with Lochnagar, left, from the approach across the River Muick (Rab Anderson)

> **Conachcraig**; *865m; (C68); L44; NO279865; abundance of rocks*

Very much overshadowed by Lochnagar to its west, both in terms of size and magnificence, Conachcraig is the hill that first catches the eye as one emerges from the trees at Linn of Muick on the approach by the single-track road up Glen Muick from Ballater. It has a 1.25km-long summit crest with three distinct highpoints of similar height, the southernmost being the actual summit. Any ascent should include all three tops to fully appreciate the hill's character and the grandstand views it affords of Lochnagar and its cliffs. This is the route described here, rather than the shorter up and down route to the summit.

Start from the end of the public road up Glen Muick, where there are pay-and-display car parks either side of the Allt Darrarie at Spittal of Glen Muick.

Follow a track through the trees past the public toilets, visitor centre and house to a junction. Take the right-hand track, which leads across the River Muick towards Allt-na-giubh-saich and Conachcraig ahead.

Don't take the Lochnagar path, but go right to join the track on the west side of the glen and follow this for 800m, then take the left fork, which swings north through the trees.

On leaving the trees, turn left and climb the heathery ridge onto Càrn an Daimh (617m), where a rough path appears, then drop to a col at 592m.

A more direct route to this col is possible by taking to a vague grassy track 300m after leaving the route to Lochnagar, then going through a gap in a wall and climbing the slope. There is no path, the terrain is rough and quite steep, and it is only some 10min or so quicker.

Beyond the col, the path continues up the slope onto a minor rise at 735m, then on to the central top (850m), which is where the OS 1:50k map places the name Conachcraig. The magnificent spectacle of Lochnagar and its great north-east corrie is now revealed ahead.

Descend north-west to gain a path and follow this across the dip, then ascend onto the rocky north-west top, Caisteal na Caillich (862m). The view

of Lochnagar is slightly better here, and moving a little to the north gains a view down Glen Gelder to Deeside and Balmoral.

Follow the path back across the dip and make the gentle ascent to the summit. The small tor to the right (north-west) is the highest point, being 40cm higher than the cairn on the large boulders first encountered, and 3m higher than the tor to the south-east (**6.75km; 570m; 2h 25min**).

Continue south-west on the path and descend steeply through boulders, then down the heathery slope beyond to gain the track through the col with Lochnagar, opposite the path off up to that mountain.

Its position close to the Lochnagar route means that Conachcraig is often climbed as a short there-and-back from this col taking 45min.

Follow the track downhill south, then east above the Clais Rathadan gorge to cross the Allt na Giubhsaich on stepping stones and continue

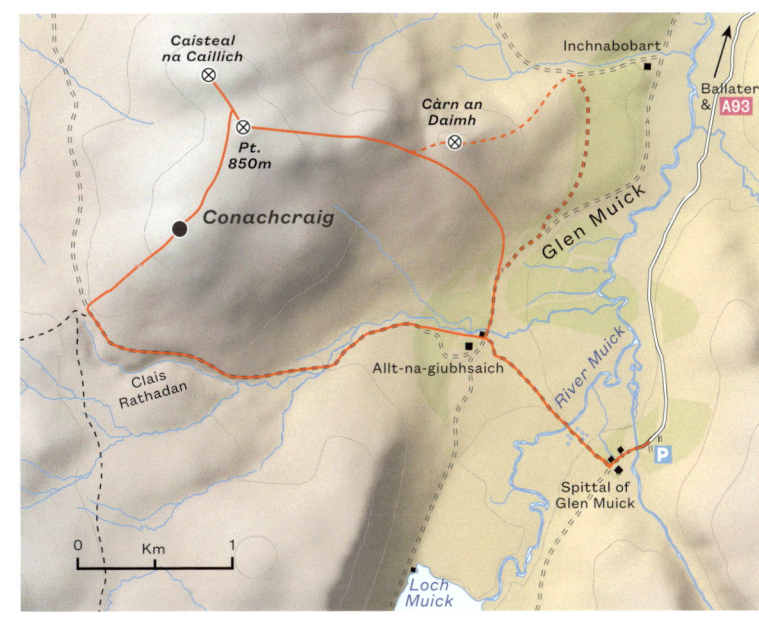

down into the trees. Leave the track for a path down through the trees to gain the track back to Spittal of Glen Muick (**12km; 590m; 3h 40min**).

If the Allt na Giubhsaich cannot be crossed, follow the line of an old path shown on maps, down above the north side to reach the track.

Across Glen Muick and Inchnabobart to Conachcraig (Rab Anderson)

North across Braeminzion in Glen Clova to Ben Tirran, with the Craigs of Loch Wharral on the left (Rab Anderson)

Ben Tirran (The Goet); 896m; (C27); L44; NO373746; *possibly hill of hillocks, (the goat)*

Ben Tirran is the highest point of the great, undulating plateau that lies between Glen Clova and Glen Esk. The OS 1:25k and 1:50k maps place the name 'The Goet' against the highest point and 'Ben Tirran' against a lower point to the south-west.

A series of scalloped corries run along the edge of the plateau overlooking Glen Clova, and two of these contain the lovely lochans, Loch Brandy and Loch Wharral. There are two principal routes which visit these lochans and go around their corries. Both start from the northern loop of the B955 around Glen Clova.

The first route has two starts: one at Wheen, from off-road parking 50m to the east of a track to Loch Wharral; the other 1km west of Wheen, from verge parking at NO353715 on the west side of the Adielinn Plantation. Both starts join above the plantation. The latter start gives the better route, and is the one described.

Go through a gate and follow a grassy track up the west side of the plantation, then go through a gate in a deer fence and follow a path uphill

to reach the left branch of the track coming up from Wheen. The quick way to the top is to go right for 100m to the main track and follow it towards Loch Wharral to pick up a path that leaves it at NO358732, then climb to the summit.

However, the better route goes up the left-hand track onto the top of Rough Craig (529m) where there is a small weather station. Just beyond the top, leave the track to take a narrow path north through the heather and across flat ground to join the line of the original stalkers' path coming up from the right. Continue uphill past a line of old stone shooting butts to meet an ATV track coming up from Loch Wharral, then follow this up the Shank of Catstae, with fine views across past the Craigs of Loch Wharral and over Loch Wharral to the summit of Ben Tirran.

There are now two options:

(i) Follow the ATV track all the way up what is called the Brae of the Rags to where the track goes through a gate in a deer fence. Turn right here then follow an indistinct path east

through peaty ground by the fence, across the head of the White Burn. Pass to the south of the small lochan on Pt.857m, then drop slightly to gain the shallow col with White Hill.

(ii) Cut the corner by leaving the ATV track to cross the White Burn and ascend pathless terrain to meet the route alongside the fence at the shallow col with White Hill.

Either way, continue alongside the fence past Stony Loch, then on up the gentle slope to reach the stone wind shelter and trig point on Ben Tirran's flat summit (**7km; 680m; 2h 40min**).

The views are fabulous. Amongst the many hills, Mount Keen stands out to the north, with Mount Battock to the north-east. West at the head of Glen Clova are Dreish and Mayar, then north-west the hills and rock faces around the Dubh Loch basin, and an unusual angle of Lochnagar, with Conachcraig to its right and distant Ben Avon between. To the south-west, hills stretch into the distance, where Stob Binnein and Ben More can be picked out just over 105km (65 miles) away.

Head south-west off the summit across featureless ground to a cairn, where the OS 1:25k and 1:50k maps show the name 'Ben Tirran'. Turn west here, picking up a path that leads down towards the track and closed bothy at the south end of Loch Wharral.

Further down, the path actually swings south-west to join the track lower down. However, it is better, certainly on a good day, to continue down to Loch Wharral to appreciate the loch and its surroundings, then go down the track from the bothy.

At the track junction lower down, straight on leads to Wheen, whilst right for 100m across the burn leads to the path used in the ascent from the west side of the Adielinn Plantation (12km; 685m; 4h).

Another good route starts from further up Glen Clova, from the public car park on the left just over the bridge, a short distance beyond the Glen Clova Hotel and its car park, which is for patrons only.

Walk back over the bridge and go up through the hotel car park, past the bunkhouse and chalets, following signs for Loch Brandy and Glen Esk. A well-built path climbs uphill towards the loch and the prow of The Snub, with the Corrie of Clova to the left.

When Loch Brandy comes into view, turn left and follow the path steeply up to the top of The Snub (837m), with fine views over Loch Brandy to Green Hill and the ridge of Broom Shank, with Ben Tirran beyond.

Now above the Craigs of Loch Brandy, follow the path along the edge above a slippage area, then down into the dip at the head of the corrie, briefly joining an ATV track.

When the track goes left, the better route follows the path up and around the rim for a way. However, since this path swings off down Broom Shank, it should be left to regain the ATV track at the cairn on top of Green Hill (870m).

Continue eastwards on the high ground and drop slightly to go over a stile in a deer fence. Leave the ATV track here, which descends the Brae of the Rags and the Shank of Catstae.

Now follow an indistinct path through peaty ground by the fence, across the head of the White Burn. Pass to the south of the small lochan

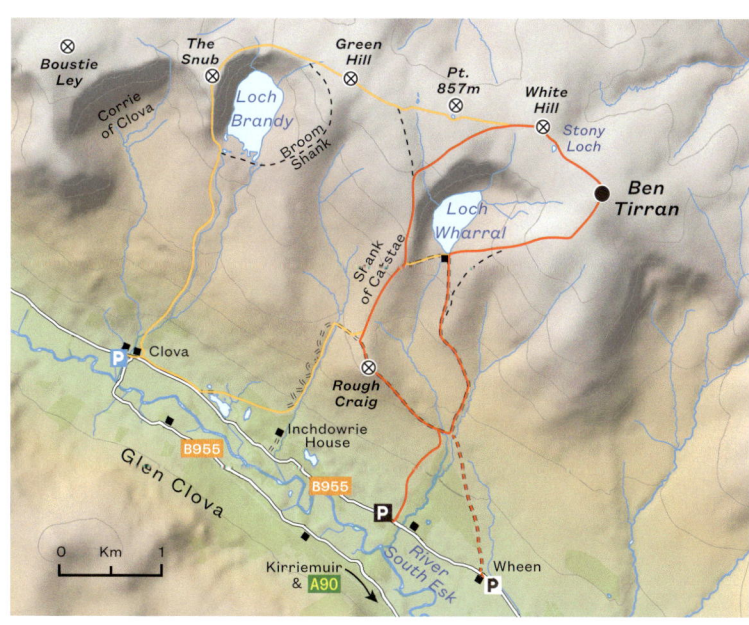

on Pt.857m, then continue alongside the fence across White Hill, then past Stony Loch, and on up to the stone wind shelter and trig point on Ben Tirran's summit (8km; 790m; 3h).

Head south-west across featureless ground to a cairn, where the OS 1:25k and 1:50k maps show the name 'Ben Tirran'. Turn west here, picking up a path which leads down towards the south end of Loch Wharral. When the main path swings away south-west towards Wheen, leave it and drop to the closed bothy by the loch.

Cross the outflow and follow an ATV track up onto the crest of the Shank of Catstae. When the track swings up right, continue ahead to pick up a

path on the far side of a line of old stone shooting butts. Follow the path downhill past the butts, then across flat ground to join a track on the north-west side of Rough Craig.

Turn right along the track and continue to its end, then step over the burn and pass through a gate in a deer fence. Follow the fence all the way down towards Inchdowrie House; the old zigzag track to the right has become a drainage line. At the bottom, continue right into birch woodland and pass to the north of some lochans to pick up a grassy track. The track leads to a gate and the road, where a footpath is followed back to the start (14.5km; 830m; 5h).

Ben Tirran above Loch Wharral (Rab Anderson)

Mount Battock with Wester Cairn, left, and Hill of Saughs, right, from Mount Een (Rab Anderson)

***Mount Battock;** 778m; (C193); L44 & L45; NO549844*

Forming the highest point in the maze of rounded hills and ridges to the east of Mount Keen, between Glen Esk and Deeside, Mount Battock is the most easterly of the higher hills of the Mounth, and also the easternmost Corbett. Its summit provides spacious views over the lowlands of north-east Scotland, as well as to the Cairngorms and the higher Mounth hills to the west.

Mount Battock lies in prime shooting country, and the exploitation of the landscape for this purpose is evidenced by the huge number of tracks that scar the hillsides hereabouts. These tracks tend to follow the lines of earlier paths up the ridges, so they are the only real means of attaining the summits. The upside is that the going underfoot is dry, and the ground is covered quickly with minimal effort.

The ascent is best made from Millden in Glen Esk to the south. On the minor road up Glen Esk, turn off right on the west side of the bridge just past Millden Lodge, onto the road to Mill of Aucheen, and park immediately on the right by the telephone kiosk. It may be possible to drive on for a further 800m, past Mill of Aucheen, to the end of the public road and park on grass on the right at the top end of a forestry plantation.

Otherwise, walk up the road past Mill of Aucheen, then from the road end, cross a cattle grid and follow the main track uphill past the farm at Blackcraigs. Continue on up the hillside past lines of shooting butts, some beautifully, but perhaps over-elaborately, constructed from stone. Go through a gate near the top then carry straight on past tracks off left and right to reach the flat top of

Mount Een, passing just to the side of the highest point at 529m.

Continue along the high ground on the main track, which swings right (northwards), past a track off left, to make a surprisingly lengthy traverse over Bennygray (558m) to reach the west side of the summit cone of Wester Cairn. Follow the track as it swings round east, to pass a track off right, then climb quite steeply to the top of Wester Cairn (717m).

Leave the main track here, which heads northwards down the other side. An ATV track is followed across a dip, then up to the summit of Mount Battock, where a gate is crossed to gain the trig point and stone windbreaks (**9km; 680m; 3h 10min**).

Go over the stile at the corner of the fence, and descend a rough path beside the fence to the dip. When the fence swings right to avoid the peat

next fence to gain the start of a track, which is followed over Hill of Saughs (656m). Pass a track off right (which also leads back, via Allrey) and continue downhill on the main track, as it swings round left then back right off Hill of Turret. At the next downhill junction, take the track that goes off at right-angles and follow this down to ford the Burn of Turret.

Continue pleasantly downhill above the burn to ford a tributary. If required, there are two bridges on the left, one over the Burn of Turret and the other over the tributary. The track leads past Muir Cottage to the road at Mill of Aucheen. Turn right if parked at the top of the plantation, or left and walk down the road to the telephone kiosk (16.75km; 715m; 5h).

If parked at the telephone kiosk, an alternative route from the foot of Hill of Turret, instead of taking the track down right, is to continue straight on, past a track off left. This track then runs down the side of Whups Craig, passing above Millden, to reach the road up Glen Esk on the east side of the bridge; about 750m shorter.

If shooting affects the route up Mount Een, the simplest option is to reverse the descent route. This is to go right just past Mill of Aucheen, then on to ford the Burn of Turret and follow the tracks over Turret Hill onto

Hill of Saughs to reach the summit beyond (7.75km; 675m; 2h 50min). Either return the same way (15.5km; 710m; 4h 40min), or take the track that descends south from the south-west side of Wester Cairn and follow this back (15.25km; 710m; 4h 35min)

An interesting long route makes an approach from the east and includes Clachnaben, one of Scotland's most outstanding lower hills. Turn west off the B974 on the south side of the bridge to the south of ruined Spital Cottage and go down a track to a parking area at NO645843 beside a bridge over the Water of Dye.

Cross the bridge, then turn right and follow the track north by the burn for just over 2km. Turn left along the route to Clachnaben, across Miller's Bog, and follow the track, then the path up the side of the forestry to gain the splendid granite tor on top (5.75km; 430m; 2h).

Now traverse west, following a path, then a track over Hill of Edendocher (577m), Sandy Hill (592m), Hill of Badymicks and a slight rise (Pt.556m), to finally climb to Mount Battock (13.75km; 780m; 4h 45min).

Return over Pt.556m, then take the track on the right, downhill into Glen Dye, and follow the track back, forking right past a small lochan, then along the river (25.25km; 840m; 7h 30min).

hags at the col, step over the fence and follow the rough path through the hags. Step over a fallen gate in the

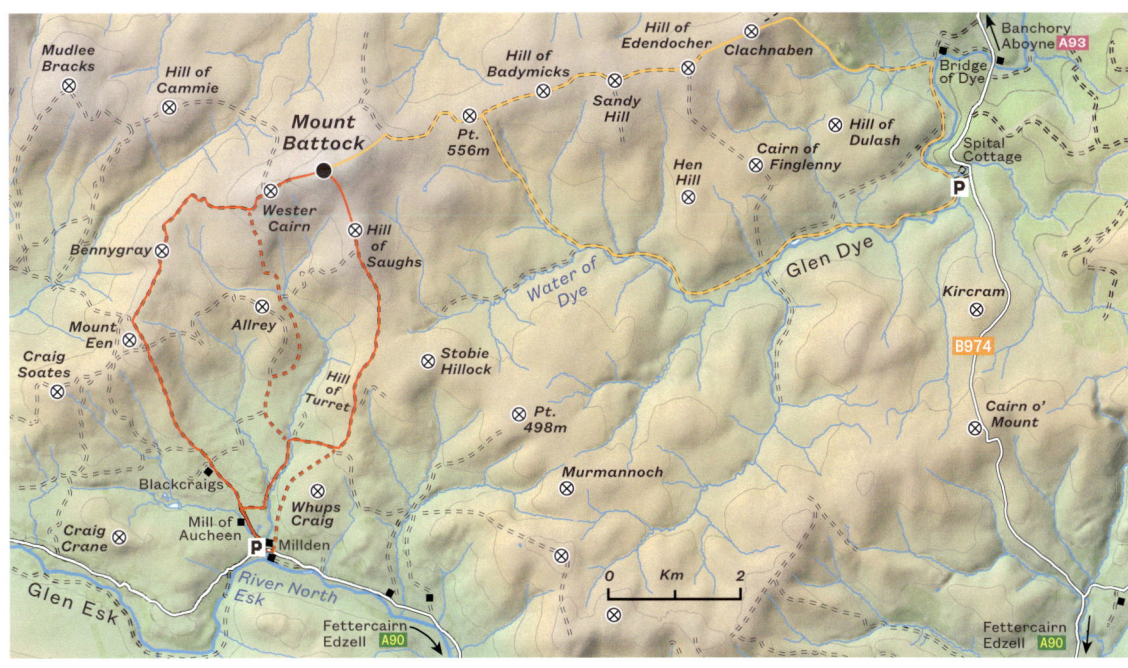

Across Glen Mòre from above the Allt Mòr to Meall a' Bhuachaille, with Creagan Gorm, Creag a' Chaillich and Creaggowrie, left (Rab Anderson)

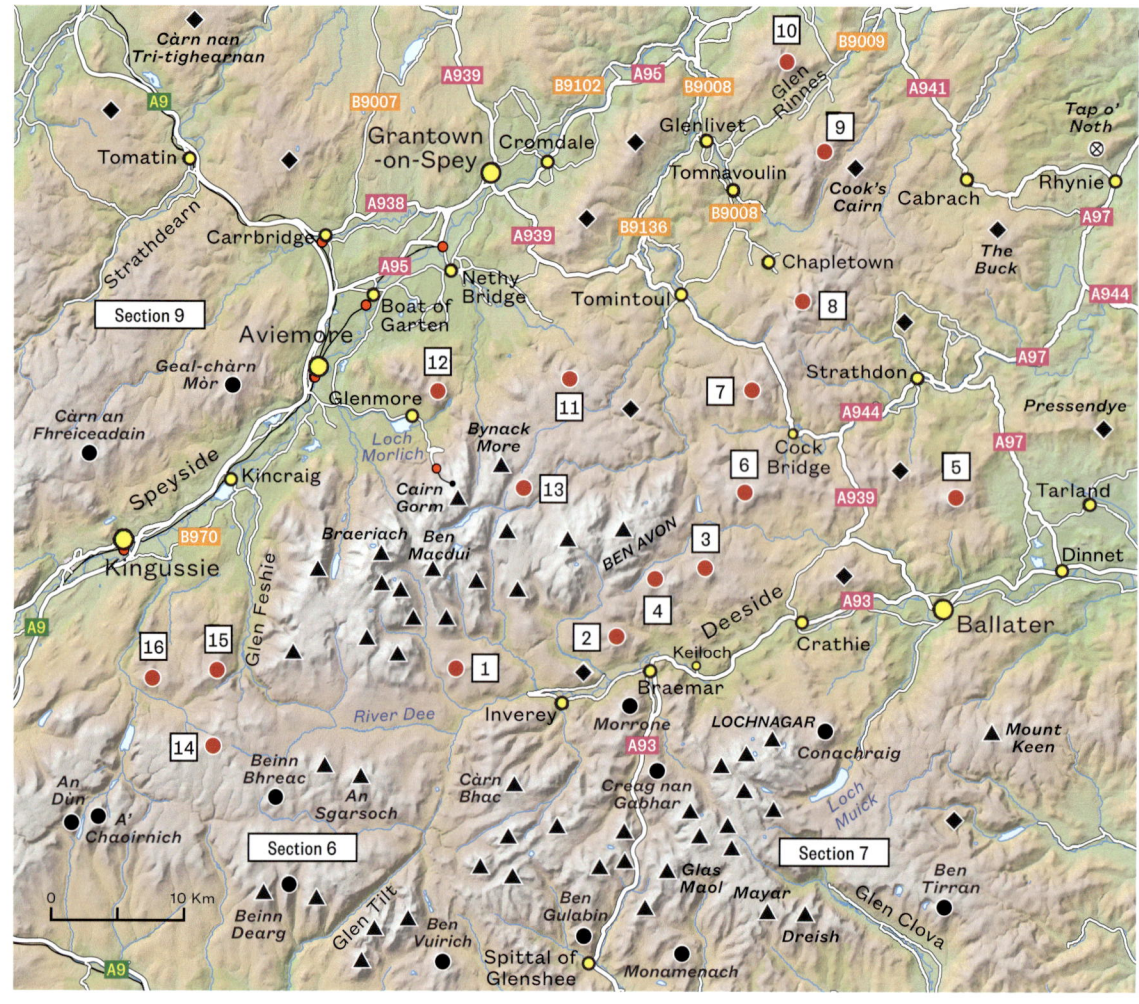

SECTION 8

Sgòr Mòr's summit, with the Devil's Point, Cairn Toul, Braeriach, the Làirig Ghru, then Càrn a' Mhàim, Ben Macdui and Derry Cairngorm forming a superb backdrop (Rab Anderson)

Sgòr Mòr; 813m; (C136); L43; NO007914; big peak

Sgòr Mòr is the highest top of the large but relatively low-lying hill mass that extends westwards from the Linn of Dee between Glen Lui and Glen Dee. The broad, 2.75km-long ridge, between the summit at the west end and its eastern top, provides a splendid elevated highway with grandstand views of Ben Macdui and the other big Cairngorm mountains.

Start from the National Trust for Scotland's Linn of Dee pay-and-display car park and toilets, accessed via the narrow road that runs west from the A93 at Braemar. The car park does fill up, and at such times, an overflow car park 500m before the Linn may have to be used.

Turn right out of the car park entrance and go along the road to follow a track west along the north side of the River Dee for almost 5km. This runs below fragmentary schistose outcrops scattered among Caledonian pines, and passes ruined settlements on the river flats before reaching White Bridge.

Leave the track here and follow a path along the north bank to the Chest of Dee, where there are some lovely pools and cascades. After a further 1.25km of pleasant walking by the river, with Beinn Bhrotain filling the view ahead, cross the first burn,

then leave the path to ascend a rough path between the burn and the side of the next burn.

At the 550m contour, cross the burn above a small basin, then climb north-north-west across rough ground to link some slabby rock and ascend to the right of a small crag. Above this, fairly flat ground leads to the final rocky rise, which is climbed to gain the flat top, where a fine pot-holed slab is crossed to reach the summit cairn (**9.5km; 460m; 2h 50min**).

Make the splendid 2.75km traverse along the broad, wind-scoured ridge to reach the wind shelter cairn and trig pillar on Sgòr Dubh (741m).

Descend south-east to gain, then follow, a rough ATV track alongside a deer fence to where the fence starts to veer away. Now follow a vague path

across rough ground to a cairn on the otherwise featureless flat top of Càrn an 'Ic Duibhe (630m).

Continue south-east to another cairn, then descend steeply through awkward terrain consisting of deep heather with hidden boulders, to gain some Caledonian pine trees. Pass leftwards through the trees and cross more deep heather, heading to the top corner of the forestry plantation, where there is a gate in the deer fence.

Go through the gate, then down the edge of the plantation for 200m or so before slanting leftwards through a break to gain a track. This track leads back to the main track, then the Linn of Dee. The Linn is worth diverting to, then following the path from there back to the road and the car park (**17km; 570m; 5h**).

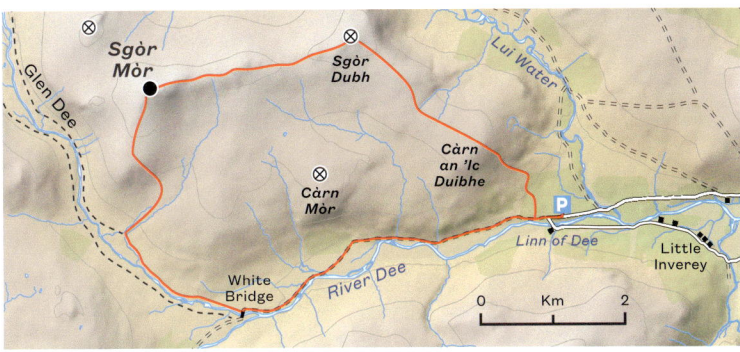

Càrn na Drochaide; 818m; (C126); L43; NO127938; cairn of the bridge

Rising from the floor of the Dee valley opposite Braemar, Càrn na Drochaide's position in front of Beinn a' Bhuird and Ben Avon makes it a splendid viewpoint for these and other surrounding hills.

Start from the National Trust's pay-and-display car park at the end of the public road at Linn of Quoich.

Walk to the end of the road, then loop round on a track across the bridge over the Quoich Water. Just before the house at Allanaquoich, go along the track on the left for 70m, then leave it and follow a rough path through the heather. This can be followed north-east all the way up the hillside, over the slight rise of Càrn Dearg, then on to the flat and stony summit, marked by a large cairn (**6.25km; 490m; 1h 35min**).

It is worth walking to the edges to expand the views a little. To the north-east the Corbetts, Creag an Dail Beag, Culardoch and Morven lie in a line. South-east is Conachcraig, then Lochnagar and the Mounth plateau, whilst south above Braemar is

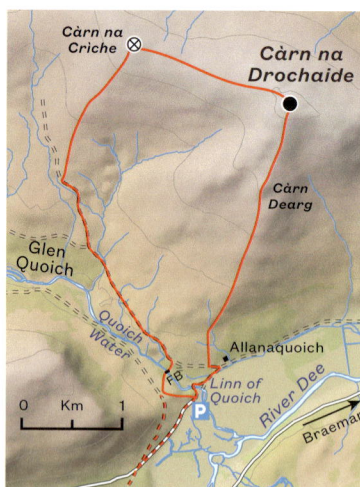

Morrone. However, it is the vast bulk of Ben Avon and Beinn a' Bhuird, with Ben Macdui and Cairn Toul to the north and north-west, that draws the eye.

Follow the path down to the west-north-west to Càrn na Crìche (737m), then descend south-south-west and south to gain a track. Go down this to gain the main track along the north

side of Glen Quoich by the forest, then follow this across a burn and down to Linn of Quoich.

Before reaching Allanquoich, cut back right on a track leading to a bridge over the river at the Linn itself, to view The Punch Bowl and its rapids. On the far side, go up the path, then at the edge of the trees, go left, then left again back to the car park (**10km; 530m; 3h 25min**).

At peak times, it has been known for the Linn of Dee road to be closed just before the Linn due to the car parks being full. In which case, a useful option is to park on the grass verge on the road on the east side of Victoria Bridge, leading to Mar Lodge.

Walk down and cross the bridge, then take the track on the right, which leads past Cragan to the road beyond, then Linn of Quoich and so up the hill (**6.25km; 510m; 2h 15min**).

On the return, instead of turning left to the car park, continue to a track then follow this to the road and cross over onto the track to Victoria Bridge (**15km; 560m; 4h 35min**).

Càrn na Drochaide above Allanaquoich and the River Dee (Rab Anderson)

Culardoch from Càrn Liath, with Geallaig Hill beyond (Rab Anderson)

Culardoch; *900m; (C23); L36 & L43; NO193988; cairn of the bridge*
Creag an Dail Bheag; *863m; (C71); L36 & L43; NO157981; crag of the little meadow*

Lying to the south-east of the huge bulk of Ben Avon, and sitting between Càrn na Drochaide and Brown Cow Hill, these two Corbetts form the divide between the upper Gairn and Dee valleys. They are separated by the Bealach Dearg at 650m, through which an old route between Braemar and Tomintoul passes, now popular with mountain bikers. This route provides a convenient approach to climb both hills. A bike can be used, and although uphill on the way in, this is offset by a downhill return and should save at least 2h on the times given for the day.

Leave the A93 to the east of Braemar and Invercauld Bridge, and go up the access road to Keiloch, to a pay-and-display car park on the right with toilets.

Exit the car park in the top left (north) corner, and follow the estate road north-west past Keiloch, signed for Linn of Quoich. After 1.75km, and just before Invercauld House, go up the first track on the right, signed to Tomintoul via Loch Buing.

After about 100m, take the left fork and continue uphill through attractive woodland, keeping straight on, heading north. Pass a track off right around Craig Leek, and emerge from the trees at the col between Creag a' Chait and Meall Gorm.

Continue across the head of the Glen Feardar basin, with Càrn Liath up to the left and Culardoch ahead, with the Bealach Dearg in between. Cross a bridge over the Allt Cùl in a dip, and carry on uphill, past a track off right, climbing more steeply for a short way. Above, continue at an easier angle to the Bealach Dearg, to where a path leaves the track on the left down by the head of the Allt na Claise Mòire.

For those using bikes, it's about 1h 25min to here, which is where they are best left (**8km; 370m; 2h 25min** on foot). Distances and times given are all on foot from the start.

Continue on up the track, past a branch off left, to a sharp bend. Take a rougher track ahead here for a short way, then a path directly up the broad crest to gain the trig point on the flat top of Culardoch. There is a grand view southwards to Lochnagar, whilst to the north is the full extent of Ben Avon (**9.75km; 620m; 3h 15min**).

Return to the bealach, then either cut across the path down the Allt na Claise Mòire, or briefly go along it from its start, to then follow a rough path up onto the bouldery top of Càrn

▶

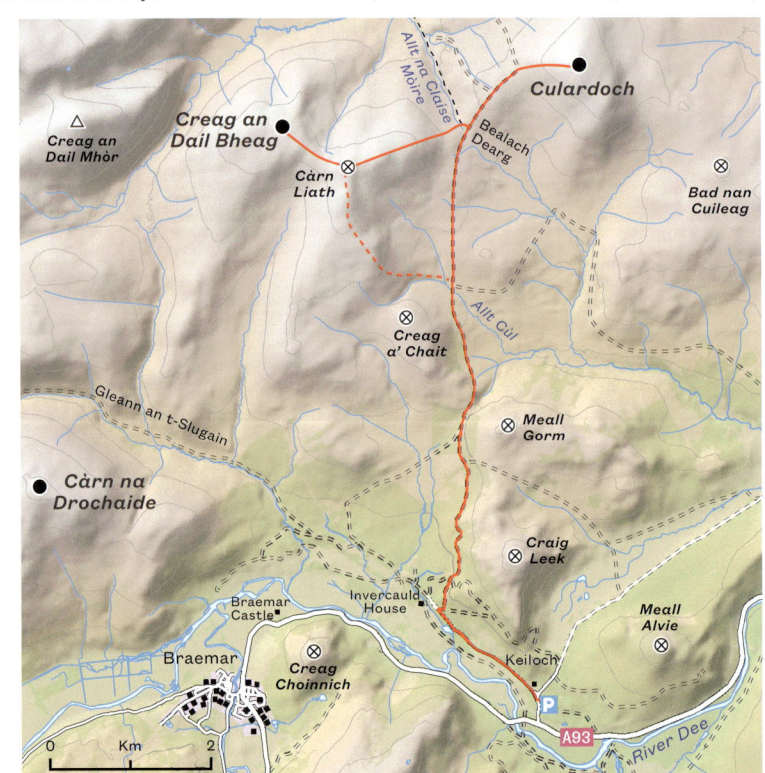

Creag an Dail Bheag and Càrn Liath with Culardoch beyond and distant Morven, from Càrn na Drochaide (Rab Anderson)

Liath. Cross a slight dip to gain the highest point at 861m, formerly the Corbett, and continue west, then north-west across the saddle, and climb to the flat top of Creag an Dail Bheag. The summit is the furthest away highpoint, marked by a cairn on a small rock outcrop (**14.25km; 880m; 4h 50min**).

Return to Càrn Liath, where there are two options:

(i) Return as for the ascent to the Bealach Dearg (especially if bikes are there), then follow the track back downhill (24.75km; 970m; 7h 35min).

(ii) Head south to a fine, but decaying, drystane dyke and follow the right side of this down the broad ridge. When the ground steepens, and the wall drops to the bealach with Creag a' Chait, go through a gap in the wall, then descend eastwards. Cross the right branch of the Allt Cùl to gain the track to the north of the bridge across this burn, then follow the track back downhill to the estate road (23.75km; 960m; 7h 20min).

Morven; 872m; (C61); L37; NJ376040; big hill

Admired by the poet Lord Byron, who spent some of his childhood in the area, Morven rises abruptly from the farmlands of Cromar in Aberdeenshire. It features in Byron's poem *When I Roved a Young Highlander.*

When I rov'd a young Highlander o'er the dark heath,
And climb'd thy steep summit, oh Morven of snow!
To gaze on the torrent that thunder'd beneath,
Or the mist of the tempest that gather'd below.

Prominent in the view to those approaching from the east, it is from that side that the most popular means of climbing the mountain is afforded. There are also routes from the south, south-west and west – the latter two enabling it to be climbed together with Mona Gowan, a Graham.

The route from the east is the shortest and most direct. Leave the A97 about 1km to the south of Logie Coldstone and take the minor road signposted to Groddie. The public road ends after 2.75km, at a fork at NJ410044, where there is parking at a sign for the Auchnerran Game and Wildlife Demonstration Farm.

Go through a gate, then follow a rough and grassy track west across undulating pastureland toward the lower slopes of Morven, to reach the ruined farmhouse of Balhennie. Go through the right-hand of two gates, then just above this, go through a pedestrian gate to gain the open hillside. Turn right to follow an initially grassy path, which develops into a narrow but clear path, and climb straight up the hillside through the heather, passing some boulders and small trees.

The ground levels off at 610m on the shoulder, where a line of old wooden fence posts is met, and flat, boggy ground is crossed. The well-travelled path leads onto the mountain's upper ridge, passing a large cairn, marked as Little Cairn on some maps. Continue along the crest, then up another steepening, passing a rock outcrop known as Mid Cairn, and make the final short climb onto the summit. To the north is a trig point with wind shelter. However, the highest point is marked by a large cairn immediately to the south, with a wind shelter on its east side, within which there is a summit book (**3.75km; 655m; 1h 55min**).

Although the quickest return (by 15min or so) is back the same way, it is perhaps more enjoyable to make a slight loop to the south for a more gentle descent of the lower slopes. To do so, partway down the descent to the shoulder from Little Cairn, take the path on the right. On reaching the boggy shoulder, the path veers away south and becomes a rough track leading to the Coinlach Burn at the col with Roar Hill. Don't take the animal track on the left here, but descend an initially grassy and boggy

▶

Morven from the A97 to the north-east (Rab Anderson)

path just above the burn. The path veers away from the burn, then descends north-east across the slope, with fine views across a patchwork of fields and woodland to Pressendye, a Graham. Rejoin the ascent route at the gate and return to the start (**8.75km; 700m; 3h 15min**).

The route from the south starts at Braehead of Tullich, about 2km along the A93 to the north-east of Ballater, either from a layby on the south side of the road by the cemetery, or the cemetery car park 100m to the east.

Walk west along the verge, then cross the road and go up the first track past the farm buildings. Go through a gate to the right of the house, then follow what was once a track and is now a path. This swings northwards past a large pond to head up the glen of the Culsten Burn, through beautiful birch and pine woods, then over into the basin of the Rashy Burn. On meeting a track at NJ318021, the driest route is to go left (west) for 600m or so along the track, crossing a burn, then head up the grassy hillside directly to the summit (**8km; 690m; 2h 55min**).

Return the same way (**16km; 710m;**

4h 50min).

The route from the south-west starts from Lary, where there is parking (NJ336002) at the end of the minor road that leaves the A93 at Bridge of Gairn, on the west side of Ballater.

Follow a track north to NJ341022, then branch right along another track, following this where it turns right at NJ344027 and is joined by an ATV track from the left from Morven Lodge. Continue for a further 1.4km, then at NJ358026, about 70m beyond a track coming up the side of Tom Garchory, break off north up an ATV track above the burn. Higher, this curves east across a flat section and carries on up to the summit (**7km; 550m; 2h 25min**).

Return the same way (**14km; 555m; 4h 10min**).

The route from the west starts from a large parking area on the north side of the A939 at NJ312027 by the Allt Glas-choille.

Walk north up the road for 230m and take the track on the right, then the first track right, which drops into Glen Fenzie. Follow the track around the side of Tom Liath to reach Morven

Lodge. At NJ339031, go right down an ATV track to cross the Morven Burn and join the route from Lary at NJ344027, then follow this to the top (**8.25km; 570m; 2h 45min**).

Return the same way (**16.5km; 690m; 5h**).

The last two routes can be extended to include Mona Gowan (749m), the Graham to the west of Morven. From Morven's summit, return west for 800m, then descend to the north-west and cross a col known as the Glac of Bunzeach. Climb over the top of Mullachdubh (681m), turning west, and drop to another col at the Slacks of Glencarvie, then ascend to the top of Mona Gowan.

For the return to Lary, descend south to a col, then follow a track down to Morven Lodge. Turn right past the lodge, then take the right-hand track at the fork to rejoin the approach route and return to Lary; an added 5km, 340m, 1h 45min.

For the return to the A939, descend west beside a fence and climb onto Cairnagour Hill (744m). Descend south off this, following a track that leads back to the road and the start; an added 2.5km, 210m, 1h.

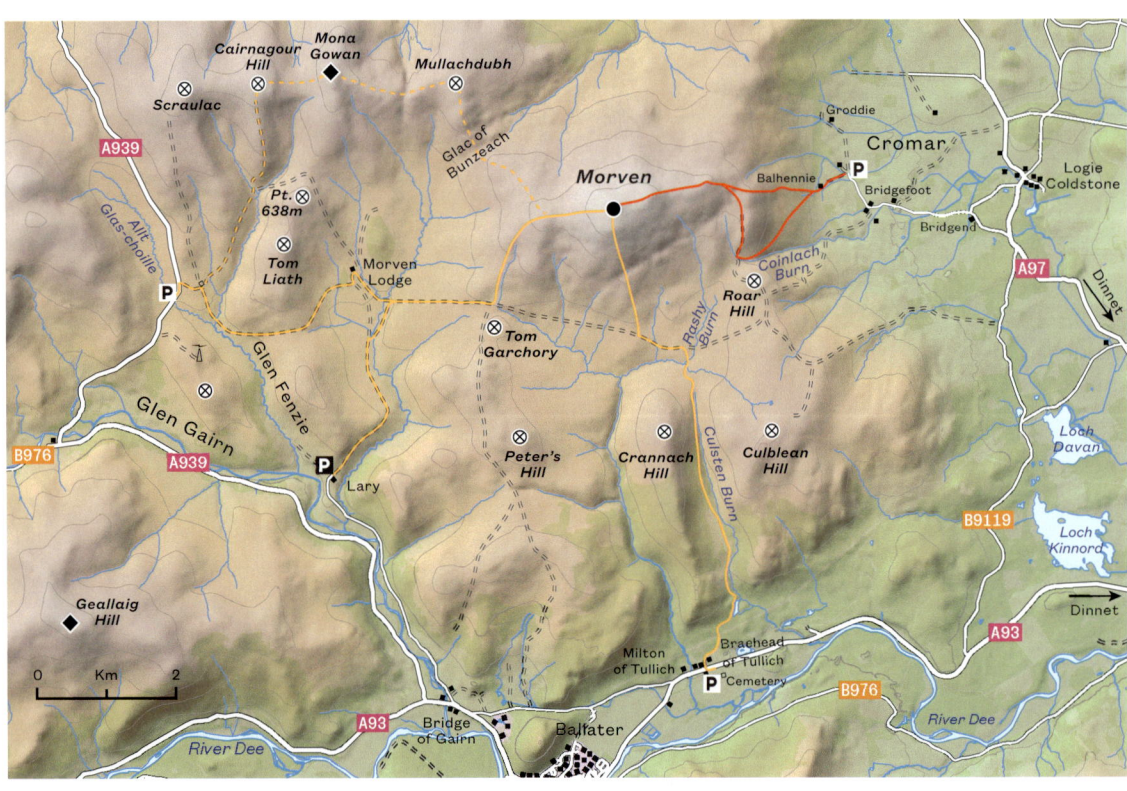

The summit crest of Brown Cow Hill, with distant Morven from Meikle Geal Chàrn to the north-west (Rab Anderson)

Brown Cow Hill; *829m; (C117); L36 & L37; NJ221044*

The vast, rounded bulk of Brown Cow Hill and its satellites fills the ground between the River Gairn to the south and the infant River Don to the north. It is separated from the equally bulky, but higher and much more interesting-looking, Ben Avon to the west by the deep trough of Glen Builg, an offshoot of Glen Avon.

Despite its dull appearance though, once on the higher ground the walking is pleasant and the views are rewarding, especially if the full extent of the high ground is traversed.

Start from the Corgarff Castle car park, signed off the A939 at Cock Bridge, through the white gate posts and 275m west along a narrow road.

Walk up the road towards the castle and go through a gate on the right into a field. Go around the back of the castle and exit the corner of the field by another gate to gain a grassy track. Either go along this track, or cut down a path, to gain the main track from Cockbridge Farm and follow this south across the slope above the Cock Burn, gaining height and passing a track off right into a forestry plantation.

Climb uphill beside a burn, then leave the track to Càrn Oighreag just below the col between it and Brown Cow Hill to follow a short track on the left to its end. Continue on an ATV track and path across boggy ground, then on up the broad, grassy spur. After the initial rise, at a small

cairn, when the path goes left to a wooden post (after which it fades), continue ahead (initially vague) to pick up the ATV track and follow it as best as possible through a haggy area. Beyond this, the ground rises and an improving path leads on up the right side of a shallow peaty basin, then on to the east top (823m), reached through a gate in a fence.

Continue west by the fence for 900m to gain the small cairn that marks the summit on the central top. The easier way is perhaps by the ATV track on the north side of the fence, which entails stepping over the fence to gain the cairn (**6.75km; 450m; 2h 15min**).

Returning the same way is quickest (**13.5km; 475m; 4h**), although from the col, it is worth following the track over Càrn Oighreag and down to the road.

However, it is better to continue west, following the ATV track to Càrn

Sawvie (820m), the west top, then downhill to the north-west. Cross the boggy col and follow a rough path up to the rocky summit of Meikle Geal Chàrn (802m), with its quartz boulder-field and a double fence just beyond.

Drop to the next col to the north-west, then either follow the fence over Little Geal Chàrn and its north top (Pt.709m) to the col above the Well of Don, or cut the corner to rejoin the fence. Either way, follow the fence up to Cairn Culchavie (726m).

Leave the fence here and go east, then north-east down an ATV track, with views ahead to Càrn Ealasaid, to gain a track in the glen below. This leads past a small, dammed lochan to reach the main track below the bothy at Inchmore. Follow this track past Delnadamph, where it becomes surfaced and leads back to the start (**18km; 595m; 5h 20min**).

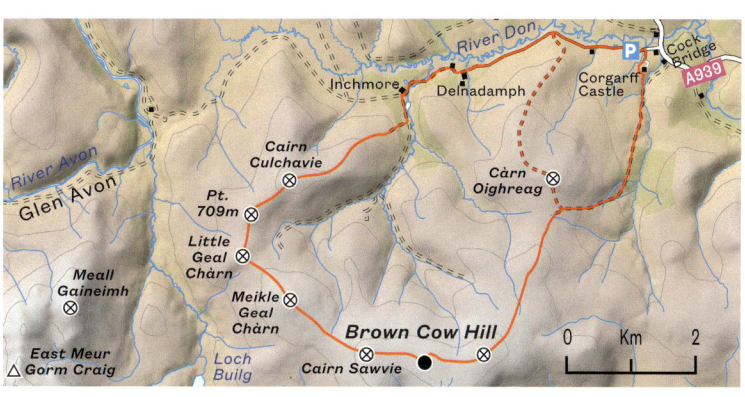

Càrn Ealasaid from Brown Cow Hill (Rab Anderson)

Càrn Ealasaid; 792m; (C171); L36 & L37; NJ227117; Elizabeth's hill

Together with westerly neighbours Tolm Bùirich and Craig Veann, Càrn Ealasaid forms a westwards extension to the Ladder Hills, which lies between Glen Avon and the A939 over the Lecht, between Cock Bridge and Tomintoul.

Although Càrn Ealasaid can be climbed quickly from a high start at the Lecht ski centre, then combined with Càrn Mòr to the north, the route is not attractive, and two other, more satisfactory routes are described.

The best ascent is from the south, where Càrn Ealasaid rises above the infant River Don, opposite the sprawling bulk of Brown Cow Hill and its satellites.

Start from the Corgarff Castle car park, reached by turning off the A939 at Cock Bridge on the south side of the bridge over the River Don and following the road for 270m.

Walk back out to the A939, turn left and follow the verge across the bridge over the River Don, then turn left at Kelvinside Academy's John Duff Lodge outdoor centre, and Briggie's Bothy. Follow the road, then the track above the River Don to just beyond the cottage at Loinherry, then take the uphill track on the right.

The track leads all the way to the summit, but initially makes a big loop, which can be cut by climbing straight up the hillside on a rough path, passing two prominent cairns at a small old quarry. Rejoin the track higher up and continue over the minor rise of Cairn Vaich, then cross fairly flat ground before rising slightly to the flat summit (**5.25km; 430m; 1h 50min**).

Brown Cow Hill lies opposite, with Ben Avon and Beinn a' Bhuird to the right, then the Loch A'an basin and the main Cairngorm massif. To the north, over Càrn Mòr, is Ben Rinnes, with Ben Wyvis visible beyond.

Either follow the track south-west off the summit, or, perhaps more pleasant, take a rough path down the crest to the left of the track to reach a prominent, tall shepherd's cairn. Below the cairn, step over a fence and descend past grouse butts to rejoin the track. Thereafter, the track leads down through a felled area to the main track along the floor of the glen, which is followed back (12km; 460m; 3h 35min).

An alternative descent can be made by going north, then north-east to Beinn a' Chruinnich (778m), then south-east past the top of the ski infrastructure to Càrn Mhic an Toisich, and down the ridge to a track leading back to Loinherry (12.75km; 530m; 3h 50min).

To maintain the grand views into the Cairngorms, the route can be extended west over Tolm Bùirich to Craig Veann, then south down the ridge to a track leading to the main track on the south side of the River Don, which leads back to the car park (18.5km; 600m; 5h 20min).

An ascent can also be made from the north, from a pull-off on the south side of the A939, almost opposite a derelict cottage 1km to the west of the access track to the car park at Well of the Lecht.

Go through a gate and follow the track above the burn as it swings up to a col on the south side of Tom Garbh-bheinne. Leave the track where it turns left, then cross the boggy col to gain the track on the far side, and follow this up onto Beinn a' Chruinnich (778m), passing a line of shooting butts and a communications aerial. The highest point is a little further on at a ski tow.

Descend to the south-west, passing through some peat hags to reach a col, then climb to the track along the top of Càrn Ealasaid, and turn left to the summit (5km; 455m; 1h 50min).

Although a circuit can be made by descending north-west, then north-wards to Blairnamarrow, this involves a 1km walk back along the road, so it is perhaps better to return by the route of ascent (10km; 545m; 3h 15min).

Càrn Mòr; 804m; (C154); L36 & L37; NJ265183; big cairn

Rising to the south-east of Chapeltown in the Braes of Glenlivet, Càrn Mòr is the highest point in the Ladder Hills. This range runs north-eastwards from the A939 Cock Bridge to Tomintoul road at The Lecht, to form the dividing line between the head of Glenlivet and Donside.

Càrn Ealasaid lies to the south-west of The Lecht, and although both hills could easily be done from a high start point at the ski centre, this is not the most attractive way of climbing either hill. So, both hills are described on their own, with more satisfactory routes. Three routes are described for the ascent of Càrn Mòr, each with its own merit.

One route climbs the hill from its north-west side, from Chapeltown, which is reached by a narrow road leaving the B9008 at Auchnarrow. Turn left just before the Chivas Brothers distillery and cross the Crombie Water to a small parking area (NJ242209) on the right at the start of a track to East Auchavaich.

Walk up the track past East Auchavaich and Corrunich, almost to Ladderfoot, where there are views north to Corryhabbie Hill. Cross the bridge over the Ladder Burn and follow the track, then path above the burn, up into a lovely, grassy corrie, and on to a col on the ridge north of Dun Muir – a point known as The Ladder. The route from Donside to the south-east arrives here.

Climb southwards onto Dun Muir, then west across the haggy dip at the head of the Ladder Burn, and swing south-west to make the final easy ascent to the trig point on the flat top of Càrn Mòr (7.25km; 530m; 2h 30min).

Head north-west off the summit to pick up a rough ATV track and drop down to a boggy area with some hags before a slight rise (Pt.721m). Continue on the ATV track, which cuts across the side of the rise and swings north down the ridge for a way, before heading towards the right side of a small forestry plantation. Pass between two fencelines, then go through a gate to regain the track, which is followed back (11.25km; 530m; 3h 35min).

This route can be extended by following the path from the summit down to the south-west to climb onto Pt.800m, Monadh an t-Sluich Leith. ▶

Càrn Mòr, with Corryhabbie Hill and Ben Rinnes beyond (Rab Anderson)

Càrn Mòr from Scalan in the Braes of Glenlivet (Rab Anderson)

Descend towards the col below Càrn Liath and take the right-hand path, which leads across the north side of the col. Traverse rightwards to a line of old wooden fence posts on Càrn Liath's north spur, and follow these, swinging westwards to two cairns.

Descend north-north-west here to pick up an ATV track and follow this down past a line of old shooting butts towards the Crombie Water and the ruins at Clash of Scalan. Continue along the track, crossing the Crombie Water to pass The Scalan.

The Scalan is an open museum with interpretive boards covering the farm buildings, mill with water wheel, and college dating back to 1716, where persecuted Roman Catholics trained as priests following the failed first Jacobite Rebellion.

Continue along the track to the road, then past the distillery back to the start (**14.75km; 570m; 4h 30min**).

For the route from Well of the Lecht to the south-west, leave the north side of the A939 at the bend to the north of The Lecht ski centre and go along a short section of track to a small parking area at NJ234152.

Walk northwards up the path into Coire Buidhe, crossing the bridge over the burn and heading towards the large building at the site of an 18th-century ironstone and manganese mine. Just before reaching this, cross the burn and follow a track up the broad ridge of Tom na Broighleig, past shooting butts. When the track ends, continue up slightly leftwards through some peat hags, on a rough path, to gain the top of Càrn Liath (792m).

Continue northwards along the fenceline to where it changes direc-tion, then follow a rough path down to the col with Pt.800m, Monadh an t-Sluich Leith, then through the hags and up the slope beyond to gain its top. Descend northwards and cross some boggy ground at the head of the West Corrie of Slochd Mòr, then make the final, easy ascent to the trig point on top of Càrn Mòr (**5.5km; 435m; 2h**).

Return to Monadh an t-Sluichd Leith, then descend towards the col with Càrn Liath via the right-hand path, which leads across the north side of the col. Traverse the slope rightwards to a line of old wooden fence posts on Càrn Liath's north spur, the continuation of the fence-line left earlier, and follow these, swinging westwards to two cairns.

Continue south-west beside the posts to another cairn to meet a path

coming up from Chapeltown. This path actually drops into the head of Coire Buidhe and can be followed. However, either go down it for about 70m, then take another path running parallel to the fenceline, or continue beside the fenceline, then cut down to meet the other path. This is the path shown on the map, which slants down across Càrn Dulack to rejoin the path in the floor of the glen close to the start (12.25km; 475m; 3h 50min).

For the route from the south-east, leave the A944 at Bellabeg and head north, signed to Glenbuchat Lodge, then branch left just before Torrancroy, signed to the Lost Gallery, to reach a parking area on the left at NJ335157, at the start of a track.

Walk up the road to its end, then go between two buildings and follow a track, known as the Ladder Route, to Aldachuie and the former Lost Gallery. Continue on the track, then ford the burn at the upper edge of the forestry to the reach the ruin at Duffdefiance. The name is said to date back to a time when a crofter, Lucky Thain, came over the hills from Glenlivet and squatted there. He was apparently able to build a house and have his lum 'reekin' before he was challenged by the local laird, Duff, and so sat there in defiance.

Leave the track by the burn and follow an ATV track northwards up onto Finlate Hill to reach a track, then continue uphill on a rougher track. Follow this track north-west to a junction, then leave it, continuing north-west to reach a col on the ridge named The Ladder, where the route from Chapeltown arrives. Turn left and follow the high ground over Dun Muir (754m), and the haggy col beyond, to reach the trig point on top of Càrn Mòr (9.5km; 580m; 3h).

Returning the same way is the simplest (19km; 680m; 5h 30min).

It is possible to make a circuit by traversing south-west over Pt.800m, Monadh an t-Sluich Leith, to Càrn Liath. From there, go east, then south-east down haggy ground to cross a boggy col and climb through hags onto The Socach to join a track.

Follow this track down to the north-east to a junction. Turn right and continue downhill, almost to a small reservoir, then go left to follow the track alongside the Quillichan Burn to reach the farm at Tolduquhill. From there, follow the track alongside the Water of Nochty to return to the start (23km; 740m; 6h 35min).

This could be shortened by descending east from Monadh an t-Sluich Leith to pick up an ATV track leading to a better track. This track leads back to Duffdefiance, but it involves multiple fordings of The Water of Nochty (20km; 670m; 6h).

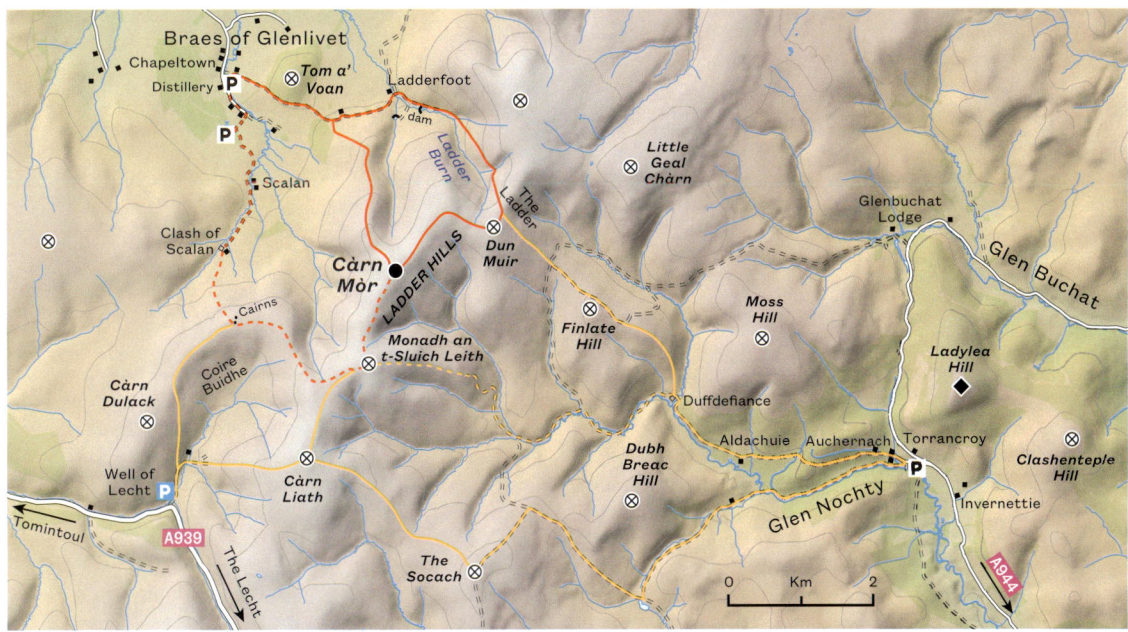

Across Mulloch Moss to Corryhabbie Hill from Glen Rinnes to the north (Rab Anderson)

Corryhabbie Hill; *781m; (C188); L36 & L37; NJ281288*

Lying to the south of the prominent and shapely landmark of Ben Rinnes is the unassuming, rounded mass of Corryhabbie Hill. It is the highest point of an elongated ridge-line between Glen Rinnes and Glenfiddich, and is best climbed from the former.

Leave the B9009 between Tomintoul and Dufftown, and turn off south-east towards Ellivreid. There is space to park at the junction at the top of the hill, on the right by the bins.

Walk south (right) along the road to Ellivreid, then go through the gate opposite the farm and follow a grassy track across the field. Pass the trees, and continue on the track as it swings up left, then right onto the spur above the Corryhabbie Burn and Shean Dhu. The track becomes less obvious here, veering right through an open gate in a fence, then left alongside the fence to a fork. Take the right fork, which snakes onto Hill of Achmore and leads to a gate in an old deer fence.

Continue on one of two rough paths across Little Lapprach. Both paths climb the steeper upper slope onto Muckle Lapprach to gain a rough track; the right-hand path goes closest to its top. Follow the track,

swinging left to avoid peat hags, then climb onto the flat top of Corryhabbie Hill, where the trig point sits within a stone shelter (**5.5km; 480m; 2h**).

Returning the same way is easiest (11km; 480m; 3h 25min).

However, a pleasant circuit can be made by continuing along the track to the north-east to meet a track coming up from the right, from the head of Glen Fiddich. This is known as Morton's Way, a shooting road built by a laird at Glenfiddich Lodge. Follow the track north-east along the crest, and down some zigzags to a col, then go left down another track above the Burn of Altavallie.

Cross the burn and go through a gate in the deer fence, then descend one of the strips between the planted trees to reach a line of mature trees. Walk left alongside the trees to reach a track, and follow this past a house, then continue down and out to a junction. Turn left to pass the ruin at the Folds of Corhabbie, then go down right on a grassy track beside the pine trees to ford the Corryhabbie Burn. Continue up the other side and go through a gate in the deer fence, then right to join the approach route, which is followed back (13km; 530m; 4h).

A longer route starts from a small car park at the end of the road from Tomnavoulin to Allanreid in Glenlivet. This is the best way of combining Corryhabbie Hill with Cook's Cairn, a Graham, to the south-east.

A mountain bike is helpful, and although it saves about an hour or more on the day, it should be noted that the biking is quite rough. Times are given on foot, though.

Follow the continuation track to where it goes uphill to Achdregnie, then go down to the River Livet, but don't cross. Instead, follow a grassy track alongside the river, then away from it to rejoin it, and cross to the other side by a footbridge. Continue along the track for 3km, which is rough in places, to reach a ford across the River Livet. Bikes are best left here.

Either ford here, or go upstream for 300m to a footbridge leading to Knochkan bothy. Continue on the track to just beyond the ruin at Suie, where it forks. Cook's Cairn is best climbed first, so ascend the right-hand track to the col in front of the first wind turbine of the Dorenell Wind Farm, then follow ATV tracks north-east up to the summit of Cook's Cairn (**10km; 480m; 3h**).

Make a steep descent to the west to gain the track junction below, then zigzag up the track onto Corryhabbie Hill, turning left at the top to gain the summit (**13.75km; 760m; 4h 30min**).

There are now three return options:

(i) Go back down the track to the junction, and turn right down Glen Suie to Suie, then return as for the approach (25.75km; 775m; 7h 30min).

(ii) Stay high, and follow the rounded ridge over Muckle Lapprach to Càrn an t-Suidhe. Continue south down the ridge for a way before swinging south-east to drop more steeply towards the bothy, then ford the burn and the River Livet, or use the bridge, and follow the track back (25km; 820m; 7h 30min).

(iii) If a bike has not been used, the shortest return is to descend the rough track towards Muckle Lapprach, and cross haggy ground to gain the dip with Pt.731m. From there, drop south-west, almost to the col with Cairn Dregnie, then head down west to follow deer tracks to a break in the forest at NJ255274. This leads to the highpoint of track, which is followed gently downhill back to the road at Allanreid (21.5km; 765m; 6h 25min).

Option (iii) also gives a there-and-back route (15.5km; 520m; 4h 25min).

An ascent can also be made via Glenfiddich, from a car park at Bridgehaugh (NJ340357), on the A941 south of Dufftown. Cross the

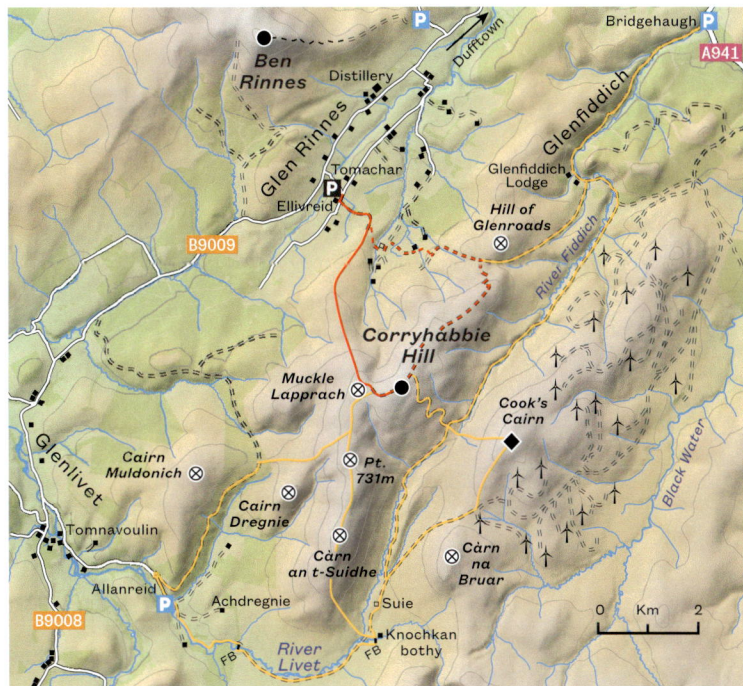

road, and go up the estate road alongside the River Fiddich to Glenfiddich Lodge. Just beyond the lodge, keep left on the main track over a burn to pass some buildings, then take the track on the right and climb uphill past a small forestry plantation. Now on Morton's Way, follow the track to the col, then up left to zigzag onto the crest. Keep straight on just below the summit, where Morton's Way turns left downhill (**11km; 550m; 3h 20min**).

Return to Morton's Way and zigzag down towards the col with Cook's Cairn, then follow the track down Glenfiddich, past the Elf House cave in the limestone just off the track at the second burn. The track leads back to Glenfiddich Lodge and the start (24.25km; 595m; 6h 45min).

Cook's Cairn could be included from the col, then descending its north ridge to drop into Glenfiddich; an added 3km, 255m, 1h.

Ben Rinnes from the summit of Corryhabbie Hill (Rab Anderson)

Ben Rinnes and its long eastern ridge from Glen Rinnes (Rab Anderson)

Ben Rinnes; *841m; (C103); L28; NJ255354; headland hill*

Rising prominently to the north-east of the main Cairngorm massif, and with an outlook over the coastal plains known as the Laich o' Moray, Ben Rinnes is a distinctive feature in the landscape. As might be expected of such a landmark, the views from its summit are expansive and far ranging. Another notable feature of the hill is its location in whisky country above the Spey Valley, and the fact that it is encircled by distilleries.

Ben Rinnes is a popular hill, and there are a number of routes to its highest point, known as the Scurran of Lochterlandoch; *scurran* meaning a peak or pinnacle. The shortest route, and therefore the most popular one, is via the prominent eastern ridge, starting from a car park at NJ284359 in a narrow glen named Glack Harnes. This is located about 500m up the minor road to Milltown of Edinvillie, which leaves the B9009 about 3 miles (5km) south-west of Dufftown.

Go through a gate and follow a wide path, which zigzags up the steep slope onto Round Hill at the start of the ridge. The path leads up the ridge over Roy's Hill (535m), then zigzags

up the steeper ridge ahead to gain the granite outcrop with trig point on top that forms the summit (**3.75km; 535m; 1h 45min**).

Far to the north across the Moray Firth, conical Morven, with humped Scaraben, to its right can be seen. To the south-west across Glenlivet are the Cairngorms, with the tors on Ben Avon identifying it, whilst closer at hand, across Glen Rinnes to the south, are the Corbett Corryhabbie Hill at the head of Glenfiddich, and the Graham Cooks Cairn, recognisable by its wind turbines. To the east of these, The Buck and Tap o' Noth stand out, with the North Sea beyond.

Return the same way (**7.5km; 545m; 2h 55min**).

A good route, which visits the fine granite tors to the north-west of the summit, ascends the hill from the Benrinnes Distillery to the north-east. There is signed parking to the rear of the distillery at NJ258396.

Follow a track southwards to exit woodland through a gate, and continue on up the broad north-east ridge. Keep an eye out for a narrow path on the left, which leaves the track at NJ247377, before it ends on what is called Baby's Hill. Follow this

narrow and quite boggy path as it makes a rising traverse up the side of the ridge to cross the Scurran Burn, then climbs more steeply across another burn and on up to the granite outcrop of Scurran of Well. This has little to see on the approach side, but on its far side, is impressive where there is quite some height to it.

Continue on to the fine tors of Lady's Chair, which the path passes through. It is worth wandering around the tors before continuing on up the path through some peat hags to join a track for the final climb to the top of Ben Rinnes (**5.5km; 620m; 2h 15min**).

Return north-west down the track to where it swings south, then continue west on an ATV track to gain the tors of Scurran of Morinsh. Now head north-north-east towards Lady's Chair on a rough path for 250m or so, to meet a rough ATV track, then follow this left (north-west) through a short section of peat hags onto a slight rise. When the ATV track swings west, follow a rough path downhill northwards, across a burn onto the broad ridge, then down to gain the start of the track. If the start of the path is missed, continue to a large cairn named Fauldgates Cairn, then head

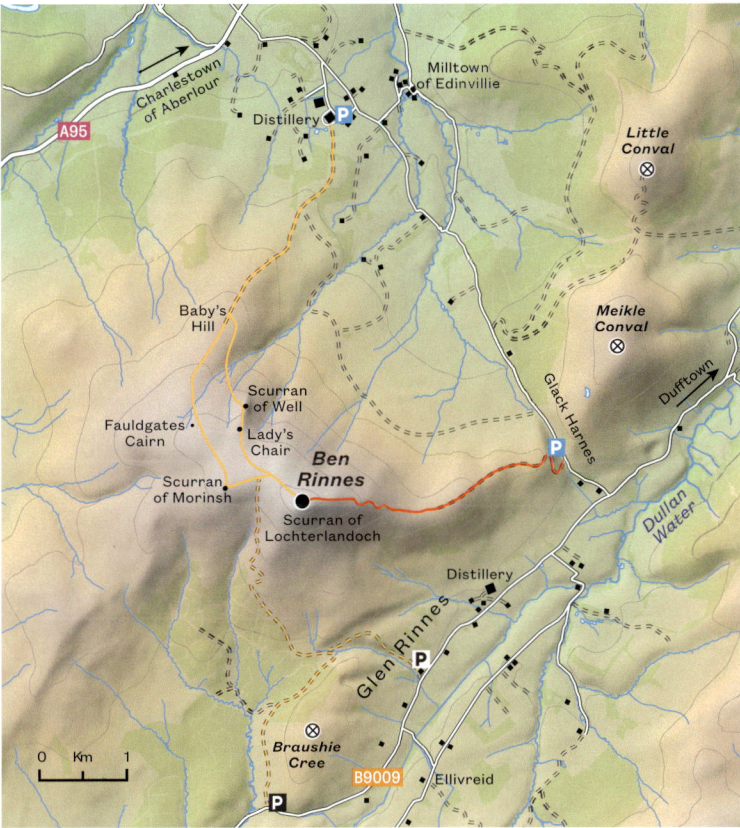

> *Geal Chàrn;* 821m; (C122);
> L36; NJ090127; white cairn

An unobtrusive hill in what is known as the Braes of Abernethy, Geal Chàrn is the highest point in an area of rolling, heathery hills to the north-east of the main Cairngorm massif, between the River Spey and the River Avon.

Start from the end of a narrow road at Dorback Lodge (NJ077168), reached by a 4.5km drive south from the link road between Nethy Bridge and the A939 to the east. A sign at the turning circle states 'no parking', but it should be possible to park considerably off the road without impeding this, or blocking the gate. There is also space on the verge for two cars just before the turning circle.

Since there is a river to ford, albeit normally straightforward, it is perhaps better left until the end of the walk, so a clockwise route is suggested.

Walk along the continuation track past disused Dorback Lodge, then a house and kennels. Take the right-hand fork, which swings right, and head south-south-east up the glen alongside the twisting Dorback Burn, which becomes the Allt Mòr. Ford a small tributary and continue to the watershed, then break off right on a rough ATV track at NJ109136, at the far end of a widening, where another track climbs the hillside on the left.

Either follow grassy ground up the left side of the small burn, now the Allt Slugan na Cloiche, or cross over and follow the rough ATV track up past a line of shooting butts. Continue up a steepening to eventually gain easier ground, which leads to the broad crest. Turn right here and head westwards beside some intermittent fence posts to reach the small quartzite cairn that marks the summit (**7.75km; 480m; 2h 30min**).

It is a surprisingly good viewpoint. South-west is Cairn Gorm, then Bynack More with Creag Mhòr to its left and Beinn Mheadhoin in between. South are Ben Avon and Beinn a' Bhuird. South-east, past the broad mass of Brown Cow Hill, is Mount Keen, and north-east is Ben

north. Follow the track back (**11km; 630m; 3h 50min**).

Routes can also be done via a track that comes up from Glen Rinnes to the south. There are two start points from the B9009, at NJ251321 and NJ268335, where there is parking. Tracks from each, pass either side of Braushie Cree, then join for the ascent onto the north-west shoulder. The route around the west side of Braushie Cree is (**11.5km; 510m; 3h 40min**), and that around the east side is (**9.5km; 535m; 3h 15min**).

The Lady's Chair tors on the northern route (Rab Anderson)

▶

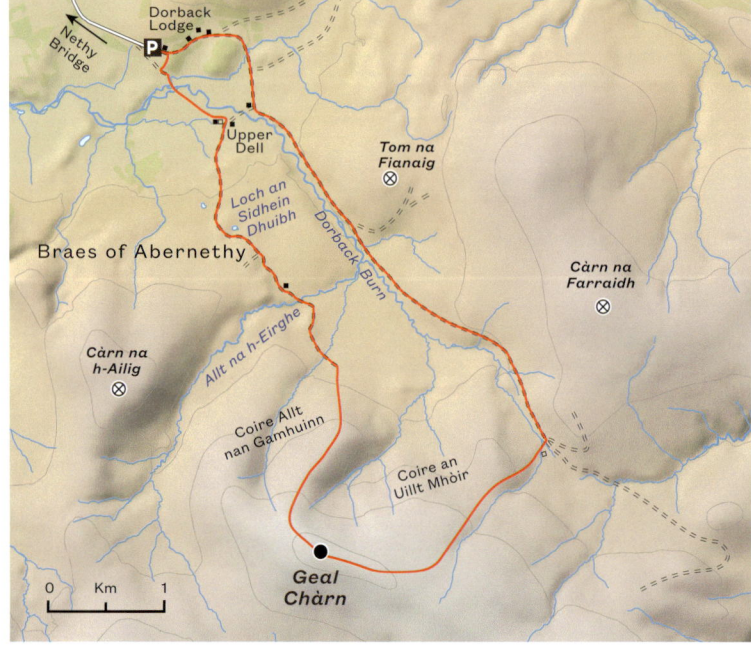

Geal Chàrn from the road to Dorback Lodge (Rab Anderson)

Rinnes. Both Morvens are also visible – the Corbett to the south-east and the Graham in the Far North.

Head north-west to pick up a path that traverses down and across the slope, then drops to a flatter section at the top of the spur between Coire an Uillt Mhòir and Coire Allt nan Gamhuinn. Continue down the spur, then towards the end, swing left and descend to the end of a track. Follow the track over the Allt nan Gamhuinn to pass a wooden hut and reach the Allt na h-Eirghe at some isolated Scots Pines.

This burn can normally be forded easily, but the wash-out on the flat floor shows how big it can get. Ascend the track on the other side, pass a small corrugated iron hut, then some kettle hole lochans, and descend to the abandoned farm at Upper Dell.

Leave the main track, which swings right, and go round past the front of the cottage. Pass through a gateway, then follow another grassy track across flat ground before heading off beside the telegraph poles to ford the

Dorback Burn. Head around the right side of a moraine mound and go through an open gate at the corner of a fence, then cross a small burn. Pass through an area of sand deposits,

and go through another gate to follow a sandy track, taking its grassy right-hand branch uphill to pass through another gate to gain the turning circle (**13.25km; 540m; 4h 5min**).

Meall a' Bhuachaille; 810m; (C140); L36; NH990115; shepherd's hill

The highest of a distinctive line of hills overlooking the north side of Loch Morlich in the Glenmore Forest Park, Meall a' Bhuachaille provides superb views of the northern Cairngorm massif. The Abernethy Forest lies to the north, and the Queen's Forest to the south, so access points are limited. The usual route is from Glen More via the Ryvoan Pass, where the hill can be climbed by its treeless eastern flank, with a descent back through the Queen's Forest for a short route, or along the ridge over its attendant summits and back through the forest for a splendid extended outing.

The ascent can be started from various points in Glenmore, the usual being the Glenmore Visitor Centre pay-and-display car park. Walk past the centre and go around a barrier to cross a side road, then go past the Cairngorm Reindeer Centre onto a narrow road. Follow the road for

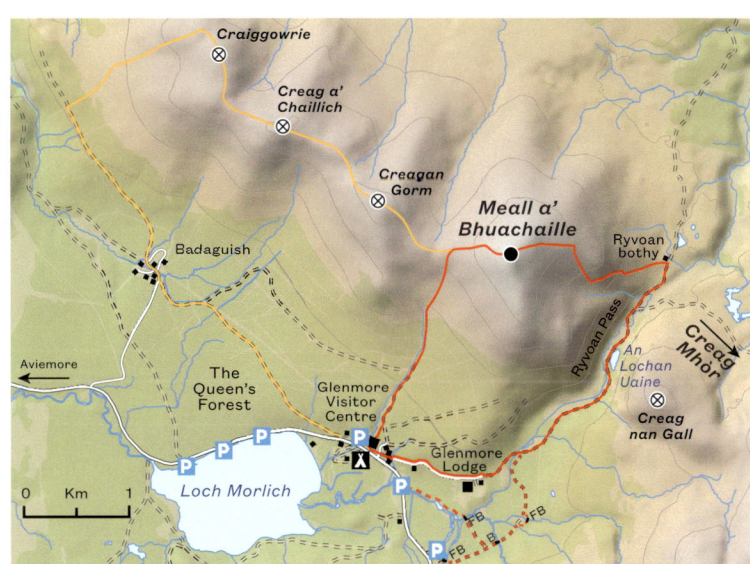

100m, then go left onto a path and cycle route, which leads alongside the road to just beyond Glenmore Lodge, Scotland's National Outdoor Training Centre, to join a track beyond a barrier at the end of the road.

Continue along the track through

▶

Across Loch Morlich to Meall a' Bhuachaille (Rab Anderson)

lovely woodland and head through the narrow gap of the Ryvoan Pass, an outflow channel for the glacier that once filled the Glen More basin. On the left, steep slopes rise to Meall a' Bhuachaille, which are covered with Scots pine and heather low down, whilst on the right, a steep, pine-clad scree slope rises to Creag nan Gall. Set within the depths of the pass is An Lochan Uaine, a little gem of a loch, which lives up to its name – *the little green loch.*

Soon after leaving the pass, take the left fork in the track, which leads to Ryvoan Bothy, overlooking the Abernethy Forest and across to Geal Chàrn. From there, a well-constructed path gives a straightforward ascent, with increasingly good views, to reach the summit of Meall a' Bhuachaille (6km; 510m; 2h 10min).

The view of the main Cairngorm massif to the south, especially Cairn Gorm and its Northern Corries, is superb. To the north-east, Ben Rinnes is prominent and in the Far North, across the Moray Firth, the cone of Morven can be identified some 70 miles (112km) away.

Descend to the west, and follow the path down towards the col with Creagan Gorm. Just above the col, keep left on the main path and descend through Coire Chondlaich, back into the Glenmore Forest Park.

The path runs down beside the burn to join a track, which is followed to where it turns left. Leave the track here, and follow a path on the right, down through woodland beside the burn, back to the Glenmore Visitor Centre (9km; 500m; 3h 5min).

The extended traverse follows the path over Creagan Gorm and Creag a' Chaillich to Craiggowrie and is very worthwhile. From Craiggowrie, a path leads downhill to the south-west into the forest, keeping left to gain a track. Follow the track to gain a road and go through the Badaguish Outdoor Centre. Beyond this, when the road sweeps right, go left past a barrier along a track, taking the right fork to reach the main road. Either take the road up behind the hostel, back to the top end of the car park, or go along the pavement beside the main road (16.75km; 740m; 5h 20min).

> *Creag Mhòr; 895m; (C31); L36; NJ057047; big crag*

Although only some twenty metres short of Munro status, Creag Mhòr looks small and insignificant in comparison to Bynack More, its western neighbour, and another four 1000m Munros, which it sits cupped between in the middle of the northern Cairngorm massif. Its location means that a long approach is required, making Creag Mhòr one of the more remote Corbetts. Despite this, the path to it is good, and on a fine day, the ascent itself is easy.

However, whilst Creag Mhòr may only be a relatively minor Cairngorm summit, its ascent should not be treated lightly, especially in adverse weather conditions. Running between it and Bynack More is an ancient drove route between Speyside and Deeside via the Làirig an Laoigh, Glen Derry and Glen Lui. The Làirig an Laoigh path is good, but it does attain a height of almost 800m on featureless terrain on the north ridge of Bynack More, and below this, careless navigation in poor visibility has seen walkers go astray to the north-east down the Water of Caiplich.

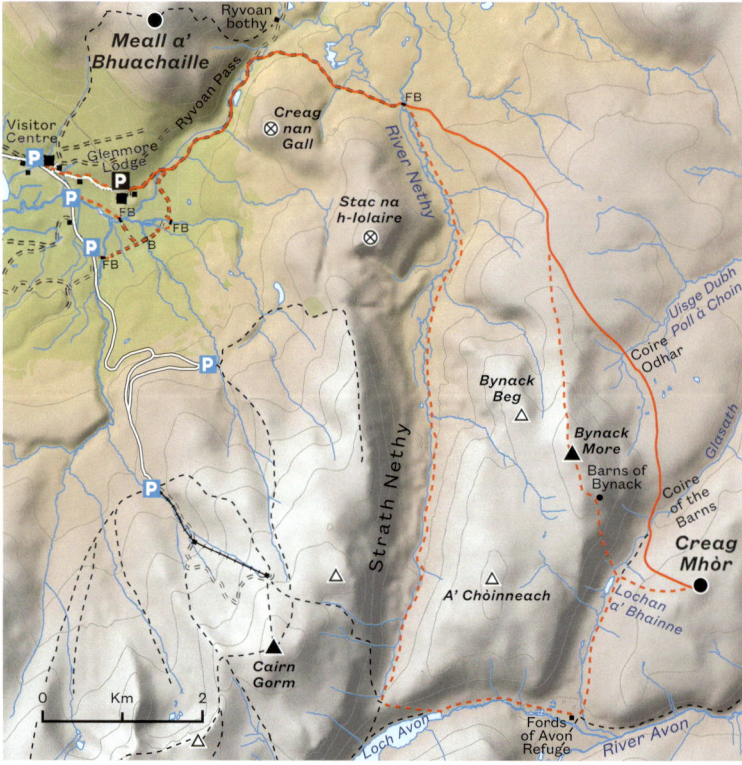

Creag Mhòr's summit, with Bynack More beyond (Rab Anderson)

A start can be made from the end of the narrow road at NH988095, just past the entrances to Glenmore Lodge, gained by leaving the Cairn Gorm access road just beyond the Glenmore Visitor Centre. Parking is limited, and particular care should be taken not to restrict access to the lodge or to the gated track beyond for rescue vehicles. If there are no spaces available, then one of the three car parks beside the main road in Glen More should be used. There is no real difference between the three, since they are all about 1.25km and 15min longer walking than parking at the road end by Glenmore Lodge. The three car parks are as follows:

(i) Glenmore Visitor Centre pay-and-display (NH976097). Gain the access road to Glenmore Lodge, then follow the path and cycleway on the left, which runs beside the road, to reach the track beyond the road end.

(ii) Allt Bàn pay-and-display (NH981094), on the left side of the Cairn Gorm access road immediately before the bridge over the Abhainn Ruigh-eunachan, 500m from the Visitor Centre; there are also roadside bays. Go upstream by the river for 600m, then 100m before a bridge, which can be crossed to join the next option, take a path on the left and follow this as it loops around Glenmore Lodge to join the track just beyond the end of the road.

(iii) Allt Mòr pay-and-display (NH983088), on the left side of the Cairn Gorm access road 1.25km beyond the Glenmore Visitor Centre, is probably the most pleasant option. From the south end of the car park, follow a path across a bridge over the Allt Mòr. Pass a track off left, cross a bridge over the Allt na Ciste, then go right at a fork on an anticlockwise loop to turn right and cross the Allt Bàn by a bridge to rejoin the track beyond a ford. Continue to meet the track from the lodge and turn right.

All starts having joined, follow the track through the narrow Ryvoan Pass beyond idyllic Lochan Uaine to where it forks left to Ryvoan bothy and Meall a' Bhuachaille. Keep right and swing round, overlooking Loch a' Gharbh-choire and the Abernethy Forest, to where the track ends at a bridge over the infant River Nethy,

4.5km from the end of the road at Glenmore Lodge and 5.75km from the other car parks. It can be biked to here to save about 1h on the day. Times and distances are given on foot from the Glenmore Lodge start.

Cross the bridge and follow a well-constructed path uphill, south-east then south, onto flatter ground on the broad north ridge of Bynack More.

The path forks at NJ039087 on featureless, wind-scoured terrain. Right is used for the ascent of Bynack More. Instead, go left on the path which ascends slightly before dropping off the ridge into Coire Odhar to cross the Uisge Dubh Poll a' Choin. The crossing is usually straightforward, but there are stepping stones a few metres upstream.

After a slight rise, where Creag Mhòr comes fully into view, drop into Corrie of the Barns and cross the Glasath burn – there are stepping stones if required. Continue for 300m, then break off left and ascend the pathless slope, steep and wet initially, to gain easier and drier, wind-scoured terrain leading to the potholed summit tor, which is the left-hand of two high-points (**12.25km; 740m; 4h**).

Returning the same way is simplest (24.5km; 930m; 7h 25min).

It is possible to make a circuit by descending south-west back to the Làirig an Laoigh path, then down to the Fords of Avon Refuge. From there, head upstream by the River Avon to gain Loch Avon, then ascend to The Saddle to descend the length of wild and rough Strath Nethy by a path down its right side to gain the bridge, then the approach track. However, although scenic this is 5km and about 1h 30min longer, with the path down the strath giving rough going.

Another option is to climb Bynack More by descending westwards to the path and cross above Lochan a' Bhainne. Make a northwards ascent across the steep slope to gain the splendid tors of the Barns of Bynack, then the Little Barns, and the summit; 2.75km, 360m, 1h 20min from Creag Mhòr. Descend the rocky north ridge to rejoin the approach route at the path fork on the broad, featureless ridge. This is only some 0.4km and 25min longer than the normal return.

Across Glen Feshie to Càrn Dearg Mòr (Rab Anderson)

Leathad an Taobhain; *912m; (C6); L43; NN822858; slope of the rafters*
Càrn Dearg Mòr; *857m; (C82); L35 & L43; NN823912; big red cairn*

These two rounded hills are reached via beautiful Upper Glen Feshie. Whilst Càrn Dearg Mòr itself doesn't require too much effort to get to, Leathad an Taobhain is one of the most remote of the Corbetts. However, a road and good tracks make the route to both hills straight-forward, especially if a bike is used, and the day is as much about the journey through Glen Feshie to reach the hills, as the ascents of the hills themselves.

Càrn Dearg Mòr overlooks Glen-feshie Lodge above the west side of the glen, opposite Mullach Clach a'

Bhlàir at the start of the Cairngorm plateau. Twin-topped Leathad an Taobhain lies 5.5km to the south in a vast tract of featureless hills and undulating plateaux between the headwaters of the River Feshie and the Minigaig Pass. The name Leathad an Taobhain has been applied by the OS to the west top, which is 10m lower than the true summit.

There are two starts from opposite sides of Glen Feshie; one for those on foot, and a slightly longer one for those using bikes. Distances and times are given on foot, but using a bike should save about 3h 30min to 4h on the day.

The on-foot approach starts from a car park on the left at NN850985, about 1km before the road up the east side of Glen Feshie ends at Achlean.

Walk towards the road end, but before reaching the estate cottage and outbuildings, go through a gate on the left; there is a sign on a boulder for All Routes and Glen Feshie. Continue on a track for 200m then, at a boulder signed for Upper Glen Feshie, go right along a path, and in a further 500m go through a gate and ford the Allt Fhearnagan; normally straightforward. In another

475m or so, take a path on the right and go down to the River Feshie, then cross what is called the Pony Bridge. Shortcut a loop in the track to gain the road on the west side of the glen.

The bike approach reaches the same point by following the road up the west side of Glen Feshie to reach a small parking area on the right at NN941999, just before a bridge over the Allt Fhearnasdail. This is where the map shows the public road ending. Bike along the track, which becomes a surfaced road, for 3.5km to join the route from Achlean.

Continue up the road past Carnachuin to where the road goes right to Glenfeshie Lodge. Take the track on the left and follow it to two solitary trees on the flat floor of the glen at Ruigh-fionntaig, where the track forks.

For those with bikes, this is perhaps the best place to leave them, although it is easy to continue for a further 1km or so to the end of a forestry plantation. Those more suited to biking, or with battery assisted power, could continue to a point just above the col between the hills, or even to its end on Meall an Uillt Chreagaich just in front of Leathad an Taobhain. However, the track is steep and gravelly in places.

Take the right fork and ascend beneath a forestry plantation into the steep-sided Slochd Mòr, and continue up past Lochan an t-Sluic to a fork just above the col between the hills.

Follow the left branch south on a gradual rise around a series of heathery corries to reach the end of the track on Meall an Uillt Chreagaich (847m). The rounded tops of Leathad an Taobhain lie ahead.

Descend a path south-south-west, to the ruin of a small stone-built bothy just above the col, then cross the col, which sits between one of the headwaters of the River Tromie and one of the headwaters of the River Feshie. A rough path leads on up the final 150m to the trig pillar on the summit of Leathad an Taobhain, where there is a grand view of the Cairngorm massif to the north-east (**15.25km; 730m; 4h 30min**).

The west top (902m) can be gained across the dip; an added 1.75km, 55m, 30min there and back.

Return to the junction just above the Slochd Mòr, then take the track on the left and cross the col to zigzag uphill. Leave the track after it has swung left to its highpoint, then follow an ATV track via its right branch, uphill to the saddle between Càrn Dearg and Càrn Dearg Mòr. Continue north-east up the rounded ridge to the flat top, where a cairn marks the summit (**22.75km; 1100m; 6h 50min**).

▶

Leathad an Taobhain from Meall an Uillt Chreagaich, with the lower west top, right (Rab Anderson)

The simplest return is back the same way, especially if a bike has been used (35km; 1150m; 9h 50min).

From the summit of Càrn Dearg Mòr, on foot it is slightly shorter by 1km and 10–15min, as well as scenic, to follow the ATV track north-north-east down the ridge above Glen Feshie to the trig point on Càrn Dearg Beag (694m). Continue north, then north-east on the ATV track, which eventually disappears, and keep on down to reach a track at a forestry plantation. Turn right along this to join the road just north of Carnachuin, and return as for the approach.

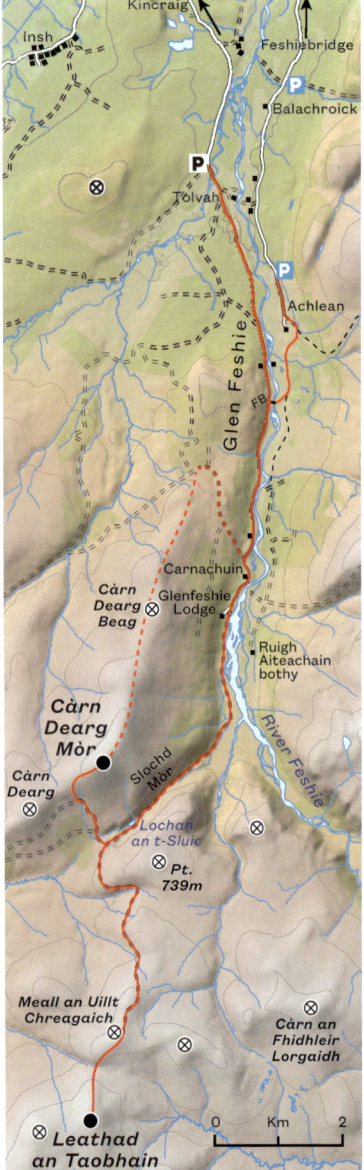

Meallach Mhòr; 769m; (C210); L35; NN776908; big hump

This reclusive hill lies well-off the beaten track between Glen Tromie and Glen Feshie, and getting to it from any direction involves a long approach. However, it lies above the historic droving route up Glen Tromie to the Gaick and Minigaig passes, and a track and road give an easy 11km approach by bike.

There is a small parking area on the left at NN791998 in the woods a short distance up the access road to Drumguish from the B970 between Kingussie and Feshiebridge. There is no parking on the B970 bend at the start of the track at Tromie Bridge.

Go up the road to Drumguish to a crossroads, then turn right down a track to gain the track along Glen Tromie. After 6.5km, at Lynaberack Lodge, this becomes a surfaced road, which runs beyond Meallach Mhòr to the dam on Loch an t-Seilich, then continues as a track.

Shortly after rounding Meallach Bheag, where the hill comes into sight, and 280m beyond unoccupied Bhran Cottage, there is a bay on the left beside a small group of trees. This is the best place to leave bikes (10.75km; 120m; about 1h by bike), (2h 35min on foot).

Times are now given on foot, from and back to this point.

A vague ATV track leaves the bay to reach a clearer ATV track that can be seen running up the side of Meallach Bheag, marked on the OS 1:50k map as a path. Whilst this is probably the best ascent route, giving a downhill through the deep heather at the end, the initial flat section can be very wet, and is perhaps best left until the end.

So, walk along the track for 330m to the other side of the Allt an Tulaich, then go up left through the heather to gain the north end of a small man-made lochan. A vague ATV track can be seen on the slope beyond. Plough through heather to gain this, and follow it parallel to the burn, then up right across the slope heading for a

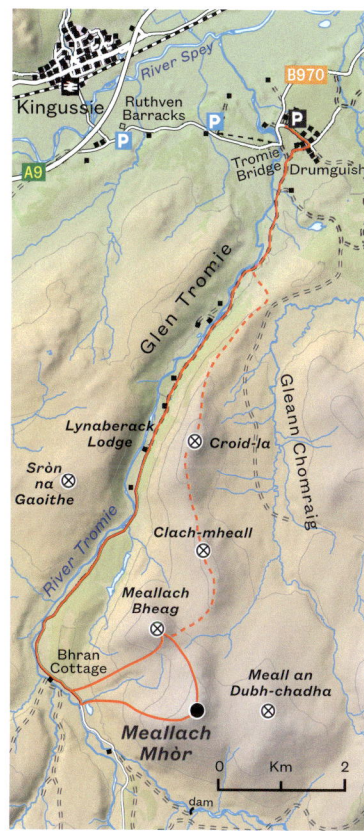

Meallach Mhòr from Meallach Bheag, with Loch an t-Seilich and the Gaick pass beyond (Rab Anderson)

large cairn. The ATV track fades and the heather becomes deeper.

Continue through heather beyond the cairn to gain the crest, then climb steeply through a small, broken band of rock to reach easier ground, where a path leads to the bouldery summit (**3km; 395m; 1h 20min**).

To the east, over the Corbett Càrn Dearg Mòr, is the main Cairngorm massif with Angel's Peak and Cairn Toul prominent, whilst to the south-east are the twin bumps of Leathad an Taobhain. To the south, there is a fine view up the Gaick trench, and to the south-west is the Munro Meall Chuaich.

Follow a path down to the north to the col, cross the ATV track, then climb to the top of Meallach Bheag. Return to the col, then follow the track back to the glen. On the flat ground at the bottom, walk over the fallen gate, then follow the now vague ATV track left across boggy ground to the small group of trees (**6.5km; 475m; 2h 30min**).

Return to Drumguish (**28km; 635m; 5h 20min** with a bike), (**7h 30min** on foot).

If on foot, rather than return along the road and track, from the col with Meallach Bheag, descend the ATV track to the north-east, then climb over Clach-mheall (626m) and continue to Croidh-la (640m). Go northwards down the long ridge to a col, then descend across the slope and drop to the track used in the approac; there is a path (**24.25km; 655m; 6h 45min**).

Meallach Mhòr from Glen Tromie (Rab Anderson)

North up Glen Roy
to Beinn Iaruinn
(Rab Anderson)

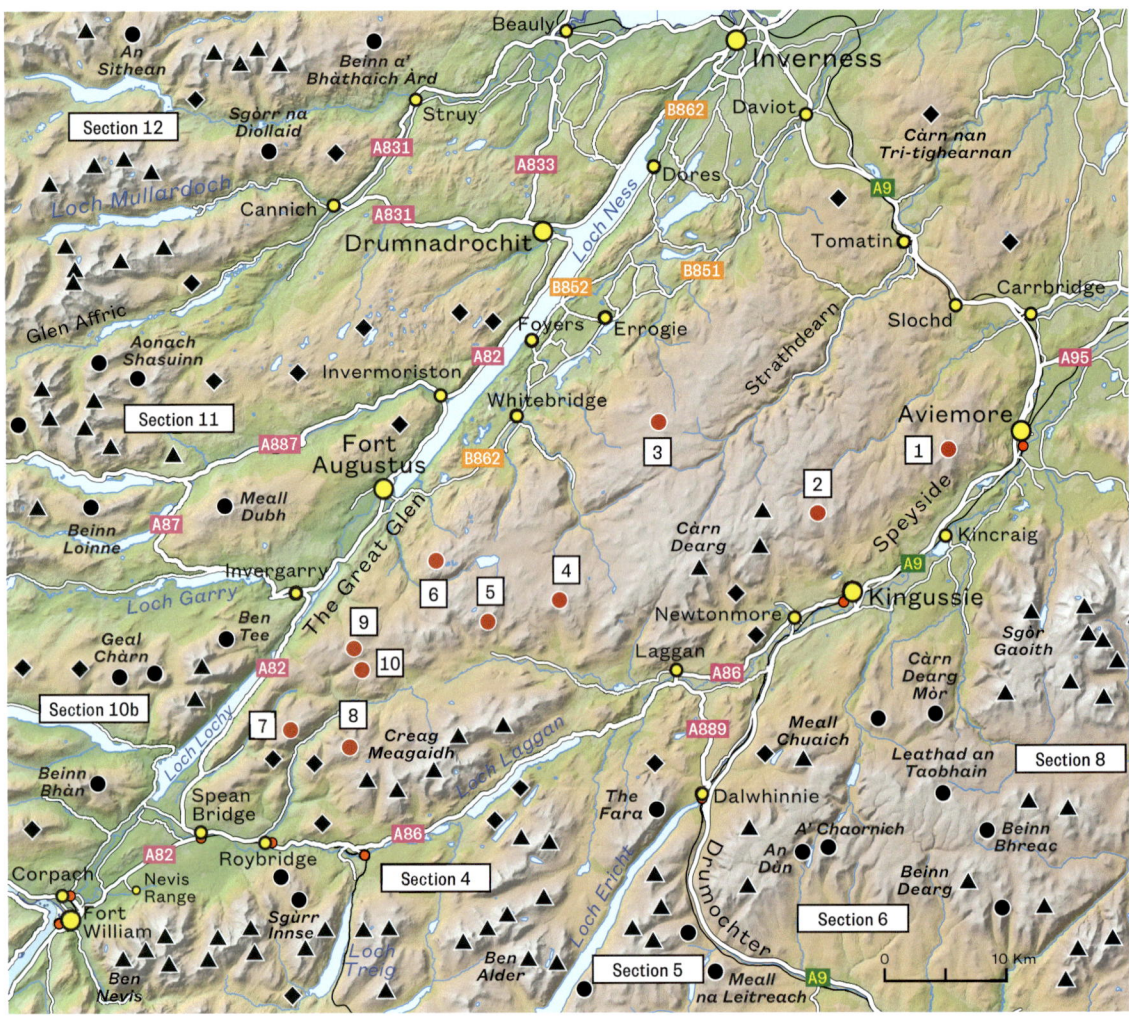

SECTION 9

Geal-chàrn Mòr across the Spey Valley from Ord Bàn (Rab Anderson)

Geal-chàrn Mòr; 824m; (C120); L35; NH836123; big white hill

Sitting above Loch Alvie and the A9 to the south of Aviemore, Geal-chàrn Mòr forms part of the extensive Monadh Liath range, which rises above the Spey Valley and extends north-westwards to Loch Ness and the Great Glen. Located towards the north-eastern end of the leading edge of the Monadh Liath, a chain of hills stretches west from the summit of Geal-chàrn Mòr across to the Corbett Càrn an Fhreiceadain above Kingussie, then past four Munros to three Corbetts, Meall na h-Aisre, Gairbheinn and Càrn a' Chuilinn.

Geal-chàrn Mòr's position means that from its slopes there are fine views across the Spey Valley to the northern Cairngorm massif.

The start is conveniently close to the A9, reached by turning off north to Lynwilg and the Kinrara Distillery, almost opposite the southern turn-off to Aviemore. There is parking on the right by the bridge across the Allt-na-Criche. There is also space 750m or so further up the narrow road where the short right fork ends at a gate.

From the bridge, walk along the road, signed as the right of way to Carrbridge via the Burma Road; apparently so called due to its construction in the 1940s by prisoners of war. Take the right fork and go through a gate, then ascend a track up wooded An Gleannan above the burn, climbing gradually for 2km to gain the open hillside. Continue up the track until it reaches its highpoint at a cairn on the watershed.

Leave the track here, then take the right-hand of two paths and climb south-west up a broad ridge, which gives pleasant walking, crossing a stile beside a gate in a fence to reach the trig point on the summit of Geal-chàrn Mòr (**6km; 600m; 2h 20min**).

Return to the track, then take the path that cuts back right and follow it southwards down the hillside below Creag Ghleannain, which is worth walking out to for the view across Loch Alvie and the Spey Valley; an added 10–15min or so.

Lower down, descend by the burn, the Caochan Ruadh, and at the bottom go through a gate to cross a field, then go through another gate onto a track. Follow this track past Ballinluig, turning right along a section of road that runs parallel to the A9.

Fork left through a gate and loop around a wooded hillock, then continue along the track back to Lynwilg (**12.75km; 600m; 4h 5min**).

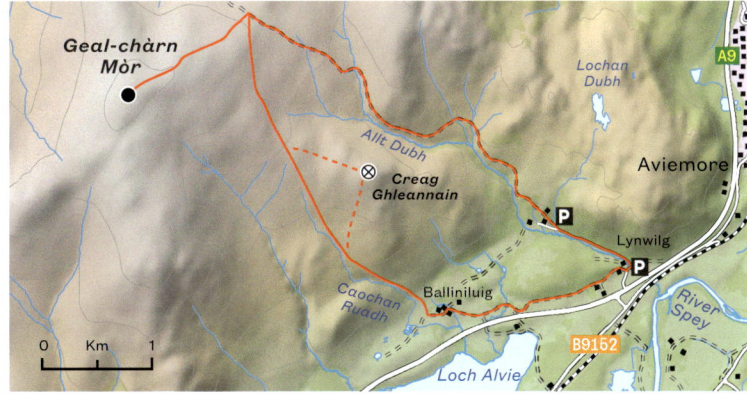

Càrn an Fhreiceadain; 878m; (C55); L35; NH725071; watcher's (lookout) cairn

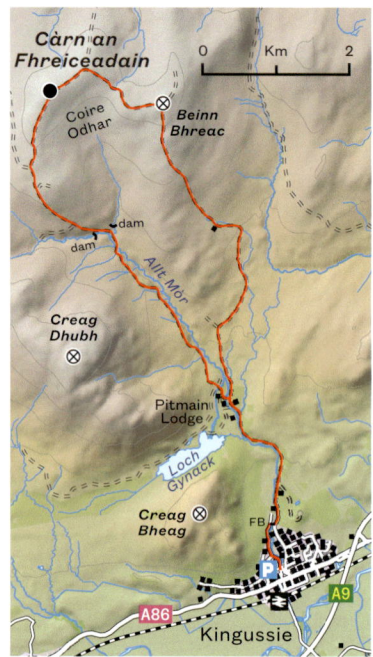

Overlooking the Spey Valley, and set back above Kingussie, Càrn an Fhreiceadain is one of the chain of rounded hills that forms the southern edge of the Monadh Liath Mountains

Turn off the A9 to Kingussie, then towards the west end of the village, at the Duke of Gordon hotel, take the turn-off signed to the golf course and parking. This is Gynack Road, where the Ardvonie Car Park is the second turn on the left, which is behind the hotel car park. The golf course car park further up the road is private, although it may be possible to park on the verge just before the entrance to this.

From the village car park, walk up the road for 800m then, just before the entrance to the golf course car park, turn off right and cross the bridge over the Gynack Burn to gain the road on the other side. Turn left along this road, then follow it through pleasant woodland and the golf course to where it crosses a bridge to Pitmain Lodge. Continue ahead on a track to reach the bridge just beyond.

Cross the bridge, over what is now the Allt Mòr, and follow the improved hydro track through the trees and up the hillside beyond, above and to the west of the Allt Mòr. The track passes around a small wooded knoll then,

crosses three bridges: the first over a small burn, the second over the Allt Mòr and third over the burn issuing from Càrn an Fhreiceadain's southern corrie, Coire Odhar. Passing dams on the right then the left, follow the track uphill, past a fork off left, then one to the right on Meall Unaig.

At the next fork, keep right on the track, which climbs the broad ridge, to pass a tall cairn just below the top. The summit of Càrn an Fhreiceadain is marked by a trig point and a low wind shelter cairn, with a stone shelter by a rock outcrop to the north (**8.75km; 685m; 3h**).

Continue on the track, which crosses a slight dip, to gain the north-east top, then turn south-east to descend across another dip and rise slightly onto Beinn Bhreac (843m).

Turn south here and follow the main track downhill, passing the Green Hut, a shooting bothy, and continue downhill to rejoin the upwards route in the woodland above Pitmain Lodge. Return to the start as for the approach (**17.75km; 735m; 5h 15min**).

Over the A9 and Kingussie to Càrn an Fhreiceadain (Rab Anderson)

Càrn na Saobhaidhe from Corriegarth Wind Farm to the west (Rab Anderson)

Càrn na Saobhaidhe; *811m; (C138); L35; NH600145; cairn of the den (fox lair)*

The northernmost Corbett in the Monadh Liath range, Càrn na Saobhaidhe forms part of a large and featureless plateau, which is now the domain of the wind turbine. Access is either from Strath Dearn, a splendid glen that bites deep into the Monadh Liath, and down which the River Findhorn flows on its way to the Moray Firth and the North Sea, or from Stratherrick, which runs parallel to Loch Ness to the north-west.

Both access points have their merits, in that they allow parts of Scotland to be visited, which the hill-walker would not routinely see. Whilst not a particularly interesting hill in itself, Càrn na Saobhaidhe has an interesting fact in that it has the greatest surface area of all Corbetts in the ground it occupies, encircled by the 150m contour. It is also unusually remote from any centre of population.

For the approach via Strath Dearn, leave the A9 just after Slochd summit if travelling north, or before Tomatin if travelling south, and follow the old A9 road to Findhorn Bridge. From there, the public road runs up Strath Dearn for some 9 miles (15km) to where it ends at a car park on the left side of the road, 250m before Coignafearn Old Lodge.

Follow the estate track for 4.5km to the newer Coignafearn Lodge, then

on for another 3.25km to the cottage of Dalbeg. It is an easy bike ride to here and bikes are probably best left at the old walls just beyond; (**7.75km; 100m; 1h 50min** on foot), (about **1h** by bike). Times are given on foot from the start, and the use of a bike should save about 2h 10min on the day.

Continue on the track, which swings west to climb beside the Allt Creagach for a further 2.5km to where the burn forks and the track heads away north. Leave the track and cross the bridge over the right fork to follow a rougher track beside what is now the Allt Odhar, heading towards Càrn na Saobhaidhe's flat top, which can be seen ahead.

When the track ends, continue on a vague path beside the burn, where the grassy sides give easier going through the haggy ground. When the burn forks, follow the right fork, then go up the final rise to gain the expansive flat summit. The cairn by the end of the track from Dunmaglass to the north has been surveyed as being lower than a point 160m to the southwest and 80m north-north-east of a wind farm mast (**14.5km; 440m; 4h**).

Return the same way (**29km; 460m; 7h 15min**).

There are two approaches from the north side.

The first leaves the B851 south of

Loch Ruthven, and west of the head of Strath Nairn, where there is limited parking at NH607245 by the bins at the Ruthven and Abersky road junction, just to the east of the entrance to Dunmaglass Lodge. There is also space on the verge to the east, on the east side of the bridge over the River Farigaig.

The route can be biked all the way, but it's by no means easy, and most may decide to give up at some point on the ascent. Times are only given on foot, but despite the uphill on the approach, there is still a good bit of flat, so bike times will be considerably quicker, especially on the return.

Walk west along the road and take the estate road to Dunmaglass Lodge, passing through a gateway by the gatehouse to where the wider wind farm access track joins from the left. Continue along this and fork right past the cottages at Achnaloddan, then keep left alongside the Allt Glac an Tùir, signed as the path to Loch Conagleann and Easter Aberchalder.

Pass beneath Dunmaglass Lodge, which is up on the right, and cross the burn by either of two bridges, then continue uphill by the Allt Uisg an t-Sìdhein on the main track. Pass a fork off left up Glac nan Gamha and swing right to rejoin the burn, passing ▶

The final approach up the Allt Odhar from the east (Rab Anderson)

a pipe bridge, then a dam, to reach a fork where the main track climbs up left to the Dunmaglass Wind Farm. Take the right fork, which drops back to the burn again, and continue alongside this for a way.

Ignore the first track on the right, which leads to a ford, then one on the left, and take the next track right to cross the burn by a bridge. Follow the track up a side valley away from the main burn to a junction, and go left to cross the watershed, past a track off

left, to reach another junction at the Aberchalder Burn.

Turn left, then follow the track by the burn, fording the burn and one of its tributaries four times. Ignore a fork off right, ford the burn again, and continue uphill on the track to a shooting bothy; the Diamond Jubilee Hut. Cross the burn again, then follow the rougher track, which has been dug into the peat, more steeply uphill. Pass a branch off left, and continue to the end of the track and a cairn on

the flat top of Càrn na Saobhaidhe. The highest point has been surveyed to lie 160m to the south-west, and 80m north-north-east of a wind farm mast on the far side (**13.5km; 650m; 4h**).

Return the same way (**27km; 720m; 6h 20min**).

The other approach from the north-west starts from the end of the road just before Garthbeg at the south end of Loch Mhòr, accessed from the B862. There is ample parking at NH514169 by the banking, just beyond the start of the access track to the Corriegarth Wind Farm.

This route utilises the track through the wind farm, which leads to within 100m of the summit. The track can be biked, and with a push over the flat top, can be linked to the route from Dunmaglass for a fine circuit, returning to Garthbeg via Conagleann and the south-east side of Loch Mhòr. Bike times are not given, but they will be quicker on the ascent where there are long stretches at a reasonable angle, and much quicker on the descent where it is all downhill.

Go up the track and cross the bridge over the River E to Garthbeg, then turn right along the track on the far side of the river. This climbs uphill to join the wind farm access track, which has made a big loop to get to this point. Continue up the track

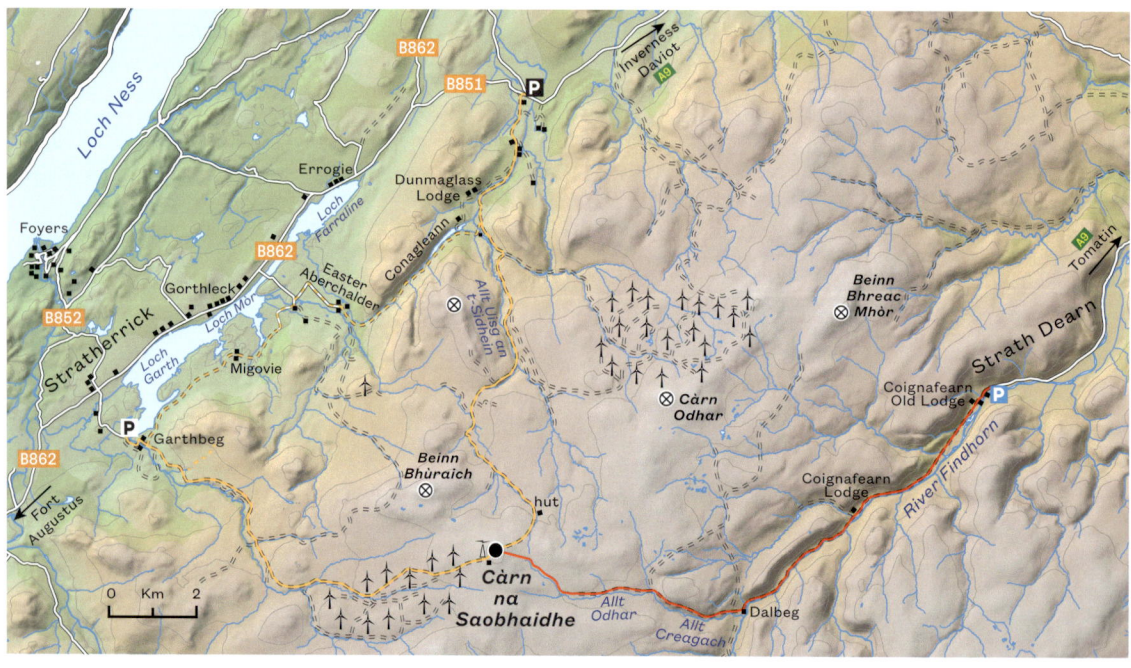

above the river, keeping to the main track past tracks off left and right, to swing round the side of another hill called Càrn na Saobhaidhe (602m), passing beneath a power station.

Keep on up to the wind turbines to reach a junction and go left. Just before the last turbine, take a track on the left and follow it past a mast to its end. The highest point has been surveyed as being 80m to the north-north-east of the mast, and 160m to the south-west of the cairn at the end of the track coming up from Dunmaglass (**11.25km; 630m; 3h 30min**).

Return the same way (22.5km; 640m; 6h).

For anyone who has biked this far, a satisfying full day can be had by descending the track to the north-

east, as used by the previous route. Pass the Diamond Jubilee Hut and go down the Aberchalder burn. At a fork, at the time of writing, the track down the burn doesn't link with the one coming up from Wester Aberchalder past a wind turbine to a dam. So, continue on the track used by the previous route, over the col and down to the Allt Uisg an t-Sìdhein, to reach the foot of the glen out in front of Dunmaglass Lodge.

Don't cross the bridge over the Allt Uisg an t-Sìdhein, but cut back sharp left on a track leading to a hydro building. In 2023 there was no bridge, so ford the Allt Uisg an t-Sìdhein (normally not a problem), to reach the building, then follow the track to Loch Conaglean. If the

crossing is a problem, go over the bridge on the main track and follow a path to cross a bridge over the outflow from the loch to gain the track.

Continue through Conaglean to Easter Aberchalder and follow a surfaced road down then left to a junction. Go left to the farm at Wester Aberchalder then right along a track to Migovie Cottage. Pass between the buildings and follow a rough track, shown on the map as a path, to rejoin the approach track to the east of Garthbeg and return over the bridge.

From the junction before Wester Aberchalder, although slightly longer, it would be easier, and probably quicker, to follow the road system back to the start, but perhaps not as much fun!

> *Meall na h-Aisre; 862m; (C76); L35; NH515000; hill of the defile*

Located in the Sherramore Forest area of the Monadh Liath, Meall na h-Aisre sits between the Corbett Gairbeinn to the west and the Munro Geal Chàrn to the east. It is a rela-

tively featureless hill, which on a dry day in summer gives a pleasant ascent through terrain covered in wild flowers.

The ascent is made from near the

end of the road leading to the Corrieyairack Pass; an ancient route through the hills linking Speyside with the Great Glen.

▶

Meall na h-Aisre and Leathad Gaothach from the Fèith Talagain near the start (Rab Anderson)

From Laggan on the A86, take the narrow road west past Spey Dam Reservoir to a parking area at Garva Bridge. This is a fine bridge across the River Spey, built in 1732 by General Wade and originally called St George's Bridge. One of the routes to the Munro Geal Chàrn also starts here.

Cross the bridge, then go north on a track and go through a gate onto the main access track to the electricity substation to the west. Cross this track, not the bridge, and pass beneath the Beauly to Denny overhead power line, then follow a rough track up the west side of the river for 300m or so to where the river forks. A bridge across the left fork, the Allt Coire Iain Oig, can be seen ahead. There are two options:

(i) If the river can be crossed dry just above the fork, then do so and follow an ATV track on the other side, which after 500m or so ascends gently uphill beside a small burn running down the hillside. When the burn swings right, continue ahead on the track to cross the second small burn running down the hillside, and follow the track up its left side.

(ii) Continue on the rough track to the bridge and cross. Follow the grassy track on the other side for 200m, then break off right and climb a slight spur of raised grassy ground, which leads towards the right-hand burn on the hillside, where the grassy ATV track is joined and followed as for option (i) above.

Further up the hillside, the track swings left, then carries on to meet a fence just below the crest. Go through an open gate and continue on the track, which after a short climb crosses a flat section, then climbs onto the top of Leathad Gaothach (844m).

With the summit now in sight, drop down the other side and follow the

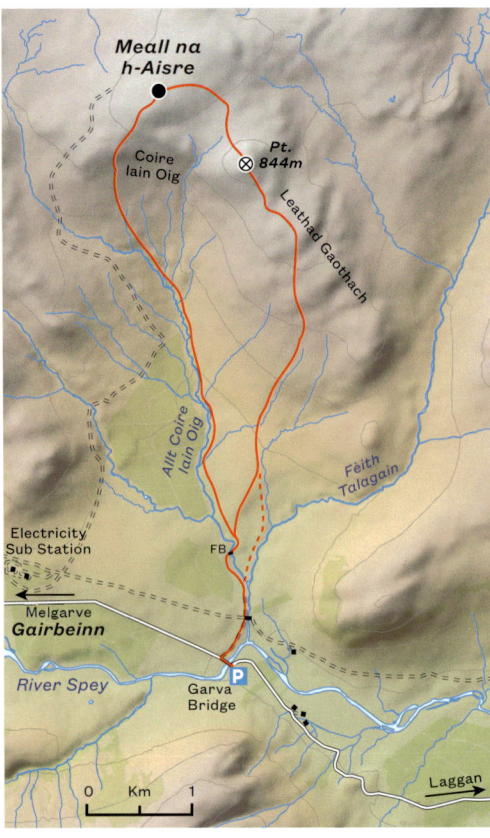

track, which becomes less distinct, across the boggy col above Coire Gorm. Continue up the other side to the trig pillar on the flat top of Meall na h-Aisre (**7km; 620m; 2h 35min**).

In the bowl to the north are the 66 turbines of the Stronelairg Wind Farm. Beyond these to the north-east is Càrn na Saobhaidhe with its wind farm, whilst westwards is Gairbeinn, then Càrn a Chuillin above the Glendoe Hydro Scheme reservoir.

The simplest return, especially if the ground is wet, is back the same way (**14km; 675m; 4h 30min**).

However, if the ground is relatively dry, follow the vague track downhill to the south-west towards a small knoll for about 400m, then go easily south down the grassy slope into Coire Iain Oig. Follow the left side of the Allt Coire Iain Oig to meet a fence level with the top edge of the forestry on the opposite side. Join a rough track and follow this through a gap in the fence, then continue alongside the burn to reach the bridge across the Allt Coire Iain Oig and return to the start (**13.5km; 630m; 4h 20min**).

> *Gairbeinn; 896m; (C30); L34; NN460985; rough hill*

Although at the time of writing the main Ordnance Survey maps give Gairbeinn and Corrieyairack Hill to its north-west the same height, information in 1997 showed Gairbeinn to be the higher hill. Since the drop between them was less than 500 feet (152.4m), Gairbeinn was confirmed as the Corbett. More recent information on the Database of British and Irish Hills shows Corrieyairack Hill to be 892m high, with a summit located 200m to the south-east of that shown on OS maps.

Although Gairbeinn is the prime objective for hill baggers, and can be climbed quickly by an up-and-down the same way route, it is better to extend the route to Corrieyairack Hill, with a return to the head of the Corriyairack Pass and down this historic route through the pass.

Linking Speyside with Fort Augustus in the Great Glen, the Corriyairack was used by drovers and travellers. It was made into a military road by General Wade's soldiers in 1731, and used by Bonnie Prince Charlie and his Jacobite army when they marched south in the 1745 rebellion. More recently it has been made into the main route bringing electricity from the north to the south with the upgrading of the Beauly to Denny overhead power line.

Whilst maps show the public road from Laggan as ending at Garva Bridge, which is where Meall na h-Aisre is climbed from, a surfaced road can be driven for a further 3.5 miles (5.75km) to a parking area at NN468959 before Melgarve.

Walk along the continuation track for 500m to one of General Wade's bridges and Melgarve bothy, then continue for a further 300m to the Caochan Bàn; the burn running down from Gairbeinn. Ascend the hillside up the left side of this burn, passing beneath the power lines, to gain the col between Meall Garbh Beag and Gairbeinn. Continue up the steepening slope to reach a rocky rib, which is followed up the narrowing ridge to the summit (**3.75km; 560m; 1h 45min**).

Go down the ridge to the north for a distance of almost 200m, to the fence posts of an old fenceline, then descend the slope to the north-west beside the posts to reach a col. Ascend the slope up the other side onto Càrn an Aonaich Odhair (833m), then follow the fence posts south-west along the crest to cross the dip and climb to Geal Chàrn (876m).

Still following the fence posts, descend north-west again to cross two narrow channels and the minor rise between, before climbing onto the broad crest of Corrieyairack Hill. Swing west along this to reach the twin rises at the far end. The summit has more recently been confirmed as the first rise at NN429995, at a height of 892m (**7.75km; 810m; 3h 15min**).

Follow ATV tracks down southwards to gain the track at the head of the Corrieyairack Pass. Descend south-east alongside the pylon line, past the General's Well, to the start of the zigzags. These are one of the defining features of the old military road, where 12 hairpin bends were required for the steep climb out of Corrie Yairack

Together with the rest of the Corrieyairack route, the zigzags form a scheduled ancient monument in the

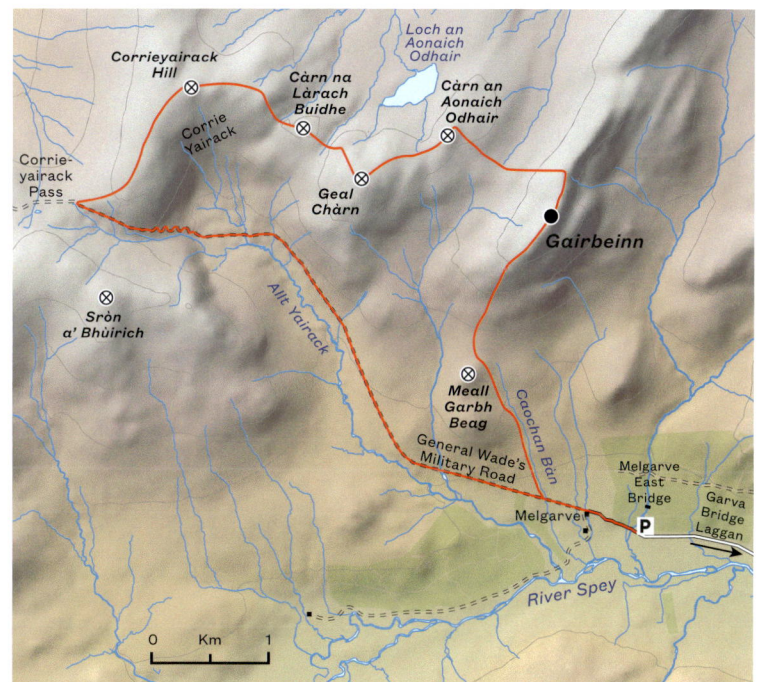

care of Historic Scotland, and users are asked not to cut the corners or damage the route and its structures in any way. The original surface has been spoiled by the passage of vehicles, now prohibited. On reaching the floor of Corrie Yairack, continue

down the track above the Allt Yairack back to Melgarve and the start (**15.75km; 820m; 5h 15min**).

Across the burn on the other side of the trees north of the parking is the fine Melgarve East Bridge, built in 1750 and restored in 1984.

Gairbeinn from Càrn an Aonaich Odhair, with Melgarve below and Càrn Liath beyond (Rab Anderson)

Càrn a' Chuilinn's summit, with Loch Garry and Ben Tee to the left (Rab Anderson)

Càrn a' Chuilinn; *817m; (C129); L34; NH416034; cairn of holly*

Whilst not having the mountainous backdrop to rival the Cruachan dam and hydro-scheme, Càrn a' Chuilinn contains a bigger, better and more modern hydro scheme in the form of the 100-megawatt-capacity Glen Doe Hydroelectric Scheme, built at a cost of £145 million.

Rising above the southern side of the Great Glen Fault above Fort Augustus on Loch Ness, Càrn a' Chuilinn sits between Glen Tarff and Glen Doe. A natural bowl has been formed in the western part of the Monadh Liath here, to the east of Càrn a' Chuilinn and north of Gairbeinn and Meall na h-Aisre. Sited within the bowl is a 1km-long dam and reservoir impounding the headwaters of the River Tarff. Water from the reservoir drops 600m down an 8km-long tunnel through the side of Càrn a' Chuilinn and down Glen Doe to a power station 250m underground, which in turn discharges into Loch Ness. A water-to-wire efficiency of nearly 90%, makes this the most efficient hydro scheme in the UK.

The Monadh Liath has become the location for numerous wind farms,

and also located within the bowl are the 66 turbines of the Stronelairg Wind Farm; more are planned.

The access track to the dam and wind farm leaves the B862 to run up Glen Doe, and is used for part of its

length to reach Càrn a' Chuilinn.

There is nowhere to park properly at the start of the access track, so start from a long layby at NH395088, on the south side of the B862, a short distance up the hill above Fort

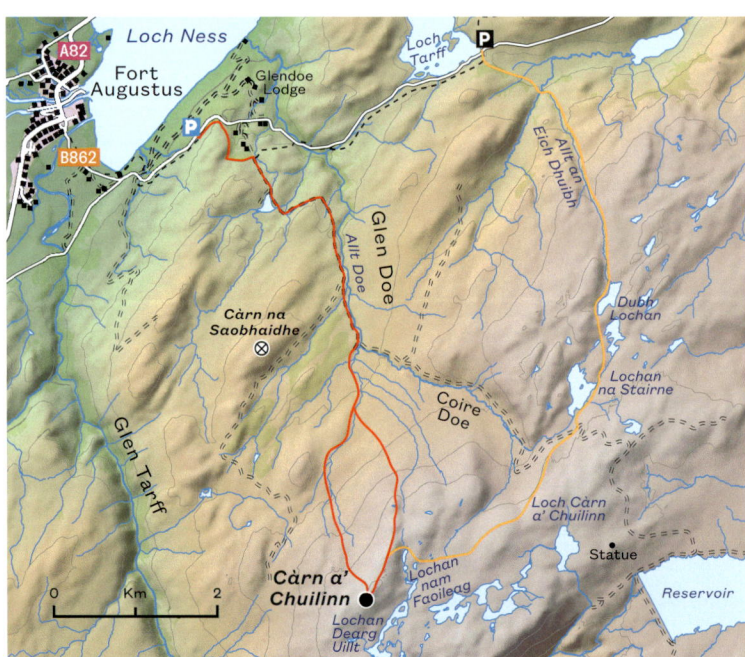

Augustus.

Go through the gate at the lower end of the layby to gain the South Loch Ness Trail path and cycleway, then follow this uphill and around a forestry plantation for 1.25km to where it crosses the access track to the dam.

Follow this wide track for just over 3km to where it crosses the Allt Doe. Break off right here and follow a short section of track, then a rough path up the right side of the tributary which drains the shallow north-east corrie beneath Càrn a' Chuilinn's summit. Initially the ground is easy-angled as it passes Càrn Doire Chaorach, but beyond this the slope steepens and the path fades out. Keep on up beside the burn to ascend the slope above, and emerge onto the crest just below the large summit cairn (**8.25km; 680m; 2h 45min**).

To return, go down the northern ridge for a way, then the slope beyond to regain the burn and return as for the approach (16.25km; 700m; 5h 15min).

An ascent can be made from a little further east along the B862, at the east end of Loch Tarf, where there is limited parking at NH431098.

Cross the road, then the South Loch Ness Trail, and follow an ATV track and stalkers' path which crosses the Allt Gleann nan Eun by ford, or a bridge downstream, then continues up the Allt an Eich Dhuibh to an unnamed lochan. Go around the left side of the lochan to reach Dubh Lochan, then Lochan na Stairne, and follow the outlet to gain the access track to the dam and wind farm.

Follow the track downhill to the right to a sharp bend, then ascend a rough track alongside the burn to where the track swings left on flat ground at the head of Coire an t-Seilich. Continue south-west to pass between the north end of Lochan Dearg Uillt and some other small lochans, then climb to the summit of Càrn a' Chuilinn (**9km; 630m; 3h**).

Either return the same way (18km; 720m; 5h 30min), or descend as for the primary route to gain the South Loch Ness Trail path and cycleway, then follow this eastwards back to the start (19.5km; 810m; 6h).

> *Beinn Iaruinn; 805m; (C153); L34; NN297900; iron hill*

This is one of four Corbetts and two Grahams located in Glen Roy, a glen internationally renowned for its geological landforms associated with glaciation; in particular, those known as the Parallel Roads. These roads are in fact three sets of parallel lines at the 260m, 325m and 350m contours, which have been scored into the steep hillsides around the glen. They are the old shorelines formed by the various levels of the loch created by dams of ice across the mouth of the glen during the Ice Age.

Leave the A86 at Roybridge in Glen Spean and follow a narrow, twisting road up the lower part of the glen through lovely wood and farmland to emerge into the upper glen at a car park and viewpoint. Beinn Iaruinn lies ahead, with Lèana Mhòr (West), a Graham, to its left, and the Parallel Roads prominent.

Continue up the glen to where the road drops down and loops across the bridge over the burn flowing from between Lèana Mhòr and Beinn Iaruinn. There is space to park on the grass on the right. The best route is the one that includes both Lèana Mhòr (684m) and Beinn Iaruinn, climbing Lèana Mhòr first via the rounded ridge to the left of narrow Coire an t-Seilich.

Walk across the bridge and go up the side of the burn to climb the steep bank on the left. Continue alongside the deer fence, then head up the hillside to climb the ridge, crossing all three Parallel Roads. At the top, go over a slight rise, then the dip beyond, and curve up north to gain the top of Lèana Mhòr (**2km; 500m; 1h 15min**).

Head north down a broad ridge to the col with Beinn Iaruinn, then climb the long, but steady whaleback of a slope, and make the final short walk around the rim of steep-sided Coire nan Eun to gain the summit cairn (**4.75km; 800m; 2h 30min**).

It is a fine viewpoint, in particular across the Great Glen to the north-west to the Loch Lochy Munros, Meall na Teanga and Sròn a Choire Ghairbh, with the distinctive, pointed Corbett, Ben Tee, to their north.

Return to the col, then follow a deer track down and across Lèana Mhòr before dropping back towards the start and crossing the burn draining ▶

Beinn Iaruinn from Lèana Mhòr to the south (Rab Anderson)

Beinn Iaruinn from its north-east ridge, with Aonach Beag, Aonach Mòr and Ben Nevis beyond (Rab Anderson)

Coire an t-Seilich (**8.5km; 810m; 3h 45min**).

Another good route starts from a small parking area on the right, opposite a communication aerial, at the end of the public road a short distance before Brae Roy Lodge.

Cross the road and follow an ATV track across flat ground, then up through a break in a brief steepening. Head across right to better ground up a slight ridge to the left of the burn, which the ATV track joins further up. At the top, swing left up a steepening to gain easy-angled ground, and follow this west-south-west to gain a rocky rib, which leads to a cairn at the start of the north-east top's rocky crest.

Continue across a slight dip, past a scattering of small lochans, to reach Pt.779m, then drop down across another dip and make the short ascent to the top of Beinn Iaruinn (**5km; 620m; 2h 10min**).

Return the same way (**10km; 655m; 3h 40min**).

A short, but steep route starts from the bridge over the burn issuing from Coire nan Eun at NN308891 where

there is room to park off the road.

Ascend the ridge up the left side of the corrie, and follow the rim round to the top (**2.25km; 605m; 1h 30min**).

Either return the same way (**4.5km; 615m; 2h 25min**), which is probably the easiest, or drop east to the dip, then descend the steep east side of Coire nan Eun past scree patches (**4km; 605m; 3h 20min**).

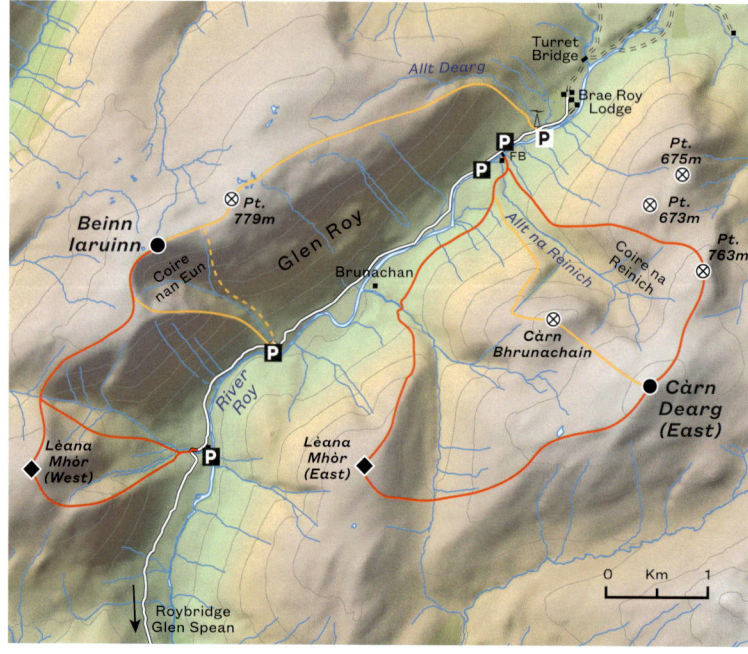

Càrn Dearg (East of Glen Roy); 834m; (C113); L34; NN345887; red cairn

Glen Roy has three hills named Càrn Dearg. This is the southern-most one, which rises above the east side of the glen opposite Beinn Iaruinn. One of its main features is the narrow corrie beneath its summit, Coire na Reinich, which bites deep into the main mass of the hill and has a fine, dissected alluvial fan at its foot.

Similar to Beinn Iaruinn, the more satisfying route is the one that includes the neighbouring Lèana Mhòr (East), a Graham. This lies to the west of Càrn Dearg and sits directly across the glen from Lèana Mhòr (West).

Start from the bridge over the River Roy at NN303909 beneath Coire na Reinich. There is space to park on the grass here, and there is also a pull-off 200m back down the road.

Climbing Lèana Mhòr first, cross the bridge and go past a small hut to ford the Allt Reinich issuing from Coire na Reinich, then climb the steep slope onto the alluvial fan terrace. Cross this diagonally south and ascend slightly to gain the lower Parallel Road on the 260m contour and follow this south-west for just over 1km until above the Allt Brunachain.

Quern-stones were quarried at Brunachan at one time, and anyone taking a lower line might come across half-made and rejected stones on the hillside behind the derelict buildings.

Drop down to the right to cross the Allt Brunachain below the trees, then climb onto the alluvial fan terrace on the other side. Go through a gate in the deer fence at NN320894, on an ATV track coming up from below, then follow this track onto the crest of the ridge. When the track leaves the crest to follow the fence, continue up the fine crest to an extensive plateau, where a small pile of stones marks the summit of Lèana Mhòr (**4km; 460m; 1h 35min**).

Head south-east off the summit, then descend steeply east to the floor of the glen. Cross a fence, then a burn, to ascend either side of a prominent straight gully and continue at a gentler angle. Pass to the right of a small lochan next to Pt.745m, and in a further 1km reach the summit of Càrn Dearg, where there are unusual views of the north side of Creag Meagaidh (**7.5km; 790m; 3h**).

Descend easily to the north-east to a saddle, then either gain the North Top (Pt.763m), or avoid it by slanting down to another dip at about 645m. From there, trend leftwards, main-taining height for another 500m, then descend the hillside on the north side of the Allt na Reinich, directly to the bridge (**11km; 820m; 4h 10min**).

A shorter route can be had by crossing the Allt Reinich to climb onto the alluvial fan and ascend the slope ahead, swinging round above a gully to cross Càrn Bhrunachain and gain Càrn Dearg (**3.25km; 660m; 1h 50min**).

Descend as for the principal route, north-east, then around the far side of Coire na Reinich (**6km; 690m; 3h**).

Map on opposite page

Across Glen Roy from Beinn Iaruinn's north-east ridge to Càrn Dearg with its dissected alluvial fan (Rab Anderson)

Càrn Dearg (North) and Càrn Dearg (South) from Beinn Iaruinn's north-east ridge (Rab Anderson)

Càrn Dearg (North of Gleann Eachach); *817m; (C130); L34; NN350966; red cairn*
Càrn Dearg (South of Gleann Eachach); *768m; (C211); L34; NN357948; red cairn*

These two hills are situated either side of Gleann Eachach, an extension of Glen Turret, which is itself an offshoot of Glen Roy beyond the road end at the head of the glen.

Separated by a col at 572m, the hills are easily combined.

Start from the end of the public road up Glen Roy, where there is a small parking area on the right, opposite a communication aerial, and before the trees at Brae Roy Lodge.

Cross the cattle grid and follow the road past the lodge and its outbuild-

ings. Càrn Dearg (south) can be seen ahead over another of the glen's renowned glacial features, the Turret Fan, an extensive sand and gravel deposit and terrace at the junction of Glen Turret with Glen Roy.

Cross the arched Turret Bridge over the river Turret and take the track on the left, which climbs onto the fan, then along it for way, before dropping off across flat ground to reach some old walls and sheep pens. Continue on the fading track, passing a bridge on the left and an old wall line on the right, to reach an isolated chimney complete with fire grate, kettle and pot. A path leads to another isolated chimney, then a wooden bridge at NN332940 over the right-hand fork in the burn, the Allt Eachach.

Cross the bridge and head uphill to an old sheep pen just below a Parallel Road.

It is possible to follow the upper of two paths above the tree-lined Allt Eachach, up steep-sided Gleann Eachach to where the angle eases

Crossing the Allt Eachach with Càrn Dearg North above (Rab Anderson)

just before the col, then head up left beside a burn to gain the summit. However, the better route is to climb steeply uphill to the right of a tiny burn onto the spur of Teanga Mhòr, then follow the easier-angled high ground through an area of easily-negotiated peat hags to pass between two minor high points and reach the cairn marking the summit (7.25km; 610m; 2h 40min).

Descend to the col, passing the distinctive subsidiary knoll of Meallan Odhar, then cross easily between the hags and climb the slope above; a solitary wooden post partway up provides something to aim for. The slope eases and the summit is easily gained (9.25km; 805m; 3h 40min).

There are various ways to return. One is to descend south-west to the imperceptible nose of Sròn a Ghoill, then to haggy ground at the watershed just beyond. From there, either take a direct line steeply down southwards, aiming for Turret Bridge, which can be seen below, to reach the flat floor close to an old sheep pen, or head south-south-east to pick up an ATV track which descends by a burn

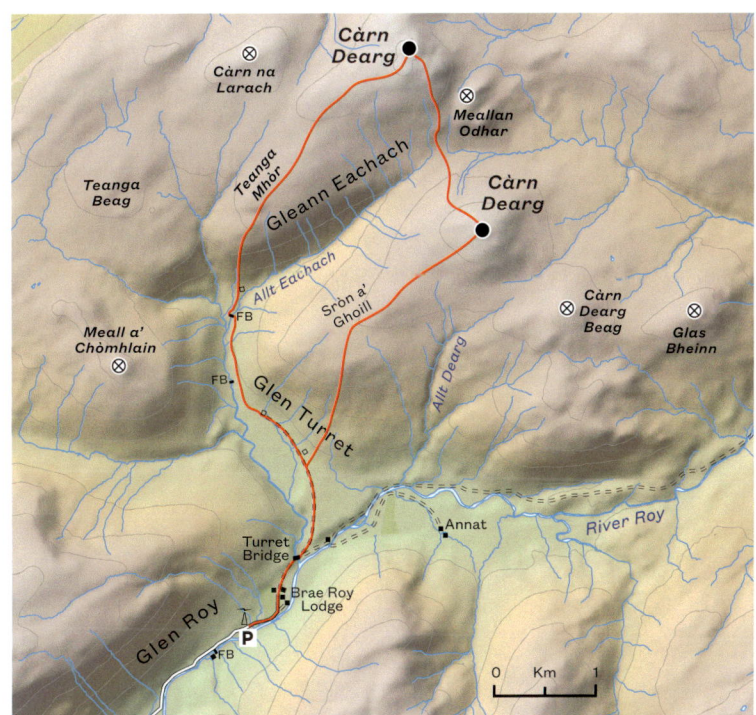

for a way before dropping south-west. Another option is to head south-west for a short way from the summit, then go down the west side of the Allt

Dearg to gain the track alongside the River Roy. All ways cross the three Parallel Roads and return over Turret Bridge (14.25km; 805m; 5h).

Càrn Dearg (South) from Càrn Dearg (North), with Creag Meagaidh, left, and Càrn Dearg (East), right, (Rab Anderson)

Càrn na Nathrach, Druim Garbh, Sgùrr Dhomhnuill,
Sgùrr na h-Ighinn and Sgùrr a' Chaorainn from
Beinn a' Chaorainn with distant Ben Nevis
(Rab Anderson)

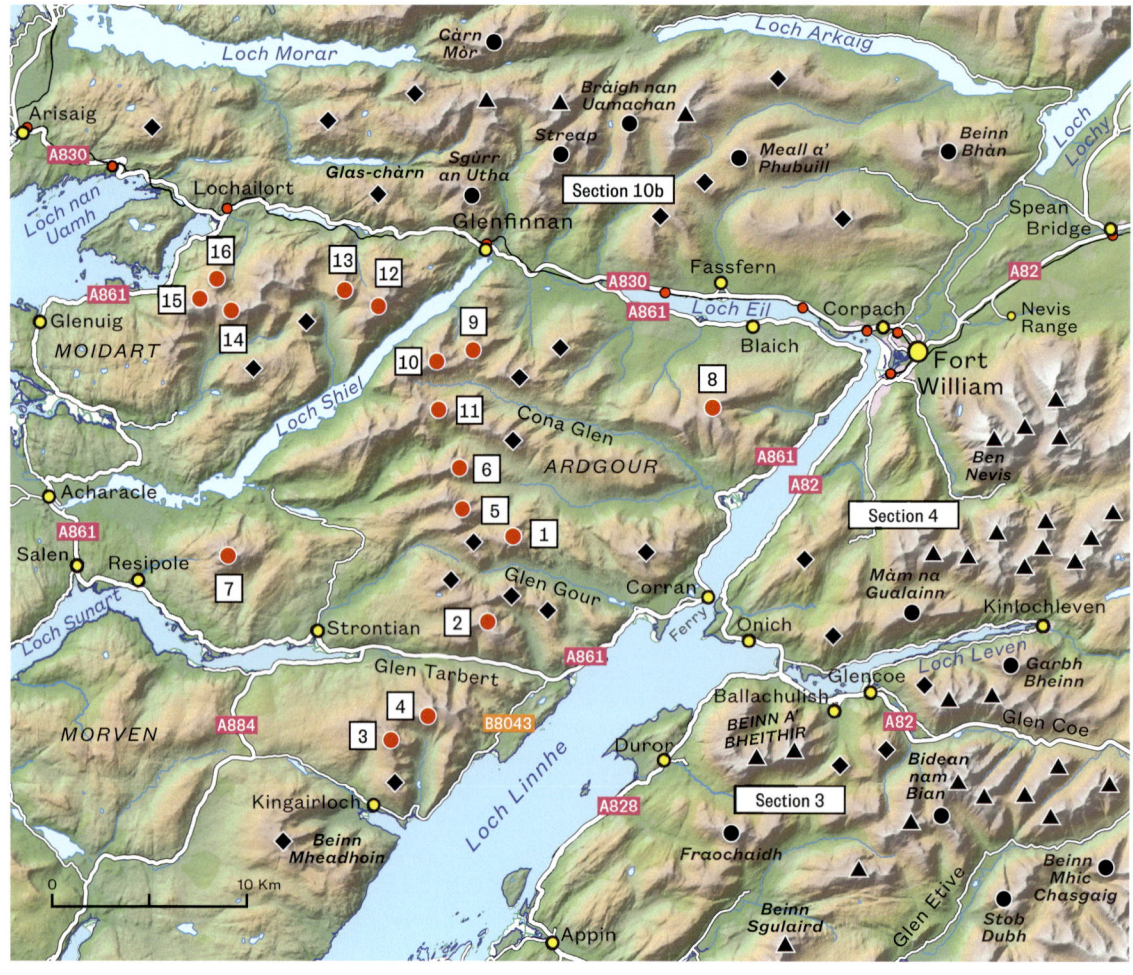

SECTION 10a

Across Loch nan Gabhar to Beinn na h-Uamha with Sgùrr a' Chaorainn to its left (David Batty)

Beinn na h-Uamha; 762m; (C222); L40; NM917664; *hill of the cave*

The lowest of the Corbetts, Beinn na h-Uamha is a remarkably rocky hill that lies in rugged terrain to the south-east of Sgùrr Dhomhnuill, the highest and most prominent peak in Ardgour.

Together with Sgùrr a' Chaorainn (761m), its twin peak and the second highest Graham, Beinn na h-Uamha forms part of a high ridge on the north side of the Glen Gour glacial trench. The south side of the glen is formed by Sgòrr Mhic Eacharna and Beinn Bheag, with Sgùrr nan Cnamh beyond; all three are Grahams.

Although it is the lowest Corbett, Beinn na h-Uamha gives a much tougher than expected ascent.

Start from Sallachan, a short distance to the south of Corran, where a section of road loops north, off and back onto the A861, across a bridge over the River Gour flowing from Glen Gour. There is space for a few vehicles to park on the north side of the bridge without blocking access to any gates.

Walk across the bridge, then go through a gate and follow the track up Glen Gour, which is signed as the right of way to Strontian. Beinn na h-Uamha and Sgùrr a' Chaorainn can be seen ahead.

The track leads past Loch nan Gabhar and the ruined building at Tigh Ghlinnegabhar to reach a stone sheepfold after almost 4km. Anyone considering using a bike should be aware that beyond this point the track becomes much rougher.

In a further 1km, when the track nears the River Gour, leave it, then go down past a dead tree and ford the river. This is normally straightforward, but could be difficult if the water was running high.

Boggy ground leads to the base of Beinn na h-Uamha's south-east ridge, whose lower crags are bypassed on the right by ascending a shallow, ▶

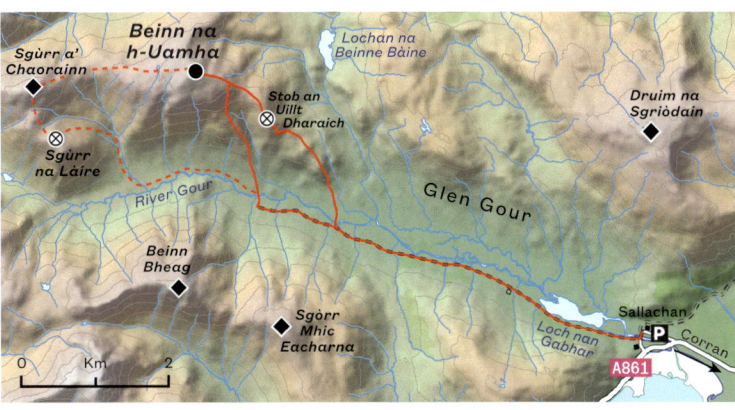

grassy gully up leftwards behind them. Above this, less steep ground leads to the rocky dome of Stob an Uillt Dharaich, which is either climbed by a steep grassy rake slanting up left then right onto the crest to gain its top (c.520m), or probably easier, around to the right with a climb up leftwards to its top.

Cross the slight dip beyond Stob an Uillt Dharaich, then continue up the ridge and cross a flatter area with some small lochans and pools. This leads to the final section of the ridge, which gives a surprisingly long climb past some more tiny lochans to reach the summit cairn on a small rise. (**8.5km; 780m; 3h 15min**).

There is a fine view of Sgùrr Dhomhnuill to the west, whilst eastwards Ben Nevis, The Mamores and Glen Coe all look grand.

Return down the ridge, almost to the flatter section to clear the rocky upper slopes, then drop south into a grassy basin at the head of Coire an Uillt Dharaich. Traverse out rightwards, then descend the broad ridge out to the right of the Allt Daraich.

At the bottom, cross a path and continue down to the River Gour, where it is forded by a rough track just above some trees. Cross to the other side to gain the start of a clearer track, and follow this back (**17.5km; 800m; 5h 40min**).

To include Sgùrr a' Chaorainn, descend easy-angled but rough terrain westwards past a lochan to the col between the hills at 556m, then climb to its summit (**11km; 990m; 4h 15min**).

To return, descend southwards to a col, then either climb to Sgùrr na Làire (624m), or avoid its top to the north and descend eastwards. If descending the broad east ridge from the top, a band of crags at the foot of the east ridge should be avoided on the left (north).

Drop down beside a burn to reach the Eas Choire na Làire, then go down the side of this to pick up an ATV track. Follow this track across the Eas Choire na Làire, and a number of other burns, to ford the River Gour and gain the start of the clearer track on the far side, which is followed back (**21.5km; 1070m; 7h 5min**).

Garbh Bheinn's south face, with Sgùrr Dhomhnuill beyond (Mike Dixon)

Garbh Bheinn; 885m; (C42); L40; NM904622; rough mountain

One of the finest mountains in the Western Highlands, Garbh Bheinn certainly lives up to its name of 'rough mountain', being surrounded by steep slopes and covered in rock. There is a grand view of Garbh Bheinn from the east, looking across Loch Linnhe from Glen Coe or Ballachulish, from where its jagged outline is clear. From closer at hand, the full extent of the crags on the various facets of its south, east and north-east faces is well-seen from the neighbouring ridges.

Despite its steep and rocky character, the ascent of Garbh Bheinn is relatively straightforward, although the mountain should be treated with due respect in adverse weather conditions.

The ascent is best made from the foot of Coire an Iubhair, where cars can be parked off the A861 on a loop of old road by the old bridge over the Abhainn Coire an Iubhair.

There are two routes. One route is an ascent of Garbh Bheinn on its

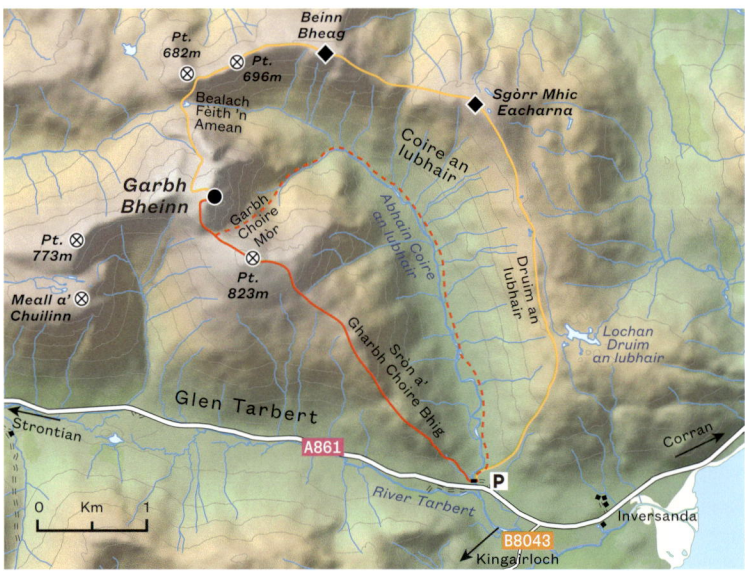

own, whilst the other is a superb, but arduous, circuit of Coire an Iubhair, which climbs the ridge on the east side of the glen to curve round over Sgòrr Mhic Eacharna and Beinn Bheag, both Grahams, before tackling Garbh Bheinn via its northern slopes.

For the ascent of Garbh Bheinn on its own, cross the bridge to the west side of the burn and follow a path up the long, but easy-angled ridge of Sròn a' Gharbh Choire Bhig. There is much bare rock, but the path weaves its way through the outcrops, and the going is easy to the cairn at the top of the Sròn (823m).

There is a grand view across the head of Garbh Coire Mòr to Garbh Bheinn's impressive south face, which holds one of Scotland's finest mountain cliffs, home to many rock climbs, atop which sits the summit. The compelling right-hand skyline edge is Great Ridge, a classic rock climb first ascended in 1897.

Descend the broad, rocky ridge to a col (748m), then climb north up the steep and rocky, but perfectly easy slope, curving round to traverse

above the precipitous south face to reach Garbh Bheinn's summit cairn, perched on the edge with superb views in all directions (**4.25km; 950m; 2h 35min**).

The easiest return is back the same way (8.5km; 1025m; 4h 15min),

However, this can be varied by returning to the 748m col at the head of Garbh Coire Mòr, then descending steeply into the corrie. There is a path down between the crags and the boulders, which leads to the burn draining the corrie. A path down the north side of the burn leads to a crossing of the Abhainn Coire an Iubhair just above the junction, where a path is then followed along the floor of the glen back to the start (9.75km; 955m; 4h 25min).

The circuit of Coire an Iubhair is described in the SMC's guidebook *The Grahams & The Donalds*, but a condensed version is given here.

Briefly follow the path up the glen, then climb the steep, but easy, grassy slope to gain the ridge on the east side of Coire an Iubhair and follow this, the Druim an Iubhair, on increas-

ingly rocky ground to the top of Sgòrr Mhic Eacharna (**4km; 640m; 2h**).

Drop to the col then, climb to Beinn Bheag (**6km; 890m; 3h**).

Follow an elevated ridge westwards across the dip, then over the West Top (Pt.696m) to a grassy col in front of Pt.682m at the end of the ridge. Go down a steep, but grassy, gully to the small Lochan Coire an Iubhair at the col with Garbh Bheinn, the Bealach Fèith 'n Amean.

Climb the break in the cliffs ahead, either by the grassy gully up its right side, or by a zigzag line up the mixed slope of grass and rock to the left of the gully. Both lead into a hanging corrie. Ascend the left side of this corrie, then either take the direct steeper, scrambly line ahead, or slant up right to the dip with Garbh Bheinn's West Top, then turn left to gain the summit (**9km; 1290m; 4h 35min**).

Follow the path west to clear the cliffs of the south face, drop to the col, then climb onto Pt.823m and follow the path down the Sròn a' Garbh Choire Bhig ridge to the start (13.5km; 1370m; 6h 15min).

Across Coire an Iubhair to Garbh Coire Mòr and Garbh Bheinn, with Creach Bheinn beyond (Iain Thow)

Fuar Bheinn; *766m; (C215); L49; NM853563; cold hill*
Creach Bheinn; *853m; (C89); L49; NM870576); hill of spoil*

Together with their lower outliers, Fuar Bheinn and Creach Bheinn form a well-defined south-facing horseshoe ridge around Glen Galmadale in Kinglairloch above Loch Linnhe. The complete traverse of this ridge is a classic hillwalk and is the best way to climb both hills.

The west side of the horseshoe over Beinn na Cille, a Graham, and Fuar Bheinn has a succession of craggy corries overlooking Glen Galmadale, although they are not that impressive when seen at close quarters. More impressive is the east side of Druim na Maodalaich, at the termination of the eastern arm of the horseshoe. This falls steeply in a long line of broken cliffs of red granite, cut by many dykes which form tree-filled gullies above the narrow B8043, the road generally used for the approach.

The traverse starts from a parking area at NM866531 on the east side of the bridge over the Galmadale River at the entrance to Glen Galmadale.

Walk across the bridge, then along the road and around the corner for a few hundred metres to the side of a forestry plantation. The quickest and shortest route is to climb up the side of the plantation, between it and a burn issuing from a ravine. Above the trees, head up and left to avoid the steeper ground to the side of the ravine, then climb the blunt ridge, named Stùchd Eas na Ceàrdaich.

Continuing along the road for just over 1km leads to a telecommunications building beyond the west end of the plantation, and from there it is a slightly less steep climb.

Either way, it is a stiff climb and feels like a long haul, with the slope of grass and granite outcrops easing slowly to the top of Beinn na Cille (**2.25km; 650m; 1h 35min**).

Descend northwards to cross the col at 460m at the head of Coire Mhic Gugain, then climb the broad ridge over Meall Coire Mhic Gugain and continue up the slope beyond to the top of Fuar Bheinn (**4.75km; 960m; 2h 45min**).

Creach Bheinn lies on the other side of the deep bowl of Coire a Chùil Mhàim, with tent-like Garbh Bheinn and pointed Sgùrr Dhomhnuill standing out beyond it. To the north-west there is also a good view of isolated Beinn Resipol.

Descend the ridge to the north-west for about 500m or so, crossing a burn, then swing north and drop more steeply for a way to gain the featureless col, the Cùl Mhàm (c.540m) at the head of the corrie. A long, but easy climb eastwards leads on up the broad ridge on the other side to the top of Creach Bheinn, marked by a low, stone wind shelter and the rusted steel pole of what remains of the trig pillar (**7.75km; 1275m; 4h**).

Head north for about 30m, then descend north-east to a slight dip, where two sets of large walls shelter the small circular walls of what

Fuar Bheinn, Creach Bheinn and Maol Odhar from Beinn na Cille (Rab Anderson)

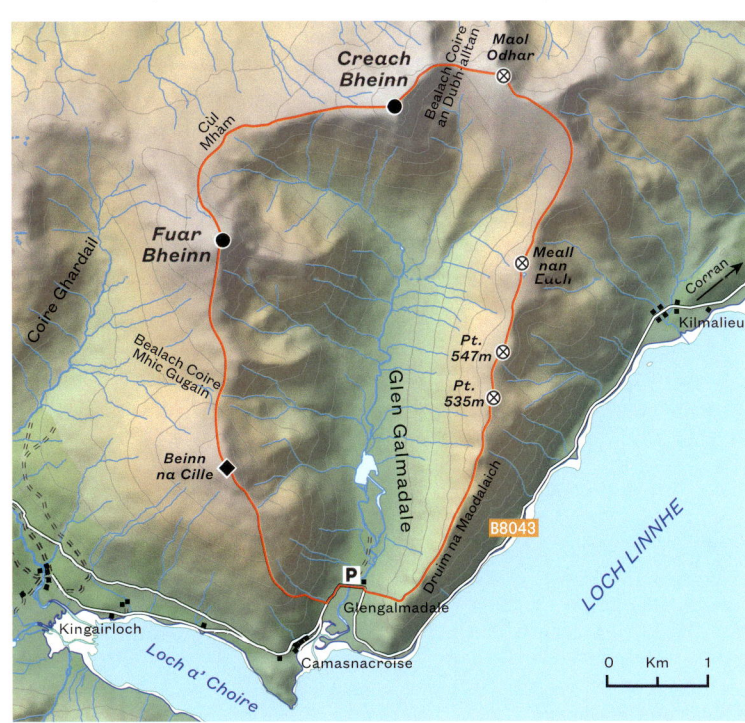

Looking up Glen Galmadale to Fuar Bheinn and Creach Bheinn (Rab Anderson)

remains of a Colby camp from the early to mid 1800s, used by the Ordnance Survey for their Trigonometrical Survey of Scotland.

Ascend onto the slight rise beyond, then descend gently north-east for 400m to where the ridge splits above An Coire Dubh on the north side. Turn right and drop east to the Bealach Coire an Dubh-alltan (714m), above the hanging corrie of the same name at the head of Glen Galmadale.

Make the short ascent up the other side onto the top of Maol Odhar (794m), where the cairn has pieces of wreckage, widely scattered hereabouts, from a USAF McDonnell F-101C Voodoo that crashed in 1964.

There is a grand view north down Coire nam Frithallt and across Glen Tarbert to Garbh Bheinn, as well as along the striking northwards-running strata to Sgùrr Dhomhnuill. With Loch Linnhe now below, the view across it from Ben Nevis, past Glen Coe, to Ben Cruachan is spectacular.

Descend grassy slopes easily south-east, swinging southwards down the other side of the glen across a 508m col, and climb onto Meall nan Each (591m), with its small

lochan of the same name. Continue down the ridge, over Pt.547m (Àirigh Mhic Bheathain), then the final slight rise of Pt.535m, and down the narrower, knolly Druim na Maodalaich

until pretty much level with the start then turn right and drop to the road (**15.25km; 1485m; 6h 30min**).

There are usually feral goats around this final section of the ridge.

Sgùrr Dhomhnuill from Sgùrr na h-Ighinn, with Càrn na Nathrach and Sgùrr Ghiubhsachain beyond (Rab Anderson)

Sgùrr Dhomhnuill; *888m; (C37); L40; NM889678; Donald's peak*

With its prominent, pointed peak, Sgùrr Dhomhnuill, the highest peak in Ardgour, is a conspicuous landmark from many distant viewpoints. It rises above the head of Strontian Glen in the rocky and rough terrain typical of the area between Loch Shiel and Loch Linnhe.

The most practicable approach to Sgùrr Dhomhnuill is from the west, and there are two routes, both from the narrow road that runs north from Strontian at the head of Loch Sunart.

The most attractive route is up Strontian Glen, from a car park at NM826633 at the entrance to the Ariundle Nature Reserve, accessed by a road off to the right, just over 1 mile (1.6km) up the road from the turn off the main road on the west side of the bridge in Strontian.

Follow a forest track through lovely natural oak woodland for 3km to a fork. Take the left branch, which leads in a further 1km to a bridge over a burn, the Allt Ruighe Spardain; it could be biked to here. On the other

side, a path continues for 900m to the abandoned Fee Donald lead mines (worked from 1727 to 1871) by the Allt Fèith Dhomhnuill.

Cross the burn at NM860663 and climb onto the attractive, long west ridge of Sgùrr na h-Ighinn, the Druim Leac a' Sgiathain. Follow this ridge to a tiny lochan at NM878669 at a height of 590m, then climb the steeper ridge beyond to the top of Sgùrr na h-Ighinn (766m).

Descend north-east to a col at 682m, then climb the south ridge of Sgùrr Dhomhnuill in two steps to the summit (**9km; 975m; 3h 40min**).

Return the same way, but at the col descend westwards and traverse beneath Sgùrr na h-Ighinn to the tiny lochan, then go down the Druim Leac a' Sgiathain (**18km; 1020m; 6h 5min**).

It is possible to include Sgùrr a' Chaorainn, the Graham to the southeast, and this is best done on the way up. From the lochan at NM878669, traverse east below the steep south face of Sgùrr na h-Ighinn. Once

beyond a band of crags, drop southeast for 100m in height past a knoll to reach a col, the Bealach Màm a' Bhearna (493m). From there, the ascent of Sgùrr a' Chaorainn's west ridge is straightforward, steep at first, then easing past a tiny lochan, with a final blocky, easy walk to the summit cairn. Return to the Bealach Màm a' Bhearna, then climb steeply to the top of Sgùrr na h-Ighinn and continue to Sgùrr Dhomhnuill; an added 2.5km, 390m, 1h 30min on the day.

The alternative route starts from the highest point of the road between Strontian and Loch Doilet, at 343m, where there is a small area to park on the west side, opposite the first of three telecommunications aerials.

Climb past the aerials and traverse east, passing to the north of the trig point on Druim Glas (435m), then head north-east across flat ground following a deer track. Continue in the same line on deer tracks to ascend up and across the rocky hillside, passing the ends of some lovely lochans to

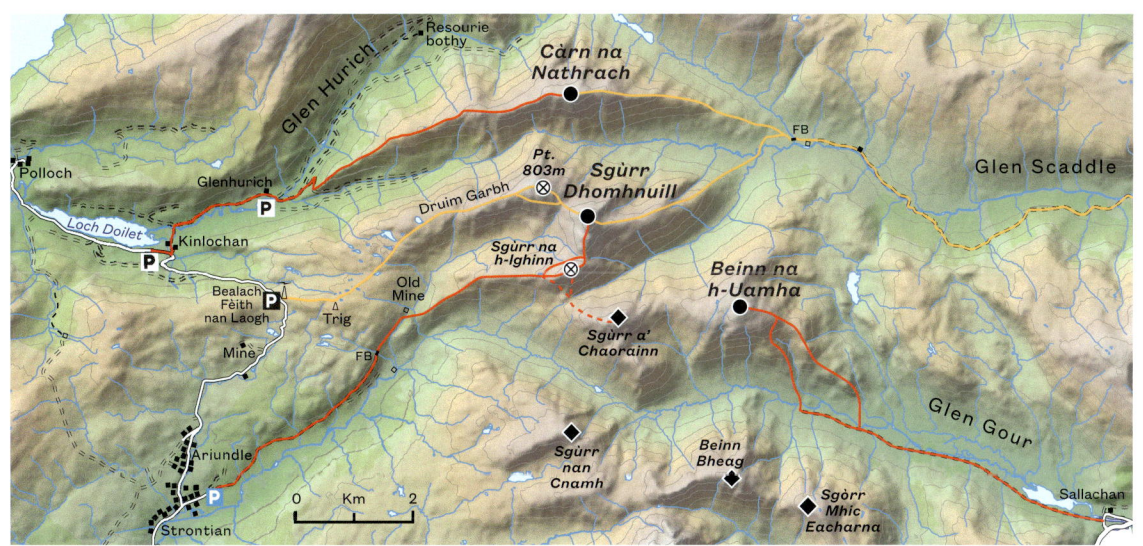

reach the crest at an upper lochan. It is remarkably rugged, but interesting terrain, which gives fairly tough going likely to be confusing in poor visibility.

Traverse across and climb the main Druim Garbh ridge to gain its highest point (803m). Weave down southeast to the Glas Bhealach, and climb Sgùrr Dhomhnuill's north-west ridge. This is very steep and rocky, but a zigzag, travelled line on grass has no difficulty (**7km; 775m; 3h 20min**).

Return the same way. From the Glas Bhealach, an easy, grassy ramp-line on the left cuts up and across the south side of the ridge, saving some effort (**14km; 950m; 5h 45min**).

An ascent can also be made from the east up Glen Scaddle, especially if a bike is used to just beyond the private Tighnacomaire bothy, which is 11.25km from where the track leaves the road, where it bends around Inverscaddle Bay on Loch Linnhe. There is parking on the west side of the bridge over the River Scaddle.

Beyond Tighnacomaire, continue on an ATV track to a bridge over the river at NM924692, and cross. Follow the track, which loops round to ford the Allt Gleann na Cloiche Sgoilte, and continue for a short way, then climb the north-east ridge of Sgùrr Dhomhnuill (Sàil a' Bhùiridh) past a small lochan on a level section, then on up to the top (**4.75km; 810; 2h 10min**).

Return to Tighnacomaire the same way (**9km; 700m; 3h 30min**), then back to Inverscaddle Bay.

Up Strontian Glen to Druim Garbh Pt.803m, Sgùrr Dhomhnuill, Sgùrr na h-Ighinn and Sgùrr a' Chaorainn (Rab Anderson)

Càrn na Nathrach; 786m; (C182); L40; NM886699; cairn of the adders

Situated in the heart of the wilds of Ardgour to the north of Sgùrr Dhomhnuill, Càrn na Nathrach is the highest point of a long ridge, to which the name Beinn Mheadhoin is given. The ridge extends eastwards from the lower reaches of Glen Hurich near Loch Doilet, over to Glen Scaddle.

Turn off the A861 on the west side of the bridge in Strontian and follow the narrow road, signed to Polloch, north over the Bealach Fèith nan Laogh and down towards the east end of Loch Doilet. At the bottom of the hill, some 320m beyond a forest track off on the right to Kinlochan, there is parking on both sides.

Walk back along the road and follow the track past Kinlochan across the bridge over the River Hurich. Turn right along the track past the house at Glenhurich, then cross a bridge back over the river.

There is space to park here, and at the time of writing there was no restriction on driving to this point, saving 2.75km (5.5km in total) and 35m (1h 10min) of walking.

Take the track on the left, then after 400m, take the right fork uphill and follow it around a sharp right-hand bend to its highpoint on the crest of the ridge, where it turns the corner. Just beyond an open area, go into the trees and follow a rough path, marked by a cairn, uphill to emerge into the open with the ridge stretching ahead.

A rough path continues up the ridge, although the lower part can be quite boggy. The going improves with height, as well as the views; to the south-west, Beinn Resipol with its northern corrie looks grand.

The ridge is surprisingly long, but continually interesting. Cross the slight rise of Pt.517m, then continue over another slight rise to negotiate a deer fence in the dip at 602m. A little further on, beyond another slight dip, there is a slabby rock step on the crest, which is easily climbed. Cross another slight rise and continue on up the undulating ridge to finally reach the cairn at the west end of the flat crest (**9km; 835m; 3h 25min**).

It is an excellent viewpoint. Aonach Mòr, Ben Nevis and The Mamores stand out to the east. To the north is Stob a' Bhealach an Sgrìodain, and peeking over the ridge that extends either side of it is Sgòrr Craobh a' Chaorainn and Sgùrr Ghiubhsachain.

To their west are the Moidart Corbetts, Beinn Odhar Bheag and Beinn Mhic Cèdidh, with Sgùrr na Bà Glaise and Rois-Bheinn to their side, then the Rum Cuillin beyond. South is pointed Sgùrr Dhomhnuill, with Beinn na h-Uamha to its side, and the Glen Coe peaks beyond.

Return the same way (18km; 855m; 6h), but 5.5km, 1h 10min shorter from the bridge just beyond Glenhurich.

As with Sgùrr Dhomhnuill, an ascent can be made up Glen Scaddle from the east, especially if a bike is used to just beyond the private Tighnacomaire bothy, which is 11.25km from where the track leaves the road where it bends around Inverscaddle Bay. There is parking on the west side of the bridge over the River Scaddle.

Beyond Tighnacomaire, continue on an ATV track to a bridge over the river at NM924692 and cross. Follow the track for 300m or so then break off and climb the ridge up Sròn Beinne Mheadhoin to Càrn na Nathrach (4.5km; 690; 2h 10min).

Return to Tighnacomaire the same way (9km; 700m; 3h 30min), then back to Inverscaddle Bay.

Map on page 211

Across Loch Doilet to Càrn na Nathrach with its long west ridge (Rab Anderson)

Beinn Resipol from the west, from the Resipole Farm approach (Rab Anderson)

Beinn Resipol; 845m; (C97); L40; NM766654; from old Norse homestead

Occupying the ground between Loch Sunart and Loch Shiel, Beinn Resipol rises prominently to the west of Sgùrr Dhomhnuill and the hills of Ardgour.

Beinn Resipol's isolated position makes its summit an outstanding viewpoint with one of the finest views along the West Highland coastline. On the seaboard side, the view extends from Dùn da Ghaoithe and Ben More on Mull, out to Barra and South Uist, over Eigg to Rum, then to the Cuillin of Skye. On the landward side, it extends from Glen Coe past the Ardgour Corbetts to Ben Nevis, then across Loch Shiel to Rois-Bheinn and the Moidart Corbetts, with Streap and a host of other peaks beyond.

The A861 runs along the north side of Loch Sunart between Strontian and Salen, and is the road used to approach the hill.

There are two principal routes: one is from Resipole near Salen on the west side of the hill, which can be quite boggy, and the other is from the Strontian side to the east, where there are three starts.

The route from Resipole starts from the Resipole Farm Holiday Park (NM724638), where it is possible (on asking) to park beside the reception building on the north side of the single-track road along Loch Sunart.

On the far side of the building, follow a path into woodland for 100m, then go right across a small bridge,

through a gate, and left along a path across flattish ground. Cross a stile onto a track, which comes up from the holiday park on the left, and follow this through oak and birch trees.

Beyond the trees, the track zigzags up and becomes a boggy ATV track, which is followed through a gate in a ▶

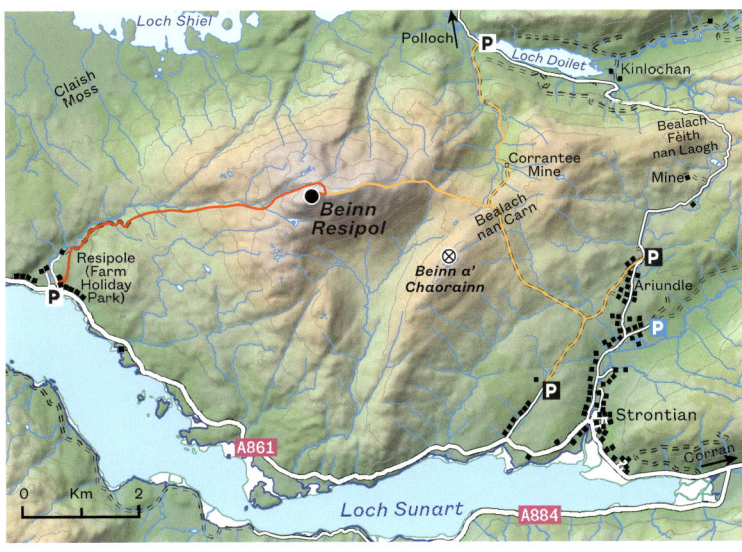

deer fence. Continue on the ATV track to meet a fence, then follow a rough path up above the Allt Mhic Chiarain and its fine ravine.

Cross a flatter section, then continue uphill beside the burn, through the bouldery and increasingly rocky, but easy, terrain of the Glac Gharbh. At the top, turn right and climb onto the summit crest, where the highest point is on the right, at the far west end, marked by a large cairn with the remains of a trig pillar next to it (**6.25km; 860m; 2h 50min**).

Return by the route of ascent (**12.75km; 875m; 4h 45min**).

The route from the Strontian side, via the eastern ridge, has three possible starts:

(i) About 1 mile (1.7km) along the A861 to the west of Strontian, turn off north and follow a narrow road past the Ben View Hotel, to where there is a small parking area at its end.

Walk along the continuation track, an old coffin road and miners' track to the Corrantee Mine. After 1.3km, turn left up a track signed to Polloch, then follow it to its highpoint at the foot of Beinn a' Chaorainn's north-east ridge, the Bealach nan Càrn.

Continue down the other side for 200m, passing an ATV track off left, to a sharp right-hand bend. Leave the track here and follow a vague path through an isolated pair of gateposts. The path finds a good way across the

Meall an t-Slugain bealach, passing through another pair of gateposts to gain Beinn Resipol.

Climb up and left across the grassy slope beneath a craggy section to gain the dip behind this, then climb the ridge and the right side of a shallow corrie. This leads up to the undulating crest, where a splendid traverse gains the summit at the far west end (**8km; 800m; 3h 10min**).

Return the same way (**16km; 845m; 5h 30min**).

(ii) A start can also be made from Ariundle, about 2 miles (3km) north up the road from the turn-off on the west side of the bridge in Strontian, where a road turns off left, signed to Heatherbank B&B. There is nowhere to park along this road, so park on the right 100m further on by some farm machinery. Follow the road to its end at Heatherbank, then continue south-west on a track to join (i) with little difference in distance.

(iii) Start at a track entrance at NM795679 at the west end of Loch Doilet, gained by a 15min drive from Ariundle over the Bealach Fèith nan Laogh. Follow the track, signed to Strontian, and ensuing path, up into then through flat-bottomed Coire an t-Suidhe. The route passes the ruins of the Corrantee Mine, opened in 1725 to mine lead, and joins the other starts at the bend below the Bealach nan Càrn; 650m shorter than these.

> ***Stob Coire a' Chearcaill; 771m; (C206); L41; NN016726; peak of the circular corrie***

Together with its subsidiary tops, Stob Coire a' Chearcaill fills the triangle of ground between Loch Linnhe and Loch Eil in the north-east corner of Ardgour. When viewed up Gleann Sròn a' Chreagain from the opposite side of Loch Linnhe just south of Fort William, Stob Coire a' Chearcaill presents an attractive sight with a distinctive rock buttress beneath its summit standing out.

The usual route of ascent is from the A861 along the south side of Loch Eil, from where uniformly featureless slopes rise to its summit. There are two routes from this side, both with limited parking.

The first route is perhaps not the best, but starts from where a hydro track leaves the road at NN012770, just to the east of Duisky and the bridge over the An Dubh Uisge. It may be possible to park at the entrance without impeding access. Failing this there is a track entrance 400m to the east that could be parked in.

Follow the hydro track to NN008760, then take the left fork to a small dam. Ascend the open hillside

Beinn Resipol from the Meall an t-Slugain bealach to the east (Rab Anderson)

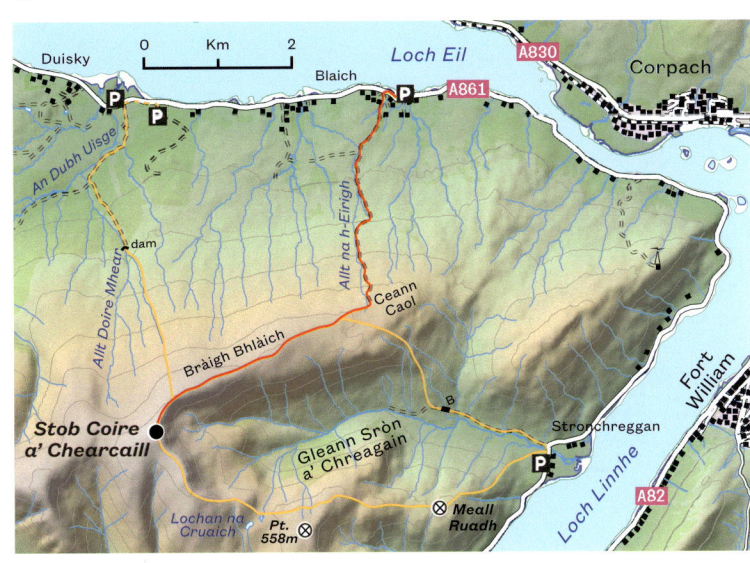

Stob Coire a' Chearcaill from the Bràigh Bhlàich ridge (Rab Anderson)

to gain the north-east ridge above Coire a' Chearcaill and continue to the huge cairn that marks the summit, a few metres from the trig point (5km; 765m; 2h 25min).

Return the same way (10km; 770m; 3h 55min).

The second route is better and starts further east at Blaich, where the gated left-hand track at a wide double track entrance leaves the road at NN048771. There is limited parking on the north verge at the bend just to the east.

Follow the track past various buildings and a yard, then past a branch off right, and continue up to 460m just before its end on Ceann Caol.

Head up right on rough ground past a cairn onto the north-east ridge, over the slight rise of Pt.609m, then on up the ridge of Bràigh Bhlàich. Swing round the head of Coire a' Chearcaill to gain the huge cairn and trig point on the summit (7km; 795; 2h 50min).

There is a grand view east down Coire a' Chearcaill and Gleann Sròn a' Chreagain to mighty Ben Nevis rising above Fort William.

Return the same way (14km; 815m; 4h 45min).

A slightly longer, but perhaps more attractive route, which is also a circuit, can be made from the east up Gleann Sròn a' Chreagain. There is space to park without impeding any access at NN070724, by a shed on the south side of the bridge over the Abhainn Sròn a' Chreagain.

Walk over the bridge and cross a stile, then follow a track west up the glen. After crossing a bridge, the track climbs to a highpoint. Leave the track here and ascend the hillside, crossing a fence; if found, there is a gate. Join the route from Blaich on Ceann Caol and continue up the Braigh Bhlàich ridge to the summit (7km; 785m; 2h 50min).

To return, follow the edge of the corrie south-south-east onto a slight rise, then swing east and drop to a col at 489m to the north of Lochan na Cruaich.

Traverse eastwards across the north side of Pt.558m then go down the broad ridge to Meall Ruadh (325m) and descend north-east back to the start (13.5km; 870m; 4h 50min).

Sgòrr Craobh a' Chaorainn and Meall na Cuartaige from the Sròn Fèith nan Còn ridge (Rab Anderson)

Sgòrr Craobh a' Chaorainn; *775m; (C199); L40; NM895758; rowantree peak*
Sgùrr Ghiubhsachain; *849m; (C94); L40; NM875751; peak of the fir-wood*
Stob a' Bhealach an Sgrìodain (Druim Tarsuinn); *770m; (C207); L40; NM874727; peak of the pass of screes*

These three mountains lie in the north-west corner of Ardgour. Sgòrr Craobh a' Chaorainn and Sgùrr Ghiubhsachain form part of a north-eastwards-running ridgeline overlooking Loch Shiel, whilst isolated Stob a' Bhealach an Sgrìodain sits on a westwards-running ridgeline between Glen Scaddle and Cona Glen. These hills are not conveniently located for the walker, and some effort is required to attain all three.

Stob a' Bhealach an Sgrìodain is not currently named on OS maps. The name Druim Tarsuinn has been applied to it by some, but this is the ridge (and 'druim' means ridge) that falls from the distinctly separate unnamed rise to the north-west, on the other side of the Bealach an Sgrìodain, between it and the ridge leading to the 770m highpoint. So, perhaps more appropriately, the name Stob a' Bhealach an Sgrìodain has been given to this highpoint and is now generally accepted.

Since Stob a' Bhealach an Sgrìodain is connected to the tail end of the Sgùrr Ghiubhsachain ridgeline by the Druim Tarsuinn ridge, the Bealach Scamodale and Meall nan Leac (755m), which sits at the head of Cona Glen, it makes some sense to climb all three in a single outing. However, this makes for a reasonably demanding outing, with a long walk back out at the end of the day, so the panel on page 218 briefly describes the options for splitting the group.

The traverse starts a short distance to the east of Glenfinnan where, at the apex of a wide bend on the A830, a track leads south to a small car park at NM924792 on the right, on the other side of the bridge over the Callop River.

Walk south on the track, past a small power station, then Callop Cottage, and continue on a hydro track up the glen. Where the track loops round to end at a dam after 2.5km, take the Cona Glen signed

path through a gate. The path loops away uphill, then swings back across the foot of the spur leading to Meall na Cuartaige, the Sròn Fèith nan Còn.

Leave the path at its highpoint and follow the Sròn Fèith nan Còn ridge over Meall na Cuartaige, then quite steeply up either side of a slabby crag on the ridge ahead; a grassy rake to the right perhaps being the most obvious line. Beyond this, easier-angled ground leads to the top of Sgòrr Craobh a' Chaorainn (**5.5km; 795m; 2h 35min**).

The western aspect below the summit terminates in a crag, which is bypassed on either side without any difficulty. Once below, follow the ridge down across a small dip, to pass the south side of a slight rise, to gain the col between the hills where there is a small lochan. Continue easily up the other side to the foot of the steep upper slopes of Sgùrr Ghiubhsachain. There is a fair amount of exposed rock on these slopes, but it is easy enough to pick a grassy line through the rock to gain the summit (**8km; 1070m; 3h 45min**).

Descend easily to the south-west, passing over a slight rise (An Sgonn) and another, then make a short climb almost to the top of Meall nan Creag Leac (755m), which can be included.

A line of old fence posts is met here and followed southwards, then south-east off the ridge to drop steeply to the Bealach Scamodale (c.511m) at the head of Cona Glen. Make a short but steep climb up the other side and follow the fence posts south-south-east up the fine, rocky, and knolly Druim Tarsuinn ridge along the edge overlooking Cona Glen, swinging south-east at the top.

Drop to the Bealach an Sgrìodain (c.655m), then make the final ascent over rough and rocky terrain next to the fence posts to gain the top of Stob a' Bhealach an Sgrìodain, which lies just south of the fenceline (**12.25km; 1390m; 5h 30min**).

Rejoin the fenceline and traverse eastwards to gain the col with Meall Mòr, the Eag a' Mhadaidh Ruaidh (656m). Descend north into Cona Glen following the prominent ridge on the left (west) side of the notched gully-line and burn. There is a fair

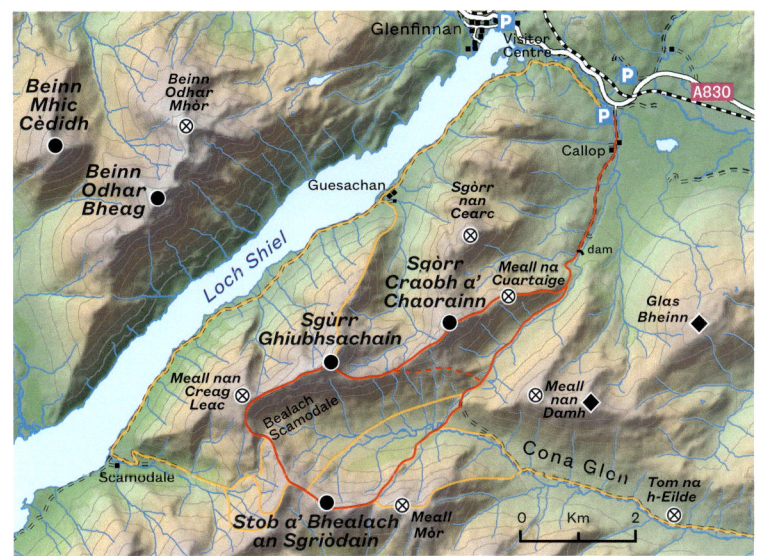

amount of slabby rock, but an easy grassy line leads down through it. Cross the burn at the bottom and go around the left side of a fenced woodland enclosure to gain the Cona River, and ford this at a prominent loop.

Climb up the other side to gain a rough track close to its end, then follow it, and the path that continues from it, through the col between Sgòrr Craobh a' Chaorainn and Meall nan Damh. The path leads down the glen to the left of the Allt Fèith nan Con to

rejoin the outward route at the foot of Sròn Fèith nan Con, which is followed back (**21.5km; 1530m; 8h 15min**).

This route can be cut short from Sgùrr Ghiubhsachain by returning east to the col with Sgòrr Craobh a' Chaorainn. From there, traverse horizontally north-north-east for about 750m to clear the burns, then descend across the hillside to gain the Cona Glen path, and follow this back (**16.25km; 1075m; 6h**).

▶

Sgùrr Ghiubhsachain from the col with Sgòrr Craobh a' Chaorainn (Rab Anderson)

Sgòrr Craobh a' Chaorainn & Sgùrr Ghiubhsachain

These two hills can be climbed together in a circuit from the Callop car park by turning right to follow the fish farm and logging extraction track north-west, then south-west along the shore of Loch Shiel for 5.5km to the foot of Sgùrr Ghiubhsachain's fine north-north-east ridge. This is a two-tiered ridge named Tom nan Dearcan Fithich and Druim an Sgriòdain, which falls from Meall a' Choire Chruinn; the steep and rocky lower part of which is avoided.

Pass the fish farm buildings at Guesachan, then cross the bridge over the burn and turn left up a track leading to a hydro building. Before reaching this, follow an ATV track for a way, to clear the steep and rocky lower part of the ridge, then traverse across and climb onto it. The ridge gives a steep ascent through rocky outcrops.

*Cross Meall a' Choire Chruinn (634m) with its tiny lochans, then climb the final steep and narrowing ridge ahead. There are crags, but from this direction the route is easily found and leads to the apparent top, from where a drop leads to the final short climb and the large cairn on the true summit (**9km; 950m; 3h 35min**).*

*Descend steeply east-south-east down awkward slabs and grass, then easily along the ridge round the head of Coire Ghiubhsachain to Sgòrr Craobh a' Chaorainn. The summit is protected by a steep and rocky west face, easily bypassed on the right (east), or by going left beneath it to cut back to the summit (**11.5km; 1165m; 4h 45min**).*

*Descend north-east, bypassing a craggy section via a grassy rake on the left, or by the slope to its right, then climb onto domed Meall na Cuartaige (566m). Descend eastwards down the Sròn Fèith nan Còn ridge to gain the path, then follow this and the track back to Callop (**17km; 1200m; 6h 25min**).*

Stob a' Bhealach an Sgriòdain

The simplest way of climbing this on its own is from the Callop car park by reversing the descent on the principal route. Follow the track south past Callop to its end (2.5km), then the Cona Glen path between Meall nan Damh and Sgòrr Craobh a' Chaorainn to meet the continuation track into Cona Glen. Descend this a very short way, then leave it and go down to cross the Cona River at an obvious loop. Go around the right side of a fenced plantation, cross the burn that flows down the obvious gully-line from the notch between Meall Mòr and Stob a' Bhealach an Sgriòdain, then climb the ridge to its right. There is a fair amount of slabby rock, but there is an easy grassy line through it.

*At the top, traverse west alongside, or out from, a line of fence posts for 750m to gain the summit (**9.25km; 915m; 3h 40min**).*

*Returning the same way is one option (**18.5km; 1070m; 6h 25min**).*

*Another option is to go down the rocky north-west ridge to the Bealach Sgriòdain, then descend into the head of Cona Glen. Cross the river, then follow the line of a path shown on the map (that doesn't appear on the ground), up and across rightwards to reach the Cona Glen path again, and return along this (**18.75km; 1020m; 6h 25min**).*

An ascent can also be made by biking up Cona Glen from Inverscaddle Bay on Loch Linnhe. There is parking at NN022686, just off the A861 at the start of a surfaced estate road.

*Follow the road and its continuation track up Cona Glen, along the base of a prominent knoll named Tom na h-Eilde, opposite Stob Mhic Bheathain, a Graham, then on to a bend in the river with a small island. This is opposite the east ridge of Meall Mòr, which is the descent route; leave bikes here (**13.75km; 265m; about 1h 40min**).*

*Continue along the track on foot, forking left along an ATV track to cross the Cona River at an obvious loop. Go around the right side of a fenced plantation, cross the burn that flows down the obvious gully-line from the notch between Meall Mòr and Stob a' Bhealach an Sgriòdain, then climb the ridge to its right. There is a fair amount of slabby rock, but there is an easy grassy line through it. At the top, traverse west alongside, or out from, a line of fence posts for 750m to gain the summit (**4.5km; 580m; 2h**), on foot from the river crossing.*

*Return east and drop to the col with Meall Mòr, the Eag a' Mhadaidh Ruaidh (656m), then climb to the top of Meall Mòr (763m). Continue east over a slight rise, then descend north-east down the ridge, turning east after a few hundred metres to gain the Cona River at the small island and cross (**8.25km; 690m; 3h 15min**), on foot from the river crossing. Bike back down the glen to Inverscaddle Bay (**35.75km; 1030m; 6h 15min**).*

*A bike approach can also be made from the Callop car park. Turn right out of the car park to follow the fish farm and logging extraction track to Loch Shiel, then along past the fish farm at Guesachan to Scamodale midway down the loch. Turn left before the bridge over the Allt Scamodale, then left again to follow the forest track that loops back on itself, and make a steady climb up the glen to reach its end at NM851733 (**14km; 315m; about 1h 30min**).*

*An ATV track leaves the right-hand corner, and is followed across a burn, then uphill through the trees to exit the forestry in the south-east corner. Drop down right on the track, cross the burn flowing from the Bealach Scamodale, and follow the track as it swings back left above the burn and fades. Continue past a gap in the deer fence (it leads to another deer fence), then climb the lower deer fence at the top corner (the wooden crossing points have rotted). Continue to the Bealach Scamodale, then ascend the Druim Tarsuinn ridge, cross the Bealach an Sgriòdain, and climb to the top of Stob a' Bhealach an Sgriòdain (**4.25km; 650m; 2h 15min**), on foot from the end of the track.*

*Return over the Bealach an Sgriòdain to the top of the Druim Tarsuinn ridge, then head south along the crest to reach the deer fence across it. Either follow this fence down westwards, then northwards, to its junction with the lower fence, then climb this and return as for the approach, or cross it then slant down south-west to follow a small burn down to gain an open gate in the lower fence at NM856727, then the ATV track (**7km; 720m; 3h 35min**), on foot from the end of the track. Bike back to Callop (**35km; 1210m; 6h 30min**).*   .

Map on page 217

Stob a' Bhealach an Sgriòdain and the Druim Tarsuinn ridge, right, from the flanks of Meall nan Damh (Rab Anderson)

Sgòrr Craobh a' Chaorainn's summit from the ridge to the south-west (Rab Anderson)

Beinn Odhar Mhòr and Beinn Odhar Bheag from Beinn Mhic Cèdidh (Rab Anderson)

> **Beinn Odhar Bheag**; *882m; (C46); L40; NM846778); little dun-coloured hill*
> **Beinn Mhic Cèdidh**; *783m; (C185); L40; NM828788; MacCedidh's hill*

This is another example where the smaller-named hill, Beinn Odhar Bheag, is actually higher than its neighbouring larger-named sibling, although Beinn Odhar Mhòr does have a greater land mass. Together with its higher sibling and Beinn Mhic Cèdidh, Beinn Odhar Bheag provides a fine circuit in the rugged north-east corner of Moidart near Glenfinnan.

The hills are bounded to the west by the Rois-Bheinn group of three Corbetts, then Loch Ailort, and to the east by the water-filled glacial trench occupied by Loch Shiel. The A830 and the railway between Fort William and Mallaig run through to their north – which is where these hills are approached from.

Start about 2.5 miles (4km) to the west of Glenfinnan, from a small pull-off (NM856813) on the south side of the road where it bends to start the descent west to Loch Eilt. Be aware that entry to the layby from the west, and the exit to the east, is across the traffic direction on a bend. The layby is immediately next to the railway and

can temporarily be busy with those waiting for a photo of the Jacobite (Hogwarts Express) steam train.

It used to be possible to cross the railway here, but the gate has been locked and a no trespass warning placed there.

Instead, walk west down the road for about 20m then go into the trees, cross the burn and go up right to emerge from the trees and cross the railway above the tunnel. Head southwards (left) around a knoll into a depression, then climb west-south-west up grassy ground heading for a notch on the skyline at NM845807 on the lower slopes of the north-north-west ridge of Beinn Odhar Mhòr at c.400m. A small burn is gained and followed to the notch, from where the broad north-west ridge gives a long and steady ascent to the top of Beinn Odhar Mhòr, marked by a cairn and broken trig pillar.

Beinn Odhar Bheag lies 1.5km to the south and is reached by descending a pleasant ridge, passing around the west side of some slight

rises, to gain the col between the hills at c.755. Follow a grassy line up the ridge ahead to the left of slabby rocks, and on up to reach the pointed summit, which is a magnificent view-point above the narrow waters of Loch Shiel (**5.5km; 900m; 2h 45min**).

Descend the grassy north-west ridge, with Croit Bheinn and Beinn Gaire, both Grahams, to the left and the Rois-Bheinn group ahead with Rum beyond, to reach the Bealach a' Choire Bhuidhe (c.485m). Grind steadily up the steeper slope on the other side, crossing flatter grassy ground at the top, to reach the summit of Beinn Mhic Cèdidh (**8km; 1195m; 4h 10min**).

There are two return options:

(i) This avoids the road walking of the traditional route. Return to the Bealach a' Choire Bhuidhe, then descend north-east into Coire Buidhe and cross the burn at the 360m contour. Make a rising traverse to the north, heading for a small crag that can be seen just before the shoulder. Pass beneath the crag, then go through a shallow col on the shoulder. Continue the northwards traverse to gain the notch on the north-north-west ridge climbed to on the initial ascent at the start of the day. Return to the road (13km; 1300m; 6h).

(i) This, the traditional route, involves a 1km section of uphill walking along a busy road on which traffic travels fast. Descend the attractive long north ridge for just over 2km, almost to the col with Sgùrr na Paite (323m), to clear a craggy section. Pick up an ATV track and follow this down to a bridge over the Allt a' Choire Bhuidhe at NM834810 and cross. The ATV track leads to an underpass beneath the railway at NM839813, then to the east end of Loch Eilt. Continue east-wards through birch woods to ford the Allt Lòn a' Mhuidhe and gain the road at NM849817. It is possible to follow the verge and the side of the crash barriers for most of the way, but there are bits where this is difficult to do (14.5km; 1310m; 6h 15min).

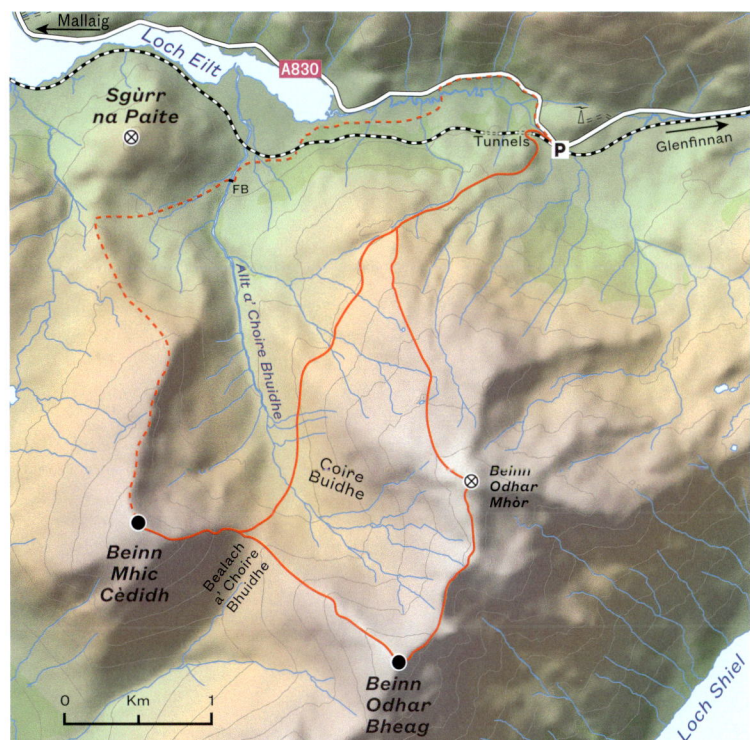

Beinn Mhic Cèdidh from Beinn Odhar Bheag, with the Rois-Bheinn group beyond (Rab Anderson)

Sgùrr na Bà Glaise; *874m; (C59); L40; NM770777; peak of the grey cow*
Rois-Bheinn; *882m; (C47); L40; NM756778; horse hill*
An Stac; *814m; (C133); L40; NM763792; the stack*

These three mountains in the north-west corner of Moidart give a superb traverse with fine ridge walking and splendid views out across the Sea of the Hebrides to Eigg, Rum, Skye and other islands.

The traverse starts at Inverailort, just off the A861 about 600m south of its junction with the A830 at Lochailort. It appears acceptable to park on the hard-standing on the left out in front of the cottages, partway down the access road to them.

Walk eastwards along the grassy track between the parking area and the cottages. When the track swings left behind the large fish factory, continue ahead on a vague path through the trees and cross a small burn. Boggy in places, the path becomes more distinct further on and climbs the south side of the knoll of Tom Odhar to join a hydro track. A drier, but longer, route continues along the initial track to join this track on the north side of Tom Odhar.

Follow the hydro track uphill for a few hundred metres, then take a

rough ATV track off left and cross the Allt a' Bhùiridh by a bridge. Continue on the ATV track, which swings left then climbs back up right. When it swings left through a shallow depression, ascend the grassy hillside of Meall Damh, which leads to the top of Beinn Coire nan Gall. It is a long and fairly brutal ascent. Either take in the summit or bypass it to the west to

gain the col between it and Druim Fiaclach, which holds a small lochan.

Climb the rocky ridge to gain the summit of Druim Fiaclach (869m) and traverse south-west along the splendid ridge. Although not a Corbett, this is possibly the finest of the group, with its narrow ridge having a number of small rock pinnacles along its undulating crest, which give the hill its name of 'toothed ridge'.

Descend steeply south off the end to the Bealach an Fhalaisg Dhuibh (c.745m). Now climb south past some lovely small pools to a tiny lochan on the crest of An t-Slat-bheinn, before turning west-south-west along the ridge to gain the top of this peak (c.830m). Descend the far side and finally climb to the summit of Sgùrr na Bà Glaise (**8.75km; 1100m; 4h**).

Descend steeply north-west to the col, Bealach an Fhìona (701m), then ascend the other side to pick up an old boundary wall at a tiny lochan and follow this to the summit of Rois-Bheinn, where bits of trig pillar form the cairn (**10.25km; 1290m; 4h 45min**).

Sgùrr na Bà Glaise, Rois-Bheinn and An Stac from Druim Fiaclach, with An Sgùrr on Eigg in the sea, right (Derek Sime)

An Stac from An t-Slat-bheinn with Eigg, Rum, the Skye Cuillin and Blàbheinn beyond (Rab Anderson)

The wall can be followed across the dip to the large cairn on the west top (878m), which, although not the highest point, gives the better views; an additional 1.2km, 100m, 30min there and back.

Return alongside the wall to the tiny lochan, then descend steeply north and north-west beside the wall before leaving it to gain the col below An Stac. Although daunting, the 255m climb proves surprisingly easy by a continually interesting route, weaving in and around the rocks, to gain this fine and isolated rocky summit (**12.5km; 1545m; 6h**).

Descend the even steeper north ridge; there are traces of path and a straightforward zigzag line gains the glaciated slabs at the bealach with Seann Chruach (521m) to the north. Although this can be climbed, the preferred option will no doubt be to take a slanting line down to the north-east from the far side of the bealach. This joins an ATV track in the floor of the glen, which leads to the end of the hydro track. Follow the hydro track to rejoin the uphill route and return to the start (**17km; 1550m; 7h 30min**).

Sgùrr na Bà Glaise from the south ridge of An Stac (Rab Anderson)

East from the summit of Beinn an Aodainn across Loch Cuaich to Gleouraich, Spidean Mialach, Meall Dubh, then Gairich, Sgurr Mòr and Sgurr Mhurlagain (Rab Anderson)

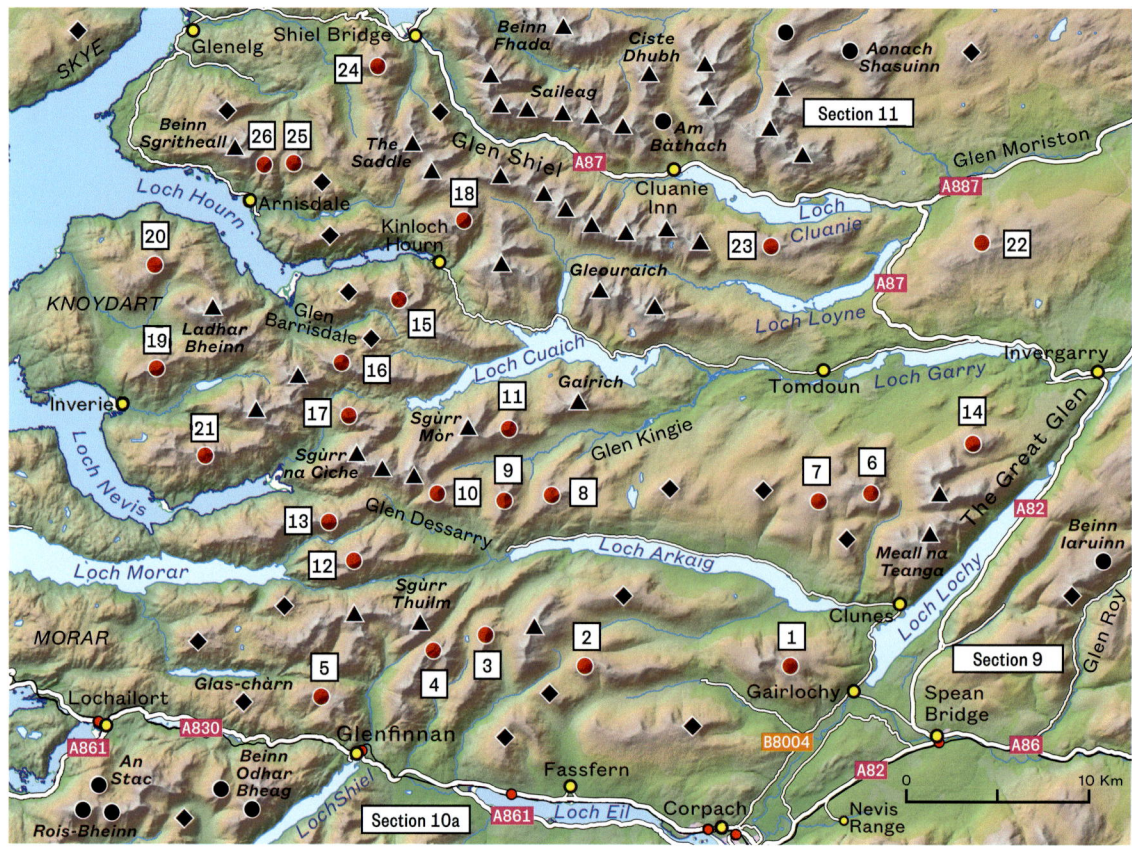

SECTION 10b

Beinn Bhàn from the Commando Memorial above Spean Bridge (Rab Anderson)

Beinn Bhàn; *796m; (C166); L34 or L41; NN140857; white hill*

Running westwards from the southern end of the Great Glen is a curving through-glen formed by Glen Loy and Gleann Sùileag, which is bounded on the north and west by a 25km-long chain of hills. Beinn Bhàn lies at the east end of this chain, with another Corbett, Meall a' Phùbuill, about two-thirds of the way along to the west, then two Grahams.

Filling the ground between Glen Loy and the ends of Loch Arkaig and Loch Lochy, Beinn Bhàn's eastern aspect is readily seen from the A82 to the south and north of Spean Bridge. However, its steep-sided south facing Coire Mhuilinn above Glen Loy remains hidden and it is by a circuit around this corrie from Inverskilavulin halfway along Glen Loy that the ascent is best made.

There is a small parking area on the left at NN125831, beside the entrance to a forest track, just before Inverskilavulin Bridge over the River Loy. This is also the parking for Stob a' Ghrianain, a Graham, on the south side of Glen Loy.

Walk across the bridge and go up the track on the right for 280m to the gate leading to Inverskilavulin and its lodges, then leave the track to follow an ATV track up left by the fence. Pass a bridge over the Allt Coire Mhuilinn, the return route, and start to climb the steepening slope on a path, which in summer can be plagued by bracken.

When the path nears the Allt Coire Mhuilinn again, at about the 300m contour, continue directly up the hillside to gain an easing of the angle overlooking the corrie. The view southwards to Ben Nevis, revealing

the full extent of its mighty North Face, is special.

Curve easily around the steep slopes dropping into Coire Mhuilinn, over two slight rises (both 771m) then drop slightly before making the final easy, short ascent south-east onto the flat summit. A sizeable cairn and a trig point sit in the far north-east corner overlooking a steep drop to Loch Arkaig, and could prove awkward to locate in poor visibility (**5km; 765m; 2h 25min**).

Situated above the junction of Loch Arkaig with The Great Glen and Loch Lochy, it is a grand viewpoint.

To return, head south-westwards across the flat summit area for about 250m before descending south through some bouldery ground. When the slope starts to steepen, curve south-westwards down grassy ground towards the Allt Coire Mhuilinn.

Pick up a path above the fence here, and follow this around the corner of the fence, then down by the falls and cascades of the Allt Coire Mhuilinn. Cross the bridge over the burn passed earlier and return to the start (**9km; 765m; 3h 40min**).

Meall a' Phùbuill; 774m; (C202); L41; NN029854; hill of the tent

Meall a' Phùbuill lies to the west of Beinn Bhàn, about two-thirds of the way along the 25km-long chain of hills on the north side of the Glen Loy and Gleann Sùileag route through to Loch Eil. Its position means that it can either be climbed from the end of the road in Glen Loy, or from Fassfern on Loch Eil at the foot of Gleann Sùileag. As well as having better parking, the advantage of the Fassfern route is that Meall a' Phùbuill can be combined with an ascent of the two Grahams to its south-west.

For the Glen Loy approach, drive up Glen Loy to Achanellan, passing Inverskilavulin and the start of the route to Beinn Bhàn. Just before the gate across the end of the public road, there is limited parking by the bins at the entrance to a forest track on the right, and a short way up it.

Go through the gate and follow the road west past the houses, then continue along the track beyond. When the forestry plantation ends, leave the track and follow an ATV track northwards up the side of the forest, which can be boggy; a line over to the left by the deer fence is drier. From the top edge of the trees,

veer north-westward and climb uphill to meet an old boundary wall running along the crest of the ridgeline. At 375m, the ascent line potentially passes an unexpected and curious deep fissure at NN08088533.

The route alongside the wall, and the two sections of fence posts linking it when it briefly stops, is a lengthy 4km scenic highway along the Druim Gleann Laoigh ridge. After passing over Pt.698m and Pt.747m, the wall ends beneath a rocky section, just above the col with Meall a' Phùbuill. Cross the col (c.645m), where the continuation fence posts turn south, then climb the grassy slope to the broad, flat top of Meall a' Phùbuill (**7.75km; 815m; 3h 10min**).

A slightly shorter, but less attractive, ascent can be made by following the track along the side of the glen to the far end of the Brian Choille native woodland, then climbing diagonally up the steep hillside to meet the wall between Pt.698m and Pt.747m.

The best return is probably the same way, although this involves a 100m climb back over Pt.747m then a 50m climb back over Pt.698m (**15.5km; 965m; 5h 40min**).

The alternative is to return towards the col with Pt.747m, then follow the fence posts south down Coire nan Laogh, passing a long water-slide of fragmental dark rock in the burn. This is the agglomerate of a volcanic vent – a rare phenomenon for the Western Highlands. Partway down, cross the burn and take a south-easterly line to gain a rough path in the floor of the glen. Follow the path, then the track back (**15.75km; 840m; 5h 40min**).

Bracken can plague the slopes of this route in summer.

For the Fassfern approach, turn off the A830 along Loch Eil and follow the short loop road to Fassfern. There is a small car park, accessed from the apex of the loop, on the west side of the An t-Sùileag burn.

Walk across the bridge, then turn left along a track signed to Glen Loy and follow it through lovely woodland by the burn to join a hydro track after 2.25km. Go right up this track for 100m, then turn left across a burn on the old track, and branch right uphill by the burn to gain a higher track. Turn left and follow this track to leave the forestry plantation and continue through an area of native trees.

Meall a' Phùbuill from Pt.747m, with Gulvain behind and distant Sgùrr Ghiubhsachain (Rab Anderson)

Leave the main track where it continues to a dam, then cross a bridge over the An t-Sùileag and go through a gate. Pass a path off right to Glensulaig bothy, 350m away, and follow the rough track quite steeply up the hillside. Shortly after crossing a bridge over the Allt Fionn Doire, leave the track and climb northward up the steepening grassy slope, which eases towards the top, to gain the flat top of Meall a' Phùbuill (**7.25km; 790m; 2h 50min**).

Return the same way (14.5km; 815m; 4h 50min).

For the inclusion of Meall Onfhaidh and Aodann Chlèireig, the two Grahams, there are two options for the descent off Meall a' Phùbuill:

(i) Go down the south-west ridge, which is very steep, and keep to the blunt crest to avoid some minor crags. Cross the rough track and the wide col, then climb quite steeply south-west to Meall Onfhaidh (**9.75km; 1090m; 4h 10min**).

(ii) Alternatively, go back down the ascent route and cross the bridge over the Allt Fionn Doire, then climb to Meall Onfhaidh, especially in winter. A rough ATV track can be followed westwards for a way up the easier-angled slope. Beyond this, veer west-north-west to gain the summit; an added 1km, 40m, 20min to (i).

Descend the steep and grassy hillside westwards, curving left towards the bottom, to gain the col, then climb the broad north shoulder of Aodann Chlèireig. Either go up a break between the crags at the top, then go right to the summit, which is on a rocky knoll, or follow a ramp up right, then cut back left above the crags (**12.5km; 1405m; 5h 30min**).

Follow the remains of a wire fence south-eastwards to where this veers off downhill, then continue down the broad ridge of Druim Beag. Cross a stile over a deer fence, then follow a rough ATV track down to the forestry area, through a break in the younger trees onto a track. Turn left along this track, then right at a junction, and descend between two ponds to follow a short link path to the car park (17.5km; 1405m; 6h 50min).

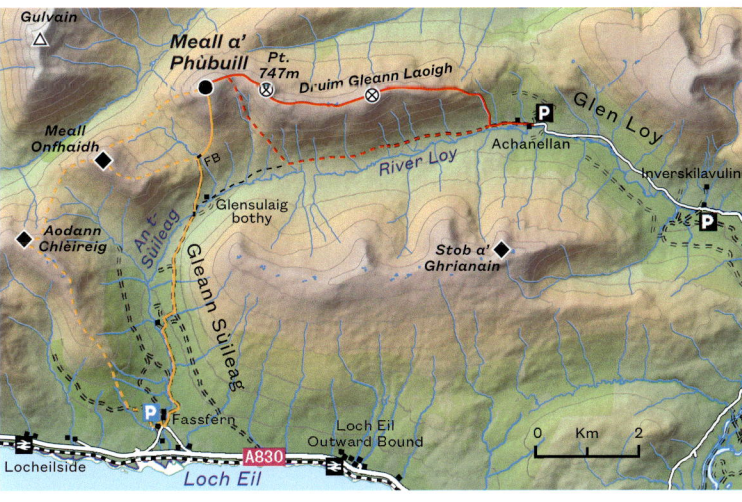

Bràigh nan Uamhachan; 765m; (C216); L40; NM975867; slope of the caves

---

Flanked either side by its higher neighbours, Streap to the west and Gulvain to the east, Bràigh nan Uamhachan is the northern highpoint of a slender, triple-topped, northward-running ridgeline.

Lying either side of the start of this ridgeline are Gleann Dubh Lighe to the west and Gleann Fionnlighe to the east. Both glens can be used to approach the summit, but the Gleann Dubh Lighe approach is by far the better since it enables all three tops on the ridge to be traversed. It also has better parking at the start, and is therefore the route described.

Whilst Bràigh nan Uamhachan may be one of the smallest of the Corbetts, it is far from being the easiest. However, the ridge is splendid and the scenery superb, making it a memorable outing.

The route up Gleann Dubh Lighe starts from the Fassfern Estate's

signposted Craigag Car Park at NM930798, a short way up an access road off the north side of the A830, some 2 miles (3km) to the east of Glenfinnan. This is the same start point as for the principal route to Streap, with both routes following the track past Dubh Lighe bothy to the edge of the forest.

Walk back to the main road and go left along the verge for 60m, then turn left up a short section of road and go through a gate onto a track. Follow the track up Gleann Dubh Lighe through mixed woodland beside the falls, cascades and pools of the Dubh Lighe river for 2.5km to where a track branches off left.

Double back downhill to the right on the main track, which crosses a bridge over the river, then continue up the other side past the Dubh Lighe bothy. In a further 1km, go through a gate to exit the forest, then leave the

track and climb steeply uphill by the fence to gain the start of the ridge.

Climb onto Na h-Uamhachan (691m) with its small lochans, picking up a line of fence posts coming up from Gleann Fionnlighe to the right, then drop to a col at c.585m to meet a wall. Continue beside the wall onto Sròn Liath (c.720m), then descend to a col at 683m.

A short way up the slope on the far side, the wall turns sharply left and drops off the ridge. Continue up the ridge to the summit where there are two highpoints some 50m apart, with the further away one being the highest (**10km; 935m; 3h 50min**).

Return the same way (20km; 1130m; 6h 40min).

The track can be biked for 3.5km or so, for a saving of about 1h on the times given, although beyond the bothy it becomes more awkward.

Map and photo on next page

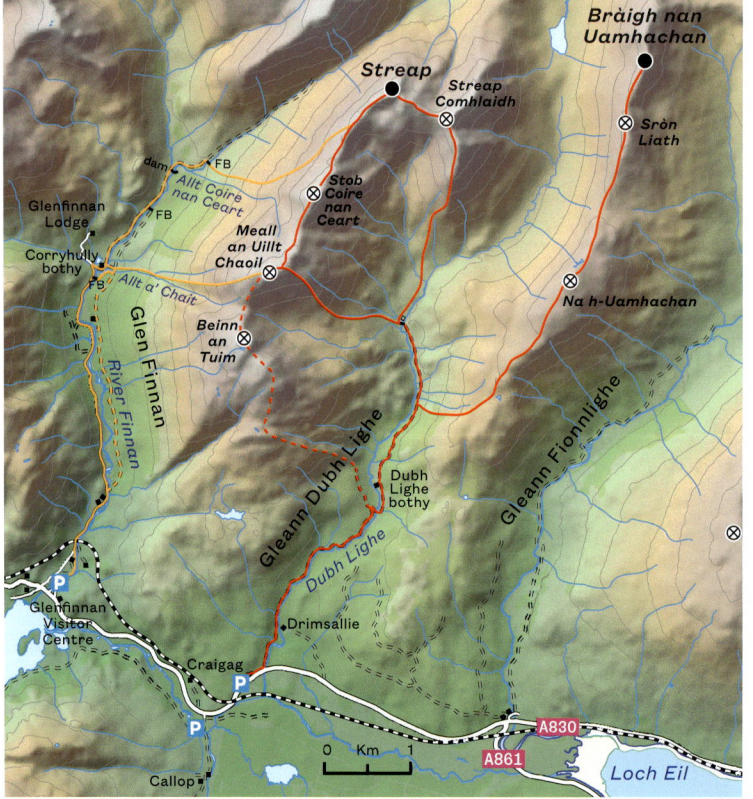

Bràigh nan Uamhachan's summit from Sròn Liath, with Sgùrr nan Coireachan, Sgùrr Còs na Breachd-laoidh, Druim a' Chùirn, Sgùrr Mòr and Sgùrr an Fhuarain beyond (Rab Anderson)

Streap; *909m; (C12); L40; NM946863; climbing hill*

Streap is the highest summit in a north-eastwards-running chain of hills between Glen Finnan and Gleann Dubh Lighe. It can be approached from either glen, but the route from Gleann Dubh Lighe, as well as having more convenient (free) parking, is perhaps more attractive and gives a better circuit, with the possibility of including some, or all, of Streap's attendant peaks.

The Glen Dubh Lighe approach starts from Fassfern Estate's Craigag car park at NM930798, signposted a short way off the north side of the A830, some 2 miles (3km) to the east of Glenfinnan. The Bràigh nan Uamhachan route starts here as well, and both routes follow the track towards Dubh Lighe bothy.

Walk back to the main road and go left along the verge for 60m, then turn left up a short section of road and pass through a gate onto a track. Follow the track up Gleann Dubh

Lighe through mixed woodland beside the falls, cascades and pools of the Dubh Lighe river for 2.5km to where a track branches off left. There are two options from here:

(i) The usual route is to double back downhill to the right on the main track, which crosses a bridge over the river, then continue up the other side past Dubh Lighe bothy. In a further 1km, go through a gate to exit the forest. This is where the route to Bràigh nan Uamhachan goes up right.

Continue on the rougher track for a further 1km, and cross a bridge over the river to reach the burn that comes off Meall an Uillt Chaoil, opposite a walled enclosure on the other side. Climb the hillside to the left of the burn, the Allt Caol, to gain the steeper ridge bounding its deep-cut upper section, then follow this to the rocky crest 200m to the east of Meall an Uillt Chaoil's summit (844m), which can easily be included if desired.

(ii) Follow the left-hand track uphill to exit the forest by a gate, then either climb over double-topped Beinn an Tuim (795m and 810m), a demoted Corbett, and drop to the col to its north, Bealach a' Chait (c.665m), or traverse north-west across the slope beneath Beinn an Tuim into Coire an Tuim, then ascend to the col. Climb over Meall an Uillt Chaoil (844m) to

join option (i). Slightly shorter, but with more ascent, so taking the same time; about 15min quicker if Beinn an Tuim is traversed across.

With both options having joined, descend the ridge northwards and cut around the left side of a rocky rise to gain the Bealach Coire nan Cearc (c.745m). Ascend the rocky, but easy, ridge onto Stob Coire nan Cearc (887m). The pointed summit of Streap lies ahead, and is gained by descending a narrowing ridge to a col, then continuing up a superb, sharp and steep-sided ridge where the drop into the head of Glen Finnan on the left creates a satisfying sense of exposure. A band of rock across the crest is easily negotiated by the path to gain the splendid summit (**9.75km; 1150m; 4h 5min**).

Descend the ridge to the south-east to cross the col at 818m, and climb to Streap Comhlaidh (898m). Go down the grassy ridge to the south and climb over the slight rise of Pt.859m, then make the long descent south down the mainly grassy ridge to join an ATV track at the bottom. The ATV track is followed across the combined burns flowing off Streap to reach the walled enclosure, where a crossing of the Allt Caol gains the approach route, which is followed back (**18.75km; 1300m; 6h 45min**).

The track can be biked for 3.5km or so, for a saving of about 1h. Beyond the bothy, it gives more difficult going.

An ascent can also be made via Glen Finnan, starting from the National Trust for Scotland visitor centre pay-and-display car park. A track from the north end of the car park leads across a bridge to join the estate road up the glen, which is followed towards Corryhully bothy.

There is no bridge across the River Finnan at the bothy, so either cross by a footbridge 350m before it, then go around the bottom of the forestry to gain a track, or continue to the bothy and ford the river to reach the track. This point can also be gained from a bridge nearer the start at NM913819, then along the track on the east side of the river.

Ascend up the side of the forestry and make a steep climb to Meall an Uillt Chaoil, where the principal route is joined and followed to Streap (**9km; 1115m; 3h 50min**).

To descend, return down the south-west ridge, then drop off right and go down a south-westwards-slanting shelf. Once clear of the steeper slopes, continue down to the upper River Finnan, which can be crossed by a bridge at NM925855, or forded. The track on the other side leads back to Corryhully (**18km; 1140m; 6h 20min**).

Streap and Streap Comhlaidh, with Sgùrr Mhurlagain beyond (Rab Anderson)

Sgùrr an Utha from Fraoch-bheinn, with Eigg, left, then Meith Bheinn and the Cuillin on Skye, right (Rab Anderson)

Sgùrr an Utha; *796m; (C168); L40; NM885839; peak of the udder*

Hidden from any roadside view by its slightly lower attendant top, Fraoch-bheinn, Sgùrr an Utha is the highest point of a well-defined west-wards-running range of rocky hills that rise steeply to the north of the A830 between Glenfinnan and Mallaig. The range is bounded to the north by the deep gash of the Caol-Ghleann and Gleann Don, then lonely Loch Beoraid, and is separated from Streap and its attendant peaks by Glen Finnan. The ascent of Sgùrr an Utha with Fraoch-bheinn gives a pleasant walk with rewarding summit panoramas.

Start from a layby on the south side of the A830 at NM873817, just west of the bridge over the Allt an Utha – the Drochaid Allt an Utha.

Walk down the inside of the crash barrier, then step over it and cross the bridge on a pavement to follow the verge, then cross to a forest track on the other side. Traffic travels fast on this stretch of road.

Step around the side of a gate, then follow the track uphill through the forestry plantation and out into the open. Just before the track crosses a bridge, take to a track on the right and follow it steeply uphill to its end at a height of 435m. A rough path continues and soon leads to a small outcrop of rock where it fades. There are two options here:

(i) Continue up the steeper slope of Druim na Brein-choille, then swing north-eastwards, either through or up the side of an obvious notch in the hillside. This gains flat ground, which is followed to the craggy upper slopes of Fraoch-bheinn, heading towards a prominent small crag, to reach a distinctive cleft before it with a burn running down it.

(ii) Go left beneath the outcrop and ascend the hillside to take a lower diagonal line up a series of grassy shelves to reach the distinctive cleft in the rock with a burn. This is a grassier, but potentially wetter line.

Ascend steep grass up the side of the cleft and continue up the rise beyond, past the crag, onto another shelf. A traverse left from here gains the col with Sgùrr an Utha. However, the better and more scenic route is to

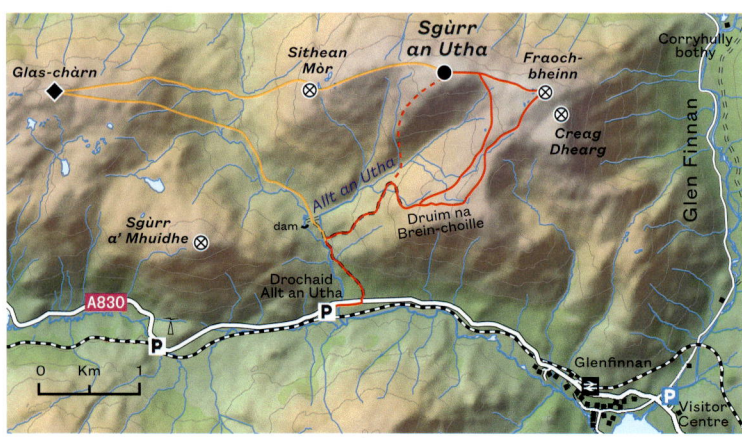

continue to the top of Fraoch-bheinn. There are two highpoints, the south-easterly of which is noted as being the highest at 790m. Drop north-west off this to a small lochan in a narrow dip, then climb past a slab of rock to gain the north-west top, which has a large boulder perched on it.

Across the steep drop into Glen Finnan, Streap and its attendant peaks look magnificent, with the distant, wind turbine-clad Meall Dubh framed in the gap between Streap and Sgùrr Thuilm. Creag Meagaidh and its window can be seen through the gap with Beinn an Tuim, then rightwards are The Aonachs, Ben Nevis and a sea of peaks stretching across Bidean nam Bian to Garbh Bheinn and Sgùrr Dhomhnuill.

Descend westwards to the col with Sgùrr an Utha, then climb over a slight rise and on up to its small, pointed rocky summit, where the cairn sits above a steep drop to the north (**5.75km; 755m; 2h 30min**).

As with Fraoch-bheinn, the views are magnificent. Westwards, the eye is led down the length of lonely Loch Beoraid to Eigg and Rum, with the hills of distant Barra between them. To the right of Rum is distant Beinn Mhòr on South Uist, then the Cuillin on Skye.

It is easier to return to the col with Fraoch-bheinn, then traverse across to pick up the higher, or lower, ascent line and follow this back to the track, then the start (**10.75km; 770m; 4h**).

A more direct return can be made from the summit by descending south-west to pick up a burn and follow this to the Allt an Utha, which is crossed to regain the track. This is quite steep and gives rough going.

An ascent can also be made by the western ridge, reached by crossing the bridge at the foot of the Allt an Utha, then climbing northwards to Sìthean Mòr and turning right up the ridge to the summit.

Sgùrr an Utha can be combined with Glas-chàrn, a Graham, to the west. However, it is best to climb Glas-chàrn first, then ascend Sgùrr an Utha by its long western ridge over Sìthean Mòr, as described in the SMC's guidebook *The Grahams & The Donalds* (**14km; 1100m; 5h 40min**).

> **Meall na h-Eilde**; *838m; (C110); L34; NN185946; hill of the hinds*
> **Geal Chàrn**; *804m; (C155); L34; NN156942; white cairn*

Lying to the west of the Loch Lochy Munros, and rising above the east end of Loch Arkaig, Meall na h-Eilde, the intermediate Meall Coire nan Saobhaidh, and Geal Chàrn form a compact group of rounded hills to the north of the smaller but bulkier Glas Bheinn, a Graham.

Meall na h-Eilde and Geal Chàrn are best climbed from Achnasaul, set back above Loch Arkaig, a short distance along the roller coaster road from its east end. A start here also enables Glas Bheinn to be included in the ascent.

There is parking in a long pull-off and passing place on the west side of the Allt Dubh, which flows down from the hills. The pull-off is just beyond the entrance to the MOWI fish farm building and the track down to the lochside, where Beinn Bhàn rises above the opposite side of the loch.

Walk back over the bridge and follow a hydro track up above the east side of the Allt Dubh to where it swings left to end at a dam beneath the steep slope rising to Glas Bheinn.

Continue on the original track up the glen between Beinn Mheadhoin and Glas Bheinn to where it peters out, then head north-east to the col (440m) to the north of Glas Bheinn, at the head of Gleann Tarsuinn.

Cross the Allt Tarsuinn then climb north-east up the prominent, steep rounded spur that falls from Pt.681m, whose top is bypassed. There is an interesting view west-north-west, through the Bealach Càrn na h-Urchaire to the side of Geal Chàrn, of a distant Druim Cosaidh ridge on the Corbett Sgùrr a' Choire-bheithe, with Ladhar Bheinn to its side. To the south-east, the Grey Corries, The Aonachs and Ben Nevis are framed between the Meall na Teanga group and Glas Bheinn. A gradual ascent leads on up north-east to the stony top of Meall na h-Eilde to meet a line of fence posts (**7km; 790m; 2h 50min**).

There is a grand view here into the northern corries of Meall na Teanga, with Sròn a' Choire Ghairbh to the north and pointed Ben Tee just showing to its side.

Descend north-west beside the fence posts to the Bealach Choire a' Ghuirein (722m), then climb onto Meall Coire nan Saobhaidh (826m). Continue west-south-west down a ▶

Meall na h-Eilde with Sròn a' Choire Ghairbh beyond (Rab Anderson)

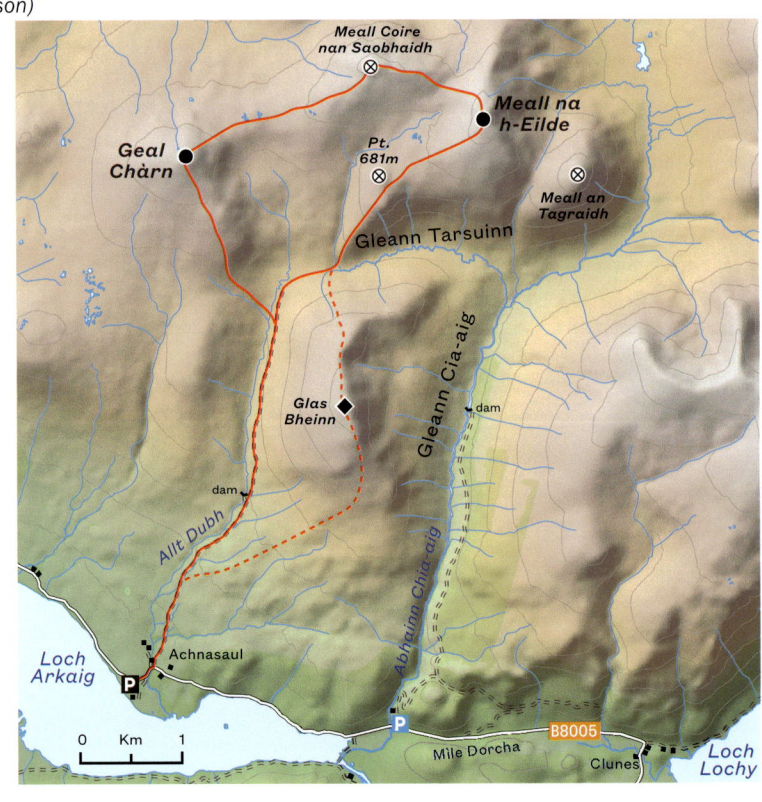

Geal Chàrn from Pt.681m (Rab Anderson)

broad ridge, passing a small lochan near the bottom, to gain the Bealach Càrn na h-Urchaire (648m), then climb south-west, still following the fence posts. There is a trig point on the summit of Geal Chàrn, and a splendid view of a multitude of peaks to the west and north-west (**10.5km; 1045m; 4h 15min**).

Head south-south-east down an easy grassy slope, which steepens towards the bottom, then drop down beside a small burn to cross the Allt Dubh and return down the track (16.5km; 1045m; 6h).

If Glas Bheinn is to be included, it is best to ascend this first by leaving the hydro track before its end to climb steeply onto the broad south ridge.

Descend easily north from the summit to where the ridge curves north-eastwards, then drop steeply north to the col at 440m at the head of Gleann Tarsuinn to ascend the spur to Pt.681 and Meall na h-Eilde, an added 0.5km, 295m, 55min.

> *Sgùrr Mhurlagain; 880m; (C49); L33; NN012944; rough-topped peaks*
> *Fraoch Bheinn; 858m; (C81); L33 & L40; NM986940; heather hill*

Forming part of a compact group of four Corbetts that lie to the north of the west end of Loch Arkaig, Sgùrr Mhurlagain and Fraoch Bheinn are conveniently climbed together. They lie close to the end of the road at the entrance to Glen Dessarry, and sit either side of the Fèith a' Bhrolaich pass, which is a route through to remote Glen Kingie.

Sgùrr Mhurlagain presents a broad grassy flank towards Loch Arkaig above the cottage at Murlaggan. Its higher rocks are unusual, being largely composed of a beautiful pale granite gneiss, marking the junction between the smooth granulite hills to the east and the rugged schist mountains to the west.

Fraoch Bheinn is perhaps the more interesting hill, particularly on its north side where narrow ridges and steep rocky corries overlook Glen Kingie and the Corbett Sgùrr an Fhuarain. It is the most easterly of the craggy schist mountains, which stretch westwards from it into the Rough Bounds of Knoydart.

The ascent begins from a good car park at the end of the wonderful 12 mile (20km) roller coaster single-track road along Loch Arkaig. There are another four Corbetts accessed from this car park, as well as four Munros and one Graham, so it can get busy; please park considerately.

Follow the continuation track for 1km around the base of Meallan Dubh at the foot of Sgùrr Mhurlagain's long south-west ridge, passing the track down to Strathan. About 50m before the bridge across the Dearg Allt, leave the track and follow a vague stalkers' path uphill beside the burn; the signposted right of way actually follows an ugly and boggy track up the far side of the burn.

After a further 1km or so, the path joins the ATV track, which comes across from the other side of the burn. Continue on the track up easier-angled ground for a short way, then break off right to climb onto, then up, Sgùrr Mhurlagain's long, but easy, south-west ridge, which affords fine views down the length of Loch Arkaig and over to Ben Nevis. The ridge broadens with height, and the final, slightly steeper slope leads to the curving summit crest, where the cairn is perched on the edge of the northern corrie, with a view across Glen Kingie to Gairich (**6km; 840m; 2h 45min**).

Return down the ridge until above the Fèith a' Bhrolaich pass between the hills, then drop down and cross flat, boggy ground (458m). This leads to the foot of the obvious broad ridge that falls from Fraoch Bheinn. It is quite a rocky ridge, but a fairly direct line up the middle, zigzagging on steep,

▶

Sgùrr Mhurlagain and its south-west ridge, with Loch Arkaig beyond, from Fraoch Bheinn (Rab Anderson)

Fraoch Bheinn and its long south ridge from the south side of Glen Dessarry over A' Chùil bothy (Rab Anderson)

but grassy ground, proves remarkably straightforward. Turn the upper rocks either side, probably easiest on the right, and continue to the summit (**10km; 1245m; 4h 35min**)

Another option for the ascent from the col, which is slightly longer, is to swing left into Coire na Cloiche Bige and take a grassy line up onto the south-south-west ridge, then turn north up this to gain the summit.

If time permits, it is worthwhile continuing north for a short way along the summit ridge across the slight dip to the north top (854m), to look down at a huge rock-slip on the east side of the hill at the head of Coire na Cloiche Moire. The slip is delimited by fissures that cut deep into the hillside.

Descend Fraoch Bheinn's long and rugged south-south-west ridge. On a slight rise at 510m, turn south-south-east, then descend again and cross an old fenceline at the bottom to gain the eroded track down the west side of the Dearg Allt. The track leads down to the main track, which is followed back (**14.5km; 1255m; 6h 15min**).

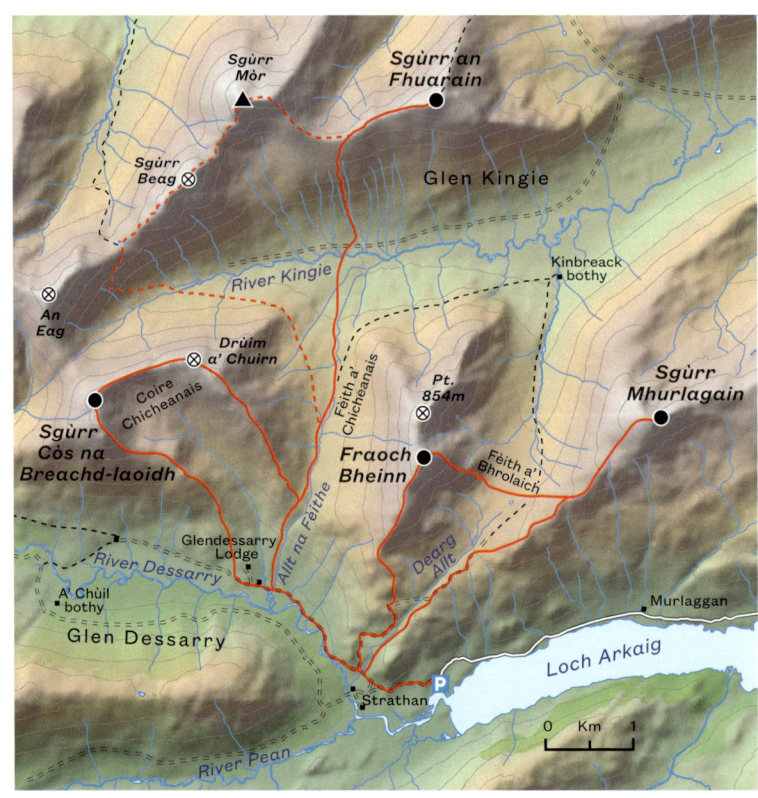

Sgùrr Còs na Breachd-laoidh; 835m; (C112); L33 or L40; NM948946; peak of the hollow of the speckled calf

One of the four closely-grouped Corbetts lying to the north of Glen Dessarry and the west end of Loch Arkaig, Sgùrr Còs na Breachd-laoidh is separated from Fraoch Bheinn and Sgùrr Mhurlagain to its east by the Fèith a' Chicheanais pass through to Glen Kingie. It is awkward to combine into a round with those two hills, and although it could be combined into a circuit around the head of Glen Kingie with Sgùrr an Fhuarain, this would entail climbing over Sgùrr Mòr (1003m), Sgùrr Beag (890m) and An Eag (873m) to get to it. As a result, it is best climbed on its own, and when climbed with the Druim a' Chùirn ridge to its east for a horseshoe circuit of Coire Chicheanais, it gives a pleasant outing amidst splendid mountain scenery.

Start from the car park at the end of the 12 mile (20km) roller coaster single-track road along Loch Arkaig. There are another five Corbetts accessed from here, as well as four Munros and one Graham, so it can get busy; please park considerately.

Walk west along the continuation track, past the track down to Strathan, around the base of the long ridges that fall from Sgùrr Mhurlagain and Fraoch Bheinn, then alongside the River Dessarry heading towards Glendessarry Lodge.

Before reaching the estate buildings that sit below Glendessarry Lodge, cross the bridge over the Allt na Fèithe, which flows down from the Fèith a' Chicheanais pass, then leave the track. Follow a vague path, which soon develops into a good stalkers' path to the side of the Allt na Fèithe, and climb uphill towards the Fèith a' Chicheanais pass.

Above a slightly steeper section, and well before the head of the pass, break off left at a group of large boulders at NM972936, then climb the grassy hillside, which is dotted with boulders. This leads to, then up, the rocky ridge, which gives a steady climb that eases towards the top to gain Pt.815m. From there, follow the remains of a fence and wall line north-westwards for 250m to gain the top of Druim a' Chùirn (Pt.822m).

Descend westwards past the prominent pinnacle of A' Chìoch to gain the lowest point (748m) at the head of Coire Chicheanais. Ascend the curving ridge ahead, following a grassy line through outcrops of rock beside the odd fence post. This leads to the summit, marked by a small cairn on a rock outcrop with some small pools of water by it, just beyond where the fence posts make a right angled turn to the north-west (**7.5km; 875m; 3h 15min**).

Follow the summit ridge to the south past some slight rises, keeping to the right side to avoid some crags, then swing south-eastwards and descend more steeply to gain the easier-angled ridge below. Continue down the ridge and the easier slopes below to gain the track to the west of the lodge, then follow this back (14km; 900m; 5h 15min).

Map on opposite page

Druim a' Chuirn, right, Sgùrr Còs na Breachd-laoidh, centre, and Bidein a' Chabair, left, from Fraoch Bheinn (Rab Anderson)

Sgùrr an Fhuarain; 901m; (C20); L33 or L40; NM987979; peak of the spring

The northern outlier of a compact group of four Corbetts to the north of Glen Dessarry and the end of Loch Arkaig, Sgùrr an Fhuarain sits at the east end of a long ridge that snakes westwards over Sgùrr Mòr and the three Glen Dessarry Munros to end on Beinn an Aodainn (Ben Aden). It lies to the west of isolated Gairich, between remote Glen Kingie and Loch Cuaich, and takes the form of a shapely pyramid, connected to Sgùrr Mòr to its west by a slender grassy ridge.

Like Sgùrr Mòr, Sgùrr an Fhuarain is a standalone mountain in its hill grouping, so it is normal to climb both together, which avoids having to ascend the daunting 510m steep slope on the north side of Glen Kingie twice in one's hillwalking days.

The easiest route to Sgùrr an Fhuarain is from the car park at the end of the 12 mile (20km) single-track road along Loch Arkaig. There are another five Corbetts accessed from here, as well as four Munros and one Graham, so it can get busy.

Walk west along the track, past the track down to Strathan, around the base of the long ridges that fall from Sgùrr Mhurlagain and Fraoch Bheinn, then alongside the River Dessarry, heading towards Glendessarry Lodge.

Before reaching the estate buildings that sit below Glendessarry Lodge, cross the bridge over the Allt na Fèithe, which flows down from the Fèith a' Chicheanais pass, then leave the track. Follow a vague path up the side of the burn, which soon develops into a good stalkers' path, and climb uphill to cross the Fèith a' Chicheanais pass (c.365m) between the hills.

At the point where the ground begins to fall away into Glen Kingie, and the path shown on the map heads north-east towards Kinbreck bothy, descend north and ford the River Kingie; it is normally possible to make the crossing dry. In high water conditions, it may be necessary to go quite far upstream to find a safe crossing place.

Rising ahead is the uniformly steep and daunting slope of Doire nan Cluainean. Choose one of the grassy ribs between the small burns and make the long and relentless 510m ascent to the saddle between Sgùrr Mòr and Sgùrr an Fhuarain. Turn right and follow the ridgeline stalkers' path easily up the pleasant grassy ridge to the top of Sgùrr an Fhuarain (**9.5km; 1020m; 3h 55min**).

Returning the same way is the quickest, if your knees will take the punishing descent to Glen Kingie (**19km; 1295m; 6h 55min**).

Much better, though, is to return to the saddle and follow the stalkers' path up onto Sgùrr Mòr (**12.25km; 1310m; 5h**), then south-eastwards down to and over Sgùrr Beag to the col beyond at 652m.

Take the path on the left and descend south-west, then east into Glen Kingie. Leave the path at a suitable point to cross the River Kingie at about the 330m contour. Once across, make a rising traverse, following deer tracks across boggy terrain, to regain the approach route at the Fèith a' Chicheanais pass, and return as for the approach (**24.25km; 1500m; 8h 45min**).

Map on page 236

Sgùrr an Fhuarain and its west ridge from across the saddle with Sgùrr Mòr (Rab Anderson)

Càrn Mòr from Pt.616m, with An Stac, left, and Bidein a' Chabair, right (Rab Anderson)

Càrn Mòr; 829m; (C116); L33 or L40; NM903909; *big cairn*

Càrn Mòr's summit is the highest point of an 11km-long ridge between Glen Pean and Glen Dessarry. The eastern half of the ridge, rising above Strathan and over Monadh Gorm (478m), lacks interest and the lower slopes are forested.

However, the western half beyond Pt.616m takes on the rugged and steep-sided character of the Knoydart peaks. The western end of the ridge above the head of Loch Morar is as rough and rocky as any of Càrn Mòr's more famous neighbours.

The approach is made from the car park at the end of the single-track road along Loch Arkaig. A bike can be used on the initial forestry track for a saving of about 1h 30min on the day.

Follow the track west, then turn left down through Strathan and cross the River Dessarry to gain a forest track on the right. Follow this track through the trees to exit the plantation above A' Chùil bothy. Bikes are best left at the fence around the forest (about **40min** by bike), (**5.5km; 135m; 1h 25min** on foot).

Cross the burn, then leave the track, and climb the hillside to the right of the burn to gain the ridge. Pass through a haggy section and follow the ridge onto the rocky top of Pt.616m. Descend the ridge gently westwards to cross a col, then follow a grassy shelf up left beneath some rock outcrops and boulders to gain Càrn Mòr's east-north-east ridge.

Take the lower, and more obvious, of two grassy rakes beneath a small band of crag, and follow this up the rocky upper section, passing some small pools in a flatter section just before the top. There are two cairned highpoints some 16m apart (**11km; 910m; 4h**), on foot from the start.

The fissured slope that falls steeply to the south is the scene of one of the largest landslips in the Highlands.

Return the same way (**22km; 1050m; 7h 5min**), (about **5h 35min** with a bike).

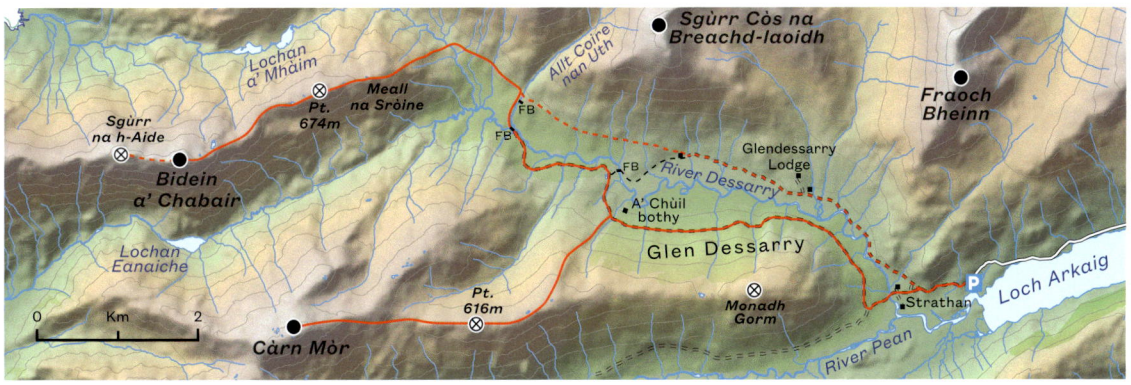

Bidein a' Chabair from the Druim Coire nan Laogh ridge with Sgùrr na h-Aide behind and Rum, right (Rab Anderson)

Bidein a' Chabair; *867m; (C66); L33 or L40; NM889930; pinnacle of the antler*

About 5km to the west of Glen-dessarry Lodge, Glen Dessarry divides into two passes, which are amongst the wildest and the most spectacular through-routes in Scotland. To the south, Gleann an Lochan Eanaiche leads to Loch Morar, whilst to the north, the Màm na Cloich' Airde leads to Loch Nevis. Between them is a steep-sided, rocky ridge, whose western end separates the upper reaches of Loch Morar and Loch Nevis. Bidein a' Chabair is the highest point of this rugged ridge, and, when seen from Loch Arkaig, it forms a sharp cone, often mistaken for Sgùrr na Cìche. It gives a superb, long, rugged and scenic ascent

The approach is from the car park at the end of the road along Loch Arkaig. There are two ways up Glen Dessarry; either by bike or on foot:

(i) The favoured way is to bike the forest track on the south side of the glen, reached by taking the track left past Strathan, then right through the forest past A' Chùil bothy and the route up to Càrn Mòr. This track leads to the junction of the Allt Coire nan Uth and the River Dessarry at

NM930934, where there is a bridge across the River Dessarry (**7.75km; 185m;** about **55min**). Distances and times are now given on foot from here.

A path on the north side leads up through the trees beside the Allt Coire nan Uth for 600m, to join the path along the north side of the glen.

(ii) This is the quickest way on foot. Follow the right of way to Loch Nevis and Inverie along the track past Glen-dessarry Lodge to the house at Upper Glendessarry on the north side of the glen, then a footpath along the top edge of the forest. It is 4.5km to Upper Glen Dessarry (which could be biked) then 2.5km to join the route from the south side of the glen.

With both routes having joined, continue along the right of way until about 200m beyond the forest, then go downhill and cross the headwaters of the River Dessarry. Climb grassy ground to the left of the rocky spur that extends from the foot of Meall na Sròine, and continue steeply uphill to its top at 600m, then on past some tiny lochans and up to Pt.674m.

Descend past a small lochan on the narrowing Druim Coire nan Laogh

ridge, which consists of rock outcrops, hummocks and hollows, to reach a small reedy pool at the lowest point. Carry on over similar ground to a larger lochan beneath the steeper upper section. Go up left here and follow a groove-line through the slabby rocks, heading towards the imposing summit prow. Tackle the prow up its left side, by a path that zigzags up steep grass to a short scramble up a rocky groove with good holds, to gain this splendid summit (**6.25km; 810m; 3h** from the bike).

On foot via the north side of the glen it is (**12.5km; 960m; 4h 40min**).

The west top, Sgùrr na h-Aide (859m), was for long shown as The Corbett, and it lies 750m away along a fine ridge without too much of an intervening drop. It is worth a visit for the fine view west; an added 1.5km, 110m, 35min there and back.

Return the same way to the bridge (**12.5km; 890m; 5h 15min**). It is about a 50min bike ride back to the start (**28km; 1185m; 7h** with a bike).

Via the north side of the glen it is (**25km; 1100m; 8h 25min** on foot).

Map on page 239

Ben Tee; 904m; (C16); L34; NN240972; fairy hill

Set apart from the Loch Lochy Munros to the south by the Bealach Easain at 548m, Ben Tee is the prominent conical hill rising above the forests in the angle where Glen Garry joins The Great Glen. From the A87 along Loch Garry, and The Great Glen to the north-east, it is the most prominent of the group. Its conical shape is also identifiable from a number of hills, near and far.

The normal route is from Kilfinnan at the north end of Loch Lochy, reached along a narrow road from just north of Laggan Swing Bridge over the Caledonian Canal. There is parking on the right at the road end, just before the bridge over the Kilfinnan Burn. This is also the parking for the Loch Lochy Munros.

Follow a rough track and path up the crest of the grassy hillside, then swing right below a steepening on a clearer section of track, heading towards a burn. At two birch trees, go steeply up left on a hill path, which then traverses back left across the hillside before turning right and climbing uphill to where Ben Tee majestically comes into view.

The path contours northwards just

below the lip, high above the Kilfinnan Burn, and, after passing through a gap in a deer fence, it swings around a bend and dips across a tributary. A few hundred metres further along, the path then climbs north-westwards away from the slope that drops to the Kilfinnan Burn, and crosses the rising moorland to climb Ben Tee's lower slopes.

After passing two boulders, the path fades for a way in the grassy terrain, but is picked up again where the route swings west-south-west up the broad and increasingly rocky ridge that leads on up to the top. The summit is further back than expected (**5km; 850m; 2h 30min**).

The view to the west and north-west of a multitude of hills and peaks is superb, and extends to the Cuillin on Skye. There is a grand perspective of The Great Glen fault with the Cairngorms to the east and Ben Nevis to the south, beyond which Ben Lawers can be picked out. The corrie to the south-west, Coire Glas, is the scene of a new pump storage hydro scheme similar to that on Ben Cruachan.

Return by the ascent route (**10km; 850m; 4h**).

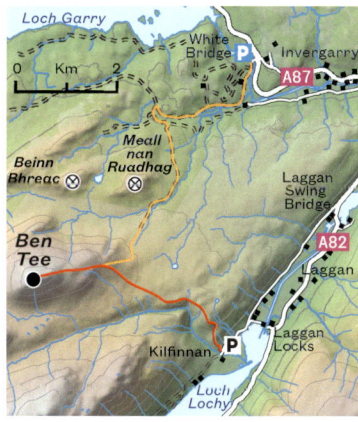

An alternative route starts from the White Bridge car park (NH283013), west of Invergarry. Follow a forestry track south by the river, then uphill to the west for 2.75km, swinging left at NH264004. Take the left-hand track after 150m, then in a further 330m, go steeply up right on a stony track to exit the forest after 2km and drop to the burn. Cross on stepping stones, and follow the track to its end, then continue up and left on a reinstated track for a way before climbing the hillside to join the Kilfinnan route on the crest (**9km; 875m; 3h 30min**). Return the same way (**18km; 910m; 6h**).

Ben Tee across Ceann Loch at the head of Loch Lochy (Robert Durran)

Sgùrr nan Eugallt from the ridge above the end of the stalkers' path (Rab Anderson)

Sgùrr nan Eugallt; *898m; (C25); L33; NG927048; peak of the furrowed rocks or precipice*

Rising above the road between the dammed waters of Loch Cuaich and the narrow sea inlet of Loch Hourn, Sgùrr nan Eugallt is the highest point of an attractive small range with a 7km-long ridgeline.

The south-western side of the range drops in uniformly steep slopes to Gleann Còsaidh and remote Sgùrr a' Choire-bheithe with its long Druim Chòsaidh ridge and the smaller, but prominent, Slat Bheinn (a Graham) in between. However, on its north-east side above the road, the range presents a series of wild and rocky corries with an outlook to Sgùrr a' Mhaoraich and Buidhe Bheinn.

It is from this single-track road, shortly before it ends at Kinloch Hourn – a 20.5 mile (33km) drive along it from the A87 in Glen Garry – that the ascent is made. The route up the hill follows a stalkers' path, which leaves the road from the north side of the bridge over the burn beside the ruin at Coireshùbh above Loch Coire Shùbh. There is parking on the right 200m before the start of the path and also 160m further on.

Follow the path, which zigzags up the slope above the burn to climb through a long and narrow, rocky gully, then on up the broad ridge beyond to make a long, rising traverse south-south-west beneath the steep slope rising to Sgùrr Dubh. Maps show the path ending at 575m, but it continues up and across a wet area at the head of a small burn, then zigzags up to end at 650m just below the ridge.

Gain the ridge, which connects Sgùrr Dubh to Sgùrr nan Eugallt and has a line of fence posts running along it, then follow it across a slight dip and on up past a tiny lochan. When the fence posts veer southwards off the ridge, continue on up the ridge with a short, steep climb at the top to gain the crest, then the trig pillar (894m). The highest point lies a further 600m to the north-west along the undulating crest, past some small pools, and is marked by a small cairn (**4.75km; 810m; 2h 25min**).

The traverse of the crest is very scenic, and it is worth continuing for a further 250m, past a small lochan, to its end on Sgùrr Sgiath Àirigh (881m) with its large cairn; an added 10min or so, there and back. There is an uninterrupted view out across Loch Hourn to the Cuillin on Skye, and over Meall nan Eun to Ladhar Bheinn and the Knoydart hills.

Return the same way. If required, the steep bit at the top can be avoided by dropping to the fence posts and following them back to the ridgeline (**9.5km; 850m; 4h 5min**).

The traverse of the ridge to Sgùrr a' Chlaidheimh is worthwhile, with a rugged but straightforward descent being made north-north-east to the road. It is down this steep hillside that Prince Charles and his small band of men slipped past the Hanoverian troops on a dark night in 1746 to escape to Glen Shiel.

Following the ascent of this hill, if there is an intention to climb Ben Aden and Sgùrr a' Choire-bheithe via the Loch Cuaich route, it is worthwhile walking down from the hydro substation to check the crossing of the Caolie Water at NG996028, which in recent times has been a short and shallow wade to the left (east) of the former bridge, due to the low waters of the loch.

Map on page 246

Sgùrr a' Choire-bheithe; 913m; (C4); L33; NG896016; peak of the birch corrie

Together with the neighbouring Beinn an Aodainn, with which it shares an awkward to-get-to location at the west end of Loch Cuaich, in an area known as the Rough Bounds of Knoydart, Sgùrr a' Choire-bheithe is one of the most remote and highly prized of the Corbett summits. It lies in an extremely rugged part of the Highlands, which also has a high rainfall, so any trip should be undertaken with due consideration for the weather, especially if the route choice includes any river crossings.

Sgùrr a' Choire-bheithe's summit lies at the west end of the splendid 7km-long Druim Chòsaidh ridge, overlooking Glen Barrisdale in Knoydart. This ridge rises gradually westwards from the end of Loch Cuaich and contains many knolls and little tops along its narrow crest. Steep and rocky slopes fall to the glens either side of the ridge, particularly below the summit, which sits above the Màm Unndalain, the pass linking routes from Loch Nevis and Loch Cuaich to Glen Barrisdale.

The easiest route itself is from Barrisdale, reached by the undulating path along Loch Hourn from the car park at Kinloch Hourn (**10.75km; 420m; 3h 10min**). The car park is at the end of a 22 mile (35km) drive along the single-track road from the A87. There is a charge and details can be found on the Lochhournhead B&B and Tea Room website.

This route will probably entail an overnight stay, either at the bothy at NG872042, or camping beside it; check the Barisdale Estate website

It may also be possible to get a boat from Arnisdale; contact Peter Fletcher on 01599 235007.

From Barrisdale, follow the track south across the bridge, past a white cottage and the ruin at Ambraigh, then leave the track before its end at a dam and cross a footbridge over the Allt Gleann Unndalain. Go up the path for 700m, then leave this at a fence around the Doire Asamaidh woodland, and ascend the 3km-long, mostly grassy, north-west ridge of Sgùrr a' Choire-bheithe, onto Pt.816m. Drop to the east and make the final ascent to the summit (**5km; 930m; 2h 40min**), from Barrisdale.

Return the same way (**10km; 950m; 4h 15min**). If a descent is to be made to the head of the Màm Unndalain

pass, it is important to return to the dip in front of Pt.816m, then descend south and south-west over a shoulder before dropping south to avoid a band of crags; about 20min longer.

Return to Kinloch Hourn (**10.75km; 430m; 3h 10min**) for a total of (**31.5km; 1800m; 10h 35min**) if walked in a day.

The other principal route is along the side of Loch Cuaich to ascend the length of the Druim Chòsaidh ridge, which on a good day is sure to be one of the most memorable days to be had in the Scottish hills.

There is space to park near the north-west corner of Loch Cuaich, at NG997034, at the entrance to an access track to a hydro substation.

Walk past the substation and go down the side of the burn to follow an old track to the remains of a bridge across the Caolie Water. In recent years it has possible to make a shallow paddle across just to the left of the former bridge; take wading footwear and leave it for the return.

If the water of the loch is ever raised, then the route will have to be made by crossing the Caolie Water further west beside the remains of a ►

Sgùrr a' Choire-bheithe's summit and Pt.816m across the River Barrisdale in Glen Barrisdale (Rab Anderson)

bridge at NG985036, then heading south-east for 1.5km to the track on the other side; parking is limited.

Beyond the paddle, follow the track, which soon disappears into the loch. It is debatable whether to follow a path above the loch, or the stony shoreline. Either way, at the headland where the Abhainn Chòsaidh enters the loch, cut inland to cross it before, or after, a small gorge. The Abhainn Chòsaidh is a notorious, rapidly rising river, so it is best to undertake this route in dry conditions.

Climb onto Meall an Spàrdain and continue along the undulating ridge over Sgùrr Àirigh na Beinne, then over and around numerous bumps and knolls towards two obvious rocky towers. The first tower requires a scramble up its slabby face – perhaps best via the centre then round right. The second tower is easier, beyond which the summit is finally gained. It is a more time-consuming traverse than expected (**12.5km; 1075m; 5h**).

Returning the same way is perhaps the easiest (25km; 1450m; 9h).

In good weather and with care, it is possible to make a steep descent northwards from the summit to clear the cliffs in Coire nan Cadha, then drop down through the corrie to head through the col with Slat Bheinn. Follow the headwaters of the Abhainn Chòsaidh across rough terrain to gain the path down the glen, then continue down this to where it crosses the Abhainn Chòsaidh. Keep on along the north side to regain the approach route, which is followed back (25km; 1285m; 8h 45min).

The longer alternative is to descend west to the dip in front of Pt.816m, then drop off the ridge by descending south and south-west over a shoulder before dropping south to avoid a band of crags. Gain the path at the Màm Unndalain and follow it down to the south-east, across the hillside, to ford the burn entering the east end of Lochan nam Breac, then continue on the path to reach Loch Cuaich. Cross the dams and follow the track back to where it disappears into the loch, then continue to recross the Abhainn Chòsaidh and return to the start (30km; 1475m; 10h).

Map on page 246

Beinn an Aodainn from the approach by canoe across Loch Cuaich, showing the dam, the east ridge and the route up Coire na Cruaiche (Anne Butler)

Beinn an Aodainn; *887m; (C38); L33 & L40; NM899986; hill of the face*

Beautifully situated in the Rough Bounds of Knoydart, in some of the most rugged and remote terrain Scotland has to offer, Beinn an Aodainn's summit is probably the most awkward of the Corbetts to attain. Along with the neighbouring Sgùrr a' Choire-bheithe, its ascent is one of the most highly valued of all Corbetts.

As with Sgùrr a' Choire-bheithe, there are a number of ways of approaching the mountain. Whatever route is chosen, pick a good day, and the experience is sure to live long in the memory.

The principal route is from the north-west tip of Loch Cuaich, reached by a 14 mile (23km) drive along the single-track road to Kinloch Hourn after leaving the A87 beside Loch Garry. A path and track lead along the side of Loch Cuaich to the dams at its west end at the foot of the mountain – a 9.5km approach before the ascent is even started.

It is possible to park at NG997034, at the entrance to a short track leading to a hydro substation by the Allt Choire nan Eiricheallach, which flows down from Sgùrr a' Mhaoraich.

Walk past the substation and go down the side of the burn to follow an old track to the remains of a bridge across the Caolie Water. In recent years, it has been possible to make a shallow paddle across just to the left of the former bridge; take wading footwear and leave it for the return. If

of Sgùrr a' Choire-bheithe's Druim Chòsaidh ridge to reach the west end of the loch. Cross first one dam above Lochan na Cruadahach, then a second dam above a small unnamed lochan to the west.

Continue on a path to the far side of a prominent rocky knoll, from where there are two options for the ascent of Beinn an Aodainn:

(i) This is the route that most take. Follow the Mam Unndalain/Barrisdale path north-west down to the far end of the unnamed lochan beneath the dam, then ascend uphill by the burn to where the path crosses it.

Leave the path here and climb uphill by the burn, Allt Coire na Cruaiche, soon crossing to the other side to continue up through wild Coire na Cruaiche. Cross the burn again below a fork, then climb up by its left branch to pass to the right of a col (Bealach a' Chàirn Deirg) to gain an obvious shallow, boulder-strewn gully that slants up through the craggy slopes. Follow the shallow gully to gain the crest just beyond a prominent knoll, then continue up the crest past another rocky knoll, and on to finally reach this most magnificent of summits. A rock 15m to the south-east of the cairn is the highest point (**13km; 950m; 4h 45min**).

After the initial crossing of the Allt Coire na Cruaiche, it is possible to gain the east-north-east ridge up on the right and ascend this with some scrambling.

(ii) Instead of following the path down to the lochan to ascend Coire na Cruaiche, climb south-west up the rocky ridge onto Meall a' Choire Dhuibh (740m). Drop west, then make a splendid traverse across rocky terrain, past a series of beautifully situated small lochans, to gain the top of Pt.717m.

Drop north-west to the col with Beinn an Aodainn (Bealach a' Chàirn Deirg) at the head of Coire na Cruaiche. Traverse across to the obvious shallow, boulder-strewn gully that slants up through the craggy slopes, and follow this as for (i); an added 0.5km; 100m; 25min or so.

The descent is made via the burn down Coire na Cruaiche, then over the dams for the long walk back beside

Loch Cuaich (**26km; 1230m; 8h 45min**).

This principal route is also possible by canoe or kayak across Loch Cuaich, with the most suitable put-in place probably being from the parking at NH004032, with a 200m carry.

Another possibility for a day ascent is to get a boat from Mallaig to the pier at Camusrory – check Western Isles Cruises (01687 462233). The route is then via the ruins at Carnoch, then up the west side of the River Carnach to ford it opposite a sheep-fold at NM886976, above where it is joined by the Allt Achadh a' Ghlinne. Climb the steepening slope on the other side north-east then north-wards, aiming to pass beneath some crags and cross the obvious gully running westwards down the hillside. This leads onto the north-west ridge above an obvious level section. Turn right and follow the ridge south-east up to the summit (**8.25km; 935m; 3h 30min**). Return the same way (**16.5km; 990m; 6h**).

An approach with an overnight stay can be made from Sourlies bothy at the head of Loch Nevis, which is a 15km walk, or a 7.75km bike ride and an 8.5km walk, from the end of Loch Arkaig. The route from the bothy follows the path to cross the bridge at Carnoch and join the route described above from the pier at Camusrory (**7.15km; 900m; 3h 15min**), (**15km; 940m; 5h 35min**).

An interesting and highly scenic day route approaches Beinn an Aodainn from the car park at the end of Loch Arkaig with the use of a bike.

Ride past Strathan and take the track on the south side of Glen Dessarry to the bridge at NM930934 (**7.75km; 185m; about 55min**).

Continue on foot by reversing the descent from Sgùrr na Cìche. This is to cross the bridge and ascend the path up the Allt Coire nan Uth to join the path on the north side of the glen, which leads to Loch Nevis and Sourlies bothy. Go along this path to just before the Bealach an Lagain Duibh, then leave it and follow a rough track on the right across a burn, then uphill. Leave the track close to its highpoint, where it turns downhill, then make a rising traverse across

the water of the loch is ever raised, then the route will have to be made by crossing the Caolie Water further west beside the remains of a small bridge at NG985036, then heading south-east for 1.5km to the track on the other side; parking is limited.

Beyond the paddle, follow the track, which soon disappears into the loch. It is debatable whether to follow a path above the loch, or the stony shoreline. Either way, at the headland where the Abhainn Chòsaidh enters the loch, cut inland to cross it before, or after, a small gorge. This can normally be done by boulder-hopping below the gorge. However, the Abhainn Chòsaidh is known for rising rapidly during rain and becoming impassable, so it is advisable to undertake this route in dry weather.

Pick up the track where it emerges from the loch and follow it along the base of Meall an Spàrdain at the start the head of Coire na Cìche to gain the prominent gully and climb this to the Feadan na Cìche col between Sgùrr na Cìche and Garbh Cìoch Mhòr.

Traverse easily across the north side of Sgùrr na Cìche on grass to gain its north-east ridge. The line is below that taken by the remains of the old wall to get to this point.

Descend the ridge, which is quite rocky, but straightforward if the correct line is chosen. There are signs of passage in places, and the line is easier to find on the return.

At the bottom, cross a narrow col, then go up the other side and traverse beneath the steeper ground of Meall nan Clach Eiteag (Meall a' Choire Dhuibh's south-west top). Continue across Meall a' Choire Dhuibh, then swing around the head of the corrie. This leads to a small lochan and a junction with option (ii) on the Loch Cuaich route. Follow this route west past the beautifully situated small lochans, then up to Pt.717m and down to the Bealach a' Chàirn Deirg.

Traverse across and climb the long, shallow, boulder-strewn gully to gain the ridge, and follow this to the top of Beinn an Aodainn (**9.5km; 1150m; 4h 15min**), from the bike.

Return the same way to Glen Dessarry (**19km; 1520m; 7h 35min**).

Bike back to Loch Arkaig (34.5km; 1815m; 9h 20min with a bike).

Buidhe Bheinn's West Top, left, and summit, right, across Loch Coire Shùbh from the Kinloch Hourn road (Rab Anderson)

Buidhe Bheinn; *885m; (C41); L33; NG963090; yellow hill*

Formerly twinned with Sgùrr a' Bhac Chaolais to the north, which it is linked to, a survey in 2012 found Buidhe Bheinn to be marginally higher, although maps show both as being the same height.

The ascent is made from the end of the single-track road at Kinloch Hourn, which is a 22 mile (35km) drive from the A87. There is a car park for walkers just beyond the car park for the Lochhournhead B&B and Tea Room. Check their website for the charge and payment details, and for their welcome seasonal tea room.

Walk 500m back along the road, then turn left across the bridge and follow the track to the lodge. Pass this to its right, then follow the track, which is the right of way to Arnisdale, steeply through the trees to join a track alongside the overhead power lines, and continue to the highpoint of the Cadha Mòr pass at 272m.

Take the second, and more obvious, of two stalkers' paths and follow this uphill by the burn, then take the left-hand branch of the path across it and the next burn. The path zigzags uphill to the north-north-east, finally swinging eastwards to end at 670m

by a boulder beside a small burn.

Climb the steeper rocky slope ahead to the side of a shallow gully to gain Buidhe Bheinn's north-west shoulder, then turn right up the ridge to the West Top (Pt.879m). Drop down a narrow rocky ridge, then cross the saddle and continue up the ridge to the summit (**6.25km; 950m; 3h**).

Both tops are superb viewpoints, especially the West Top with its outlook down Loch Hourn and across

to Ladhar Bheinn on Knoydart.

Return the same way over the West Top (12.5km; 1010m; 4h 50min).

Alternatively, from the West Top, go down the south-east ridge above Coire Làir to a lochan at NG959081, then descend the steeper slope westwards for 250m to pick up the head of another stalkers' path by a burn. Follow this path, taking the left branch lower down, back to the Cadha Mor; the same distance and time.

Buidhe Bheinn's summit from the saddle with the West Top (Rab Anderson)

Sgùrr Coire Chòinnichean's West Top and summit, with Beinn Sgritheall, left, and Luinne Bheinn, right (Rab Anderson)

Sgùrr Coire Chòinnichean; *796m; (C169); L33; NG791011; peak of the mossy corrie*

Shapely Sgùrr Coire Chòinnichean dominates Inverie Bay, and its cone sits centre stage as the approach is made by ferry boat to the village of Inverie on the Knoydart peninsula from Mallaig. The panel below right gives the Knoydart access information.

Since the hill rises above Inverie, it is conveniently climbed from there, either as a short final hill for a multi-day trip to Knoydart, or as a day trip to easily fit in with the ferry times.

Directions for the ascent are given from the pier. From there, either follow the road on the right, or the path through the bushes on its right which joins it, towards the village.

At a waymark post in front of The Old Forge inn, take to a track signed Knoydart in a Nutshell and follow this uphill past a parking area and some houses to gain a forest track. Turn right along the track and continue uphill, passing a path off right, which leads to the road near the campsite, and can be used by anyone making an approach from there.

In a further 200m, in front of some log stacks, turn off left and follow a path uphill through the trees. Ignore a grassy path off left and continue

uphill, looping around through a felled area, to pass through the old wall that rises up the hillside, then ascend to a ladder stile and cross this to gain the open hillside.

The path now follows the fence to the right for a short way before swinging away to climb steeply up the hillside, then runs up the side of the impressive cleft formed by the Slochd a' Mhogha gorge, with the enticing sight of the upper ridge rising beyond. Cross grassy ground at the head of the gorge, where there is a fine view down its length, then follow the path up some wetter ground to gain the rocky upper ridge.

A short way up, a little groove in a band of rock gives a hands-on pull over two wedged blocks; avoidable on grass to the left. Thereafter, the slender ridge provides a splendid, and in places airy, route to the grassy West Top (779m). Cross the dip beyond and make the short climb onto the main summit (**4km; 820m; 2h 15min**).

It is a superb viewpoint which includes all of the Knoydart Corbetts and Munros, as well as a huge number of other mountains, including Ben Nevis. On the western seaboard, the mountains on the island of Rum

and the Cuillin on the Isle of Skye stand out, with Canna between and the hills of South Uist on the horizon.

It is possible to contrive a circuit by continuing along the ridge to either descend into wet and haggy Coire Chòinnichean to the west, or on the south side via bracken slopes to the Gleann an Dubh-Lochain track. However, it is better to return the same way, with Inverie Bay at your feet and the islands of Eigg and Rum floating in the sea beyond. Any time to kill is better spent savouring these views, as well as the refreshments and eating options available in the village (**8km; 840m; 3h 35min**).

Map opposite

Knoydart Peninsula
Three of the Knoydart Corbetts are accessed from Inverie, reached by boat from Mallaig. Entering Mallaig on the A830 from Fort William, there is a car park with toilets on the left, opposite the railway line and station. This is a 5 minute walk from where the boat leaves. Western Isles Cruises www.westernislescruises.co.uk (01687 462233) is the sole operator.

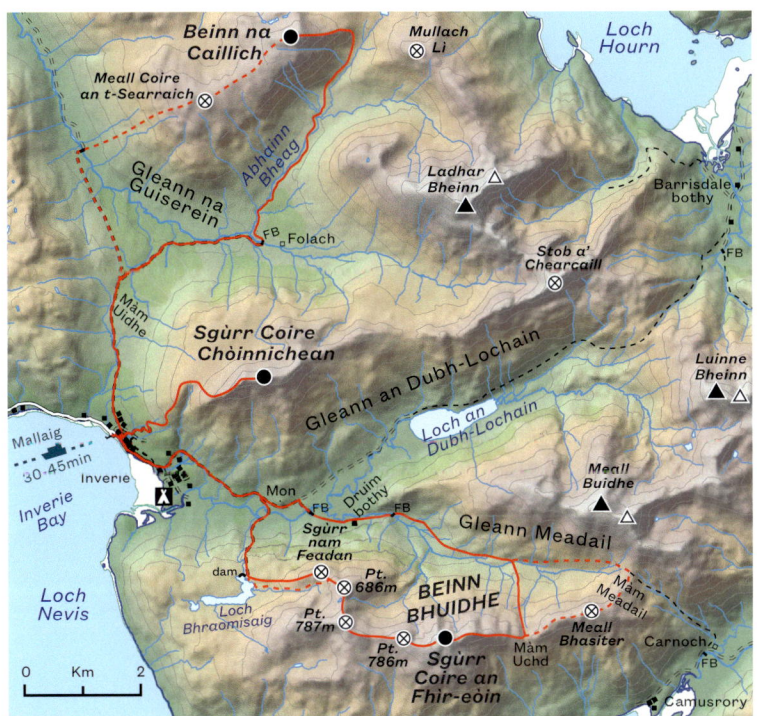

Beinn na Caillich; *785m; (C184); L33; NG796067; hill of the old woman

A long with its attendant summits, Beinn na Caillich fills the wild and uninhabited north-west corner of the Knoydart peninsula.

It lies some 7km to the north of Inverie (see panel opposite) and is approached by the Màm Uidhe track, reached from the pier by crossing straight over the shoreline road to go left along the track through the forest and out into the open by the Allt a' Mhuilinn. Take the north-east branch through forestry down into Gleann na Guiserein, then go alongside the river. Either ford the river above the junction to shortcut the loop, or continue to cross a bridge near the ruin of Folach and go down the other side.

Briefly boggy, the path improves and runs up the side of the Abhainn Bheag, with its waterfalls and cascades. Ford the river at NG799051 and start to climb towards the Màm Li pass. At about the 350m contour, climb up to the base of the slabby ribs on the rough east ridge of Càrn Dubh. Either climb these ribs, or swing round behind them and continue west uphill to the summit of Beinn na Caillich. There are excellent views over the sea to the west, south-east towards Ladhar Bheinn, and east to Loch Hourn (**11.25km; 860m; 4h**).

Return the same way (**22.5km; 960m; 7h**).

Alternatively, descend south-west and climb onto Meall Coire an t-Searraich (686m), then continue in the same direction and descend to the bridge below, and follow the track back (**21.25km; 1040m; 7h**).

Beinn na Caillich from the approach up the Abhainn Bheag (Rab Anderson)

Sgùrr Coire an Fhìr-eòin from Sgùrr Coire nan Gobhar – then, from left to right, Beinn an Aodainn, Gairich, Sgùrr Mòr, Sgùrr na Cìche, Garbh Chìoch Mhòr, and far right, Bidean a' Chabair (Rab Anderson)

BEINN BHUIDHE; yellow hill

Sgùrr Coire an Fhìr-eòin; 855m; (C87); L33 or L40; NM821967; peak of the notable bird

---

The southern part of Knoydart is occupied by a single massive mountain, Beinn Bhuidhe, which forms a long, undulating ridge, whose main spine runs for some 6km over five named tops, with Sgùrr Coire an Fhìr-eòin near the centre.

Long grassy slopes fall south from this ridge into Loch Nevis, whilst to the north a fine series of rugged corries overlooks Gleann Meadail, with the Munro Meall Buidhe rising opposite, which Beinn Bhuidhe is connected to at its east end by the Màm Meadail pass at c.545m.

Start from the pier at Inverie; see the panel on page 248 for ferry information. Follow the road through the village to its end, and continue on the track to Strathan, which climbs uphill through woodland, then loops around and descends south-east. Pass a track on the right, which can be seen zigzagging up the hillside beside the Allt Dubh (the return route), then round the corner beneath Tòrr a' Bhalbhain and take the track on the right.

Cross the footbridge over the Inverie River and continue on a good path past Druim bothy into Gleann Meadail. Cross a bridge over the Allt Gleann Meadail and ascend up the side of the glen. When the path comes close to the burn at NM832980, there are two options:

(i) Leave the path and cross the burn to climb the hillside southwards past a prominent upright boulder. Go up a grassy gully right of a burn, then through a small upper corrie to gain the Màm Uchd col (574m) on Beinn Bhuidhe's ridge between Meall Bhasiter and Sgùrr an t-Sagairt. Times and distances are given for this shorter route.

(ii) Continue on the path to reach the Màm Meadail pass at the head of the glen, then turn right to climb over the Pt.610m knoll, then over Meall Bhasiter (718m), and descend the ridge to the Màm Uchd col; an added 3km, 150m, 1h.

Climb westwards up the broad, stepped ridge to gain the top of Sgùrr an t-Sagairt (802m) by steep grass and boulders up the left side of the craggy nose. Cross the slight dip, and climb easily to the summit of Sgùrr Coire an Fhìr-eòin, with its broken trig pillar and superb views (**11.5km; 965m; 4h 15min**).

Continue westwards down the grassy ridge onto Sgùrr a' Choire Ghuirm (786), then down across the Bealach Buidhe (696m) and climb to Sgùrr Coire nan Gobhar (787m). Turn north here, then weave down the rocky ridge to a small lochan, and climb onto Pt.686m above grassy Coire Chomhlaich.

Go north a short way, then turn west and drop to a col, then climb onto and along the rocky crest of Sgùrr nam Feadan (598m). Descend the west ridge past numerous rock outcrops to gain the dam at the north end of Loch Bhraomisaig. Don't be tempted to leave the ridge early and take a more direct line down by a burn to the bridge over the Inverie River; the terrain is tortuous.

If time is pressing, an easier descent can be made to Loch Bhraomisaig from the col with Sgùrr nam Feadan, down by the burn in Coire nan Gobhar.

Descend the track, then cross the bridge over the river to regain the approach route and follow this back (**22.25km; 1190m; 7h 35min**).

With regard to ferry times, bear in mind that this is a worked-out time that does not include for stops, and that it is 3km and 1h longer if the ascent is made via the Màm Meadail.

Map on page 249

Meall Dubh; 789m; (C177); L34; NH245078; black hill

Standing in an isolated position to the west of the Great Glen, Meall Dubh is the highest point of an extensive area of high moorland between Loch Garry and Glen Moriston. Its position here makes it an exceptional viewpoint for the mountains of Lochaber and the Western Highlands.

Meall Dubh is also the location of the Millennium and Beinneun Wind Farms, with turbines situated as high as the 700m contour.

Start from a long layby on the north side of the A887, at NH254116, opposite the gated entrance to the Millennium Wind Farm. This is 3 miles (4.75km) east of the A87 Fort William road junction. The summit of Meall Dubh and its huge cairn can be seen from here.

Cross the road and go through a pedestrian gate on the left, then follow the main wind farm track uphill into a forestry plantation. Loop round past a track off right, and continue uphill to exit the plantation. Leave the main track here and follow the track on the right uphill into Coire an Eòin.

Leave this track about 100m

beyond its highpoint, immediately after it crosses a small burn before it descends to the main burn, the Allt Coire na Gaoith an Ear. There is a large cairn on the right here.

Traverse round the hillside to reach the Allt Coire na Gaoith an Ear below a small waterfall, then cross over, either above or below the fall. Continue up easier heathery ground, then swing round onto Meall Dubh's ill-defined north-east ridge and follow this up through rockier terrain to its top. Traverse south-west on level ground, then make the final 50m ascent to the summit of Meall Dubh. The highest point sits on a thin ridge of rock 40m to the south of the huge cairn (**5.75km; 670m; 2h 25min**).

It is easiest to return the same way (11.5km; 680m; 3h 55min).

The return can be varied by descending north to climb Beinn an Eòin (660m), taking in a minor top on the way. The terrain on the descent is quite rugged and there is a small band of rock to negotiate on the drop to the col, which is best done to the right (east). A short 45m ascent gains

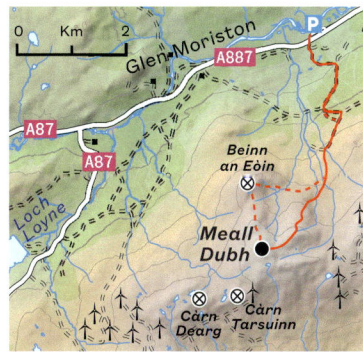

the top of Beinn an Eòin. To descend, it is probably easiest to head down east and cross the burn at the corrie lip, then drop down through heather to gain the upward route just above the waterfall (12.25km; 725m; 4h 20min).

It used to be possible to climb Meall Dubh from the west, from the side of the A87 just beyond the end of Loch Loyne. The route started at a gate into the felled forest above the River Loyne at NH207081. Unfortunately, boulders have been placed at the edges of the track entrance, so there is now no room to park.

Meall Dubh with Beinn an Eòin, left, from below Cluanie Dam to the west (Rab Anderson)

Beinn Loinne, West Top, right, above Loch Cluanie from the approach, with distant Meall Dubh beyond (Rab Anderson)

Beinn Loinne (West Top); 790m; (C175); L33 & L34; NH131077; *elegant hill*

Sandwiched between the flooded glens now occupied by Loch Loyne to the south and Loch Cluanie to the north, Beinn Loinne takes the form of a long, triple-topped ridgeline. The OS has applied the name to the Central Top, perhaps due to its apparent prominence. However, it is the West Top that is the summit.

The normal route starts from the west end of Loch Cluanie, 200m to the east of the Cluanie Inn, where the old road to Tomdoun in Glen Garry leaves the A87. There is limited space to park at various points along the start of this road.

Follow the road across the inflow to the loch, then uphill above Cluanie Lodge and cross an old stone bridge, the Drochaid an Uillt Ghiubhais. Continue to the highpoint at 435m on the flat ground of the Mullach Màm Chluainidh beneath Creag a' Mhàim at the start of the South Glen Shiel Ridge (**5.5km; 230m; 1h 35min**).

It can be biked to here in about 40min, for an overall saving of about 1h 40min on the day. Times and distances are on foot from the start.

Leave the old road and cross the flat and potentially boggy ground to the east-north-east onto drier, rocky terrain on a small rise (Pt.540m),

then go over this. Cross the watery flat ground to the south-east to gain firmer, dry ground on the broad and rocky Druim nan Cnàmh ridge, which leads to the trig pillar on the flat summit. The highest point is 18m to the west of the trig (**9.25km; 595m; 3h**).

Return the same way (**18.5km; 625m; 5h 15min**).

Another route starts from the A87 to the east, at NH213091, from a wide entrance to a gated forest track. This is 1 mile (1.75km) beyond the gated access track leading to Loyne Dam at the north end of Loch Loyne, where there is no parking.

If the gate is locked, climb it, and follow the forest track to the Allt Coire na Creadha, then up beside this to its end at a small lochan after 4.25km.

Continue uphill by the burn and climb onto Beinn Loinne's Central Top, then descend west to a col and climb onto the West Top (**9.5km; 715m; 3h 20min**).

Return to the col, then make a descending traverse to the flat ground between Meall Coire na Creadha and the Central Top. Follow the Allt Coire na Creadha back to the track, and return along this (**19km; 750m; 5h 45min**).

On this route, all three tops can be climbed by leaving the approach track at NH192082 and following an ATV track to Ceann Druim na Garbh-leitir. Leave the track before a communications aerial to climb the rocky Druim na Garbh-leitir ridge over the East Top (748m/750m); an added 1km, 70m, 20min or so.

Sgùrr Mhic Bharraich; *779m; (C191); L33; NG917173; peak of the son of Maurice*

Looming large above the seaward entrance to Glen Shiel at the head of Loch Duich, Sgùrr Mhic Bharraich is a great lump of a hill. It is the first in a chain that stretches south-eastwards over The Saddle and another eight Munros that line the south side of this most magnificent of glens.

A complex web of spurs, ridges and corries radiate from its summit, and when viewed across Loch Duich, the steep slopes that rise above the loch lend the hill an air of impregnability. The breach in the hills defences lies on its south side above a col at 462m, which connects it to The Saddle's northern ridge. It is via this col and the narrow Gleann Undalain, which runs southwards from Shiel Bridge on the A87, that the ascent is made.

Start from the car park at the entrance to Glenshiel Campsite, which is located down the short road to the side of the coffee shop.

Walk down the road towards its end and go through a gate, then follow a track along the back of the campsite by the Allt Undalain. The track climbs over the rock bar across the entrance to Gleann Undalain and descends to

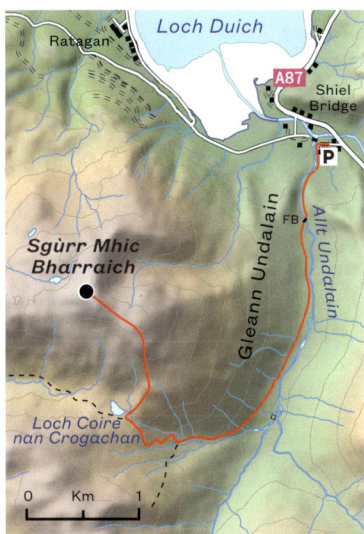

a bridge over the burn, which is crossed.

Continue on a wide path and rough track along the base of Sgùrr Mhic Bharraich, then take the path on the right after 2.25km. The path swings westwards, uphill above another burn, the Allt na h-Innse Gairbhe, which is crossed. Pass an old stalkers' path off to the left and zigzag uphill between the burns to reach Loch Coire na Crogachan, nestling just below the col between the hills.

Leave the path here and cross the outflow from the loch, then climb onto a small spur. Ascend the slope above this, with a steeper section to pass around the right side of some scree and a rock outcrop. Easier-angled ground leads to a flat section, which is crossed for a final easy climb north-west to the broad summit, where the cairn sits on an outcrop of rock (**6km; 800m; 2h 40min**).

The views across to the Five Sisters of Kintail, and of The Saddle with its great northern corrie, are outstanding. To the south-west is Beinn Sgritheall, with the Corbetts, Beinn nan Caorach and Beinn na h-Eaglasie on one side,

and in the distance on the other side, the Cuillin, whilst closer at hand to the north, on the other side of Loch Duich, is Sgùrr an Airgid.

Whilst a quicker return can be made directly down the long east shoulder from the far side of the flat area below the summit, it is probably more enjoyable to return by the ascent route (**12km; 825m; 4h 30min**).

Sgùrr Mhic Bharraich and the head of Loch Duich across Glen Shiel from Sgùrr Fhuaran (Grahame Nicoll)

Beinn na h-Eaglaise from Beinn nan Caorach, with Pt.906m and Beinn Sgritheall beyond (Mike Dixon)

Beinn nan Caorach; *774m; (C201); L33; NG871121; hill of the rowan berries*
Beinn na h-Eaglaise; *805m; (C152); L33; NG854120; hill of the church*

Situated on the Glenelg peninsula, on the opposite side of Loch Hourn from Knoydart, Beinn nan Caorach and Beinn na h-Eaglaise are the eastern outliers of Beinn Sgritheall. Steep slopes fall to Loch Hourn from the south side of this group, but when viewed from their north side, a series of long ridges flanking deep corries gives them a finely sculpted appearance.

The route could be extended to include Beinn Sgritheall, but the descent north-west from Beinn na h-Eaglaise to the Bealach Arnasdail is not straightforward. Better would be to include Beinn Clachach, the Graham to the south of Beinn nan Caorach, for a more logical round, and a description for this is given.

The ascent starts from a car park just before the bridge over the river to Corran on the south side of Arnisdale, reached by a 20 mile (32km) drive along the single-track road that leaves the A87 at Shiel Bridge.

Walk back along the road towards Arnisdale for 400m, then take the track on the right up Glen Arnisdale to where it crosses a bridge over the River Arnisdale, and a branch continues ahead to ford the burn flowing from the hills, the Allt Utha. There is a footbridge upstream, so cut across open ground on the left and go up the side of the burn, then cross the bridge to gain the track on the other side.

Follow the track, which after a short climb makes a rising traverse above the burn, to then zigzag up and traverse across above the Eas na Cuingid waterfall. There is a fine view across the fall to the slope failure on the east side of Beinn Bhuidhe, with the steep Coire an Eich Chàim on Beinn na h-Eaglaise beyond.

Leave the track a short distance beyond the waterfall and cross the burn at a suitable point, either before or after the track fords it. Ascend the broad and pathless south-south-west ridge of Beinn nan Caorach, which has a few steeper steps, but no difficulty. The summit is marked by a cairn and a line of fence posts (**6km; 780m; 2h 40min**).

If Beinn Clachach is to be included, it is best climbed first by following the above route to above the waterfall. The OS map places the name Beinn Clachach against Pt.618m, the West Top, however, the highest point is the East Top (643m), which lies to the east across a saddle. The best route is to climb to Pt.618m and traverse across to the East Top, then descend the ridge to the north to gain the col between the hills (415m). From there, climb onto the east-south-east ridge of Beinn nan Caorach, passing over, or around, a knoll at its start, then follow this to the top; an added 3km, 290m, 1h 20min.

From Beinn nan Caorach, follow the line of fence posts north for 350m, initially down the ridge, then off it, downhill to the north-west where the posts become intermittent. Cross a broad, grassy col (Bealach Dhruim nam Bò), then turn south-west beneath the slight rise at the top of the Druim nam Bò ridge to cross the dip. Follow the unsightly posts up the elegant ridge onto Beinn na h-Eaglaise, easily passing what initially appears as a step blocking the way (**8.75km; 1025m; 3h 50min**).

Just beyond the summit, a line of fence posts heads off north-west-wards down the ridge that links to Beinn Sgritheall via the Bealach Arnasdail. This becomes very steep and is craggy at the bottom, so should be avoided. If Beinn Sgritheall is to be included, it should be climbed first, so a route to the side of this ridge, avoiding the rock, can be seen.

For the descent from Beinn na h-Eaglaise, head south-south-east down the ridge beside another line of spaced fence posts. When these head off down to the right, continue out along the ridge and make the slight rise onto Beinn Bhuidhe (639m) at the end of the summit shoulder. From there, drop to a nicely situated small lochan in front of another slight rise. There are two options from here:

(i) Go down to the left (east) of the

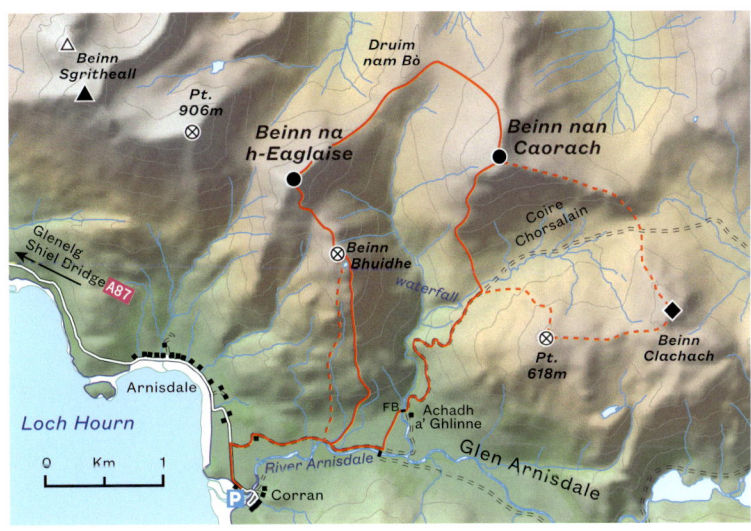

lochan, then descend south beneath some crags to gain the crest of the south ridge and make the long descent down this to pass through a break in the wall at the bottom and regain the track by the river.

(ii) Pass the right (west) side of the lochan, then continue south down the right side of the ridge on grassy ground, and make the long descent down this, and the burn that appears, to pass through the wall and regain the track at the bottom,

Follow the track back (**13km; 1045m; 5h 20min**).

The route described above is for the traditional anticlockwise round, which is easily reversed if the preference is to tackle the steep slope at the start of the day.

Including Beinn Sgritheall, which is best climbed first to then climb Beinn na h-Eaglaise, would add about 3.75km, 515m, 2h. This would open up the possibility of an unusual Munro, Corbett, Graham combination.

Beinn nan Caorach from the lochan on Beinn Bhuidhe, with The Saddle and Sgùrr na Sgìne beyond (Mike Dixon)

Loch Cluanie with snow-capped Aonach Meadhoin and Sgùrr an Fhuarail, then Am Bàthach (Rab Anderson)

SECTION 11
Glen Shiel to Loch Mullardoch

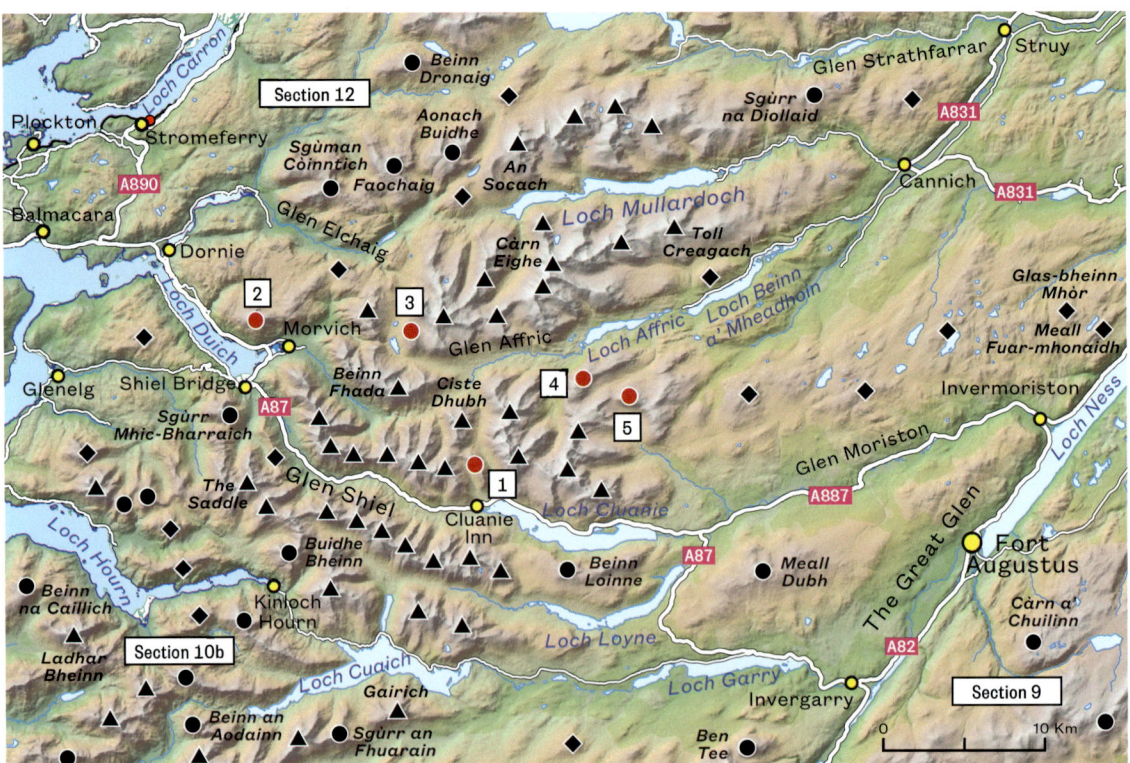

SECTION 11

Across Loch Cluanie to Am Bàthach with Ciste Dhubh beyond (Rab Anderson)

Am Bàthach; *798m; (C162); L33; NH073143; the byre*

Prominent in the view on the approach to the Cluanie Inn at the west end of Loch Cluanie, is the long and undulating, steep-sided, grassy north-westwards running ridge of Am Bàthach. Sandwiched between the long, steep slopes rising to Sgùrr an Fhuarail to its west and A' Chràileag to its east, Am Bàthach's form is further enhanced by the narrow, parallel-running glens, An Caorann Beag and An Caorann Mòr, that separate it from these peaks.

Am Bàthach is commonly climbed as a prelude to the ascent of, or as a finale to the descent from, the Munro Ciste Dhubh, which can be glimpsed in the distance beyond its north end. However, climbed for its own sake, it also gives an excellent short day, its ridge providing an airy highway from which to appreciate the surroundings and its bigger neighbours.

Start from a long pull-off beneath a felled plantation on the north side of the A87, about 1.5km to the east of the Cluanie Inn.

Walk east along the verge and go through an old gateway to follow a path up the south-east ridge of the hill, beside the felled plantation. The narrow crest is gained at the 650m contour and leads over the south top, Pt.734m. With grassy slopes falling steeply away on both sides, continue across the saddle and on up to the summit (**3.25km; 615m; 1h 45min**).

Returning the same way is easiest and driest (6.5km; 655m; 2h 55min).

Alternatively, head north-west down the ridge, passing a flat slab of rock, to reach the lower part of the boggy Bealach a' Chòinich (c.565m).

To return to the road, follow a path down south into the head of An Caorann Beag, and continue along the obvious, but boggy, path down the east side of the Allt a' Chaorainn Bhig to reach the road 400m to the west of the start (8.5km; 615m; 3h 15min).

To include Ciste Dubh, follow the path up to the higher part of the Bealach a' Chòinich, then on up past pointed An Cnapach (877m) and over

Pt.929m to gain the splendid summit (**6.5km; 1050m; 3h 20min**).

Return to the Bealach a' Chòinich and follow the boggy path down An Caorann Beag (13km; 1070m; 5h 5min).

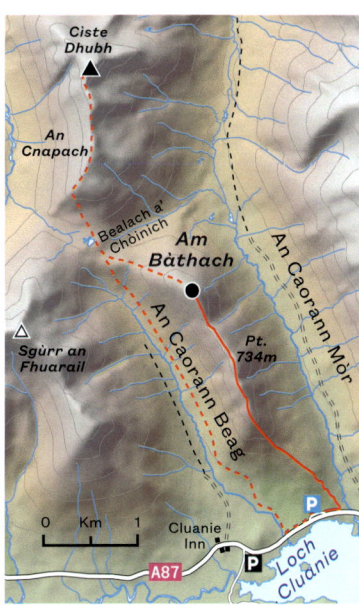

Sgùrr an Airgid; *841m; (C102); L25 or L33; NG940227; peak of silver*

Rising prominently and steeply above the head of Loch Duich, Sgùrr an Airgid sits directly above the north end of the causeway which takes the A87 across the head of the loch. There is a fine view of the hill on rounding the corner beyond Shiel Bridge when travelling north.

The ascent is short, suitable for an easy second day, shorter daylight hours, or short weather windows. However, the reward on a good day is a fine view of the higher peaks of Kintail in one direction, and the western lochs and Skye in the other.

On the north side of the causeway across Loch Duich, take the road signed to Morvich and park on the right after 300m, as for the Clachan Duich Burial Ground and old church.

Cross the road, then go through a walkers' gate and follow a rough track, which zigzags rightwards up the hillside, to where it is joined by the original stalkers' path from Lienassie, whose start is difficult to locate. Continue uphill, passing through a gate in a deer fence, now

on a path, and zigzag up onto the shoulder of Beinn Bhuidhe.

Head west across the col, the Màm na Dubharaiche, and climb the right-hand of two ridges to gain the fine crest leading to the broken trig pillar. The highest point is a rock outcrop 25m to the north-east of the trig (**4.75km; 835m; 2h 30min**).

To the south, there is a grand view of the jagged nature of the Five

Sisters of Kintail ridge and its steep slopes, with the hooded bulk of Ben Nevis beyond. To the south-east, the elusive top of Beinn Fhada is revealed over the top of its notched western ridge, and to its side Sgùrr Gaorsaic and the route to it through the Bealach an Sgàirne. To the north east is Sgùman Còinntich, with pointed Bidein a' Choire Sheasgaich beyond, and to the side. Moving south 100m or so opens up the view down to Loch Duich; definitely a hill worth saving for a good day, and savouring.

Return the same way (**9.5km; 840m; 3h 55min**).

From the summit, it is worthwhile dropping to the west and making the 400m crossing to Sgùrr na Seamraig (824m), from where there are better views west to Skye; an added 0.8km, 55m, 15min there and back.

For anyone seeking a little extra, a short climb can be made from the far side of the Màm na Dubharaiche to the summit of Beinn Bhuidhe (703m); an added 1.5km, 110m, 40min there and back.

Sgùrr an Airgid across Loch Duich from Sgùrr an t-Searraich (Iain Thow)

Sgùrr Gaorsaic from the approach path around Loch a' Bhealaich (Rab Anderson)

Sgùrr Gaorsaic; *839m; (C107); L25 or L33; NH036219; peak of horror*

Surrounded by higher mountains, elusive Sgùrr Gaorsaic sits in splendid isolation above the watershed between the waters that flow into Glen Affric and the northward-flowing waters that plunge down the Falls of Glomach into Glen Elchaig.

Despite being walled-in by the surrounding mountains, the views are good. The day is as much about the journey to the hill as the ascent itself.

The shortest route is from Strath Croe at the head of Loch Duich, where there is parking at the National Trust for Scotland centre at Morvich. This is on the right at the first buildings, and just before the entrance to the Caravan Club site. It may be possible to find one of a few spaces further along before the end of the road. However, with the routes for Beinn Fhada and A' Ghlas-bheinn also starting here, others will be seeking these limited spaces too.

Walk along the road to its end at the turning circle by the bridge to Innis a' Chròtha. Cross the bridge, then, after about 80m, take the path on the right, which goes up Gleann Chòinneachain, passing through the gates of two fenced-in areas and traversing beneath the impressively

steep northern spurs of Beinn Fhada. The path climbs away from the river to reach the Allt a' Choire Chaoil, which can usually be crossed without a problem, although there will be times when this is not the case.

Continue up to the top of the zigzag section, then go left where the path to Beinn Fhada goes right. The path leads to the Bealach an Sgàirne, the splendid narrow pass between A' Ghlas-bheinn and Beinn Fhada.

Descend from the pass and follow the path around the south end of Loch a' Bhealaich. Shortly after crossing the inflow, leave the path and climb north-north-east directly up the steep slopes of Sgùrr Gaorsaic, following a line of fence posts onto the flat and rocky summit area. When

the fence posts veer off to the right at the remnants of what maps show as a lochan, continue for a further 150m to the summit cairn at the north end, with some large boulders just beyond (**10.5km; 950m; 4h 5min**).

The rocks 65m to the north could be as high, and should be included.

There is a fine view north to the Torridon peaks, from Beinn Dearg to Liathach, but to the east the view is blocked by the West Top of Sgùrr nan Ceathramhnan. To the south-east, Mullach Fraoch-choire and A' Chràileag look grand, whilst west through the Bealach an Sgàirne, beyond Sgùrr an Airgid, there is a view of the full Cuillin ridge.

Return the same way (**21km; 1150m; 7h 5min**).

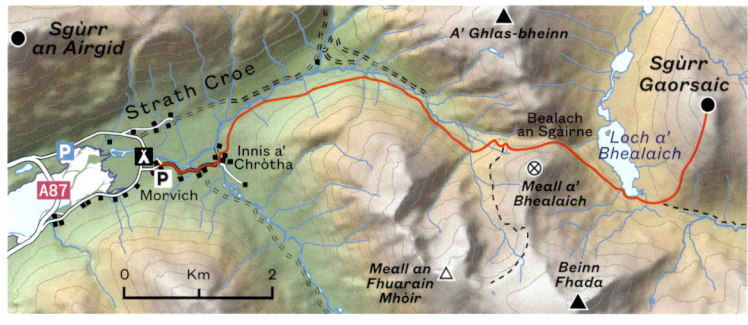

Càrn a' Choire Ghairbh from Càrn a' Choire Ghuirm, with the Màm Sodhail and Càrn Eige group behind (Rab Anderson)

Càrn a' Choire Ghairbh; 865m; (C69); L25 & L34; NH136188; cairn of the rough corrie
Aonach Shasuinn; 888m; (C35); L25 & L34; NH173180; height of the Saxon (sassenach)

These two Corbetts lie to the south of Loch Affric in Glen Affric, forming a group of lower hills to the north of the Sgùrr nan Conbhairean group of three Munros and their associated Tops above Loch Cluanie.

Càrn a' Choire Ghairbh rises above the western end of Loch Affric, above Athnamulloch, whilst Aonach Shasuinn lies hidden away above the Allt Garbh, which flows into the southern end of Loch Affric.

Glen Affric is one of Scotland's longest and most beautiful glens, and it contains one of the best preserved remains of the old Caledonian pine forest, in a beautiful, tranquil setting of loch and mountain. The day spent traversing these two hills is quite long, but the terrain is generally good, the scenery superb and the expedition memorable.

Start from Forestry and Land Scotland's River Affric pay-and-display car park at the end of the single-track public road in Glen Affric.

Head west from the car park and follow the track across the bridge over the River Affric and through the Pollan Buidhe forest, passing Affric Lodge on the other side of Loch Affric. Shortly after passing a cottage, then a short stub of track off left, there is a path on the left, signed to Cougie, just before the track crosses the Allt Garbh. The return route arrives here via this path.

The path shown on the 1:50k map up the west side of the Allt Garbh no longer exists, and the original route onto Càrn Glas Iochdarach is boggy, overgrown and fenced-in, so this no longer provides a suitable route.

Continue on the track above Loch Affric to NH143210, above a small chalet and pier at the west end of the loch, then leave the track. Follow a good, but overgrown, grassy stalkers' path, which zigzags up the hillside above the forest overlooking Athnamulloch, with increasingly fine views west up the glen.

The path ends at the 650m contour on the broad, but shallow, ridge bounding Coire Cròm. Continue south-west up the ridge on stony, upturned rock strata to meet an old line of fence posts leading towards the top of Càrn a' Choire Ghairbh, which lies to the left of the posts on a ridge of rock (**10.75km; 720m; 3h 35min**).

Drop south-westwards for 250m to reach a large cairn next to the fence-line (which heads off right lower down). Continue south-south-west down to the col, the Cadha Riabhach, below the slope leading up to a minor top, Càrn a' Choire Ghuirm, and above that the Munro Top, Tigh Mòr na Seilge. On this descent, there are fine views across Gleann na Cìche into the eastern corries of A' Chràileag and Mullach Fraoch-choire.

Ascend south-eastwards up the grassy slope and broad ridge ahead, passing to the right side of the slight rise of Càrn a' Choire Ghuirm (743m), then swing round eastwards and cross flat ground to the north of Loch a' Chòinich. Keep to the higher, stony ground, and traverse north-east above a shallow, peaty basin to gain a small rise (Pt.862m) at the top of the ridge of An Elric.

Descend this narrow ridge to the Bealach an Amais (651m). Pass through some hags, then climb the grassy slope to gain stony ground and the cairn on the slight rise of Pt.873m, Aonach Shasuinn's west top. There is a grand view here of Màm Sodhail and Càrn Eighe, with their long ridges and associated tops.

Continue south-south-east for 600m or so, with a slight rise to the top where there is a tall cairn with a wind shelter 70m beyond it. The highest point lies midway between these, and 10m or so out to the south from them (**17.75km; 1180m; 6h 15min**).

There are two descent options:

(i) Descend north to the Allt Garbh. However, the steep headwall of Coire Gorm needs to be avoided, so return to the west top (Pt.873m), then descend north, then north-east down the broad ridge of Ceann Aonach Shasuinn to reach the Allt Garbh near Loch an Sguid. Cross the burn flowing from the corrie and continue to a dam and hydro track.

Follow the track through a gate, then after 650m, when it swings right through a col at NH188212, take the path on the left. The path leads down towards the Allt Garbh, then through lovely woodland to emerge onto the Glen Affric track, which is followed back (**26.75km; 1280m; 8h 30min**).

(ii) Better, but longer, is to continue the horseshoe around the corrie, Toll Odhar, by traversing double-topped Càrn nan Coireachan Cruaidh (872m

& 862m). Drop north and climb onto Cnap na Stri (724m), then descend north and north-west to follow a fence around a fenced area down to the Allt

Garbh hydro track. Go through the gate to gain the path at NH188212, and finish as for option (i) above (**27.5km; 1380m; 8h 50min**).

Aonach Shasuinn from Tigh Mòr na Seìlge, with Pt.862m, left, and Loch Beinn a' Mheadhoin beyond (Mike Dixon)

*Across the head of Loch Long to
Ben Killilan and Sgùman Còinntich
(Rab Anderson)*

SECTION 12
Loch Mullardoch to Glen Carron

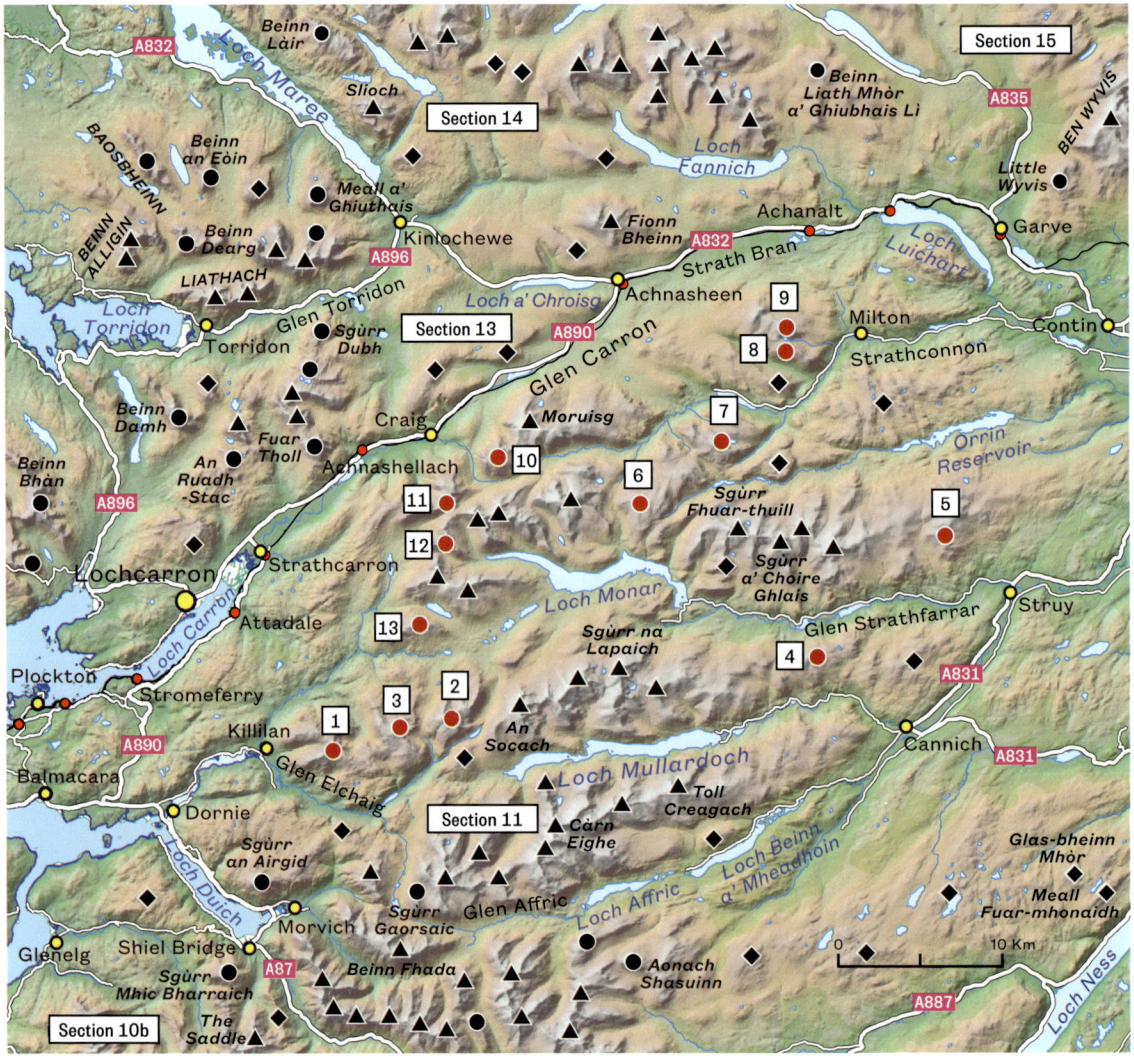

SECTION 12

Sgùman Còinntich from its west ridge (Mike Dixon)

Sgùman Còinntich; *879m; (C53); L25; NG977303; mossy peak*

The westernmost of a chain of three Corbetts on the north side of Glen Elchaig, Sgùman Còinntich, with Ben Killilan to its left, creates a picturesque backdrop on the drive along the road up the north side of Loch Long from Dornie.

Faochaig and Aonach Buidhe lie further east, and although Faochaig can be included with Sgùman Còinntich (see panel on page 269), it is better climbed with Aonach Buidhe, especially if a bike is used along Glen Elchaig, as is usual nowadays. Sgùman Còinntich is then a useful single hill, which is easy to access and gives a quick ascent for short days. It can be combined with Ben Killilan to give a longer outing.

Turn off the A87 on the north side of the bridge at Dornie (signed to Killilan) and follow the narrow road for 8.75km to a car park on the left at NG940303, at the start of a surfaced private estate road to Killilan, where the public road makes a right-angled turn towards Camus-luinie.

Walk along the road to Killilan to the bridge over the Allt a' Choire Mhòir, which flows down Coire Mòr between Ben Killilan and Sgùman Còinntich. Turn off left here and go up the left side of the burn, between it and a building, to pick up a path.

Follow the path uphill by the trees, then on to join a track where it forks, and take the main left branch. When the angle starts to ease around the 450m contour, leave the track and cross the burn to ascend the rough but uncomplicated slope to gain the ridge a short distance to the south-south-west of the summit. Make the final ascent up the ridge to gain the cairn and a trig pillar held in place by its steel legs (**5km; 880m; 2h 35min**).

It is easiest to return the same way (10km; 880m; 4h 15min).

An alternative return is to go down the north-east ridge, then a short way down the south-east ridge before descending south, out to the east of the main burn draining the hillside, to pick up an ATV track. This drops into An Glas-choire and becomes clearer on the line of a stalkers' path shown on the map. On reaching the floor of Glen Elchaig, it is a 3.25km walk back along the road (13.5km; 900m; 5h)

From Sgùman Còinntich's summit, the route can be extended to Ben Killilan. However, the direct route involves finding a line down through the crags guarding the col between the hills, the Bealach Mhic Bheathain. This can be avoided by returning a short way down the south-west ridge, then going down the side of the craggy north-west face and making a north-eastwards traverse beneath this face towards the bealach. Either continue the traverse below Pt.788m, the small top to the north of the bealach, or go over this.

The 2.5km-long crest of Ben Killilan has three highpoints over 750m. The East Top is thought to be the highest at 757m; the central top is actually given the name the West Top and is given 754m, and the actual west top is named Sgùrr na Cloiche (c.752m) on maps.

To descend from Sgùrr na Cloiche, it is probably best to return partway along the ridge, then descend to the track and return to the start (15km; 1150m; 5h 45min).

If the plan is to climb Ben Killilan, then it is perhaps best done first by leaving the track up Coire Mòr around the 450m contour and climbing north. From the East Top, traverse across to Bealach Mhic Bheathain. The line through the rocks is easily found in ascent. From a large boulder, a diagonal grassy line slants right through the lower band of crag, then a broad grassy ledge leads below the upper band. **Map on page 269**

> **Aonach Buidhe**; 899m; (C24); L25; NH057324; yellow ridge
> **Faochaig**; 868m; (C64); L25; NH021317; the whelk

Forming the central and eastern-most of the three Corbetts in the range on the north side of Glen Elchaig, these two hills are best climbed together.

Aonach Buidhe occupies an isolated position at the head of Glen Elchaig, and is the highest of the three. It is a finely shaped hill with distinctive spurs on all sides, and is separated from its neighbours by deep passes to the west and south-east. These passes carry the stalkers' path from Glen Elchaig to the Maol-bhuidhe bothy, which crosses between Faochaig and Aonach Buidhe, and the right of way to Pait Lodge on the shore of Loch Monar, which crosses between Aonach Buidhe and An Socach at the west end of the Mullardoch Munro chain.

Faochaig, although not as high, is more sprawling, and throws out ridges and spurs from its flat summit to create a series of deep corries.

The use of a bike on the estate road and track up Glen Elchaig saves about 3h 20min on the day.

Turn off the A87 on the north side of the bridge at Dornie (signed to Killilan) and follow the narrow road for 8.75km to a car park on the left at NG940303, at the start of an estate road to Killilan, where the public road makes a right-angled turn.

Walk along the estate road to Killilan and follow the surfaced road, then track past the path off to the Falls of Glomach gorge on the right. Continue along Loch na Leitreach to Carnach, crossing the bridge over the Allt Domhain to where a rough track comes off the hill on the left (north); the return route. Bikes are best left here (**10.75km**; **165m**; about **1h**), (**2h 40min** on foot). Times are now given on foot from and back to here.

Continue on the track along the glen, passing the track on the right to Iron Lodge, and follow the track up the hillside for a further 480m to a fork. Go right and cross the bridge over the An Crom-allt, which flows from between Faochaig and Aonach Buidhe. In a further 300m, leave the track at a boulder and climb the long south-west ridge of Aonach Buidhe, which, after an initial steep section, leads easily to the large summit cairn (**6km**; **820m**; **2h 40min**).

A vague ATV track, which becomes clearer further down, can be followed west from the summit, then down south-south-west to swing north-west to the col between the hills. If located, it provides a route to follow. Otherwise, traverse westwards above the head of the big northern corrie onto a minor top, then turn south-south-west and go down the broad ridge, which curves west above Coireag nan Each, then south-west. Towards the bottom, the slope steepens. Either drop straight down to an old wall, or cross a burn, then drop down and cut back over to recross the burn to reach the wall. The wall leads to the col, named Rèidh Leum na Fèithe, and a small ruin where the track on the line of the stalkers' path leads through to the Maol-bhuidhe bothy.

Head north along the track for 430m to a fork by a burn, then take the left fork and cross the burn. Leave the track and follow the burn west for about 50m to find the start of a stalkers' path, then follow this to zigzag up one steepening, across an easing, and up another steepening.

The path can be followed to the

Aonach Buidhe across the head of Glen Elchaig from above Iron Lodge (Grahame Nicoll)

Faochaig from Aonach Buidhe (Rab Anderson)

800m contour, a little further than the map shows. Continue past some small lochans onto a slight rise at the north-east end of Faochaig's sizeable summit plateau, then traverse south-west for 500m past some more tiny lochans to reach the summit cairn on an area of slanting rock outcrops (**11.5km; 1260m; 4h 50min**).

Descend the slope to the south to cross the main burn draining the hill-side, then follow this down into the corrie, Slochd Mòr, to meet a track where the burns join to form the Allt Domhain. Follow the track downhill, then across the slope above the burn to NH023292.

Leave the track here and drop towards the burn on the original stalkers' path, in a series of zigzags. Continue pleasantly down the path, which rejoins the track for the final descent to Carnach in Glen Elchaig (**16km; 1265m; 6h 10min**).

Return to Killilan (**37.5km; 1515m; 8h** with a bike), (**11h 20min** on foot).

Another option, with the aid of a bike, is to bike on from Carnach for a further 10–15min or so to where the track turns off right to Iron Lodge. Leave bikes here and climb both hills, returning to the col between them, then back to Iron Lodge. Although the timings are almost the same, the route is perhaps easier.

Sgùman Còinntich & Faochaig

*To climb these together, follow the route described on page 267 and climb to the top of Sgùman Còinntich (**5km; 880m; 2h 35min**).*

*Go down the north-east ridge for about 700m, then turn and go south-eastwards down the ridge above Coire Caol and Coire Shlat to a col at 638m, then climb north-east onto Sròn na Gaoithe (724m). Traverse east, then north-east above Coireag Searrach to the col with Faochaig, then climb northwards by a burn and on up to the summit (**11km; 1200m; 4h 45min**).*

*Return as for the descent route in the column opposite: south to cross the burn to gain the track and stalkers' path leading to Carnach, then make the 10.75km walk back along the track and road (**26km; 1290m; 8h 45min**).*

Aonach Buidhe

*For the ascent of Aonach Buidhe on its own, follow the road and track along Glen Elchaig to where a track turns off to Iron Lodge (**12.75km; 210m; 1h 10min** by bike), (**3h 10min** on foot).*

*Climb Aonach Buidhe as described on the page opposite; across the An Crom-alt and up its southern ridge (**4km; 770m; 2h 15min**) from Iron Lodge.*

*Descend to the col with Faochaig, as described opposite, then follow the track southwards back to Iron Lodge (**9.25km; 780m; 3h 45min**) and return to Killilan (**34.75km; 1080m; 6h** with a bike), (**10h** on foot).*

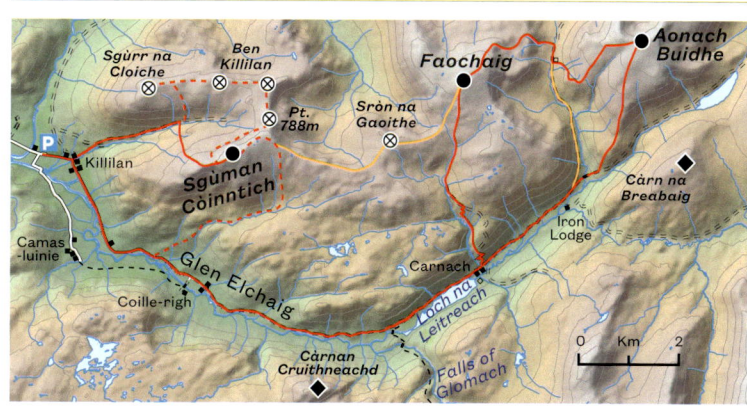

Sgòrr na Dìollaid's west top with Sgùrr na Lapaich, left, then Lurg Mhòr and the Monar Munros (Hugh Munro)

> *Sgòrr na Dìollaid*; 818m; (C127); L25; NH281362; peak of the saddle

Located towards the eastern end of the Mullardoch range of hills between Glen Cannich and Glen Strathfarrar, Sgòrr na Dìollaid is a fine hill with two distinctive rocky knolls

forming its scenic summit.

It provides an excellent short day, with particularly good views of the Mullardoch, Strathfarrar and Glen Affric hills; worth saving for a fine day.

The ascent is best made from Glen Cannich to the south, about halfway along the narrow road from Cannich village to Loch Mullardoch dam.

Start to the east of Muchrachd, on the east side of the bridge over the River Cannich. There is ample space to park on the left 150m before the bridge, and 50m up the track on the left just before it.

Cross the bridge to gain the Muchrachd track entrance; please don't park here since it is required for farm vehicles turning.

A prominent knoll can be seen at 490m on the lower hillside. From the track entrance, climb a slight ridge to pass the left side of the knoll, and

continue up the hillside beyond. Cross the right side of a flat, boggy area, then climb onto the rocky south top, Pt.786m.

Drop down and cross the narrow corrie in between, Coire Gorm, then climb up to the left of the right-hand (eastern) of the two prominent rocky points that can be seen from Pt.786m. This is the summit, and it is easily gained. Traverse the narrow crest to the spectacular western point, which is a photogenic location, sitting above a steep drop into Glen Strathfarrar (**3.75km; 680m; 2h**).

Return to the foot of the summit rocks, then head south-south-west across Coire Gorm and climb onto Pt.777m, the west top. Descend to the south-east, then cross the west side of the flat area to rejoin the approach route and follow this back downhill (**8.5km; 720m; 3h 25min**).

Beinn a' Bhàthaich Àrd; *862m; (C74); L26; NH360434; hill of the high byre*

Rising prominently above the north side of Glen Strathfarrar near its junction with Strath Glass at Struy, Beinn a' Bhàthaich Àrd is the easternmost highpoint of a range that, further west, rises to the four Strathfarrar Munros. It is a triple-topped hill, well seen from points to the east, such as the Kessock Bridge over the mouth of the Beauly Firth. Being slightly removed from the nearby bigger hills, its summit commands extensive views.

The approach to it is made from Inchmore at the entrance to Glen Strathfarrar, a short distance along the narrow road from the A831 on the north side of Struy Bridge. There is a car park on the left, just before the vehicle access controlled gate to the road up Glen Strathfarrar.

Walk along the road up the glen for 1.75km to the Culligran Power Station, then leave the road and follow a track west-south-west through pleasant birch woods. On emerging from the trees after 1.5km at an electricity pylon, there are two options:

(i) Better and more scenic, though more rugged, is to head north up the hillside which, although heathery and initially craggy, has no difficulty. Pass west of Càrn Coire na Muic (329m) and follow the lower south ridge of the hill, past a prominent survey post, then on over a small rise, Càrn Mòr (487m). Ascend the steeper slope beyond, passing Cnoc an Duine (617m) to its west, then a notch beyond to its east, and continue up the ridge to beneath the final slope.

(ii) Easier, if you prefer track walking, is to continue on the track for a further 3km, swinging right past a dam to climb uphill to where an ATV track leaves the track shortly after crossing a small burn. This is before the track ends at an upper dam. Follow this ATV track a short way, and although it does swing right towards the summit, it is probably best to leave it and simply head north-north-east to steeper ground, then the ridge leading to the final slope.

Climb the final short, but steeper slope to gain the stone trig point on the summit (**7.5km; 840m; 3h 15min**).

Continue north-north-east along the broad ridge over Pt.835m, then north-east to the flat summit of Sgùrr a' Phollain (855m), the third of the

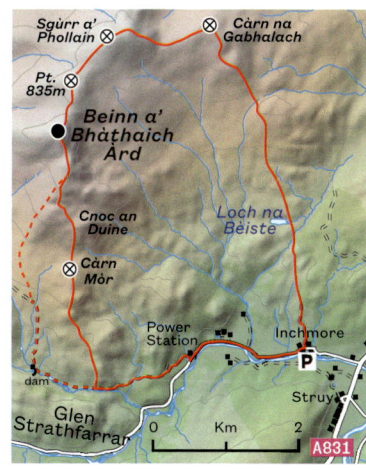

hill's triple tops. Follow a stalkers' path briefly north-east, then more steeply down south-east in zigzags, before heading north-east along a broad ridge for 600m onto the slight rise of Càrn na Gabhalach (713m).

Make an initial south-eastwards descent and follow the path, which disappears in places, to reach the east side of Loch na Beiste. Continue on down via the path and a track, through attractive birch woods, back to Inchmore (**16km; 950m; 5h 45min**).

Beinn a' Bhàthaich Àrd from the A831 at Struy (Rab Anderson)

Across Loch Monar to An Sìthean, distant left, with Meall Dubh na Caoidhe, centre (Hugh Munro)

An Sìthean; *814m; (C132); L25; NH171453; fairy hill*

Standing in the rarely-frequented tract of wilderness to the north of Loch Monar, known as the East Monar Forest, An Sìthean is a remote hill with few marked features. Its position between the west end of the Strathfarrar Munros and Maoile Lunndaidh makes it a little awkward to access.

There are two routes: one from the north, from the end of the road along Strathconon, which is longer and rougher, and the other from the south, from the Monar Dam in Strathfarrar, which is the more popular route since it follows better paths and is perhaps more scenic. This is described first.

The road along Glen Strathfarrar is private, with an access-controlled gate at its start at Inchmore. For the current access information, check Mountaineering Scotland's website. Generally, during the summer months, the gate is open from 9am to between 6–8pm, depending on the month. It is closed all day Tuesday and until 1.30pm on Wednesday. Winter access has to be arranged in advance through Mountaineering Scotland.

Drive up the glen and park on the left just before Monar Dam. It is nearly 14 miles (22km) to here from the gate, and 30min should be allowed for the drive there, and 30min back. Plan this into the day.

Continue on foot along the road, then the track, where the hill can be seen looking some distance away, for 1km to Monar Lodge. On the north side of the buildings, go through a gate and follow a stalkers' path that traverses the hillside above the loch to climb through the pass between the small knoll of Creag Dubh (315m) and Creag a' Chaobh (474m).

Descend the other side and follow the path across bridges over the Allt nan Euan, then the Allt a' Choire Dhomhain. Continue along just above the loch and cross a bridge over the Allt na Cois, which flows down the side of An Sìthean.

Leave the path along the loch here and follow the path that climbs above this burn, then swings away from it across the hillside to reach another small burn, the Alltan Fearna. Cross the head of this burn, then continue for 200m or so before leaving the

path to climb the broad, rounded ridge ahead to the easier upper slopes, where the shoulder of Mullach a' Gharbh-leathaid is followed to the summit (**9km; 750m; 3h 15min**).

Rather than return the same way, descend south-east past a series of small pools and lochans, then make a steeper descent to the col with Meall Dubh na Caoidhe. This is the Clach a' Chomharraidh between the head of the Allt na Cois to the south and Glen Orrin to the north.

Cross the stalkers' path and climb 30m up the other side, then contour eastwards around the north side of Meall Dubh na Caoidhe and drop down by one of the burns to pick up the head of a stalkers' path.

Follow this path downhill to the south, joining another path, and continue down Coire Domhain above the Allt a' Choire Dhomhain to rejoin the lochside path. Cross back over the bridge and return through the pass to Monar Lodge and the start (**17.5km; 920m; 5h 45min**).

The Strathconon route starts from the end of the public road along the glen and avoids the restrictions imposed by the gate times for access to and from Glen Strathfarrar.

Start from the parking area on the right towards the west end of Loch Beannacharain. The principal route to Bac an Eich starts here too, and the determined walker could include both hills; brief details are given at the end.

Walk along the road, then branch left along the track that passes beneath Scardroy Lodge. Continue to a fork at a cottage before the bridge over the River Meig. Take the right fork here, which soon crosses a tributary, then swings away up beside this, before turning southwards across a col to rejoin the River Meig.

Continue alongside the river, with another brief section away from it, then pass beneath the steep Creag na h-Iolaire. Just before, or after, the Allt na Criche joins from the right, find an appropriate place to ford the River Meig; it is perhaps worth carrying suitable lightweight footwear for this purpose.

Follow the rough ATV track on the other side, which climbs south-west beside the Allt an Amise up Gleannan Allt an Amise. Just below the Torran Ceann Liath col, take the more obvious track that zigzags up left, and follow this south-south-east up the hillside. It is not so clear in a few places, but it does carry on up to the 700m contour. From there, continue to the summit (**12km; 680m; 4h**).

The easiest return is back the

same way (**24km; 710m; 7h**).

Another option is to descend east, then traverse over Pt.768m and Sgùrr Coire na Eun. An unmarked stalkers' path starts at NH205478, and this can be followed down to the col with Bac an Eich, the Drochaid Coire Mhadaidh. From there, descend the

track down Coire Mhòraigein to the ruins at Corriefeol and return to the start (**24.75km; 810m; 7h 25min**).

Bac an Eich can be climbed from the Drochaid Coire Mhadaidh, with a descent down the Allt Coire na Feòla, reversing the ascent route described on page 274 (**25.5km; 1110m; 8h 15min**).

An Sìthean's lonely summit cairn with Maoile Lunndaidh beyond (Rab Anderson)

Bac an Eich; 849m; (C91); L25; NH222489; bank of the horse

Like An Sìthean to its south, with which it shares a tract of rugged wilderness, Bac an Eich is another infrequently climbed Corbett. It, together with its attendant tops, rises to the south of Loch Beannarachain at the end of the road in the upper reaches of Strathconon. Its summit is a particularly fine viewpoint; another hill worth saving for a good day.

There are two routes, both starting towards the end of the single-track road through Strathconon, some 20 miles (33km), or so from the A835.

The better route starts from a large parking area on the right towards the west end of Loch Beannacharain, shortly before the public road ends.

Walk to the end of the road, passing through a gate, and take the main left-hand track to pass beneath Scardroy Lodge. Continue past the estate buildings and a forestry plantation to Corrievuic cottage, then take the track on the left and cross the bridge over the River Meig to reach the ruins at Corriefeol.

The ravine of the Allt Coire na Feòla lies ahead. Follow a rough path through the heather up the left side of the ravine to gain a section of track that can be seen from the approach. Follow this track and a path, then another section of track to its end.

Climb up and right across rough ground to a large wooden post on the edge of the upper part of the ravine at NH213501. This, and a post on the opposite side, marks the crossing point where a narrow, gravelly path leads steeply down into the ravine for a step across the burn and a climb back up the other side.

Wade uphill through the heather, then make a short, but steep climb onto the ridge above An Leth-chreag and follow this pleasantly up to the stone shelter enclosing the stone trig point on top of Bac an Eich (**6.25km; 730m; 2h 40min**).

It is a superb viewpoint which includes the Strathfarrar, Mullardoch, Monar, Torridon, Fisherfield and Fannaich Munros and Ben Wyvis, as well as the Corbetts An Sìthean to the south, Sgùrr nan Ceannaichean to the west, and Meallan nan Uan and Sgùrr a' Mhuilinn to the north.

Descend south-westwards off the summit, down open slopes and a slight spur, to reach the col between the hills; the Drochaid Coire Mhadaidh. Cross the col. If found, a

Bac an Eich from Creag Coire na Feòla, with the Strathfarrar Munros beyond (Rab Anderson)

rough ATV track runs across it to a track on the far side, which leads to one (not shown on maps) that can be seen zigzagging up the opposite side.

Turn right and follow this track pleasantly down Coire Mhòraigein beside the burn. Towards the bottom, when the vehicle tracks break off left, continue on the path around the base of Creag Coire na Feòla to ford the Allt Coire na Feòla to reach the ruins at Corriefeol, and return to the start (15.25km; 745m; 5h).

The other route starts from a little further back along the road opposite Inverchoran, where there is limited parking on the verge where the access track to Inverchoran leaves the road at NH261508.

This is also the parking for the Grahams Meall na Faochaig above the road to the north, and Beinn Mheadhoin to the south, which sits on the east side of Gleann Chorainn,

Summit view to the Torridon mountains, left, and Fisherfield, right (Rab Anderson)

separating that hill from Bac an Eich. The initial part of the approach is the same as for Beinn Mheadhoin.

Walk down the track and cross the bridge over the River Meig, then circumnavigate Inverchoran farm by a track on the left across a bridge, then ford the tributary burn to gain the track on the other side. Continue south on the track up Gleann Chorainn, passing the track off left up Beinn Mheadhoin, to the far end of the forestry, then ford the burn. There are now two options:

(i) Make a rising traverse west-south-west to cross the Allt Toll Lochain, which flows from Loch Toll Lochain, above a ravine in the steep lower hillside.

(ii) Continue on the grassy track and the original stalkers' path just above to cross the Allt Toll Lochain, then ascend the steep hillside.

Either way, ascend the spur of Sgùrr Toll Lochain, which is steep and rocky, but with an easy way up the centre avoiding any difficulties. At the top, follow the ridge round north-west above the steep headwall of Coire an Lochain, which plunges into the lochan, to gain the trig point and wind shelter (6km; 730m; 2h 35min).

Descend, south then south-east between the burns to reach the top of a short stalkers' path and go down this to join the stalkers' path through the col (Torran Ceann Liath) at the head of Gleann Chorainn. Go north-eastwards for 200m to pick up the track coming up from Loch na Caoidhe in Glen Orrin, then follow this track and the stalkers' path down the glen, crossing the river to regain the approach route, which is retraced back to Inverchoran and the road (14km; 770m; 4h 50min).

Map on page 273

West up Strathconon to Creag Ruadh, left, Meallan nan Uan, centre, and Sgùrr a' Mhuilinn, right (Rab Anderson)

Meallan nan Uan; *838m; (C109); L25; NH263544; little hill of the lambs*
Sgùrr a' Mhuilinn; *879m; (C54); L25; NH264557; peak of the mill*

Rising above the bend in Strathconon, a short distance to the west of Milton, is an attractive group of compact hills, which has this pair as its highest points. There are six well-defined summits in the group, with Meallan nan Uan and Sgùrr a' Mhuilinn sitting in the centre 2km apart, either side of Coire a' Mhuilinn with its small lochan.

The group is visible from the A835 and the A9 on the west side of the Black Isle. To their north, long slopes fall to Strath Bran and the A832 west, from where Meallan nan Uan can be seen, although it is its pyramidal outlier, Sgùrr a' Choire-rainich, that catches the eye, then from further west its twin Sgùrr a' Ghlas Leathaid.

Access is from the A835 by a 14

mile (23km), or so, drive along the single-track road up Strathconon. There is space to park beneath the start of the route at NH294544, on the right (west) side of the road at Strathanmore, just beyond Milton; either by the walled enclosures, or in a small grassy pull-off 30m further on.

Ascend south-west by the fence around the woodland then continue steeply up the grassy and, in summer, bracken-covered slopes, heading for the burn up on the right; the Allt an t-Srathain Mhòir. Ascend close to this burn to reach an unlocked gate in a deer fence across the hillside at NH282546, shortly before where a burn, Allt Luachrach, flows in from the other side. A more direct line towards Creag Ruadh leads to a locked gate 250m or so to the south-east. Once through the open gate, turn southwards and climb to the top of Creag Ruadh (734m).

A pleasant walk then leads northwest along a narrow ridge, with the two Corbetts appearing positioned either side of the intermediate rise of

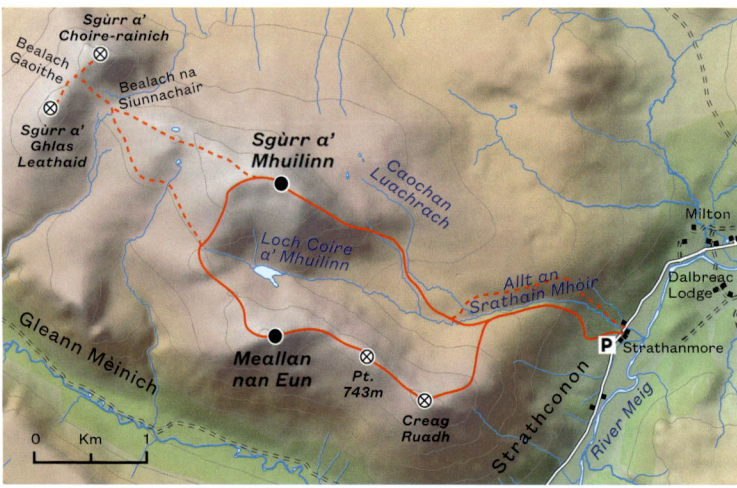

Pt.743m, which is crossed. There are grand views down the steep slope on the left across Gleann Mèinich, a fine example of a U-shaped valley, to Meall na Faochaig, a Graham, on the far side. A final, steeper 120m climb gains the summit of Meallan nan Uan (**3.75km; 785m; 2h 10min**).

Drop west off the summit and scramble easily down through some rocks, then head north-west down a broad ridge to a col. Either climb over the small rise of Càrnan Fuar (715m) at the head of Coire a' Mhuilinn, or bypass it to the right, to gain another col and climb to the summit of Sgùrr a' Mhuilinn (**6km; 1000m; 3h 10min**).

If time, weather and legs permit, it is worth climbing the other two principal hills in the group. These are the twins of Sgùrr a' Ghlas Leathaid and Sgùrr a' Choire-rainich, which are so prominent in the view from the A832 near Achnasheen.

To do this, contour north-west across the slopes of Sgùrr a' Mhuilinn to another col at c.705m, Bealach na Siunnachair. From there, ascend the hills in turn, which are separated by a col at c.785m, Bealach Gaoithe.

Return to Bealach na Siunnachair then follow a broad ridge south-eastwards past a pool in a peaty area, shown as a lochan on maps, to gain the top of Sgùrr a' Mhuilinn; an added

Sgùrr a' Mhuilinn from Strathconon (Rab Anderson)

4km, 205m, 1h 15min.

To descend from Sgùrr a' Mhuilinn, go down the steep south-east ridge. At the bottom, follow the green line of a minor watercourse through a peaty area to the right of another burn, the Caochan Luachrach. Cross the Allt an t-Srathain Mhòir, which flows from Loch Coire a' Mhuilinn, and descend the south side to rejoin the ascent line at the gate and continue down to the road (**10km; 1000m; 4h 25min**).

If the water is running high and a crossing of the Allt an t-Srathain Mhòir cannot be made higher up,

then one may be forced to continue down the north side, since a crossing lower down is likely to be difficult. There is a gate in the upper deer fence at NH288550. On reaching the deer fence around the woodland, climb it close to the burn, then drop down through the trees to a TV aerial and water tank. Continue down the narrow strip between a fence around the house and the burn. This leads to a small gate onto the road next to the bridge over the burn. There is also a gate on the other side of the fence around the house.

Pt.743m with Meallan nan Uan, left, and Sgùrr a' Mhuilinn, right, from Creag Ruadh (Tom Prentice)

Sgùrr nan Ceannaichean; 913m; (C3); L25; NH087480; peak of the merchants

Sgùrr nan Ceannaichean sits at the end of a westwards-running, multi-topped ridgeline forming the south side of upper Glen Carron, which has Moruisg, a Munro, as its highest point. Sgùrr nan Ceannaichean was formerly a Munro, but following a height survey in 2009, it was demoted to Corbett status. It is commonly climbed together with Moruisg, which adjoins it to the east, and a description for that route can be found in the SMC's guidebook *The Munros*. The two routes described here are for Sgùrr nan Ceannaichean alone.

Start in Glen Carron, from a layby at NH081521 on the A890, 7 miles (11km) south of Achnasheen and 1 mile (1.5km) to the west of Loch Sgamhain.

Go through the gate at the west end of the layby and cross the River Carron by a bridge, then go through a low underpass beneath the railway to gain open moorland. Follow the path west-south-west to reach the burn, Alltan na Feòla, and continue uphill alongside this, heading for the corrie between the hills, Coire Toll nam Bian.

Soon after passing through a gated, fenced area of regenerating woodland, cross the Alltan na Feòla and follow a path out onto the north ridge, passing

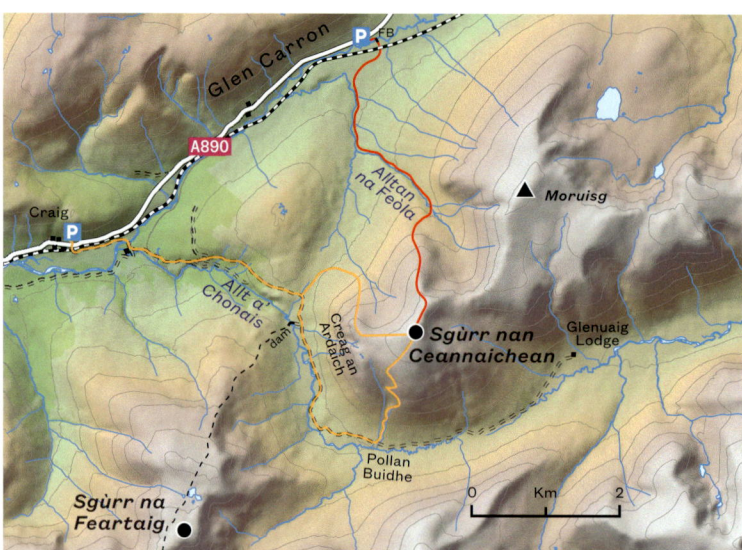

to the right of a rocky bluff. Continue up the ridge to the summit, which lies to the south of the first cairn encountered (**5.5km; 780m; 2h 30min**).

Return the same way (**11km; 790m; 4h 5min**).

An ascent can also be made from Craig (see opposite for parking) by following a track around to the Pollan Buidhe at the back of the mountain to ascend a stalkers' path. This starts to the right of a burn at NH081466 and zigzags up almost the full height

of the slope to the right of the streamway. When the path ends, continue to the west ridge, then the summit (**9.75km; 900m; 3h 40min**).

A descent can be made down the west ridge, then steeply down northwards between the rocky west face, Creag an Ardaich, and the burn draining Am Fliuch-choire. Continue almost to the fence around the fenced-in area, before turning west to rejoin the track to return to Craig (**15.75km; 930m; 5h 25min**).

Sgùrr nan Ceannaichean and Creag an Ardaich from Strath Carron to the west (Mike Dixon)

Beinn Tharsuinn with Bidein a' Choire Sheasgaich to its left, from the ridge to Sgùrr Choinnich (Mike Dixon)

Beinn Tharsuinn; *863m; (C72); L25; NH055433; transverse hill*
Sgùrr na Feartaig; *862m; (C73); L25; NH055454; peak of the sea-pink (thrift)*

Lying to the south-east of Achnashellach in Glen Carron, these two hills are to some extent neglected due to the proximity of the higher and more popular mountains that surround them.

Were it anywhere else, Beinn Tharsuinn would probably receive attention for itself, but its position, tucked out of sight on the most direct route to Bidein a' Choire Sheasgaich and Lurg Mhòr, means that for many it is simply viewed as an obstacle to overcome to get to these Munros. However, when paired with Sgùrr na Feartaig to its north, the route gives a varied and scenic outing.

Sgùrr na Feartaig is actually quite an attractive hill, which forms a long, level ridge with steep corries on its northern side overlooking Glen Carron. Its ascent provides fine views of the mountains around Coire Làir and of the Torridonian giants beyond.

The ascent of both hills is made from Craig in Glen Carron, just over 10 miles (16km) along the A890 from Achnasheen and 2 miles (3.5km) to

the east of Achnashellach Station. The Achnashellach Forest car park at NH040493 provides the start, and is located up a short track on the north side of the A890.

There are plans to create a new car park in a better location on the south side of the road to the east at some point.

Cross the road opposite the car park entrance and go over the level crossing, then follow the track, which runs parallel to the railway, for 750m before turning south across a bridge over the River Carron.

Take the left fork and follow this up the glen between the hills, above the Allt a' Chonais. Continue past forks on the right to where a track loops left, then take the higher track up the side of the glen to exit the forestry.

Continue over the highpoint to the north of a small knoll named Cona Mheallain (298m) on some maps, and descend past a track to a dam. If the river is running high, to avoid the crossing further on, it is possible to cross at the dam, or by the rickety

suspension bridge 100m upstream, then follow the west side of the river.
▶

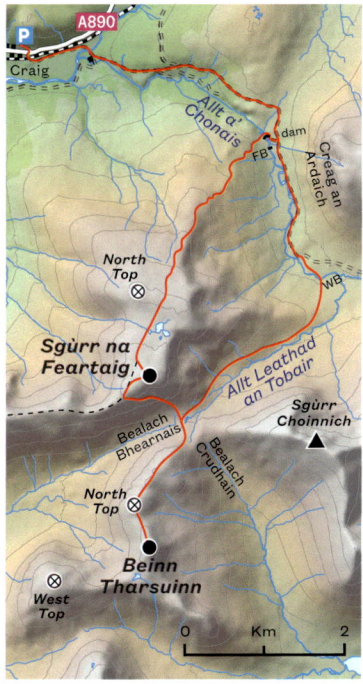

Bealach Bhearnais, left, and Sgùrr na Feartaig (Mike Dixon)

Otherwise, continue along the track to where it makes a left turn and starts to climb at the bend in the glen.

Leave the track here and follow a stalkers' path to the river, which is crossed by a two-strand wire bridge at NH074467; the wires alternate between being usable and unusable. On the far side, continue on a section of track, then the original path, climbing south-west above the Allt Leathad an Tobair to reach the Bealach Bhearnais (596m).

Climb south-west, passing to the side of a higher col, Bealach Crudhain, with Sgùrr Choinnich, then ascend steeply onto the north-east ridge of Beinn Tharsuinn. Follow this broad and grassy ridge over a minor rise, then the North Top (817m), and continue up the crest to the summit (**10.5km; 860m; 3h 45min**).

Return to the Bealach Bhearnais at the foot of the steep slope falling from Sgùrr na Feartaig's summit. The most straightforward option is to simply take a direct line up the slope to gain the summit, which is marked by a large cairn (**13.25km; 1170m; 5h**).

Another option is to take an easier, but less direct, line by following the broad grassy slope on a rising traverse up left (west) to reach a stalkers' path along Sgùrr na Feartaig's western ridgeline a few hundred metres south-west of the summit; an old stalkers' path takes this line and, once found, provides something to follow. If this line is taken, once on the ridgeline, go along the path a short way then leave it, since it bypasses the summit to the west, and climb to the top.

To descend, head northwards to pick up the stalkers' path leading past the west side of Loch Sgùrr na Feartaig in the dip with the North Top. The path is not so clear beyond the loch, but follow the line shown on the map and, once over the crest, the path becomes clear and leads all the way down to the dam across the Allt Chonais.

Either cross below the dam, or go 100m upstream to the wood slatted, wobbly suspension bridge and cross this. Gain the main track and follow this back to Craig (**21.75km; 1240m; 7h 15min**).

For anyone who has already climbed Beinn Tharsuinn en route to Lurg Mhòr, for the ascent of Sgùrr na Feartaig on its own, simply go up and back down the stalkers' path from the dam (**8.5km; 870m; 3h 20min**), (**17km; 940m; 5h 35min**).

> **Beinn Dronaig**; *797m; (C163); L25; NH037381; hill of the knoll or ragged hill*

One of the most remote and awkward to get to Corbetts, Beinn Dronaig sits squat in the outback of the Attadale Forest to the east of Loch Carron. On foot, from Attadale by Loch Carron, or Achintee in Strathcarron, the ascent involves a long approach walk of 12.25km, or 9.75km, just to reach Bendronaig Lodge and bothy below it.

However, good tracks on the Attadale approach make this ideal for a single-day approach using a bike, which is how most walkers now approach this hill.

Turn off the A890 along the east side of Loch Carron, signed to Attadale Gardens, to a car park immediately on the right at NG924387.

Walk along the road to the entrance to the gardens and turn right along the road, taking the right fork past a cottage, then the holiday homes at Strathan. Now on a track, continue ahead and turn round the head of the glen across a bridge over the River Attadale. The track climbs to join a hydro track, which leads

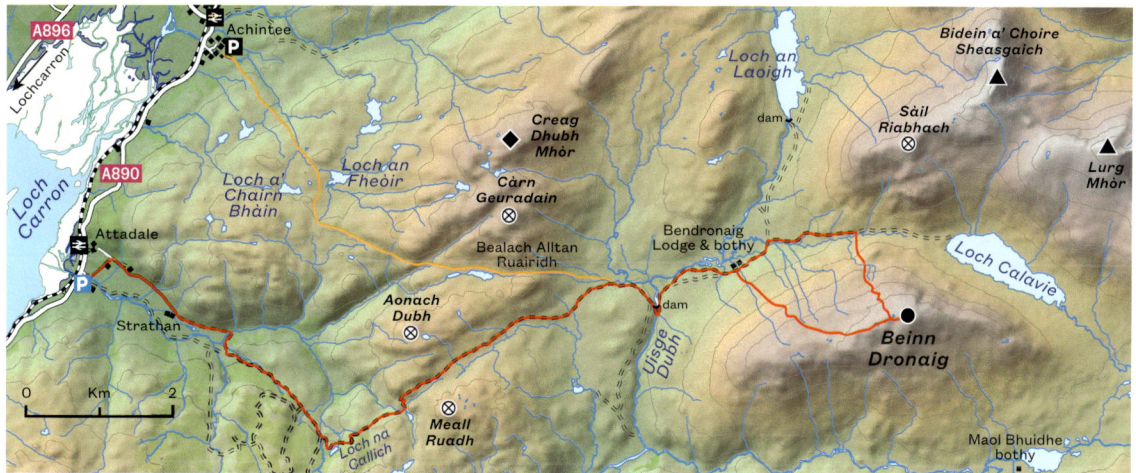

uphill for a way before easing. Swing left past Loch an Droighinn and continue on the track, which climbs to the north end of Loch na Caillich, then zigzag steeply up (perhaps with some pushing) to pass through the watershed between the hills.

With Beinn Dronaig now in sight ahead, make the long descent down Srath Fèith a' Mhadaidh, taking the second track on the right before the dam to cross a bridge over the Uisge Dubh. Turn left up the other side, then take either fork (the left is better to bike) to reach the track down to Bendronaig Lodge and the open estate bothy. Bikes are best left here (**12.25km; 400m; 1h 45min**), (**3h 20min** on foot). The distance and time is now given on foot, from and back to here.

Walk north-east along the track to cross either of the bridges over the Allt Coire na Sorna, then take the track that climbs uphill. Follow this to just before it levels off, where an old fenceline meets the track, at the point the main burn is joined by a burn coming off Sàil Riabhach on the left, which the track crosses.

Step over both burns, then climb the hillside steeply up the right side of a craggy knoll. Cross a burn and continue in the same direction, with increasingly good views behind to Bidein a' Choire Sheasgaich and Lurg Mhòr. Veer left at the top of the final steepening to reach the trig pillar on the summit, where there are magnificent views of the encircling wilderness (**4.25km; 580m; 1h 55min**).

Rather than return the same way, head south-west along the broad crest to drop down a steeper section, and head west-north-west across a flatter area with the Achnashellach hills in view ahead. When the bothy comes into view, drop steeply down the grassy hillside to it, avoiding two steep steps (**7.25km; 585m; 2h 55min**).

Make the long return to Attadale (**28.75km; 1150m; 5h 15min** with a bike), (**8h 15min** on foot).

For the route from Achintee, go left then right to park by the substation at NG942417. Follow the stalker's path up the hillside through the Bealach Alltan Ruairidh to join the hydro track, and follow it past the dam to the bothy (**9.75km; 400m; 2h 50min**).

Climb Beinn Dronaig and return to the bothy (**4.25km; 580m; 1h 55min**).

Return to Achintee as for the approach (**26.75km; 1215m; 8h 15min**).

Beinn Dronaig from Creag Dhubh Mhòr, with Loch Calavie, left, and Aonach Buidhe, right (Rab Anderson)

Across the Horns of Alligin from Sgùrr Mòr to Beinn Dearg, middle right, with flat-topped Stùc Loch na Cabhaig, left, Beinn Eighe beyond with Meall a' Ghiuthais, left, and the distant Fannaichs. (Robert Durran)

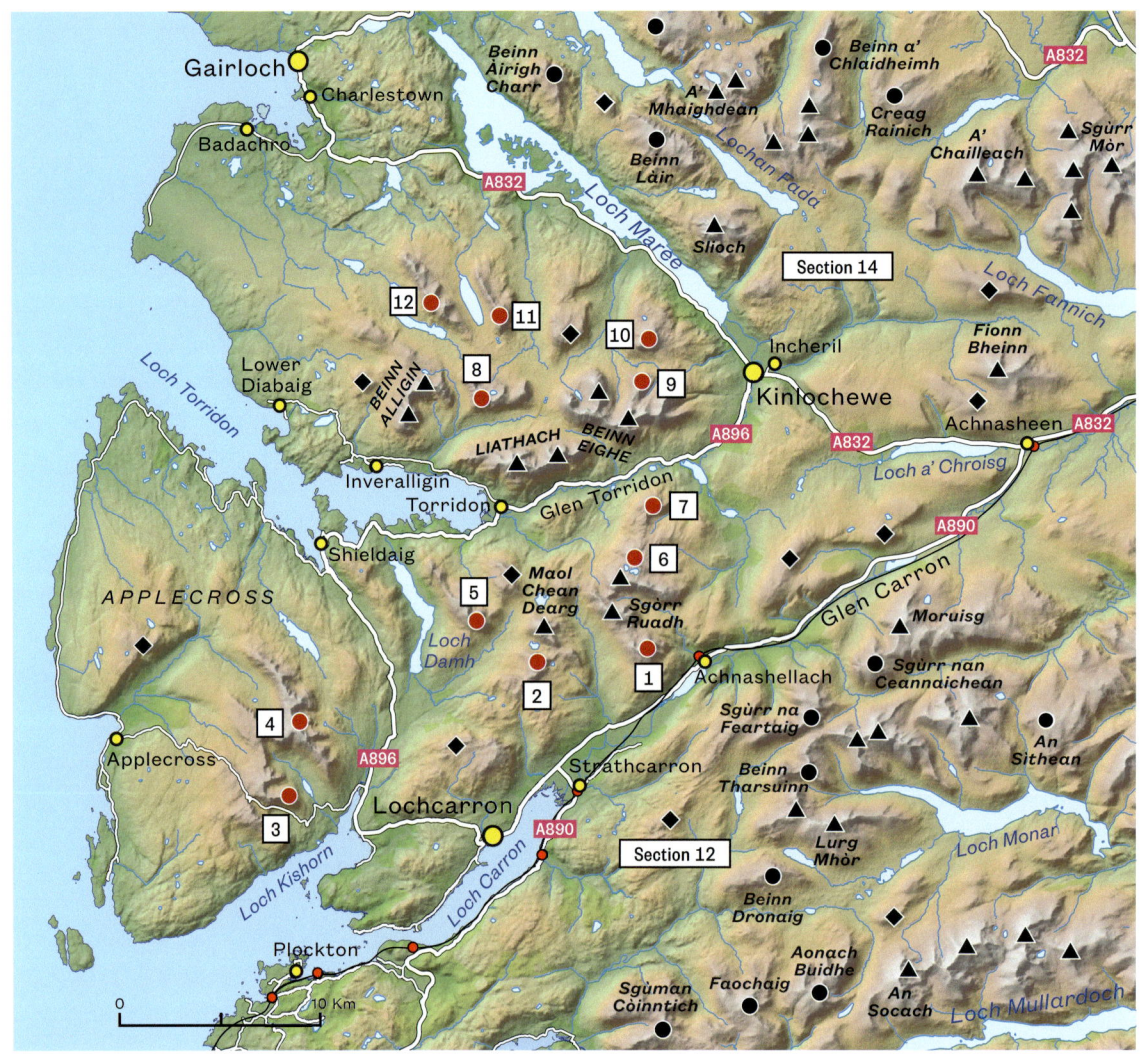

SECTION 13

Fuar Tholl and Mainreachan Buttress from the Bealach Mòr with Sgòrr Ruadh (Derek Sime)

Fuar Tholl; 907m; (C13); L25; NG975489; cold hole

Rising at the head of Strath Carron, Fuar Tholl is a fine and craggy mountain whose triple-topped skyline profile, when seen from either side of Loch Carron, resembles the upturned face of the Duke of Wellington. From these points, the tip of Mainreachan Buttress is prominent and gives rise to the local name Wellington's Nose.

Although the quickest way up Fuar Tholl is from Coulags or Balnacra on the A890 to the south, the ascent is steep and rather dull. A better way of appreciating the mountain and its grand surroundings starts at Achnashellach, several kilometres further up Glen Carron. From there, great sweeps of red Torridonian sandstone tower over tiny Achnashellach railway station, a request stop on ScotRail's Highland Line railway.

This is the same start point for the traverse over the Munros Beinn Liath Mhòr and Sgòrr Ruadh. It is common to include Fuar Tholl for a full traverse of Coire Làir, brief details of which are given in the panel at the end.

Start from a rough layby at NH005483, on the south side of the A890, almost opposite the access

track to the station.

The approach is by the right of way from Achnashellach to Torridon, which passes through Coire Làir. Walk up the access road to the station, cross the railway line and go through the gate opposite on a track leading to a crossroads. Turn sharp-left and follow a forestry track with fine views to Fuar Tholl. After about 600m, keep an eye out for a path that cuts back left, and follow this to go through a gate. Continue alongside the River Làir, then climb steadily through the forest onto the more open hillside, where scattered pines cling to the

steep sides of the ravine, through which the river plunges.

At an elevation of 370m, with Coire Làir opening out, the gradient eases and the path divides at NG990501. Take the left fork and cross the River Làir. A wade might be required, so it may be worth carrying suitable footwear for this. A small island downstream a little can give an easier crossing point. If the river is running too high, a crossing will have to be made further up the corrie, and a return made that way, as there are no better crossing places lower down.

▶

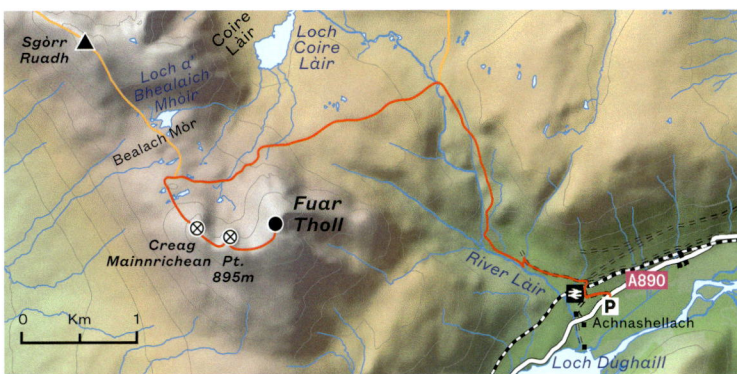

Continue up the path out in front of Coire Mainnrichean, at the back of which sits the superb and imposing Mainreachan Buttress. Whilst a direct route on grass then scree can be taken up the corrie to the left of the buttress, it is better to continue on the main path for a short way to climb the north-west ridge above the corrie.

After passing a small lochan to the right of the path, a short climb gains the crest between Fuar Tholl and Sgòrr Ruadh. Turn left to pass between some small lochans, then ascend a stony and rocky slope onto Creag Mainnrichean (857m). Climb up and cross the slope below the top of Pt.895m, Mainreachan Buttress, (although it is worth going to the top), then drop slightly to the col at the head of the corrie. A final easy 50m climb gains the summit shelter and what remains of the trig point (**8km; 960m; 3h 25min**).

It is best to return the same way (**16km; 1015m; 5h 40min**).

A more direct line can be taken down the scree in the corrie. A direct descent via the south-east ridge is very rough and not recommended.

> ### Coire Làir Round
> *For the complete round of Coire Làir, where the path divides at NG990501, take the right-hand path then, at a fork in another 100m, take the right fork again. In a further 300m, take the left fork then climb onto and along the undulating 2km-long ridge to the summit of Beinn Liath Mhòr (**7.25km; 1040m; 3h 20min**).*
>
> *Drop to a small lochan, negotiating a sandstone band, then traverse down and across the south side of Pt.769m to gain the main path through the corrie at a small lochan. Leave this path at the north end of the lochan and climb to the summit of Sgòrr Ruadh (**10km; 1360m; 4h 50min**).*
>
> *Descend to the Bealach Mòr to gain the stalkers' path then cross to the far side and climb the ridge over the top of Mainreachan Buttress to the summit of Fuar Tholl (**13km; 1665m; 6h 10min**).*
>
> *Return to the stalkers' path and follow this back as for the normal descent (**21km; 1720m; 8h 25min**).*

> **An Ruadh-Stac**; *892m; (C33); L25; NG921480; the red conical hill*

Located a short distance to the west of Fuar Tholl is the splendid quartzite cone of An Ruadh-Stac, which thrusts itself into the rugged Torridonian terrain between Strath Carron and Glen Torridon. Standing beside its bigger neighbours, it creates an equally impressive sight. Immediately to its north is the similarly-shaped, but sandstone-capped, Maol Chean-dearg, with which it is often paired; a brief description of which is given in the panel at the end.

Start from the lower part of Strath Carron, from a small parking area on the north side of the A890, at NG956451, just west of Coulags Bridge over the Fionn-abhainn.

Walk across the bridge over the Fionn-abhainn and take the signed right of way to Torridon, passing through a gate and along a track. After 140m, go left along another track, then a path which rejoins the main track again, and follow this for a further 300m to a bridge. Leave the track here, as it goes to a hydro building, then take the old track on the right, which leads to a dam.

Continue on a path and cross the bridge over the Fionn-abhainn just above the dam. The path leads past Coire Fionnaraich bothy to the Clach nan Con-fionn, the stone to which the mythological hero Fionn chained his hunting dogs.

In a further 500m, leave the path through the glen and take the path that climbs steeply uphill under the craggy nose of Meall nam Ceapairean to gain the Bealach a' Choire Ghairbh at 587m between Meall nan Ceapairean and Maol Chean-dearg.

The great north face of An Ruadh-Stac lies ahead and creates a magnificent sight, with cliffs

An Ruadh-Stac from Maol Chean-dearg, with Beinn Bhàn right (Derek Sime)

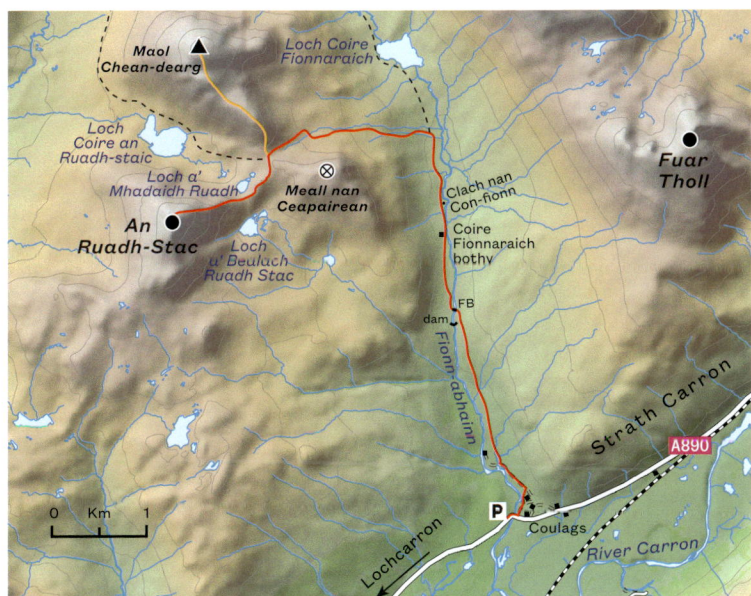

Sgùrr a' Chaorachain; 792m;
(C173); L24; NG796417; peak of
the little sheep

Sitting between Meall Gorm and Beinn Bhàn, with the splendid Coire na Bà to its left and the even bigger Coire nan Arr (the giants' corrie) to its right, Sgùrr a' Chaorachain creates an impressive sight rising above Loch Kishorn. Its great sandstone cliffs and buttresses are a spectacular example of Torridonian mountain architecture. The most impressive feature of the mountain is Na Ciòchan, a steep tower that rises above Coire nan Arr and is connected to the main mass of the mountain by a distinctive narrow, serrated ridge.

Sgùrr a' Chaorachain's upper parts form a horseshoe around a splendid narrow, north-east facing hanging corrie, Coire a' Chaorachain, which overlooks Coire nan Arr, with the highest point being at the east end of the southern arm opposite Na Ciòchan. Towards the middle of the horseshoe is a lower top (776m), which has an aerial on its summit and a rough track leading to it from the top of the Bealach na Bà road 1km to the west. This narrow, twisting road links Kishorn with Applecross and climbs steeply round the south side of Sgùrr a' Chaorachain through Coire na Bà to a height of 625m, making this hill one of the most easily accessible Corbetts.

It is a very short route, which in good visibility can be extended around the head of Coire nan Arr to include Beinn Bhàn to the north, although this involves crossing very rough, but interesting, terrain.

Start from a car park in the bleak terrain just to the north of the track to the aerial, at the highest point of the Bealach na Bà road.

Follow the access track to the aerial on the north top above Coire a' Chaorachain, then head south down rough ground. Swing south around the rim of the corrie to pass over the top of a short rise with a cairn, where the easiest descent is by a path to the right (south). Continue east over the next small rise and make the ►

---

harbouring various lochans, each one at a different level. Head south for 200m to the Bealach an Ruadh-Stac, then traverse south-west along a

knobbled rocky ridge with lochans on either side and descend to the foot of the mountain's steep and rocky east ridge.

The initial section is climbed over lovely smooth quartzite slabs at an easier angle than expected, and leads up right onto the crest. Steeper ground above proves to be quite broken and is easily climbed to gain the flat summit, where a large cairn marks the highest point (**8.25km; 935m; 3h 30min**).

Return by the route of ascent (16.5km; 1000m; 5h 50min).

Maol Chean-dearg & An Ruadh-Stac

For the ascent with Maol Chean-dearg, most walkers normally climb the Munro first, then the Corbett.

*Follow the route described above to the Bealach a' Choire Ghairbh, then climb north-west by a rough path up quartzite screes and grassy patches to reach a level shoulder. Continue along this and climb the final dome of Maol Chean-dearg, which resembles a great pile of sandstone boulders (**8.25km; 950m; 3h 25min**).*

*Return to the bealach then climb An Ruadh-Stac as described above (**11.25km; 1305m; 5h 5min**)*

Return by the route of ascent (20.5km; 1370m; 7h 25min).

Sgùrr a' Chaorachain's final tower with the summit beyond (Iain Thow)

ascent out along the ridge to the summit, climbing over, or round, a tower, then on up the final grassy slope (**3.25km; 290m; 1h 15min**).

Return the same way (**6.5km; 410m; 2h 25min**).

For the extension to Beinn Bhàn, from the aerial, descend rough terrain north to a small lochan. Continue north along the ridge above the cliffs dropping into Coire nan Arr, and swing round the head of the corrie on a terrace across the slope below Càrn Dearg to reach the Bealach nan Arr.

Pass between two tiny lochans and follow a path up the bouldery slope beyond, over a slight rise, then continue up the centre of the broad and featureless ridge ahead to gain the summit (**9.5km; 770m; 3h 45min**).

Return the same way to the lochan beneath the aerial, then cut across the slope to regain the track close to the road (**14.5km; 890m; 5h 30min**).

A stalkers' path, which is shown on maps, starts at NG781441 and can be followed west for 2.25km to the road. This path is the alternative high-level route to Beinn Bhàn, see page 290. A 2km walk up the road regains the car park for a longer, but perhaps easier, return (**16.25km; 1005m; 6h**).

Sgùrr a' Chaorachain can be climbed by a more substantial route from partway up the Bealach na Bà road above Loch Kishorn. There is limited parking off the road at the

bridge over the Russell Burn, the Drochaid Coire nan Arr (NG814412), or 270m further up the road where a track leaves it at a bend; take care not to block the track entrance.

Follow the track to the dam on Loch Coire nan Arr, then go along the west side of the loch over rough ground and make a rising traverse towards the great tower of Na Ciòchan. Continue west-south-west up the burn flowing from the inner corrie, which is enclosed by Sgùrr a' Chaorachain's towering sandstone cliffs, to reach a little lochan; there is a rough path in places. From there, climb south-west up a steep slope of

grass and boulders to reach the col on the summit ridge, where the previous route is joined and followed to the top (**3.75km; 685m; 2h 15min**).

To descend, head east-south-east along the broad ridge, which becomes steeper and is crossed by small cliffs and terraces. Provided one stays on the crest of the ridge, on a bearing south-east as it steepens, there are no serious obstacles. Scramble down a succession of short, easy walls with grassy ledges between them until the angle eases, and a walk east down the rough lower slopes leads back to the road near the start (**5.75km; 685m; 3h 15min**).

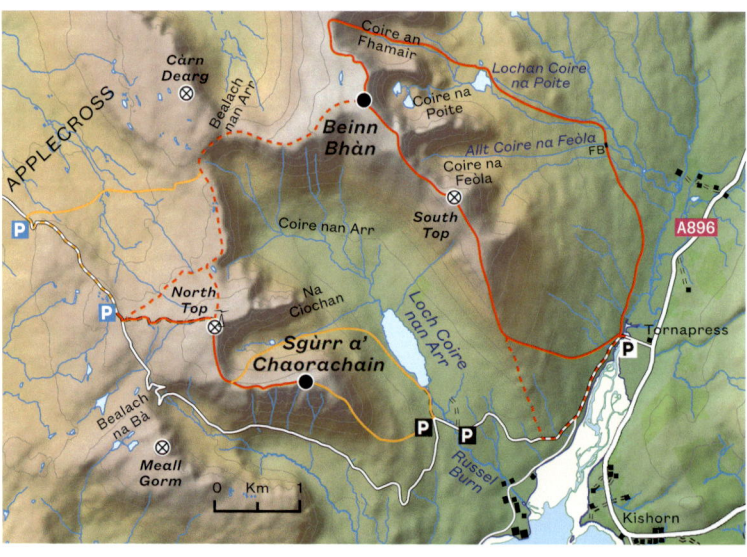

Beinn Bhàn; 896m; (C28); L24; NG803450; white hill

The highest and most imposing summit in Applecross is Beinn Bhàn, a great 8km-long north-west-wards running ridge whose eastern aspect forms an eye-catching series of six corries, typically Torridonian in their architecture of terraced cliffs and dark gullies.

The best view of the mountain and its corries is the panorama from the A896 a few kilometres north of Loch Kishorn, and south from Shieldaig. In complete contrast, the western side of the mountain is a long slope of grass, scree and low-terraced cliffs. The summit lies about a third of the way north along the narrow ridge between these east and west-facing slopes, sitting above the head of the magnificent cliff-lined bowl of Coire na Poite.

The normal, and best, way of climbing Beinn Bhàn starts from the bridge over the River Kishorn at the head of Loch Kishorn. This is known as the Drochaid Mhòr, and it lies 500m along the Bealach na Bà road to Applecross from Tornapress on the A896. There is limited parking on the

left, just before the bridge.

The slopes above the start, which drop from the south end of the mountain, look dull and featureless, and their ascent is similar in character, although giving the shortest route to the summit.

It is debatable whether it is best to climb the mountain in a clockwise, or an anti-clockwise, direction, but the description here is for an anti-clockwise circuit since this perhaps gives the better direction for catching the morning light in the corries.

Leave the bend in the road on the north side of the bridge, then follow a rough track and path across the hillside to cross a bridge over the Allt Coire na Fèola, which issues from Coire na Fèola. In a further 400m, after crossing the Allt Coire na Poite, and just before the next burn, leave the path and follow another path between the two burns. This leads up the hillside to the largish Lochan Coire na Poite, out in front of the magnificent bowl of Coire na Poite, which is framed by the ridge spurs of A' Chìoch on the left, and A' Phoit on

the right, both are graded rock climbs.

Go around the north side of the lochan and climb into Coire an Fhamair (*the Giant's corrie*), crossing a burn to follow the Allt Coire an Fhamhair past A' Phoit into the inner recesses of this corrie, backed by a steep and impressive cliff, which is split by a great cleft called Gully of the Gods.

Ascend a grassy line up the back of the corrie, between the scree and boulder slopes, to gain the rim just above, and to the south of, Loch na Beinne Bàine. Follow the edge of the corrie south above the cliffs, passing the head of Gully of the Gods, to reach the stone trig pillar and wind shelter on the summit overlooking Coire na Poite (**7.5km; 905m; 3h 15min**).

To descend, head south-east down the narrowing plateau, along the top of Coire na Feola, then over Pt.763m and on down south-east above Coire Each. The easiest line is to keep on southwards down the broad ridge to reach the road just over 1km to the south of the start, although a more ▶

Beinn Bhàn - A' Chìoch, left, then A' Phoit with the snow-fringed summit, centre, then Coire an Fhamair (Jamie Hageman)

Beinn Bhàn and Coire na Poite from A' Chìoch (Iain Thow)

BEINN DAMH; hill of the stag
Spidean Coire an Laoigh; *903m;
(C17); L24 & L25; NG892502;
peak of the corrie of the calf*

Another superb Torridonian Corbett, Beinn Damh rises steeply above the south side of Loch Torridon to the craggy top of Sgùrr na Bana-Mhoraire. From there, a 3km-long high-level ridge runs gracefully south-east over Meall Gorm and Pt.868m, which maps have placed the name Beinn Damh against, to the highest peak, Spidean Coire an Laoigh, almost encircled by steep slopes at the southern termination.

Despite the impregnable-looking nature of the mountain, and it being one of the higher Corbetts starting from close to sea-level, the ascent via Toll Bàn, the north-facing corrie, is on a good path and remarkably straight-forward.

Beinn Damh's position between the Applecross, Torridon and Strath Carron hills, means its ridge is a spectacular and rewarding viewpoint.

direct descent can be made down the wide slope (12.5km; 945m; 5h 40min).

Beinn Bhàn can also be climbed from the north side of the Bealach na Bà, a short way down the road from its summit, on the descent to Apple-cross. There is a parking area at NG763436, just below a sharp bend.

This is a quick, but inferior, route. If one chooses to climb the hill from this side, it is better combined with Sgùrr a' Chaorachain, as an extension to the principal route for Sgùrr a' Chaorachain, as described on page 287, for a more satisfactory outing.

For the short route, though, walk downhill for 80m, then follow an ATV track, then the path that continues from it, east-north-east across the bleak and featureless Coire nan Cuileag to where it ends at NG781441, just below the rim of Coire nan Arr.

Continue to the edge of the corrie and traverse around its head on a terrace, across the slope below Càrn Dearg, to reach the Bealach nan Arr.

Pass between two tiny lochans, then follow a path up the bouldery slope beyond, over a slight rise, and continue up the centre of the broad and featureless ridge ahead to gain the stone trig point on the summit (5km; 510m; 2h).

Return the same way (10km; 585m; 3h 35min).

Map on page 288

Start from the large car park for the Beinn Bar (NG889541); signposted Walking Routes at the entrance off the A896 Torridon to Shieldaig road. There is also space to park at a bend in the road, just before and after the bridge over the Allt Coire Roill. The initial part of the route is the same as that for Beinn na h-Eaglaise, a Graham.

Walk west past the inn through the rear courtyard and cross a bridge over the Allt Coire Roill. Turn left and follow a path signed Beinn Damh Viewpoint Trail through woodland to go through a gate and cross the road.

Continue on a stalkers' path up through beautiful native Caledonian pines and planted firs, with the Allt Coire Roill roaring down on the left in a gorge. At the head of this gorge, the river makes a spectacular 30m plunge over a sandstone cliff, which may be glimpsed from the path.

On emerging from the forest onto the open hillside, take the right fork in the path and climb south-west into the corrie of Toll Bàn. Higher up, the path becomes rougher, and a steeper eroded section at the top leads to

easier ground on the ridgeline forming the broad col that separates Meall Gorm and Sgùrr na Bana-Mhoraire from the main mass of the mountain.

Continue south-east on the path, which ascends easily up the ridge and cuts across the slope beneath Pt.868m, heading for Spidean Coire an Laoigh. The path splits into various branches below the boulder field here, but they all quickly rejoin for a short way before the path disappears into the main mass of boulders leading to the ridgeline, and a small rise named Spidean Toll nam Biast, which sits above the splendid corrie of Toll nam Biast.

Follow the rocky ridge around the head of the corrie and make the final easy ascent to the prominent summit, where the crowning cairn is perched on the brink of the very steep east-facing Corrie an Laoigh; a spectacular viewpoint (**6km; 925m; 2h 50min**).

It is best to return the same way (12km; 955m; 4h 40min).

However, from Spidean Toll nam Biast, it is worth climbing the boulder field to gain the top of Pt.868m

(Creagan Dubh Toll nam Biast), and from there descending the bouldery ridge to meet the path a short distance from the broad col above Toll Bàn; an added 15min or so.

From the col, it is also well worth continuing on the ridgeline path onto Meall Gorm (675m), then crossing the dip beyond to follow the path that slants across the steep slope and cuts back to the top of Sgùrr na Bana-Mhoraire (687m), with its stone trig point and more superb views.

Whilst a way can be found down the very steep ridge to the north, it is easier to return the same way. Regain the path at the broad col with the main mass of the mountain, then go back down this; an added 2.5km, 190m, 1h.

The north-east ridge of Spidean Coire an Laoigh, called Stùc Toll nam Biast, is an alternative route of ascent, which gives a good but easy scramble from the Drochaid Coire Roill, the pass between Beinn na h-Eaglaise and Beinn Damh. The left fork of the approach path is taken on emerging from the forest, to cross the Allt Coire Roill, and is followed for a further 2.5km to the pass, giving grand views of the gullied north-east cliffs of the mountain. From the pass, climb a rocky ridge south-west, then more steeply west up a buttress to reach the short north-east ridge of Spidean Coire an Laoigh. Any difficulties on the buttress can be avoided on the left (**6.5km; 955m; 3h 10min**).

Return as for the normal descent route (12.5km; 985m; 5h).

Beinn Damh from Maol Chean-dearg - Spidean Coire an Laoigh, left (Derek Sime)

Stùc Loch na Cabhaig, left, and Beinn Dearg, right, from The Horns of Alligin (Grahame Nicoll)

Beinn Dearg; *914m; (C2); L19, L24 & L25; NG895608; red hill*

Falling short of Munro status by a mere 70cm, and lying tucked away from general sight behind Liathach, between Beinn Alligin and Beinn Eighe, Beinn Dearg is a hidden gem, left by many as their final Torridonian peak. It is a fabulous hill, and like its neighbours, is comprised of more than one summit connected by a ridgeline, making its ascent an airy, scenic and particularly rewarding experience.

Start from the Coire MhicNòbaill car park at NG869576 on the west side of the bridge across the Abhainn Coire Mhic Nòbuil, just over 2 miles (3.5km) along the road on the north side of Loch Torridon from Torridon village. This is where the route to Beinn Alligin also starts.

Walk across the bridge and follow the path signposted to Coire Dubh through lovely mixed woodland to emerge into the open above the Abhainn Coire Mhic Nòbuil, with Beinn Dearg ahead and Beinn Alligin to the left. Cross the bridge over the river, then in a further 170m, at a fork, take the left-hand branch, which crosses a

bridge over the Allt a' Bhealaich, and continue uphill towards the foot of the ridge leading to Na Rathanan and the Horns of Alligin.

At a fork in front of some slabby rocks, where the left-hand path heads for the foot of Na Rathanan, go right and follow this path close under the steep slope, heading for the col at the head of the glen. The path becomes rougher, boggier and less distinct.

At a suitable point, leave the path and cut across the glen, crossing the burn, to gain the far (north) side of the boulder field that spews from the foot of the broad west ridge of Stùc Loch na Cabhaig, which has a prominent large block near its top.

Climb steeply up the left side of the boulder field and slant up rightwards to above the large block. Zigzag up the grassy slope above, towards a band of rock, then go out left onto the ridge proper, which, although rocky, gives a straightforward zigzag ascent to reach a minor top on the shoulder.

Cross the shoulder, then follow the lovely, narrow upper ridge to gain the summit of flat-topped Stùc Loch na

Cabhaig (882m), which is a spectacular viewpoint, with Baosbheinn and Beinn an Eòin to the north, and Beinn Alligin to the west.

Drop down to the south to gain the narrow connecting ridge with Beinn Dearg, and follow this across to, then up, the rocky and airy ridge beyond to the summit. A short rock step at the top of the ridge can be taken on the left, or perhaps easier on rock steps to the right. The summit is also surprisingly level-topped and provides yet more breathtaking views (**7.25km; 960m; 3h 20min**).

The ridge that continues has a short rock step, which involves a scrambling Grade 1 descent. Whilst this is not too difficult, there are some who may prefer to avoid it. There is a bypass, but this is potentially more dangerous than the rock step. If this section is to be avoided, then it is best to return the same way, resisting the temptation of any apparent short-cuts (**14.5km; 1045m; 5h 40min**).

To continue the traverse, head south-east down an easy ridge, which in 200m turns east with a short and steep descent to a col. The ridge then rises again over Pt.840m for a short distance and becomes narrow and rocky, giving a pleasant scramble along the exposed crest above Loch a' Choire Mhòir to the north. Although easy, the scramble is generally avoided by a traverse path along a grassy shelf beneath the crest on the south side.

Either way leads to a triple-stepped rocky nose, or tower, at the end, which has to be downclimbed. Although this can be bypassed on the south side via steep, grassy ledges, there is a big drop below. The bypass line is also not that obvious, and the ground is steep and uncomfortable, with some awkward steps; a slip would have consequences.

In reality, it is probably easier to descend the rocky crest. The first two steps are easier than the final step, a short corner-groove on which the holds are good. A scrambling grade of 1 is given to this section of the ridge. Under cover of snow and ice, a rope is probably advisable.

Reversing the route to tackle the tower in ascent will be easier, but to descend, one will have to follow the ascent description for Stùc Loch na

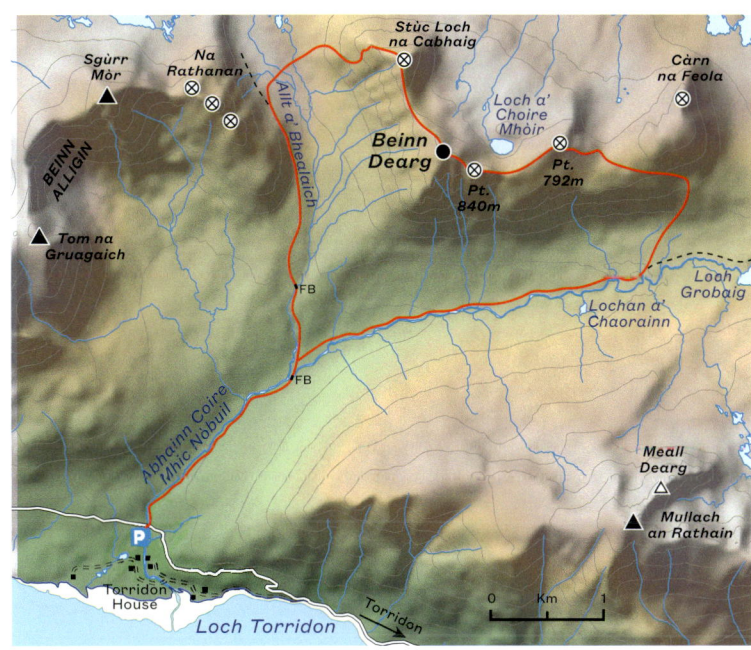

Cabhaig in reverse carefully.

Continue easily along the ridge over the slight rise of Pt.792m, then drop to the sandstone pavement and boulder-strewn col with Càrn na Feola (761m) at the east end.

This final summit on the ridge can be climbed by a there-and-back detour; an added 2km, 100m, 45min.

From the col, descend diagonally across the hillside to the south-east for a distance of 600m to a pavement on top of a small crag. Go down the side of the crag and continue down to the main path through the glen, which is followed back beneath Beinn Dearg to the bridge and the start (**16km; 1005m; 6h 20min**).

Beinn Dearg from Coire MhicNòbaill, living up to it's name bathed in the evening light (Rab Anderson)

Sgòrr nan Lochan Uaine; 871m; (C62); L25; NG969531; peak of the little green loch
Sgùrr Dubh; 782m; (C187); L25; NG979558; black peak

Lying on the south side of Glen Torridon opposite Beinn Eighe, these two hills occupy a large part of the Coulin Forest. This is the wild and open country between Loch Clair and Loch Coulin to the north-east, and the Coire Làir peaks to the south.

They are well seen, but rarely identified from the Achnasheen to Kinlochewe road, where the more famous Torridonian peaks draw the eye. Whilst they lack the height and grandeur of their neighbours on the opposite side of Glen Torridon, they provide a remarkably rugged outing, with a fine appreciation of Torridonian terrain and scenery.

Both hills are climbed together from a start at the main car park at the foot of Coire Dubh, on the single-track road through Glen Torridon.

Walk east along the road for 100m, then follow a good stalkers' path south past Lochan an Iasgair and the Ling Hut. The path continues south-west close to the Allt Frianach,

passing a fine waterfall and entering Coire a' Cheud Chnoc (*corrie of a hundred hillocks*), filled with innumerable moraine mounds of regular proportions. The path steers a course through this maze of hillocks, and is followed for about 3km, crossing a level section above Loch na Frianach, then climbing until almost opposite the top of Sgòrr nan Lochan Uaine.

At a cairn at NG9519 5349, the path starts to deteriorate. Continue for 100m to a smaller cairn at a flattening, then break off left across rough ground to reach a small burn.

Either cross this burn and another burn that flows down from Lochan Uaine, then climb the rough hillside beyond, or follow it to a small lochan blocked by boulders, then cross the burn from Lochan Uaine and cut across the rough hillside.

Either way, cross a third burn, which flows down a more defined streamway from the side of Sgòrr nan Lochan Uaine, then climb the slope

beyond to gain the crest of the ridge to the north-west of the summit. Finally, zigzag up the steep and bouldery cone to the top (**6.25km; 810m; 2h 50min**).

The crossing to Sgùrr Dubh is remarkably rough and rugged, and is likely to prove awkward in poor visibility. Descend to the north to gain grassier ground down the side of a broad and bouldery ridge, then follow this down to first one small lochan, then another.

Continue north-north-east down grassier ground in a shallow runnel between slabby rocks on the left and broken, craggier rocks on the right to gain a tiny lochan. Drop down and cross a slight rise, then pass between two small lochans at the lowest point between the hills at c.565m.

Continue up a slight rise, then cross flat ground past another small lochan and climb the hillside beyond to follow the ridge past more lochans down on the left. Bypass a prominent rocky knoll on its right side via a path

Sgùrr Dubh across Loch Coulin from Glen Torridon (Mike Dixon)

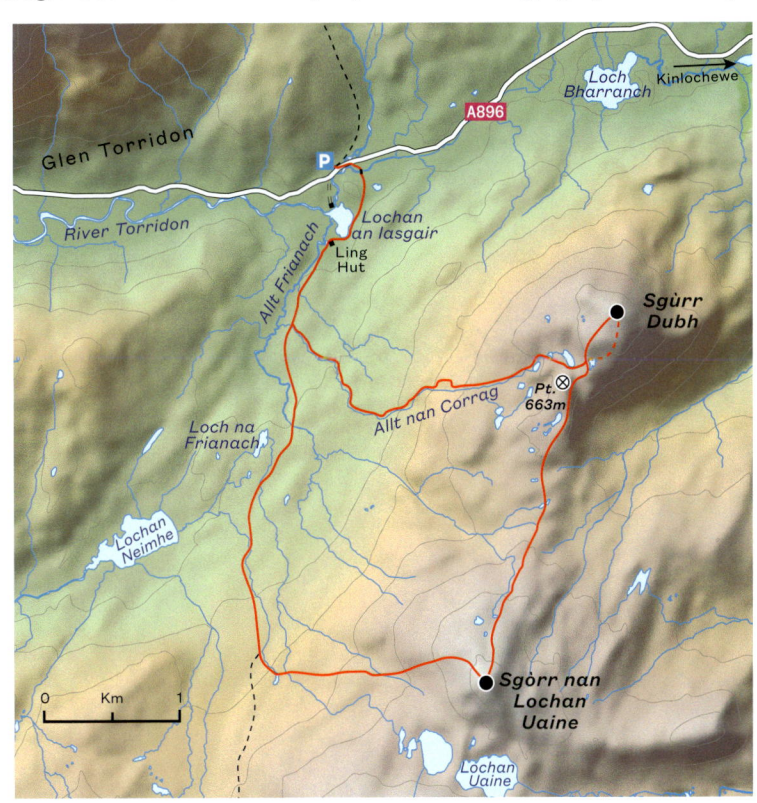

Sgòrr nan Lochan Uaine from the col with Sgùrr Dubh – Beinn Liath Mhòr, left, Maol Chean-dearg, right (Rab Anderson)

down a grassy break between slabs, then cross just below the col linking the knoll to the top of Sgùrr Dubh. Climb onto a slanting rocky ridge, then ascend to a small lochan and continue north up the ridge to easier ground, turning north-east to gain the summit (**9.75km; 990m; 4h 30min**).

There are superb views across Glen Torridon to Liathach and Beinn Eighe, with Baosbheinn framed in between.

Return to the north end of the small lochan, either the same way, or by a path to the south, then a traverse. From there, descend a stony gully through the band of slanting cliff to reach the lochan below. Go around the west side of this lochan, then follow the outflow, the Allt nan Corrag, downhill past more lochans, crossing to the north side.

Continue down the north side of an impressive rocky gorge, through which the burn flows, negotiating a rock step lower down, and follow the burn through the moraine maze to the stalkers' path, which is followed back (**15.25km; 1010m; 6h 45min**).

Ruadh-stac Beag from the col, with Spidean Coire nan Clach, left, and Ruadh-stac Mòr, right (Rab Anderson)

Ruadh-stac Beag; 896m; (C29); L19; NG973613; small red peak
Meall a' Ghiuthais; 887m; (C39); L19; NG976634; M22; hill of the fir tree

These two fine hills are located within the stunning Beinn Eighe & Loch Maree National Nature Reserve, where they provide another superb and rugged Torridonian outing.

Mirroring Ruadh-stac Mòr to its west, the highest peak in the Beinn Eighe massif, Ruadh-stac Beag sits hidden to the north of the main Beinn Eighe ridge, clasped by its eastern arm at the end of an offshoot ridge.

Meall a' Ghiuthais lies to the north, on the other side of the Toll a' Ghiuthais. It is a more identifiable peak, which reveals itself straight ahead on the approach to Kinlochewe at the foot of Glen Docharty on the A832 from Achnasheen, as well as on the drive through the village. As one enters Kinlochewe this way, the top of Ruadh-stac Beag briefly shows itself, appearing to the left of Meall a' Ghiuthais, beyond Creag Dhubh at the start of the Beinn Eighe ridge.

The hills are best climbed together from a start at the Coille na Glas-Leitir car park beside Loch Maree; 2.5 miles (4km) from the Torridon turn-off in Kinlochewe. The Glas Leitir Woodland and Mountain Trails start here, with the route to the hills using the Mountain Trail for the approach and descent through the splendid Caledonian pine forest which clads the hillside. There is an interpretation board at the car park, and it is worth picking up a leaflet for the many points of interest on the trail. The hills can either be climbed as a clockwise or an anticlockwise circuit, but are described here as a clockwise circuit.

Follow the path through the underpass beneath the road to a bridge over the burn, the Allt na h-Airighe. Instead of crossing, keep on ahead alongside the burn for a short way, climbing southwards through the forest, with splendid views back across Loch Maree to mighty Slioch.

Cross a bridge over the next burn, the Alltan Mhic Eogheinn, and continue up slabby rocks above the treeline to the highpoint of the trail on a small rise named Leathad Buidhe, overlooking the two lochans of Loch Allt an Daraich.

Leave the Mountain Trail here and descend to the south-west to gain the col between the hills, crossing the burn flowing from Loch Allt an Daraich then the Pony Path, which comes up from the Beinn Eighe Visitor Centre. There are two tiny lochans here.

Continue south-south-west to pick up a rough path beside the Allt Toll a' Ghiuthais, then follow this up between Creag Dhubh at the start of the main ridge of Beinn Eighe and Ruadh-stac Beag. The path leads beneath Ruadh-stac Beag's steep scree slopes, heading for the col between it and Spidean Coire nan Clach, Beinn Eighe's other Munro.

Before reaching the col, cross the burn then climb grassy slopes to gain the foot of Ruadh-stac Beag's south ridge, close to the smaller of two lochans at the col. A path leads up the ridge through scree and boulders to a surprisingly flat and bouldery plateau, which is crossed to gain the summit (**7.5km; 990m; 3h 30min**).

Return down the south ridge and cross the Allt Toll a' Ghiuthais. Either follow the same path by the burn to regain the col between the hills, or take the path that briefly contours east to take a higher descending line to join the other path before the col.

Cross the Pony Path again, then

ascend the gradually steepening hillside beyond, swinging westwards to gain the dip between the north-east top and the south-west summit. A short climb to the south gains the large cairn marking the highest point of Meall a' Ghiuthais, which sits above a steep drop with a grand view across the Toll a' Ghiuthais to Ruadh-stac Beag's truncated north face and Beinn Eighe (**13km; 1430m; 6h**).

The north-east-top of Meall a' Ghiuthais is easily included by a short detour, for the view down Loch Maree.

Return partway down the slope, then swing north-eastwards, heading for the north end of a small lochan not named on maps, but called the Lunar Loch. Pick up the northern leg of the Mountain Trail here, which is followed downhill above the Allt na h-Àirighe gorge. When the Woodland Trail loop is reached at a viewpoint, go right and follow this path back to the start (**17.25km; 1430m; 7h 35min**).

Climbing both hills from the Beinn Eighe Visitor Centre via the Pony Path is longer (**20.25km; 1360m; 7h 50min**).

Ruadh-stac Beag is best climbed on its own from the visitor centre via the Pony Path (**8.5km; 910m; 3h 35min**), with a return the same way (**17km; 950m; 6h**).

Meall a' Ghiuthais is best climbed

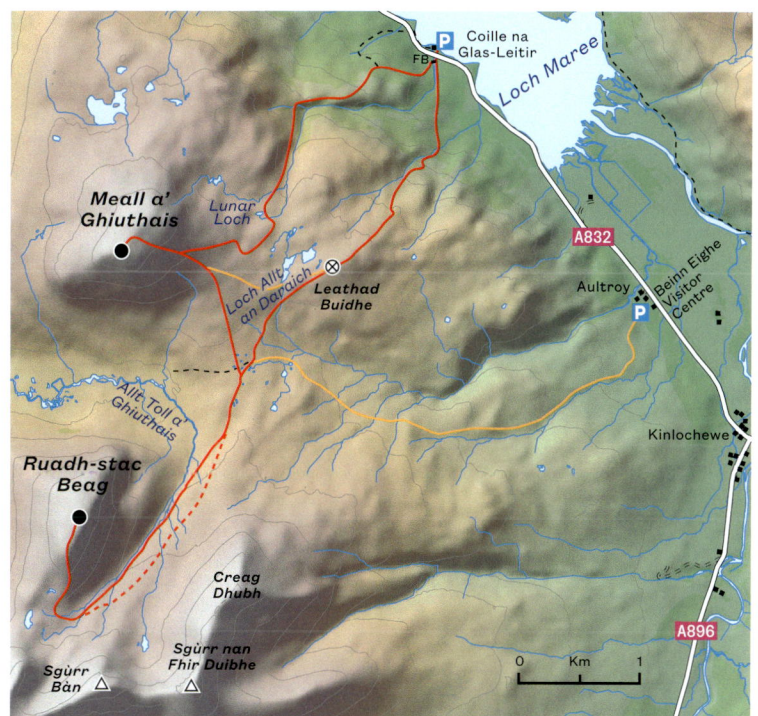

on its own from the Coille na Glas-Leitir car park via the Mountain Trail. Follow this to the highpoint on Leathad Buidhe, as described in the principal route, then continue past Loch Allt an Daraich to the north side of Lunar Loch. Leave the trail here and follow a rough path uphill, which

disappears, and climb to the top of Meall a' Ghiuthais (**4.75km; 920m; 2h 45min**). Return to the Lunar Loch and descend the northern leg of the Mountain Trail, above the Allt na h-Àirighe gorge, to the Woodland Trail loop, then go right and follow this back (**9km; 920m; 4h 20min**).

Meall a' Ghiuthais from the higher path beneath Creag Dhubh (Rab Anderson)

Beinn an Eòin and Loch na h-Oidhche from Beinn Dearg, with Beinn Àirigh Charr, right (Rab Anderson)

***Beinn an Eòin**; 855m; (C86); L19; NG905646; hill of the bird*
*BAOSBHEINN; hill of the forehead; **Sgòrr Dubh**; 875m; (C57); L19; NG870654; black peak*

Another tough Torridonian duo, Beinn an Eòin and Baosbheinn form multi-topped northwards-running ridgelines either side of Loch na h-Oidhche in the Flowerdale Forest. Lying some distance from the nearest road, they are wild and lonely hills set amongst grand scenery to the north of Beinn Dearg and the main Torridon group.

They are best climbed together to provide a memorable outing. It is a big day, and, whilst the map suggests that the approach track could be biked all the way to Loch na h-Oidhche, the surface is rough and stony, with uphill climbs. In practice, only 4km or so prove relatively easy to bike, and even then there is not much difference in the walking time.

It is worth noting that there are two potentially major, though short, river crossings 6km from the start, on the way in, and on the way out. There are stepping stones, but they are not always clear; it may be worth carrying lightweight wading footwear.

Start from a small car park at NG856720 by a green shed (known locally as the Red Barn) between the north end of Loch Bad an Sgalaig and the small Am Feur-Loch, close to the highpoint of the A832 between

Gairloch and Loch Maree.

Cross the road and follow a track across the bridge over the river between the lochs, then on through a

gate leading into the Bad an Sgalaig Native Pinewood. A million trees have been planted here as part of the Millennium Forest project to recreate

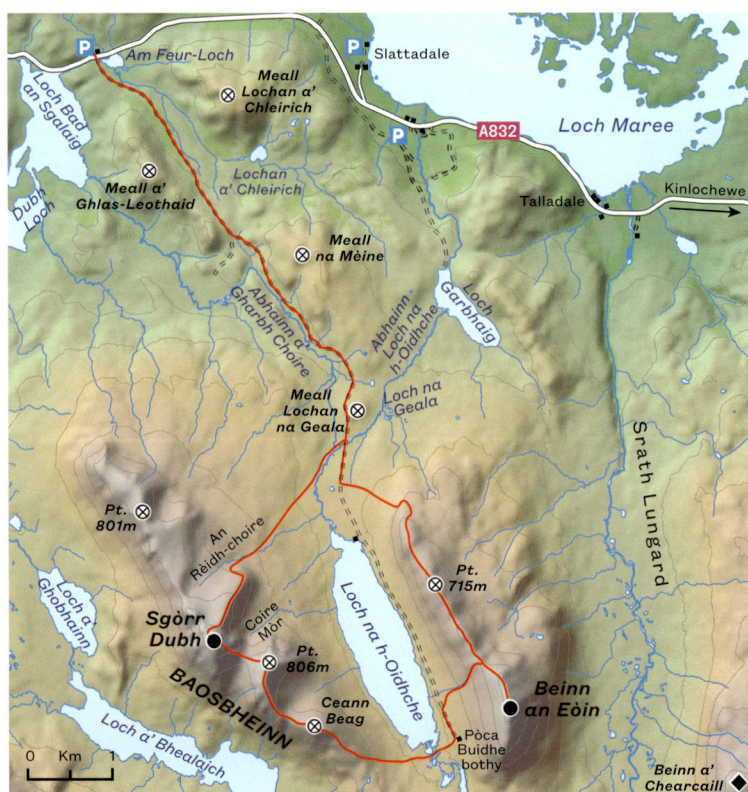

the Caledonian forest.

The track climbs uphill to a height of 260m, then drops past a branch off right to traverse the hillside before running alongside a river, the Abhainn a' Gharbh Choire. Pass the Grouse Stone boulder, where shot grouse were left for collection, then pass through a gate out of the fenced area.

The track now worsens and climbs uphill around the side of a knoll, Meall Lochan na Geala, to reach the Abhainn Loch na h-Oidhche, just down from its divergence from the Abhainn a' Gharbh Choire, created to help prevent flooding in Kerrysdale.

Once over, continue up the track for 400m to reach two large boulders at a levelling. Leave the track here and cross rough ground, heading for the left (north) side of the steep rocks forming the base of Beinn an Eòin's north ridge. Ascend a grassy ramp and shallow gully up the left side of these rocks, then climb up right onto the north ridge.

The ridge provides a superb and scenic 4km-long boulder-strewn traverse, crossing sandstone pavements and three minor tops, with a steeper climb and final narrow crest to reach the wind shelter cairn and place where the trig point once sat on the summit. A rock 15m to the north is the highest point (**10.5km; 865m; 4h**).

With steep drops on all but the approach side, it is a grand and airy viewpoint. Especially notable is the view into Beinn Eighe's Coire Mhic Fhearchair, at the back of which sits the iconic Triple Buttress.

It is possible to descend off the end of the ridge by heading south for 400m or so, then west to gain the now closed Pòca Buidhe bothy at the end of Loch na h-Oidhche. However, there are bands of rock to negotiate, and it is very steep. It is better to return along the ridge and go down to a large boulder near the foot of the steep climb, then turn left (west) to find the head of a grassy gully and go down this. Partway down, it is easier to move out onto the left side, then go down this for a way before cutting across the slope to gain the track along Loch na h-Oidhche, which is followed for 400m or so to the bothy.

From the bothy, head downhill past large boulders, then cross the inflow to the loch and ascend the boulder-strewn hillside to gain a broad ridge just north of a small lochan. Ascend the ridge onto Ceann Beag (705m) at the start of Baosbheinn's long ridge, then make a steep, though straight-forward descent off the end to reach a boulder-strewn col.

A climb of 180m leads on up the narrower ridge beyond, which curves northwards onto Baosbheinn's unnamed East Top (806m). There are fine views back over Loch a' Bhealaich to the Horns of Alligin and Sgùrr Mòr, and over Beinn Dearg to jagged Liathach behind.

Drop down 100m in height and cross the col beyond, then make the final 170m climb up the edge of the stony slope above the drop into Coire Mòr to the north. This leads to the surprisingly grassy flat top of Sgòrr Dubh; a slab 15m to the west of the cairn is the highest point (**16.75km; 1545m; 7h**).

To descend, drop briefly north-west to a col, then go down the north-east ridge above Coire Mòr to a rocky steepening near the bottom. Traverse left (west) and drop into An Rèidh-choire to go down the west side of the steepening. Rather than make two crossings of the river, it is best to follow it to where it forks, then make a single short crossing there to regain the track, which is followed back (**26km; 1610m; 9h 30min**).

Beinn an Eòin climbed on its own, and returning the same way, is (**21km; 990m; 7h**). Sgòrr Dubh climbed up and back the same way from the river divergence is (**18.5km; 890m; 6h**).

Baosbheinn - Ceann Beag, extreme left, then Pt.806m (East Top) and Sgòrr Dubh, with Coire Mòr, centre (Robert Durran)

Beinn Àirigh Charr across Loch Maree,
Spidean nan Clach, left, and Meall
Chnàimhean, right (Rab Anderson)

SECTION 14
Loch Maree to Loch Broom

SECTION 14

Beinn Àirigh Charr across Loch nan Dailthean, with Martha's Peak, left, and Meall nan Chnàimhean, right (Mike Dixon)

Beinn Àirigh Charr; *792m; (C174); L9; NG930761; hill of the rough shieling*

Well seen across Loch Maree and from the low-lying coastal area around Loch Ewe, Beinn Àirigh Charr stands in a prominent position at the western edge of the Letterewe and Fisherfield forests, one of the finest wilderness areas in Scotland.

A characteristic feature of Beinn Àirigh Charr is the steep tower on its rocky north face, named Martha's Peak after a legendary shepherdess who fell to her death on the cliffs.

Approaches into this area are long, and many walkers opt to stay at, or in the vicinity of, the barn at Carnmore, or the bothy at Shenavall. Beinn Àirigh Charr is the most accessible of the Corbetts here, but it is still some distance from the nearest public road at Poolewe, especially since it is not possible to drive the private road to Inveran. However, it is a pleasant and relatively easy bike ride along the road, then an estate track, to get to the foot of the path up the mountain above the side of Loch Maree, for a saving of about 1h 40min on the day.

Turn south off the A832 on the east side of the bridge over the River Ewe in Poolewe, onto the road that runs alongside the river, to a car park immediately on the left.

Walk, or bike, south-east past Poolewe Primary School on what soon becomes a private road. When the road surface ends, take the track on the left and continue past Inveran, swinging round to cross a bridge over the Inveran River. There are now two options:

(i) On foot, in a further 300m, just beyond Loch an Doire Ghairbh, take a path on the right at a small cairn. Follow the path uphill, then across flat ground to the south-east for 1.25km to rejoin the track from Kernsary to Ardlair. This is 1.5km shorter than the route along the track.

(ii) The route on the track loops around, passing the track off left across the bridge to Kernsary, then climbs south, initially by the burn, to where it is joined by the path.

Both options having joined, in a further 1km, after a descent and a flat section, leave the track where the walls of an old stone sheep fold can be seen up to the left (**7.75km; 160m; about 50min** by bike), (**6.5km; 160m; 1h 40min** on foot). Distances and times are now given on foot, from and back to here.

Follow a grassy path to the sheepfold, then a short section of track. Continue on a good stalkers' path to ford a burn and enter a little gorge, then start climbing gently uphill by the burn to reach a fork in the path. Take the right-hand path and follow it up into Coire nan Dearcag to where the stalkers' path ends on flat ground at the head of the corrie.

Cross the burn here, then slant up and across the hillside on the left to pick up a rough path, which crosses a stony patch to rejoin the burn above. Continue through the col between Spidean nan Clach on the left and Meall nan Chnàimhean on the right.

Swing round a slabby bluff, where the summit comes into view, and follow a gentle grassy slope up a shallow corrie to the col between

▶

Beinn Àirigh Charr's summit with Spidein Moirich (Martha's Peak), left, from Spidean nan Clach (Rab Anderson)

Spidean nan Clach and the summit. Make a steep climb up a stony, shale-like slope to gain easy ground leading to the rocky crown, passing the trig pillar stump to reach the summit cairn (**4.75km; 715m; 2h 15min**).

Return the same way to the track (**9.5km; 750m; 3h 40min**)

From the summit, it is worth crossing the dip to the rise beyond for a slightly expanded view.

It is also worthwhile descending the slope, then the ridge northwards from the dip between the two highpoints to gain the top of Spidein Moirich (Martha's Peak). This juts out above an impressive drop and is one of the mountain's defining features. If this is done, it is best to make the 90m climb all the way back to the summit, rather than attempt to follow what looks like a path across the steep and unpleasantly loose slope across the head of Coire nan Laogh for a direct route to the col with Spidean nan Clach.

It is also worthwhile making the short diversion to the top of Spidean nan Clach. These diversions add 1.5km, 140m, 40min to the route.

Return to Poolewe (**25km; 970m; 5h 5min** with a bike), (**22km; 950m; 6h 45min** on foot).

Map on pages 306 & 307

> ***Beinn Làir;*** *859m; (C78); L19; NG981732; hill of the mare*

A hill of two contrasting aspects, Beinn Làir's south-west side consists of long slopes of grass and heather that fall at a fairly gentle angle to the wooded shore of Loch Maree, whilst on its north-east side a 5km-long line of cliffs drops precipitously to Gleann Tùlacha and Lochan Fada. These cliffs are one of the finest, and probably the longest, mountain walls in the Highlands. Between these two aspects, the broad summit ridge extends for 5km, with the highest point near the middle, and the slightly lower top of Sgùrr Dubh 1km to its south-east.

Beinn Làir is almost equidistant from Poolewe and Kinlochewe, a long way from both villages. The Poolewe approach is shorter, especially if a bike is used on the initial road and track for a saving of about 1h 40min on the day.

Start from the small parking area on the left at the start of the road down the east side of the River Ewe.

Walk, or bike, past Poolewe Primary School on what becomes a private road alongside the river. When the road surface ends, take the track on

the left and continue past Inveran, swinging round to cross a bridge over the Inveran River and past the path off to Beinn Àirigh Charr. In a further 1.5km, take the track on the left over a bridge across the River Kernsary to reach Kernsary.

Pass the buildings and, in a further 500m, take a track on the right, then go through a gate into Kernsary Forest where the track deteriorates.

Unless it has been dry for some time, bikes are best left here (**6km; 80m;** about **35min** by bike), (**1h 25min** on foot). Distances and times are now given on foot, from and back to here.

Continue along the track through the forest for another 1.5km, almost to its end, then follow a path to exit the forest by a gate and stile at NG910789. Older maps do not show the line of this higher stalkers' path, which runs up the side of the valley above the Allt na Creige.

Ascend gently uphill on the path to cross the watershed and drop slightly to Loch an Doire Crionaich, which sits beneath Spidein Moirich (Martha's

Peak), the impressive tower that juts out from Beinn Àirigh Charr.

Continue along the north side of the loch to Srathan Buidhe, the southerly glen that separates Beinn Àirigh Charr from Meall Mhèinnidh, and take the shortcut path over the burn; there is a bridge 400m upstream if required.

Ascend past a small lochan, then make a gradual descent below the north-east face of Meall Mhèinnidh towards Fionn Loch, with Beinn a' Chàisgean Mòr, the impressive crag on Càrn Mòr and domed Sgùrr na Laocainn prominent on the other side.

On reaching a path junction at Poll Fraochan, in front of the rocky Creag Poll Fraochain, take the path on the right and climb to the Bealach Mhèinnidh between Beinn Làir and Meall Mheinnidh. At the end of a band of crag, leave the path and climb onto the ridge of Beinn Làir, north-east at first, then south-east. This leads all the way along the edge of the stupendous cliffs and gullies overlooking Fionn Loch and Gleann Tùlacha.

At 830m there is a promontory that juts out over the north face to give fine views of the cliffs and lochs below, as well as across to A' Mhaighdean, the Fisherfield peaks and An Teallach. The summit is a wide, featureless dome, although the huge cairn is unmistakable (**13.5km; 950m; 4h 35min**).

Return the same way to Kernsary (**27km; 1100m; 8h 10min**).

Return to Poolewe (**39km; 1220m; 9h 15min** with a bike), (**10h 55min** on foot).

From the Bealach Mhèinnidh it is easy enough to climb Meall Mhèinnidh (722m), a Graham, via a 230m ascent up its south-east ridge, past a little lochan just above mid-height. Descend the north-west ridge, which has some short slabby cliffs low down that are easily avoided. Towards the foot of the ridge, drop into Srathan Buidhe to the path, cross the burn by a bridge and return to Kernsary; 1.25km shorter, an added 150m of ascent, but only 15min or so longer.

Map on pages 306 & 307

Beinn Làir from Meall Mhèinnidh, with A' Mhaighdean and The Fisherfield peaks, left, and Slioch, right (Rab Anderson)

Braes of
Ullapool

A835

Badcaul

Little Loch Broom

Badrallach

Ardessie

Camusnagaul

Loch Broom

Sàil
Mhòr

Dundonnell

Ruigh
Mheallain

Corrie
Hallie

Bidein a'
Ghlas Thuill

AN TEALLACH

Sgùrr
Fiòna

Loch Toll
an Lochain

Pt.
392m

Loch na Sealga

Sàil
Liath

Beinn
Dearg
Bheag

Loch Coire
Chaorachain

Beinn
Dearg
Mòr

FB

Shenavall

FB

Larachantivore

Achneigie

Loch Beinn
Dearg

Strath
na Sealga

Gleann na
Muice Beag

Gleann na Muice

A832

Beinn a'
Chlaidheimh

Meall an
t-Sithe

Ruadh
Stac Mòr

Am
Briseadh

Loch a'
Bhrisidh

Bristeadh a'
Mhill Dhuibh

Creag
Rainich

P

Sgùrr
Bàn

Meall
Dubh

Loch
an Nid

Mullach Coire
Mhic Fhearchair

Loch a' Bhraoin

Beinn
Tarsuinn

Lochivraon
bothy

Feinasheen

0   Km   2

Beinn a' Chàisgein Mòr with Càrn Mòr and Sgùrr na Laocainn across Fionn Loch (Rab Anderson)

Beinn a' Chàisgein Mòr; *856m; (C85); L19; NG982785; big forbidding hill*

Like many of the hills in the great wilderness area between Loch Maree and Little Loch Broom, Beinn a' Chàisgein Mòr is an awkward hill to access, and any route to it involves long approaches from the roads around the perimeter. Located in the Fisherfield Forest between Beinn Dearg Bheag and Beinn Dearg Mòr to its north-east, and the chain that includes Beinn Àirigh Charr and Beinn Làir to its south-west, it is an extensive, flat-topped hill that rises above the east side of the Fionn Loch. To the south of its summit, above the lodge and barn at Carnmore, it holds impressive, large cliffs on Càrn Mòr and Sgùrr na Laocainn.

There are two principal approaches to the hill, both starting from the A832 along the coast to the west. One starts from the Gruinard River to the north-west, and the other from Poolewe to the west. Both are long and can be made more reasonable with the use of a bike along estate tracks. The most practicable day approach is via the Gruinard River, which also enables Beinn a' Chàisgein Beag, the Graham to the north-west, to be included. Many walkers approaching from Poolewe opt for a multi-day trip, and camp at the head of the Fionn Loch, or stay in Carnmore

barn, an option that allows Beinn Làir to be included in the trip.

The route from the Gruinard River starts on the west side of the river, from verge parking at NG961911 on the south side of the A832. Most of the approach is the same as for the route to Beinn Dearg Bheag and Beinn Dearg Mòr. Using a bike saves about 1h 45min on the day, although the track is quite rough.

Follow the track along the west side of the river, dropping down to flat ground at Guisachan and a bridge over the Allt Loch Ghiubhsachain where it joins the Gruinard River. Bikes are best left by the ruin on the right (**7.5km**; **100m**; about **1h** by bike), (**1h 50min** on foot). Distances and times are now given on foot, from and back to here.

Cross the bridge and follow the east bank of the Allt Loch Ghiubhsachain above a gorge section, then cross it after 1.5km at NG998840, just past a burn running down the opposite hillside. The east bank gives easier walking than the west bank, but if the water is running high, it may be necessary to go up the west bank.

Ascend the steep hillside and traverse south-westwards to gain a stalkers' path that starts at the foot of a rock outcrop at NG994833.

Follow this path round to where Beinn a' Chàisgein Beag comes into view, then drop down and cross the Uisge Toll a' Mhadaidh on stepping stones.

Continue uphill for 1km, past an unlikely chalet off to the left, to reach the col below Beinn a' Chàisgein Beag. This Graham can easily be included by a there-and-back diversion, best climbed first if the intention is to make the circuit around Toll a' Mhadaidh; an added 1.75km, 180m, 45min. The highest point is some 50m south-east of the stone trig point.

For the route to Beinn a' Chàisgein Mòr, leave the stalkers' path at the col and climb southwards up a rounded ridge to pass over Frithmheallan (680m) above Loch Toll a' Mhadaidh. Cross the dip beyond, then make the long and gentle, gradual ascent across grassy ground studded with boulders to reach the flat summit, where rocks 25m to the east of the cairn form the highest point (**9km**; **880m**; **3h 30min**).

The easiest route is to return the same way (**18km**; **980m**; **6h**).

Return to the start (**33km; 1130m; 7h 50min** with a bike), (**9h 35min** on foot).

There are another two options for the return to the track:

(i) A scenic return across rugged

terrain can be made by heading north, then north-north-east down to the col between Loch Toll a' Mhadaidh and Lochan na Bearta, to climb onto Creag-mheall Mòr (628m). Continue northwards along the rocky ridge over another rise (628m), then descend north towards the end of the ridge and go north-north-east down a grassy depression. Cross the stalkers' path and descend to the Allt Loch Ghiubhsachain as for the approach, then return to the track. This is 500m shorter, with 100m of ascent, but takes roughly the same time.

(ii) Go east, then north-east and descend to the south end of Lochan na Bearta. Follow the outflow down into Srath Beinn Dearg and continue beneath Na Bearta Buttress to the south end of Loch Ghiubhsachain. It is probably easier to cross the inflow and go down the east side of the loch, then follow the river back to the track. This is 500m longer than (i), with 40m of ascent, but takes the same time.

The route from Poolewe starts from the same place as for the ascents of Beinn Àirigh Charr and Beinn Làir, from a small car park at the start of the road down the east side of the River Ewe. Most of the approach is the same as for Beinn Làir, and using a bike on the initial road and track saves about 1h 40min on the day.

Walk, or bike, past Poolewe Primary School on what becomes a private road alongside the river. When the road surface ends, take the track on the left and continue past Inveran, swinging round to cross a bridge over the Inveran River and past the path off to Beinn Àirigh Charr. In a further 1.5km, take the track on the left over a bridge across the River Kernsary to reach Kernsary.

Pass the buildings and, in a further 500m, take a track on the right, then go through a gate into Kernsary Forest, where the track deteriorates. Unless it has been dry for some time bikes are best left here (**6km; 80m;** about **35min** by bike), (**1h 25min** on foot).

Distances and times are now given on foot, from and back to here.

Continue along the track through the forest for another 1.5km, almost to its end, then follow a path to exit the forest by a gate and stile at NG910789. Older maps do not show the line of this higher stalkers' path, which runs up the side of the valley above the Allt na Creige.

Ascend gently uphill on the path to cross the watershed and drop slightly to Loch an Doire Crionaich, which sits beneath Spidein Moirich (Martha's Peak), the impressive tower that juts out from Beinn Àirigh Charr.

With Beinn a' Chàisgein Mòr laid out on the other side of Fionn Loch, continue along the north side of Loch an Doire Crionaich to Srathan Buidhe, the southerly glen that separates Beinn Àirigh Charr from Meall Mhèinnidh. Drop down and take the short-cut path across the burn here; there is a bridge 400m upstream if required.

Ascend past a small lochan, then make a gradual descent below the north-east face of Meall Mhèinnidh towards Fionn Loch, with Beinn a' Chàisgean Mòr, the impressive Càrn Mòr and its crag, and domed Sgùrr na Laocainn prominent on the other side.

On reaching a path junction at Poll Fraochan, in front of the rocky Creag Poll Fraochan, take the path on the left and follow it around the head of Fionn Loch to cross the causeway between it and Dubh Loch, then continue to within 100m of the lodge at Carnmore (**11.5km; 300m; 3h**).

Take the path on the right, which makes a rising traverse east below the cliffs of Sgùrr na Laocainn, then north-east up the Allt Bruthach an Easain opposite Càrnan Bàn. Leave the path at its highpoint above Lochan Fèith Mhic'illean, just before the path off to Ruadh Stac Mòr and A' Mhaighdean. Now climb north-west-wards for just over 2km, up an open hillside with no features except for a small lochan at a flattening on the left halfway up, to reach the summit (**16.5km; 960m; 5h 15min**).

Return to Kernsary (**33km; 1130m; 9h 25min**).

Return to Poolewe (**45km; 1260m; 10h 30min** with a bike), (**12h 10min** on foot).

Map on pages 306 & 307

Beinn a' Chàisgein Mòr from Beinn Dearg Bheag, with Loch Ghiubhsachain, bottom right (Rab Anderson)

Beinn Dearg Bheag; 820m; (C124); L19; NH020811; little red hill
Beinn Dearg Mòr; 906m; (C15); L19; NH032799; big red hill

Occupying a remote location deep in the Fisherfield Forest, these two Corbetts are separated from the Beinn a' Chàisgein Mòr massif to their south-west by the deep and narrow, steep-sided trench of Srath Beinn Dearg. To their north-east, they rise grandly above the wider, but equally deep and steep-sided trench formed by Loch na Sealga and Strath na Sealga, which separates them from the magnificent An Teallach massif. Their awkward-to-reach location and the beauty of their setting make them two of the most highly prized of the Corbetts.

There are two principal routes from the A832 around the perimeter of this wilderness area. One is from the coast to the north-west via the Gruinard River, where the approach is the same as for Beinn a' Chàisgein Mòr, and the other is from Corrie Hallie in Strath Beag at the head of Little Loch Broom, where the approach is the same as for the

traverse of An Teallach, as well as the northern route to Beinn a' Chlaidheimh.

The Corrie Hallie route is the shorter of the two, but long enough that many walkers stay at, or camp in the vicinity of, the bothy at Shenavall.

Although the Gruinard River route is longer, an estate track can be biked for 8.75km to Loch na Sealga, which makes it the more practicable day route. This route also enables Beinn Dearg Bheag's north-west ridge to be climbed, which, when combined with the ascent of Beinn Dearg Mòr, ranks the outing as another one of Scotland's finest mountain days. There is some scrambling on this ridge and, whilst not particularly difficult, an easier way of attaining both summits is to go up and back down the described return route through Coire Toll an Lochain and climb them via the col between them.

The route from the Gruinard River starts on the west side of the river, from verge parking at NG961911 on

the south side of the A832. Using a bike saves about 2h on the day, although the track is quite rough.

Follow the track along the west side of the river, dropping to flat ground at Guisachan to cross the bridge over the Allt Loch Ghiubh-sachain. This is where the route to Beinn a' Chàisgein Mòr leaves the track. Continue to the end of the track at the head of Loch na Sealga.

Bikes can be left here, or around the corner by a solitary tree at an old slipway where the map shows a non-existent boat house; (**8.75km; 110m; 1h 5min** by bike), (**2h 5min** on foot).

Distances and times are now given on foot, from and back to here.

Follow the lochside path, which after 1km rises above some trees to avoid a craggy section. Leave the path after dropping slightly and crossing a burn, then make a rising ascent across the hillside, aiming for the foot of Beinn Dearg Bheag's north-west ridge. Pass below and to

Beinn Dearg Mòr and Beinn Dearg Bheag from the Gruinard River track to the north-west (Rab Anderson)

Beinn Dearg Mòr, with the summit, centre, and Beinn Dearg Bheag, far right, from Shenavall (Anne Butler)

the east of Pt.392m to reach a small boulder field beneath the imposing craggy nose at the foot of the ridge.

Tackle the nose on its left side by climbing up and right through the boulders, then traversing left to zigzag steeply up to reach grassy ground. Continue up this and turn the rocks above on the left, passing beneath a large perched boulder, then cutting up right above it by the easier left-hand of two options.

Now on easy ground, ascend the bouldery crest with fine views opening up on both sides, then climb a rocky steepening to gain a minor top, Pt.707m. A slight drop is followed by a level section leading to a climb onto another small top, at the end of which there is a descent on the left to avoid a small crag.

The crest then leads to an ascent onto another top, on the far side of which there is a drop and a band of rock to negotiate. Either go down steep, heathery steps on the left, or descend a slabby groove in the rock on the right. Beyond this, pass over another small top and make a short climb to gain the summit of Beinn Dearg Bheag (**5.5km; 795m; 2h 50min**).

Descend to the col with Beinn Dearg Mòr, then climb the broad ridge and bouldery slope beyond via a zigzag path past some slabby rock outcrops. Turn left at the top to gain the summit (**8km; 1110m; 4h 10min**).

Most walkers will want to continue around the narrow, steep-sided summit corrie to the slightly lower and spectacular twin top, gained by an easy, but exposed, climb.

Return to the col with Beinn Dearg Bheag then, towards the far side, go down right (north-eastwards) onto a slabby spur. Cut back right here to avoid rocky ground below to gain easy ground, then descend Coire Toll an Lochain to superbly situated Loch Toll an Lochain. Go around the left side of the lochan and descend beside the outflow for a short way, then take a direct line northwards away from the burn. This crosses another burn to gain a good, but overgrown, stalkers' path above Loch na Sealga.

The path leads north-west to a ruined shieling. After this, the path becomes difficult to follow in places, at one point disappearing. A slight descent to the right, marked with cairns, finds the path again. In a

further 500m, join the approach route and return to the head of the loch (**16.75km; 1200m; 6h 40min**).

Return along the track to the start (**34.25km; 1380m; 8h 45min** with a bike), (**10h 45min** on foot).

An approach can be made through Coire Toll an Lochain to climb both hills via the col between them, thereby avoiding Beinn Dearg Bheag's rocky north-west ridge.

Climb Beinn Dearg Mòr first (**8.5km; 890m; 3h 25min**), then cross to Beinn Dearg Bheag (**11.25km; 1130m; 4h 45min**). Regain the col, then return to the head of the loch the same way (**19.5km; 1180m; 7h 15min**). Return to the start (**37km; 1360m; 9h 20min** with a bike), (**11h 20min** on foot).

The route from Corrie Hallie starts from a long layby on the east side of the A832 at NH114851, about 2 miles (3.5km) south of Dundonnell.

Follow the rough track opposite the south end of the layby for 3km, through the birches of Gleann Chao-rachain, to the highpoint above Loch Coire Chaorachain. Take the path on the right, which leads downhill to the south-west, across the foot of Sàil

▶

Liath to Shenavall in Strath na Sealga (7.5km; 380m; 2h 15min).

Distances and times are now given from, and back to, Shenavall.

The direct route from here heads straight for Larachantivore, fording the Abhainn Srath na Sealga, then a kilometre of boggy ground to ford the Abhainn Gleann na Muice to reach the estate bothy and chalet at Larachantivore. This crossing can cause problems if the water is high. An easier crossing can be made by following the path to the mouth of the loch to paddle across the shallows, then follow a track to Larachantivore; an added 2km and 30min.

Follow the path south by the river for a short way, then make a rising traverse up the steep slope on the right (south-west) to gain the shallow corrie between Beinn Dearg Mòr's ridges. Go up the centre of this corrie then swing round onto the crest at the top to gain the summit (4.5km; 810m; 2h 30min).

Drop around the narrow, steep-sided summit corrie to gain the slightly lower and spectacular twin top by an easy, but exposed, climb.

Traverse back to the summit crest, then cut down across the slope to pass between two slabby rock outcrops and descend the bouldery slope by a zigzag path to gain the col. An easy climb up the steepening ridge leads to the top of Beinn Dearg Bheag (7.25km; 1050m; 3h 50min).

Return to the col, then drop off left into Coire Toll an Lochain and go a short way down a slight spur, cutting back right to avoid slabby rocks to gain easy ground. Continue down to superbly situated Loch Toll an Lochain, and go around its left side, then follow the burn for a short way and cross it.

Go down the side of the burn to clear the foot of Beinn Dearg Mòr's north ridge, then cut down and across the slope to gain the path alongside Loch na Sealga. Follow the path and paddle across the inflow at the mouth of the loch to gain the path on the far side, and follow this back to Shenavall (14.25km; 1090m 5h 50min).

Return to the Corrie Hallie layby (29.25km; 1690m; 10h 15min).

Map on pages 306 & 307

Sàil Mhòr; 767m; (C212); L19; NH033887; big heel

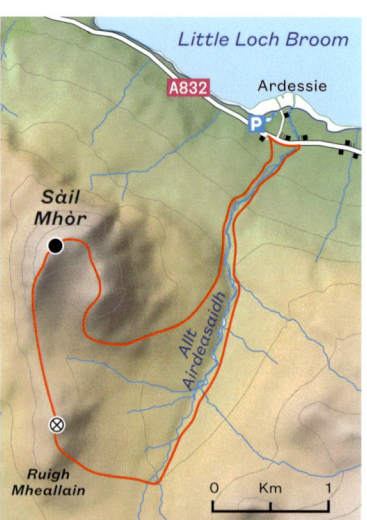

Living up to its name, Sàil Mhòr is a big lump of a hill rising from the elevated moorland several kilometres to the north-west of An Teallach. The hills northern slopes drop steeply to Little Loch Broom, and it is from that side that the ascent is made, starting at the foot of the Allt Airdeasaidh, the Ardessie Burn.

There is a layby 200m to the west of the bridge over the burn, next to Scottish Water's Badcaul Water Treatment Works, behind which Sàil Mhòr's summit can be seen

The main path up the burn is on the further away east side, reached by walking along the verge. This gives the better route, but the burn – actually more of a river – has to be crossed higher up, so if it has been wet and the water is running high this is likely to prove problematic. In which case, it would be better to follow the prepared path to the side of the water treatment works and continue up the rougher path on the right side.

The splendid falls and cascades of the Ardessie Falls are the first point of interest on the climb, also popular with tourists. Beyond these, the main path up the left side runs above the upper gorge into the flatter upper valley opposite Sàil Mhòr. A section has been washed away where a tributary burn flows down from the left. Either plough through this, or keep to the higher ground to avoid it.

The quickest route onto the hill is to ford the river at NH045875, where another burn flows down from the left, opposite the burn on the other side that flows down from the shallow corrie between Sàil Mhòr and Ruigh Mheallain to its south. This burn can be followed to the col between the hills, from where a path leads up the south ridge of Sàil Mhòr.

However, the better route is to keep on up the east side of the river to NH042868, until just beyond Ruigh Mheallain, then make the crossing above where a burn joins on the other side. From there, an easy climb gains the top of Ruigh Mheallain (594m), which has a huge boulder sitting on it.

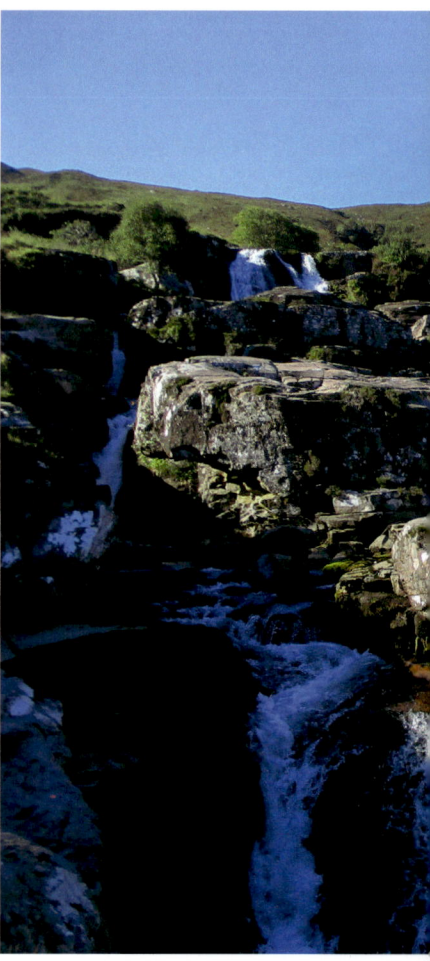

Sàil Mhòr from Ruigh Mheallain (Rab Anderson)

Sàil Mhòr from the Ardessie Falls (Mike Dixon)

As well as the view up Coire Mòr an Teallaich to the An Teallach range, there is a good view to Beinn Dearg Mòr, Beinn Dearg Bheag and Beinn a' Chàisgein Mòr to the south.

Drop to the col, then follow a rough path up the south ridge above the steep west face to reach the top of Sàil Mhòr with its more expansive views (**7km; 825m; 3h**).

Rather than go back down the same way, it is more interesting to head north-east for 130m to a wind shelter above the steep drop to Little Loch Broom. This is apparently 2m lower than the summit. From there, descend the stony, solifluction-terraced slope to the south-east. At the bottom, cross a flat col, then go over a minor rocky top (706m) and on past some rock outcrops to another minor rocky top (690m).

From there, drop down to the right (south-west) and go down the slope, turning left at the bottom to cut across the slope and pick up a rough path above the Allt Airdeasaidh. This is followed downhill above the upper gorge and its falls, of which there are some fine views. Keep an eye out for the wild goats that roam these parts. Continue down to the lower falls, then follow the path leading to the water works and the layby at the start (**11.5km; 845m; 4h 30min**).

Beinn a' Chlaidheimh; 914m; (C1); L19; NH061775; hill of the sword

Formerly a Munro, Beinn a' Chlaid-heimh is now the highest Corbett, having been demoted following a survey in 2012. It lies 3km to the north of the Munro Sgùrr Bàn, over-looking beautiful Strath na Sealga, and is the first peak on one of Scot-land's great hillwalking challenges, a circuit known as the Fisherfield Six. This was six Munros, but even with the demotion of Beinn a' Chlaidheimh, for the sake of less than half a metre it should still retain the Fisherfield Six title. A description for the Fisherfield Six is given in the SMC's guidebook *The Munros*. The route described here is for an ascent of Beinn a' Chlaidheimh on its own, or perhaps with neighbouring Sgùrr Bàn.

Beinn a' Chlaidheimh is more of a sandstone mountain than its two quartzite southern neighbours, and it shows the characteristic terracing of this rock type. The summit ridge is narrow and extends for 2km above the 800m contour, on the western side of which, the slope plunges steeply into Gleann na Muice.

Perhaps the best route for an ascent of Beinn a' Chlaidheimh on its own is from the Corrie Hallie layby on the east side of the A832, to the south of Dundonnell in Strath Beag, at the head of Little Loch Broom.

Cross the road at the south end of the layby and take the rough track southwards up beautifully wooded Gleann Chaorachain, following it over the lochan-studded moorland, past the path off right to Sàil Liath for the An Teallach traverse, and to the bothy at Shenavall.

Continue down the track into Strath na Sealga to where the track loops north towards Achneigie opposite Beinn a' Chlaidheimh's east ridge above Creag Ghlas. Leave the track here and ford the Abhainn Loch an Nid. There is no bridge, and it is a sizable river. If the water is running high, the crossing is likely to be difficult or impassable.

Once over, climb westwards up the slope onto Beinn a' Chlaidheimh's

Beinn a' Chlaidheimh and An Teallach from Creag Rainich (Rab Anderson)

north-east shoulder to reach a flattish section above Creag Ghlas. Avoid the crags on the steeper upper part of the mountain by a grassy rake on the left, then climb steeply to the narrow crest, which leads over two lower tops to the summit at the southern end (**11.5km; 1165m; 4h 40min**).

Returning the same way is perhaps the easiest option (**23km; 1465m; 8h 10min**).

Another descent is possible by heading south from the summit for about 50m or so to descend the short, curving east ridge and the slope below to reach the Abhainn Loch an Nid. Find a suitable place to cross, then follow the path back to the track and return to Corrie Hallie (**23km; 1450; 8h 10min**).

An ascent can also be made from Loch a' Bhraoin, via the bothy at Lochivraon, then around the foot of Creag Rainich to Loch an Nid. The use of a bike to the bothy makes this route more feasible. The best route is one that climbs the 'rivers' of slab on

the east face of the Munro Sgùrr Bàn to traverse to the col with Beinn a' Chlaidheimh, or better to climb all the way to Sgùrr Bàn's summit.

Start from the layby on the A832 at NH161761, at the top of a wide bend on the west side of the road, 4 miles (6km) west of Braemore Junction.

Head southwards along the road for 100m and follow the track on the right, which leads down towards Loch a' Bhraoin. Go right at a three-way junction and continue along the track on the north side of the loch to reach Lochivraon cottage and the open estate bothy. The track along Loch a' Bhraoin has been improved, and biking it offers a saving of about 1h 20min on the day (**6km; 20m; 40min by bike**), (**1h 20min on foot**).

Distances and times are now given on foot, from and back to the bothy, and via the summit of Sgùrr Bàn.

Continue along the track to where it ends after 700m, then follow an ATV track and a path alongside the meandering burn. Just over 1km

right from here to gain the col with Beinn a' Chlaidheimh at c.645m, or continue west up the summit dome of Sgùrr Bàn, which is covered in white boulders (**7.5km; 820m; 3h**).

Descend north to the col at 650m, Am Briseadh, with its small lochans, then ascend the ridge ahead over Pt.815m to gain the col beyond (787m), where there are some small lochans. The summit cone of Beinn a' Chlaidheimh lies ahead and is climbed by a path up its left side (**11.25km; 1120m; 4h 40min**)

To descend, return over Pt.815m to Am Briseadh, then descend south-east beneath some crags to reach the north end of Loch An Nid. Cross the outflow to regain the path, which is followed back to the bothy (**21.25km; 1260m; 7h 30min**).

Return to the road (**33.25km; 1325m; 8h 55min** with a bike), (**10h 15min** on foot).

Omitting the Sgùrr Bàn slabs for a there-and-back the same way route from the north end of Loch an Nid and the Am Briseadh col should give a slightly shorter and quicker route by about 1.25km, 325m, 1h.

Also see map on page 307.

further on, at NH101728, the burn swings rightwards towards the hillside and a path follows it. Instead of following these, cross the burn here, then continue west, following the ATV track and path on the other side to cross another burn and reach a ruined building known as Feinasheen, with Mullach Coire Mhic Fhearchair rising beyond. This is where the route to Creag Rainich leaves the path.

Follow the path around the hillside and down to Loch an Nid. The 'rivers' of quartzite slab on Sgùrr Bàn are an amazing feature, extending from around the 800m contour and falling almost all the way to Loch an Nid to give a route 1500m long. In the dry, the walk up them is easy, but in the wet more care is needed.

Cross the burn flowing into the loch and make a rising traverse to gain the first and lowest tongue of slab. Ascend the tongue almost to the top of the more extensive sheet of slab from which the tongues fall at the 650m contour. Either traverse

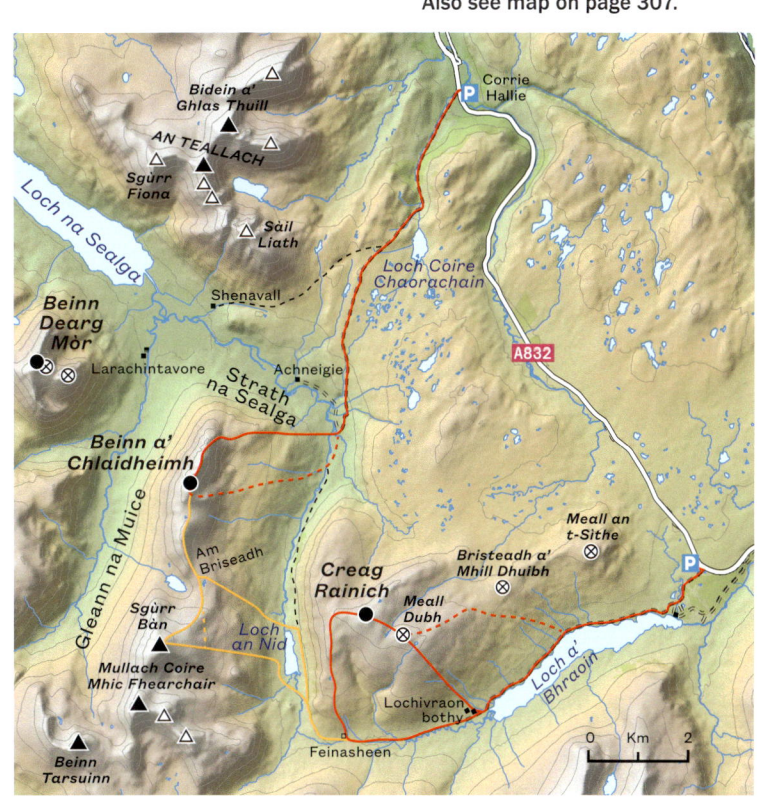

Creag Rainich and Loch an Nid from from below Sgùrr Dubh on Mullach Coire Mhic Fhearchair (Rab Anderson)

Creag Rainich; *807m; (C147); L19 & L20; NH096751; bracken crag*

Snaking through from the A832 near Corrieshalloch to Gruinard Bay is a glacial trench that holds Loch a' Bhraoin, Loch an Nid and Loch na Sealga. Creag Rainich rises above a sharp bend in this trench, and its location between the Fannaich, the Fisherfield, An Teallach and the Beinn Dearg ranges, makes its summit an outstanding viewpoint.

The usual start is from 'The Destitution Road', the name given to what is now the A832 as it sweeps over the bare moorland from Braemore Junction to Dundonnell. This road was originally built to provide employment in exchange for food during the Highland Potato Famine of 1846–56.

The road passes close to the northern end of Loch a' Bhraoin, where there is parking in a layby at NH161761. This is at the top of a wide bend, on the west side of the road, just over 4 miles (6km) to the west of Braemore Junction.

Head southwards along the road for 100m and follow the track on the right, which leads down towards Loch a' Bhraoin. At a three-way junction, go right and continue along the track on the north side of the loch to reach Lochivraon cottage and the open estate bothy. The track along Loch a' Bhraoin has been improved and biking it offers a saving of about 1h 20min on the day (**6km; 20m; 40min** by bike), (**1h 20min** on foot).

Distances and times are now given on foot, from and back to the bothy.

Continue along the track to where it ends after 700m, then follow an ATV track and path beside the meandering burn. Just over 1km further on, at NH101728, the burn swings rightwards towards the hillside and a path follows it. However, cross the burn at this point, and continue west, following the ATV track and path on the other side to cross a burn and reach a ruined building known as Feinasheen, with Mullach Coire Mhic Fhearchair rising beyond.

Climb north-west up the broad ridge by the burn, which soon disappears. A line of fence posts runs up the ridge, although the better route, certainly higher up, is closer to the edge overlooking the trench holding Loch an Nid. At the top, turn right to gain the flat summit area. The highest point lies 60m to the west of the stone trig point, formed by three slabs of rock (**6km; 550m; 2h 15min**).

Descend south-east to a col with some small lochans, then climb over Meall Dubh (748m) to another small lochan, and continue south-east down the slope by the burn back to Lochivraon (**9km; 580m; 3h 15min**).

Return to the road (**21km; 645m, 4h 40min** with a bike), (**6h** on foot).

If on foot, from the lochan, the crest can be followed north-east towards a col to take a diagonal line down to the loch further along. A higher line can also be taken to descend from Meall an t-Sìthe.

Map on previous page & 307

Beinn Liath Mhòr a' Ghiubhais Lì; 766m; (C213); L20; NH281713; big grey hill of the coloured pines

Standing above Loch Glascarnoch, Beinn Liath Mhòr a' Ghiubhais Lì is an outlier of the Fannaichs. Except for a growing forest on its north-west flanks, it is a featureless dome of mainly rough grass and heather.

There are two starts, the best being from the Torrandhu Bridge parking area at NH277742, just off the south side of the A835, west of Torrandhu Bridge, beneath which the Abhainn an Torrain Duibh flows before entering Loch Glascarnoch. This is next to an automated meteorological station. It is also the parking for some of the Fannaich Munros to the south-west, and for Am Faochagach to the north-east, so it can get busy. There is another start with a short route described at the end.

Walk carefully south-east over the bridge across the Abhainn an Torrain Duibh (there is no pavement, and traffic travels fast), then along the verge for 260m to cross a bridge over a burn, the Allt an Odhar Mòr.

Follow a track through a gate, then on up through the Altan Wood plantation to ford the Allt an Odhar Mòr, normally easy. Continue for a further 600m to an open strip of hillside at

NH272731 between the plantings, and just before the next burn, which flows beneath the track in two pipes.

Leave the track here and follow an ATV track uphill beside the burn to pass through a wide, open gap in the deer fence at NH272725, then continue up onto a flattening named Cnap a' Ghiubhais Lì. Pass through an area of peat hags and climb south-east up the slope to the summit (**4.25km; 505m; 1h 50min**).

The view is remarkably fine, for on one side is the whole length of the Fannaich chain, whilst to the north is the Beinn Dearg group.

None of the old pines that gave the hill its name survive, but upper parts show some of the best examples of solifluction boulder ramparts to be found in Scotland. They may be the relics of a time when the summit of the hill protruded from the glacier ice.

It is easiest to return the same way (8.5km; 510m; 3h).

Another route starts from a parking area on the Loch Glascarnoch side of the road at NH288736. Cross the road, then head across boggy ground to climb beside a fence around a forestry plantation, crossing a gate. Leave the fence to climb over the minor rise of Meall Daimh (533m), which protrudes from Beinn Liath Mhòr a' Ghiubhais Lì, and continue up the slope beyond to the summit (3km; 540m; 1h 35min).

Return the same way (6km; 570m; 2h 30min).

It is possible to combine these routes to make a circuit, but this involves a 1km section alongside a busy road with fast moving traffic.

Beinn Liath Mhòr a' Ghiubhais Lì with Meall Daimh, left, across Loch Droma (Rab Anderson)

Seana Bhraigh, Creag an Duine,
Ben More Coigach, Beinn an Eòin,
Stac Pollaidh, Cùl Beag, Cùl Mòr,
Suilven, Canisp and Quinag from
Càrn Bàn (Rab Anderson)

SECTION 15

Loch Broom to the Cromarty Firth

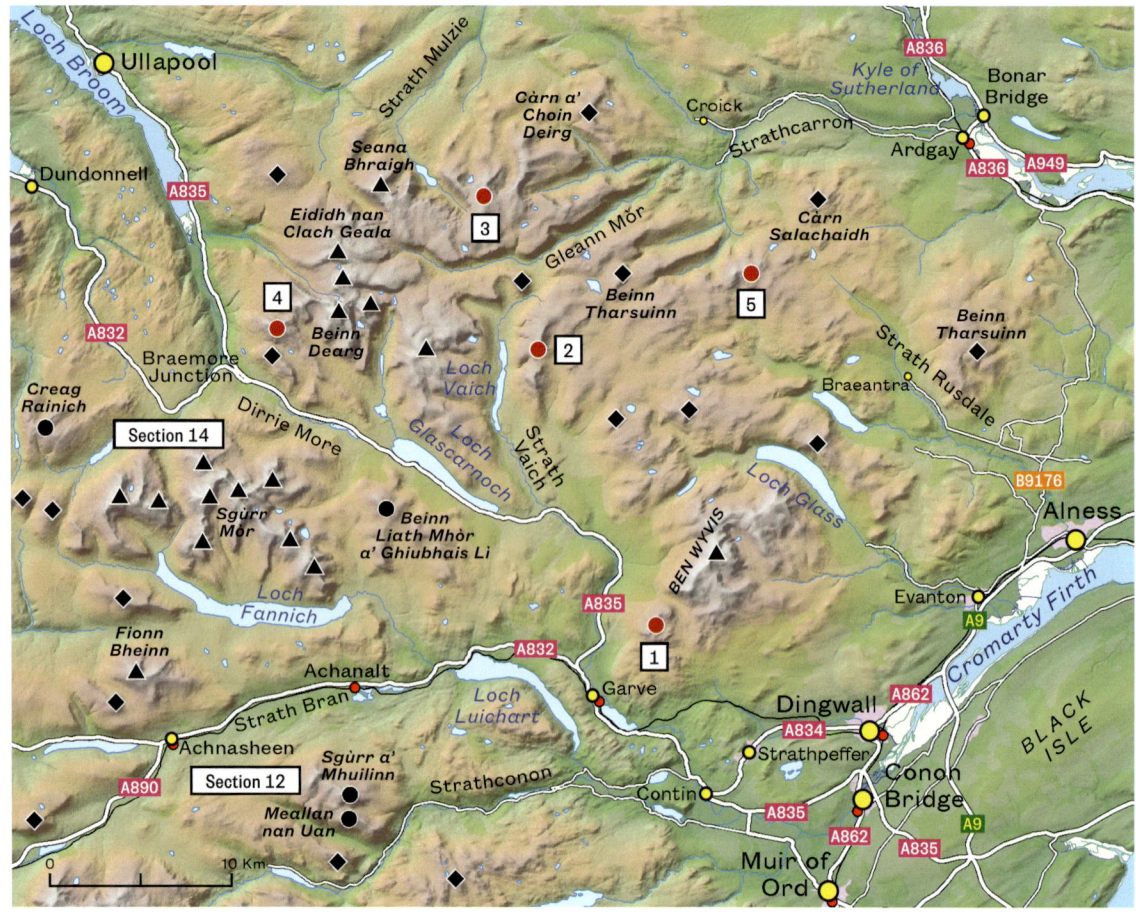

Little Wyvis from Strath Rannoch near Inchbae (Rab Anderson)

Little Wyvis; *763m; (C221); L20; NH429645; little awesome hill*

In keeping with its name, Little Wyvis, the second lowest of the Corbetts, looks small sat beside the bigger bulk of Ben Wyvis, which dominates it to the north-east. Rising above Garve and the A832 turn-off to Torridon from the A835 to Ullapool, Little Wyvis gives an accessible and easy short climb, useful for a short day.

There are two approaches, both from the A835 a short distance to the north of Garve. One starts from the signed parking area and toilets on the west side of the road at Silverbridge, 1.25 miles (2km) north of the Torridon turn-off, whilst the other starts 2.25 miles (3.5km) further north, from Forestry and Land Scotland's sign-posted Ben Wyvis car park on the east side of the road south of Garbat.

The route from Silverbridge follows a track all the way to the summit, which gives an easier way, though arguably less aesthetic, and for that reason the Garbat route is probably the better, although the car park can get very busy with walkers heading for Ben Wyvis.

For the route from Garbat, leave the north end of the Ben Wyvis car park on a well-built path to cross a bridge over the Allt a' Bhealaich Mhòir, and follow the path uphill beside the burn through the Garbat Forest. Cross a forestry track and continue uphill to emerge from the forest with the Bealach Mòr ahead, the steep-sided ▶

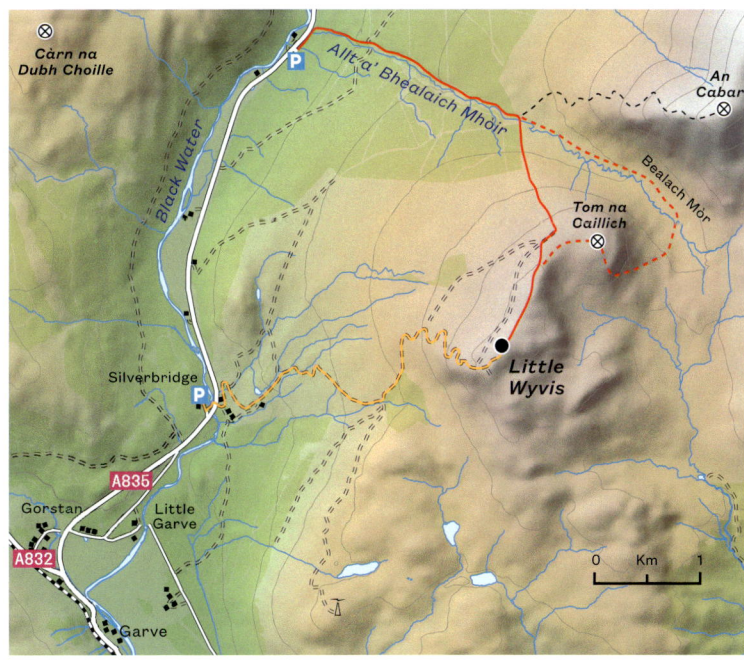

pass that separates Little Wyvis from Ben Wyvis.

There are two options from here:

(i) Easiest is to cross the burn and follow the edge of the forest, then a line of old fence posts, uphill to gain the end of a track at 635m. Go right along this for 80m to its junction with another track at a sharp bend, then leave the track and climb onto the crest just west of Tom na Caillich. Continue over a slight rise beside a line of intermittent old fence posts, and go up the final rise to the summit of Little Wyvis (**4.75km; 640m; 2h 5min**).

Return by the ascent route (9.5km; 650m; 3h 30min).

(ii) A short circuit can be made by continuing on the Ben Wyvis path to where it swings left and zigzags up onto An Cabar. Carry on through the Bealach Mòr on an ATV track and old stalkers' path to climb Tom na Caillich from behind. At the point the burn and ATV track turn left uphill to Ben Wyvis, cross the burn and rough ground to pick up a line of old fence posts, then follow these steeply up onto Tom na Caillich (705m); the slope further left is easier-angled. Cross the dip, then climb to the summit of Little Wyvis; an additional 2.25km, 35m, 35min. Return via ascent option (i), back towards the dip with Tom na Caillich, then down north to the forest.

For the Silverbridge route, cross the old bridge over the Black Water (*Allt Dubh*) falls, which provide a fine sight when in full flow, and continue ahead to the main road. Cross carefully, for it is a fast stretch of road, and go up the road on the other side, signed to Silverbridge Lodge.

At a three-way junction, go left through a gate then follow a track, which loops back on itself, and climb uphill past a barn and a small lochan. Pass a branch off left and zigzag up to a junction, then go left through woodland to where the main track loops right.

Take the track ahead along the top edge of the trees, passing a track off left, to zigzag sharply, and more steeply, uphill before turning around left and heading north-east up to the summit (**5.25km; 655m; 2h 15min**).

Return the same way (10.5km; 660m; 3h 45min).

Beinn a' Chaisteil; 787m; (C179); L20; NH370801; castle hill

Lying some 9km to the north of the A835 between Inverness and Ullapool, Beinn a' Chaisteil forms the highest point of a northwards running ridgeline above the east side of Loch Vaich and Strath Vaich.

The summit sits above the north end of Loch Vaich, 2.5km to the north of the other hill on the ridgeline, Meall a' Ghrianain (772m), which it is separated from by a col at c.645m.

The hills have uniformly steep, heathery slopes, but their upper ridges consist of stony ground, which gives easy walking. Both hills can be climbed, particularly if the whole route is undertaken on foot.

A private road, which leads to Strathvaich Lodge and the dam at the south end of Loch Vaich, then a good track, run all the way along the east side of the loch through to Gleann Beag and Gleann Mòr. The road and the track can be biked, and are also used for the southern approach to Càrn Bàn (page 324), and for two Grahams, Meall a' Chaorainn and Beinn Tharsuinn. The use of a bike enables the two Grahams to be combined with Beinn a' Chaisteil, as described in the SMC's guidebook *The Grahams and The Donalds*. Using a bike for the ascent of Beinn a' Chaisteil itself saves over 2h on the day.

The approach is made from Black Bridge, where there is parking on the north side of the A835 at the start of the private road up Strath Vaich.

Follow the road past the cottages and through a gate for 3.5km to where it turns left across the Abhainn Srath a' Bhàthaich to Strathvaich Lodge and the dam. Continue ahead on a track past woodland, then through a gate and across a bridge over a burn to pass a track off right.

If the route is being done on foot, this is where the optional return over Meall a' Ghrianain arrives, which is now in view ahead. Bikes could also be left here for this purpose.

Continue up the track, which swings round onto the small Cnoc na h-Iolare (324m), where there is a view up Loch Vaich over Meall a' Chuaille and Meall a' Chaorainn to the distant

Meall a' Ghrianain and Beinn a' Chaisteil from the north-east (Rab Anderson)

high ground of Càrn Bàn. Beinn a' Chaisteil's upper ridge remains hidden behind Meall a' Ghrianain, but the line of ascent up its lower slopes above the red-roofed buildings at Lubachlaggan can be seen.

The track now makes a gradual descent to enter a gated area planted with natural forestry, which it then exits above the two derelict buildings at Lubachlaggan. Cross the bridge over the burn, then leave the track before it enters another gated area.

This is where bikes should be left if only doing the Corbett (**8.75km; 160m; about 1h** by bike), (**2h 10min** on foot).

Distances and times are now given on foot, from and back to here.

Follow an old stalkers' path uphill between the burn and the fence to zigzag quite steeply up the rounded lower spur. The path ends at a small cairn at about 530m. Continue up the spur past a large cairn to gain level ground on the shoulder at the 670m contour, then cross stony ground and a wetter section to climb an easier-angled slope onto the ridgeline crest above a steep drop into Coire a' Chùndrain. Follow the edge to gain the wind shelter cairn and stone trig

point on the summit (**3.25km; 515m; 1h 35min**).

There are fine views of Seana Bhraigh to the north-west, with the extensive undulating mass of Càrn Bàn to its right, and Suilven in between. Càrn Chuinneag with its twin tops stands out to the north-east, whilst to the south-east Ben Wyvis is clear with Little Wyvis to its side.

Return to Lubachlaggan (**6.5km; 515m; 2h 35min**), then to Black Bridge (**24km; 760m; 4h 25min** with a bike), (**6h 50min** on foot).

For the route on foot over Meall a' Ghrianain, return south down the ridge and drop to the col at c.645m then climb up the other side to the top; 2.75km, 130m, 50min from Beinn a' Chaisteil (**14.75km; 805m; 4h 35min**) from Black Bridge.

Descend southwards on steepening ground to pick up some zigzags, then cross a haggy section, following a line of old fence posts down the broad ridge. At the haggy dip before the rise to Meallan Donn (397m), either drop down left to a track and follow this around Meallan Donn, or drop down to the right to pick up the track on the west side of Meallan Donn, after it

has looped around it.

If the left-hand option is taken, at the apex of the track around Meallan Donn, it is possible to take a short cut by following an old path, marked on the map, south-west down past woodland towards Lubriach to go through a gate and join the road where it turns across the bridge to the lodge.

Return to Black Bridge (**23.25km; 830m; 6h 45min**).

The route including the two Grahams is not described here, but is shown on the map below and on page 325 (**44km; 1180m; 8h 45min** with a bike), (**12h 15min** on foot).

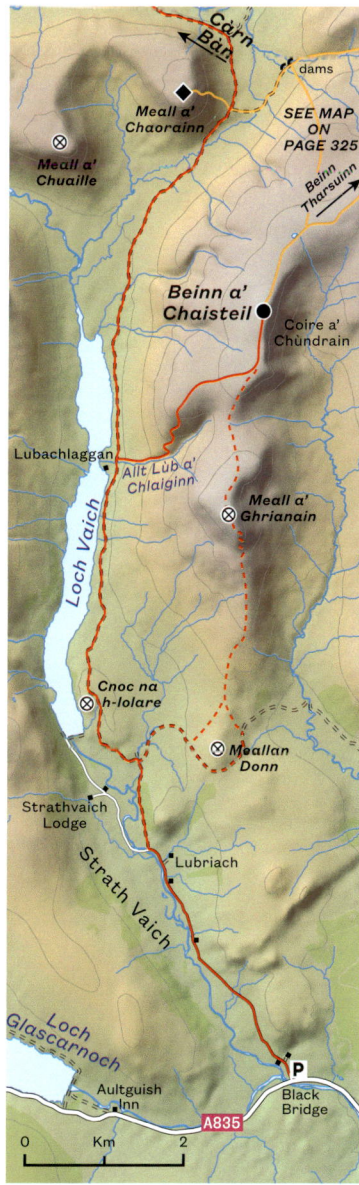

Loch Vaich and the southern approach to distant Càrn Bàn, with Meall a' Chaorainn, right (Rab Anderson)

Càrn Bàn; *842m; (C99); L20; NH338875; white cairn*

Forming the continuation eastwards of the Seana Bhraigh plateau, Càrn Bàn's dome-shaped summit and its numerous satellite tops make up the great hill mass of the Freevater Forest, lying between Gleann Beag and Gleann Mòr in the south, and Strath Mulzie and Glen Einig to the north. This is one of the more remote parts of Scotland and therefore the approaches to it are all lengthy.

Although it is possible to walk-in then climb the hill, it is assumed that most walkers will approach by bike.

Two principal approaches are described, both leading to Gleann Beag then following the same route to the summit. The first approach is via Strath Vaich to the south, whilst the other is via Gleann Mòr from the north-east. A third approach, which is not described, can be made from Strath Mulzie to the north, as for the approach to Seana Bhraigh described in *The Munros,* perhaps utilising the bothies at NH305888 (Coiremor MBA east end and Magoo's west end) to climb the hill by its north-west ridge.

The Strath Vaich approach from the south, although slightly longer, is probably the easiest for most to reach. This starts at Black Bridge (NH373708) near the south-eastern end of Loch Glascarnoch, where there is parking on the north side of the A835 between Inverness and Ullapool, at the start of a private road up Strath Vaich.

The route to Beinn a' Chaisteil on page 322 also starts here, as well as that to the two Grahams, Meall a' Chaorainn and Beinn Tharsuinn. The map opposite shows the northern part of the route, whilst the map on page 323 shows the start and the southern part of route up Strath Vaich.

Follow the tarmac road through a locked gate then, after 3.5km where the road swings left over a bridge to Strathvaich Lodge and a dam on Loch Vaich, continue ahead on a rough track. Shortly after passing through another gate and crossing a bridge, keep to the main track, which swings left, then climbs to a highpoint at 316m on Cnoc na h-Iolaire.

Loch Vaich stretches ahead here with Meall a' Ghrianan and Beinn a'

Chaisteil to its right. The high ground of Càrn Bàn is visible in the far distance beyond Meall a' Chuaille and Meall a' Chaorainn.

Continue downhill along the track, passing through a number of gates in fences around planted areas, then ascend to a highpoint at 369m beneath Meall a' Chaorainn where a track branches off to the right. Keep straight on and descend into the head of Gleann Mòr, with Deanich Lodge visible in the glen below. Pass a track off to the right and continue downhill to cross a bridge over the river, then turn onto a track on the right where bikes are best left by a boulder (**16km; 250m; about 1h 50min** by bike), (**4h** on foot).

The Gleann Mòr approach from the north-east, whilst shorter, is perhaps a more awkward and time-consuming start for most to reach. From Ardgay at the head of the Dornoch Firth, take the road signed to Croick, then turn left at the telephone box just before Croick. Pass Annat Lodge to reach the end of the public road at the Glencalvie Lodge track junction,

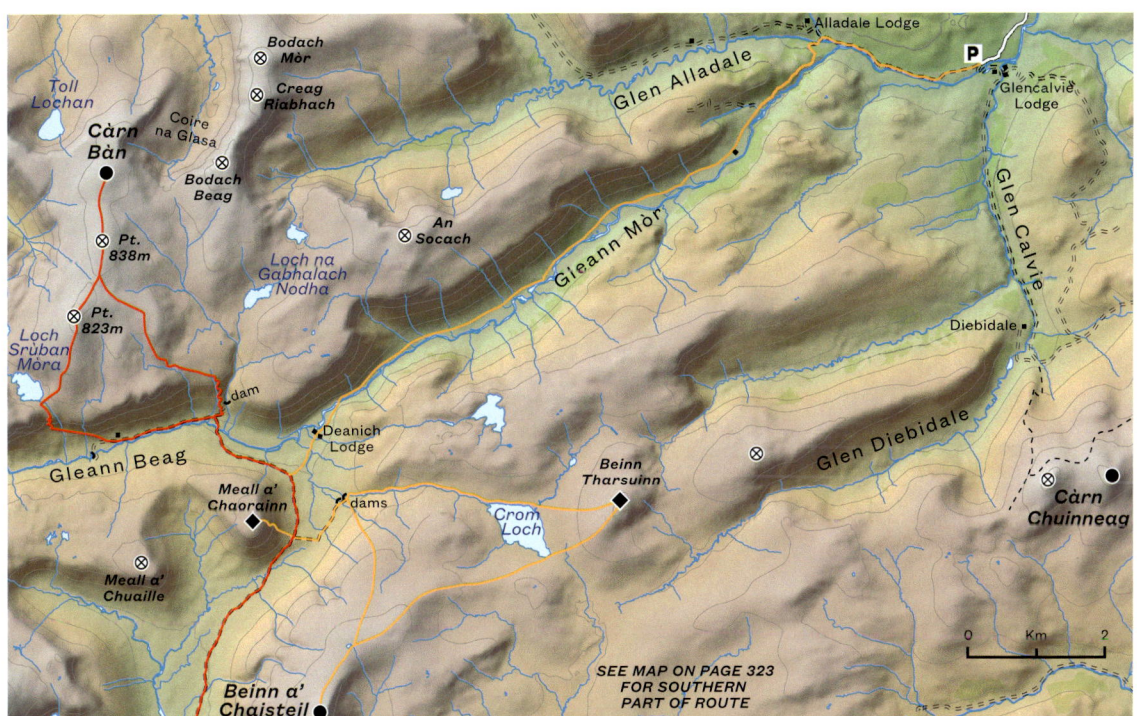

SEE MAP ON PAGE 323
FOR SOUTHERN
PART OF ROUTE

where there is parking on the right (NH464891). The route to Càrn Chuinneag on page 328 starts here.

Head west along the track towards Alladale through Caledonian pinewoods, then after 3.5km, at a three-way junction, turn down left and take the track over the bridge across the river. Continue on this track through Gleann Mòr, passing through a number of gated, fenced areas. For anyone on foot, where the track crosses a bridge to gain Deanich Lodge, a path (boggy in places) continues ahead to cut the corner. Otherwise, stay on the track past the lodge and climb uphill to join the Strath Vaich track. Follow this downhill, then over the bridge, and turn right onto another track where bikes are best left by a boulder; (**14.5km; 205m; about 1h 40min** by bike), (**13.75km; 180m; 3h 20min** on foot).

With both approaches having joined, distances and times are now given on foot, from and back to here.

Follow the right-hand track, which zigzags uphill, then leave it at the final bend where it continues a short way to a dam. Now gain a stalkers' path, which zigzags steeply uphill then makes a long traverse westwards across the boggy hillside. As it nears

the burn, the path turns north-west and is followed to its end at a height of about 680m. In places the path is not always immediately obvious, but the line is marked by cairns.

From the end of the path, either continue ahead and curve round, heading for the dip between the southern and central tops of Càrn Bàn, crossing some haggy ground, or cut up right to drier, stony ground before curving round; again, there are some cairns. From the dip, climb north following a rough path onto the stony central top (838m), marked by some distinctive white rocks, then drop north across another dip and climb to the cairn on the flat, stony top of Càrn Bàn (**5.25km; 560m; 2h 5min**).

The view is superb. Lined up to the north-west are the hills of Coigach and Assynt, whilst to the west Seana Bhraigh presents a striking sight with the Beinn Dearg group to the south-west and An Teallach in between. The vastness of Càrn Bàn is obvious, especially to the east where its satellite tops of Bodach Beag (837m), Creag Riabhach (833m) and Bodach Mòr (821m) all appear to look higher than the 842m summit does.

Although returning the same way is the quickest (**10.5km; 580m; 3h 30min**),

it is better to make a circuit by returning over the central top (838m) to the dip, then continuing southwards onto the bouldery southern top (823m). From there, descend south-south-west through the summit boulder field, then down a grassy slope to gain the south end of Loch Srùban Mòra. Cross the outflow, then go up onto the shoulder to a cairn that marks the start of a stalkers' path.

Follow this path, which zigzags down a remarkably steep slope before making a descending traverse across the outflow from the loch, where it is joined by another stalkers' path that has come down the east side of the burn. If found, this other path could also be used to descend from the shoulder on the east side of the loch. Cross a section of landslip to pick-up the path on the far side, then continue down to gain the track in the floor of the glen, which is followed back to the bike (**12.25km; 620m; 4h 5min**).

For the approach from the south, return to Black Bridge (**44.25km; 1020m; 7h 30min** with a bike), (**11h 50min** on foot).

For the approach from the northeast, return to the Glencalvie Lodge track junction (**41.25km; 860m; 7h** with a bike), (**10h 30min** on foot).

Beinn Enaiglair and Meall Doire Fàid from the A832 near Braemore Junction (Rab Anderson)

Beinn Enaiglair; *889m; (C34); L20; NH225805; hill of timid birds*

A western outlier of the Beinn Dearg group of hills, Beinn Enaiglair rises to the north-east of Braemore Junction at the head of the Corrieshalloch Gorge on the A835 between Inverness and Ullapool. It gives a good ascent on its own, but is easily combined with Meall Doire Fàid, the Graham that sits between it and the A835. There is no view of the hill from the A835. However, on the approach to Braemore Junction along the A832 from Poolewe and Gairloch, there is a good view of it with Meall Doire Fàid to the right.

Start from the large car park on the north side of the road, directly opposite Braemore Junction. Leave the east end of the car park through some trees on a path, and go through a gate next to the road. Climb uphill on a rough path to the side of a felled area of forestry, and continue across moorland to pass the east side of Home Loch. Cross a footbridge over the inflow and join a track.

Follow the track uphill by the burn for 275m, then take a path off on the right, up beside the burn. At a fork in a further 180m, go left and follow a stalkers' path north onto the base of

the broad north-west ridge. Leave the path here and climb the ridge, passing over the north-west top with its large cairn, to reach the broad summit (**6km; 725m; 2h 30min**).

Whilst the quickest descent is steeply south to the Bealach nam Bùthan between Beinn Enaiglair and Meall Doire Fàid, it is perhaps more enjoyable to go down the south-east ridge where there are two options:

(i) Go all the way down the ridge to reach the stalkers' path around the north side of the hill, as used on the approach to the north-west ridge, and follow this to a junction. Take the right-hand path through the Bealach nam Bùthan to rejoin the approach route, which is followed back.

(ii) Slightly longer is to go down the ridge a short way, then drop off the north side at a level section at NH228804 on a stalkers' path that zigzags down to a burn. This leads to the stalkers' path around the north side of the hill and joins option (i) at the foot of the ridge to return as for that (**14km; 750m; 4h 45min**).

A longer ascent route can be had by continuing on the stalkers' path around the north-west ridge, past a

large boulder (Clach na h-Aide), into the grassy corrie beneath Beinn Enaiglair's steep north face. Ascend by the burn, crossing it, then recrossing it higher up, to zigzag up above the col with Iorguill. Drop into the shallow eastern corrie, then leave the main path just before the burn draining the corrie. Follow another stalkers' path, initially vague, to cross the burn higher up, and zigzag up to a flattening on the south-east ridge just below the summit, which is easily gained (**8km; 740m; 3h**).

To descend, return to the stalkers' path around the hill, either as for the ascent, or all the way down the south-east ridge and follow this back through the Bealach nam Bùthan (**16km; 765m; 5h 15min**).

The other options are to make the short, but steep, direct descent to the Bealach nam Bùthan, or go down the north-west ridge back to the approach.

From any of the descents to the Bealach nam Bùthan, it is worthwhile making the short climb to the summit of Meall Doire Fàid. A zigzag line up right, then left, then back up right is required to avoid craggy ground. Returning to the bealach makes this an added 1.75km, 175m, 50min, whilst making a direct descent south-west to the gate by the road is 1.5km shorter, but with an added 175m in ascent for an added 10min or so.

Another way of climbing Meall Doire Fàid and Beinn Enaiglair is by a fine circuit of Coire Leacachain to the south-east. This starts from a long pull-off on the west side of the road at NH229765, about 2km to the east of Braemore Junction.

Cross the road, go up the left side of a forestry plantation, then veer left and ascend to the ridge ahead. The initial steep section is probably best bypassed by easier ground on the left to gain the crest. Thereafter, continue up the ridge, passing over Meall nan Doireachan (713m) to reach Meall Doire Fàid (**3.5km; 520m; 1h 45min**).

Descend to the Bealach nam Bùthan by going right (east) to bypass cliffs beneath the summit, then back left (west) and down right to bypass craggy terrain above the bealach. Make an initially steep ascent directly to the summit of Beinn Enaiglair (**5.5km; 850m; 3h**).

Descend the south-east ridge to the stalkers' path around the hill, and follow this southwards to a junction, then go left and follow that path south-east along the side of a broad ridge to Meallan Mhurchaidh (625m).

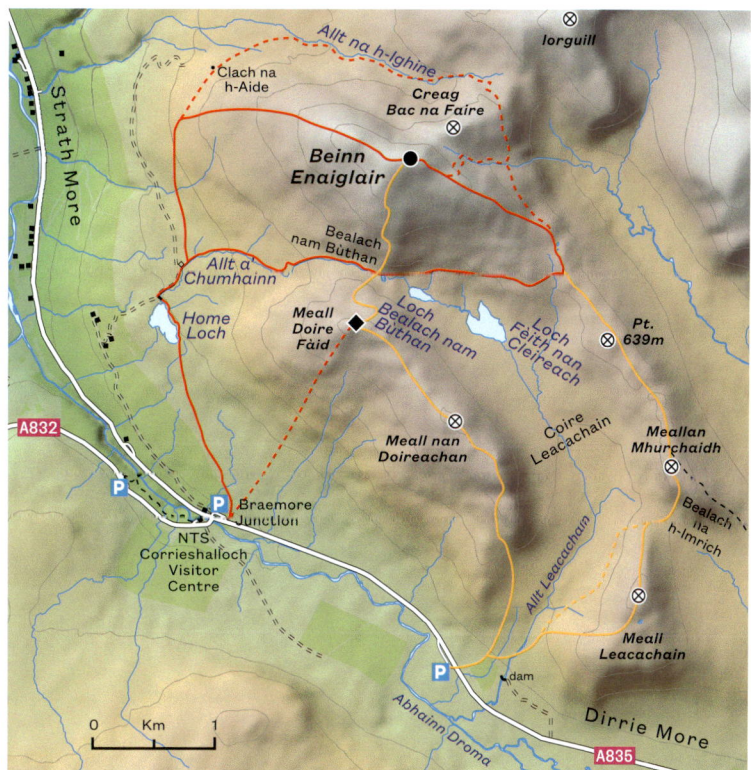

Leave the path here, then cross the highpoint and descend a grassy rake to avoid some craggy ground and scree to gain a broad col, Bealach na h-Imrich. There are now two options:

(i) Climb Meall Leacachain (621m) and descend south, then west, to cross the burn above a dam to regain the start (**12.5km; 1015m; 5h 15min**).

(ii) Shorter, is to pick up a rough ATV track marked with intermittent white posts, and follow this beneath Meall Leacachain to then cross the Allt Leacachain above the dam.

Beinn Enaiglair, Iorguill and Beinn Dearg across Loch Fèith nan Cleireach from Meall nan Doireachan (Rab Anderson)

The distinctive twin tops of Càrn Chuinneag from Beinn nan Eun to the south-west (Rab Anderson)

Càrn Chuinneag; *839m; (C108); L20; NH483833; hill of the churn (bucket)*

With its distinctive twin tops, Càrn Chuinneag enjoys an isolated position amongst the rolling hills and deer forests of Easter Ross. Its location here makes its summit an outstanding viewpoint.

The ascent is made via Glen Calvie to the north, which is reached from Ardgay at the head of the Dornoch Firth by taking the road along the north side of Strathcarron, signed to Croick. At The Craigs, turn off left (south) at the red telephone box to reach a parking area on the right where the public road ends and continuations lead ahead to Alladale and left to Glencalvie Lodge.

Cross over and go down the road

Càrn Chuinneag's summit from the west top, with the Graham Beinn Tharsuinn beyond (Rab Anderson)

across the bridge above the river to Glencalvie Lodge. Follow the track around the lodge and head south up Glencalvie beside the Water of Glencalvie, which is crossed by a bridge about 1.5km from the lodge.

Continue up the track through birch woods, with Càrn Chuinneag's West Top in view ahead, finally swinging left away from the river, uphill to where a track branches off right to Diebidale Lodge. In a further 40m, leave the track and take the stalkers' path that starts on the west side of the burn, and zigzag up the side of the nose of A' Chìoch onto its top.

After a long flattish section, this fine path zigzags up the broad and bouldery ridge of the West Top, then makes a rising traverse up right to a junction marked by a cairn.

Take the left-hand path, which is climbed to its highpoint below the col between the two tops. Leave the path here and slant up left across the slope to cross the col, then ascend to the East Top's rocky summit. Marked by a stone trig point within a stone wind shelter, this is 8m higher than the West Top (**9km; 740m; 3h 15min**).

The fabulous view extends from Ben Wyvis in the south, across the Fannaichs to the Beinn Dearg group and Seana Bhraigh, then over Càrn Bàn to the peaks of Coigach and Assynt. North are Ben Hope and Ben Loyal, whilst beyond Ben Klibreck, Morven in the far north-east is visible.

Cross the col and climb to the West Top (830m). The easiest descent is to return to the col to regain the path used in the ascent and go back down this to follow the track back to the start (**18.5km; 825m; 5h 45min**).

A saving of about 1h 30min can be achieved by biking the initial 5km.

From the West Top, it is possible to descend to the south-west to gain the right-hand branch of the stalkers' path, which traverses around the west side of the hill from the junction. However, boulder fields here are likely to make this more trouble than it's worth. The best line is slightly to the left, linking grassy areas to gain the stalkers' path just above its lowest point, where there is a ruined building. It would perhaps be easier to ascend this way.

An ascent can be made from the north-east, from the track that runs between Càrn Chuinneag and Càrn Salachaidh, a Graham that can easily be included. The approach is made by bike from Braeantra to the south, at the end of the road up Strath Rusdale (NH567780). Follow the continuation track north-west to NH506853, where the eastern end of the stalkers' path that traverses Càrn Chuinneag leaves the track at a stile (**10.5km; 220m; 1h 30min** by bike). Follow this stalkers' path past Loch Chuinneag to below the col between the tops, then climb each in turn and return by the path (**9.25km; 510m; 3h 15min** on foot).

Climbing the West Top first enables a varied return over Càrn Maire.

Return to Strath Rusdale (**30.25km; 730m; 5h 40min** with a bike).

Càrn Salachaidh is included via a short section of track to the north of the stile; an additional 5.5km, 250m, 1h 50min there and back.

Foinaven – Stob Cadha na Beucaich, Lord Reay's Seat, A' Chèir Ghorm, Ganu Mòr & Ceann Garbh from An t-Sàil Mhòr (Rab Anderson)

SECTION 16

Loch Broom to the Pentland Firth

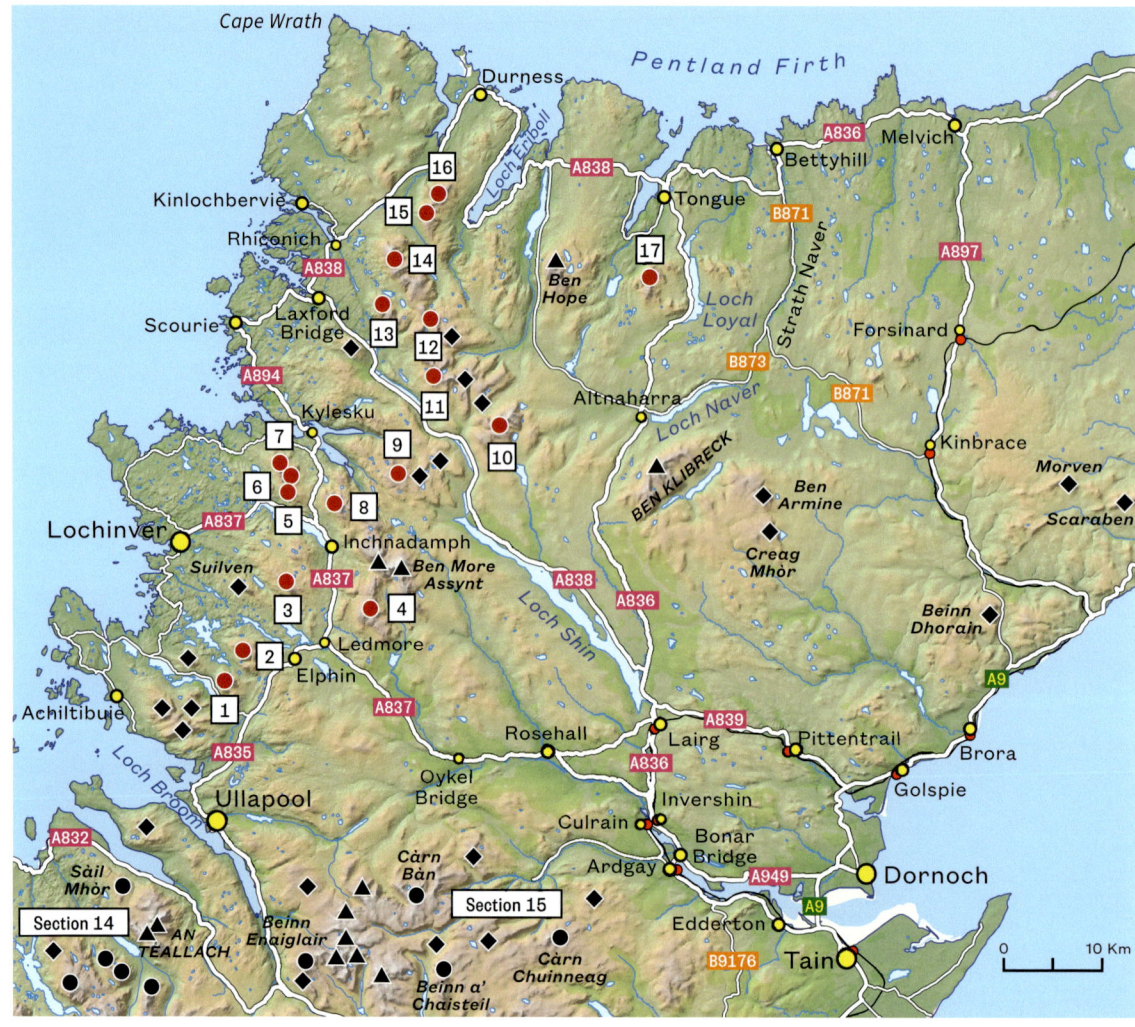

SECTION 16

Cùl Beag above Loch Lurgainn from the road to Achiltibuie to the west (Hugh Munro)

Cùl Beag; *769m; (C209); L15; NC140088; small back*

Sitting between Ben More Coigach and its big brother Cùl Mòr, with jagged Stac Pollaidh to its side, Cùl Beag struggles to impress when seen from the A835 to the south. However, when seen from the west, and from Knockan Crag to the north, it presents a different, and much finer, spectacle.

There are two routes. One starts from the west, from the single-track road to Achiltibuie, which runs along the north side of Loch Lurgainn. The other starts from the east, from the A835. Both routes have their merits. The route from the east can also be incorporated into an ascent with Cùl Mòr for a magnificent traverse of both Corbetts, which is described in the panel on page 335.

The route from the west follows a good stalkers' path, which leaves the road from the north end of a passing place at NC126088, 500m east of Linneraineach, to ascend north past a small group of Scots pine trees.

There are various places to squeeze a car in off the road close to the start of the path without blocking passing places. However, the best place is about 150m west of Linneraineach, some 650m from the start of the stalkers' path.

Cùl Beag's lower slopes rise steeply above the approach down the road from the A835, blocking any view of its features until beyond it. The upper part of the mountain contains bands of sandstone cliff, which face west and north, and the route climbs a gap between these to reach the top.

Gain the stalkers' path and follow it for almost 1km to just beyond the southern tip of Lochan Fhionnlaidh, which lies in the broad col between Stac Pollaidh and Cùl Beag. Leave the path here and follow a rough path east-south-east up the steep slope to reach a shallow col on the north ridge of Cùl Beag, between it and the top of a steep nose called Cìoch a' Chùil Bhig. Turn south and zigzag steeply up the broad ridge between the cliffs of the west and north faces to reach the summit (**3.25km; 700m; 1h 55min**).

Returning the same way is quickest (**6.5km; 700m; 3h**), but it is better to make a traverse by descending southwards above the cliffs of the west face to a slight rise. From there, drop south-east to a col at the head of a westward-running gully, then continue south up a small rise onto Pt.518m.

Descend southwards on less steep ground to an easing, then head south-west to bypass the end of the lower crags and reach the road. Walk north along the road for 2km or so back to the start (**8.25km; 730m; 3h 30min**).

The route from the east starts from a pull-off on the east side of the A835 at NC184078, opposite a loop of the old road, or another pull-off on the west side 200m further on. The loop leaves the road a little further to the north and can be driven to a couple of parking places.

Walk along the old road, then follow a rough track, which loops round to the south end of Lochan Fada, and cross the inflow. In a further 420m, where the track turns sharp right to Loch nan Ealachan, continue ahead on a path to cross a fence and ascend across the side of Creag Dhubh, or along its crest. Climb more steeply onto Meall Dearg (657m), then drop west to the col with Cùl Beag. Pass the north end of a small lochan, Lochan Uaine, and climb to the summit (**5.25km; 640m; 2h 20min**).

Return the same way (**10.5km; 750m; 4h**).

Map on next page

Cùl Mòr; 849m; (C93); L15; NC162119; big back

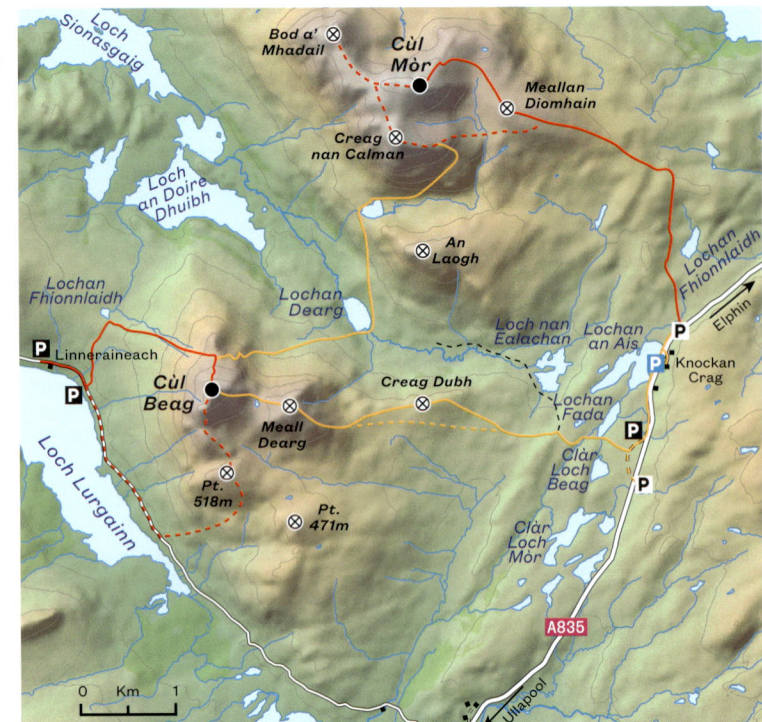

The highest of the Assynt Corbetts, Cùl Mòr and its attendant peak of Creag nan Calman provide one of the great landmarks of the North West.

Rising to the north of Cùl Beag, its smaller sibling, the mountain's southern, western and northern flanks are steep and craggy, and protected by a moat of lochans. Fortunately its south-eastern aspect is easier-angled and gives a straightforward ascent from a start height of 230m on the A835 across its foot.

The route can be extended to include Cùl Beag for a magnificent walk; see panel opposite.

Start from a pull-off on the west side of the road at NC188093, about 500m north of the Knockan Crag National Nature Reserve visitor centre and toilets. If the pull-off is full, park at Knockan Crag.

Cùl Mòr across Loch an Doire Dhuibh from Stac Pollaidh (Iain Young)

Creag nan Calman with Cùl Mòr behind from Creag Dhubh (Rab Anderson)

Cùl Mòr & Cùl Beag

The traverse of Cùl Mòr and Cùl Beag gives a magnificent day's walk. However, the terrain between the two is rough, and the time required may be more than the distance suggests, especially with the lowest point between the mountains being 108m, which is lower than the start and finish.

Start from either the Knockan Crag National Nature Reserve visitor centre car park and toilets, or the pull-off 500m further north up the road on the left.

*Follow the route described opposite for the ascent of Cùl Mòr, via the path over Meallan Dìomhain and the north-east ridge (**5.5km; 660m; 2h 25min**).*

Descend west a short way, then drop to the col and climb onto pointed Creag nan Calman (828m). Descend the south-south-east ridge to clear the steep ground of the southern slopes, then turn down south-west and west beneath a line of cliff to gain beautifully situated Lochan Dearg a' Chùil Mhòir.

Go around the north side of the loch, cross the outflow, then descend south, down and across the slope under the prow of An Laogh, to reach the south end of Lochan Dearg in Gleann Laoigh, where a 660m ascent awaits.

*Cross the inflow and the lovely sands, then ascend westwards across the slope beneath the north-facing cliffs to gain the col between Cìoch a' Chùil Bhig and Cùl Beag where the normal route from Loch Lurgainn arrives. Continue via the path up the north ridge to gain the top of Cùl Beag (**12.25km; 1385m; 5h 35min**).*

*Now descend the route described on page 335 for the ascent of Cùl Beag from the east. This is east down to the col with Lochan Uaine, then over Meall Dearg and across Creag Dubh to the rough track. On reaching the old road loop, go north to the main road and follow this back to the start (**19km; 1550m; 7h 45min**).*

Go through a gate in the fence, and follow a good path northwards above Lochan Fhionnlaidh to reach the mountain's ill-defined eastern ridge. Continue west-north-west up the broad ridge onto Meallan Dìomhain (609m), then drop to the north and cross a broad col. Ascend north towards a small lochan and swing round onto the north-east ridge, then follow the path steeply up this and on through a boulder field to gain the summit, marked by a trig point and wind shelter above a steep drop into Coire Gorm (**5.5km; 660m; 2h 25min**).

Returning the same way is easiest (**11km; 695m; 4h**).

However, it is worth going west then, north-west down the ridge of Sròn Gharbh and up the slight rise onto the splendid viewpoint at the end, Bod a' Mhadail (758m). Return up the ridge, then drop to the col with Creag nan Calman and make the short ascent onto the top of this fine, pointed peak.

Return to the col, then descend into the eastern corrie by the burn to either traverse across to join the ascent route for the climb over Meallan Diomhain, or traverse its south side to rejoin the path (**13.25km; 850m; 5h**).

Canisp with Suilven to its left from Breabag (Derek Sime)

Canisp; 847m; (C96); L15; NC203187; white hill

Like Suilven, its near neighbour, Canisp rises abruptly from a table-land of Lewisian gneiss. Also like Suilven, Canisp takes the form of a steep-sided ridge running from south-east to north-west. However, although higher by a considerable 115m, Canisp lacks the steepness and sharply serrated spine of Suilven, which makes the latter such an outstanding hill. Nevertheless, because of its isolation, Canisp gives a good ascent with excellent views of the other, more shapely Assynt hills and their rugged, watery landscape.

An approach can be made from either end of Canisp's whaleback ridge, although the route from Lochinver to the north-west is much longer. As a result, the standard route is from the A837 to the south-east.

Start from the north end of Loch Awe about 2.5 miles (4km) north of Ledmore, where there is a signed layby on the west side of the A837.

Follow a normally wet path south-west to cross a bridge over the outflow from Loch Awe. Continue by a boggy ATV track, which heads right-wards for a short way before swinging round over a slight rise to cross the flat ground beyond and ford the Allt Mhic Mhurchaidh Ghèir at an area of distinctive white stony ground.

The slope ahead is broad, and there are two lines to take. Perhaps best is to continue directly ahead by the path up the gentle slope, heading directly towards the summit. A line on the right leads towards the burn and is probably best used for the return.

The path leads up onto a small rise (Pt.307m), then rightwards across its top to drop down and follow a clear path to a section of slabs. Either climb the slabs or, if wet, the ground to the side, and continue in the same direction. The line soon becomes less distinct, but veers slightly right uphill across bouldery terrain, heading for the flat ground to the west of Meall Diamhain (562m). This is immediately left of its name on the OS map. Once there, a grassy line can be followed uphill between the scree and boulder fields to pass beneath an obvious low

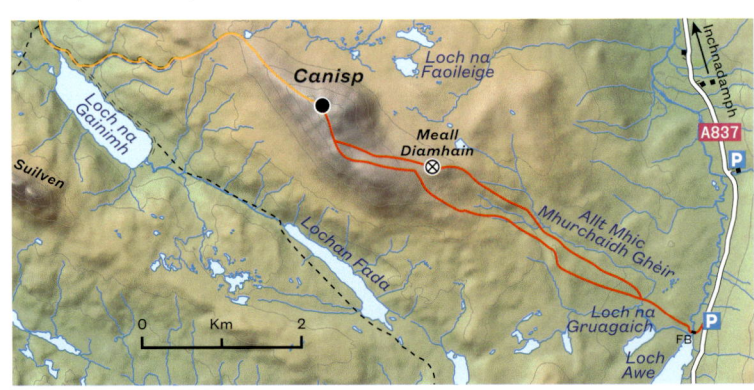

line of crag on the skyline to gain the left-hand ridge.

Continue over a small rise at 750m, then the dip beyond, and follow the path up the broad ridge to the summit boulder field and small cairn marking the highest point. The fine wind shelter 50m further on is lower, but being perched on the edge of the drop into the northern corrie, it offers the best views, especially of Suilven (**6.5km; 720m; 2h 45min**).

Return to the flat ground west of Meall Diamhain, either by the line of ascent, or by the grassy corrie and crossing the burn. Once there, either return via the ascent route, or better, climb onto Meall Diamhain, then descend east off this to follow a pleasant line down through slabby rocks and cross the burns just above where they join. A clear path then leads beneath Pt.307m and continues down above the cascading burn to join the approach line for the crossing of the Allt Mhic Mhurchaidh Ghèir (**13km; 750m; 4h 45min**).

The route from the north-west starts from the walkers' car park at NC107220, at the end of the public road from Lochinver to Glencanisp Lodge. This is also the starting point for some low-level walks, as well as the northern route to Suilven, of which there are some splendid views, so it can be busy.

Walk along the road to Glencanisp Lodge and pass behind this to follow the main track, past a path off left (The River Inver Loop). After 4.5km, pass the path off left to Suileag bothy and continue for 2km to cross a bridge over the river.

In another 700m, pass the path off right to Suilven, then cross back over the river by a bridge. In a further 430m, at a fork above Loch na Gainimh, go left and follow the fading track to where it effectively ends at a flat, boggy area at NC188194, almost beneath Canisp's north ridge.

Continue on a much vaguer grassy track, which leads to a small lochan at the foot of the ridge, then climb the ridge to the summit, passing from sandstone rock to quartzite rock (**11.75km; 940m; 4h 10min**).

Return the same way (**23.5km; 1080m; 7h 15min**).

Looking up the Allt nan Uamh past Creag nan Uamh to Breabag (Rab Anderson)

Breabag; 815m; (C131); L15; NC286157; *little height*

Lying to the south-west of Conival and Ben More Assynt, Breabag forms a 6km-long broad ridgeline between the upper reaches of Glen Oykel to the east and the A837 from Ledmore to Inchnadamph to the west. The highest point of this ridge-line sits towards the centre and currently has no name against it on the OS 1:50k map, apart from Creag Liath (*grey cliff*). However, this name applies to the crags and scree slopes to the south-west that make Breabag's rounded mass identifiable on the approach by road from Elphin to Ledmore, and from the entrance to the marble quarry just north of there.

These grey screes, and the broken cliffs of Breabag's hidden eastern corries, are composed of quartzite, however, the approach to the hill from the west passes through the glen of the Allt nan Uamh, where Durness limestone predominates.

There is a car park at NC253179, just off the A837 on the north side of the bridge across the Allt nan Uamh, at the entrance to the glen. This is also the parking for the Bone Caves of Creag nan Uamh some 2km up the

glen, which are a popular tourist attraction gained by a well-used and, in places, improved path.

Bones of long-extinct mammals were found in the caves, providing evidence of the presence of early man. The caves are shallow, but it is perhaps worth taking a torch to have a look on the return. There is a more substantial cave system in the Allt nan Uamh (*burn of the caves*) streambed, and cave entrances on the hillside above, which are of interest to speleologists, who may be spotted disappearing into, and emerging from, holes in the ground.

Follow the path uphill past a waterfall and the tumbling Allt nan Uamh, soon crossing the Fuaran Allt nan Uamh resurgence. This is a fine feature where the burn wells up from underground.

With Breabag rising ahead, continue on the path past where the main streambed becomes dry. Pass the path off right up to the Bone Caves in the cliff of Creag nan Uamh, then continue to a fork in the glen. On the right is another dry streambed and

▶

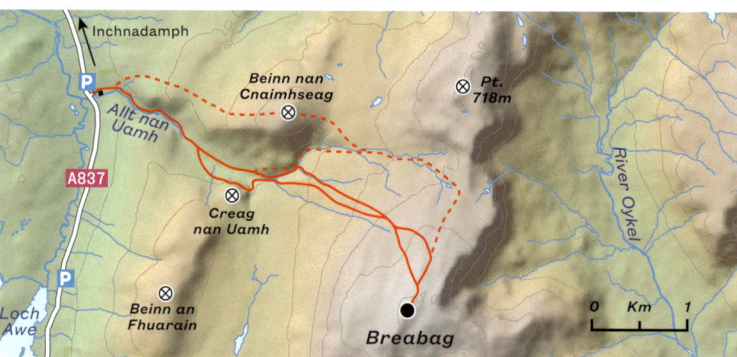

the location of An Claonaite, the longest cave system in Scotland.

Cross to the other side here, as for the loop path to the Bone Caves. It is possible to go up the spur above the loop path to access the hill, but the better route continues left up the main streambed in the narrowing, steep-sided glen, crossing a burn on the right after 250m. The north side of this burn is used by the descent, but it can be ascended for an easier route, especially if it's wet, to avoid water and slippery boulders in the streambed.

Continuing up the main streambed, though, and crossing from one side to the other, for a further 200m gains the small entrance hole to the Allt na Uamh Stream Cave on the left. This leads into one of the most complex subterranean mazes and best known sporting caves in Scotland.

In a further 100m, having crossed a small burn on the right, a rock step with a fine waterfall prevents further progress up the streambed.

Ascend steeply up the right side, away from the fall, to follow the small burn eastwards. Pass the left side of a boulder field, then swing gradually south-east to ascend steepening ground to the left (north) of a slabby escarpment with a waterfall. This leads into a shallow basin called the Fuarain Ghlasa.

Continue up through bouldery terrain to gain the crest and follow this to the right (southwards), passing two lower knolls, which lie to the left, to reach the summit cairn with a wind shelter just to its south (**5km; 675m; 2h 20min**).

Return almost the same way. It is possible to follow less stony ground on the east side of the crest before

swinging round back down past the waterfall to the lower boulder field. Pass either side of this and continue down between the two burns to go around the edge of a large sinkhole, then descend the side of the southern burn to the Allt nan Uamh. Return to the start, perhaps utilising the loop path to visit the Bone Caves (**10.5km; 755m; 4h**, including caves).

A longer route provides a circuit by continuing down the ridge northwards from the summit for 1.4km to gain the bealach at 631m with the North Top (Pt.718m). There are small lochans below this, to the east and west. Descend to the north-west past the small lochan there and go down the upper reaches of the Allt nan Uamh, where there are two options:

(i) Continue down beside the burn as it swings south and pick up a path or animal track on the west side, which is then followed across the slope above the rock step with the waterfall. Take the higher, or lower, traverse line across the slope, then drop to the main approach path and return along this (**11.25km; 675m; 4h**).

(ii) Traverse out north-west towards the col with Beinn nan Cnaimhseag at 459m then climb to its 570m summit. Descend westwards, crossing flat ground at the bottom, then swing round and drop west down the lower slopes to join the path just before the car park (**10.75km; 790m; 4h 15min**).

Breabag's North Top (Pt.718m) is worth including for the rugged terrain and views of the eastern corries, but unless the traverse is to be continued to Inchnadamph, which requires transport between start and finish, a way will have to be found down the craggy western slopes, or a return made to the bealach to descend.

An eye-catching spectacle from any direction, Quinag, with its three distinct peaks, is one of the great mountains of the North West. Its prows, rocky features and steep slopes give the mountain a formidable appearance. However, its three summits can be gained with relative ease to give a memorable experience, and one of the best mountain traverses in Scotland.

One of the most dramatic views of Quinag is from the north, where the rock prows of Sàil Gharbh and Sàil

Gorm tower above the sea at Kylesku. From the west, it appears as a long wall of cliff, and it is only to the south-east where there is a chink in the mountain's armour, and it is from there, at the convenient highpoint of the A894 between Loch Assynt and Kylesku, that the ascent is made.

There is a large car park on the east side of the road at NC233274 beneath Glas Bheinn, 40m to the north of the start of a stalkers' path on the opposite side. Traffic travels fast on this road, and care should be taken when leaving the car park.

Spidean Còinich, the first peak on the traverse, faces the car park, and the line of ascent can be clearly seen up its broad south-east ridge, whose northern edge is marked by crags.

Cross the road and follow the stalkers' path to the top of the initial rise, where the angle eases, then traverse left on a path past a small lochan to reach the east ridge.

▶

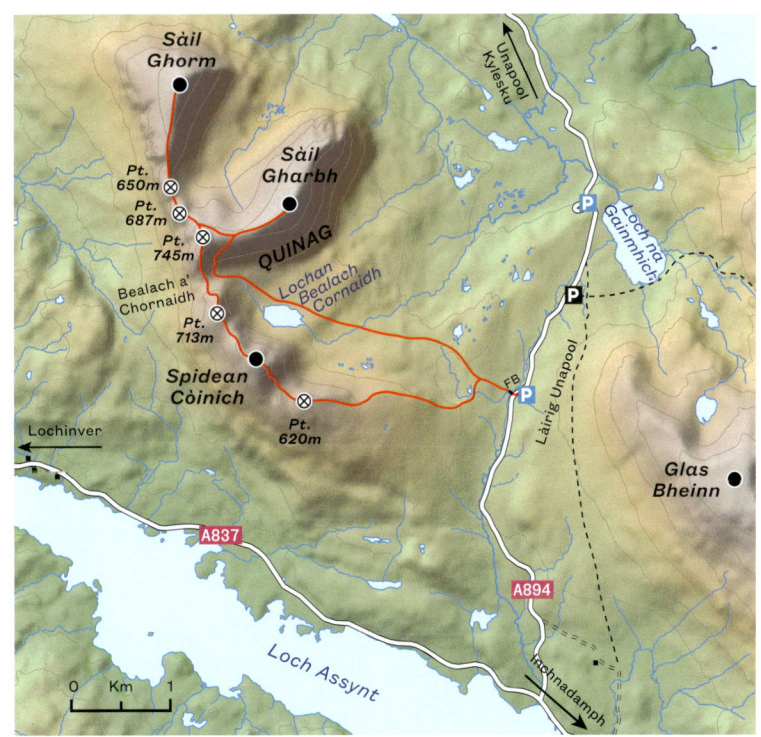

Quinag's western ramparts – Sàil Ghorm, Sàil Gharbh and Spidean Còinich (Robert Durran)

Spidean Còinich, Pt.713m, Pt.745m and Sàil Gharbh from the initial approach (Robert Durran)

The ascent is a delight, linking sections of lovely, smooth, slabby rock on the tilted quartzite strata, in places littered with boulders. Cross the bouldery top of Pt.620m and go through a gap in a band of rock, then cross the dip beyond and zigzag steeply, but easily, up the final cone to the splendid top of Spidean Còinich. This sits above cliffs to the north-east with a big drop to idyllic Lochan Bealach Cornaidh (**3.75km; 550m; 1h 50min**).

Head southwards for about 30m, then drop steeply west off the summit on a path, which turns north, and go down the ridge to cross a col above a small lochan, Lochan Ruadh. Climb onto the North Top (Pt.713m), then go along the airy crest and follow a twisting path steeply down to the left, then straight on down to the Bealach a' Chornaidh (c.575m).

Continue on the path, which zigzags steeply up to pass through a band of sandstone, then climb more easily across the slope onto Sàil Gharbh's West Top (Pt.745m). This is the central point of the Quinag massif, from which the arms of its three ridges radiate out to the north, east and south.

Head north-west and zigzag down to another col to the side of the steep, sandstone-terraced south face of Pt.687m, which has a grassy flat top. It is possible to make an easy climb to the top of this, but a return will have to be made the same way to avoid its craggy north side. Traverse across the east side of Pt.687m on the path, then make a short scramble down through rocks to another col.

Continue across the slight rise of Pt.650m, and the dip beyond, before finally following the easy ridge past the head of a gully and on up to the top of the spectacular prow of Sàil Ghorm (**7.25km; 950m; 3h 50min**).

It is worth continuing a little further north to appreciate the steep drop to the sea at Loch a' Chàirn Bhàin and the Kylesku Bridge, as well as for the view north to Foinaven and Arkle.

Spidean Còinich, Sàil Gharbh and Sàil Ghorm from the north-east (Rab Anderson)

Spidean Còinich and Pt.713m from the ascent to Pt.745m, with Conival, left, and Canisp, right (Rab Anderson)

Return the same way and climb partway up Pt.745m, then take the path that traverses up and left across the slope. This gains the broad saddle with Sàil Gharbh, from where a pleasant ascent over flat sandstone boulders leads to its quartzite-capped summit and the highest point of Quinag. The boulder 15m to the north-west is higher than where the trig point sits (**10.25km; 1160m; 5h**).

Return to the saddle, then follow the path down and across the slope towards the Bealach a' Chornaidh, and the imposing sight of Spidean Còinich with its pointed North Top.

Just before the bealach, the path loops round and descends into the corrie out to the north of Lochan Bealach Cornaidh for a pleasant walk back (**15km; 1165m; 6h 30min**).

Sàil Ghorm from Sàil Gharbh (Rab Anderson)

Glas Bheinn across Loch na Gainmhich (Rab Anderson)

Glas Bheinn; *776m; (C195); L15; NC254264; grey hill*

Being surrounded by the grander peaks of Assynt means that Glas Bheinn is often overlooked. This is a pity, for the walk to its summit and the views obtained make it a very worthwhile and pleasant outing.

Although seen ahead when travelling north towards Inchnadamph on the A837, it is the shapely Quinag to its left that catches the eye. However, when travelling southwards past Quinag on the A894, Glas Bheinn reveals its attractive side.

There are two routes, a shorter one from the road to the north and a longer one from Inchnadamph to the south. Both have their merits.

For the route from the north, start from a pull-off on the east side of the road at NC238284, where a path leaves the road and there is space for about three cars. This is opposite the south end of Loch na Gainmhich, and just north of the highest point of the A894 between Loch Assynt and Kylesku, 1.25km north of the car park for Quinag. There is another pull-off on the west side of the road 270m to the north, and on the right a further 400m to the north.

Head east on the path, which goes around the south end of Loch na Gainmhich, but leave it after 140m and follow another path south for about 500m. Leave this path and climb a grassy runnel up the steep hillside to gain the crest of the ridge; there is a rough path. Follow the fine crest up the edge overlooking Coire Dearg and curve round above the back wall of this corrie before heading south-east across flat ground to gain the large cairn on the bouldery summit (**3km; 525m; 1h 30min**).

Returning the same way is the quickest (6km; 525m; 2h 25min).

However, a circuit can be made by heading south-east to the edge of Coire Gorm, then following this round to descend a path north-east down the ridge to reach a col, Bealach na h-Uidhe. The stalkers' path from Inchnadamph arrives here and crosses over. Follow this path, initially down to the north, then eastwards above a small lochan before turning north-eastwards to reach the north end of a small lochan. When the path forks on the far side of the lochan, take the left-hand path and follow it down north, then north-west, up and over a rise to reach a burn issuing from another small lochan.

Glas Bheinn's north ridge above Coire Dearg (Rab Anderson)

From here, it is possible to make a there-and-back diversion to view the Eas a' Chùal Aluinn, Britain's highest waterfall, by following a path down this side of the burn. Don't take the path down the far (north) side that's marked on the map, since this leads to the lip of the fall and only gives a limited view. The path down the south side leads to a better, and a safer, viewpoint; an added 1.75km, 100m, 40min detour.

Continuing the descent, cross the burn and make a 155m climb uphill on the path, west-north-west, then drop to Loch Bealach a' Bhùirich. Descend above the burn issuing from the loch and keep an eye out for where the path forks, then go left (south) across the burn and follow that path across the south end of Loch na Gainmhich back to the start (**12.25km; 755m; 4h 15min**).

The route from the south starts from the car park next to the Inchnadamph Hotel on the east side of the A837. The first kilometre is the same as for the approach to Conival and Ben More Assynt.

Follow the A837 verge north to cross the bridge over the River Traligill, then go up the road on the right. Pass Inchnadamph Lodge and the houses, then continue on a track.

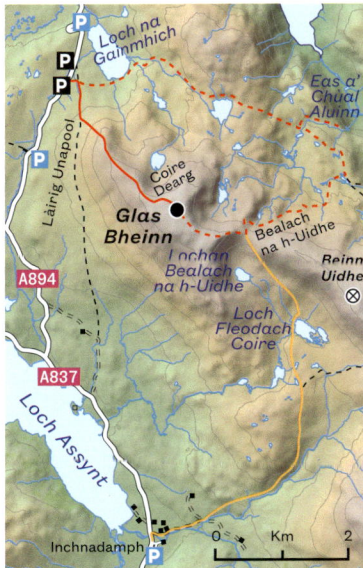

About 30m past a track off to the left, and before the track crosses the Allt Poll an Droighinn, follow a path up the grassy hillside on the left. The path becomes more defined a short way on, and is a good stalkers' path that runs all the way across the east side of Glas Bheinn. It is also the path followed by the Cape Wrath Trail long-distance walk.

The path makes a gradual ascent above the Allt Poll an Droighinn before swinging away north onto the

shoulder of Cnoc an Droighinn, where Glas Bheinn comes into view and the path forks at a small shelter. Take the left-hand path and continue past a small lochan on the left, then another on the right, to climb over a slight rise and drop to the west end of Loch Fleodach Coire. There is some wet ground here and two burns to cross.

Leaving the loch, the path climbs again and is clear for a short way. Where it becomes indistinct, it veers slightly right on wet ground. The path is there though, and it soon swings leftwards, becoming clearer, to make a rising traverse up the hillside; there are two path lines, with the higher one being better. On the traverse above Loch Bealach na h-Uidhe keep below a boulder field and continue up grassy ground to its left to gain the col. This is the Bealach na h-Uidhe, where the path drops over the other side.

Follow a zigzag path up the narrowing ridge on the left, through scree and boulders, to gain the plateau, then follow the edge of the corrie to the north, Coire Gorm, for a way. Cross a dip, then ascend north-west over increasingly bouldery ground to reach the large cairn on the summit (**8km; 770m; 3h**).

Return the same way (**16km; 835m; 5h 10min**).

Glas Bheinn from the Inchnadamph path to the Bealach na h-Uidhe (Tom Prentice)

Beinn Leòid from the approach over the foot of Meallan a' Chuail's north ridge (Rab Anderson)

Beinn Leòid; *792m; (C170); L15; NC320295; McLeod's hill*

Only partly visible from the road-side in a few places along the A894 in the vicinity of Unapool and Kylesku, Beinn Leòid lies tucked away in a tract of remote hill country between the heads of Glen Coul and Gleann Dubh, to the north-east of the distinctive Stack of Glencoul.

Despite Beinn Leòid's elusive nature, the approach is relatively straightforward, linking stalkers' paths, although the section between these can give quite rough going if the best line is missed.

Start from the A838 single-track road, just west of its highest point at 126m between Loch More and Loch Merkland. There is a small parking area at NC358333 on the south side of the road at a passing place. This is the same start point for the route to Meall an Fheur Loch and Meallan a' Chuail, both Grahams, and since the route to Beinn Leòid passes these, they can be included.

Walk west for 100m and cross a wooden bridge over a small burn to follow a stalkers' path which zigzags south up the steep hillside. The path levels-out and drops slightly across a shallow basin between the Grahams, passing the south end of a tiny lochan, Lochain a' Chuail. The path then rises slightly again, turning past some pools, to end at the start of Meallan a' Chuail's broad north ridge.

Beinn Leòid can be seen to the south-west, but to reach the stalkers' path leading to it, which comes up the glen below, Srath nan Aisinnin, rough ground has to be crossed.

The best line, which is easier to find on the return, is to head south up the high ground of the ridge for about 500m to the 480/490m contour. Drop off the ridge from there to make a diagonal traverse down and across the hillside to the south-south-west via a grassy ramp-line. Towards the bottom, pass to the left of a small hummock and continue to join the stalkers' path. Follow this path past Loch Dubh and zigzag up to the Drochaid Beinn Leòid col (546m),

between Meallan a' Chuail and Beinn Leòid, where the stalkers' path ends.

A rough hill path leads on up the long, but easy, east ridge of Beinn Leòid, past a tall cairn, then on up to the stone trig point sat within a stone wind shelter on the bouldery summit above north facing Glas Choire (**8km; 760m; 3h 10min**).

It is another splendid viewpoint, with the range from Ben More Assynt and Conival in the south, past Glas Bheinn, to Quinag in the west being particularly notable, along with the view to the north and north-east, which includes all five of the Reay Forest Corbetts.

Returning the same way is the simplest option, ensuring that at the col the correct path is taken leading to the descent back to Loch Dubh (**16km; 850m; 5h 30min**).

The other option is to follow the path across the col and ascend the increasingly bouldery slope to the top of Meallan a' Chuail. Descend the north ridge, then towards the bottom, swing round and traverse past the south end of Loch Cùl a' Mhill, and climb to Meall an Fheur Loch. Descend north-north-west to rejoin the stalkers' path for the descent to the road (**17km; 1140m; 6h 30min**).

A lengthy approach can be made along the north side of Loch Glendhu, from the car park just off the A894 at Kylestrome. A track can be biked easily for some 4km, but then it becomes rougher with ups and downs where it runs beside the loch, which walker-bikers are unlikely to appreciate. The track passes Glendhu bothy and continues up Gleann Dubh to end in haggy ground north of Beinn Leòid. Ascend the north ridge over Sàil na Slataich (**15km; 950m; 5h** on foot) and return the same way (**30km; 1150m; 9h** on foot).

It may also be possible to approach Beinn Leòid via Glen Coul by boat up Loch Glencoul from Kylesku. Enquire at the pier by the hotel.

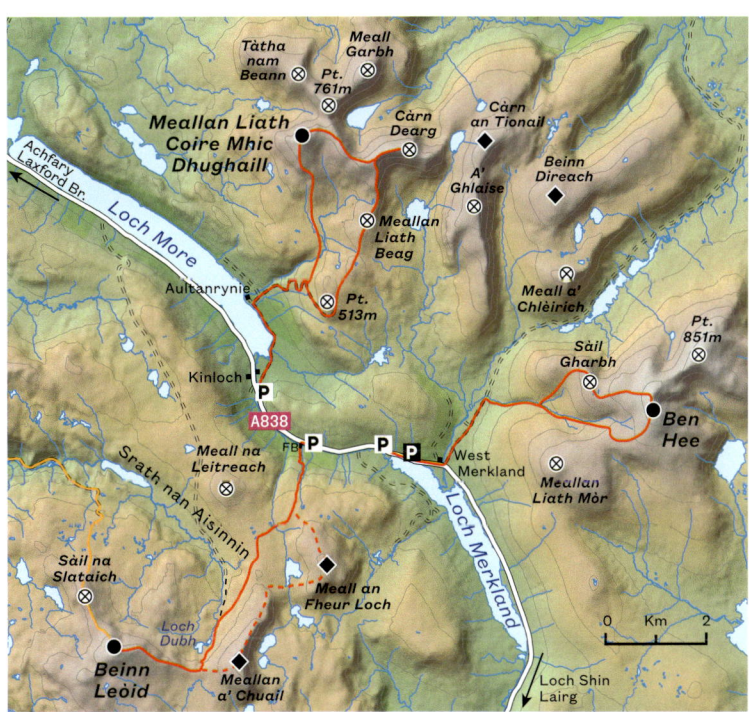

Ben Hee; 873m; (C60); L16; NC426339; fairy hill

Appearing as a big rounded hill from most viewpoints, Ben Hee and its subsidiary tops rise above Loch Merkland at the eastern edge of the Reay Forest. It is from West Merkland, towards the north end of Loch Merkland, that the approach is made to ascend the hill via its long western corrie, Coire a' Chruiteir.

The approach track leaves the A838 single-track road at the cottage at West Merkland, but there is no parking there. The nearest suitable parking is 1km to the west at the north end of Loch Merkland where there is a sizeable parking area on the north side of the road at NC373331. There is a single off-road space on the north side, 500m closer to the start. The parking and the track are also used for the ascent of Càrn an Tionail and Beinn Direach, the Grahams that lie to the north-west of Ben Hee.

Walk down the road past the cottage and cross the bridge over the Allt nan Albannach, then go through a gate and follow the track uphill for 1.5km. About 80m before the track crosses the burn issuing from Coire a' Chruiteir, take to a stalkers' path on the right and follow this uphill beside the Allt Coire a' Chruiteir. It is quite rough and boggy in places, and the path crosses some sections that have been washed out.

The path emerges into the shallow upper part of the corrie, to effectively end at a flattening. A rough hill path leads on for a way, up and across the slope ahead, to emerge onto the shoulder of the hill above the Drochaid Coire nam Mang; the col with Meallan Liath Mòr to the south-west and Coire nam Mang to the south.

With views opening out, continue up towards the large, rounded dome of the upper section and climb this. Higher up the ground changes to extensive areas of remarkably flat scree and boulders, which lead to the trig point enclosed within a small stone wind shelter, on the edge of the drop into An Gorm-choire, the great eastern corrie, with the 851m North-East Top on the far side. The cairn some 30m or so to the north-west is apparently lower (**6.75km; 765m; 2h 45min**).

It is a fine panoramic viewpoint.

South is Ben Wyvis, then closer at hand Ben More Assynt and Conival and the tops of the Assynt hills including Suilven. Closer is Beinn Leòid with Glas Bheinn beyond and Quinag to its side, then to the north-west Ben Stack and the other Reay Corbetts; Meallan Liath Coire Mhic Dhughaill, Arkle, Foinaven and Meall Horn. There is also a good view north down Strath More to Ben Hope with Ben Loyal off to the right and finally east to Ben Klibreck.

Although the simplest return is by the route of ascent, or over Meallan Liath Mòr to make a direct descent to West Merkland, it is perhaps better to descend the stony slope north-west then west to a shallow col with some small pools. From there, make a slight ascent north onto Sàil Gharbh (677m), then weave west down through stony ground towards the col with Pt 582m, until easier grassy ground is reached, then descend southwards and ford the burn (normally easy) to regain the stalkers' path, which is followed back (**13.5km; 780m; 4h 35min**).

Map above, photo next page

Ben Hee from Sàil Gharbh (Rab Anderson)

Meallan Liath Coire Mhic Dhughaill from north of Pt.513m on the approach, with Arkle, left (Rab Anderson)

Meallan Liath Coire Mhic Dhughaill; 801m; (C159); L15 & L16; NC357391; grey hill of MacDougall's corrie

Filling the high ground above and to the north-east of Loch More, from where its summit appears as a broad dome, Meallan Liath Coire Mhic Dhughaill is the highest point of a complex hill massif of radiating spurs, tops and corries. Its remote and finely sculpted northern corries are lined with crags, but the approach from the south is more accommodating and gives pleasant walking.

Start to the south of Kinloch at the south-east end of Loch More, where a track leaves the A838 single-track road at NC348343. There is space to park on the south side of the track entrance, or off the road at the second passing place to the south.

Follow the track to Aultanrynie, passing the small Cladh an Lòin Lèith burial ground, and with Ben Stack prominent in the view up the loch. Just before reaching the house, go up a wide track on the right to where it crosses a bridge to traverse the hillside. Go up right here and follow an old grassy track which zigzags uphill, then makes a long rising traverse to the south-east before curving around Pt.513m to climb north to end at a cairn and small stone wind shelter.

Traces of an ATV track can now be followed for a short way. Traverse up and across the side of the next minor rise, then cross a dip to climb over Pt.527m, the South Top of Meallan Liath Beag, with its tiny lochan.

Drop to a narrow col (Bealach Fir Ashair), then climb up and along the broad crest of Meallan Liath Beag (567m). Cross the slight dip beyond, then ascend the fine ridge ahead, weaving through minor rock outcrops to reach the stony crest.

It is worth making the detour eastwards to the top of Càrn Dearg (797m), where there are fine views south down the steep headwall into the corrie holding Loch Ulbhach Coire, as well as east to the Graham Càrn an Tionail.

Return westwards and descend the broad ridge, across a mix of grass and ground littered with flat slabs of rock, to a broad saddle at the head of lovely Coire a' Phris to the north, which holds the finely situated Coire Loch. Go over the slight rise of Pt.741m, then cross more stony ground and grass at a broad saddle to swing round and climb the stone-strewn north-east ridge. This runs above west facing Coire Mhic Dhughaill and leads to the trig point and stone wind shelter on top of Meallan Liath Coire Mhic Dhughaill (**10.75km; 940m; 4h**).

Descend by heading south-west then south, down easy and mainly grassy slopes on the left side of the south ridge, which kinks to the left partway down. At the bottom, cross the flat ground of the Poll an Reinidh via a raised rocky pavement. Cross a small burn, passing through some minor peat hags, and keep heading in the same direction to cross the Allt an Reinidh before it flows through a narrow gorge. It is a fairly substantial burn, but under normal conditions the crossing should be straightforward. Ascend the other side, cross flat ground, then descend grassy slopes to regain the approach track just before the zigzags and return to the start (17.75km; 960m; 6h).

Map on page 345

Meallan Liath Coire Mhic Dhughaill from the descent off Càrn Dearg (Rab Anderson)

Meall Horn; 777m; (C194); L9; NC352449; hill of the eagle

One of the Reay Forest group of Corbetts located in North-West Sutherland, Meall Horn sits between and behind its more shapely neighbours – Foinaven, Arkle and Meallan Liath Coire Mhic Dhughaill – which serve to shield its bland and rounded features from view. It does provide a good outing though, with splendid views of its neighbours, and the route can be adjusted to include Sàbhal Beag, the Graham to the east, or extended to include Arkle for an arduous two-Corbett day.

The start point is the same as for Arkle, at the southern tip of Loch Stack, 750m to the north of Achfary where a track leaves the east side of the A838 single-track road. There is parking about 100m down this track beside the bridge over the river.

Cross the bridge and follow the surfaced estate road to Airdachuilinn, then the continuation track past a barn and across the bridge to the derelict cottage at Lone.

Whilst only 3km, a bike can be used to here to provide a rapid approach and return, saving about 50min on the overall time given.

At the fork in the track, go right and follow the track beside the Abhainn an Lòin for 1.5km, up to the gap in the craggy ridge ahead. Leave the track here and climb north up grassy slopes, then follow the broad, easy-angled ridge, curving round to climb the steeper ridge of Sàil an Taghain. This leads to a pleasant traverse along the 1km-long crest of Creachan Thormaid.

At the end of the crest, drop to the rocky Cadha Cumhann col with its two small lochans, then climb the broad and mainly grassy slope to gain the flat summit crest of Meall Horn. The cairn lies a short way to the left, above a steep drop into the wild and rugged Coire Lochan Ulbha (**9.5km; 830m; 3h 30min**).

Notable in the view to the north-east is the great whaleback of Ben Hope. To the north is Loch Eriboll with Cranstackie and Beinn Spionnaidh to the left, then a fine view north-west along the Foinaven ridge. Arkle looks splendid, as does Meallan Liath Coire Mhic Dhughaill with its attendant peaks and surrounding corries to the south-east.

Descend north-west towards Creagan Meall Horn, down a delightful slope of thin slabs of rock, to reach a broad col. It is worth making the 15min or so there-and-back diversion to the top of Creagan Meall Horn (731m).

From there, it is possible to descend to the north-west to gain the track at the Bealach Horn, but the slope is steep and shale-like, and care should be taken to keep north-west towards Foinaven to avoid the craggy slopes to the west. Although not that difficult, this is probably an easier slope to negotiate in ascent.

For the standard descent from the col between Meall Horn and Creagan Meall Horn, descend the grassy slope south-west, following the drainage line to pass the end of a rocky band that extends northwards to form the crags on the west side of Creagan Meall Horn. The best line from here is to then slant down north-west across the slope, aiming to gain the track coming down from the Bealach Horn

Meall Horn with Creagan Meall Horn to its left, from the long crest of Creachan Thormaid (Rab Anderson)

Meall Horn from Creagan Meall Horn with Meallan Liath Coire Mhic Dhughaill, right (Rab Anderson)

at a flat section in front of an unnamed lochan. Follow the track above the Allt Horn back to Lone then the start (**19km; 860m; 6h**).

A quick alternative route is to go up the Allt Horn track from Lone; it can be biked to the boulders in front of a small plantation. At the flat section in front of the unnamed lochan, the easiest option is to slant up right around the rocky band to gain the summit and return the same way.

However, a better route is to continue up the track to the Bealach Horn. Follow the track around the base of the slope a short way to just in front of some boulders, then climb the slope above, up left initially, to zigzag up onto the top of Creagan Meall Horn. This slope is easier than it looks at first and, although quite steep, there is no real difficulty.

Drop down and climb to Meall Horn (**10.5km; 840m; 3h 45min**).

Descend as for the principal route, back to the col, then down and around the foot of the rocky band to regain the track at the unnamed lochan and return (**20.25km; 870m; 6h 15min**).

To include Arkle from either of the above routes, from the unnamed lochan, ascend the bouldery ridge to pass south of Loch na Faoileige and climb to Meall Aonghais, then to

Pt.758m and the summit of Arkle.

Return to Pt.758m, descend south to the track, and return to the start; an added 6.25km; 610m; 2h 35min.

The inclusion of Sàbhal Beag, the Graham to the east, with Meall Horn is a very good and less arduous outing. To do so, follow the track from Lone eastwards alongside the Abhainn an Lòin to the Bealach na Fèithe, then climb to 732m-high Sàbhal Beag (**11km; 750m; 3h 40min**).

Head north-westwards, then descend to the Bealach Eadar da Shàbhal and climb to Sàbhal Mòr (703m). From there, head north then north-west along the ridge to Meall Horn (**14.25km; 980m; 5h**).

Descend as for the principal route (**23.75km; 1010m; 7h 30min**).

See the end of the Arkle route description on page 351 for the note on the hidden gem of the Eas Allt Horn, which lies a short distance off the path and is worth viewing on the return from Meall Horn.

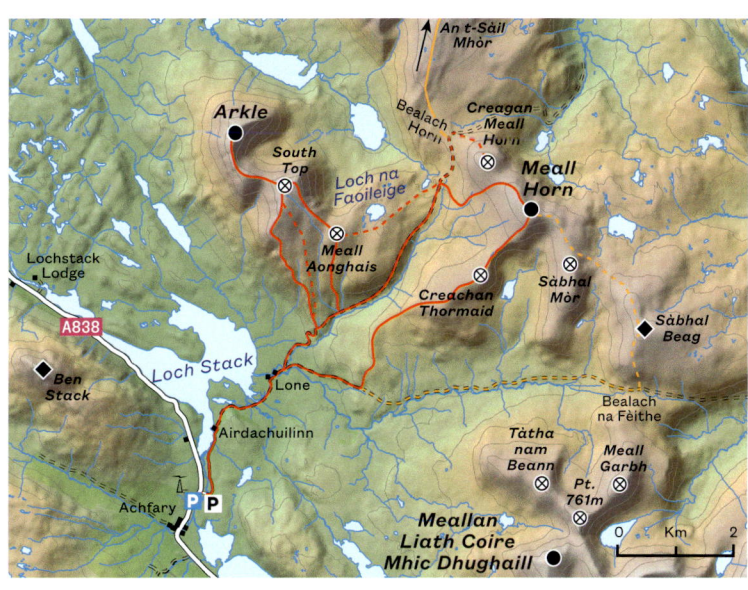

Arkle across Loch Stack (Rab Anderson)

Arkle; *787m; (C180); L9; NC302461; peak of the chest*

Scoured by glaciation and the processes of weathering, Arkle rises majestically above Loch Stack opposite Ben Stack. It is a beautiful mountain and one of the highlights of walking in the Far North. Despite its steep and impregnable-looking nature when viewed from the north and west, the route of ascent up its tapered southern flank is quite straightforward, passing through satisfyingly rugged terrain.

The start point is the same as for Meall Horn, at the southern tip of Loch Stack, 750m to the north of Achfary, where a track leaves the east side of the A838 single-track road. There is parking about 100m down this track, by the bridge over the river.

Cross the bridge and follow the surfaced estate road to Airdachuilinn then the continuation track past a barn and across the bridge to the derelict cottage at Lone. At the fork, take the left-hand track leading to a small forestry plantation and pass between two huge boulders forming a gateway. Whilst only 3.5km, a bike can be used to here to provide a rapid approach and return, saving about 1h on the overall time given.

Beyond the trees, the track zigzags steeply uphill, then swings round over the start of the western escarpment and levels off. A small cairn here marks the start of a rough path which climbs left up grassy ground. At the lowest rocks the path forks, and if going up this way, the better option is the less-travelled route up left to follow the edge of the escarpment, rather than the cairned route up the right side of a shallow basin. However, whilst an ascent can be made up either of these, a better circuit is described, with a descent being made this way.

Continue on the track, immediately crossing one burn, then in a further 450m crossing another; the Allt na Dige Mòire. Leave the track immedi-ately after crossing, then follow a rough path up the hillside between this burn and another to the east. The path peters out in rocky ground, which is climbed to gain the top of Meall Aonghais (581m) where Foinaven is splendidly revealed across An Garbh-choire and Loch an Easain Uaine. There is also a fine view across the high Lochan na Faoileige to Creagan Meall Horn and Meall Horn in rounded contrast.

Over to the left, the eroded and washed-out quartzite streambed of the upper Allt na Dige Mòire resem-bles a track running up the hillside. Drop to a shallow col and ascend the slight ridge to the right of the streambed, passing the head of an impressive deep and narrow gully plunging into An Garbh-choire, to gain the flat-topped South Top (758m).

The summit can now be seen on the far side of the deep glacial bowl of Am Bàthaich, and there is an even better view of Foinaven.

Descend a path north-west to the saddle between the tops and continue up the other side over a minor top. Curve around the back wall of the corrie, following the narrow blocky crest to the summit with some sense of exposure, at one point passing along a splendid flat pavement (**9km; 900m; 3h 40min**).

Return to the saddle and climb back to the South Top. Whilst it is possible to descend south from the saddle via Coire Uairidh and traverse beneath the cliffs of the western escarpment, it is better to stay high as long as possible to appreciate this special mountain and the views it offers. Head south along the crest for about 350m to its end, where there are two options:

(i) Perhaps the easiest is to head slightly left and descend, linking grassy patches leading to a rocky rib forming the left side of a shallow basin through which a small burn flows, the Allt Eason an t-Siabaidh; there is a rough, cairned path.

(ii) However, the better route drops slightly to the right, following a rough path close to the edge, to descend the length of the escarpment which is the defining feature of the mountain. En route, the heads of some gullies

Arkle's summit ridge pavement, with Loch Stack below (Rab Anderson)

are passed and there are fine views down to the cliffs and across Loch Stack to Ben Stack. It is possible to keep pretty much to the crest, although there are times when it is easier to follow grassy rakes to the side; there are traces of path here and there the whole way. Lower down, the route swings down and across the Allt Eason an t-Siabaidh at the foot of a shallow basin to join the route down the other side for the last little bit on

heathery and grassy ground to gain the track, which is followed back (**18km; 1010m; 6h 15min**).

On entering the small forestry plantation, it is worth going left to the Allt Horn to view the Eas Allt Horn waterfall, another fall lower down and a natural rock bridge; a hidden little gem. There is a vague path down the side, which rejoins the track just before the two boulders.

Map on page 349

Arkle's summit across Am Bàthaich from the South Top (Rab Anderson)

Looking up Coire Dùail to Ganu Mòr and Ceann Garbh (Rab Anderson)

FOINAVEN (FOINNE BHEIN); white hill
Ganu Mòr; (C8); 911m; L9; NC315507; big wedge or head

Sharing some similarities with mighty Beinn Eighe, Foinaven is another of Scotland's finest mountain massifs. Like Beinn Eighe, it too comprises a high-level ridge containing six principal peaks and, from its narrow crest, great sweeps of pale quartzite scree fall down uniformly steep slopes to give the mountain an air of impregnability. It is also similar in respect of what remains hidden from view from the roadside, for along the length of the mountain's eastern flanks above Srath Dionard, a series of spurs project from the main ridge to contain some large and fabulous corries. This grand mountain architecture is further enhanced along this eastern side by an abundance of rock and some massive cliff faces.

Ganu Mòr is the highest point, which sits towards the northern end of the main ridge. Two routes are described for gaining this summit, and two are described in the panel on page 354 for a fabulous traverse of all six principal summits on the ridge. Three of the routes start from the A838 single-track road between Rhiconich and Durness, which passes the mountain's northern end. The other route is a traverse from the A838 near Achfary to the south, passing

between Arkle and Meall Horn, which can be done either as a linear traverse or as a traverse with a return back the same way along the ridge.

The best route for attaining the summit of Ganu Mòr starts about 300m to the north of Gualin House, where there is space for a few cars in a pull-off on the west side of the road. A bike is useful for the initial 7km approach along an estate track.

Walk towards Gualin House and go through a gate, then along a section of track, and turn left down the track that drops into Srath Dionard to run alongside the River Dionard. The track passes beneath the cliffs of Cnoc a' Mhadaidh, then runs out in front of Coire Dùail, at the head of which Ganu Mòr can be seen.

Leave the track just before it crosses the Allt Coire Dùail (**7km; 70m; 50min** by bike), (**1h 40min** on foot). Distances and times are now given on foot, from and back to here.

Follow a rough path up the north side of the Allt Coire Dùail, which flows down the hillside in a series of lovely cascades and waterslides, to reach the lochan occupying the floor of Coire Dùail; although unnamed on maps, it is probably Lochan Dùail.

A decision now has to be made on whether to make a clockwise circuit

from here or an anticlockwise circuit. Although both ways are easier in ascent, an anticlockwise circuit is perhaps best, since the descent from the summit of Ganu Mòr is probably easier that way, albeit this is down a scree-covered ridge. The descent off Ceann Garbh is steeper, and the boulder fields towards its foot are probably more awkward in descent.

For the anticlockwise circuit, walk along the north side of the lochan, then follow either side of the inflow uphill, above a fine ravine with a waterfall, to reach a shallow basin. Follow the burn for a short way, then climb towards the foot of Ceann Garbh's east ridge by an obvious line up right beneath a band of rock. The best way through the initial boulder field, and another just above it, is slightly further to the right (north) on the broad lower part of the ridge, where there is grassier ground to link.

Above the boulder fields, the ridge narrows and steepens, making the route up it more defined and easier to follow. On the left, steep slopes plunge into the hanging corrie of Glas-Choire Grànda with its small lochan, and there are views across to Ganu Mòr. Towards the top, pass some large boulders, cross a grassy dip and curve round to the top of

Ceann Garbh (902m).

Descend the rocky crest south-wards, then curve eastwards and climb onto the level crest of Ganu Mòr. There are two cairns 150m or so apart; the first (western) cairn is the highest point (**5km; 880m; 2h 45min**).

Continue to the larger eastern cairn, which is a splendid viewpoint, and go down the narrow scree and block-strewn north-east ridge. There are traces of path and, although the angle is reasonable, progress is slow due to the unstable nature of the scree. When the scree ends, leave the north-east line down the ridge and go south-eastwards down a broad shelf interspersed with slabby rocks and boulders, making a traverse above the cliffs at the head of Coire Dùail. Drop down around the east end of the cliffs and follow a spur down next to the burn to reach the east end of the lochan and cross the outflow. Return down the path to the track (**9.25km; 880m; 4h 15min**).

Return to the road (**23.25km; 1100m; 6h** with a bike), (**7h 40min** on foot).

If not using a bike, a shorter route is possible from Gualin House by approaching via the Srath Dionard track and following the above route to the lochan in Coire Dùail. Take the clockwise option, which is to reverse the route described above. This crosses the outflow from the lochan, after passing the main burn flowing downhill to join it, then ascends the spur beside the burn. Ascend the broad shelf above the cliffs and climb the narrow scree-covered north-east ridge to the summit of Ganu Mòr (**11.25km; 880m; 4h 15min**).

Traverse across to Ceann Garbh and descend the broad slope of grass and boulders to the north-west, ensuring that a band of crags at the 440m contour are bypassed to the left (west). Once below these crags, take a direct line towards Gualin House, keeping to the higher and rockier ground. Thread through the pools and small lochans, then pass between Loch Tarbhaidh and Lochan Sgeireach to reach the road (**18.25km; 980m; 6h 30min**).

Another option, which is the quickest way of attaining the summit, is to park at NC284548, in small pull-

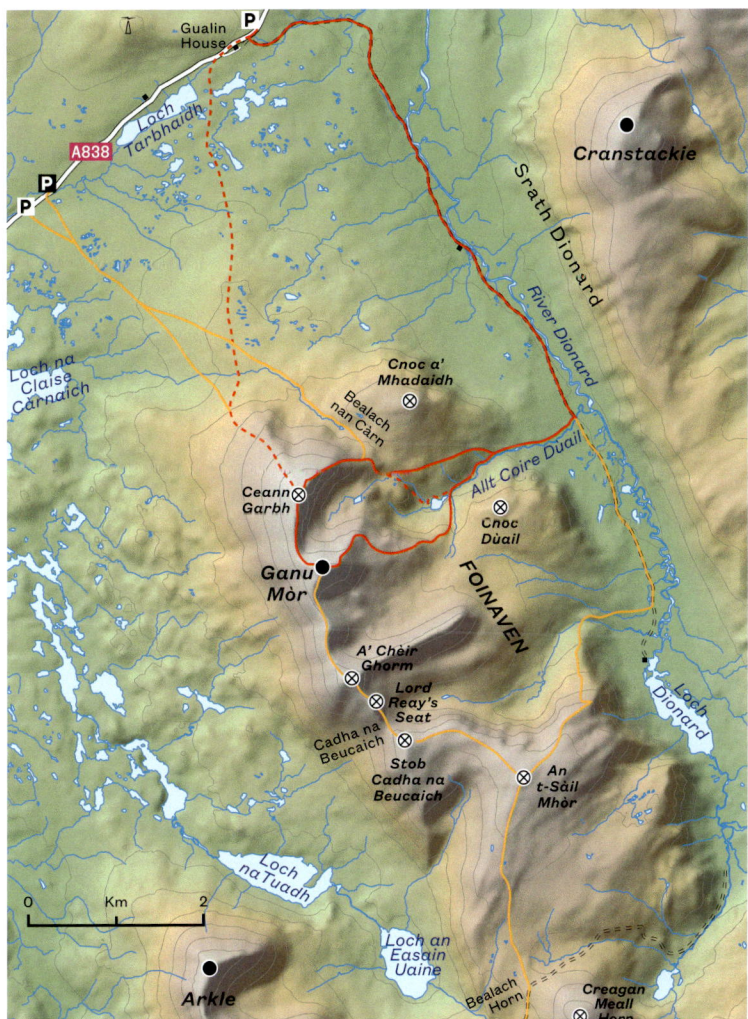

off on the west side of the road immediately north of the bridge over the Allt Loch Tarbhaidh, to the south of Loch Tarbhaidh and Gualin House. There is another pull-off on the east side of the road a few hundred metres to the south.

Walk across the bridge, then drop down and go through an area of old peat cuttings. Go up a rise, then cross flat ground past a small lochan, taking a direct south-easterly line across the moor. The ground is peppered with pools and tiny lochans, but after a week or so of dry weather it is possible to pick a way across and remain dry. The worst bit is the initial 200m after the rise above the road.

Continue across the moor, passing to the south of a cluster of lochans, and head to a small rock island at NC290540. From there, head south-

east, just above a shallow and wet basin into which a burn drains, aiming for an isolated large boulder on the slope ahead at NC298533.

Beyond the boulder, maintain the same direction for a short way, then gradually swing south across the Allt na Claise Càrnaich. Either ascend around the right side of the rocky ground ahead, or find a way through it by one of the steep heather and grass breaks. Above, firm ground gives good walking up the side of rocky ribs in the broad ridge descending from Ceann Garbh. Continue through the stony and bouldery upper slopes on grass to finally reach the top of Ceann Garbh.

Head south along the crest, descending gently to a point above the head of the deep bowl of Glas- ▶

Ceann Garbh, Ganu Mòr and A' Chèir Ghorm from Achriesgill to the north-west

Choire Grànda, then curve round and ascend easily to the summit. The highest point is the smaller first cairn, but it is worth making the 150m stroll to the larger cairn (**6km; 840m; 3h**).

Returning the same way is quickest and easiest, but from Ceann Garbh another option is to head north-east across a grassy dip to follow traces of rough path steeply down the north-east ridge towards Cnoc a' Mhadaidh below; initially through the boulders then down steep grass. Lower down, veer left to find the shortest way through the lower boulder fields, then swing northwards and descend into the narrow corrie beneath the Bealach nan Càrn. Pass a large boulder and tiny lochan, then follow the Allt na Claise Càrnaich (crossed earlier on the walk) for just over 1km until it veers away, and maintain the same north-west line, keeping to the higher ground to pass some 300m north of the isolated large boulder passed on the approach. Rejoin the approach line past the small rock island and return to the start (**13.5km; 900m; 5h 15min**).

This quicker route can also be done from Gualin House by reversing the descent route to there from Ceann Garbh as described on page 353, then descending the north-east ridge to the Bealach nan Càrn to rejoin the approach; perhaps 30min longer.

The traverse of all of Foinaven's tops is a superb expedition that ranks amongst the best of Scotland's mountain walks. There are two routes: one from the north, which is a circuit, and the other from the south, which is essentially a linear south-to-north traverse, although it can be done as a there-and-back the same way route.

Foinaven Circuit

*The circuit from the north starts as for the standard route from the pull-off just north of Gualin House. It is best undertaken with the aid of a bike for the initial 7km of track. Bike down into Srath Dionard and follow the track to the bridge across the Allt Coire Dùail (**7km; 70m; 50min** by bike), (**1h 40min** on foot). Distances and times are now given on foot, from and back to here.*

Continue along the track for another 2.4km, until just past a small lochan, then either slant up the hillside, or continue a little further, then ascend, making for the main burn issuing from Coire na Lurgainn. The objective is to ascend the broad north ridge of An t-Sàil Mhòr, which lies between the Creag Urbhard cliffs on the left and Coire na Lurgainn on the right. Although the line through the upper band of rock is not obvious at this point, and looks steep and intimidating, the way up the left side of a scree slope falling from the 550m contour can be seen.

Level with the base of the broad ridge, drop into the ravine carrying the Allt Coire Lurgainn and cross this burn, likely to be problematic in high water conditions. Ascend the other side, up and right, on deer tracks and continue up the ridge on deer tracks here and there, through heather and boulders, heading for the left side of the scree slope.

On reaching the scree, follow a more distinct line that slants rightwards up its left side to pass around the end of a band of rock, then zigzag up and slightly leftwards. Leave the scree and follow a rough line up left towards a perched boulder at the base of the upper rocks. The line continues more steeply, but easily, up a shallow depression in tight zigzags for 25m or so. Break out left on a line that leads to a rock ledge, then slant easily up left across the face with no handwork or exposure to reach a levelling on the skyline edge at the top.

*Continue rightwards up the edge with stupendous views to reach a minor unmarked 700m summit overlooking the corrie. Descend across the top of the grassy basin above the waterfall that drops into the corrie, then go up the other side and continue to the circular walled cairn on top of boulder-strewn An t-Sàil Mhòr, 778m, (**6km; 700m; 2h 45min**).*

Descend north-west across a broad saddle (716m) and cross stony ground, curving round towards Pt.808m; it is worth diverting to the edge now and again for the view into the corrie with its glacially sculpted floor and grand rock architecture. Ascend easily to the top of Pt.808m, Stob Cadha na Beucaich (**7.75km; 800m; 3h 20min**).

Carefully descend the boulder and scree-covered ridge to the north-west by a path. Just above the Cadha na Beucaich col, a small rock band is easily outflanked on the left (looking down) by a path, with the only real problem being the prospect of dislodging loose rock onto anyone below. A path leading to the centre, top and bottom, of the rock band indicates that many get led to a direct scramble that way.

Cross the col (c.685m) and follow the path steeply, but easily, up to gain the top of the impressive monolith of Lord Reay's Seat, which sits above a steep east-facing cliff. Descend the other side, then continue to the top of Pt.869m, A' Chèir Ghorm. This sits at the head of the fine and slender ridge which, along with Lord Reay's Seat, has captured the eye for much of the route (**9km; 1010m; 4h 15min**).

Descend to the north-west and follow the delightful ridge crest over a minor rise at the head of Bràigh a' Choire Leacaich, and curve round then up right to the large eastern cairn on top of Ganu Mòr. The highest point is the smaller cairn 150m or so to the west along the crest (**11km; 1150m; 5h**).

To complete the traverse, drop down and swing around the head of the deep bowl of Glas-Choire Grànda, then ascend to Ceann Garbh (902m), the final summit (**12km; 1215m; 5h 20min**).

To descend, swing round right across a grassy dip and up past a small tor-like outcrop, then follow a vague path, which weaves down through the upper rocks to reach grassier ground. Zigzag steeply down the grassy slope to the lower boulder field and head slightly left on grass to find the shortest and easiest route through this, then cut back right and descend grassier ground. Pick up a minor burn and descend a vague path down beside this, beneath rock outcrops, to gain the basin where the burn issuing from the corrie is joined.

There are now two options:

(i) Leave the burn and cross the basin, then traverse across the hillside beyond, below the boulder field, continuing down and across heathery ground. At a suitable point further along, cut down right to pick up the rough path alongside the Allt Coire Dùail and follow this pleasantly down past waterslides and cascades to the track.

(ii) Follow either side of the burn down above a gorge with a fine waterfall to reach the lochan, then traverse its north side and go down the rough path from the outflow to the track (**16km; 1225m; 6h 50min**).

Return to the road (*30km; 1345m; 8h 35min* with a bike), (*10h 15min* on foot).

If the entire circuit is done on foot from Gualin, from Ceann Garbh at the end of the ridge, it is quicker and shorter, by 5km, to descend the broad slope of grass and boulders to the north-west, ensuring that a band of crags at the 440m contour are bypassed to the left (west). Once below these, take a direct line towards Gualin House, keeping to the higher and rockier ground. Thread through the pools and small lochans to finally pass between Loch Tarbhaidh and Lochan Sgeireach to gain the road (*25km; 1320m; 9h*).

Foinaven Traverse

For the route from the south, start at the southern tip of Loch Stack, 750m to the north of Achfary, where a track leaves the east side of the A838 single-track road. There is parking about 100m down this track beside the bridge over the river. This is the starting point for the routes to Arkle and Meall Horn.

Cross the bridge and follow the surfaced estate road to Airdachuilinn, then the continuation track past a barn and across the bridge to the derelict cottage at Lone. Take the left-hand track leading to a small forestry plantation and pass between two huge boulders forming a gateway. If a return is to be made the same way, a bike can be used to here to provide a rapid approach and return, saving about 1h on the overall time given.

Follow the track through the trees and all the way to the Bealach Horn. Leave the track, then head northwards across boggy ground peppered with pools, to ascend a grassy line to the right (east) of the crest to avoid the boulder fields and gain the top of 778m-high An t-Sàil Mhòr (**11km; 780m; 3h 45min**).

From there, follow the route to Ganu Mòr as described in the above circuit (**16km; 1230m; 6h**).

Continue across the head of Glas-Choire Grànda to Ceann Garbh (**17km; 1295m; 6h 20min**).

For the linear route, descend the broad slope of grass and boulders to the north-west, ensuring that a band of crags at the 440m contour are bypassed to the left (west). Once below these, take a direct line towards Gualin House, keeping to the higher and rockier ground. Thread through the pools and small lochans to finally pass between Loch Tarbhaidh and Lochan Sgeireach to gain the road (*23km; 1330m; 8h 15min*).

Alternatively, once below the band of crags, head for a large boulder at NC298533, then direct to a pull-off by the bridge at NC284548 via a rock island at NC290540, as for the short route on page 353; about 10min quicker.

For a return to Lone and Achfary, reverse the route along the ridge, passing down the side of Lord Reay's Seat. After descending from Pt.808m to the col with An t-Sàil Mhòr, bypass this top to its right (west) by following a grassy line to the right of the crest, past a small lochan, to regain the Bealach Horn. Follow the track back to Lone, then the road (*33.5km; 1420m; 10h 10min* on foot); reduced by 2km, 140m 40min if the there-and-back to Ceann Garbh is not made, and by about 1h if a bike is used.

Map on page 353

Cranstackie across Calbhach Coire, with Foinaven beyond (Rab Anderson)

Cranstackie; *801m; (C158); L9; NC350556; rugged hill*
Beinn Spionnaidh; *773m; (C203); L9; NC362573; hill of strength*

Lying to the north of Foinaven, and rising steeply above the deep trench of Srath Dionard, which lies in between, these are the most northerly Corbetts and the most northerly high ground of any consequence in Britain. They are well seen from the A838 between Rhiconich and Durness, where the road descends from its highpoint past the entrance to Srath Dionard and the isolated house at Carbreck.

Cranstackie is the higher and more distinctive of the two hills, and is separated from Beinn Spioinnaidh to its north by a deep col, which provides the link between them.

Start from a pull-off on the north side of the road at NC330590, some 290m to the south-west of Carbreck and a track leading to the cottage and farm buildings at Rhigolter.

Walk down the road to the house and follow the track across the bridge over the River Dionard to Rhigolter. Pass through a pedestrian gate to the side of a small wooden building, and follow the track uphill to its end at a gate in a fence in front of a large boulder.

Beinn Spionnaidh and Cranstackie above Rhigolter Rab Anderson)

Cross the fence by a stile, then ascend to the upper fence. This fence has a top strand of barbed wire, so either go up left to pass through the northern gate in it, or go up right to pass through the southern gate.

Either way, ascend the slope beyond, up rightwards into Calbhach Coire. The left-hand gate leads to slightly higher ground on the left side of the corrie, whilst the right-hand gate leads one across the floor of the corrie, which is potentially a little boggier. There is no difference in distance, and both ways cross the burn, the Allt Chalbhach Coire, then join for the steeper climb beside the burn to gain the col between the hills. On this climb, a steep section in the middle can be passed either side. There are few signs of passage from the end of the track to this point.

Ascend the ridge on the right to meet a vague path leading down to the col on the left, then follow the path up and along a level section above the crags overlooking Calbhach Coire. Continue up the increasingly

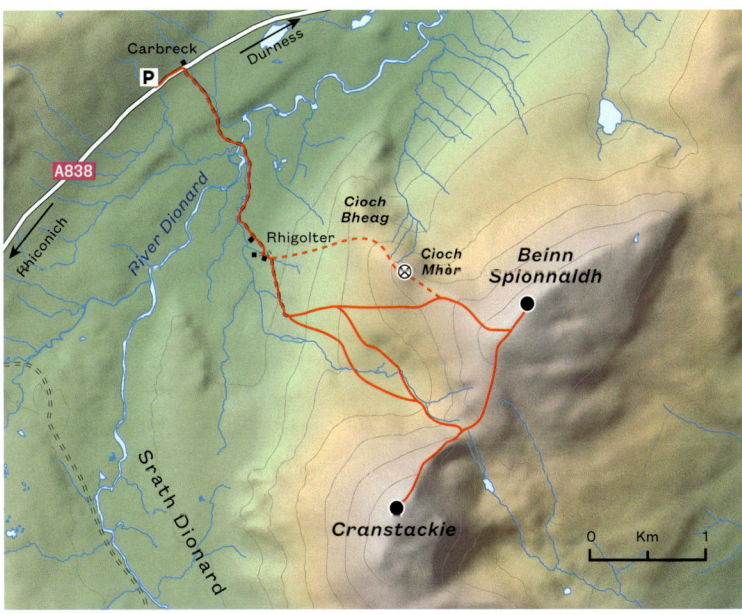

rocky slope ahead to weave up through a large boulder field onto the flatter summit area, then boulder-hop across this to the large summit cairn (**6km; 790m; 2h 55min**).

Return the same way to cross the

right side of the col (c.565m) between the hills and ascend the slope on the far side. Clamber through the boulder field at the top to reach a cairn on a slight rise, then continue across the flat top for a further 500m of boulder-hopping to reach the small stone wind shelter and trig point on the summit (**8.5km; 1005m; 4h 15min**).

Return towards the cairn on the slight rise and find a way down through the boulder field to the north-west to reach easier grassy slopes leading towards the col at 520m with pointed and grassy Cìoch Mhòr. There are two options here:

(i) Simply drop westwards down the easier-angled grassy slopes and go through the northern gate in the fence to regain the track, then follow this back to Rhigolter.

(ii) Ascend to the top of Cìoch Mhòr (c.550m), then drop quite steeply down the other side to pass through gates and rejoin the track at Rhigolter; little, if any difference in time.

Return along the track to the start (**14km; 1055m; 6h**).

An ascent of these hills can be made from the east, via the fish farm at Polla, starting from where the A838 loops round the head of Loch Eriboll. Parking in the vicinity of the track to Polla is limited, and the section of single-track road on the NC500 that runs around Loch Eriboll is also a pain to drive when busy.

Ben Loyal and all of its tops, with An Caisteal, centre, from Cnoc an Daimh Mòr to the south-west (Hugh Munro)

BEN LOYAL; law hill
***An Caisteal**; 764m; (C217); L10; NC578488; the castle*

Regarded as another of Scotland's finest mountains, Ben Loyal lies between Ben Hope to the west and Loch Loyal to the east, and about 7km south of the village of Tongue on the north coast. Its striking appearance and isolated position more than compensate for its lack of height, only just sufficient for Corbett status.

The distinctive outline of Ben Loyal's four granite peaks is best seen across the Kyle of Tongue, from where they create a formidable sight. This belies their difficulty though, and the ascent to the highest point, and indeed the subsidiary tops, is actually fairly straightforward.

Ben Loyal is normally climbed from the north, for that route shows the best of the mountain. There is a shorter alternative from the A836 along Loch Loyal to the east, but this is dull by comparison, and the ground there is often wet and boggy.

Leave the A836 at the sharp bend in Tongue and take the minor road south signed to Tongue Village. Follow this road for 1.4 miles (2.25km) with Ben Loyal in view ahead, then turn off left onto the track to Ribigill and a car park on the left at NC584547.

Walk up the track towards Ribigill, taking the left fork to pass through some farm buildings, and continue towards the mountain on a rougher track. After crossing the second of two burns, the track worsens and becomes boggier. Cross a third burn and pass well out to the right of the enclosure and deserted building at Cunside, on a path heading towards the Bealach Clais nan Ceap between Ben Hiel on the left and the formidable-looking Sgòr Chaonasaid on the right.

Go up the right side of a burn for a way, then cross it to continue uphill to an easing by another burn. Swing right here and climb the steep grass and heather slope up the left side of the rocky prow of Sgòr Chaonasaid to gain the crest left of its twin peaks.

The scattered remains of an RAF Hampden, which crashed in 1943, lie on the slope out to the left.

A detour to the right can be made to climb onto Sgòr Chaonasaid's 712m top, gained by a path on the west side, then an easy scramble.

Continue south across a dip and climb past the rocks of the intervening

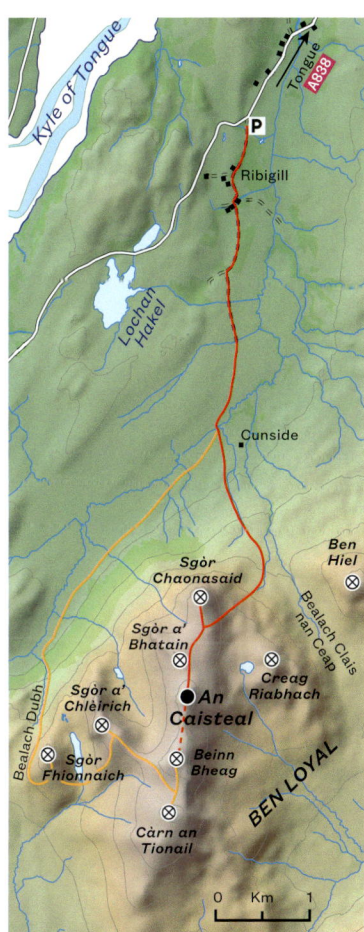

Sgòr a' Bhatain (700m) on its east side to reach the blocky granite tor of An Caisteal, which is climbed on its west side to reach the stone trig point on top (**6.75km; 830m; 3h**).

It is easier to return the same way, perhaps cutting down and across the slope from the dip between Sgòr a' Bhatain and Sgòr Chaonasaid (13.25km; 870m; 4h 50min).

However, it is worth continuing south to Beinn Bheag (744m); an added 30min or so there and back.

A much longer traverse can be made by climbing either or both of Càrn an Tionail (716m) to the south and Sgòr a' Chlèirich (642m), which juts out to the north-west.

There is no suitable descent to the north from Sgòr a' Chlèirich, so a descent should be made down to the burn issuing from Loch Fhionnaich below Sgòr Fhionnaich (568m), which could be included for completeness. Either way, go around the south and west flank of Sgòr Fhionnaich, following deer tracks to about the 400m contour to gain the Bealach Dubh. From there, a rough path can be followed down by the burn through the trees, then an ATV track north-east back to Cunside and the approach (20km; 1130m; 7h for all the tops).

Ben Loyal from Ben Hiel to the north-east – An Caisteal, centre, Sgòr Chaonasaid, right, Ben Hope beyond (Mike Dixon)

*Mullach Buidhe, North Goatfell, Goatfell
and Cir Mhòr, with Beinn a' Chliabhain and
A' Chir, far right, from Caisteal Abhail
(Tom Prentice)*

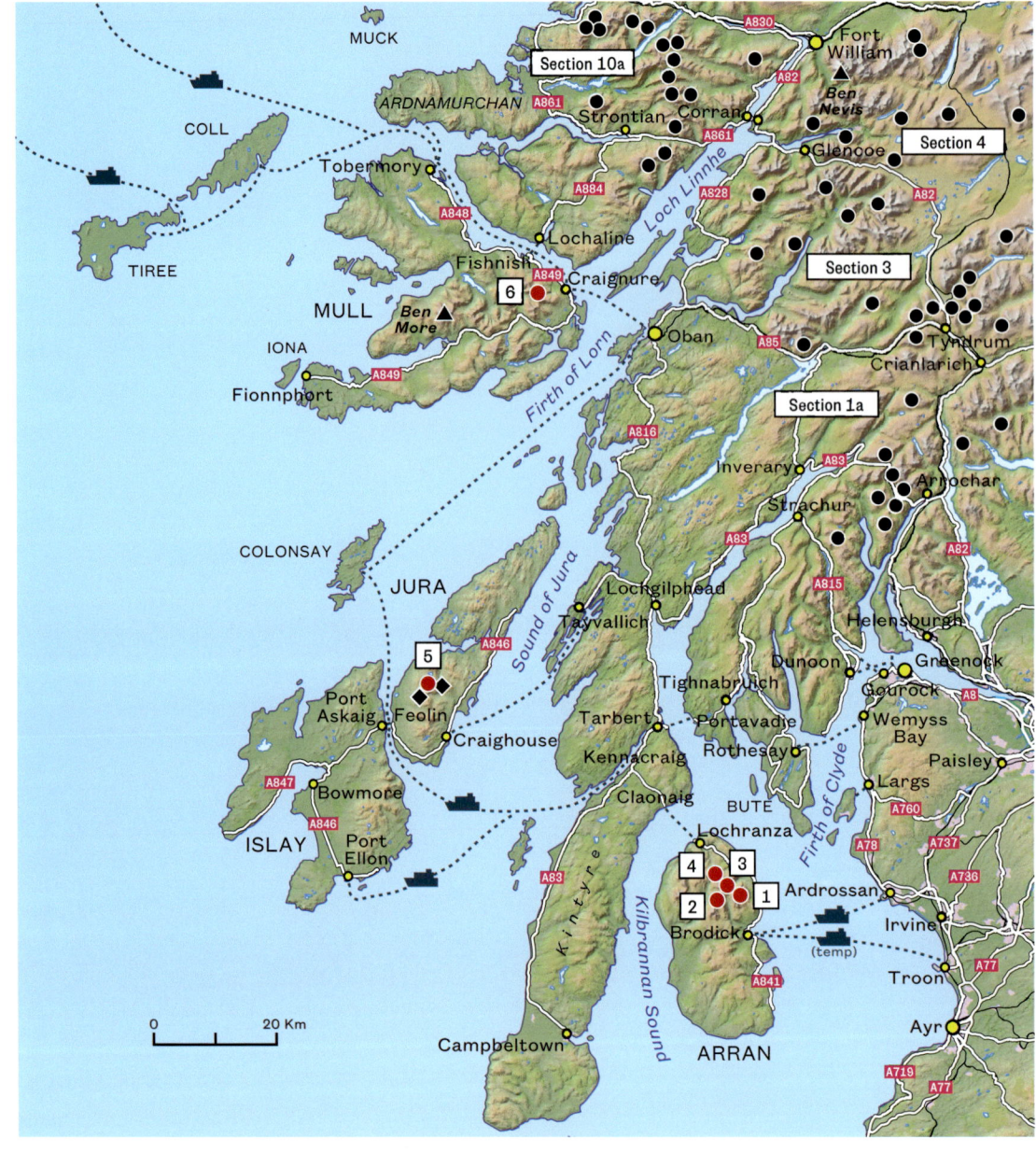

SECTION 17

THE ISLANDS

Caledonian MacBrayne (CalMac) is the major operator of ferries to the islands calmac.co.uk. Highland Council operate a few small crossings, and there are some private companies running services. Online searches for ferry crossings to the island name should reveal the relevant information. In addition to the standard crossings, CalMac offer a multiple journey island-hopping ticket which covers various ferry crossings to, from, and between the islands; valid for a limited period. Routes and timetables are liable to change, so check online for current details.

ARRAN & THE INNER HEBRIDES

The Isle of Arran and the group of islands known as the Inner Hebrides contain a total of eight Corbetts on four islands. Arran has four Corbetts, Jura has one, Mull has one and Rum has two.

ARRAN *is reached by CalMac ferry from Ardrossan, or Troon (temporary) to Brodick. Another CalMac ferry crosses from Claonaig on the Kintyre Peninsula to Lochranza. At the time of writing, an 11h 25min window Monday to Saturday enables most Corbetts to be climbed as day trips, both as foot/bike passengers or with a vehicle. The Sunday window is 8h 40min. Note that route description times are based on Naismith's Rule and don't include stops.*

A number 324 bus operated by Stagecoach stagecoachgroup.com runs between Brodick and Blackwaterfoot. It is timed to meet with the ferry – on the northward run it stops at Cladach (10min trip), Corrie, Glen Sannox (20min) and North Glen Sannox, which covers all of the hillwalking starts except Glen Rosa Campsite.

JURA *is reached by CalMac ferry from Kennacraig at the northern end of the Kintyre Peninsula, either to Port Ellen or Port Askaig on Islay. Another ferry crossing is required from Port Askaig to Feolin on Jura, run by ASP Ship Management Ltd; details on isleofjura.scot, through the Argyll & Bute Council website and in the CalMac timetable. A passenger-only ferry crosses directly to Craighouse on Jura from Tayvallich (NR742782) on Knapdale, details on jurapassengerferry.com and on calmac.co.uk. Bikes can be taken on both crossings, but check first though. Further information on Jura and accommodation can be found on isleofjura.scot.*

MULL *can be reached by ferry from Oban to Craignure. If only the Corbett is to be climbed, then this can be done as a foot passenger on this crossing. If longer is to be spent on the island, then it may be more convenient and less expensive to use the crossing to Fishnish on Mull, from Lochaline on Morvern (probably gained via the Corran ferry operated by Highland Council). There is an end of March to end of September crossing to Tobermory from Kilchoan on Ardnamurchan. The Mull crossings are operated by CalMac, where details of the Corran ferry can also be found.*

RUM *has two Corbetts, and the island can be reached by ferry crossing from Mallaig via the Caledonian MacBrayne Small Isles service. It used to be possible to climb the Corbetts in the day on a Saturday, but a change to the ferry timetable means that this is not possible at the time of writing, so at least one or two nights will need to be spent on the island to fit in with the ferry timetable. Check isleofrum.com for information on accommodation and the island.*

ISLE OF SKYE

The Isle of Skye contains two Corbetts, and most walkers will choose to arrive on the island via the Skye Bridge from Kyle of Lochalsh. However, the Kylerhea ferry crossing from near Glenelg is an alternative. This ferry is seasonal and it takes vehicles. The ferry is operated by the Isle of Skye Ferry Community Interest Company skyeferry.co.uk – details of which are also on the CalMac website, as well as their own Mallaig to Armadale service on Skye.

THE OUTER HEBRIDES

Despite their size and hilly nature, the islands of the Outer Hebrides only contain one Corbett: An Cliseam on Harris. There are also three Grahams on Harris and one Graham on South Uist. CalMac is the sole ferry operator.

ISLE OF HARRIS *can be reached from Uig on Skye by ferry to Tarbert. A ferry also crosses from Ullapool on the mainland to Stornoway on the Isle of Lewis, which is joined to the Isle of Harris. There is also a ferry between Leverburgh on Harris and the island of Berneray, which is connected to the Uists by causeway, from where there is a ferry between Lochmaddy and Uig on Skye, as well as a ferry between Lochboisdale and Oban.*

Rum from Mallaig (Rab Anderson)

Goatfell and Brodick Castle from the Ardrossan to Brodick ferry (Mike Dixon)

ARRAN
Goatfell; *874m; (C58); L69; NS991415; goat hill*

Dominating the eastern side of Arran with an outlook across the sea to the mainland, shapely Goatfell captures the eye as one approaches the island. Rising to the north of Brodick, the capital and main ferry port, it is the highest peak on Arran and, together with North Goatfell and Mullach Buidhe to its north, forms a barrier that hides the spectacular peaks and connecting ridges that lie beyond it.

Goatfell probably receives more ascents than any other island peak, its commanding situation and ease of access making it an irresistible attraction. Three main ridges radiate from its lofty summit. To the north is the pinnacled Stacach ridge, which links it to North Goatfell and the connecting ridges to the rest of the range. To the south and east are the ridges that give the mountain its distinctive pyramidal shape, and it is up Coire nam Meann between these ridges that the principal route to the summit climbs to gain the east ridge.

The main route of ascent starts at Cladach, about a 3km walk, or 3.5km drive, to the north of the pier at Brodick. See bus information in the panel opposite. The walk follows the start of the Arran Coastal Way and the Fisherman's Walk, signposted from the Co-op at the north end of the seafront. The approach by road is along the seafront road to a car park on the right at Cladach, opposite the Cladach Centre and Arran Brewery.

The route to Goatfell is signposted. Cross the road and go up the track opposite past the Cladach Centre, to curve left past the brewery into the castle grounds, and cross a road to enter the woodland of Cnocan Wood.

Continue past tracks and paths on either side then, where the track swings right, follow a path ahead to exit Cnocan Wood into scattered birch woodland above the Cnocan Burn. Cross a track and continue uphill to meet a wide path coming up from the right, then cross a footbridge over a burn and go through a gate onto the open hillside.

Ascend through Coire nam Meann and swing up left onto Goatfell's east ridge to meet the path of the alternative ascent route coming up from Corrie down to the east. The ground now steepens and a quite narrow rocky ridge leads to the summit of Goatfell, which is adorned with a trig pillar, a viewpoint indicator and several perched boulders (**5.5km; 870m; 2h 40min**).

Sitting above the drop into Glen Rosa, with the ridges and peaks beyond revealed, and with the outlook across the sea to the mainland, it is a spectacular viewpoint.

Return the same way (**11km; 870m; 4h 15min**).

An alternative descent can be made by continuing down the east ridge on the path to Corrie. The path swings north across Coire Lan to cross

▶

the Corrie Burn, then descends beside this to gain the road to High Corrie, which leads to the main road; there is a bus stop to the north opposite the houses (9.75km; 870m; 4h).

It is also possible to walk back to Cladach from Corrie, following the Arran Coastal Way. On reaching the main road, turn right and walk the verge south for 340m, then go up a forest track into Maol Donn Wood. The track climbs uphill then traverses the hillside below Maol Donn to pass through Merkland Wood and join the ascent route in Cnocan Wood, which is followed back down to Cladach (16.25km; 970m; 5h 45min).

An ascent can also be made from Corrie, climbing to North Goatfell then following the Stacach ridge to the summit. It may be possible to drive up the narrow road towards High Corrie, signposted for Goatfell, forking left to park by the water works. Failing

this, there is parking on the main road opposite the houses, or opposite the village hall a little further along.

From the water works, follow the track a short way then take the Goatfell-signed path off right and follow this above the Corrie Burn through birch woodland between the forestry plantations. Pass through two gates onto the open hillside and continue uphill on the path, passing a path off left across the burn, which is the return.

A good path leads up through Coire Lan to below the headwall, where the path deteriorates. Ascend a rougher path up the headwall to gain the ridge between North Goatfell and Mullach Buidhe.

Mullach Buidhe (829m) can be climbed by an easy and worthwhile there-and-back diversion; an added 0.75km, 80m, 20min.

North Goatfell (818m) can be

avoided by a path on its left (east) side. However, it is best to climb it by following the path up to where a path drops west to The Saddle and Cìr Mhòr. From there, the rocky summit is gained by an easy short scramble. There is a trickier descent beyond, which can be avoided by returning off the summit the same way, then following a path beneath the west side of the summit. Beyond, an eroded path drops quite steeply to the col with the Stacach ridge.

Either scramble over the pinnacles on the ridge, or avoid them by a path on the left (east) side, and climb through a boulder field to the top of Goatfell (5.5km; 940m; 3h).

Descend the east ridge, past the path off to Cladach, and swing left at the bottom to cross the Corrie Burn, then follow the path used in the ascent back down to Corrie (9.75km; 940m; 4h 20min).

Goatfell and the pinnacled Stacach ridge from North Goatfell, with the east ridge on the left (Tom Prentice)

Beinn Tarsuinn and Cìr Mhòr from Beinn Nuis (Derek Sime)

ARRAN

Beinn Tarsuinn; *826m; (C119); L69; NR959412; traverse hill*

Cìr Mhòr; *799m; (C161); L69; NR973431; great comb*

These two hills comprise part of the superb granite ridge that forms a southward-facing horseshoe around Glen Rosa. Beinn Tarsuinn lies on the west side of the glen, whilst the magnificent rock spire of Cìr Mhòr sits at its head, connected to Goatfell on the east side by a narrow ridge.

The full round of Glen Rosa is one of the best mountain walks in the country and is described in the panel on page 372. However, the principal route described here is a less arduous undertaking of Beinn Tarsuinn and Cìr Mhòr, with a possible extension to include the fourth of Arran's Corbetts, Caisteal Abhail, which lies to the north of Cìr Mhòr.

Following the true ridgeline between Beinn Tarsuinn and Cìr Mhòr involves some scrambling and basic rock climbing skills on the A' Chir Ridge, which includes the descent of the infamous bad step known as Le Mauvais Pas. The SMC's guidebook *Highland Scrambles South* describes this traverse and has photos showing how best to descend Le Mauvais Pas.

The route described here takes a bypass path on the west side that has no difficulty.

Start from the end of the road by the Glen Rosa Campsite where there is limited parking. This is 4km from the ferry terminal and an easy bike ride.

Follow the track up Glen Rosa for 2.25km to the bridge over the Garbh Allt; it can be biked this far.

An alternative route to this point can be made from the car park at Cladach by following the Goatfell track past the brewery to the road in the castle grounds. Turn left along the road to gain a track that loops round right, then go left on a path that traverses through the bottom of woodland and out into the open. Continue along the path on the east side of Glen Rosa to cross a bridge over the Glenrosa Water to the north of the Garbh Allt bridge, then go back down the other side for 180m to that bridge; an added 1.5km, 60m, 25min.

Follow the path westwards, up beside the Allt Garbh, soon passing a path off right, which heads up onto

Beinn a' Chliabhain. At a fork in the burn, the original route crossed over to go up the far side. However, the main path now keeps on up the right side for 400m to ford the burn at a small gorge. Continue uphill, then exit the planted area through a gate to gain the open hillside.

The path leads on up the side of shallow Coire na Cuiseig onto the shoulder at the top of the south ridge of Beinn Nuis. There is a fabulous view across the cliffs that fall from the summit of Beinn Nuis, across Coire nam Meann and Coire a' Bhradain to Beinn Tarsuinn and its cliffs, with Cìr Mhòr beyond.

Continue up the path above the impressive cliffs of the east face, Creag na h-Iolaire, to gain the summit of Beinn Nuis (792m).

Descend the ridge northwards, skirting the rocky Flat Iron Tower, to reach a col (709m), then continue up the ridge on the far side above the Full Mead Tower and over several false tops, passing a rock feature known as the Old Man of Beinn

Tarsuinn, to reach Beinn Tarsuinn's summit (**7.25km; 920m; 3h 10min**).

It is a splendid viewpoint with the A' Chir ridge below and the great grey comb of Cìr Mhòr beyond, then Goatfell on the other side of Glen Rosa over the top of Beinn a' Chliabhain.

Make a steep descent of the northeast ridge to Bealach an Fhir-bhogha (*pass of the bowmen*) above Coire Daingean. Some care is required as the path twists and turns to avoid a number of rocky sections, including one called the Consolation Tor, which has paths around either side.

At the col, the path ahead splits, with the right branch leading onto the famous A' Chir ridge where some rock climbing skills are required. Instead, take the path on the left and traverse beneath the base of A' Chir's slabby west face. There is only a slight loss of height, and the ridge is regained a short distance before the col at 591m with Cìr Mhòr.

Continue up the main path with magnificent views of the massive architecture of the Rosa Pinnacle on the south flank of Cìr Mhòr to gain the very small and very airy summit of one of Scotland's finest peaks (**10km; 1205m; 4h 30min**).

It is a wonderful position at the head of Glen Rosa, forming the hub at the centre of the Arran range with ridges radiating out in three directions to connect with the other peaks.

Reluctantly leave the summit and return to the col, then take a good path on the left and descend through Fionn Choire into Glen Rosa. There are superb views back with Cìr Mhòr and the Rosa Pinnacle looking truly alpine. Follow the path alongside the Glenrosa Water back to the start (**17.75km; 1225m; 6h 30min**).

It is an added 3km, 120m, 50min if the start was made from the Cladach car park and the return is made to there, back across the footbridge.

To include Caisteal Abhail, from a short distance below the summit of Cìr Mhòr, take the right-hand path and go down the north ridge with splendid views back to Cìr Mhòr's awesome dark, dank northern precipice. At the bottom, cross the narrow ridge forming the lowest point between the peaks at 624m, and ascend the curving ridge beyond. This is known as the Hunters' Ridge and it leads easily up to Caisteal Abhail, passing some cairned springs and overlooking the wilds of Coire na h-Uaimh to the east.

The summit area, in keeping with the mountain's alternative name of The Castles, features several rocky castellations. To attain the highest one, follow the path around its left (north) side to easily gain the summit (**11.75km; 1440m; 5h 25min**).

Return down the Hunters' Ridge, cross the narrow ridge between the peaks, then take the path on the right, which cuts across the slope to regain the col between Cìr Mhòr and A' Chir. Follow the path down Fionn Choire into Glen Rosa and return to the start (**20.5km; 1485m; 7h 50min**).

It is an added 3km, 120m, 50min if the start was made from Cladach, and the return is made to there.

Map on page 367

Cìr Mhòr and the Rosa Pinnacle (Tom Prentice)

ARRAN
Caisteal Abhail; *859m; (C79); L69; NR969443; forked keep*

Forming the northernmost of Arran's four Corbetts, Caisteal Abhail is a complex mountain from whose castellated summit four ridges radiate. A short ridge to the south, the Hunters' Ridge, connects Caisteal Abhail to Cìr Mhòr, which enables it to be linked with that hill and Beinn Tarsuinn, as described in the extension to that route on page 369. This ridge also enables Caisteal Abhail to be climbed as an extension to the superb Glen Rosa Horseshoe, which is described on page 372, enabling all four Arran Corbetts to be climbed in one long outing. The Hunters' Ridge also allows Caisteal Abhail and Cìr Mhòr to be climbed together as part of the equally good Glen Sannox Horseshoe, as described in the panel on page 373.

However, as a stand-alone hill, it is via its three northern ridges that Caisteal Abhail is described here, to give an enjoyable and scenic outing. Two of these northern ridges arc round to cup a great northward-facing crater-like bowl, which is split into two corries, Garbh-Choire and Coire nan Ceum, by the third ridge

between them. The burns that emanate from these corries flow north then east to form the North Glen Sannox Burn, which runs down the glen of the same name to the North Glen Sannox Bridge, crossed by the A841 between Brodick and Lochranza. There is a car park on the south side of this bridge, which is from where the approach is made; the bus stops here, see page 364.

Follow a well-constructed path up the glen beside the lovely burn, entering forestry by a gate, then exiting it after 2km by another gate. Caisteal Abhail is fully revealed here at the head of the glen, with the obvious cleft of the Ceum na Caillich, or the Witch's Step as it is more commonly known, prominent in the jagged ridge to the left.

Leave the path up the glen and ford the burn, which can normally be done dry, but could be a problem if the water was running high. Once across, follow a rough path westwards up the hillside and swing round onto the start of the long ridge that arcs around the corrie. The path becomes clearer, leading over Sàil

an Im and above the cliffs of Creag Dubh, on terrain that becomes more stony and dotted with boulders. There are grand views across to the summit and its tors, with the hill's other name of The Castles apparent.

Swing round at the top and weave past numerous boulders, rock formations and tors to reach the summit at the far (eastern) end. Taking the form of a large tor made up of slanting granite blocks, the top is easily gained by following the path around its left (north) side, then climbing onto it (**6km; 810m; 2h 40min**).

The view southwards to Cìr Mhòr and the other Arran peaks is spectacular, as is the surrounding view across the sea, which encompasses Ireland, the Paps of Jura and the Highlands.

There are three return options, by each of the three northward ridges:

(i) The easiest is back the same way (**12km; 820m; 4h 20min**).

(ii) Head east from the summit for a short way to the top of the central ridge, which splits the bowl into its two corries, then go down a grassy slope through rock and boulders and

Caisteal Abhail across the head of Garbh-Choire from the north-west ridge (Rab Anderson)

Caisteal Abhail's imposing summit (Tom Prentice)

descend the ridge. At the bottom, follow the burn flowing from Garbh-Choire to where it meets the burn flowing from Coire nan Ceum, and cross above the junction. A path leads down the other side to the good path of the outward route, which is followed back (10.75km; 820m; 4h 5min).

(iii) The more difficult return, but the most rewarding, is to traverse eastwards and cross the Ceum na Caillich (*Witch's Step*) then follow the north-east ridge with a direct descent

to the car park. From the summit, follow the path along the ridge and its right side through interesting rocky terrain, passing to the right of a rocky pinnacle (Pt.758m), then a blocky section. From there, a steep and gravelly descent leads down into the Ceum na Caillich, which requires care. The direct route out the other side either involves a climb, or a scramble. Instead, go down the gully on the left (north) for a short way to find an obvious line leading up right

with some easy scrambling back onto the ridge beyond. A path leads pleasantly along the ensuing narrow ridge, across a dip, then up onto Suidhe Fhearghas (c.660m). Descend the ridge, north-east then north, dropping quite steeply to take the left-hand path across flat ground to the left of the small rise of Cnocan Donna. A direct descent down the hillside to the right of a burn leads to the car park (10.5km; 950m; 4h 30min).

Map on page 367

Caisteal Abhail and the Hunters' Ridge from the north ridge of Cìr Mhòr (Tom Prentice)

Glen Rosa Horseshoe

This ranks as one of Scotland's finest hillwalks, climbing the three Corbetts around Glen Rosa: Goatfell, Cìr Mhòr and Beinn Tarsuinn, with the possibility of including Caisteal Abhail, the fourth Arran Corbett.

Climbing Goatfell first, start from Cladach as described on page 365 and follow the signed route through Cnocan Wood, then up by the Cnocan Burn and Coire nam Meann to gain the summit (**5.5km; 870m; 2h 40min**).

Descend to the north and climb over, or bypass as required, the three squat pinnacles of the Stacach ridge, and climb onto North Goatfell, either scrambling directly onto the summit block or, bypassing it to the left (west), then gaining it easily from the far side.

Drop off North Goatfell's summit and take the left-hand path, then carefully descend the fine ridge to the north-west. Initially this is bouldery, and then it is loose and gravelly in places with some easy scrambling required to reach The Saddle at 432m between Goatfell and Cìr Mhòr.

Climb Cìr Mhòr by a path that zigzags up the line of weakness to the left of the buttress forming the right-hand edge, which can look a little intimidating. However, although there is loose rock and some easy scrambling, with care there should be no real difficulty. Easier ground leads to the summit rocks, which are bypassed on the left (south) to gain the other side, from where the top of this magnificent peak is easily gained (**8.75km; 1300m; 4h 30min**).

Leave the summit briefly north-west and take the left-hand path, which leads easily down the broad south-west ridge to gain the col at 591m at the head of Fionn Choire with the foreboding-looking A' Chìr ridge ahead.

If Caisteal Abhail is to be included, shortly after leaving the summit of Cìr Mhòr, take the right-hand path, which swings round to descend the north ridge. Cross the narrow ridge between the peaks, then climb the curving Hunters' Ridge past some springs.

Once on the castellated top, go round the far side of the summit block to gain its top. Return to the col on the narrow ridge with Cìr Mhòr, ascend slightly, then follow a traverse path that cuts across to the col at the head of Fionn Choire; an added

2.75km, 260m, 1h 20min on the day.

Ascend slightly to gain the base of the A' Chìr ridge, then take the bypass path on the right (west), which drops down and traverses beneath the rocks without any difficulty, before ascending to regain the ridge beyond at Bealach an Fhir-bhogha.

Anyone wishing to climb the A' Chìr ridge should refer to the SMC guide *Highland Scrambles South*, where there is a detailed description together with pictures of the Mauvais Pas (bad step), which in this direction of travel is graded at least V.Diff for the initial moves off the ground. Interestingly, it's actually easier in descent coming the other way for anyone doing a clockwise round of Glen Rosa. From Bealach an Fhir-bhogha, follow the path around Consolation Tor, and climb to the top of Beinn Tarsuinn (**11.5km; 1620m; 5h 55min**).

Descend south along the ridge past the Old Man of Tarsuinn, then over a slight rise and continue down to a col at 709m. Now climb past the Flat Iron Tower to gain the top of Beinn Nuis, the final hill.

Follow the path south-south-east down the steepening above the summit cliffs to the shoulder, and continue down the path, which veers off the main ridge to descend south-east to the Garbh Allt. Cross this, and follow the path down to Glen Rosa.

Don't cross the bridge over the Garbh Allt, but go left on the path up Glen Rosa for 180m, then cross a bridge over the Glenrosa Water to follow a path back down the other side. This enters woodland to gain a track, then a path leading to a road in the grounds of Brodick Castle. Go along the road a short way to meet the Goatfell route, which crosses it, and go back down this to the start (**20.25km; 1800m; 8h 30min**).

If Caisteal Abhail is included (**23km; 2060m; 9h 50min**).

Cìr Mhòr from across The Saddle on the descent from North Goatfell. Caisteal Abhail beyond on the other side of Glen Sannox with Ceum na Caillich (Witch's Step), right (Tom Prentice)

follows a steep path that zigzags up the line of weakness to the left of the buttress forming the right-hand edge, which can look quite intimidating. However, although there is loose rock and some easy scrambling, with care there should be no real difficulty.

Easier ground above leads to the summit rocks, which are bypassed on the left (south) to gain the other side, from where the top of this magnificent peak is easily gained (**8km; 1330m; 4h 25min**).

Leave the summit to the north-west and take the right-hand path, which swings round to descend the north ridge. Cross the narrow ridge between the peaks, then climb the curving Hunters' Ridge past some springs. Once on the castellated crest of Caisteal Abhail, go round the far side of the summit block to gain its top (**9.75km; 1565m; 5h 20min**).

Follow the path east along the ridge and its right side, through rocky terrain, passing to the right of a pinnacle (Pt.758m), then a blocky section and make a steep, gravelly descent into the deep cleft of the Ceum na Caillich (Witch's Step), which requires care.

The direct routes up the other side either involve a climb or a scramble. Instead, go down the gully on the left (north) for a short way to find an obvious line leading up right with some easy scrambling back onto the ridge beyond.

A path leads pleasantly along the ensuing narrow ridge, across a dip, then up onto Suidhe Fhearghas (c.660m). Descend the ridge, north-east then north, and drop quite steeply towards a flat section.

Go right when the path forks, and descend eastwards across the slope towards Sannox to some old mine workings. Continue downhill past the workings to the Glen Sannox Burn, and follow this to a bridge, which is crossed to gain the track, then the car park (**16km; 1705m; 7h 25min**).

Map on page 367

Glen Sannox Horseshoe

A superb circuit of the ridges around Glen Sannox, which takes in the peaks of Cìr Mhòr and Caisteal Abhail that sit at the head of the glen.

Start from either of two car parks at Sannox, on the seaward side of the A841 between Brodick and Lochranza, just before the bridge over the Sannox Burn; there is a bus stop here.

Walk up the lane next to the cottage, signposted to Glen Sannox, and follow the continuation track to some old mine workings where a burn comes down from the left, the Allt a' Chapuill.

Leave the track and ascend a rough footpath beside the burn until above a ravine. Cross the burn, and continue on the path up the other side, heading towards the imposing bulk of Cìoch na h-Oighe, with its massive clean wall of rock called The Bastion near its top.

When the slope starts to steepen at the 350m contour below Coire na Cìche, known as The Devil's Punch-bowl, follow a path up right onto the broad and rocky north-east ridge. Traverse up rightwards to some slabs, then scramble up these to follow a path that weaves its way up through splendid rocky terrain to reach the top of Cìoch na h-Oighe (661m).

Traverse along the lovely narrow and airy crest, crossing a rocky pinnacle (665m), then Pt.692m without any difficulty, and continue up the broad ridge over the North Top of Mullach Buidhe (823m), then on to its 829m summit (**5km; 905m; 2h 45min**).

Descend the ridge south-west and cross the side of a slight rise, then climb to North Goatfell (818m) where the path splits just in front of its summit, easily gained by a quick there-and-back. Follow the path carefully down the ridge to the north-west, initially through boulders, then loose terrain with some easy scrambling to reach The Saddle (432m).

The onward ascent of Cìr Mhòr

Across the Imir an Aonaich from Beinn Shiantaidh to Beinn an Oir (Iain Thow)

JURA
Beinn an Oir; *785m; (C183); L61; NR498749; hill of gold*

The island of Jura lies off the west coast of Scotland in a southerly position level with the Central Belt. At some 44km in length, Jura is a surprisingly long island, though not of any great width. Almost split in two through its middle by Loch Tarbert, both parts contain some wild and rugged hills. Those in the northern part of the island are not high, and rarely frequented, whilst those in the south form the renowned Paps of Jura.

There are actually three hills, one Corbett and two Grahams, not two as might be expected from the Gaelic translation of breasts from paps.

They are particularly wild and rugged hills, covered in scree and rock, and they have a well-justified reputation for toughness, similar to the Cuillin of Rum, described later in this section.

Beinn an Oir is the Corbett and therefore the highest, and it sits between the two Grahams, Beinn a' Chaolais to its south and Beinn Shiantaidh to its east. Their distinctive

shape, domed or conical depending on viewpoint, and their separation from each other make them stand out in the views to the western seaboard from many of the hills in the Southern and Central Highlands, as well as from Arran.

Whilst the premise of this book is the Corbetts, it is assumed that most people making the trip to Jura will be interested in taking up the challenge of climbing all three hills for a superb and memorable round, so this is the principal route described here. For those only interested in Beinn an Oir, a brief Corbett-only description is given at the end.

Start from the A846 on the south side of the bridge over the Corran River (NR544720). There is a small car park on the north side of the bridge opposite the minor road to Knockrome. This is nearly 3½ miles (5.5km) from the hotel and campsite at Craighouse, which itself is just over 8 miles (13.25km) from Feolin, where the ferry from Islay arrives.

Drop down to the side of the bridge parapet, cross a stile and follow a path then an ATV track on the west side of the Corran River, first north-north-west, then north-west, towards Loch an t-Sìob'. The route is very boggy in places and leads to stepping stones at the east end of Loch an t-Sìob', which are crossed.

Leave the lochside path here and climb northwards up the steepening lower slopes of Beinn Shiantaidh, following vague paths through heather and tongues of scree. Continue up to the west side of the rounded south-east ridge, where the main mass of scree that falls from the summit is reached. A path becomes more obvious here and there are two options. After a left traverse, one option heads up the left side of the ridge to the summit, whilst the other option gains the ridge and follows it to a levelling, which leads south-west over grass and scree mounds to the large summit cairn (**4.75km; 745m; 2h 30min**).

Leave Beinn Shiantaidh's summit and descend the ridge to the west, which broadens into a mixture of scree and grass. About halfway down, where the ridge steepens, break through a band of rock by a gully-line a little to the right, then continue down to pass to the south of the col (Imir an Aonaich) between the hills.

Follow a path that traverses west-wards across the flanks of Beinn an Oir to reach a small burn draining the shallow corrie formed by the obvious rake that slants up rightwards across the side of the mountain. Turn north beside the burn and follow a path up the rake into the upper corrie to reach a stone shelter where the scree starts. There are now two options:

(i) Easiest is to continue up the rake into a depression, then onto the north-east ridge. Turn south-west past a cairn, then climb the ridge and cross the slight rise of the North-East Top (763m) to reach the remains of a building, then another just beyond in the dip before the summit. These are the remains of a Colby Camp occupied by the Ordnance Survey during the first Triangulation of Great Britain in the first half of the 19th century.

(ii) Ascend grass between the scree slopes, directly below an obvious small tor formed by an igneous sill. This leads directly to the building in the dip between the summit and the north-east top; shorter by 500m and about 7min.

A stone pathway leads to the trig point (7.5km; 1100m; 4h).

Head south and go down a splendid ridge of blocky quartzite with fine views west to Islay and south-west to Beinn a' Chaolais. After about 300m, turn south-west and drop down onto a subsidiary ridge, then weave down this through scree and crags to pass above the south end of the lochans of Na Garbh-lochanan, then cross the broad col between the hills, the Màm an t-Sìob.

There are two options for the ascent of Beinn a' Chaolais:

(i) Simply climb directly up the left side of the scree that starts to the right of some minor rock outcrops to gain the east ridge about halfway up.

(ii) Traverse left around the crest, then ascend easier-angled scree, heather and rock to gain the crest; slightly longer but perhaps easier.

Either way, continue up the ridge to the top (9.75km; 1460m; 5h 45min).

Go back down the east ridge and take the easier right-hand line, linking grass and heather to reach the bottom, then drop into Gleann an t-Sìob. Pick up a wet and muddy path along the southern edge of Loch an t-Sìob to reach the east end, then follow the path used in the approach back (16.5km; 1470m; 7h 45min).

To climb Beinn an Oir on its own, follow the route described above to the stepping stones at the east end of Loch an t-Sìob and cross. Follow a path around the north side of the loch, which at the mid-point starts to rise across the hillside. Once below the col between the hills, start climbing towards Beinn an Oir, crossing the main burn coming down from the col. Continue uphill to meet the path from Beinn Shiantaidh, then follow this up the slanting rake to gain the summit of Beinn an Oir by either of the options described in the principal route (7km; 785m; 2h 50min).

Return the same way (14km; 795m; 4h 40min).

These mountains can also be approached from their west side, from the Feolin Ferry. Follow the bike-able track north above the shore through woodland to a crossroads. Take the track that leads east, uphill to the dam on Lochan Gleann Astaile, then continue along the track to a burn where bikes are probably best left (7.25km, 185m 1h 55min on foot).

Climb to the summit of Beinn a' Chaolais via its south-west ridge (9.5km; 770m; 3h 25min). Distances and times are on foot from the start.

Descend the east ridge to its base, then traverse north to the Màm an t-Sìob col between the hills.

▶

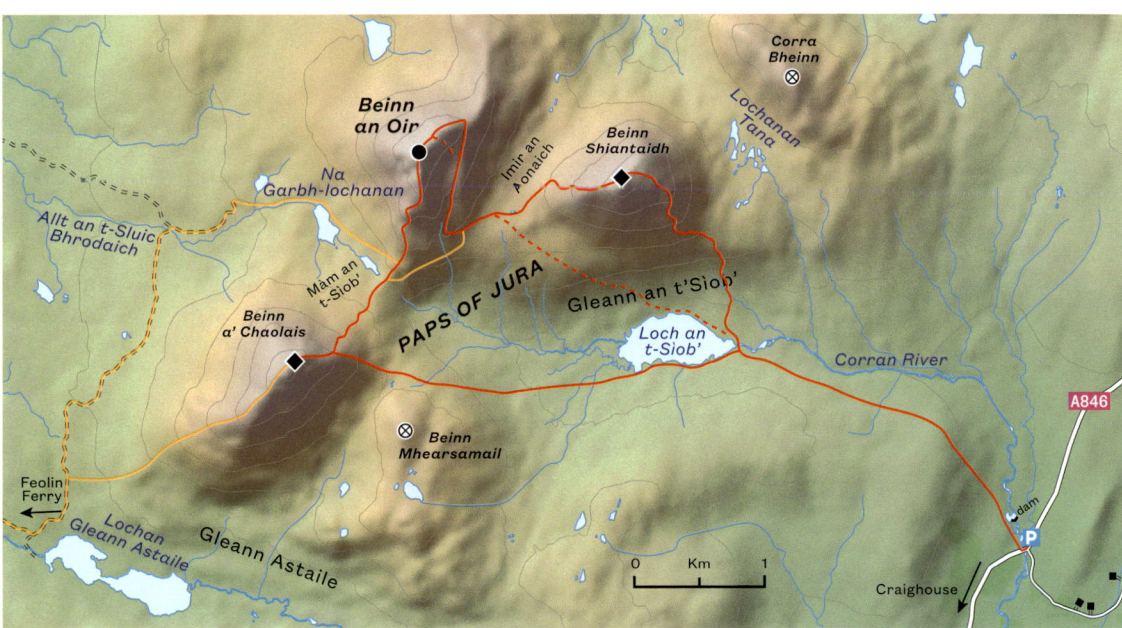

Across the Màm an t-Sìob' from Beinn a' Chaolais to Beinn an Oir and Beinn Shiantaidh (Tom Prentice)

It is probably best to climb Beinn Shiantaidh next, since the way ahead avoiding the scree and rock at the base of Beinn an Oir is easier to see. Drop down about 50m to traverse below this area, then climb up to the col with Beinn Shiantaidh and climb to the summit via the path up the gully (**12.75km; 1225m; 5h 20min**).

Return to the col, then follow the path northwards up the slanting rake and climb to the top of Beinn an Oir as described in the standard route on page 375 (**15km; 1570m; 6h 50min**).

Descend the path down the ridge, south, then south-west, to above the Na Garbh-lochanan. Skirt these lochans on their west side, cross the outflow and descend to a track. Follow the track down to cross back over the burn, and take the left-hand track to rejoin the approach route, which is followed back (**28.25km; 1650m; 10h 15min**).

The use of a bike should save about 2h on the day for this route.

MULL

Dun da Ghaoithe; *766m; (C214); L49; NM672362; fort of the two winds*

With its lovely curving north-east corrie, Dùn da Ghaoithe is an attractive hill overlooking Craignure, at the meeting of the Sound of Mull with the Firth of Lorn and Loch Linnhe. It is the first of Mull's fine hills to catch the eye when arriving by ferry from the mainland, either on the shorter and cheaper Lochaline to Fishnish crossing, or the principal crossing from Oban to Craignure.

The ascent is best made from Craignure, which means that it can be undertaken as a foot passenger from Oban. The only inconvenience is finding parking in Oban, which for speed might be best in one of the pay-and-display car parks.

On disembarking at Craignure, turn right, then walk north-west on the pavement alongside the road for 700m. Cross over to the start of a track into Forestry and Land Scotland's Scallastle Forest and follow the track south-west through the forestry for 2km with views ahead to Dùn da

The Paps of Jura, with Beinn an Oir, left, across the Sound of Islay (Mike Dixon)

Ghaoithe. When the track ends, continue on a path and cross a bridge over the Scallastle River, which flows from the big north-eastern corrie. This corrie is actually made up of three corries: Coire Mòr, Coire nan Each and Coire nan Dearc.

Turn left and follow the track on the other side next to the river to its end beside a footbridge, then continue on a rough ATV track and path to exit the forestry area by a gate in a deer fence. Climb diagonally up the grassy hillside above Coire Mòr onto the broad east ridge of Maol nan Damh, then follow this easily to the steeper upper section of scree and boulders, which has two small bands of crag running across it.

Ascend through the break in the centre of the lower band of crag, then zigzag up through the scree keeping to the grass and climb through the middle of the upper band. This is short but steep and would require care in the wet. If necessary, it should be possible to bypass this second band towards its right end. The easier upper slope leads south-west, then south to the large cairn on the summit (**6.25km; 790m; 2h 45min**).

Descend south, then cross the

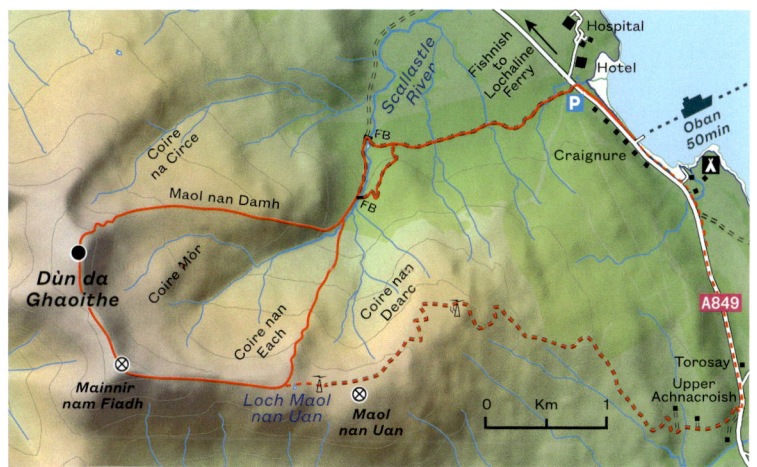

saddle and climb to the slightly lower south top, Mainnir nam Fiadh (757m), with its nearby trig point.

Continue down the ridge to the east for just over 1km, along the edge of the corrie, to tiny Loch Maol nan Uan, just above an aerial and the access track to it.

Turn northwards here and go down the grassy ridge between Coire nan Each and Coire nan Dearc, weaving through a number of minor rock outcrops, to reach the Scallastle River just before the deer fence around the forestry area. The river can normally

be crossed without getting wet feet.

Go through the gate, then back along the path to cross the upper footbridge and zigzag uphill on a track. Follow the track to join the track used in the approach, then return along this and the road to Craignure (**13.75km; 905m; 5h**).

It is possible to go down the track from the aerial to the road, then follow this back for 2.5km to the pier. The road is single-track for 1.2km or so, there is a verge in places, and after 1.4km there is a pavement (**16.75km; 880m; 5h 30min**).

Across Coire Mòr to Dùn da Ghaoithe and the Sound of Mull from Pt.757m (Colin Moody)

> **RUM**
>
> **Askival**; 812m; (C137); L39;
> NM393952; hill of the spear
>
> **Ainshval**; 781m; (C189); L39;
> NM378943); rocky ridge hill

Together with the Paps of Jura, the Glen Rosa Horseshoe, the Foinaven circuit and probably Quinag, the traverse over Askival and Ainshval in the Rum Cuillin rates as one of the best of all Corbett expeditions, giving a route of exceptional toughness, character and beauty.

Askival and Ainshval are the highest points on a ridge of five distinct peaks that bear some comparison with their larger and more celebrated neighbours across the sea to the north. Whilst the Black Cuillin of Skye may be higher, more numerous and more starkly rocky, the Rum peaks have their own charm and individuality.

As with walkers visiting Jura and traversing all three paps rather than just climbing the Corbett there, it is expected that those visiting Rum will be interested in climbing all five hills on the ridge. Accordingly, this is the main route described here.

The changed ferry timetable means that it is no longer possible to climb these hills as a day trip, so time will need to be spent on the island; see page 364. The start for the route is therefore described from the bunkhouse and campsite, which is a brisk 10min walk from the pier.

Walk along the track to Kinloch Castle (5min), then go left alongside it and left through a gate into woodland, passing an old bridge over the river. Pass to the left of a powerhouse building onto the end of a track, then follow an engineered path uphill to its end at a hydro dam.

Continue uphill on a rougher path into Coire Dubh to reach a causeway breached by the burn, then cross. This is the old dam that once supplied Kinloch Castle with water to generate electricity, the first Scottish castle to be lit this way.

The path forks here with both branches becoming less distinct. The right branch continues up the corrie to Bealach Bairc-mheall, which is the

return route if coming back via Atlantic Corrie. Take the left branch, which veers left, and follow it up beside a small burn to a col named Cnapan Breaca, then ascend the rocky hillside to gain the lower north-west ridge of Hallival, just above Bealach Bairc-mheall. Ascend the ridge, initially grassy then steeper and rocky, to reach Hallival's 723m summit (**5km; 730m; 2h 20min**).

There are fine views north to Skye, the Cuillin and Blàbheinn, then south-wards to Askival and over the island of Eigg floating in the sea to the hills of Mull beyond. The ground is covered

in Manx Shearwater burrows; a large portion of the world's population breed here on Rum.

Descend the crest south from Hallival, negotiating a steeper section via a series of rocky steps, which may require care early in the day if damp, then drop through boulders to gain the col (599m) between the hills.

Continue up and along an amazing narrow grassy ridge to the first rocks of Askival's rocky crest. The Askival Pinnacle can be seen ahead, which is actually more of a slab than a pinnacle. Follow the path left here and make a rising zigzag ascent up

Across Nameless Corrie to Ainshval and Askival with Hallival then the Isle of Skye beyond (Rab Anderson)

the easier ground to the left of the crest. At the top, a trickier move gains easy ground, then the stone trig point on Askival's bouldery summit (**6.25km; 945m; 3h 20min**).

Make a surprisingly long and tiring descent of the steep and gravelly west ridge to gain the Bealach an Oir (455m) at the head of Atlantic Corrie to the north. Be wary of being drawn too far down left on the initial part of the descent from the summit.

Trollabhal and its east ridge lie ahead, and the decision has to made whether to climb this first or later, depending on the choice of route for the return. If the return is to be made via Atlantic Corrie, which is both shorter and recommended, then Trollabhal can be climbed on the return from Askival, probably giving easier route finding that way.

If bypassing Trollabhal, a vague traverse path can be followed below the rocks at its base to gain the Bealach an Fhuarain below Ainshval.

However, to climb Trollabhal first, ascend easily up the broad and grassy lower section to the narrow upper section which, despite its rocky profile, is straightforward. The easiest line is just right of the crest and leads to the slightly lower south-east top. The main summit lies some 50m further on to the north-west across a gap, reached by a short descent, then an exposed scramble up rock and grass to gain an impressive and airy summit (**8km; 1200m; 4h 35min**).

Return to the south-east top and go down to the south-east for a short

▶

way before descending more steeply down the broad south ridge. Initially this is down the left side (facing out) of rocks, then by a weaving line between small rock steps to reach the Bealach an Fhuarain (c.511m); there is a worn route to follow.

Avoid the rock buttress at the foot of Ainshval's north ridge by traversing right (west) for a short way, then zigzag up through boulders and scree to gain a grassy col on the ridge.

Although the ridge ahead can be scrambled up (tricky when wet), it is normally bypassed to the left by a small path up the edge of the corrie, Grey Corrie. A couple of minor slabby rock steps and some loose ground near the top lead to the grassy ridge a short distance from the large cairn that marks the summit of Ainshval

(**9.25km; 1480m; 5h 40min**).

With the main summits climbed, a return can be made from here. However, unless pressed for time, it is better to complete the traverse. To do so, descend the grassy ridge south above Forgotten Corrie to a col, then follow a pleasantly airy ridge up and over the broad Pt.759m (Leac a' Chaisteil) above Nameless Corrie and on to Sgùrr nan Gillean at the end of the ridge. The view back is spectacular (**10.75km; 1595m; 6h 15min**).

There are three principal ways back to Kinloch from Sgùrr nan Gillean:

(i) Perhaps the best is via Atlantic Corrie, which is easier than expected and pleasant in the early evening sun. Return to Ainshval (**12.25km; 1730m; 6h 50min**), then down to the Bealach an Fhuarain. Drop into the

head of Glen Dibidil, then traverse north-east below the rocks at the base of Trollabhal on a vague path to regain the Bealach an Oir.

Drop into Atlantic Corrie, losing 100m in height, either north down grass then north-north-east, or by a more direct north-easterly line. From the 350m contour, make a long and gradual rising traverse north beneath Askival and Hallival. There is a rough path in places. It is important to drop low enough to only make a short crossing over the boulders at the foot of the large boulder field and fairly recent rockfall. Beyond this, a rising ascent on rough paths gains the Bealach Bairc-mheall (466m).

Descend into Coire Dubh and follow the path back to Kinloch then the track behind the castle to the shop (**19.75km; 1870m; 9h 30min**).

The shop offers refreshments: ice cream, soft drinks and a well-earned beer. Note that the shop is 10min from the bunkhouse and 1.5km, 20min from the pier.

(ii) Many of those undertaking the traverse return via Dibidil bothy and the path above the eastern coast. To do so, from the summit of Sgùrr nan Gillean, go down the south ridge for about 600m to where the ground flattens at a tiny lochan at NM381925.

The last 100m can involve scrambling down short rocky gullies and requires care. Head east from the flatter ground to pick up the burn draining the east face, then follow it eastwards to gain the path above Dibidil bothy. Follow this path around the coast, which is rough and boggy in places and involves more ascent than expected. The path leads to the bunkhouse (**21.5km; 1870m; 9h 40min**).

It should be noted that Sgùrr nan Gillean's east ridge looks tempting as a direct descent, but it leads to steep and rocky ground and is not recommended. Other than (ii) or (iii), the only safe route into Glen Dibidil is into its head from Bealach an Fhuarain.

(iii) Easier but longer to the bothy is to return to the col between Sgùrr nan Gillean and Pt.759m, then descend south-west and south to cross the Papadil Burn and gain the coastal path to Dibidil and Kinloch (**24.25km; 1950m; 10h 25min**).

Askival with its north ridge, left, and west ridge, centre, from Trollabhal (Rab Anderson)

Ainshval and its north ridge from Trollabhal (Iain Thow)

Belig, left, and Garbh-bheinn with its north ridge in the foreground, from Marsco to the west (Tom Prentice)

SKYE

Garbh-bheinn; *808m; (C145); L32; NG531232); rough hill*

Although Skye is renowned for the Cuillin, the island contains many other fine hills worthy of attention. This becomes evident to anyone travelling the A87 between Broadford and Portree, where it loops around Loch Ainort, for the hills that encircle the head of the loch make an impressive sight with their bold outlines, contrasting red screes and dark gabbro cliffs.

Garbh-bheinn is the highest of these hills, and is the northern peak of a long ridge that extends from Loch Scavaig in the south over Blàbheinn to Loch Ainort in the north. Belig is a pointed outlier to the north-east, and is separated from Garbh-bheinn by the Bealach na Bèiste at 456m with the north facing Coire na Seilg between them. It is normal to climb both hills as a circuit around this corrie.

The traverse is started from a long layby at NG534267 in front of the Eas a' Bhradain waterfall, just around the bend where the A87 straightens for the uphill climb.

Cross the road and go along a path beside the crash barrier to cross the Allt Coire nam Bruadaran in front of the waterfall. Go through a gate in the fence and follow a path beside the waterfall and the river for a short way. Soon head up left on rough, but gently rising ground, aiming for the foot of the obvious spur, Druim Eadar Dà Choire, which extends from Garbh-bheinn's north ridge. A path soon appears by some boulders, leading to the ridge, then up to its top at 489m, where a line of old fence posts is met.

Descend south-east beside the fence posts to the col with the north ridge of Garbh-bheinn, where the rock changes from red granite to black gabbro, then follow the path up the increasingly rocky ridge. There is some easy scrambling, avoidable on the right, before the ridge turns left at the top to gain the rocky crown. This can be taken direct, or avoided on the right, to gain the splendid and airy summit (**4.25km; 850m; 2h 30min**).

It is a fabulous viewpoint: west to the Cuillin, northwards from Marsco to the ridge running over Beinn Dearg Mhòr to Glamaig, east to the other Beinn Dearg Mhòr and Beinn na Caillch above Broadford, then south to Clach Glas and Blàbheinn.

If only climbing Garbh-bheinn, then it is best to return the same way (**8.5km; 920m; 4h**).

To continue the traverse across to Belig, make a brief descent to the east, then drop steeply down to the north to gain some pinnacles at the start of the north-east ridge. The ridge leads down more easily to a scree slope, which is descended to then weave through an area of minor rock outcrops on grass to reach the Bealach na Bèiste between the hills.

Continue up the other side through rock and scree to meet an old wall, then follow this up to the grassy summit of Belig (**6.25km; 1095m; 3h 45min**).

Descend the north ridge to the 530m contour, where the ridge steepens into its craggy termination. Cut down to the left (west) here and descend quite steep scree to gain easier ground below, which leads north to the Abhainn Ceann Loch Ainort flowing from Coire ne Seilg between the hills. Follow this burn to where it is joined by the Allt a' Mheadhoin, then cross this and follow the combined burns to reach the road. Walk back along the side of the road. At the cutting where there is limited verge, it is probably best to keep clear of cars speeding round the bend by walking above the cutting on the north-east side of the road (9.5km; 1115m; 4h 50min).

A circuit of Garbh-bheinn and Belig can also be made from the south-east, from the B8083 where it loops around the head of Loch Slapin just beyond Torrin. This is perhaps best done in an anti-clockwise direction, starting with Belig, which also allows for variations at the end of the day.

Either park at NG561224 on a loop of old road where a rough path heads across to the south-east ridge of Belig, or in the main car park used for the ascent of Blàbheinn, then walk north along the road to this point.

Walk north to join an ATV track and cross the Allt Aigeinn's gravel beds, then gain the fine south-east ridge of Belig and follow it to the summit (2.75km; 705m; 1h 50min).

Descend Belig's south-west ridge to Bealach na Bèiste, then ascend the north-east ridge of Garbh-bheinn to reach its summit (4.25km; 1055m; 3h 5min).

Go down the rocky south-east ridge, which has some avoidable Grade 1 scrambling, to reach the col (636m) with Sgùrr nan Each. This peak can be skirted by a traverse south to reach the col with Matterhorn-like Clach Glas, where a descent east down steep scree leads into Choire a'

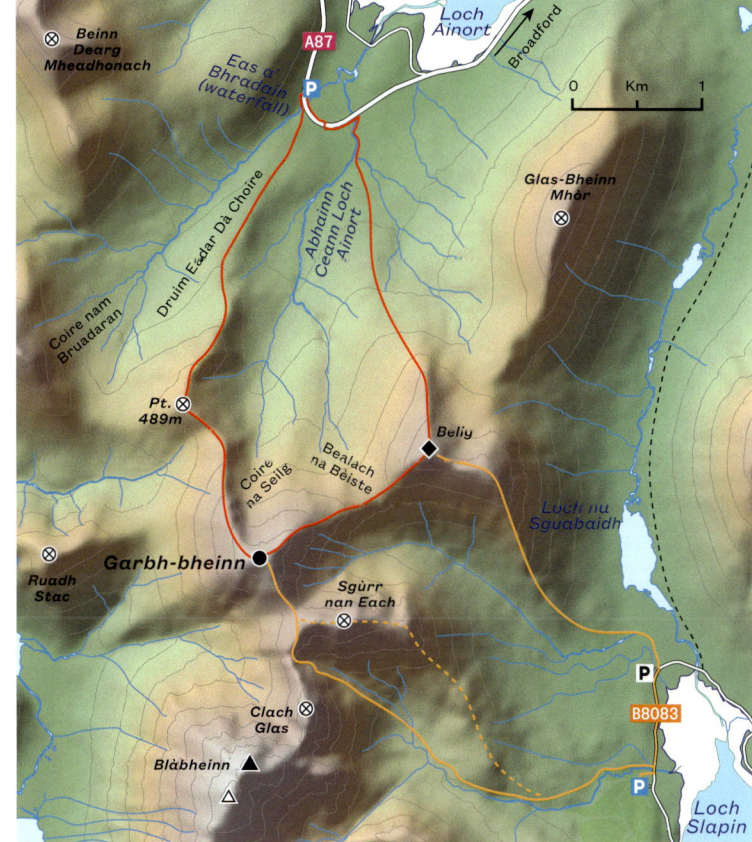

Càise to gain the Blàbheinn path where it runs down the Allt na Dunaiche. Follow this path back to the road (9km; 1090m; 4h 40min).

If Sgùrr nan Each is included, the ridge beyond its West Top (c.705m)

gives some Grade 1/2 scrambling leading to the summit (720m). Drop east to a dip, and climb onto the East Top (Pt.623m), then go down the south-east ridge to join the Blàbheinn path (9km; 1160m; 4h 50min).

Garbh-bheinn and Coire na Seilg, with the north ridge rising from Druim Eadar Dà Choire on the right (Tom Prentice)

Sgùrr Mhairi then Beinn Dearg Mhòr, Beinn Dearg Mheadhonach, Garbh-bheinn and Marsco (Robert Durran)

SKYE
GLAMAIG; greedy woman
Sgùrr Mhairi; *775m; (C198); L32; NG513300; Mary's Peak*

Appearing as a huge pyramidal cone rising above the entrance to Glen Sligachan opposite Sgùrr nan Gillean and the northern termination of the Cuillin ridge, Sgùrr Mhairi creates a compelling sight. Named after a girl who was killed while searching for a lost cow, its steep slopes of grass, capped with scree, rise to one of the most outstanding summit viewpoints on Skye.

Sgùrr Mhairi forms the northernmost of a chain of hills known as the Red Cuillin. It is often climbed with the smaller, though equally shapely, Beinn Dearg Mhòr (a Graham) to its south, from which it is separated by a col at 415m. This is the route that is recommended, although the short route is briefly described first. Another route from the north-east is also briefly described, which is the best way of climbing the hill on its own.

The two routes from the west start from a car park just off the A87 at the head of Loch Sligachan, on the east side of the bridge over the River Sligachan in front of the Sligachan Hotel. This is beside the entrance of the road to a self-catering bunkhouse and cottages.

The direct line can be seen and studied from here and presents no real problem other than one of unrelenting steepness, scree and some brutality. In 1899, a Gurkha ran from the Sligachan Inn to the summit and back in 55min, apparently barefoot. This route, although short, now forms one of Scotland's toughest hill races, with the record at the time of writing being set in 2018 at a staggering 44min, 22sec.

Ascend grass then scree to the left of the main mass of scree to gain a slight ridge and follow this to the top (**2.75km; 770m; 1h 55min**)

For the walker, returning the same way is probably best and safest (5.5km; 770m; 2h 50min).

The route can be extended along a ridge to An Coileach (673m) to the east-north-east; an added 2.5km, 180m, 50min there and back.

The descent to Sligachan can also be made by way of the Bealach na Sgàirde to the south, although the descent to there is steep too. This is actually the descent described for the recommended route, which includes Beinn Dearg Mòr, as follows.

Walk along the old road towards the picturesque old bridge and take the Loch Coruisk footpath past the statue of Cuillin pioneers Mackenzie and Collie, keeping to the left-hand path. In a further 200m, when the path forks, go left through a gate and follow the path up the side of the Allt Daraich gorge.

Pass a hummock to its left, then go through a gate on the left and follow the path as it crosses boggy ground and curves round to the base of the ridge. After the initial steepening, the ridge provides a fine highway leading to the final slopes of red-coloured scree, up which the path zigzags onto Beinn Dearg Mheadhonach (651m).

The top lies a short way to the south-east and is worth including for the view (**4.5km; 660m; 2h 5min**).

Head northwards around the edge of the eastern corrie, whose slopes plummet steeply to the road below, then descend to the Bealach Mosgaraidh. Climb the steep summit cone by a path that zigzags up through scree and juniper to reach the top of Beinn Dearg Mhòr (**6.25km; 880m; 3h**).

Descend north and continue along the shoulder overlooking Coire nan Laogh on the right, heading for a small cairn at the end. Once there, turn left towards Sligachan and drop down to pick up paths which descend steeply through the scree to the Bealach na Sgàirde (415m).

Glamaig's long and very steep southern shoulder rises dauntingly upwards from here. This gives a steep and stony climb linking areas of grass to avoid as much of the scree as

possible. The angle eases at the top, and the summit of Sgùrr Mhairi lies a short distance to the north-west (**8.25km; 1240m; 4h 15min**).

If the East Top of An Coileach (673m) is to be included, just before reaching the summit, turn right and follow a line of old fence posts across the dip and up the slight rise to its top; an added 2.4km, 155m, 45min there and back.

Although the punishing direct descent can be made towards Sligachan, it is perhaps easier to return to the Bealach na Sgàirde. From there, follow a path down south-westwards across to a spur, Teanga Mhòr, between the burns and descend this to where the burns join at NG505292. Either cross over to briefly follow the left bank, then cut across to the upward route, or cross to the right-hand burn and follow its right bank, then cut the corner to ▶

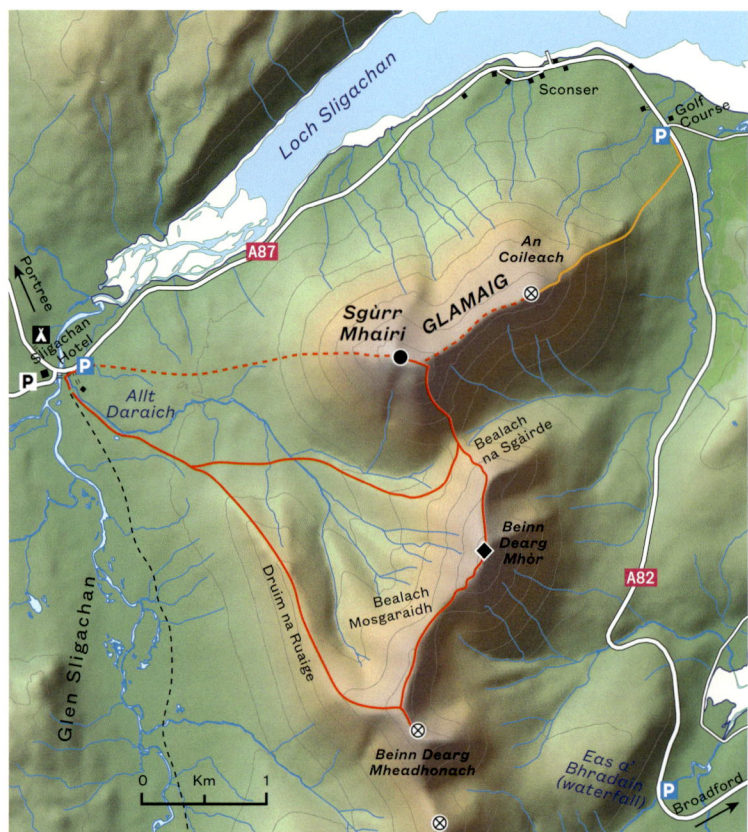

regain the car park more directly
(13.25km; 1250m; 5h 45min).

For the route from the north-east,
park in a layby at NG535317 on the
west side of the A850, just south of
the road off to the Golf Club and Moll.

Walk south along the roadside
verge for 300m and go through a
gate, then follow a fenceline straight
up the hillside. Most of the height is
gained on very steep grass.

Pass to the left of the lower crags,
on a path through the heather close
to the fence posts. Continue up
grassy ground to the foot of a run of
scree, which falls from a gully in the
middle of the next crags, and bypass
the crags on their left. The angle
eases for a way and leads to the
upper craggy section where the fence
posts are followed up a grassy break,
then on up to the top of 673m-high
An Coileach (*the cockerel*).

Continue pleasantly along a fine
and scenic ridge, crossing the dip,
then ascending easily and curving
round to the summit of Sgùrr Mhairi
(3km; 790m; 2h 5min).

It is easiest to return the same way
(6km; 830m; 3h 15min).

Across Loch Sligachan to Glamaig, with An Coileach and its north-east ridge, left, and Sgùrr Mhairi, right (Tom Prentice)

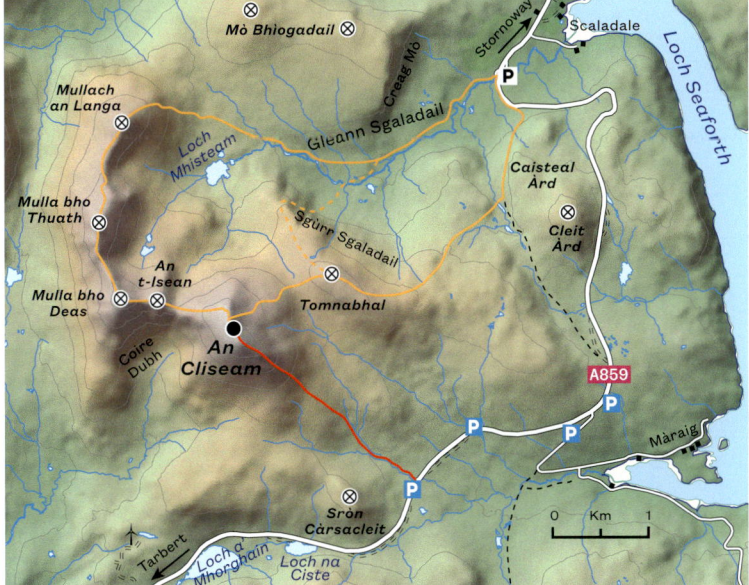

Mulla bho Thuath, Mulla bho Dheas and An Cliseam across Loch Bun Abhainn Eadarra (Rab Anderson)

HARRIS
An Cliseam (Clisham); 799m; (C160); L13 or L14; NB155073); rocky hill

---

There is only one Corbett in the entire 210km-long chain of islands that make up the Western Isles, or Outer Hebrides, and this is An Cliseam (Clisham) on the Isle of Harris. The name 'isle' is a bit of a misnomer, because Harris is not a separate island, and is joined to the Isle of Lewis to the north, so together they make up one single large island.

The separation between the two 'islands' is formed by the long sea inlet of Loch Seaforth in the east, and running westwards to Loch Rèasort, the rugged North Harris Hills.

An Cliseam is the highest point of these hills, and it overlooks the only road between Harris and Lewis, the A859, which runs between the hills and Loch Seaforth. This road climbs to a height of 155m beneath An Cliseam's south-eastern slopes, where a small car park and long pull-off on a section of the old road at NB174057 provide a convenient start point for the standard route of ascent. The Abhainn Mhàraig flows down from the hill here to run under the car park and the road.

It is only a short route, so a longer, more satisfying circuit of An Cliseam and the fine hills around Gleann Sgaladail to the north is described in the panel on page 388.

Leave the layby and follow a rough path up the right (north) side of the ▶

An Cliseam from the approach up the Abhainn Mhàraig to the south-east (Rab Anderson)

burn. A path up the left side is usually wetter. Cross at the fork and continue uphill beside the right branch for about 500m, then head more directly up towards the hill's stony upper cone. This lower section can be wet.

The upper section tapers to an increasingly rocky and bouldery ridge with a final short walk along a flat crest to the large circular walled cairn surrounding the trig point, which is perched above a steep drop to the north-east (**2.5km; 645m; 1h 40min**).

The views are superb. To the north-west over the three Grahams and assorted tops of the North Harris hills are the Uig hills on Lewis. South-east is Skye, with the hills of Wester Ross, Coigach and Assynt on the mainland beyond and to the east. South-west-wards across South Harris and a scattering of islands are the Uists, whilst out to the west is St Kilda on the edge of the Continental Shelf.

Return the same way (**5km; 645m; 2h 30min**).

The Sgaladail Horseshoe

An Cliseam, together with its immediate neighbours, Mulla bho Dheas and Mulla bho Thuath, and the lower hills Mullach an Langa and Tomnabhal, form a fine and prominent north-east facing horseshoe enclosing Loch Mhisteam and Gleann Sgaladail. This horseshoe gives a superb traverse.

Start from the north side of the bridge over the Abhainn Sgaladail at NB182099, where the A859 between Tarbert and Stornoway drops back down towards sea level on Loch Seaforth after passing between the hills, or, coming the other way, starts the climb up the hill. There is parking on sections of the old road either side of the main road. The impressive cliffs of Creag Mò are obvious close at hand to the west, whilst An Cliseam can be seen to the south-west over the top of another big, dank-looking cliff, Sgùrr Sgaladail, and to the side of Tomnabhal, the first objective.

There are two ways of attaining the summit of Tomnabhal, each of interest and each of the same distance and time:

*(i) Walk southwards along the road and up the hill for 600m to the start of a path that climbs across the hillside of Caisteal Ard. Signed to Màraig. This is the old post road, now part of the Harris Walkway network. Follow the path up and across the hillside into a small glen. When the path starts to flatten out, break off right, then head across boggy ground past the start of a small lochan, the lowest and most northerly of three lochans. Skirt around the south side of a small knoll, then climb south-west up the flanks of Tomnabhal to reach the long ridge running towards its summit, where the ground becomes firmer and rockier. Follow a long, grassy shelf just below a rocky escarpment and continue to the top of Tomnabhal (**4.25km; 520m 1h 50min**).*

*(ii) The alternative way to Tomnabhal is to follow a rough path up Gleann Sgaladail on the right (north) side of the Abhainn Sgaladail, passing beneath Creag Mò, to where the burn bends west below Sgùrr Sgaladail and the path fades. Find a suitable crossing point, then cross flattish ground and climb steeply up the obvious break in the lower slope to gain the slanting grass shelf beneath the cliff towards its right end. Follow the shelf up rightwards to pass around the north end of the cliff, then climb easily south-east above the cliff, up the side of Coire na h-Aonaig Mòire, passing a small lochan to gain the top of 552m high Tomnabhal (**4.25km; 520m 1h 50min**).*

*Leave Tomnabhal's summit and drop west to the col, then climb south-west and zigzag up the steepening slope on grass between the boulders, heading for an obvious notch in the battlement-like summit crest of An Cliseam. Climb through the notch to emerge onto the crest about 80m or so to the north-west of the summit; although steep at the top, there is no difficulty (**5.75km; 845m; 2h 45min**).*

Clamber northwards over the boulders, down and along the summit crest towards its end, then descend westwards to the narrow col with Mulla bho Dheas, picking up a rough path. Continue up the narrow ridge over the minor top of An t-Isean, then on up to Mulla bho Dheas (743m). The final rocky ridge can be tackled directly with some scrambling up the narrow crest, or more easily by a path on the right which cuts diagonally up beneath the rocks on the north-east side overlooking Coire Loch nan Eang. A large cairn marks the summit on the surprisingly flat crest.

*Swing north-west and go down the narrow and bouldery ridge with Uisgneabhal Mòr and Tèileasbhal prominent across the steep drop to the west. A steeper rocky section in the middle, above a crag to the east and steep slopes to the west, is easily negotiated. The fine ridge continues easily on up to Mulla bho Tuath (720m), which is a grand place from which to survey the route so far (**8km; 1075m; 4h**).*

Descend the ridge northwards to cross a col, then ascend over boulders to reach the flat top of the final summit, Mullach an Langa (614m), with the large Loch Langabhat stretching ahead into Lewis and a great inland wilderness system of lochs.

*Go down to the north-east for a short way, then swing eastwards and drop to easier-angled slopes to the north of Loch Misteam to gain its outflow, the Abhainn Sgaladail. Follow a rough path beside this burn down into Gleann Sgaladail to pass out in front of the long, vegetated dank cliffs of Sgùrr Sgaladail, to pick up a better path which runs alongside the burn beneath the cliffs of Creag Mò and back to the start (**14km; 115m; 5h 45min**).*

Heading northwards from the summit of An Cliseam, with Skye beyond (Rab Anderson)

Corbett's List

Scottish Mountains of 2500 feet (762m) and under 3000 feet (914.4m) in height with a reascent of 500 feet (152.4m) on all sides

The Table that follows lists 222 Scottish mountains that are over 2500ft (762m) in height and less than 3000ft (914.4m) in height, which have a reascent (drop, or prominence) of 500 feet (152.4m) on all sides.

The Table came into being following the publication in the Scottish Mountaineering Club's (*SMC*) Journal in 1952 of John Rooke Corbett's *List of Scottish Mountains 2500ft and Under 3000ft in Height*. Unlike Munro before him, whose Table of Scottish 3000ft mountains was published in 1891, Corbett set a height separation criterion to illustrate how distinct each hill on his list was from those hills around it. This was based on a set number of map contour rings, which was subsequently interpreted to mean that hills on his list had to involve a reascent (or drop) of 500ft (152.4m) on all sides, thereby illustrating their prominence.

Given the historic nature of The Munros, The Corbetts and The Donalds hill listings, the traditional method of grouping hills into their original imperial measurement height bands in feet has prevailed, despite the metrication of UK mapping, albeit that this creates odd metric equivalents for use with contemporary maps.

The Ordnance Survey (OS) is the national mapping authority responsible for the maintenance of the definitive record of Britain's geographic features. The OS produces the most widely-used maps for hillwalkers, and in order that this guidebook aligns with these maps, OS hill heights are used in the Table and throughout walk descriptions. The SMC recognises the ongoing survey work by others, so has included the height information held in the Database of British and Irish Hills (*DoBIH*) where it is different, or more accurate, than that on OS maps. The SMC hopes that the results of valid independent surveys can be incorporated into the OS database for potential inclusion in future mapping for the benefit of all walkers.

Table/Column Explanations

Section Number & Name: The Tables have been grouped into geographical Sections that correspond to the established Sections numbered 1-17, as used by the SMC for The Munros. Since there are no Munros in The Southern Uplands, a Section 0 was introduced to include the seven Lowland Corbetts. The addition of sixteen Corbetts in Morvern, Sunart, Ardgour and Moidart, an area of the Western Highlands that has no Munros, when added to the twenty-seven in the existing Section 10, would have meant that Section would have contained a disproportionate number of Corbetts, so it was sub-divided into Section 10a and Section 10b. Similarly, Section 1 has now been now sub-divided into Section 1a containing ten Corbetts and Section 1b containing twelve Corbetts; the division occurring either side of Loch Lomond, which was a division in Corbett's original list. Another amendment is that Meallach Mòr, Càrn Dearg Mòr and Leathad an Taobhain, which were included in Section 6 of the previous edition of Corbetts List, have now been moved to Section 8, where they sit more logically since they are most easily approached from Speyside to their north.

As with previous SMC Tables, the Sections here are ordered in a snake-like south to north progression through Scotland, finishing with The Islands. Some hill listings have hills listed in descending order of height, or in a strict OS grid location order. However, for ease of use in connection with this book and the way the text has been laid out, the Table here lists hills in a geographic order that generally relates to the way in which they are approached by road. This also has the advantage of having hills that are generally linked and climbed together appearing together in the Table.

Name: The name is generally that according to the OS. When there are two hills with the same name, standard brackets give a relevant location. When there is an overall name for a hill massif, or a second or an alternative name for a hill, this is shown in square brackets.

Height: This is in metres and taken from OS maps. Figures in brackets next to these indicate heights taken from the DoBIH that differ from and may be more accurate than the OS heights.

C No: Corbetts in order of height, (C1) being the highest, which is Beinn a' Chlaidheimh (914m), and C222 being the lowest, which is Beinn na h-Uamha (762m). A list of Corbetts in order of height is given on page 392.

OS Map & Grid: The first two digits refer to the relevant OS 1:50k Landranger series map which covers the hill. Some hills appear on two maps with the route to the summit shown complete, or in part. An eight-figure OS grid reference, prefixed by two grid letters, is given in the following Table, which provides the location of a summit to within 10m. A six-figure grid reference has been given in the text, which provides the location of a summit to within 100m.

Munro's Tables and Donald's Tables both included Tops. As a result Munro's Tables lists a total of 508 summits, of which 282 are classed as separate mountains, or Munros, and 226 are classed as subsidiary Munro Tops. Donald did the same, and there are 89 Donalds and 52 Donald Tops. Corbett did not do this, so Corbett Tops are not listed here. A list of some 450 Corbett Tops was produced in 1999 with a 30m drop criterion. More recently this listing has been rationalised and they, together with other hills in Britain & Ireland above 600m with a 30m drop, have been named SIMMS (Six Hundred Metre Mountains).

Name	Height (DoBIH)	C No	OS Map	Grid Ref	Page	Date climbed
SECTION 0 – Galloway & The Borders						
The Merrick	843	C98	77	NX 4276 8555	16	
Shalloch on Minnoch	775 (774.2)	C200	77	NX 4076 9056	19	
Corserine	814	C134	77	NX 4978 8706	21	
Cairnsmore of Carsphairn	797	C164	77	NX 5944 9800 (a)	23	
Hart Fell	808	C146	78	NT 1136 1357	25	
White Coomb	821	C123	79	NT 1632 1509	28	
Broad Law	840 (840.1)	C105	72	NT 1464 2353	30	
SECTION 1a – Loch Fyne to Loch Lomond						
The Cobbler [Ben Arthur]	884	C43	56	NN 2596 0582	35	
Beinn Luibhean	858 (859.7)	C80	56	NN 2428 0791	37	
The Brack	787 (787.5)	C178	56	NN 2457 0305	39	
Cnoc Còinnich	764 (763.5)	C220	56	NN 2335 0075	41	
Ben Donich	847	C95	56	NN 2184 0431	42	
Beinn an Lochain	901 (901.7)	C19	56	NN 2181 0789 (b)	44	
Stob Coire Creagach	817 (817.8)	C128	56/50	NN 2306 1091	45	
Caisteal Dubh [Beinn Bheula]	779	C190	56	NS 1548 9832	46	
Meall an Fhùdair	764	C218	56/50	NN 2707 1924	48	
Beinn Chùirn	880	C48	50	NN 2803 2923	50	
SECTION 1b – Loch Lomond to Loch Tay						
Beinn a' Choin	770 (768.7)	C208	56/50	NN 3543 1302	55	
Ben Ledi	879	C50	57	NN 5624 0977	56	
Benvane	821	C121	57	NN 5352 1372	58	
Beinn Each	813	C135	57	NN 6017 1580	60	
Beinn Stacach	771 (771.8)	C205	57	NN 4744 1632	61	
Stob a' Choin	869	C63	56	NN 4172 1597	62	
Creag Mac Rànaich	809 (808.6)	C144	51	NN 5456 2556	64	
Meall an t-Seallaidh	852 (852.7)	C90	51	NN 5421 2340	64	
Meall na Fearna	809 (810)	C141	57	NN 6508 1868	66	
Auchnafree Hill	789 (787.4)	C176	52	NN 8086 3080	67	
Creag Uchdag	879 (878.8)	C51	51/52	NN 7083 3232	68	
Creagan na Beinne	888 (889.1)	C36	51/52	NN 7444 3685	71	
SECTION 2 – Loch Tay to Rannoch Moor						
Meall Tairneachan	787	C181	52	NN 8075 5437	75	
Farragon Hill	783 (782.4)	C186	52	NN 8403 5530	75	
Meall nam Maigheach	779 (778.9)	C192	51	NN 5859 4359 (c)	77	
Beinn nan Oighreag	909 (909.6)	C10	51	NN 5417 4119	79	
Beinn Dearg	830	C115	51	NN 6087 4975 (d)	81	
Cam Chreag (Glen Lyon)	862	C75	51	NN 5368 4912	82	
Meall nan Subh	806	C151	51	NN 4608 3974	84	
Meall Buidhe	910 (908.4)	C9	51	NN 4269 4495	85	
Sròn a' Choire Chnapanaich	837 (835)	C111	51	NN 4560 4529	85	
Beinn nan Imirean	849	C92	51	NN 4193 3094	87	
Cam Chreag (Glen Lochay)	884 (883.6)	C44	50	NN 3755 3466	88	
Beinn Chaorach	818	C125	50	NN 3589 3281	88	
Beinn Odhar	901 (900.8)	C22	50	NN 3374 3388	90	
Beinn a' Chaisteil	886	C40	50	NN 3472 3640	92	
Beinn nam Fuaran	806	C149	50	NN 3611 3818	92	
SECTION 3 – Glen Orchy to Loch Linnhe						
Beinn a' Bhùiridh	897 (898.4)	C26	50	NN0944 2837 (e)	97	
Beinn Mhic Mhonaidh	796	C165	50	NN2087 3501 (f)	98	
Beinn Udlaidh	840 (840.4)	C104	50	NN2803 3326	99	
Beinn Bhreac-liath	802	C157	50	NN3028 3391	99	
Beinn a' Chrùlaiste	857	C83	41	NN 2463 5667	101	
Beinn Mhic Chasgaig	864	C70	41/50	NN2215 5022 (g)	102	
Stob Dubh	883	C45	41/50	NN1664 4882	103	

Name	Height (DoBIH)	C No	OS Map	Grid Ref	Page	Date climbed
Beinn Maol Chaluim	907 (906.3)	C14	41/50	NN 1350 5258	106	
Beinn Trilleachan	840	C106	50	NN 0865 4389	108	
Meall Lighiche	772	C204	41	NN 0948 5283	109	
Fraochaidh	879	C52	41	NN 0291 5170	110	
Creach Bheinn	810	C139	50	NN 0238 4223	112	
Garbh Bheinn	867	C67	41	NN 1693 6009	113	

SECTION 4 - Loch Linnhe to Loch Ericht

Name	Height (DoBIH)	C No	OS Map	Grid Ref	Page	Date climbed
Mam na Gualainn	796 (796.5)	C167	41	NN 1151 6254	117	
Glas Bheinn	792	C172	41	NN 2590 6411	119	
Leum Uilleim	909 (906.5)	C11	41	NN 3307 6413	120	
Meall na Meoig [Beinn Pharlagain]	868 (867.3)	C65	42	NN 4482 6420 (h)	122	
Cruach Innse	857	C84	41	NN 2799 7636	123	
Sgùrr Innse	809	C142	41	NN 2903 7481	123	
The Fara	911	C7	42	NN 5983 8425	124	

SECTION 5 – Loch Ericht to Drumochter

Name	Height (DoBIH)	C No	OS Map	Grid Ref	Page	Date climbed
Beinn a' Chuallaich	892 (892.2)	C32	42	NN 6846 6176	129	
Stob an Aonaich Mhòir	855 (855.6)	C88	42	NN 5375 6942	130	
Beinn Mholach	841 (841.8)	C101	42	NN 5875 6548	131	
Meall na Leitreach	775 (777.1)	C197	42	NN 6398 7029 (i)	132	
The Sow of Atholl [Meall an Dobharchain]	803 (798.9)	C156	42	NN 6248 7412 (j)	132	

SECTION 6 – Drumochter to Glen Shee

Name	Height (DoBIH)	C No	OS Map	Grid Ref	Page	Date climbed
An Dùn	827 (827.4)	C118	42	NN 7165 8013	137	
	827 (827.4)			NN 7173 8049 (k)		
A' Chaoirnich [Maol Creag an Loch]	875 (875.7)	C56	42	NN 7352 8070	137	
Beinn Bhreac	912 (912.4)	C5	43	NN 8684 8207 (l)	139	
Beinn Mheadhonach	901 (900.9)	C21	43	NN 8801 7589	140	
Ben Vuirich	903	C18	43	NN 9972 7000	142	
Ben Vrackie	841 (842.2)	C100	43	NN 9508 6323	144	
Ben Gulabin	806	C150	43	NO 1004 7220	146	
Morrone [Morven]	859 (859.5)	C77	43	NO 1321 8863	147	

SECTION 7 – Glen Shee to Glen Esk

Name	Height (DoBIH)	C No	OS Map	Grid Ref	Page	Date climbed
Monamenach	807	C148	43	NO1760 7066	151	
Creag nan Gabhar	834	C114	43	NO 1546 8410	152	
Conachcraig	865	C68	44	NO 2795 8651	154	
Ben Tirran [The Goet]	896 (897)	C27	44	NO 3734 7461	156	
Mount Battock	778	C193	44/45	NO 5496 8446	158	

SECTION 8 – Deeside to Speyside

Name	Height (DoBIH)	C No	OS Map	Grid Ref	Page	Date climbed
Sgòr Mòr	813	C136	43	NO 0073 9142	163	
Càrn na Drochaide	818	C126	36/43	NO 1274 9383	164	
Culardoch	900	C23	36/43	NO 1935 9882	165	
Creag an Dail Bheag	863	C71	36/43	NO 1573 9815	165	
Morven	872	C61	37	NJ 3768 0399	167	
Brown Cow Hill	829	C117	36/37	NJ 2210 0444	169	
Càrn Ealasaid	792	C171	36/37	NJ 2277 1177	170	
Càrn Mòr	804	C154	36/37	NJ 2657 1834	171	
Corryhabbie Hill	781 (781.3)	C188	36/37	NJ 2809 2886	174	
Ben Rinnes	841	C103	28	NJ 2550 3544	176	
Geal Chàrn	821	C122	36	NJ 0905 1269	177	
Meall a' Bhuachaille	810	C140	36	NH 9908 1153	179	
Creag Mhòr	895	C31	36	NJ 0574 0477	180	
Leathad an Taobhain	912 (911.7)	C6	43	NN 8217 8582	182	
Càrn Dearg Mòr	857 (857.4)	C82	35/43	NN 8232 9118	182	
Meallach Mhòr	769	C210	35	NN 7766 9087	184	

Name	Height (DoBIH)	C No	OS Map	Grid Ref	Page	Date climbed
SECTION 9 – Speyside to the Great Glen						
Geal-chàrn Mòr	824	C120	35	NH 8364 1232	189	
Càrn an Fhreiceadain	878	C55	35	NH 7256 0712	190	
Càrn na Saobhaidhe	811 (811.1)	C138	35	NH 6003 1449 (m)	191	
Meall na h-Aisre	862 (862.1)	C76	35	NH 5154 0005	193	
Gairbeinn	896 (895.5)	C30	34	NN 4605 9851	194	
Càrn a' Chuilinn	817	C129	34	NH 4167 0339	196	
Beinn Iaruinn	805	C153	34	NN 2970 9003	197	
Càrn Dearg (East of Glen Roy)	834	C113	34	NN 3450 8869	199	
Càrn Dearg (North of Gleann Eachach)	817 (816.5)	C130	34	NN 3500 9662	200	
Càrn Dearg (South of Gleann Eachach)	768	C211	34	NN 3572 9487	200	
SECTION 10a – Loch Linnhe to Glenfinnan						
Beinn na h-Uamha	762 (762.4)	C222	40	NM 9172 6641	205	
Garbh Bheinn	885	C42	40	NM 9044 6220	206	
Fuar Bheinn	766	C215	49	NM 8535 5634	208	
Creach Bheinn	853	C89	49	NM 8706 5764	208	
Sgùrr Dhomhnuill	888 (888.4)	C37	40	NM 8896 6788	210	
Càrn na Nathrach	786	C182	40	NM 8863 6987	212	
Beinn Resipol	845	C97	40	NM 7665 6545	213	
Stob Coire a' Chearcaill	771	C206	41	NN 0169 7267	214	
Sgòrr Craobh a' Chaorainn	775	C199	40	NM 8956 7578	216	
Sgùrr Ghiubhsachain	849	C94	40	NM 8756 7512	216	
Stob a' Bhealach an Sgrìodain	770	C207	40	NM 8747 7273	216	
Beinn Odhar Bheag	882 (883.3)	C46	40	NM 8466 7786	220	
Beinn Mhic Cèdidh	783	C185	40	NM 8283 7881	220	
Sgùrr na Bà Glaise	874 (874.1)	C59	40	NM 7704 7773 (n)	222	
Rois-bheinn	882 (882.4)	C47	40	NM 7561 7783	222	
An Stac	814	C133	40	NM 7631 7928 (o)	222	
SECTION 10b – Glenfinnan to Glen Shiel						
Beinn Bhàn	796 (795.9)	C166	34/41	NN 1406 8570	227	
Meall a' Phubuill	774 (772.7)	C202	41	NN 0294 8541	228	
Bràigh nan Uamhachan	765	C216	40	NM 9754 8671	229	
Streap	909	C12	40	NM 9466 8636	230	
Sgùrr an Utha	796	C168	40	NM 8851 8397	232	
Meall na h-Eilde	838 (837.2)	C110	34	NN 1855 9462	233	
Geal Chàrn	804	C155	34	NN 1562 9426	233	
Sgùrr Mhurlagain	880	C49	33	NN 0126 9446	235	
Fraoch Bheinn	858 (857.3)	C81	33/40	NM 9861 9403	235	
Sgùrr Còs na Breachd-laoidh	835	C112	33/40	NM 9488 9467	237	
Sgùrr an Fhuarain	901	C20	33/40	NM 9874 9797	238	
Càrn Mòr	829 (830)	C116	33/40	NM 9031 9093 (p)	239	
Bidein a' Chabair	867 (867.5)	C66	33/40	NM 8891 9305	240	
Ben Tee	904	C16	34	NN 2406 9719	241	
Sgùrr nan Eugallt	898 (897.5)	C25	33	NG 9272 0486	242	
Sgùrr a' Choire-bheithe	913 (913.3)	C4	33	NG 8960 0158	243	
Beinn an Aodainn [Ben Aden]	887	C38	33/40	NM 8994 9861 (q)	244	
Buidhe Bheinn	885 (885.5)	C41	33	NG 9634 0904	247	
Sgùrr Coire Chòinnichean	796	C169	33	NG 7908 0109	248	
Beinn na Caillich	785	C184	33	NG 7960 0669	249	
Sgùrr Coire an Fhìr-eòin [Beinn Bhuidhe]	855	C87	33/40	NM 8218 9671	250	
Meall Dubh	789	C177	34	NH 2454 0784 (s)	251	
Beinn Loinne, West Top	790 (789)	C175	34	NH 1308 0768 (r)	252	
Sgùrr Mhic Bharraich	779	C191	33	NG 9177 1735	253	
Beinn nan Caorach	774	C201	33	NG 8715 1211	254	
Beinn na h-Eaglaise	805	C152	33	NG 8544 1200	254	

Name	Height (DoBIH)	C No	OS Map	Grid Ref	Page	Date climbed
SECTION 11 – Glen Shiel to Loch Mullardoch (Glen Cannich)						
Am Bàthach	798 (798.1)	C162	33	NH 0733 1433	259	
Sgùrr an Airgid	841 (841.2)	C102	25/33	NG 9405 2270 (t)	260	
Sgùrr Gaorsaic	839	C107	25/33	NH 0359 2186 (u)	261	
Càrn a' Choire Ghairbh	865 (862.5)	C69	25/34	NH 1369 1887	262	
Aonach Shasuinn	888	C35	25/34	NH 1733 1801	262	
SECTION 12 – Loch Mullardoch (Glen Cannich) to Glen Carron						
Sgùman Còinntich	879	C53	25	NG 9770 3035	267	
Aonach Buidhe	899	C24	25	NH 0576 3245	268	
Faochaig	868	C64	25	NH 0219 3170	268	
Sgòrr na Dìollaid	818 (817.9)	C127	25	NH 2818 3625	270	
Beinn a' Bhàthaich Àrd	862	C74	26	NH 3606 4347	271	
An Sìthean	814	C132	25	NH 1711 4538	272	
Bac an Eich	849	C91	25	NH 2222 4894	274	
Meallan nan Uan	838 (838.3)	C109	25	NH 2637 5446	276	
Sgùrr a' Mhuilinn	879 (878.8)	C54	25	NH 2647 5574	276	
Sgùrr nan Ceannaichean	913 (913.4)	C3	25	NH 0873 4805	278	
Beinn Tharsuinn	863 (861.2)	C72	25	NH 0552 4334	279	
Sgùrr na Feartaig	862 (863)	C73	25	NH 0552 4540	279	
Beinn Dronaig	797	C163	25	NH 0371 3817	280	
SECTION 13 – Glen Carron to Loch Maree						
Fuar Tholl	907	C13	25	NG 9755 4893	285	
An Ruadh-Stac	892 (890.4)	C33	25	NG 9215 4805	286	
Sgùrr a' Chaorachain	792	C173	24	NG 7966 4174	287	
Beinn Bhàn	896	C28	24	NG 8036 4503	289	
Spidean Coire an Laoigh [Beinn Damh]	903	C17	24/25	NG 8926 5019	290	
Beinn Dearg	914 (913.7)	C2	19/24/25	NG 8953 6081	292	
Sgòrr nan Lochan Uaine	871	C62	25	NG 9691 5314	294	
Sgùrr Dubh	782	C187	25	NG 9791 5578	294	
Ruadh-stac Beag	896	C29	19	NG 9728 6133	296	
Meall a' Ghiuthais	887	C39	19	NG 9761 6341	296	
Beinn an Eòin	855	C86	19	NG 9051 6462 (v)	298	
Sgòrr Dubh [Baosbheinn]	875	C57	19	NG 8703 6541 (w)	298	
SECTION 14 - Loch Maree to Loch Broom						
Beinn Àirigh Charr	792	C174	19	NG 9303 7617	303	
Beinn Làir	859	C78	19	NG 9816 7327	304	
Beinn a' Chàisgein Mòr	856	C85	19	NG 9825 7854	308	
Beinn Dearg Bheag	820	C124	19	NH 0200 8112	310	
Beinn Dearg Mòr	906 (906.3)	C15	19	NH 0322 7993	310	
Sàil Mhòr	767	C212	19	NH 0330 8870	312	
Beinn a' Chlaidheimh	914 (913.9)	C1	19	NH 0614 7757	314	
Creag Rainich	807 (807.9)	C147	19/20	NH 0960 7514 (x)	316	
Beinn Liath Mhòr a' Ghiubhais Lì	766	C213	20	NH 2808 7130	317	
on OS 1:25k map as Beinn Liath Mhòr a' Ghiuthais Lì						
SECTION 15 – Loch Broom to the Cromarty Firth						
Little Wyvis	763	C221	20	NH 4296 6448	321	
Beinn a' Chaisteil	787	C179	20	NH 3700 8010	322	
Càrn Bàn	842 (843.3)	C99	20	NH 3385 8757	324	
Beinn Enaiglair	889 (890)	C34	20	NH 2250 8051	326	
Càrn Chuinneag	839	C108	20	NH 4836 8332	328	

Name		Height (DoBIH)	C No	OS Map	Grid Ref	Page	Date climbed

SECTION 16 – Loch Broom to The Pentland Firth

Name	Height (DoBIH)	C No	OS Map	Grid Ref	Page
Cùl Beag	769	C209	15	NC 1404 0882	*333*
Cùl Mòr	849	C93	15	NC 1621 1191	*334*
Canisp	847	C96	15	NC 2031 1876	*336*
Breabag	815	C131	15	NC 2866 1572	*337*
Spidean Còinich [Quinag]	764	C219	15	NC 2061 2772	*338*
Sàil Ghorm [Quinag]	776	C196	15	NC 1983 3043	*338*
Sàil Gharbh [Quinag]	809	C143	15	NC 2093 2919	*338*
Glas Bheinn	776	C195	15	NC 2548 2649	*342*
Beinn Leòid	792	C170	15	NC 3203 2949	*344*
Ben Hee	873	C60	16	NC 4265 3394	*345*
Meallan Liath Coire Mhic Dhughaill	801 (800.8)	C159	15/16	NC 3572 3914	*347*
Meall Horn	777 (776.7)	C194	9	NC 3526 4491	*348*
Arkle	787	C180	9	NC 3027 4618	*350*
Ganu Mòr [Foinaven]	911	C8	9	NC 3153 5070	*352*
Cranstackie	801	C158	9	NC3506 5559	*356*
Beinn Spionnaidh	773	C203	9	NC 3620 5730	*356*
An Caisteal [Ben Loyal]	764 (764.2)	C217	10	NC 5781 4885	*358*

SECTION 17 – The Islands: Arran, Jura, Mull, Rum, Skye & Harris

Name		Height (DoBIH)	C No	OS Map	Grid Ref	Page
Goatfell	(Arran)	874 (875)	C58	69	NR9914 4154	*365*
Beinn Tarsuinn	(Arran)	826	C119	69	NR9596 4120	*368*
Cir Mhòr	(Arran)	799 (798.1)	C161	69	NR9728 4310	*368*
Caisteal Abhail	(Arran)	859	C79	69	NR9691 4432	*370*
Beinn an Oir	(Jura)	785	C183	61	NM4981 7494	*374*
Dùn da Ghaoithe	(Mull)	766	C214	49	NM6725 3621	*376*
Askival	(Rum)	812	C137	39	NG3931 9521	*378*
Ainshval	(Rum)	781	C189	39	NG3785 9432	*378*
Garbh-bheinn	(Skye)	808 (808.3)	C145	32	NG5313 2323	*382*
Sgùrr Mhairi [Glamaig]	(Skye)	775	C198	32	NG5136 2999	*384*
An Cliseam [Clisham]	(Harris)	799 (800)	C160	13/14	NB1547 0731	*387*

(a) Cairnsmore of Carsphairn - boulder 12m north-west of trig is apparently the highest point.

(b) Beinn an Lochain - highest point is on the further away south-west knoll, 100m from the north-east knoll.

(c) Meall nam Maigheach - large rock 50m to the east-south-east of the cairn at NN5855 4359 is the highest point.

(d) Beinn Dearg - rock 35m north-north-west of the southern cairn is the highest point.

(e) Beinn a' Bhùiridh - rock 20m north-north-east of the cairn is the highest point.

(f) Beinn Mhic Mhonaidh - rock 50m east-south-east of the cairn is the highest point.

(g) Beinn Mhic Chasgaig - boulder 60m north-east of cairn at NN2211 5017 is the highest point.

(h) Meall na Meoig - slab 40m north-north-west of cairn is the highest point.

(i) Meall na Leitreach - small cairn at NN6405 7026 is the higest point; just before larger cairn, 100m east-south-east of track and where the OS show it.

(j) The Sow of Atholl - cairn on boulder at NN6252 7411, some 40m east-south-east of where OS show summit.

(k) An Dùn - surveys have determined that the south summit at NN7165 8013 (a tiny cairn 29m north-north-west of the main cairn) and the north summit, some 430m away at NN7173 8049 (small cairn), are the same height.

(l) Beinn Bhreac - embedded boulder 25m north-east of the cairn is the highest point.

(m) Càrn na Saobhaidhe - the cairn by the end of the Dunmaglass track to the north has been surveyed as being lower than a point at NN5990 1440, which lies 160m to the south-west and 80m north-north-east of a windfarm mast.

(n) Sgùrr na Bà Glaise - outcrop 26m south-east of the cairn is the highest point.

(o) An Stac - outcrop 25m east-north-east of the cairn is the highest point.

(p) Carn Mòr - small cairn on outcrop 16m to south-south-west of main cairn has been found to be the highest point.

(q) Beinn an Aodainn - rock 15m to south-east of the cairn is the highest point.

(r) Beinn Loinne - highpoint is 18m to the west of the trig pillar.

(s) Meall Dubh - rock 40m south of the large cairn has been found to be higher.

(t) Sgùrr an Airgid - rock outcrop 25m north-east of the broken trig pillar is the highest point.

(u) Sgùrr Gaorsaic - rock 65m to the north of the cairn could be as high.

(v) Beinn an Eòin - rock 15m north of wind shelter is the highest point.

(w) Sgòr Dubh (Baosbheinn) - slab 15m west of cairn is the highest point

(x) Creag Rainich - slabby rock 60m west of the trig is the highest point.

C No.	Name	Height	Page	C No.	Name	Height	Page
C1	Beinn a' Chlaidheimh	914	314	C60	Ben Hee	873	345
C2	Beinn Dearg (Torridon)	914	292	C61	Morven (Cromar)	872	167
C3	Sgùrr nan Ceannaichean	913	278	C62	Sgòrr nan Lochan Uaine	871	294
C4	Sgùrr a' Choire-bheithe	913	243	C63	Stob a' Choin	869	62
C5	Beinn Bhreac	912	139	C64	Faochaig	868	268
C6	Leathad an Taobhain	912	182	C65	Meall na Meoig [Beinn Pharlagain]	868 *	122
C7	The Fara	911	124	C66	Bidein a' Chabair	867 *	240
C8	Ganu Mòr [Foinaven]	911	352	C67	Garbh Bheinn (Loch Leven)	867	113
C9	Meall Buidhe	910 *	85	C68	Conachcraig	865	154
C10	Beinn nan Oighreag	909 *	79	C69	Càrn a' Choire Ghairbh	865 *	262
C11	Leum Uilleim	909 *	120	C70	Beinn Mhic Chasgaig	864	102
C12	Streap	909	230	C71	Creag an Dail Bheag	863	165
C13	Fuar Tholl	907	285	C72	Beinn Tharsuinn (West Monar)	863 *	279
C14	Beinn Maol Chaluim	907 *	106	C73	Sgurr na Feartaig	862 *	279
C15	Beinn Dearg Mòr	906	310	C74	Beinn a' Bhàthaich Àrd	862	271
C16	Ben Tee	904	241	C75	Cam Chreag (Glen Lyon)	862	82
C17	Spidean Coire an Laoigh [Beinn Damh]	903	290	C76	Meall na h-Aisre	862	193
C18	Ben Vuirich	903	142	C77	Morrone [Morven] (Cromar)	859 *	147
C19	Beinn an Lochain	901 *	44	C78	Beinn Làir	859	304
C20	Sgùrr an Fhuarain	901	238	C79	Caisteal Abhail	859	370
C21	Beinn Mheadhonach	901	140	C80	Beinn Luibhean	858 *	37
C22	Beinn Odhar	901	90	C81	Fraoch Bheinn	858 *	235
C23	Culardoch	900	165	C82	Càrn Dearg Mòr	857	182
C24	Aonach Buidhe	899	268	C83	Beinn a' Chrùlaiste	857	101
C25	Sgùrr nan Eugallt	898	242	C84	Cruach Innse	857	123
C26	Beinn a' Bhùiridh	897 *	97	C85	Beinn a' Chàisgein Mòr	856	308
C27	Ben Tirran [The Goet]	896 *	156	C86	Beinn an Eòin	855	298
C28	Beinn Bhàn	896	289	C87	Sgùrr Coire an Fhìr-eòin [Beinn Bhuidhe]	855	250
C29	Ruadh-stac Beag	896	296	C88	Stob an Aonaich Mhòir	855 *	130
C30	Gairbeinn	896	194	C89	Creach Bheinn (Morvern)	853	208
C31	Creag Mhòr	895	180	C90	Meall an t-Seallaidh	852 *	64
C32	Beinn a' Chuallaich	892	129	C91	Bac an Eich	849	274
C33	An Ruadh-Stac	892 *	286	C92	Beinn nan Imirean	849	87
C34	Beinn Enaiglair	889 *	326	C93	Cùl Mòr	849	334
C35	Aonach Shasuinn	888	262	C94	Sgùrr Ghiubhsachain	849	216
C36	Creagan na Beinne	888 *	71	C95	Ben Donich	847	42
C37	Sgùrr Dhomhnuill	888	210	C96	Canisp	847	336
C38	Beinn an Aodainn [Ben Aden]	887	244	C97	Beinn Resipol	845	213
C39	Meall a' Ghiuthais	887	296	C98	The Merrick	843	16
C40	Beinn a' Chaisteil (Auch)	886	92	C99	Càrn Bàn	842 *(i)	324
C41	Buidhe Bheinn	885 *	247	C100	Ben Vrackie	841 *	144
C42	Garbh Bheinn (Ardgour)	885	206	C101	Beinn Mholach	841 *	131
C43	The Cobbler [Ben Arthur]	884	35	C102	Sgùrr an Airgid	841	260
C44	Cam Chreag (Glen Lochay)	884	88	C103	Ben Rinnes	841	176
C45	Stob Dubh	883	103	C104	Beinn Udlaidh	840	99
C46	Beinn Odhar Bheag	882 *	220	C105	Broad Law	840	30
C47	Rois-bheinn	882	222	C106	Beinn Trilleachan	840	108
C48	Beinn Chuirn	880	50	C107	Sgùrr Gaorsaic	839	261
C49	Sgùrr Mhurlagain	880	235	C108	Càrn Chuinneag	839 (ii)	328
C50	Ben Ledi	879	56	C109	Meallan nan Uan	838	276
C51	Creag Uchdag	879	68	C110	Meall na h-Eilde	838 *	233
C52	Fraochaidh	879	110	C111	Sròn a' Choire Chnapanich	837 *	85
C53	Sgùman Còinntich	879	267	C112	Sgùrr Còs na Breachd-laoidh	835	237
C54	Sgùrr a' Mhuilinn	879	276	C113	Càrn Dearg (East of Glen Roy)	834	199
C55	Càrn an Fhreiceadain	878	190	C114	Creag nan Gabhar	834	152
C56	A' Chaoirnich [Maol Creag an Loch]	875 *	137	C115	Beinn Dearg (Glen Lyon)	830	81
C57	Sgòrr Dubh [Baosbheinn]	875	298	C116	Càrn Mòr (Glen Dessarry)	829 *	239
C58	Goat Fell	874 *	365	C117	Brown Cow Hill	829	169
C59	Sgùrr na Bà Glaise	874	222	C118	An Dùn	827	137

C No.	Name	Height	Page
C119	Beinn Tarsuinn (Arran)	826	368
C120	Geal-chàrn Mòr	824	189
C121	Benvane	821	58
C122	Geal Chàrn (Dorback)	821	177
C123	White Coomb	821	28
C124	Beinn Dearg Bheag	820	310
C125	Beinn Chaorach	818	88
C126	Càrn na Drochaide	818	164
C127	Sgòrr na Dìollaid	818	270
C128	Stob Coire Creagach	817 *	45
C129	Càrn a' Chuilinn	817	196
C130	Càrn Dearg (North of Gleann Eachach)	817	200
C131	Breabag	815	337
C132	An Sìthean	814	272
C133	An Stac	814	222
C134	Corserine	814	21
C135	Beinn Each	813	60
C136	Sgòr Mòr	813	163
C137	Askival	812	378
C138	Càrn na Saobhaidhe	811	191
C139	Creach Bheinn (Loch Creran)	810	112
C140	Meall a' Bhuachaille	810	179
C141	Meall na Fearna	809 *	66
C142	Sgùrr Innse	809	123
C143	Sàil Gharbh [Quinag]	809	338
C144	Creag Mac Rànaich	809	64
C145	Garbh-bheinn (Skye)	808	382
C146	Hart Fell	808	25
C147	Creag Rainich	807 *	316
C148	Monamenach	807	151
C149	Beinn nam Fuaran	806	92
C150	Ben Gulabin	806	146
C151	Meall nan Subh	806	84
C152	Beinn na h-Eaglaise	805	254
C153	Beinn Iaruinn	805	197
C154	Càrn Mòr (Ladder Hills)	804	171
C155	Geal Chàrn (Loch Arkaig)	804	233
C156	The Sow of Atholl [Meall an Dobharchain]	803 *	132
C157	Beinn Bhreac-liath	802	99
C158	Cranstackie	801	356
C159	Mcallan Liath Coire Mhic Dhughaill	801	347
C160	An Cliseam [Clisham]	799 *	387
C161	Cir Mhòr	799 *	368
C162	Am Bàthach	798	259
C163	Beinn Dronaig	797	280
C164	Cairnsmore of Carsphairn	797	23
C165	Beinn Mhic Mhonaidh	796	98
C166	Beinn Bhàn (Great Glen)	796	227
C167	Mam na Gualainn	796 *	117
C168	Sgùrr an Utha	796	232
C169	Sgùrr Coire Chòinnichean	796	248
C170	Beinn Leòid	792	344
C171	Càrn Ealasaid	792	170
C172	Glas Bheinn (Kinlochleven)	792	119
C173	Sgùrr a' Chaorachain	792	287
C174	Beinn Àirigh Charr	792	303
C175	Beinn Loinne, West Top	790 *	252
C176	Auchnafree Hill	789 *	67
C177	Meall Dubh	789	251
C178	The Brack	787 *	39
C179	Beinn a' Chaisteil (Strath Vaich)	787	322
C180	Arkle	787	350
C181	Meall Tairneachan	787	75
C182	Càrn na Nathrach	786	212
C183	Beinn an Oir	785	374
C184	Beinn na Caillich	785	249
C185	Beinn Mhic Cèididh	783	220
C186	Farragon Hill	783 *	75
C187	Sgùrr Dubh	782	294
C188	Corryhabbie Hill	781	174
C189	Ainshval	781	378
C190	Beinn Bheula [Caisteal Dubh]	779	46
C191	Sgùrr Mhic Bharraich	779	253
C192	Meall nam Maigheach	779	77
C193	Mount Battock	778	158
C194	Meall Horn	777	348
C195	Glas Bheinn (Assynt)	776	342
C196	Sàil Ghorm [Quinag]	776	338
C197	Meall na Leitreach	775 *	132
C198	Sgùrr Mhairi [Glamaig]	775	384
C199	Sgòrr Craobh a' Chaorainn	775	216
C200	Shalloch on Minnoch	775 *	19
C201	Beinn nan Caorach	774	254
C202	Meall a' Phubuill	774 *	228
C203	Beinn Spionnaidh	773	356
C204	Meall Lighiche	772	109
C205	Beinn Stacach	771 *	61
C206	Stob Coire a' Chearcaill	771	214
C207	Stob a' Bhealach an Sgrìodain	770	216
C208	Beinn a' Choin	770 *	55
C209	Cùl Beag	769	333
C210	Meallach Mhòr	769	184
C211	Càrn Dearg (South of Gleann Eachach)	768	200
C212	Sàil Mhòr	767	312
C213	Beinn Liath Mhòr a' Ghiubhais Lì	766	317
C214	Dùn da Ghaoithe	766	376
C215	Fuar Bheinn	766	208
C216	Bràigh nan Uamhachan	765	229
C217	An Caisteal [Ben Loyal]	764	358
C218	Meall an Fhùdair	764	48
C219	Spidean Còinich [Quinag]	764	338
C220	Cnoc Còinnich	764	41
C221	Little Wyvis	763	321
C222	Beinn na h-Uamha	762	205

* Denotes a summit where, following independent survey information, the Database of British and Irish Hills (*DOBIH*) gives a different height to that shown on OS maps and that used in this book - see Corbetts List page 391.

(i) OS 1:25k map has 842m, and 1:50k map has 845m.

(ii) OS 1:25k map has 839m, and 1:50k map has 838m.

Beinn Trilleachan above Loch Etive, with distant Ben Cruachan from Sgùrr na h-Ulaidh (Tom Prentice)

Sàil Mhòr and Beinn Dearg Bheag, with Beinn Dearg Mòr between, and A' Mhaighdean beyond, right (Iain Young)